COCKTAIL HANDBOOK

A Grown-Up's Guide to Making Mixed Drinks

Noah J. Wright

200 recipes

WINE

ISBN 978-1-70-3173994

CONTENTS

INTRODUCTION

"I drink to make other people more interesting."
– Ernest Hemingway

Some of the best cocktails were created over a century ago. These are the timeless favorites that have tantalized and whetted the palates of generations of drinkers.

Sure, the modern cocktail scene is filled with many great drinks that will astound and amaze the most refined palates. Yet, these classic cocktails have stood up to the tests of time, survived Prohibition, and witnessed amazing changes in the booze that is poured into them. We keep going back to them, and for very good reasons: they are simply great drinks.

Unless you're still an undergrad, it's time to move on from making rum and Cokes or vodka sodas at the bar. After all, you're a grown-up, and you should be drinking grown-up drinks. In this book you will find recipes of most popular bar drinks that you can make.

Follow the recipes in this book, then experiment and tweak them to your own liking. Drinks are not a one-size-fits-all experience and these are simply a foundation that you can use to build a true appreciation for everything the cocktail world has to offer.

COCKTAIL MAKING TECHNIQUES

Here are some techniques you need to know to make cocktails from this book.

Building is simply the process of making a cocktail in the glass we're going to serve it in. Depending upon the individual cocktail it is usually coupled with other methods like stirring or churning.

There are two main reasons why we might want to do this: efficiency; and because the style of cocktail demands it.

For example I could make a Dark and Stormy or a Negroni in a mixing glass and then pour it into the glass I intend to serve it in. But there is no special need to do this and I'm just making my life harder. Instead making the cocktail in the glass I'm going to serve it in and mixing it along the way is faster. So why not?

Some cocktails, however, pretty much require to be built. Anything served over crushed ice needs to be built. Because if you were to shake or stir (and so chill/dilute) it first then the further dilution of the quickly melting crushed ice would make the drink so weak and watery it would lose its punch.

Stirring is pretty self-explanatory. You put your ingredients in a container with ice and then you...stir them. Usually with a bar spoon or a dedicated stirrer to be left in the drink, but a straw works just as well. While many techniques for stirring have been proposed by self-proclaimed experts, the science behind all stirring remains pretty much the same. Stirring mixes a drink more gently than shaking does. This mean it takes longer to reach the Equilibrium of Temperature associated with chilling and dilution, but still reaches it all the same. Stirring is typically done in two ways:

Since stirring is slower than shaking we typically only do it when there is a good reason to. In conjunction with building a drink is one. Making large quantities of a cocktail for a party is another. And reducing the aeration of a drink during mixing is a third.

Shaking is the method by which you use a cocktail shaker to mix ingredients together and chill them simultaneously. The object is to almost freeze the drink whilst breaking down and combining the ingredients. Normally this is done with ice cubes three-quarters of the way full. When you've poured in the ingredients, hold the shaker in both hands, with one hand on top and one supporting the base, and give a short, sharp, snappy shake. It's important not to rock your cocktail to sleep. When water has begun to condense on the surface of the shaker, the cocktail should be sufficiently chilled and ready to be strained.

Blending is an appropriate way of combining ingredients, creating a smooth ready to serve mixture. Some recipes will call for ice to be placed in the blender, in which case you would use a suitable amount of crushed ice. An electric blender is needed for recipes containing ingredients which do not break down by shaking.

GLASSWARE

If you've ever tried to stock a bar cart or set up a home bar, you've probably been confused by all of the different types of cocktail glasses. You will need these ten types of cocktail glasses to make cocktails from this book.

Cocktail glass. Also known as a martini glass, this was one of the first glasses in which cocktails were served without ice. Before serving, the glass must be chilled, and the long stem prevents the cocktail from warming up in the hand. Standard capacity: 3-5 oz.

Cognac glass. A classic glass for drinking cognac or brandy. Standard capacity: 5-13 oz.

Collins glass. A tall glass for long and mixed drinks. Named after the classic "Tom Collins" cocktail. Standard capacity: 10-13 oz.

Copper mug. A must have. It has become the "Trojan horse" for vodka in America and vessel of choice for the "Moscow Mule." Standard capacity: 10-13 oz.

Coupe glass (champagne saucer). A glass with a tall stem and wide bowl. According to legend, it was designed to resemble the silhouette of one of the King of France's mistresses. Used to serve champagne and tiki cocktails. Standard capacity: 7-10 oz.

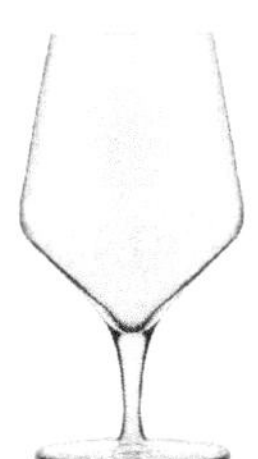

Goblet glass. A royal glass with thick walls, permitting the clinking of glasses while drinking without the risk of breaking. Standard capacity: 6-10 oz.

Flute glass. A high-society glass for cocktails featuring champagne or sparkling wine. The long, narrow form is reminiscent of a tulip and holds the bubbles in the cocktail, allowing it to remain fizzy for longer. Standard volume: 6-8 oz.

Highball glass. A tall glass for water, juice or club mixes. Mixes are built right in the glass. Standard capacity: 10-13 oz.

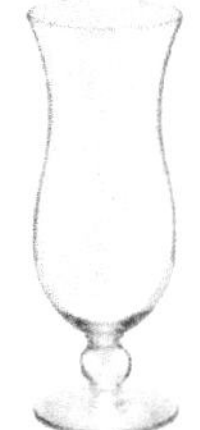

Hurricane glass. An old-fashioned glass resembling a kerosene lamp, used for serving tropical drinks, named in honor of Pat O'Brien's cocktail of the same name. Standard capacity: 10-15 oz.

Margarita glass. In a past life, it was a simple container for guacamole, but now it is the signature glass for serving the most famous tequila-based cocktail in the world. Standard capacity: 8-12 oz.

Rocks glass. A Wide glass with a thick bottom, used to serve strong spirits or cocktails in a pure, undiluted form. Standard capacity: 6-10 oz.

Sling glass. The quintessential glass for serving the eponymous cocktail, which would become the calling card of the Raffles Hotel. Standard capacity: 7-10 oz.

Wine glass. A classic, slightly curved glass. Traditionally taller than a white wine glass. Standard capacity: 6-10 oz.

GADGETS

Bar spoon. This indispensable bartender's tool is used for preparing cocktails in a mixing glass and for making layers in shots, as well as to measure ⅛ oz. portions of liquids or dry ingredient

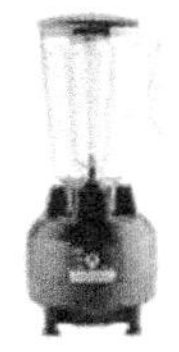

Blender. Invented in 1922 by Stephen Poplawski, this electric appliance is indispensable for making tiki cocktails, smoothies and frozen drinks

Clothespins. A decorative accessory used to hold garnishes to the glass

Cocktail skewer. A decorative accessory for serving olives in martinis and cocktail cherries in Manhattans. First appeared in bars at the end of the 19th century, thanks to the marketing genius Charles Forster

Drinking straws. In 1888, Marvin Stone, the owner of a paper mouthpiece factory, invented the best accessory for drinking drinks from glasses. Joseph Friedman then made a fortune by developing flexible drinking straws. The final step was to make straws from plastic

Jigger. Ensures accurate and ideal portions in cocktails. The best bartenders always have a range of sizes in their arsenal: ½-1 oz., ¼-¾ oz. and 1-2 oz.

Mixing glass. Used to prepare strong, masculine drinks without added juices, herbs or jams. Ice keeps its form and does not melt, maintaining the drink's strength. Standard capacity 16-30 oz.

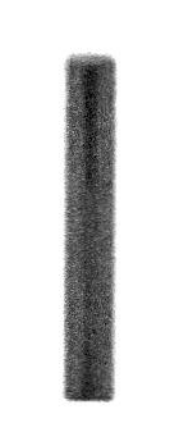

Muddler. An indispensable accessory for tropical cocktails, this crushes berries and fruits either in the shaker or directly in the glass

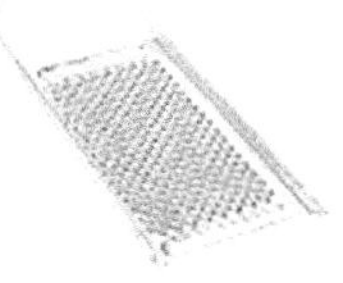

Nutmeg grater. A useful accessory for preparing nutmeg or chocolate powder, or even zest from citrus fruits

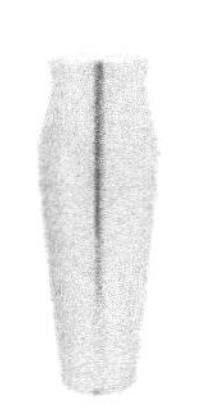

Shaker. It took its current form at the end of the 1800s, and earned especial popularity in the 1920s and 1930s through dozens of different styles and forms. They are divided into categories: cobbler shakers, which have a built-in strainer; French shakers, without a strainer; and Boston shakers, which consist of two equal-sized cups. Standard capacity 15-25 oz.

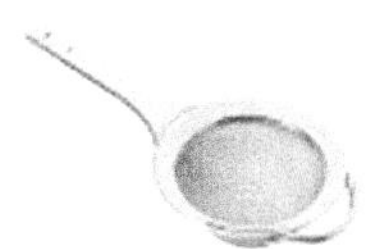

Sieve. Used together with shakers and strainers for double filtration of cocktails when pouring them from the shaker into the glass. With a finer net than a strainer, it does not allow even the smallest fruit seeds and bits of ice to fall into the drink

Strainer. An accessory indispensable when working with Boston or French shakers. Used for filtering fruit pits, pieces of ice and other undesired ingredients out of drinks

Squeezer. An indispensable tool for squeezing juice from limes and lemons. Despite the fact that most popular establishments nowadays use pre-prepared juice, freshly-squeezed juice is a mark of higher quality

Zest knife. A bartending tool sourced from the Japanese culture of carving. Used to cut off thin layers of zest, or make rings or twists from apples

THE CLASSICS

You can't go wrong with a classic cocktail. Whether you're craving a tried-and-true Old Fashioned, a traditional whiskey-and-vermouth Manhattan or James Bond's famous Vesper, the classic cocktail recipes below are anywhere from centuries to decades old and were invented all over the world.

AMERICANO

technique: build | time total: 5 min | serves: 1

rocks glass, jigger, bar spoon, drinking straws

- **1½ oz. red vermouth**
- **1½ oz. red bitter**
- **1½ oz. club soda**
- **Ice**
- **Orange zest**

1. Fill a rocks glass to the top with ice cubes
2. Pour in 1½ oz. of red bitter and 1½ oz. of red vermouth
3. Top up with club soda and stir gently
4. Garnish with an orange wheel

BICICLETTA

technique: build | time total: 3 min | serves: 1

wine glass, jigger, bar spoon, drinking straws

- **3 oz. dry white wine**
- **2 oz. red bitter**
- **2 oz. soda water**
- **Ice**
- **Orange wheels**

1. Fill a wine glass to the top with ice
2. Pour in 3 oz. of dry white wine and 2 oz. of red bitter and stir
3. Top up with a soda water
4. Garnish with 2 orange wheels

BLACK RUSSIAN

technique: build | time total: 3 min | serves: 1

rocks glass, jigger, bar spoon, drinking straws

- **2 oz. vodka**
- **1 oz. coffee liqueur**
- **Ice**

1. Fill a rocks glass to the top with ice
2. Pour in 1 oz. of coffee liqueur and 2 oz. of vodka
3. Stir gently

BOULEVARDIER

technique: build | time total: 3 min | serves: 1

rocks glass, jigger, bar spoon, zest knife

- **1½ oz. bourbon**
- **1 oz. red vermouth**
- **1 oz. red bitter**
- **Ice**
- **Orange zest**

1. Fill a rocks glass to the top with ice cubes
2. Pour in 1 oz. of red vermouth, 1 oz. of red bitter and 1½ oz. of bourbon
3. Stir gently
4. Garnish with orange zest

CUBA LIBRE

technique: build | time total: 5 min | serves: 1

- **2 oz. gold rum**
- **½ oz. lime juice**
- **5 oz. cola**
- **Ice**
- **Lime wheels**

highball glass, jigger, squeezer, bar spoon, drinking straws

1. Fill a highball glass to the top with ice
2. Pour in ½ oz. of lime juice and 2 oz. of gold rum
3. Top up with cola and stir gently
4. Garnish with 2 lime wheels

DARK'N'STORMY

technique: build | time total: 5 min | serves: 1

- **2 oz. black rum**
- **3 oz. ginger beer**
- **½ oz. lime juice**
- **Ice**
- **Lime**

highball glass, jigger, squeezer, bar spoon, drinking straws

1. Fill a highball glass to the top with ice
2. Pour in ½ oz. of lime juice, 3 oz. of ginger beer and 2 oz. of black rum
3. Stir gently
4. Garnish with a lime wedge

GIN AND TONIC

technique: build | time total: 3 min | serves: 1

highball glass, jigger, bar spoon, drinking straws

- **1½ oz. gin**
- **5 oz. tonic**
- **Ice**
- **Lime**

1. Fill a highball glass to the top with ice
2. Pour in 1½ oz. of gin
3. Top up with tonic and stir gently
4. Garnish with 2 lime wheels

GIN RICKEY

technique: build | time total: 3 min | serves: 1

highball glass, jigger, squeezer, bar spoon, drinking straws

- **2 oz. gin**
- **½ oz. fresh lime juice**
- **5 oz. soda water**
- **Ice**
- **Lime wheels**

1. Fill a highball glass to the top with ice
2. Pour in ½ oz. of lime juice and 2 oz. of gin and stir
3. Top up with a soda water
4. Garnish with 2 lime wheels

HORSE'S NECK

technique: build | time total: 3 min | serves: 1

highball glass, jigger, bar spoon, zest knife

- **2 oz. Cognac**
- **5 oz. ginger ale**
- **Angostura bitters**
- **Lemon zest**
- **Ice**

1. Fill a highball glass to the top with ice cubes
2. Pour in 2 oz. of Cognac and 1 dash of Angostura bitters
3. Top up with ginger ale and stir gently
4. Garnish with long lemon zest

MINT JULEP

technique: build | time total: 5 min | serves: 1

copper mug, muddler, jigger, bar spoon, drinking straws

- **1½ oz. bourbon**
- **½ oz. still water**
- **Mint**
- **Caster sugar**
- **Crushed ice**

1. Place 10 mint leaves and 2 bar spoons of caster sugar into a copper mug
2. Pour in ½ oz. of still water and muddle gently
3. Fill the mug to the top with crushed ice
4. Pour in 1½ oz. of aged bourbon and stir gently
5. Top up with crushed ice
6. Garnish with a mint sprig

MOJITO

technique: build | time total: 5 min | serves: 1

highball glass, muddler, jigger, bar spoon, drinking straws

- **2 oz. white rum**
- **½ oz. simple syrup**
- **3 oz. club soda**
- **Lime**
- **Mint**
- **Crushed ice**

1. Place 3 lime wedges into a highball glass and muddle
2. Take 10 mint leaves and "clap" them between your hands
3. Place the mint into the highball glass
4. Fill the highball glass to the top with crushed ice
5. Add ½ oz. of simple syrup and 2 oz. of white rum
6. Top up with club soda and stir gently
7. Top up with crushed ice
8. Garnish with a mint sprig

HOW TO MAKE: SIMPLE SYRUP

Ingredients:

- 1 cup white sugar
- 1 cup water

Directions:

1. In a medium saucepan combine sugar and water
2. Bring to a boil, stirring, until sugar has dissolved
3. Allow to cool

MOSCOW MULE

technique: build | time total: 5 min | serves: 1

cooper mug or rocks glass, jigger, bar spoon, squeezer

- **2 oz. vodka**
- **5 oz. ginger beer**
- **¼ oz. lime juice**
- **Ice**
- **Lime wedge**
- **Mint leaves**

1. Fill a copper mug to the top with ice
2. Pour in ¼ oz. of lime juice
3. Pour in 2 oz. of vodka
4. Top up with ginger beer and stir gently
5. Garnish with a lime wedge and mint leaves

NEGRONI

technique: build | time total: 3 min | serves: 1

rocks glass, jigger, bar spoon

- **1 oz. gin**
- **1 oz. red vermouth**
- **1 oz. red bitter**
- **Ice**
- **Orange**

1. Fill a rocks glass to the top with ice
2. Pour in 1 oz. of red vermouth, 1 oz. of red bitter and 1 oz. of gin
3. Stir gently
4. Garnish with an orange wheel

OLD FASHIONED

technique: build | time total: 3 min | serves: 1

rocks glass, jigger, muddler, bar spoon

- **2 oz. bourbon**
- **Angostura bitters**
- **Orange**
- **Cane sugar cubes**
- **Maraschino cherry**
- **Ice**

1. Place an orange wedge and a red Maraschino cherry into a rocks glass
2. Add a cane sugar cube soaked in 1 dash of Angostura bitters and muddle
3. Fill the rocks glass with ice cubes
4. Pour in 2 oz. of bourbon and stir gently

RUSTY NAIL

technique: build | time total: 3 min | serves: 1

rocks glass, jigger, bar spoon

- **2 oz. Scotch whisky**
- **1 oz. Drambuie**
- **Ice**

1. Fill a rocks glass to the top with ice cubes
2. Pour 1 oz. of Drambuie and 2 oz. of Scotch whisky into the rocks glass and stir

CAMBRIDGE UNIVERSITY PRESS
Cambridge, New York, Melbourne, Madrid, Cape Town, Singapore,
São Paulo, Delhi, Dubai, Tokyo, Mexico City

Cambridge University Press
79 Anson Road, #06-04/06, Singapore 079906

www.cambridge.org

This Japan bilingual edition is based on
Grammar in Use Intermediate with Answers, Third edition,
ISBN 978-0-521-73477-6 first published by Cambridge University Press in 2009.

First published 2009
Japan bilingual edition 2010

Printed in Singapore by Craft Print International Ltd

ISBN 978-4-902290-23-3 paperback Japan bilingual edition

Book design and layout: Adventure House, NYC
Cover design: Kenji Okazaki and K's counter

CAMB

Grammar in use Intermediate

マーフィーのケンブリッジ英文法

（中級編）新訂版

Raymond Murphy 著

William R. Smalzer 執筆協力

渡辺 雅仁 訳

目次

本書の巻末（p. 319）には「診断テスト」が用意されています。
まず「診断テスト」を受けて，自分の学習すべきユニットを見つけてください。

if と wish

受動態

間接話法

疑問文と繰り返しを避ける助動詞

動名詞（-ing）と不定詞（to + 動詞の原形）

冠詞と名詞

本書の巻末（p. 319）には「診断テスト」が用意されています。
まず「診断テスト」を受けて，自分の学習すべきユニットを見つけてください。

代名詞と限定詞

関係詞節

形容詞と副詞

接続詞と前置詞

本書の巻末（p. 319）には「診断テスト」が用意されています。
まず「診断テスト」を受けて，自分の学習すべきユニットを見つけてください。

前置詞

句動詞

本書の巻末（p. 319）には「診断テスト」が用意されています。
まず「診断テスト」を受けて，自分の学習すべきユニットを見つけてください。

日本語版出版にあたって

本書『マーフィーのケンブリッジ英文法（中級編）』は，2009年にアメリカのケンブリッジ大学出版局から出版された *Grammar in Use Intermediate* third edition（アメリカ英語版）に基づいた「日英バイリンガル第2版（新訂版）」です。
レイモンド・マーフィー（Raymond Murphy）による Grammar in Use シリーズは，1985年にイギリスで刊行された *English Grammar in Use*（イギリス英語版）以来，四半世紀にわたって，長く世界の英語学習者からコミュニケーションに「使える」実用文法書として高い評価を得てきました。

現在，Grammar in Use シリーズは中級の学習者を対象とする *English Grammar in Use* を核に，イギリス英語版とアメリカ英語版，初級—中級—上級の分化とともに，各国の学習者の母国語で解説を記述するバイリンガル版の刊行等を通じて，ますます多くの読者を増やしています。

Grammar in Use シリーズの最大の特長は，以下の3点に集約されます。

1. 統一された「見開き2ページ構成」によって，辞書を引くように学習したい文法項目がすぐに見つかる。
   実用性の高い多様な文法事項が，すべて，左ページに「文法解説と例文」，右ページに「練習問題」といった共通のレイアウトによって配置されています。
2. 「文法解説」より「例文」が豊富
   学習者による，より主体的な文法学習を推進するために専門用語に依存した文法解説は最小限にとどめ，直感による理解を推進するイラストや，中学校卒業程度の英語力があれば十分理解できる平易な例文を多数配置しています。
3. コミュニケーションにおける実用性の高い例文
   「文法解説」および「練習問題」中の「例文」は，大半が1つのピリオドや疑問符で終わる単文ではなく，自然な文脈や会話を構成する複数の文の中に置かれています。これにより，文法を英語が実際に使われる場面や会話の中で学ぶことができます。

本書「日英バイリンガル第2版（新訂版）」でも，オリジナルの *Grammar in Use Intermediate* 同様，左ページに「文法解説と例文」，右ページに「練習問題」という統一レイアウトを用いています。また，すぐれた例文をできるだけ多く読みながら文法理解の確認ができるように，以下の原則に基づいて解説の日本文を作成しました。

1. 学習者が自問自答しながら，理解について確認できるような質問事項とその答えを配置した。
2. 学習者がなるべく多くの例文を自分の力で読みこなせるように，本文中の例文の全訳は行わない。日本語訳を行う場合には，例文中でポイントとなる部分についてのみ訳出した。
3. 原著に準じて，文法の専門用語はなるべく用いないで解説を行った。一方で原著に登場する，日本の中学校や高校における英語学習には普通登場しない文法用語については，必要に応じて解説を加えて訳出した。

本書は「日英バイリンガル版」ですが，すべて英語で記述されている「オリジナル版」と同様，イラストや例文の主体的な学習は欠かすことができません。本書を通じて英文法のより深い，直感的な学習が可能になり，ひとりでも多くの学習者の方がコミュニケーションに「使える」英文法力を獲得されることを願っています。

2010年初夏　横浜にて　　　　訳者

学習者の皆さんへ

あなたは，英文法がわからなくなることはありませんか？ 本書は，そのような時に，あなたが英語の先生に頼らずに自分で英文法が学べるように作られています。

例えば，次の質問にきちんと答えられますか？ いずれの答えも本書から見つかります。

- I did（過去形）と I have done（現在完了形）は，どのように異なりますか？
- どのような時に，will を用いて未来を表しますか？
- I wish の後には，どのような構文がきますか？
- used to do と used to doing は，どのように異なりますか？
- どのような状況で定冠詞の the を使いますか？
- like と as は，どのように異なりますか？

本書には，このほかさまざまな文法項目が解説されていて，見開き 2 ページの項目ごとに，理解を確認する右ページの「練習問題（Exercises)」も付いています。

読者の対象レベル

本書は，「中級」レベルの学習者を対象に書かれています。また，中学校から高校 1，2 年程度の英語の初級文法を終えて，さらに英文法を学びたいと考えている「中級」レベルの学習者が「英語で言ってみたい。でも間違っていないか心配」と思うような構文を多く取り上げています。さらに，英語をそれなりに使えるものの，もっと文法を詳しく学びたいと考えている「上級」レベルの学習者にも役立ちますが，英語を学び始めた小学生や中学生のような「初級」の学習者にはお勧めできません。

本書の構成

本書は「1 つのユニットに 1 つの文法事項」を原則として，全体で 142 ユニットで構成されていますが，「現在完了形」や「定冠詞の the」などのように，より詳しい解説が必要な項目は複数のユニットで解説されています。それぞれのユニットで扱っている文法項目については「目次」で確認してください。

各ユニットはすべて見開き 2 ページで構成されています。左のページには「文法説明と例文」，右のページには「練習問題 (Exercises)」が配置されています。練習問題の正解は巻末の「Exercises 解答」(pp. 328-357) で確認してください。

また，巻末には「付録」(pp. 286-295) として次の 7 項目がまとめられています。

1. 規則動詞と不規則動詞
2. 現在時制と過去時制
3. 未来
4. 法助動詞（can/could/will/would など）
5. 短縮形（I'm/you've/didn't など）
6. つづり
7. アメリカ英語とイギリス英語

さらに詳細な「索引」(pp. 363-373) では，文法項目と重要語句の確認ができます。

本書の使い方

本書は，最初から終わりまでのユニットを 1 つずつ順番に学習する必要はありません。ユニットは，易しいものから難しいものへと難易度順に構成されているわけではないからです。「本書の構成」でも触れたように，「1 つのユニットに 1 つの文法事項」の原則によって，学習者が自分なりに「難しい，よくわからない」と感じる文法項目を選択して学習できるのです。

例えば，次のように学習します。

- ■ 本書の巻末（pp. 319–327）には「診断テスト」が用意されています。まず，この「診断テスト」を受けてください。テストは全158題の選択式問題で，1時間程度で終了します。このテストの結果から，自分が十分に理解していないユニットが明らかになります。また「目次」や「索引」から学習すべきユニットを探してみるのもよいでしょう。
- ■ 選択したユニットの左ページの文法解説をよく読みます。解説だけを拾い読みするのではなく，例文やイラストが表す状況について理解しましょう。例文は，中学校レベルの英語力があれば十分理解できる平易な語句で記述されています。
- ■ 本文中の以下の記号に注意します。
  - ☆ 文法について考えるべきポイントです。多くは質問形式になっていますので，質問に答えられるかどうか確認してから読み始めます。
  - ➤ ☆の質問への解答がまとめられています。
  - ⇒ 解釈の難しい構文の理解を助けるヒントです。例文の日本語訳ではないことに注意してください。
  - ⇔ 左右の構文を比較し，どのように異なるかを考えます。
  - × 文法上正しくない構文を表します。なぜ正しくないかを考えます。
  - = 左右の構文が同じであることを表します。
  - ➲ 参照すべきユニットを表します。指示されたユニットを適宜参照して理解を確認します。
- ■ 選択したユニットの右ページの「練習問題（Exercises）」に取り組みます。なぜ，その答えとなるのかを考えながら解答します。
- ■ 巻末の「Exercises 解答」（pp. 328-357）で正解を確認します。
- ■ 間違えた問題は，なぜ間違えたかをユニット左ページの文法解説を読み直して確認します。間違えた問題は後で復習できるよう問題番号をメモしておきます。場合によっては「練習問題（Exercises）」はやらずに，左のページの文法解説だけを目次や索引から辞書を引くように参照してもよいでしょう。

補充問題

巻末には「補充問題」（pp. 296-318）が用意されています。この「補充問題」は関連する複数のユニットをまとめた，より広い出題範囲の中から作られています。例えばp. 305の「補充問題16」は，25～34までのユニットを出題範囲として作られています。各ユニットを学習した後で「補充問題」に取り組めば，ユニットを超えたより幅広い範囲で，短時間に文法の理解が確認できます。

先生方へ

本書『マーフィーのケンブリッジ英文法（中級編）』は，学習者がひとりで学べる自学自習用の文法書として作成されたものですが，高校や大学などの英語の授業でもテキストや参考資料として十分活用できます。ことにコミュニケーションを重視しつつ，英文法についてより詳しく学習させたい場合に役立ちます。

中学校の文法を理解した「中級」の学習者や，高校までの文法を理解した「中上級」の学習者を対象としていますので，このレベルの学習者であれば，本文中のほぼすべての項目について問題なく理解できます。学習者に，すでに学んだ文法事項を復習させることも，新しい構文を導入して練習させることも可能です。また，高校の英語を十分に習得し，さらに高度な英語力を目指す「上級」レベルの学習者にも，英文法でわからないことがあった際に辞書を引くように文法項目を参照させたり，練習させたりできます。しかし，小学生や中学生のような「初級」の学習者にはお勧めできません。

「目次」にあるように，それぞれのユニットは「現在形と過去形」「冠詞と名詞」「前置詞」といった文法上の分類によってまとめられています。この分類は易しいものから難しいものへと配置されているわけではありません。したがって，本書は「目次」にある順番ですべてのユニットを1つずつ学習する必要はありませんので，先生方の授業における文法学習のシラバスや学習者のレベルや学習状況などに応じて，柔軟にユニットを選択することができます。

本書は，文法事項を新しく導入し，ただちに定着させる際にも，一定の期間の後に復習したり，学習者の弱い部分に焦点を当てて強化する際にも役立ちます。また，一斉授業においてクラス全体で使用することも，学習者に応じて個別学習させることも可能です。文法の解説と例文は，もともとは英文法の自学自習のために書かれたものですが，教員が授業を行う際のヒントや参考資料にもなります。学習者にとって左のページは授業で学んだことの記録となり，授業の後も繰り返して参照できます。右のページの「練習問題（Exercises）」は，学習者への自習課題としても，クラスでの全体学習としても，授業の前提としての自宅学習としても取り組ませることができます。また，ある文法項目について，特定の学習者の理解が十分ではない場合には，その学習者に学習すべきユニットを個別に指定して取り組ませることもできます。ここでも，複数のユニットをまとめ，より広い出題範囲の中から作られた巻末の「補充問題」が役に立ちます（「学習者の皆さんへ」も参照してください）。

本書中の英語表現は，大半が標準的な口語の北アメリカ英語として実際に使われ，広く受け入れられているものです。英語の母国語話者の中には，例えば，目的格代名詞としての who や，he or she（彼もしくは彼女）の意味で用いる they について「正しくない」とする人たちもいますが，本書ではこのような用法は問題のない標準的なものとして取り上げています。

「日本語版出版にあたって」でも触れたように，本書は，2009 年にアメリカのケンブリッジ大学出版局から出版された *Grammar in Use Intermediate* third edition に基づいたもので，原著の 2009 年版は 2000 年に出版された第 2 版の改訂版です。原著の第 3 版では，2000 年の第 2 版に対して以下のような主要な改訂を行っています。

- 第2版では，Unit 133として1つのユニットで「句動詞」を取り上げていましたが，第3版では，これを Units 134–142（句動詞 1〜句動詞 9）の 9 ユニット構成に強化しています。また，wish についての新しいユニットを追加しました（Unit 39）。これにより，Units 40–133 まで，第 2 版に比べて 1 つずつ番号が繰り下がっています。
- 記載事項については，ほぼすべてのユニットにおいて改訂および改編を行っています。
- 巻末の「補充問題」を拡張しました。新たに 14–16, 25, 30–31, 37–41 の問題を追加しました。
- すべてのイラストをフルカラーにしました。

Grammar
in use
Intermediate

マーフィーの
ケンブリッジ英文法
（中級編）新訂版

UNIT 1

現在進行形 (I am doing)

A

☆ イラストの状況について考えなさい。どのような形の動詞が使われていますか？

Sarah は車に乗っていて，仕事に行くところです。

She **is driving** to work.

話し手が話をしている瞬間（現在時）に，彼女は車を運転しています。運転は終了していません。

➤ am/is/are + -ing の形は現在進行形と呼ばれます。

I	**am**	(= I'**m**)	driv**ing**
he/she/it	**is**	(= he'**s** など)	work**ing**
we/you/they	**are**	(= we'**re** など)	do**ing** など

B

「…している最中」のように，現在時に進行中で終わっていない動作は現在進行形 (**I am doing** …) で表します。この動作は**単純現在形** (**I do**) では書き換えられません。

- Please don't make so much noise. **I'm trying** to work. (× I try)
- "Where's Mark?" "He'**s taking** a shower." (× He takes a shower)
- Let's go out now. It **isn't raining** any more. (× It doesn't rain)
- 〔パーティーで〕Hello, Jane. **Are** you **enjoying** the party? (× Do you enjoy)
- What's all that noise? What'**s going** on?（⇒ 何が起こっているの？）

☆ 下のイラストの現在進行形は，上の例文中の現在進行形とどのように異なりますか？

Steve は電話で友達と話をしています。

I'm reading a really good book at the moment. It's about a man who . . . .

話をしている時，Steve は電話をしています。本を読んでいるわけではありません。「本は読み始めたが，まだ読み終えていない。本を読んでいる途中である」と言いたいのです。

➤ 現在進行形が話をしている瞬間に進行していない動作を表すことがあります。

同様に以下の例文中の**現在進行形**も，動作は話の最中に進行していません。

- Kate wants to work in Italy, so she'**s studying** Italian.
  （⇒ イタリア語を学習している。たった今，学習しているわけではない）
- Some friends of mine **are building** their own house. They hope to finish it next summer.

C

today / **this week** / **this year** などの現在を含む語句は，**現在進行形**とともに用います。

- *A:* You'**re working** hard **today**. (× You work hard today)
  B: Yes, I have a lot to do.
- The company I work for **isn't doing** so well **this year**.

D

現在を含む期間の中で進行する変化は**現在進行形**で表します。この意味を持つ動詞には以下のようなものがあります。

get	**change**	**become**	**increase**	**rise**
fall	**grow**	**improve**	**begin**	**start**

- **Is** your English **getting** better? (× Does your English get better?)
- The population of the world **is increasing** very fast. (× increases)
- At first I didn't like my job, but **I'm beginning** to enjoy it now. (× I begin)

現在進行形と単純現在形の違い ➲ Units 3–4　未来を表す現在進行形や単純現在形 ➲ Unit 18

Exercises

1.1 以下から適切な動詞を選び，正しい形に変えて文を完成しなさい。

get happen look lose make start stay try ~~work~~

1. "You *'re working* hard today." "Yes, I have a lot to do."
2. I __________ for Christine. Do you know where she is?
3. It __________ dark. Should I turn on the light?
4. They don't have anywhere to live at the moment. They __________ with friends until they find a place.
5. Things are not so good at work. The company __________ money.
6. Do you have an umbrella? It __________ to rain.
7. You __________ a lot of noise. Can you be quieter? I __________ to concentrate.
8. Why are all these people here? What __________ ?

1.2 (　) 内の動詞を適切な形に変えて，文を完成しなさい。否定形となる場合もあります。

1. Please don't make so much noise. I *'m trying* (try) to work.
2. Let's go out now. It *isn't raining* (rain) any more.
3. You can turn off the radio. I __________ (listen) to it.
4. Kate called me last night. She's on vacation in Quebec. She __________ (have) a great time and doesn't want to come home.
5. I want to lose weight, so this week I __________ (eat) lunch.
6. Andrew has just started evening classes. He __________ (study) German.
7. Paul and Sally had an argument. They __________ (speak) to each other.
8. I __________ (get) tired. I need a break.
9. Tim __________ (work) this week. He has a week off.

1.3 (　) 内の語句を正しい形に変えて，対話を完成しなさい。

1. *A:* I saw Brian a few days ago.
   B: Oh, did you? *What's he doing* these days? (what / he / do)
   A: He's in college now.
   B: __________ ? (what / he / study)
   A: Psychology.
   B: __________ it? (he / enjoy)
   A: Yes, he says __________ a lot. (he / learn)
2. *A:* Hi, Liz. How __________ ? (your new job / go)
   B: Not bad. It wasn't so good at first, but __________ better now. (it / get)
   A: What about Jonathan? Is he OK?
   B: Yes, but __________ his work at the moment. (he / not / enjoy) He's been in the same job for a long time, and __________ to get bored with it. (he / begin)

1.4 以下から適切な動詞を選び，正しい形に変えて文を完成しなさい。

begin change get ~~increase~~ rise

1. The population of the world *is increasing* very fast.
2. The world __________ . Things never stay the same.
3. The situation is already bad and it __________ worse.
4. The cost of living __________ . Every year things are more expensive.
5. The weather __________ to improve. The rain has stopped, and the wind isn't as strong.

UNIT 2

単純現在形 (I do)

A

☆ イラストの状況について考えなさい。どのような形の動詞が使われていますか？

Alex はバスの運転手です。今，彼は寝ている最中でバスは運転していません。

この状況は以下の 2 通りで表せます。

He is not driving a bus. （⇒ 眠っている最中）
⇔ He **drives** a bus. （⇒ 眠っていてもバスの運転手）

➤ **drive(s)/work(s)/do(es) などの形は単純現在形と呼ばれます。**

I/we/you/they	**drive/work/do** など
he/she/it	**drives/works/does** など

B

「…するものだ，いつも…する」のように，常時成立していたり，繰り返して生じる出来事や一般的に真となる事柄は**単純現在形**で表します。

- Nurses **take** care of patients in hospitals.
- I usually **leave** for work at 8 a.m.
- The earth **goes** around the sun.
- The coffee shop **opens** at 7:30 in the morning.

☆ **主語が変わると，単純現在形の動詞はどのように変化しますか？**

I **work** … ⇔ He **works** … They **teach** … ⇔ My sister **teaches** …

(-s, -es) のつづり ➲ 付録 6

C

単純現在形の疑問文や否定文は，**助動詞**としての **do/does** を用いて作ります。

do **does**	I/we/you/they he/she/it	**work?** **drive?** **do?**

I/we/you/they he/she/it	**don't** **doesn't**	**work** **drive** **do**

- I come from Japan. Where **do** you **come** from?
- I **don't go** to church very often.
- What **does** this word **mean**? (✕ What means this word?)
- Rice **doesn't grow** in cold climates.

以下の例文中には，**主動詞**としての **do** （…をする）も生じています。

- "What **do** you **do**?" "I work in a department store."
- He's always so lazy. He **doesn't do** anything to help.

D

頻度を表す語句は，**単純現在形**とともに用います。

- I **get** up at 8:00 **every morning**.
- **How often** do you **go** to the dentist?
- Julie **doesn't drink** tea **very often**.
- Robert usually **plays** tennis **two or three times a week** in the summer.

E

I promise … / **I suggest** … など，ことばを発することで動作が行われる場合，**単純現在形**を用います。例えば **I promise** … と言うことによって「**約束**」，**I suggest** … と言うことによって「**提案**」という動作が行われます。

- **I promise** I won't be late. (✕ I'm promising)
- "What do you **suggest** I do?" "**I suggest** that you spend less money."

I advise … / **I insist** … / **I refuse** … / **I suppose** … なども同じように用います。

現在進行形と単純現在形の違い ➲ Units 3–4 未来を表す現在進行形や単純現在形 ➲ Unit 18

Exercises

2.1 以下から適切な動詞を選び，正しい形に変えて文を完成しなさい。

cause(s) connect(s) drink(s) live(s) open(s) ~~speak(s)~~ take(s)

1. Tanya _speaks_ German very well.
2. I don't ________ much coffee.
3. The swimming pool ________ at 7:30 every morning.
4. Bad driving ________ many accidents.
5. My parents ________ in a very small apartment.
6. The Olympic Games ________ place every four years.
7. The Panama Canal ________ the Atlantic and Pacific Oceans.

2.2 （ ）内の動詞を適切な形に変えて，文を完成しなさい。

1. Julie _doesn't drink_ (not / drink) tea very often.
2. What time ________ (the banks / close) here?
3. I have a TV, but I ________ (not / watch) it much.
4. "Where ________ (Ricardo / come) from?" "He's Cuban."
5. "What ________ (you / do)?" "I'm an electrician."
6. It ________ (take) me an hour to get to work. How long ________ (it / take) you?
7. Look at this sentence. What ________ (this word / mean)?
8. David isn't in very good shape. He ________ (not / exercise).

2.3 以下から適切な動詞を選び，正しい形に変えて文を完成しなさい。否定形となる場合もあります。

believe eat flow ~~go~~ ~~grow~~ make rise tell translate

1. The earth _goes_ around the sun.
2. Rice _doesn't grow_ in Canada.
3. The sun ________ in the east.
4. Bees ________ honey.
5. Vegetarians ________ meat.
6. An atheist ________ in God.
7. An interpreter ________ from one language into another.
8. Liars are people who ________ the truth.
9. The Amazon River ________ into the Atlantic Ocean.

2.4 Liz に，本人や家族のことを尋ねる疑問文を作りなさい。

1. You know that Liz plays tennis. You want to know how often. Ask her.
   How often _do you play tennis_ ?
2. Perhaps Liz's sister plays tennis, too. You want to know. Ask Liz.
   ________ your sister ________ ?
3. You know that Liz reads a newspaper every day. You want to know which one. Ask her.
   ________ ?
4. You know that Liz's brother works. You want to know what he does. Ask Liz.
   ________ ?
5. You know that Liz goes to the movies a lot. You want to know how often. Ask her.
   ________ ?
6. You don't know where Liz's grandparents live. You want to know. Ask Liz.
   ________ ?

2.5 以下から空所に入れるのにふさわしいものを選び，文を完成しなさい。

I apologize I insist I promise I recommend ~~I suggest~~

1. It's a nice day. _I suggest_ we go for a walk.
2. I won't tell anybody what you said. ________ .
3. I won't let you pay for the meal. ________ that you let me pay.
4. ________ for what I did. It won't happen again.
5. The new restaurant downtown is very good. ________ it highly.

UNIT 3

現在進行形と単純現在形 1 (I am doing と I do)

A

☆ 現在進行形と単純現在形は，どのように異なりますか？

I am doing（現在進行形）

➤ 現在進行形は「…している最中」のように，話をしている時やその周辺で生じている出来事を表します。動作は完了していません。

I am doing

過去　現在　未来

- The water **is boiling**. Can you turn it off?
- Listen to those people. What language **are** they **speaking**?
- Let's go out. It **isn't raining** now.
- "I'm busy." "What **are** you **doing**?"
- **I'm getting** hungry. Let's eat.
- Kate wants to work in Italy, so she**'s learning** Italian.
- The population of the world **is increasing** very fast.

➤ 現在進行形は一時的な状況を表します。

- **I'm living** with some friends until I find a place of my own.
- *A:* You**'re working** hard today.
  B: Yes, I have a lot to do.

現在進行形 ➲ Unit 1

I do（単純現在形）

➤ 単純現在形は「いつも…する」のように，一般的な物や人の性質や，繰り返し生じる出来事を表します。

I do

過去　現在　未来

- Water **boils** at 100 degrees Celsius.
- Excuse me, **do** you **speak** English?
- It **doesn't rain** very much in summer.
- What **do** you usually **do** after work?
- I always **get** hungry in the afternoon.
- Most people **learn** to swim when they are children.
- Every day the population of the world **increases** by about 200,000 people.

➤ 単純現在形は永続的な状況を表します。

- My parents **live** in Vancouver. They have lived there all their lives.
- John isn't lazy. He **works** hard most of the time.

単純現在形 ➲ Unit 2

B

I always do (…) と I'm always doing (…)

I always do … は「いつも…する」という習慣を表します。

- **I always drive** to work. (✕ I'm always driving)

☆ イラストの **I'm always doing (…)** は，どのような状況を表しますか？

I've lost my key again. **I'm always losing** things.

➤ ***I'm always losing* things.** は，「物を失くしてばかりいる」を表します。**I'm always doing …** は，「…してばかりいる，よく…して困る」のような困った状況を表します。

☆ 例文はどのような状況を表していますか？

- You**'re always watching** television. You should do something more active.
  (⇒ テレビの見過ぎ)
- Tim is never satisfied. He**'s always complaining**. (⇒ 文句の言い過ぎ)

上記以外の現在進行形と単純現在形の違い ➲ Units 3–4　　未来を表す単純現在形 ➲ Unit 18

Exercises

3.1 下線部の動詞の用法について誤りがあれば訂正しなさい。

1. Water boils at 212 degrees Fahrenheit. _OK_
2. The water boils. Can you turn it off? _is boiling_
3. Look! That man tries to open the door of your car. ____________
4. Can you hear those people? What do they talk about? ____________
5. The moon goes around the earth in about 27 days. ____________
6. I have to go now. It gets late. ____________
7. I usually drive to work. ____________
8. "Hurry up! It's time to leave." "OK, I come." ____________
9. I hear you've got a new job. How does it go? ____________
10. Paul is never late. He's always getting to work on time. ____________
11. They don't get along well. They're always arguing. ____________

3.2 (　) 内の語句を現在進行形もしくは単純現在形に変えて，空所に入れなさい。

1. Let's go out. It _isn't raining_ (not / rain) now.
2. Julia is very good at languages. She _speaks_ (speak) four languages very well.
3. Hurry up! Everybody ____________ (wait) for you.
4. "____________ (you / listen) to the radio?" "No, you can turn it off."
5. "____________ (you / listen) to the radio every day?" "No, just occasionally."
6. The River Nile ____________ (flow) into the Mediterranean.
7. The river ____________ (flow) very fast today – much faster than usual.
8. We usually ____________ (grow) vegetables in our garden, but this year we ____________ (not / grow) any.
9. *A:* How's your English?
   B: Not bad. I think it ____________ (improve) slowly.
10. Rachel is in New York right now. She ____________ (stay) at the Park Hotel. She always ____________ (stay) there when she's in New York.
11. Can we stop walking soon? I ____________ (start) to feel tired.
12. *A:* Can you drive?
    B: I ____________ (learn). My father ____________ (teach) me.
13. Normally I ____________ (finish) work at five, but this week I ____________ (work) until six to earn a little more money.
14. My parents ____________ (live) in Taipei. They were born there and have never lived anywhere else. Where ____________ (your parents / live)?
15. Sonia ____________ (look) for a place to live. She ____________ (stay) with her sister until she finds a place.
16. *A:* What ____________ (your brother / do)?
    B: He's an architect, but he ____________ (not / work) right now.
17. 〔パーティーで〕I usually ____________ (enjoy) parties, but I ____________ (not / enjoy) this one very much.

3.3 以下の対話の B の発言を現在進行形 (always -ing) を用いて完成しなさい。

1. *A:* I've lost my keys again.
   B: Not again! _You're always losing your keys_.
2. *A:* The car has broken down again.
   B: That car is useless. It ____________.
3. *A:* Look! You made the same mistake again.
   B: Oh no, not again! I ____________.
4. *A:* Oh, I forgot my glasses again.
   B: That's typical! ____________.

UNIT 4

現在進行形と単純現在形 2 (I am doing と I do)

A

They **are eating**. や It **is raining**. などのように，始まったものの完了していない動作や出来事は**現在進行形**で表します。

know や **like** のような動詞は，I **am knowing** や they **are liking** のような**進行形**にはできません。たった今の事柄についても，I **know**，they **like** のような**単純現在形**を用います。普通，**進行形にしない動詞**には次のようなものがあります。

like	love	hate	want	need	prefer	
know	realize	suppose	mean	understand	believe	remember
belong	fit	contain	consist	seem		

- I'm hungry. I **want** something to eat. (× I'm wanting)
- **Do** you **understand** what I **mean**?
- Ann **doesn't seem** very happy.

B

think

think が「…と思う」のように，**believe** や **have an opinion** の意味を持つ場合，**進行形**にはなりません。

➲Unit 4A

- I **think** Mary is Canadian, but I'm not sure. (× I'm thinking)
- What **do** you **think** about my plan? (⇒ ～についてどう思う？)

think が「…と考える」のように，**consider** のようなより積極的な意味を持つ場合，**進行形**になります。

- **I'm thinking** about what happened. I often **think** about it.
- Nicky **is thinking** of quitting her job. (⇒ ～を（真剣に）考えている)

C

He is selfish と He is being selfish

He's being ... は「…のようにふるまっている，…のふりをしている」の意味を持ちます。

- I can't understand why he**'s being** so selfish. He isn't usually like that.
  (**being** selfish = behaving selfishly at the moment)
- He never thinks about other people. He **is** very selfish. (× He is being ...)
  (= He is selfish generally, not only at the moment)

am/is/are being ... は「（人が）…のようにふるまっている」の意味を持つ場合のみ使えます。この意味を持ちえない場合は，**進行形**にはなりません。

- It**'s** hot today. (× It's being hot)
- Sarah **is** very tired. (× is being tired)

D

see, hear, smell, taste

活動に積極性の乏しい，身体の知覚を表す動詞（**知覚動詞**）は普通，**単純現在形**で用い，**進行形**にはしません。

- **Do** you **see** that man over there? (× Are you seeing)
- This room **smells**. Let's open a window.

can + see〔**hear/smell/taste**〕のように，**知覚動詞**は助動詞 **can** とともによく用います。

- I **can hear** a strange noise. **Can** you **hear** it?

E

look と feel

「…のように見える / …と思われる」の意味を持つ **look** と **feel** は，**単純現在形**でも**現在進行形**でも用います。

- You **look** good today. = You**'re looking** good today.
- How **do** you **feel** now? = How **are** you **feeling** now?

しかし以下のように，「いつも…を感じる」のように，現在に限定されずに感じていることは**単純現在形**を用います。

- I usually **feel** tired in the morning. (× I'm usually feeling)

現在進行形と単純現在形 1 ➲ Unit 3　have ➲ Unit 16　未来を表す単純現在形 ➲ Unit 18

Exercises

4.1 下線部の動詞の用法に誤りがあれば訂正しなさい。

1. Nicky <u>is thinking</u> of giving up her job. _OK_
2. <u>Are</u> you <u>believing</u> in God? ______
3. <u>I'm feeling</u> hungry. Is there anything to eat? ______
4. This sauce is great. It<u>'s tasting</u> really good. ______
5. <u>I'm thinking</u> this is your key. Is it? ______

4.2 (　) 内の語句を用いて文を完成しなさい。必要に応じて Unit 3 も復習すること。

4.3 (　) 内の動詞を現在進行形もしくは単純現在形の適切な形にして，文を完成しなさい。

1. Are you hungry? _Do you want_ (you / want) something to eat?
2. Don't put the dictionary away. I ______ (use) it.
3. Don't put the dictionary away. I ______ (need) it.
4. Who is that man? What ______ (he / want)?
5. Who is that man? Why ______ (he / look) at us?
6. Alan says he's 80 years old, but nobody ______ (believe) him.
7. She told me her name, but I ______ (not / remember) it now.
8. I ______ (think) of selling my car. Are you interested in buying it?
9. I ______ (think) you should sell your car. You ______ (not / use) it very often.
10. Air ______ (consist) mainly of nitrogen and oxygen.

4.4 be 動詞の単純現在形 (am/is/are) か現在進行形 (am /is/are being) を用いて，文を完成しなさい。

1. I can't understand why _he's being_ so selfish. He isn't usually like that.
2. Sarah ______ very nice to me these days. I wonder why.
3. You'll like Debbie when you meet her. She ______ very nice.
4. You're usually very patient, so why ______ unreasonable about waiting 10 more minutes?
5. Why isn't Steve at work today? ______ sick?

UNIT 5

単純過去形 (I did)

A

☆ 単純過去形はどのような状況で用いられますか？

Wolfgang Amadeus Mozart was an Austrian musician and composer. He **lived** from 1756 to 1791. He **started** composing at the age of five and **wrote** more than 600 pieces of music. He **was** only 35 years old when he **died**.

➤ **lived/started/wrote/was/died** のような「…した」を表す動詞の形は，単純過去形と呼ばれます。単純過去形はモーツァルトの人生のように，過去において完結した出来事を表します。

B

単純過去形の多くは動詞の語尾に **-ed** を付加して作ります。このような動詞は**規則動詞**と呼ばれます。

- I work in a travel agency now. I **worked** in a department store before.
- We **invited** them to our party, but they **decided** not to come.
- The police **stopped** me on my way home last night.
- Laura **passed** her exam because she **studied** very hard.

sto**pp**ed や stud**i**ed などの語のつづり ➲ 付録 6

以下のように，**単純過去形**の語尾に **-ed** を付加して作れない動詞は**不規則動詞**と呼ばれます。

write	→	**wrote**	■ Mozart **wrote** more than 600 pieces of music.
see	→	**saw**	■ We **saw** Rose at the mall a few days ago.
go	→	**went**	■ I **went** to the movies three times last week.
shut	→	**shut**	■ It was cold, so I **shut** the window.

不規則動詞一覧 ➲ 付録 1

C

単純過去形の疑問文や否定文は **did/didn't**（**助動詞**）**＋ 動詞の原形**（enjoy/see/go など）を用いて作ります。

I	enjoy**ed**
she	**saw**
they	**went**

did	you	**enjoy**?
	she	**see**?
	they	**go**?

I	**didn't**	**enjoy**
she		**see**
they		**go**

- *A:* **Did** you **go** out last night?
  B: Yes, I **went** to the movies, but I **didn't enjoy** the film much.
- "When **did** Mr. Thomas **die**?" "About 10 years ago."
- They **didn't invite** her to the party, so she **didn't go**.
- "**Did** you **have** time to write the letter?" "No, I **didn't**."

did … do / didn't do の形を含む以下の例文中には，**主動詞**としての **do**（…をする）も生じています。

- What **did** you **do** on the weekend? (✕ What did you on the weekend?)
- I **didn't do** anything. (✕ I didn't anything)

D

was/were は **am/is/are**（**be 動詞**）の**過去形**です。

I/he/she/it	**was/wasn't**
we/you/they	**were/weren't**

was	I/he/she/it?
were	we/you/they?

was/were（**be 動詞の過去形**）が生じている時，否定文と疑問文中に **did** は生じません。

- I **was** angry because they **were** late.
- **Was** the weather good when you **were** on vacation?
- They **weren't** able to come because they **were** so busy.
- Did you go out last night, or **were** you too tired?

単純過去形と過去進行形 ➲ Unit 6　現在完了形と単純過去形の違い ➲ Units 12–13

Exercises

5.1 職場での Debbie の 1 日は普通，次のように過ぎていきます。昨日，彼女はいつも通りの勤務をしました。Debbie が昨日したこと，しなかったことを答えなさい。

I usually get up at 7:00 and have a big breakfast. I walk to work, which takes me about half an hour. I start work at 8:45. I never have lunch. I finish work at 5:00. I'm always tired when I get home. I usually cook dinner a little later. I don't usually go out. I go to bed around 11:00, and I always sleep well.

Debbie

1. *She got up at 7:00.*
2. She ______ a big breakfast.
3. She ______ .
4. It ______ to get to work.
5. ______ at 8:45.
6. ______ lunch.
7. ______ at 5:00.
8. ______ tired when ______ home.
9. ______ dinner a little later.
10. ______ out last night.
11. ______ at 11:00.
12. ______ well last night.

5.2 以下から適切な動詞を選び，正しい形に変えて文を完成しなさい。

buy catch cost fall hurt sell spend teach throw ~~write~~

1. Mozart *wrote* more than 600 pieces of music.
2. "How did you learn to drive?" "My father ______ me."
3. We couldn't afford to keep our car, so we ______ it.
4. Dave ______ down the stairs this morning and ______ his leg.
5. Jim ______ the ball to Sue, who ______ it.
6. Ann ______ a lot of money yesterday. She ______ a dress that ______ $200.

5.3 James に休暇の過ごし方を尋ねる疑問文を作りなさい。全体で 1 つの対話となっています。

Hi. How are things?

Fine, thanks. I've just had a great vacation.

1. Where *did you go* ?
   We went on a trip from San Francisco to Denver.
2. How ______ ? By car?
   Yes, we rented a car in San Francisco.
3. It's a long way to drive. How long ______ ?
   Two weeks.
4. Where ______ ? In hotels?
   Yes, small hotels or motels.
5. ______ ?
   It was very hot – sometimes too hot.
6. ______ the Grand Canyon?
   Of course. It was wonderful.

5.4 (　) 内の動詞を肯定または否定の適切な形に変えて，文を完成しなさい。

1. It was warm, so I *took* off my coat. (take)
2. The movie wasn't very good. I *didn't enjoy* it very much. (enjoy)
3. I knew Sarah was very busy, so I ______ her. (disturb)
4. I was very tired, so I ______ the party early. (leave)
5. The bed was very uncomfortable. I ______ very well. (sleep)
6. The window was open and a bird ______ into the room. (fly)
7. The hotel wasn't very expensive. It ______ very much. (cost)
8. I was in a hurry, so I ______ time to call you. (have)
9. It was hard carrying the bags. They ______ very heavy. (be)

UNIT 6

過去進行形 (I was doing)

A

☆ 次のイラストの状況について考えなさい。どのような形の動詞が使われていますか？

昨日，Karen と Jim はテニスを 10 時に始め 11 時半に終えました。この状況は次のように表すことができます。

At 10:30, they **were playing** tennis.

この文は次の事柄を表します。
1）ふたりはテニスをしている最中であった。
2）テニスは終わっていなかった。

➤ was/were -ing のような形は過去進行形と呼ばれます。

I/he/she/it	**was**	play**ing**
we/you/they	**were**	do**ing**
		work**ing** など

B

I **was doing** の形の**過去進行形**は「…していた」のように，過去の一時点において何かをしていた最中であったことを表します。動作や状況はこの一時点の少し前から始まったものの，まだ完了していません。

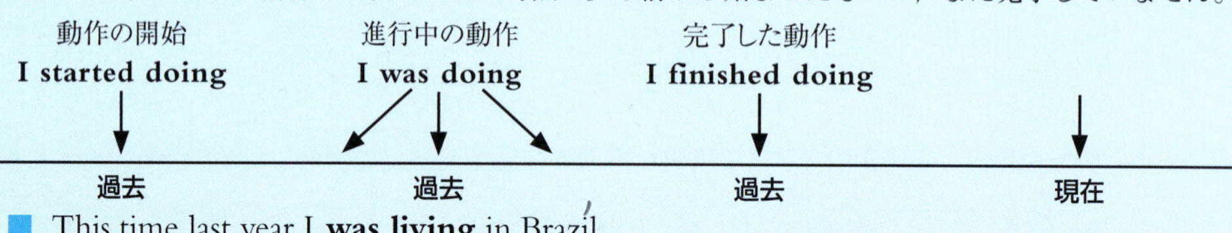

- This time last year I **was living** in Brazil.
- What **were** you **doing** at 10:00 last night?
- I waved to Helen, but she **wasn't looking**.

C

☆ 以下の例文の過去進行形（I was doing）と単純過去形（I did）は，どのように異なりますか？

➤ 過去進行形は過去の一時点で進行中の動作
- I **was walking** home when I met Dave.
- Kate **was watching** television when we arrived.

➤ 単純過去形は過去において完了した動作
- I **walked** home after the party last night.
- Kate **watched** television a lot when she was sick last year.

D

単純過去形と**過去進行形**を合わせて用いて，「…していた時に～した」のように，ある出来事が別の出来事の最中に起こったことを表します。この意味では **while** が**過去進行形**の前によく用いられます。

- Matt **burned** his hand while he **was cooking** dinner.
- It **was raining** when I **got** up.
- I **saw** you in the park yesterday. You **were sitting** on the grass and **reading** a book.
- I **hurt** my back while I **was working** in the garden.

単純過去形が連続すると，1つの出来事が別の出来事に引き続いて起こったことを表します。

- I **was walking** downtown when I **saw** Dave. So I **stopped**, and we **talked** for a while.

☆ 以下の例文が表す状況はどのように異なりますか？ ⇒ に注目して時を表す直線上で考えます。

- When Karen arrived, we **were having** dinner.（⇒ 到着する前に夕食は始まっていた）
- When Karen arrived, we **had** dinner.（⇒ 到着してから夕食を始めた）

E

know や **want** のような動詞は，過去に進行中であっても普通，**進行形**にはしません。
普通，進行形にしない動詞のリスト ➲ Unit 4A

- We were good friends. We **knew** each other well.（✕ We were knowing）
- I was having a good time at the party, but Chris **wanted** to go home.（✕ was wanting）

Exercises

6.1 指示されているそれぞれの時間にあなたは何をしていましたか？ 自分自身のことで答えなさい。ただし 2 番目のように，必ずしも過去進行形を使う必要はありません。

1. (at 8:00 last night) *I was having dinner.*
2. (at 5:00 last Monday) *I was on a bus on my way home.*
3. (at 10:15 yesterday morning) ______
4. (at 4:30 this morning) ______
5. (at 7:45 last night) ______
6. (half an hour ago) ______

6.2 過去進行形を用いて，自分なりに文を完成しなさい。

1. Matt burned his hand while he *was cooking dinner* .
2. The doorbell rang while I ______ .
3. We saw an accident while we ______ .
4. Lauren fell asleep while she ______ .
5. The television was on, but nobody ______ .

6.3 ( ) 内の動詞を過去進行形もしくは単純過去形の適切な形にして，文章を完成しなさい。

1\. I *saw* (see) Sue in town yesterday, but she ______ (not / see) me. She ______ (look) the other way.

2\. I ______ (meet) Tom and Jane at the airport a few weeks ago. They ______ (go) to Boston and I ______ (go) to Montreal. We ______ (talk) while we ______ (wait) for our flights.

3\. I ______ (ride) my bicycle yesterday when a man ______ (step) out into the street in front of me. I ______ (go) pretty fast, but luckily I ______ (manage) to stop in time and ______ (not / hit) him.

6.4 ( ) 内の動詞を過去進行形もしくは単純過去形の適切な形にして，文を完成しなさい。

1. Jane *was aiting* (wait) for me when I *arrived* (arrive).
2. "What ______ (you / do) at this time yesterday?" "I was asleep."
3. " ______ (you / go) out last night?" "No, I was too tired."
4. How fast ______ (you / drive) when the accident ______ (happen)?
5. Sam ______ (take) a picture of me while I ______ (not / look).
6. We were in a very difficult position. We ______ (not / know) what to do.
7. I haven't seen David for ages. The last time I ______ (see) him, he ______ (try) to find a job in Miami.
8. I ______ (walk) along the street when suddenly I ______ (hear) footsteps behind me. Somebody ______ (follow) me. I was scared and I ______ (start) to run.
9. When I was young, I ______ (want) to be a pilot.
10. Last night I ______ (drop) a plate while I ______ (do) the dishes. Fortunately it ______ (not / break).

補充問題 1 (p. 296)

UNIT 7

現在完了形 (I have done)

A

☆ 次の対話の状況について考えなさい。どのような形の動詞が使われていますか？

Dave: **Have** you **traveled** a lot, Jane?
Jane: Yes, **I've been** to lots of places.
Dave: Really? **Have** you ever **been** to China?
Jane: Yes, **I've been** to China twice.
Dave: What about India?
Jane: No, I **haven't been** to India.

現在までの Janeの人生

過去　現在

➤ **have/has + traveled/been/done（過去分詞）などの形は現在完了形と呼ばれます。**

I/we/they/you **have** (= **I've**など)	**traveled** **been** **done** など
he/she/it **has** (= he**'s**など)	

過去分詞は travel**ed**/decid**ed** などのように，その多くは動詞の語尾に **-ed** を付加して作ります。しかし，日常重要な動詞の多くは **been/done/written** などのように，不規則に作られます。

不規則動詞一覧 ➲ 付録 1

B

「今までに…したことがある」のように，過去から始まり，現在まで継続している期間について話題とする場合に**現在完了形**を用います。上の **A** の対話では，Jane が現在までの彼女の人生（⇒ 過去から始まり，現在まで継続した期間）で訪問したことのある場所についての話をしています。以下の例文でも同様の期間を表します。

- **Have** you ever **eaten** caviar?〔これまでのあなたの人生において〕
- We**'ve** never **had** a car.
- "**Have** you **read** *Hamlet*?"　"No, I **haven't read** any of Shakespeare's plays."
- Susan really loves that movie. She**'s seen** it eight times!
- What a boring movie! It's the most boring movie **I've** ever **seen**.

C

recently / **in the last few days** / **so far** / **since breakfast** などの語句とともに，「…から今まで」のように過去から始まり，現在まで継続している期間を話題にする場合も**現在完了形**を用います。

- **Have** you **heard** from Brian **recently**?
- **I've met** a lot of people **in the last few days**.
- Everything is going well. We **haven't had** any problems **so far**.
- I'm hungry. I **haven't eaten** anything **since breakfast**.
- It's nice to see you again. We **haven't seen** each other **for a long time**.

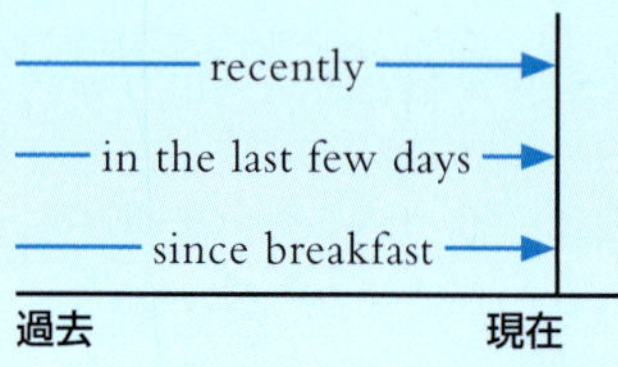

D

today / **this morning** / **this year** などの語句は，それぞれが意味する期間が発話時にまだ終わっていない場合に**現在完了形**とともに用います。

- **I've drunk** four cups of coffee **today**.
- **Have** you **had** a vacation **this year** (yet)?
- I **haven't seen** Tom **this morning**. **Have** you?
- Rob **hasn't studied** very hard **this semester**.

today

過去　現在

E

It's the (first) time ~ has done の形で，「…したのは(1)回目」を表します。

- Don is taking a driving lesson. It's his first one. It's the first time he **has driven** a car. (✕ drives)
- = He **has never driven** a car **before**.
- Sarah has lost her passport again. This is the second time this **has happened**. (✕ happens)
- Bill is calling his girlfriend again. That's the third time he**'s called** her **tonight**.

This is the first time **I've driven** a car.

現在完了形と過去形の違い ➲ Units 8–9　現在完了進行形 ➲ Units 10–11

Exercises

7.1 ( ) 内の語句と ever を用いて，今までの人生においてしたことがあるかどうかを尋ねる疑問文を作りなさい。

1. (ride / horse?) *Have you ever ridden a horse?*
2. (be / Mexico?) Have ______
3. (run / marathon?) ______
4. (speak / famous person?) ______
5. (most beautiful place / visit?) What's ______

7.2 以下の動詞を肯定または否定の適切な形に変えて，A の質問に対する B の答えの文を完成しなさい。

be be eat happen have ~~meet~~ play read see see try

	A	B
1.	What's Mark's sister like?	I have no idea. *I've never met* her.
2.	How is Diane these days?	I don't know. I ______ her recently.
3.	Are you hungry?	Yes. I ______ much today.
4.	Can you play chess?	Yes, but ______ in ages.
5.	Are you enjoying your vacation?	Yes, it's the best vacation ______ for a long time.
6.	What's that book like?	I don't know. ______ it.
7.	Is Sydney an interesting place?	I have no idea. ______ there.
8.	Mike was late for work again today.	Again? He ______ late every day this week.
9.	Do you like caviar?	I don't know. ______ it.
10.	I hear your car broke down again yesterday.	Yes, it's the second time ______ this week.
11.	Who's that woman by the door?	I don't know. ______ her before.

7.3 today / this year / this semester などの語句を用いて，文を完成しなさい。

1. I saw Tom yesterday, but *I haven't seen him today* .
2. I read a newspaper yesterday, but I ______ today.
3. Last year the company made a profit, but this year ______ .
4. Tracy worked hard at school last semester, but ______ .
5. It snowed a lot last winter, but ______ .
6. Our football team won a lot of games last season, but we ______ .

7.4 例にならい，状況を把握したうえで適切な語句を用いて文を完成しなさい。

1. Jack is driving a car, but he's very nervous and not sure what to do.
   You ask: *Have you driven a car before?*
   He says: *No, this is the first time I've driven a car.*
2. Ben is playing tennis. He's not good at it, and he doesn't know the rules.
   You ask: Have ______
   He says: No, this is the first ______
3. Sue is riding a horse. She doesn't look very confident or comfortable.
   You ask: ______
   She says: ______
4. Maria is in Los Angeles. She has just arrived, and it's very new for her.
   You ask: ______
   She says: ______

UNIT 8

現在完了形と過去形* 1 (I have done と I did)

A

「最近〔たった今〕…した」のように，今までではなく最近起こった出来事は**現在完了形** (I **have done**) で表します。

- **I've lost** my keys. **Have** you **seen** them?
- "Is Sally here?" "No, she**'s gone** out."
- The police **have arrested** two people in connection with the robbery.

同じことは**単純過去形** (I **lost** ..., she **went** ... など) でも表せます。

- I **lost** my keys. **Did** you **see** them?
- "Is Sally here?" "No, she **went** out."
- The police **arrested** two people in connection with the robbery.

B

新しく話題にする出来事は，**現在完了形** (I **have done**) もしくは**単純過去形** (I **did**) で導入します。

- Have you heard? Bill and Sarah **have won** the lottery!
  (= Bill and Sarah **won** . . .)
- The road is closed. There**'s been** (there **has been**) an accident.
  (= There **was** an accident)

最近起こったとは考えられない過去の出来事には，**単純過去形**しか使えません。

- Mozart **was** a composer. He **wrote** more than 600 pieces of music.
  (× has been . . . has written)
- My mother **grew** up in Chile. (× has grown)

☆ 単純過去形と現在完了形は，どのように異なりますか？

- Shakespeare **wrote** many plays.
- My brother is a writer. He **has written** many books. (⇒ 今も本を書いている)

C

現在完了形は，現在と何らかのつながりがあります。

- I'm sorry, but **I've forgotten** your name. (⇒ 今も思い出せない)
- Sally isn't here. She**'s gone** out. (⇒ 今も外出中)
- I can't find my bag. **Have** you **seen** it? (⇒ 今どこにあるのか知っていますか？)

上の例文では，いずれも**単純過去形**（I **forgot** your name. など）も用いることができます。
過去と現在で状況が異なる場合には，**単純過去形**のみを用い，**現在完了形**は用いません。

☆ 現在完了形と単純過去形は，どのように異なりますか？

- It **has stopped** raining, so you don't need the umbrella. (⇒ 今も止んでいる)
  It **stopped** raining for a while, but now it's raining again. (⇒ 今は止んでいない)

D

just, **already**, **yet** といった語は，**現在進行形**と**単純過去形**の両方とともによく用います。

just :「たった今，ほんの少し前に」

- *A:* Are you hungry?
  B: No, I **just had** lunch = **I've just had** lunch.
- *A:* Why are you so happy?
  B: I **just heard** some good news. = **I've just heard** some good news.

already :「もう，すでに〔予想よりも早く出来事が起きた〕」

- *A:* Don't forget to mail the letter.
  B: I **already mailed** it. = **I've already mailed** it.
- *A:* What time is Mark leaving?
  B: He **already left**. = He**'s already left**.

yet :「もう…したか？（**疑問文**）／まだ … していない（**否定文**）」
〔話し手は出来事が起きることを期待している。疑問文と否定文においてのみ用いられる〕

- **Did** it **stop** raining **yet**? = **Has** it **stopped** raining **yet**?
- I wrote the letter, but I **didn't mail** it **yet**. = . . . I **haven't mailed** it **yet**.

* 通常「過去形」とは「単純過去形」と「過去進行形」の 2 つの形について言及しますが，この Unit 8 では「単純過去形」の例文しか現われません。

単純過去形 ➲ Unit 5 現在完了形 ➲ Unit 7 現在完了形と過去形 2 ➲ Unit 9 イギリス英語の用法 ➲ 付録 7

Exercises

8.1 (　) 内の動詞を適切な形に変えて，文を完成しなさい。過去形にしなければ文法的に誤りとなる場合を除き，可能な限り現在完了を用いること。

1. It _has stopped_ (stop) raining, so you don't need your umbrella.
2. *before* *now* The town is very different now. It ________ (change) a lot.
3. I meant to call you last night, but I ________. (forget).
4. Mary ________ (go) to Peru for a vacation, but she's back home in Austin now.
5. Are you OK? Yes. I ________ (have) a headache, but I feel fine now.
6. You look great! You ________ (lost) weight.

8.2 文法的に正しい文は **a)** ですか，**b)** ですか？　あるいはその両方ですか？

1. a) My mother has grown up in Chile. b) My mother grew up in Chile. _b_
2. a) Did you see my purse? b) Have you seen my purse? _両方正しい_
3. a) I already paid the gas bill. b) I've already paid the gas bill. ________
4. a) The Chinese invented paper. b) The Chinese have invented paper. ________
5. a) Where have you been born? b) Where were you born? ________
6. a) Ow! I cut my finger. b) Ow! I've cut my finger. ________
7. a) I forgot Jerry's address. b) I've forgotten Jerry's address. ________
8. a) Did you go to the store yet? b) Have you gone to the store yet? ________
9. a) Albert Einstein has been the scientist who has developed the theory of relativity. b) Albert Einstein was the scientist who developed the theory of relativity. ________
10. a) My father was raised by his aunt. b) My father has been raised by his aunt. ________

8.3 全体の状況をよく読み，現在完了形もしくは単純過去形と **just**，**already**，**yet** を用いて適切な文を作りなさい。

1. After lunch you go to see a friend at her house. She says, "Would you like something to eat?" You say: No, thank you. _I've just had lunch_ OR _I just had lunch_. (have lunch)
2. Joe goes out. Five minutes later, the phone rings and the caller says, "Can I speak to Joe?" You say: I'm sorry, ________. (go out)
3. You are eating in a restaurant. The waiter thinks you have finished and starts to clear the table. You say: Wait a minute! ________. (not / finish)
4. You are going to a restaurant tonight. You call to reserve a table. Later your friend says, "Should I call to reserve a table?" You say: No, ________. (do it)
5. You know that a friend of yours is looking for a place to live. Perhaps she has been successful. Ask her. You say: ________? (find)
6. You are still thinking about where to go on vacation. A friend asks, "Where are you going on vacation?" You say: ________. (not / decide)
7. Linda went to the bank, but a few minutes ago she returned. Somebody asks, "Is Linda still at the bank?" You say: No, ________. (come back)
8. Yesterday Carol invited you to a party on Saturday. Now another friend is inviting you to the same party. You say: Thanks, but Carol ________. (invite)

UNIT 9

現在完了形と過去形* 2 (I have done と I did)

A

yesterday / 10 minutes ago / in 1999 / when I was a child のように，現在と関連のない過去の時を指定する語句とともに**現在完了形** (I **have done**) を用いることはできません。**過去形**を用います。

- It **was** very cold **yesterday**. (× has been)
- Paul and Lucy **went** out **10 minutes ago**. (× have gone)
- **Did** you **eat** a lot of candy **when you were a child**? (× have you eaten)
- I **got** home late **last night**. I **was** very tired and **went** straight to bed.

When ...? や **What time ...?** のように，「いつ…しましたか？」と尋ねる時も**単純過去形**を用います。

- **When did** your friends **get** here? (× have . . . gotten)
- **What time did** you **finish** work?

☆ 動詞が表す出来事は左右の例文で，どのように異なりますか？

➤ 現在完了形と単純過去形が同じように使える	➤ 単純過去形しか使えない
■ Tom **has lost** his key. He can't get into the house. (= Tom **lost** . . .)	■ Tom **lost** his key **yesterday**. He couldn't get into the house.
■ Is Carla here or **has** she **left**? (= **Did** she **leave**?)〔最近の出来事〕	■ **When did** Carla **leave**?〔現在と関連しない過去の出来事〕

B

☆ 例文と下の図で考えます。現在完了形と単純過去形は，それぞれどのような期間で用いますか？

現在完了形 (I have done)

- I**'ve done** a lot of work **today**.

➤ 現在完了形は today / this week / since 1999 などのように，現在まで継続し，まだ終わっていない期間に関して用います。

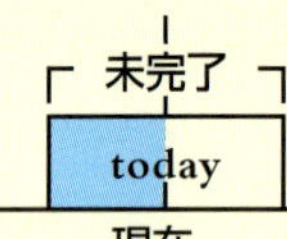

- It **hasn't rained this week**.
- **Have** you **seen** Lisa **this morning**? (⇒ 今はまだ午前中)
- **Have** you **seen** Tim **recently**?
- I don't know where Lisa is. I **haven't seen** her. (⇒ 最近会っていない)
- We**'ve been waiting for an hour**. (⇒ まだ待ち続けている)
- John lives in Los Angeles. He **has lived** there **for seven years**.
- I **have never played golf**. (⇒ 今まで)
- 〔長期休暇の最終日に〕 It's been a really good vacation. I**'ve** really **enjoyed** it.

単純過去形 (I did)

- I **did** a lot of work **yesterday**.

➤ 単純過去形は yesterday / last week / from1999 to 2005 などのように，過去において完了した期間に関して用います。

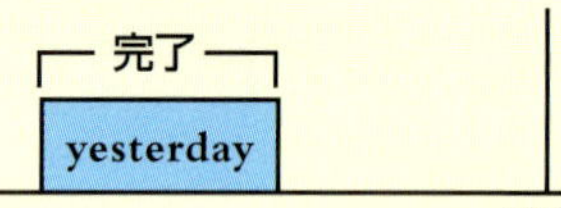

- It **didn't rain last week**.
- **Did** you **see** Lisa **this morning**? (⇒ もう午前中は終わった)
- **Did** you **see** Tim **on Sunday**?
- *A:* **Was** Lisa at the party **on Sunday**? *B:* I don't think so. I **didn't see** her.
- We **waited** (= **were waiting**) **for an hour**. (⇒ もう待っていない)
- John **lived** in New York **for 10 years**. Now he lives in Los Angeles.
- I **didn't play** golf **last summer**.
- 〔長期休暇が終わり職場に戻って〕 It **was** a really good vacation. I really **enjoyed** it.

* ここでは「過去形」の「単純過去形」と「過去進行形」の 2 つの形について言及します。➲ Unit 8

単純過去形 ➲ Unit 5　現在完了形 ➲ Unit 7　現在完了形と過去形 1 ➲ Unit 8　現在完了進行形 ➲ Units 10–11

Exercises

9.1 下線部について文法的に正しいかどうかを答え，誤りがあれば正しい形に変えなさい。

1. I've lost my key. I can't find it anywhere. — *OK*
2. Have you eaten a lot of candy when you were a child? — *Did you eat*
3. I've bought a new car. You have to come and see it. ______
4. I've bought a new car last week. ______
5. Where have you been last night? ______
6. Maria has graduated from high school in 2004. ______
7. I'm looking for Mike. Have you seen him? ______
8. "Have you been to Paris?" "Yes, many times." ______
9. I'm very hungry. I haven't eaten much today. ______
10. When has this book been published? ______

9.2 (　) 内の語句を用いて，動詞を現在完了形もしくは単純過去形の適切な形にして文を完成しなさい。

1. (it / not / rain / this week) *It hasn't rained this week.*
2. (the weather / be / cold / recently) The weather ______
3. (it / cold / last week) It ______
4. (I / not / read / a newspaper yesterday) I ______
5. (I / not / read / a newspaper today) ______
6. (Kate / make / a lot of money / this year) ______
7. (she / not / make / so much / last year) ______
8. (you / take / a vacation recently?) ______

9.3 (　) 内の動詞を現在完了形もしくは単純過去形の適切な形にして，文を完成しなさい。

1. I don't know where Lisa is. *Have you seen* (you / see) her?
2. When I ______ (get) home last night, I ______ (be) very tired, so I ______ (go) straight to bed.
3. *A:* ______ (you / eat) at the new sushi place on Joe's birthday?
   B: No, but ______ (we / be) there twice this month.
4. There was a bus drivers' strike last week. There ______ (not / be) any buses.
5. Mr. Lee ______ (work) in a bank for 15 years. Then he quit.
6. Kelly lives in Toronto. She ______ (live) there all her life.
7. *A:* ______ (you / go) to the movies last night?
   B: Yes, but it ______ (be) a mistake. The movie ______ (be) awful.
8. My grandfather ______ (die) before I was born. I ______ (never / meet) him.
9. I don't know Karen's husband. I ______ (never / meet) him.
10. It's nearly lunchtime, and I ______ (not / see) Martin all morning. I wonder where he is.
11. *A:* Where do you live?
    B: In Rio de Janeiro.
    A: How long ______ (you / live) there?
    B: Five years.
    A: Where ______ (you / live) before that?
    B: In Buenos Aires.
    A: And how long ______ (you / live) there?
    B: Two years.

9.4 (　) 内の指示通りに，自分自身のことを記述しなさい。

1. (something you haven't done today) *I haven't eaten any fruit today.*
2. (something you haven't done today) ______
3. (something you didn't do yesterday) ______
4. (something you did last night) ______
5. (something you haven't done recently) ______
6. (something you've done a lot recently) ______

補充問題 2–4 (pp. 297–298) / 14–15 (pp. 304–305)

UNIT 10

現在完了進行形 (I have been doing)

A

It has been raining.

☆ イラストの状況について考えなさい。どのような形の動詞が使われていますか？ 今はどうなっていますか？

Is it raining?（まだ雨が降っていますか？）
No, but the ground is wet.（いいえ，でも地面はぬれています）

It **has been raining**.（雨がずっと降っていました）

➤ **have/has been -ing の形は現在完了進行形と呼ばれます。雨は少し前にやんでいます。今は降っていません。**

I/we/they/you	**have**	(= I**'ve** など)	**been**	do**ing**
he/she/it	**has**	(= he**'s** など)		wait**ing** play**ing** など

「少し前まで…していた」のように，最近やほんの少し前に終わった出来事には**現在完了進行形**を用います。**現在完了進行形**には，常に現在とのつながりがあります。

- You're out of breath. **Have** you **been running**?（⇒ 今，息を切らしていることからわかる）
- Jason is very tired. He**'s been working** very hard.（⇒ 今，疲れていることからわかる）
- Why are your clothes so dirty? What **have** you **been doing**?
- 〔電話で〕I'm glad you called. I**'ve been thinking** about calling you . . .
- Where have you been? I**'ve been looking** everywhere for you.

B

It has been raining for two hours.

☆ イラストの状況について考えなさい。今はどうなっていますか？

➤ **2 時間前から雨が降り始めて，今も降り続いています。**

How long **has** it **been raining**?
It **has been raining** for two hours.

現在完了進行形は，**how long ...**，**for ...**，**since ...** といった表現とともによく用います。出来事は「ずっと…し続けて，今も…している」のように，まだ続いている場合もあれば，ちょうど今，終わった場合もあります。

- **How long have** you **been studying** English?（⇒ まだ勉強は続いている）
- Tim is still watching television. He**'s been watching** television **all day**.
- Where have you been? I**'ve been looking** for you **for the last half hour**.
- Christopher **hasn't been feeling** well **recently**.

現在完了進行形は「今まで（何度も）…してきた」のように，一定の期間の間に繰り返される動作を表します。

- Debbie is a very good tennis player. She**'s been playing since she was eight**.
- Every morning they meet in the same café. They**'ve been going** there **for years**.

C

☆ **I am doing の現在進行形（➲Unit 1）と I have been doing の現在完了進行形は，どのように異なりますか？**

➤ **現在を中心に少し前から始まり，まだ終わっていない**

I am doing
現在進行形
現在

- Don't bother me now. I**'m working**.
- We need an umbrella. It**'s raining**.
- Hurry up! We**'re waiting**.

➤ **現在まで続いている / 現在の少し前に終わった**

I have been doing
現在完了進行形
現在

- I**'ve been working** hard. Now I'm going to take a break.
- The ground is wet. It**'s been raining**.
- We**'ve been waiting** for an hour.

単純現在完了形と現在完了進行形の違い ➲ Units 11–12　　for/since と現在完了形 ➲ Units 12–13

Exercises

10.1 イラストの人物がしていた活動や，イラストの状況について現在完了進行形を用いて記述しなさい。

1. *earlier* *now*
They *'ve been shopping.* ________

2. *earlier* *now*
She ________

3. *earlier* *now*
They ________

4. *earlier* *now*
He ________

10.2 （　）内の語句を用いて，それぞれの状況について質問する疑問文を作りなさい。

1. You meet Paul as he is leaving the swimming pool.
You ask: (you / swim?) *Have you been swimming?*
2. You have just arrived to meet a friend who is waiting for you.
You ask: (you / wait / long?) ________
3. You meet a friend at the store. His face and hands are very dirty.
You ask: (what / you / do?) ________
4. A friend of yours is now working at a gym. You want to know how long.
You ask: (how long / you / work / there?) ________
5. A friend tells you about his job – he sells computers. You want to know how long.
You ask: (how long / you / sell / computers?) ________

10.3 それぞれの状況を説明する文を完成しなさい。

1. It's raining. The rain started two hours ago.
It *'s been raining* for two hours.
2. We are waiting for the bus. We got to the bus stop 20 minutes ago.
We ________ for 20 minutes.
3. I'm studying Spanish. I started classes in December.
I ________ since December.
4. Jessica is working in Tokyo. She started working there on January 18.
________ since January 18.
5. Our friends always spend their summers in the mountains. They started going there years ago. ________ for years.

10.4 （　）内の動詞を現在進行形もしくは現在完了進行形の適切な形にして，文を完成しなさい。

1. *Maria has been studying* (Maria / study) English for two years.
2. Hello, Tom. ________ (I / look) for you all morning. Where have you been?
3. Why ________ (you / look) at me like that? Stop it!
4. Linda is a teacher. ________ (she / teach) for 10 years.
5. ________ (I / think) about what you said, and I've decided to take your advice.
6. "Is Kim on vacation this week?" "No, ________ (she / work)."
7. Sarah is very tired. ________ (she / work) very hard recently.

UNIT 11

現在完了進行形と単純現在完了形 (I have been doing と I have done)

A

☆ イラストの状況について考えなさい。どのような形の動詞が使われていますか？

Lingの服にはペンキがついています。

She **has been painting** the ceiling.

➤ **has been painting の形は現在完了進行形と呼ばれます。**

現在完了進行形では「ずっと…し続けてきた」のように，活動そのものが話題の中心になっています。何かが完了したかどうかは重要ではありません。Lingはまだペンキを塗り終えていません。

以前白かった天井は，今，すべて赤くなりました。

She **has painted** the ceiling.

➤ **has painted の形は単純現在完了形と呼ばれます。**

単純現在完了形では「…し終えた」のように，活動が終わったことが重要になります。Lingはペンキを塗り終えました。その結果，今，天井は余すところなく赤くなりました。活動が完了した結果が話題の中心となっていて，活動そのものは重要ではありません。

☆ 例文が表す状況は，現在完了進行形と現在完了形でどのように異なりますか？

現在完了進行形

- My hands are very dirty. **I've been fixing** the car.
- Joe **has been eating** too much recently. He should eat less.
- It's nice to see you again. What **have** you **been doing** since the last time we saw you?
- Where have you been? **Have** you **been playing** tennis?

単純現在完了形

- The car is OK again now. **I've fixed** it.
- Somebody **has eaten** all my candy. The box is empty.
- Where's the book I gave you? What **have** you **done** with it?
- **Have** you ever **played** tennis?

B

進行中の動作について，**How long …?**を用いて期間を質問したり答えたりする際には，**現在完了進行形**を用います。

- How long **have** you **been reading** that book?
- Lisa is still writing her report. She**'s been writing** it **all day**.
- They**'ve been playing** tennis **since 2:00**.
- I'm studying Spanish, but I **haven't been studying** it very long.

完了した動作について，**How much …?**, **How many …?**, **How many times …?**を用いて量や個数や回数を質問したり答えたりする際には，**単純現在完了形**を用います。

- How much of that book **have** you **read**?
- Lisa **has written** 10 pages today.
- They**'ve played** tennis three times this week.
- I'm studying Spanish, but I **haven't learned** very much yet.

C

know/like/believe といった動詞は，期間について話題にする場合でも普通，進行形にはしません。

- **I've known** about it for a long time. (✕ I've been knowing) ➲ Unit 4A

普通は進行形にしない **want** と **mean** は，**現在完了進行形**で用いられることがあります。

- **I've been meaning** to phone Pat, but I keep forgetting.

単純現在完了形 ➲ Units 7–8　現在完了進行形 ➲ Unit 10　for/since と現在完了形 ➲ Units 12–13

Exercises

11.1 例にならい（　）内の語句を用いて，状況を説明する文を 2 通り作りなさい。

1. Luis started reading a book two hours ago. He is still reading it, and now he is on page 53.
(read / for two hours) _He has been reading for two hours._
(read / 53 pages so far) _He has read 53 pages so far._
2. Min is from Korea. She is traveling around Asia right now. She began her trip three months ago.
(travel / for three months) She ______________________
(visit / six countries so far) ______________________
3. Jimmy is a tennis player. He began playing tennis when he was 10 years old. This year he is national champion again – for the fourth time.
(win / the national championships / four times) ______________________
(play / tennis since he was 10) ______________________
4. When they graduated from college, Lisa and Amy started making movies together. They still make movies.
(make / five movies since they finished college) They ______________________
____
(make / movies since they finished college) ______________________
____

11.2 （　）内の語句を用いて，状況について質問する疑問文を作りなさい。

1. You have a friend who is studying Arabic. You ask:
(how long / study / Arabic?) _How long have you been studying Arabic?_
2. You have just arrived to meet a friend. She is waiting for you. You ask:
(wait / long?) Have ______________________
3. You see somebody fishing by the river. You ask:
(catch / any fish?) ______________________
4. Some friends of yours are having a party next week. You ask:
(how many people / invite?) ______________________
5. A friend of yours is a teacher. You ask:
(how long / teach?) ______________________
6. You meet somebody who is a writer. You ask:
(how many books / write?) ______________________
(how long / write / books?) ______________________
7. A friend of yours is saving money to take a trip. You ask:
(how long / save?) ______________________
(how much money / save?) ______________________

11.3 （　）内の語句を単純現在完了形もしくは現在完了進行形に変えて，文を完成しなさい。

1. Where have you been? _Have you been playing_ (you / play) tennis?
2. Look! ______________ (somebody / break) that window.
3. You look tired. ______________ (you / work) hard?
4. " ______________ (you / ever / work) in a factory?" "No, never."
5. 〔電話で〕"Hi, is Sam there?" "No, he ______________ (go) for a run."
6. My brother is an actor. ______________ (he / appear) in several films.
7. "Sorry I'm late." "That's all right. ______________ (I / not / wait) long."
8. "Is it still raining?" "No, ______________ (it / stop)."
9. ______________ (I / lose) my cell phone. ______________ (you / see) it anywhere?
10. ______________ (I / read) the book you lent me, but ______________ (I / not / finish) it yet. It's very interesting.
11. ______________ (I / read) the book you lent me, so you can have it back now.

UNIT 12

How long have you (been) ...?

A

☆ イラストの状況について考えなさい。どのような形の動詞が使われていますか？

Bob と Alice は結婚しています。ふたりはちょうど 20 年前に結婚しました。今日がふたりの 20 回目の結婚記念日です。この現在の状況は，以下のように**現在完了形**と**単純現在形**を用いて表現できます。

They **have been** married for **20 years**.（現在完了形）

They are married.（単純現在形）

How long have they **been** married?（現在完了形）
(✕ How long are they married?)

They **have been** married for **20 years**.（現在完了形）
(✕ They are married for 20 years)

➤ 現在完了形は，「ずっと…し続けてきた」のように，過去に始まり現在時まで継続している出来事を表します。ことに how long，for，since といった期間を表す語句とともに現在完了形を用います。

☆ 以下の例文において，現在形* と現在完了形はどのように異なりますか？ 時を表す直線上で考えます。

■ Bill is in the hospital.
⇔ He **has been** in the hospital **since Monday**.
(✕ Bill is in the hospital since Monday)

■ **Do** you **know** each other well?
⇔ **Have** you **known** each other **for a long time**?
(✕ Do you know)

■ She'**s waiting** for somebody.
⇔ She'**s been waiting all morning**.

■ **Do** they **have** a car?
⇔ **How long have** they **had** their car?

過去形 ——— 現在形
現在完了形
現在

B

現在完了形には，I **have known/had/lived** などの**単純現在完了形**と I **have been learning** / **been waiting** / **been doing** などの**現在完了進行形**があります。**How long ...?** のように期間を質問したり答えたりする場合には，**単純現在完了形**よりも**現在完了進行形**の方がよく用いられます。➲ Unit 10

■ **I've been studying** English **for six months**.
■ **It's been raining since lunchtime**.
■ Richard **has been doing** the same job **for 20 years**.
■ "**How long have** you **been driving**?" "Since I was 17."

know/like/believe のような動詞は期間について話題にしている場合でも，**現在完了進行形**にはなりません。

■ How long **have** you **known** Emily? (✕ have you been knowing)
■ **I've had** a stomachache all day. (✕ I've been having)

普通，進行形にしない動詞 ➲ Unit 4A　現在完了進行形 ➲ Unit 10C　動詞 have の用法 ➲ Unit 16A

C

live や **work** のような動詞は，**現在完了進行形**でも**単純現在完了形**でも同じように用います。

■ John **has been living** / **has lived** in Montreal for a long time.
■ How long **have** you **been working** / **have** you **worked** here?

しかし，動詞に **live** や **work** を使っても，**always** が現れると**単純現在完了形**のみ用います。

■ **Have** you **always lived** in the country? (✕ always been living)

D

I haven't done ~ since/for ... のような**単純現在完了形**をよく用います。単純過去形との対比に注意。

■ I **haven't seen** Tom **since** Monday. (⇒ Monday was the last time I saw him)
■ Sue **hasn't called for** ages. (⇒ The last time she called was ages ago)

*「現在形」とは，「単純現在形」と「現在進行形」の 2 つの形について言及します。

I haven't done ~ since/for ... ➲ Unit 7C　現在完了進行形 ➲ Units 10–11　for と since の用法 ➲ Unit 13

Exercises

12.1 下線部について文法的に正しいかどうかを答えなさい。誤りがあれば訂正しなさい。

1. Bob is a friend of mine. <u>I know him</u> very well. ___*OK*___
2. Bob is a friend of mine. <u>I know him</u> for a long time. ___*I've known him*___
3. Sue and Scott <u>are married</u> since July. ______
4. The weather is awful. <u>It's raining</u> again. ______
5. The weather is awful. <u>It's raining</u> all day. ______
6. I like your house. How long <u>are you living</u> there? ______
7. Gary <u>is working</u> in a store for the last few months. ______
8. <u>I don't know</u> Tim well. We've only met a few times. ______
9. I quit drinking coffee. I <u>don't drink</u> it for a year. ______
10. That's a very old bike. How long <u>do you have</u> it? ______

12.2 (　)内の語句を用いて，状況について質問する疑問文を作りなさい。

1. John tells you that his mother is in the hospital. You ask him:
(how long / be / in the hospital?) ___*How long has your mother been in the hospital?*___
2. You meet a woman who tells you that she teaches English. You ask her:
(how long / teach / English?) ______
3. You know that Erica is a good friend of Carol's. You ask Erica:
(how long / know / Carol?) ______
4. Your friend's brother moved to Costa Rica a while ago. You ask your friend:
(how long / be / in Costa Rica?) ______
5. Chris drives a very old car. You ask him:
(how long / have / that car?) ______
6. You are talking to a friend about Scott. Scott now works at the airport. You ask your friend:
(how long / work / at the airport?) ______
7. A friend of yours is taking guitar lessons. You ask him:
(how long / take / guitar lessons?) ______
8. You meet somebody on a plane. She says that she lives in Chicago. You ask her:
(always / live / in Chicago?) ______

12.3 A の質問に対する B の答えを完成しなさい。

	A	B
1.	Amy is in the hospital, isn't she?	Yes, she ___*has been*___ in the hospital since Monday.
2.	Do you see Ann very often?	No, I ___*haven't seen*___ her for three months.
3.	Is Margaret married?	Yes, she ______ married for 10 years.
4.	Are you waiting for me?	Yes, I ______ for the last half hour.
5.	You know Linda, don't you?	Yes, we ______ each other a long time.
6.	Do you still play tennis?	No, I ______ tennis for years.
7.	Is Jim watching TV?	Yes, he ______ TV all night.
8.	Do you watch TV a lot?	No, I ______ TV for ages.
9.	Do you have a headache?	Yes, I ______ a headache all morning.
10.	George is never sick, is he?	No, he ______ sick since I met him.
11.	Are you feeling sick?	Yes, I ______ sick all day.
12.	Sue lives in Miami, doesn't she?	Yes, she ______ in Miami for the last few years.
13.	Do you go to the movies a lot?	No, I ______ to the movies for ages.
14.	Would you like to go to Taiwan one day?	Yes, I ______ to go to Taiwan. (*use* **always / want**)

UNIT 13

for と since
When ...? と How long ...?

A

☆ for も since も，ともに出来事がある期間継続していることを表します。それぞれどのように異なりますか？

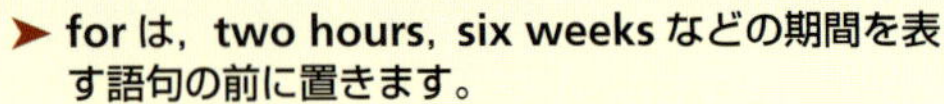

➤ for は，two hours，six weeks などの期間を表す語句の前に置きます。

■ I've been waiting **for two hours**.

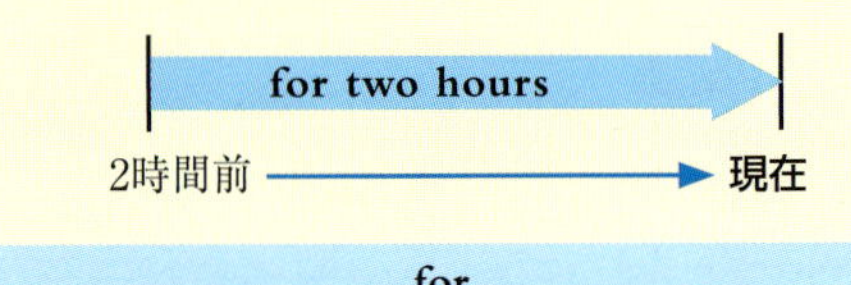

	for	
two hours	a long time	a week
20 minutes	six months	ages
five days	50 years	years

■ Kelly has been working here **for six months**. (× since six months)

■ I haven't seen Tom **for three days**.

➤ since は，8:00，Monday，1999 などの期間の始まりを表す語句の前に置きます。

■ I've been waiting since **8:00**.

	since	
8:00	April	lunchtime
Monday	1985	we arrived
May 12	Christmas	yesterday

■ Kelly has been working here **since April**. (= from April until now)

■ I haven't seen Tom **since Monday**.

前置詞 for は省略できます。**否定文**中では **for** は省略できません。

■ They've been married (**for**) **10 years**.（for は省略可能）

■ They **haven't had** a vacation **for 10 years.**（for は省略できません）

all day，**all my life** などのように，**all** で始まる**名詞句**の前には **for** は置けません。

■ I've lived here **all my life**. (× for all my life)

否定文では **for** の代わりに **in** を使うこともできます。

■ They **haven't had** a vacation **in 10 years**.

B

以下のイラストの状況は，**When ...**（**＋単純過去形**）**?** と **How long ...**（**＋現在完了形**）**?** の 2 通りで表現できます。

A: **When** did it start raining?
B: It started raining **an hour ago** / **at 1:00**.

A: **How long** has it been raining?
B: It's been raining **for an hour** / **since 1:00**.

A: **When** did Joe and Carol first meet?
B: They first met { a long time **ago**. / **when** they were in high school.

A: **How long** have they **known** each other?
B: They**'ve known** each other { **for** a long time. / **since** they were in high school.

C

It's (= It has) **been a long time** / **two years since ～ did** は「～してから…経過した」を表します。**for** を用いた文との対比に注意。

■ **It's been two years since** I saw Joe. (⇒ I **haven't seen** Joe for two years)

■ **It's been ages since** we went to the movies. (⇒ We **haven't gone** to the movies for ages)

出来事が起こってからの期間の長さは **How long has it been since ...?** で尋ねます。**when＋単純過去形**との対比に注意。

■ **How long has it been since** you saw Joe? (⇒ When did you last see Joe?)

■ **How long has it been since** Mrs. Hill died? (⇒ When did Mrs. Hill die?)

How long have you (been) ...? ➲ Unit 12

Exercises

13.1 空所に for もしくは since を入れて，文を完成しなさい。

1. It's been raining __since__ lunchtime.
2. Sarah has lived in Chicago ________ 1995.
3. Joe has lived in Dallas ________ 10 years.
4. I'm tired of waiting. We've been sitting here ________ an hour.
5. Kevin has been looking for a job ________ he graduated.
6. I haven't been to a party ________ ages.
7. I wonder how Joe is. I haven't seen him ________ last week.
8. Jane is away at college. She's been away ________ last August.
9. The weather is dry. It hasn't rained ________ a few weeks.

13.2 状況に合うように，How long ...? と When ...? の 2 通りの疑問文を作りなさい。

1. It's raining.
   (how long?) __How long has it been raining?__
   (when?) __When did it start raining?__
2. Kate is studying Japanese.
   (how long / study?) ________
   (when / start?) ________
3. I know Jeff.
   (how long / you / know?) ________
   (when / you / meet?) ________
4. Rebecca and David are married.
   (how long?) ________
   (when / get?) ________

13.3 状況に合うように，空所に適切な語句や表現を入れて文を完成しなさい。

1. It's raining. It's been raining since lunchtime. It __started raining__ at lunchtime.
2. Ann and Sue are friends. They met years ago. __They've been friends for__ years.
3. Mark is sick. He got sick on Sunday. He has ________ Sunday.
4. Mark is sick. He got sick a few days ago. He has ________ a few days.
5. Sarah is married. She's been married for a year. She got ________ .
6. You have a headache. It started when you woke up.
   I've ________ I woke up.
7. Megan has been in France for the last three weeks.
   She went ________ .
8. You're working in a hotel. You started six months ago.
   I've ________ .

13.4 (　) 内の語句を用いて，A に対する B の発言を完成しなさい。

1. *A:* Do you take vacations often?
   B: (no / five years) __No, I haven't taken a vacation for five years.__
2. *A:* Do you see Laura often?
   B: (no / about a month) ________
3. *A:* Do you go to the movies often?
   B: (no / a long time) ________
4. *A:* Do you eat out often?
   B: (no / ages) ________

上の B の発言を It's been 〜 since ... の形で書き換えなさい。

5. (1) __No, it's been five years since I took a vacation.__
6. (2) No, it's ________
7. (3) No, ________
8. (4) ________

UNIT 14 過去完了形 (I had done)

A

☆ イラストの状況について考えなさい。どのような形の動詞が使われていますか？

Sarah は先週パーティーに出かけました。Eric もパーティーに参加したのですが，ふたりは出会うことができませんでした。Eric は 10 時半に帰り，Sarah は 11 時に到着したからです。Sarah が到着した時，Eric はパーティー会場にはいませんでした。この状況は次のように表せます。

He **had gone** home.

➤ **had gone のような形は（単純）過去完了形と呼ばれます。**

I/we/they/you he/she/it	**had**	(= **I'd** など) (= he**'d** など)	**gone** **seen** **finished** など

過去完了形は **had + 過去分詞**（gone/seen/finished など）で作ります。
「…した」のように，過去において起こったことは**単純過去形**で表します。

- Sarah **got** to the party.

この過去の出来事が基準点となります。ここで，「すでに…していた」のように，基準点より以前の出来事は**過去完了形**（**had + 過去分詞**）で表します。

- When Sarah arrived at the party, Eric **had** already **gone** home.

以下の例においても**過去完了形**は，過去の基準となる出来事より前の出来事を表しています。

- When we got home last night, we found that somebody **had broken** into our house.
- Karen didn't want to go to the movies with us because she**'d** already **seen** the film.
- At first I thought **I'd done** the right thing, but I soon realized that **I'd made** a big mistake.
- The man sitting next to me on the plane was very nervous. He **hadn't flown** before.
  = . . . He **had** never **flown** before.

B

☆ 現在完了形と過去完了形は，それぞれどのような期間を話題としていますか？ 時を表す直線上で考えます。

現在完了形

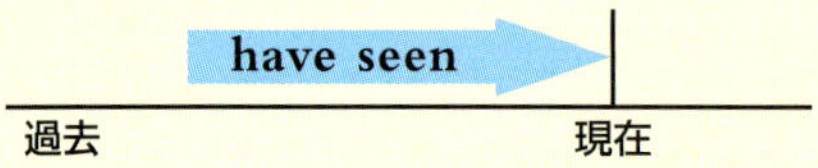

- Who is that woman? **I've** never **seen** her before. (⇒ 現在より前に…)
- We aren't hungry. We**'ve** just **had** lunch.
- The house is dirty. They **haven't cleaned** it for weeks.

過去完了形

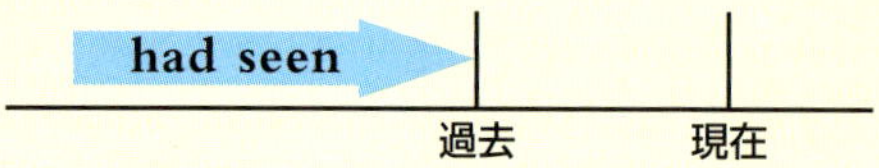

- I didn't know who she was. **I'd** never **seen** her before. (⇒ その時より前に…)
- We weren't hungry. We**'d** just **had** lunch.
- The house was dirty. They **hadn't cleaned** it for weeks.

C

☆ 単純過去形と過去完了形は，それぞれどのような期間を話題としていますか？ 時を表す直線上で考えます。

単純過去形

- *A:* Was Tom there when you arrived?
  B: Yes, but he **left** a little later. (⇒ その後…)
- Amy **wasn't** at home when I called.
  She **was** at her mother's house.

過去完了形

- *A:* Was Tom there when you arrived?
  B: No, he **had** already **left**. (⇒ すでに…)
- Amy **had** just **gotten** home when I called.
  She **had been** at her mother's house.

現在完了進行形 ➲ Unit 15　不規則変化する過去分詞（had gone, had seen など）➲ 付録 1

Exercises

14.1 状況に合うように，（　）内の語句を正しい形にして文を完成しなさい。

1. You went to Jill's house, but she wasn't there.
(she / go / out) *She had gone out.*
2. You went back to your hometown after many years. It wasn't the same as before.
(it / change / a lot) ______
3. I invited Rachel to the party, but she couldn't come.
(she / make / plans to do something else) ______
4. You went to the movies last night. You got there late.
(the movie / already / begin) ______
5. It was nice to see Daniel again after such a long time.
(I / not / see / him in five years) ______
6. I offered Sue something to eat, but she wasn't hungry.
(she / just / have / breakfast) ______

14.2 状況に合うように，（　）内の語句を用いて never ... before で終わる文を完成しなさい。

1. The man sitting next to you on the plane was very nervous. It was his first flight.
(fly) *He had never flown before.*
2. A woman walked into the room. She was a complete stranger to me.
(see) I ______ before.
3. Sam played tennis yesterday. He wasn't very good at it because it was his first game.
(play) He ______ before.
4. Last year we went to Mexico. It was our first time there.
(be there) We ______ before.

14.3 左欄の文を用いて右欄の文章を完成しなさい。左欄のそれぞれの文は番号順に生じていますが，右欄では，左欄の下線の引かれた出来事が最初に現れるので，適宜，過去完了形に変える必要があります。

1. (1) Somebody broke into the office during the night. (2) We arrived at work in the morning. (3) We called the police.	We arrived at work in the morning and found that somebody *had broken* into the office during the night. So we ______ .
2. (1) Laura went out this morning. (2) I tried to call her. (3) There was no answer.	I tried to call Laura this morning, but ______ no answer. She ______ out.
3. (1) Jim came back from vacation a few days ago. (2) I met him the same day. (3) He looked relaxed.	I met Jim a few days ago. ______ just ______ vacation. ______ relaxed.
4. (1) Kevin sent Sally lots of e-mails. (2) She never answered them. (3) Yesterday he got a phone call from her. (4) He was very surprised.	Yesterday Kevin ______ from Sally. He ______ very surprised. He ______ lots of e-mails, but she ______ .

14.4 （　）内の動詞を過去完了形もしくは単純過去形に変えて，文を完成しなさい。

1. "Was Ben at the party when you got there?" "No, he *had gone* (go) home."
2. I felt very tired when I got home, so I ______ (go) straight to bed.
3. The house was very quiet when I got home. Everybody ______ (go) to bed.
4. Sorry I'm late. My car ______ (break) down on the way here.
5. We were driving on the highway when we ______ (see) a car that ______ (break) down, so we ______ (stop) to help.

補充問題 5–8 (pp. 298–301)

UNIT 15

過去完了進行形 (I had been doing)

A

☆ イラストの状況について考えなさい。どのような形の動詞が使われていますか？

Yesterday morning

昨日の朝起きて窓の外を見たら，太陽は輝いていたものの，地面はとてもぬれていました。この状況は次のように表せます。

It **had been raining**.

➤ **had been -ing の形を過去完了進行形と呼びます。**

I/we/you/they he/she/it	**had**	(= I'**d**など) (= he'**d**など)	**been**	do**ing** work**ing** play**ing**など

B

以下の例文中の**過去完了進行形**も同じような状況を表します。

- When the boys came into the house, their clothes were dirty, their hair was messy, and one of them had a black eye. They'**d been fighting**.
- I was very tired when I got home. I'**d been working** hard all day.
- When I went to Tokyo a few years ago, I stayed with a friend of mine. She'**d been living** there only a short time but knew the city very well.

C

「〜した時まで…し続けていた」のように，ある出来事がもう一つの出来事が起こる以前に一定期間継続して生じていた場合，**過去完了進行形 (had been -ing)** を用いて表します。

- We'**d been playing** tennis for about half an hour when it started to rain hard.
- Jim went to the doctor last Friday. He **hadn't been feeling** well for some time.

☆ **現在完了進行形 (have been -ing) と過去完了進行形 (had been -ing) は，どのように異なりますか？**

現在完了進行形

I have been -ing

過去　現在

- I hope the bus comes soon. I'**ve been waiting** for 20 minutes.
(⇒ 現在より前に…)
- James is out of breath. He **has been running**.

過去完了進行形

I had been -ing

過去　現在

- The bus finally came. I'**d been waiting** for 20 minutes.
(⇒ バスが来るまで…)
- James was out of breath. He **had been running**.

D

☆ **過去進行形 (was -ing) と過去完了進行形 (had been -ing) は，どのように異なりますか？**

- It **wasn't raining** when we went out. The sun **was shining**. But it **had been raining**, so the ground was wet. (⇒ 雨は降ってはいなかったが，少し前まで降っていた)
- Stephanie **was sitting** in an armchair resting. She was tired because she'**d been working** very hard.

E

know や **like** のような動詞は，過去のある時まで動作が継続していても，普通は**過去完了進行形**にはしません。

- We were good friends. We **had known** each other for years. (✕ had been knowing)

普通，進行形にしない動詞 ➲ Unit 4A

現在完了進行形 ➲ Unit 10　過去完了形 ➲ Unit 14

Exercises

15.1 状況に合うように，( ) 内の語句を用いて文を完成しなさい。

1. I was very tired when I got home.
(I / work / hard all day) *I'd been working hard all day.*
2. The two boys came into the house. They had a soccer ball, and they were both very tired.
(they / play / soccer) ____________
3. I was disappointed when I had to cancel my vacation.
(I / look / forward to it) ____________
4. Ann woke up in the middle of the night. She was scared and didn't know where she was.
(she / dream) ____________
5. When I got home, Mike was sitting in front of the TV. He had just turned it off.
(he / watch / a DVD) ____________

15.2 状況に合うように，空所に適切な語句や表現を入れて文を完成しなさい。

1. We played tennis yesterday. Half an hour after we began playing, it started to rain.
We *had been playing for half an hour* when *it started to rain* .
2. I had arranged to meet Robert in a restaurant. I arrived and waited for him. After 20 minutes I suddenly realized that I was in the wrong restaurant.
I ____________ for 20 minutes when I ____________
____________ the wrong restaurant.
3. Sarah got a job in a factory. Five years later the factory closed down.
When the factory ____________ , Sarah ____________
____________ there for five years.
4. I went to a concert last week. The orchestra began playing. After about 10 minutes a man in the audience suddenly started shouting.
The orchestra ____________
when ____________

自分自身のことについて考え，文を完成しなさい。

5. I began driving home from work. I ____________
when ____________

15.3 状況に合うように，( ) 内の動詞を過去進行形，過去完了形，過去完了進行形のいずれかに変えて文を完成しなさい。

1. It was very noisy next door. Our neighbors *were having* (have) a party.
2. We were good friends. We *had known* (know) each other for years.
3. John and I went for a walk. I had trouble keeping up with him because he ____________ (walk) so fast.
4. Sue was sitting on the ground. She was out of breath. She ____________ (run).
5. When I arrived, everybody was sitting around the table with their mouths full. They ____________ (eat).
6. When I arrived, everybody was sitting around the table and talking. Their mouths were empty, but their stomachs were full. They ____________ (eat).
7. Jim was on his hands and knees on the floor. He ____________ (look) for his contact lens.
8. When I arrived, Kate ____________ (wait) for me. She was upset with me because I was late and she ____________ (wait) for a long time.
9. I was sad when I sold my car. I ____________ (have) it for a long time.
10. We were exhausted at the end of our trip. We ____________ (travel) for more than 24 hours.

補充問題 5–8 **(pp. 298–301)**

UNIT 16

have と have got

A

have と **have got** は「…を持つ」「…がいる」「…（病気）にかかる」などを表します。
have got と got を持たない **have** との間には意味の違いはありません。

- They **have** a new car. = They**'ve got** a new car.
- Nancy **has** two sisters. = Nancy **has got** two sisters.
- I **have** a headache. = **I've got** a headache.
- He **has** a few problems. = He**'s got** a few problems.
- Our house **has** a big yard. = Our house **has got** a big yard.

I **have** a new cell phone.
I**'ve got** a new cell phone, too.

have や **have got** が上のような意味（所有，関係，病気など）を表す時，たった今持っていることであっても is having / are having などの進行形にはなりません。

- We're enjoying our vacation. We **have** / **have got** a nice room in the hotel. (× We're having)

have と **have got** では，**疑問文**と**否定文**の作り方が異なります。

Do you **have** any questions? I **don't have** any questions.	**Have** you **got** any questions? I **haven't got** any questions.
Does she **have** a car? She **doesn't have** a car.	**Has** she **got** a car? She **hasn't got** a car.

B

have と **have got** の**過去形**はいずれも **had** となります。

- Ann **had** long hair when she was a child.

過去形 had の**疑問文**と**否定文**は **did/didn't** を用いて作ります。

- **Did** they **have** a car when they were living in Miami?
- I **didn't have** a watch, so I didn't know what time it was.
- Ann **had** long hair, **didn't** she?

C

have breakfast / have trouble / have a good time など

以下のように，**have** はさまざまな動作や体験と結び付きます。

have	**breakfast** / **dinner** / **a cup of coffee** / **something to eat** **a party** / **a safe trip** / **a good flight** **an accident** / **an experience** / **a dream** **a look** (at something) **a conversation** / **a discussion** / **a talk** (with somebody) **trouble** / **difficulty** / **fun** / **a good time** など **a baby** (= give birth to a baby : 出産する) / **an operation**

上の枠の中の動作や体験には **have got** を用いることはできません。

- Sometimes I **have** (= eat) a sandwich for lunch. (× I've got)
- ⇔ **I've got** / I **have** some sandwiches. Would you like one?

上の枠の中の動作や体験は**進行形**（**am having** など）になります。

- We're enjoying our vacation. We**'re having** a great time. (× We have)
- Mike **is having** trouble with his car. He often has trouble with his car.

上の枠の中の動作や体験は **do/does/did** を用いて**疑問文**や**否定文**にします。

- I **don't** usually **have** a big breakfast. (× I usually haven't)
- What time **does** Ann **have** lunch? (× has Ann lunch)
- **Did** you **have** any trouble finding a place to live?

have to ... ➲ Unit 30

Exercises

16.1 ( )内の語句を用いて，動詞 have の否定文で書き換えなさい。can't の場合には現在形，couldn't の場合には過去形にします。

1. I can't get into the house. (a key) *I don't have a key.*
2. I couldn't read the letter. (my glasses) *I didn't have my glasses.*
3. I can't climb up on the roof. (a ladder) ____________
4. We couldn't visit the museum. (enough time) We ____________
5. He couldn't find our house. (a map) ____________
6. She can't pay her bills. (any money) ____________
7. I can't fix the car tonight. (enough energy) ____________
8. They couldn't take any pictures. (a camera) ____________

16.2 動詞 have を用いて文を完成しなさい。状況に合わせて，現在形もしくは過去形にします。

1. Excuse me, *do you have* a pen I could borrow?
2. Why are you holding your face like that? ____________ a toothache?
3. ____________ a lot of toys when you were a child?
4. *A:* ____________ the time, please?
   B: Yes, it's ten after seven.
5. I need a stamp for this letter. ____________ one?
6. When you took the test, ____________ time to answer all the questions?
7. *A:* It started to rain very hard while I was taking a walk.
   B: Did it? ____________ an umbrella?

16.3 自分のことについて答えなさい。( )内の事物について，今持っているか 10 年前に持っていたかを考えます。前者の場合には I have / I don't have で，後者の場合には I had / I didn't have で記述します。

	Now	*10 years ago (or 5 if you're young)*
1.	(a car) *I have a car.* OR *I've got a car.*	*I didn't have a car.*
2.	(a bike) I ____________	I ____________
3.	(a cell phone) ____________	____________
4.	(a dog) ____________	____________
5.	(a guitar) ____________	____________
6.	(long hair) ____________	____________
7.	(a driver's license) ____________	____________

16.4 以下から適切な語句を選び，必要ならば動詞を適切な形にして文を完成しなさい。

have a baby	**have a dream**	**have a talk**	**have trouble**	**have a good flight**
have a look	~~**have lunch**~~	**have a party**	**have a nice time**	**have dinner**

1. I don't eat much during the day. I never *have lunch* .
2. If you're angry with your friend, it might be a good idea to sit down and ____________ with her.
3. We ____________ last week. It was great – we invited lots of people.
4. Excuse me, can I ____________ at your newspaper, please?
5. Jim is on vacation in Hawaii. I hope he ____________ .
6. I didn't sleep well last night. I ____________ about my exam.
7. *A:* ____________ finding the book you wanted?
   B: No, I found it OK.
8. Crystal ____________ a few weeks ago. It's her second child.
9. *A:* Why didn't you answer the phone?
   B: We ____________ with friends.
10. *You meet your friend Sally at the airport. She has just arrived. You say:*
    Hi, Sally. How are you? ____________ ?

UNIT 17

used to ＋ 動詞の原形

A

☆ イラストの状況について考えなさい。どのような形の動詞が使われていますか？

David は大好きだったジョギングを 2 年前にやめてしまいました。今はもう走っていません。

He **used to jog** three miles a day.

➤ **He used to jog は，過去において繰り返し習慣的にジョギングしていましたが，現在はジョギングしていないことを表します。**

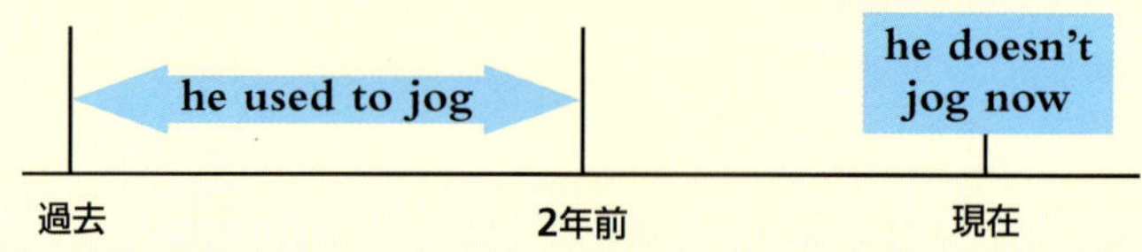

B

～ used to ＋ 動詞の原形は「よく…したものだ」のように，過去に**習慣**としていたが現在はしていない**動作**を表します。

- I **used to play** tennis a lot, but I don't play very often now.
- David **used to spend** a lot of money on clothes. These days he can't afford it.
- "Do you go to the movies much?" "Not any more, but I **used to**." (= I used to go)

used to ＋ 動詞の原形は「昔は…だった」のように，現在とは異なる**過去の状態**を表すことがあります。

- This building is now a furniture store. It **used to be** a movie theater.
- I **used to think** Mark was unfriendly, but now I realize he's a very nice person.
- I've started drinking coffee recently. I never **used to like** it before.
- Nicole **used to have** very long hair when she was a child.

C

I used to ＋ 動詞の原形は過去の習慣を表します。I use to ＋ 動詞の原形のような現在形はありません。**現在の習慣や状態は単純現在形** (I **do**) で表します。

過去 現在	he **used to play** he **plays**	we **used to live** we **live**	there **used to be** there **is**

- We **used to live** in a small town, but now we **live** in Chicago.
- There **used to be** four movie theaters in town. Now there **is** only one.

D

used to ＋ 動詞の原形の**疑問文**は **Did** (you) **used to ＋ 動詞の原形？**で作ります。

- **Did** you **use to eat** a lot of candy when you were a child?

used to ＋ 動詞の原形の**否定文**は **didn't used to ＋ 動詞の原形**で作ります。

- I **didn't use to like** him.

E

I **used to ＋ 動詞の原形**と I **was -ing**（**過去進行形**）は意味的に異なります。

- I **used to watch** TV a lot when I was little.（⇒ 子どもの頃はよくテレビを見たが，今はあまり見ていない）
- I **was watching** TV when Mike called.（⇒ テレビを見ていた）

F

I **am used to -ing**（…するのに慣れている）（➲ Unit 59）は I **used to ＋ 動詞の原形**と似ていますが，形も意味も異なります。

- I **used to live** alone.（⇒ かつてはひとり暮らしをしていたが，今はもうしていない）
- I **am used to living** alone.（⇒ 長くひとり暮らしをしてきたのでもう慣れた）

過去進行形 (I was doing) ➲ Unit 6　　used to ＋ 動詞の原形と同様に過去の習慣を表す would ➲ Unit 34C
be/get used to … ➲ Unit 59

Exercises

17.1 状況に合うように，used to に適切な動詞を付け加えて文を完成しなさい。

1. David quit jogging two years ago. He *used to jog* three miles a day.
2. Liz ______ a motorcycle, but last year she sold it and bought a car.
3. We moved to Spain a few years ago. We ______ in Paris.
4. I seldom eat ice cream now, but I ______ it when I was a child.
5. Tracy ______ my best friend, but we aren't friends anymore.
6. It only takes me about 40 minutes to get to work now that the new highway is open. It ______ more than an hour.
7. There ______ a hotel near the airport, but it closed a long time ago.
8. When you lived in New York, ______ to the theater very often?

17.2 Matt は自分の生活を変えるために，以下のような事柄をやめたり始めたりしました。

He stopped { ~~studying hard~~ / going to bed early / running three miles every morning }

He started { ~~sleeping late~~ / going out every night / spending a lot of money }

Matt のこの状況を，used to と didn't use to を用いて書き表しなさい。

1. *He used to study hard.*
2. *He didn't use to sleep late.*
3. ______
4. ______
5. ______
6. ______

17.3 Karen の 5 年前の発言と今日の発言を比較しなさい。

Karen がこの 5 年間でどのように変わったかを，used to / didn't use to / never used to のいずれかを用いた形を but の前後の空所に入れて，全体を完成しなさい。

1. *She used to travel a lot*, but *she doesn't take many trips these days.*
2. She ______, but ______
3. She ______, but ______
4. She ______, but ______
5. She ______, but ______
6. She ______, but ______
7. She ______, but ______
8. She ______, but ______
9. She ______, but ______
10. She ______, but ______

補充問題 9 (p. 301)

UNIT 18

未来の意味を表す現在時制* (I am doing / I do)

A

☆ イラストの状況について考えなさい。どのような形の動詞が使われていますか？

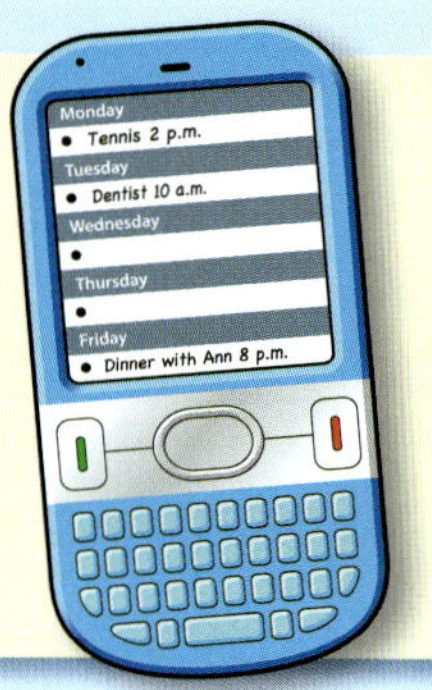

電子手帳には Ben のスケジュールが表示されています。

He **is playing** tennis on Monday afternoon.
He **is going** to the dentist on Tuesday morning.
He **is having** dinner with Ann on Friday.

Ben はすでに電子手帳に表示された事柄を決定し，必要な準備や打ち合わせを済ませています。

➤「…することになっている」のように，すでに決心し準備を終えた未来の活動は現在進行形 (I am doing) で表します。

- *A:* What **are** you **doing** Saturday night? (× What do you do)
  B: **I'm going** to the theater. (× I go)
- *A:* What time **is** Cathy **arriving** tomorrow?
  B: At 10:30. **I'm meeting** her at the airport.
- **I'm not working** tomorrow, so we can go out somewhere.
- Sam **isn't playing** football next Saturday. He hurt his leg.

上の例文は，いずれも I'm **going to (do)** の形を用いて書き換えられます。

- What **are** you **going to do** Saturday night?

しかし，あらかじめ準備された活動については**現在進行形**を用いるのがより自然です。➲ Unit 19B
あらかじめ準備された活動について will を用いることはできません。

- What **are** you **doing** tonight? (× What will you do)
- Eric **is getting** married next month. (× will get)

「今，まさに…しようとしていた」活動についても**現在進行形**で表します。ことに **go/come/leave** などの移動を表す動詞とともに**現在進行形**が用いられた際に，この意味が生じます。

- I'm tired. **I'm going** to bed now. Goodnight. (× I go to bed now)
- "Tina, are you ready yet?" "Yes, **I'm coming**." (× I come)

B

未来の意味を持つ単純現在形 (I do)

交通機関の時刻表や映画のプログラムなどのように，予定が組まれている未来の出来事は**単純現在形**を用いて表します。

- My flight **leaves** at 11:30, so I need to get to the airport by 10:00.
- What time **does** the movie **begin**?
- **It's** Wednesday tomorrow. / Tomorrow **is** Wednesday.

未来に生じる人の活動を**単純現在形**を用いて表すと，その活動があたかも時刻表のように決められて変更しにくいことを意味します。

- I **start** my new job on Monday.
- What time **do** you **finish** work tomorrow?

個人的に計画や準備をした活動には**現在進行形**を用います。

- What time **are** you **meeting** Ann tomorrow? (× do you meet)

☆ 例文で考えます。現在進行形と単純現在形では表す未来について，どのように異なりますか？

現在進行形	単純現在形
What time **are** you arriving?	What time **does** the plane **arrive**?
I'm going to the movies tonight.	The movie **starts** at 8:15 (tonight).

* ここでの「現在時制」は，「単純現在形」と「現在進行形」の 2 つの形について言及します。

I'm going to＋動詞の原形 ➲ Units 19, 22　will ➲ Units 20–22　when/if 内の単純現在形 ➲ Unit 24

Exercises

18.1 あなたの友達が長期休暇をとろうとしています。この友達に，休暇の計画について吹き出し中のことばが答えとなるように，（　）内の語句を用いて尋ねる疑問文を作りなさい。

1. (where / go?) *Where are you going?*
2. (how long / stay?) ______
3. (when / leave?) ______
4. (go / alone?) ______
5. (travel / by car?) ______
6. (where / stay?) ______

Quebec.
Ten days.
Next Friday.
No, with a friend.
No, by plane.
In a hotel.

18.2 Ben から会いたいという連絡が来ましたが，あなたは忙しくて会いに行けません。自分のスケジュールを電子手帳で確認して，会いに行けない理由を Ben に説明する文を完成しなさい。

Monday
- Volleyball 7:30 p.m.

Tuesday
- Work late until 9 p.m.

Wednesday
- Theater

Thursday
- Meet Julia 8 p.m.

Friday
-

Ben: Can you come over on Monday night?
You: Sorry, but *I'm playing volleyball* . (1)
Ben: What about Tuesday night then?
You: No, not Tuesday. I ______ . (2)
Ben: And Wednesday night?
You: ______ . (3)
Ben: Well, are you free on Thursday?
You: I'm afraid not. ______ . (4)

18.3 あなたは（　）内で指定された期日に何か予定がありますか？ 自分のことで答えなさい。

1. (tonight) *I'm going out tonight.* OR *I'm not doing anything tonight.*
2. (tomorrow morning) I ______
3. (tomorrow night) ______
4. (next Sunday) ______
5. (*choose another day or time*) ______

18.4 状況に合わせて，（　）内の動詞を現在進行形もしくは単純現在形に変えて文を完成しなさい。

1. I *'m going* (go) to the movies tonight.
2. *Does the movie begin* (the movie / begin) at 3:30 or 4:30?
3. We ______ (have) a party next Saturday. Would you like to come?
4. The art exhibit ______ (open) on May 3.
5. I ______ (not / go) out tonight. I ______ (stay) at home.
6. "______ (you / do) anything tomorrow morning?" "No, I'm free. Why?"
7. We ______ (go) to a concert tonight. It ______ (start) at 7:30.
8. I ______ (leave) now. I came to say good-bye.
9. *A:* Have you seen Liz recently?
   B: No, but we ______ (meet) for lunch next week.
10. *You are on the train to Boston and you ask another passenger:*
    Excuse me. What time ______ (this train / get) to Boston?
11. *You are talking to Julie:*
    Julie, I ______ (go) to the store now. ______ (you / come) with me?
12. *You and a friend are watching television. You say:*
    I'm bored with this show. What time ______ (it / end)?
13. I ______ (not / use) the car tonight, so you can have it.
14. Sue ______ (come) to see us tomorrow. She ______ (fly) from Seattle, and her plane ______ (arrive) at 10:15 a.m.

補充問題 10–13 (pp. 302–304)

(I'm) going to (do)

A

I am going to do（動詞の原形）は，「私は…するつもり」のように，これからすることをすでに決めている場合に用います。

- *A:* **Are** you **going to watch** the football game on TV tonight?
  B: No, **I'm going to go** to bed early. I'm tired from my trip.
- *A:* I heard Lisa won some money. What **is** she **going to do** with it?
  B: She**'s going to buy** a new car.
- **I'm going to make** a quick phone call. Can you wait for me?
- This cheese smells awful. **I'm not going to eat** it.

B

I am doing と I am going to do

I am doing（**現在進行形**）は，「私は…することになっている」のように，誰かと待ち合わせしたり，どこかに出かけたりする場合のように，すでに準備したり計画を立てている場合に用います。

- What time **are** you **meeting** Amanda tonight?
- **I'm leaving** tomorrow. I already have my plane ticket.

I am going to do は，すでに決めているものの，具体的な準備はまだしていない場合に用います。

- "The windows are dirty." "Yes, I know. **I'm going to wash** them later."
  （⇒ 洗おうと思っているが，まだ準備ができていない）
- I've decided not to stay here any longer. Tomorrow **I'm going to look** for another place to live.

実際にはこの両者の間にはほとんど違いがないため，多くの場合，両者は同じように用いられています。

C

☆ イラストを見て考えます。(be) going to do はどのような出来事を表しますか？

左のイラストでは，男性は目の前の壁が見えません。このままでは壁にぶっかってしまいます。

He **is going to walk** into the wall.

➤ **He is going to walk into the wall. は，「まもなく壁にぶっかってしまうでしょう」を意味します。(be) going to do は，現在の状況から確実に予想できる未来の出来事を表します。**

現在の状況　　予想される未来

以下の例文においても，現在の状況から確実に予測できる未来が表されています。

- Look at those dark clouds! It**'s going to rain**. （⇒ 今，黒い雲が集まっているから）
- I feel awful. I think **I'm going to be sick**. （⇒ 今，ひどく気分が悪いから）
- The economic situation is bad now, and things **are going to get** worse.

D

I was going to do ... は「…するつもりだった」のように，過去に計画していたが実現しなかった動作を表します。

- We **were going to fly** to New York, but then we decided to drive instead.
- Peter **was going to take** the exam, but he changed his mind.
- I **was** just **going to cross** the street when somebody shouted, "Stop!"

～ was going to do は「…しそうだった」のように，実際には起こらなかった過去の出来事を表します。

- I thought it **was going to rain**, but it didn't.

I'm doing（未来を表す現在進行形）➲ Unit 18A　I will と I'm going to ➲ Unit 22

Exercises

19.1 状況に合うように，(be) going to＋動詞の原形を用いた疑問文を作りなさい。

1. Your friend has won some money. You ask:
   (what / do with it?) *What are you going to do with it?*
2. Your friend is going to a party tonight.
   You ask: (what / wear?) ____________
3. Your friend has just bought a new table.
   You ask: (where / put it?) ____________
4. Your friend has decided to have a party.
   You ask: (who / invite?) ____________

19.2 状況に合うように，(be) going to＋動詞の原形を用いて対話を完成しなさい。

1. You have decided to clean your room this morning.
   Friend: Are you going out this morning?
   You: No, *I'm going to clean my room.*
2. You bought a sweater, but it doesn't fit you very well. You have decided to return it.
   Friend: That sweater is too big for you.
   You: I know. ____________
3. You have been offered a job, but you have decided not to take it.
   Friend: I hear you've been offered a job.
   You: That's right, but ____________
4. You have to call Sarah. It's morning now, and you intend to call her tonight.
   Friend: Have you called Sarah yet?
   You: No, ____________
5. You are in a restaurant. The food is awful and you've decided to complain.
   Friend: This food is awful, isn't it?
   You: Yes, it's disgusting. ____________

19.3 (　) 内の語句を用いて，状況から予測できることを記述した文を完成しなさい。

1. There are a lot of dark clouds in the sky.
   (rain) *It's going to rain.*
2. It is 8:30. Tom is leaving his house. He should be at work at 8:45, but it takes him 30 minutes to get there. (late) He ____________
3. There is a hole in the bottom of the boat. A lot of water is coming in through the hole.
   (sink) The boat ____________
4. Erica and Chris are driving in the country. There is very little gas left in the tank. The nearest gas station is miles away.
   (run out) They ____________

19.4 was/were going to に以下の動詞を続けて，状況に合うように文を完成しなさい。

buy　call　~~fly~~　have　play　quit

1. We *were going to fly* to New York, but then we decided to drive instead.
2. I ____________ some new clothes yesterday, but I was very busy and didn't have time to go shopping.
3. Joshua and I ____________ tennis last week, but he hurt his ankle.
4. I ____________ Jane, but I decided to e-mail her instead.
5. *A:* The last time I saw Bob, he ____________ his job.
   B: That's right, but in the end he decided not to.
6. We ____________ a party last week, but some of our friends couldn't come, so we changed our minds.

UNIT 20

will 1

A

I'll (= I will) は、話している時点で「私は…する，…しよう」と決めたことに用います。

- Oh, I left the door open. **I'll go** and **shut** it.
- "What would you like to drink?" "**I'll have** some orange juice, please."
- "Did you call Julie?" "Oh no, I forgot. **I'll call** her now."

I'll (= I will) がこの意味で用いられる時，I do / I go などの**単純現在形**にすることはできません。

- **I'll go** and **shut** the door. (× I go and shut)

will は，I think I'll ... や I don't think I'll ... のような形でよく用います。相手を配慮した丁寧な主張になります。I think I won't ... のような形はありません。

- I am a little hungry. **I think I'll have** something to eat.
- **I don't think I'll go** out tonight. I'm too tired. (× I think I won't go out . . .)

話しことばでは，will の否定形は普通 will not ではなく **won't** [wóunt] と発音されます。

- I can see you're busy, so **I won't stay** long.

B

話す前にすでに決心していたり，計画を立てたりしていることには will を用いません。➲ Units 18–19

- **I'm going** on vacation next Saturday. (× I'll go)
- **Are** you **working** tomorrow? (× Will you work)

C

☆ will をよく用いる状況にはどのようなものがありますか？

➤「…します」提案したり申し出たりする。

- That bag looks heavy. **I'll help** you with it. (× I help)

➤「はい，…します」相手からの要請を承諾する。

- *A:* Can you give Tim this book?
  B: Sure, **I'll give** it to him when I see him this afternoon.

➤「必ず…します」約束する。

- Thanks for lending me the money. **I'll pay** you back on Friday.
- I **won't tell** anyone what happened. I promise.

➤「…していただけますか？」相手に依頼する。

- **Will you** please **be** quiet? I'm trying to concentrate.
- **Will you shut** the door, please?

☆ イラストや例文は，どのような状況を表していますか？

- I've tried to give her advice, but she **won't listen**.
- The car **won't start**. (⇒ the car "refuses" to start)

➤ いくら手を施しても，「どうしても… しない」状況は won't で表します。

D

Shall I . . . ? / Shall we . . . ?

「…しましょうか？」のように，周りの人の意向を聞く際に **Shall I ...? / Shall we ...?** の**疑問文**を用います。ことに自分から提案したり，申し出たりする場合に用います。C の I'll を用いた提案より丁寧になります。

- **Shall I open** the window? (⇒ Do you want me to open the window?)
- "Where **shall we have** lunch?" "Let's go to Marino's."

同じことは **should** でも表せ，should の方がよく使われます。

- **Should I open** the window? (⇒ Do you want me to open it?)
- Where **should we have** lunch?

will 2 ➲ Unit 21　I will と I'm going to ➲ Unit 22　イギリス英語の用法 ➲ 付録 1

Exercises

20.1 状況に合うように，**I'll** に適切な動詞を付け加えて文を完成しなさい。

1. I'm too tired to walk home. I think *I'll take* a taxi.
2. "It's a little cold in this room." "You're right. ________ on the heat."
3. "We don't have any milk." "We don't? ________ and get some now."
4. "Can I wash the dishes for you?" "No, that's all right. ________ it later."
5. "I don't know how to use this computer." "Don't worry, ________ you."
6. "Would you like tea or coffee?" "________ coffee, please."
7. "Good-bye! Have a nice trip." "Thanks. ________ you a postcard."
8. Thanks for letting me borrow your camera. ________ it back to you on Monday, OK?
9. "Are you coming with us?" "No, I think ________ here."

20.2 状況に合うように，**I think I'll ...** もしくは **I don't think I'll ...** で始まる文を完成しなさい。

1. It's a little cold. The window is open, and you decide to close it. You say:
   I think I'll close the window.
2. You're tired, and it's getting late. You decide to go to bed. You say:
   I think ________
3. A friend of yours offers you a ride in his car, but you decide to walk. You say:
   Thank you, but I think ________
4. You arranged to play tennis today. Now you decide that you don't want to play. You say:
   I don't think ________
5. You were going to go swimming. Now you decide that you don't want to go. You say:
   ____

20.3 下線部の正しい方を選んで，文を完成しなさい。➲ **Units 18–19**

1. "Did you call Julie?" "Oh no, I forgot. ~~I call~~ / I'll call her now." (I'll call が正しい)
2. I can't meet you tomorrow. I'm playing / ~~I'll play~~ tennis. (I'm playing が正しい)
3. "I meet / I'll meet you outside the hotel in half an hour, OK?" "Yes, that's fine."
4. "I need some money." "OK, I'm lending / I'll lend you some. How much do you need?"
5. I'm having / I'll have a party next Saturday. I hope you can come.
6. "Remember to get a newspaper when you go out." "OK. I don't forget / I won't forget."
7. What time does your plane leave / will your plane leave tomorrow?
8. I asked Sue what happened, but she doesn't tell / won't tell me.
9. "Are you doing / Will you do anything tomorrow night?" "No, I'm free. Why?"
10. I don't want to go out alone. Do you come / Will you come with me?

20.4 状況に合うように，**I'll / I won't / Shall I / Shall we** に適切な動詞を付け加えて文を完成しなさい。

1. *A:* Where *shall we have* lunch?
   B: Let's go to that new restaurant on North Street.
2. *A:* It's Mark's birthday soon, and I want to get him a present.
   What ________ him?
   B: I don't know. I never know what to give people.
3. *A:* Do you want me to put these groceries away?
   B: No that's OK. ________ it later.
4. *A:* Let's go out tonight.
   B: OK, where ________ ?
5. *A:* What I've told you is a secret. I don't want anybody else to know.
   B: Don't worry. ________ anybody.
6. *A:* I know you're busy, but can you finish this report this afternoon?
   B: Well, ________ , but I can't promise.

補充問題 10–13 (pp. 302–304)

UNIT 21

will 2

A

未来に起こるように，あらかじめ計画したり決心していることは**現在進行形**や **(be) going to ＋ 動詞の原形**で表します。この場合，**will** は使えません。➲ Units 18–19

- Ann **is working** next week. (× Ann will work)
- **Are** you **going to watch** television tonight? (× Will you watch)

しかし，「〜だろう」のように，あらかじめ計画したり決心していないことが未来の出来事として話題になる場合もあります。

☆ **イラストはどのような未来の状況を表していますか？**

Joeと友人が映画館の入り口で並んでいます。

Joe

We'll get in. には「あらかじめ映画館に入ることを決めていた」という意味はありません。Joe は自分が起きることを知っていたり，起きるだろうと思う出来事を話しています。Joe は出来事が起きることを「予測」しています。

➤ **「…するだろう / …しないだろう」のように，未来の出来事や状況をその場で予測する際に，will/won't を用います。**

以下の例文も同じように，未来の出来事の予測をしています。

- Jill has lived abroad for a long time. When she comes back, she**'ll find** a lot of changes here.
- "Where **will** you **be** this time next year?"　"**I'll be** in Japan."
- That plate is hot. If you touch it, you**'ll burn** yourself.
- Tom **won't pass** the exam. He hasn't studied hard enough.
- When **will** you **find out** how you did on the exam?

B

以下のような語句は，よく **will ('ll)** とともに用います。**will** だけの場合と比べて丁寧になります。

probably	I'll **probably** be home late tonight.
I expect	**I expect** the test **will** take two hours.
I'm sure	Don't worry about the exam. **I'm sure** you**'ll** pass.
I think	**Do you think** Sarah **will** like the present we bought her?
I don't think	**I don't think** the exam **will** be very difficult.
I guess	*A:* What are you doing after dinner? *B:* I don't know. **I guess I'll** read the paper.
I suppose	When **do you suppose** Jan and Mark **will** get married?
I doubt	**I doubt** you**'ll** need a heavy coat in Las Vegas. It's usually warm there.
I wonder	I worry about those people who lost their jobs. **I wonder** what **will** happen to them.

I hope ...（…してほしい）の後では普通，**現在形**を用います。

- **I hope** Kate **passes** the exam.
- **I hope** it **doesn't rain** tomorrow.

will 1 ➲ Unit 20　I will と I'm going to ➲ Unit 22　will be -ing と will have ＋ 過去分詞 ➲ Unit 23
未来 ➲ 付録 3

Exercises

21.1 下線部の正しい形もしくは，より自然な形を選びなさい。

1. Diane isn't free on Saturday. ~~She'll work~~ / She's working. (She's working が正しい)
2. I'll go / I'm going to a party tomorrow night. Would you like to come, too?
3. I think Amy will get / is getting the job. She has a lot of experience.
4. I can't meet you tonight. A friend of mine will come / is coming over.
5. *A:* Have you decided where to go on vacation?
   B: Yes, we'll go / we are going to Italy.
6. Don't be afraid of the dog. It won't hurt / It isn't hurting you.

21.2 状況に合うように，will ('ll) の後に以下の動詞を続けて文を完成しなさい。

come get like live look ~~pass~~ see take

1. Don't worry about the exam. I'm sure you *'ll pass* .
2. Why don't you try on this jacket? It ______________ nice on you.
3. I want you to meet Brandon sometime. I think you ______________ him.
4. It's raining. Don't go out. You ______________ wet.
5. Do you think people ______________ longer in the future?
6. Good-bye. I'm sure we ______________ each other again soon.
7. I invited Sue to the party, but I don't think she ______________ .
8. When the new road is finished, I expect that my trip to work ______________ less time.

21.3 状況に合うように，will ('ll) もしくは won't を用いて文を完成しなさい。

1. Can you wait for me? I *won't* be very long.
2. You don't need to take an umbrella along. It __________ rain.
3. If you don't eat anything now, you __________ be hungry later.
4. I'm sorry about what happened yesterday. It __________ happen again.
5. I've got some incredible news! You __________ never believe what happened.
6. There's no more bread. I guess we __________ have to go shopping before we eat.
7. Don't ask Amanda for advice. She __________ know what to do.
8. Jack doesn't like crowds. I don't think he __________ come to our party.

21.4 設問で指定された時間に自分がどこにいるかを以下から適切な表現を選び，適宜補って記述しなさい。

I'll be … I'll probably be … I don't know where I'll be … I guess I'll be …

1. (next Monday night at 7:45)
   I'll be at home. or *I guess I'll be at home.* or *I don't know where I'll be.*
2. (at 5:00 tomorrow morning)
   ____
3. (at 10:30 tomorrow morning)
   ____
4. (next Saturday afternoon at 4:15)
   ____
5. (this time next year)
   ____

21.5 状況に合うように以下から適切な動詞を選び，Do you think ～ will … ? の文を完成しなさい。

be back cost end get married happen ~~like~~ rain

1. I bought Rosa a present. *Do you think she'll like it* ?
2. The sky is dark and cloudy. Do you ______________________________ ?
3. The meeting is still going on. When do you ______________________________ ?
4. My car needs to be fixed. How much ______________________________ ?
5. Sally and David are in love. Do ______________________________ ?
6. "I'm going out now." "OK. What time ______________________________ ?"
7. The future is uncertain. What ______________________________ ?

補充問題 10–13 (pp. 302–304)

UNIT 22

I will と I'm going to

A

☆ イラストはどのような状況を表していますか？ **will ('ll)** と **(be) going to** の使われている状況と，上下のイラストの時間的な流れに注意します。

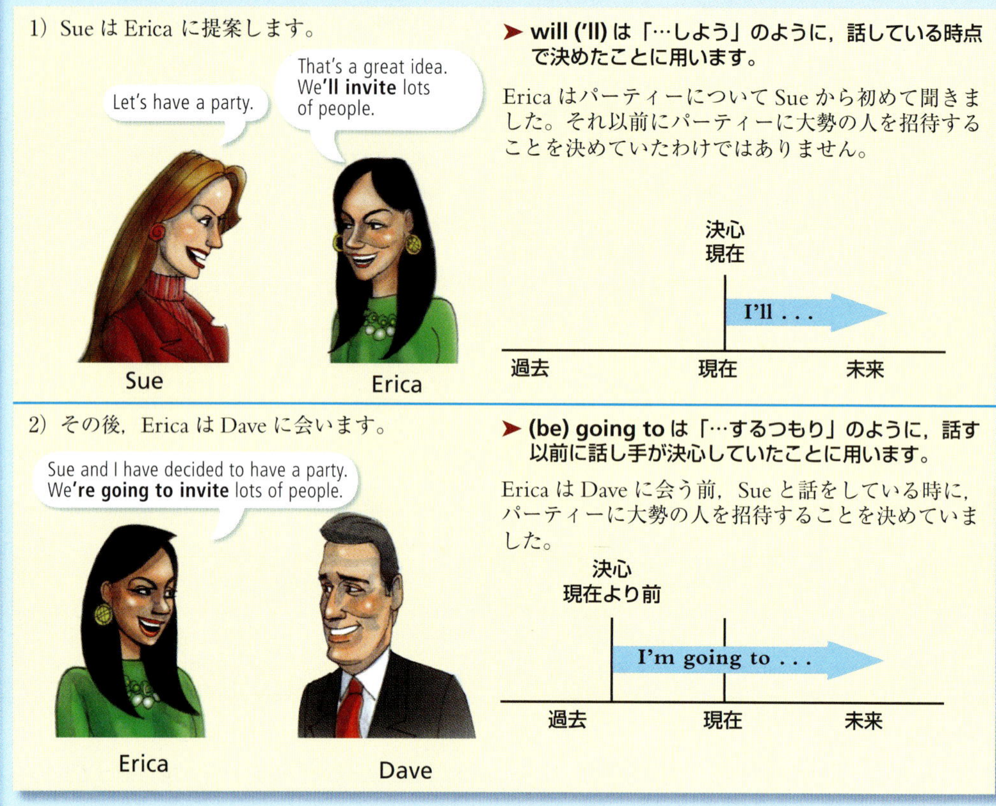

1）Sue は Erica に提案します。
Let's have a party.
That's a great idea. We'll invite lots of people.
Sue
Erica
➤ will ('ll) は「…しよう」のように，話している時点で決めたことに用います。
Erica はパーティーについて Sue から初めて聞きました。それ以前にパーティーに大勢の人を招待することを決めていたわけではありません。
決心
現在
I'll . . .
過去
現在
未来
2）その後，Erica は Dave に会います。
Sue and I have decided to have a party. We're going to invite lots of people.
Erica
Dave
➤ (be) going to は「…するつもり」のように，話す以前に話し手が決心していたことに用います。
Erica は Dave に会う前，Sue と話をしている時に，パーティーに大勢の人を招待することを決めていました。
決心
現在より前
I'm going to . . .
過去
現在
未来

以下の例文も，**will ('ll)** と **(be) going to** の使われる状況の違いを示しています。

- "Daniel called while you were out." "OK. I**'ll call** him back."
  "Daniel called while you were out." "Yes, I know. I**'m going to call** him back."
- "Anna is in the hospital." "Oh really? I didn't know. I**'ll go** and visit her."
  "Anna is in the hospital." "Yes, I know. I**'m going to visit** her tonight."

B

未来の出来事や状況の予測に関して，**will ('ll)** と **(be) going to** との間に大きな違いはありません。以下の例文では「…だろう」のように，ほぼ同じ意味になります。

- I think the weather **will** be nice later.
- I think the weather **is going to** be nice later.

現在の状況から未来の出来事が確実に予測できる場合，**(be) going to** を用い，**will** は用いません。➲ Unit 19C

- Look at those black clouds. It**'s going to rain**. (✕ It will rain)
  (⇒ 今，空に見える雲から雨が降ることが明らか)
- I feel terrible. I think I**'m going to be** sick. (✕ I think I'll be sick)
  (⇒ 今，吐いてしまいそうなくらい気分が悪い)

上のような状況がなく，「…だろう」と予測する場合には **will ('ll)** を用います。

- Tom **will** probably **get** here at about 8:00.
- I think Jessica **will like** the present we bought for her.
- These shoes are very well made. They**'ll last** a long time.

I'm going to ➲ Unit 19 will ➲ Units 20–21 未来 ➲ 付録 3

Exercises

22.1 状況に合うように，will ('ll) もしくは (be) going to のいずれかと（　）内の語句を組み合わせて対話を完成しなさい。

1. *A:* Why are you turning on the television?
   B: _I'm going to watch_ the news. (I / watch)
2. *A:* Oh, I just realized. I don't have any money.
   B: You don't? Well, don't worry. ______________ you some. (I / lend)
3. *A:* I have a headache.
   B: You do? Wait a second and ______________ an aspirin for you. (I / get)
4. *A:* Why are you filling that bucket with water?
   B: ______________ the car. (I / wash)
5. *A:* I've decided to paint this room.
   B: Oh, really? What color ______________ it? (you / paint)
6. *A:* Where are you going? Are you going shopping?
   B: Yes, ______________ some things for dinner. (I / buy)
7. *A:* I don't know how to use this camera.
   B: It's easy. ______________ you. (I / show)
8. *A:* Did you mail that letter for me?
   B: Oh, I'm sorry. I completely forgot. ______________ it now. (I / do)
9. *A:* The ceiling in this room doesn't look very safe, does it?
   B: No, it looks as if ______________ down. (it / fall)
10. *A:* Has Dan decided what to do when he finishes high school?
    B: Yes. Everything is planned. ______________ a few months off. (he / take) Then ______________ classes at the community college. (he / start)

22.2 状況に合うように，will ('ll) もしくは (be) going to のいずれかと（　）内の語句を組み合わせて文を完成しなさい。

1. The phone rings and you answer. Somebody wants to speak to Jim.
   Caller: Hello. Can I speak to Jim, please?
   You: Just a minute. _I'll get_ him. (I / get)
2. It's a nice day, so you have decided to take a walk. Just before you go, you tell your friend.
   You: The weather's too nice to stay indoors. ______________ a walk. (I / take)
   Friend: Good idea. I think ______________ you. (I / join)
3. Your friend is worried because she has lost an important letter.
   You: Don't worry about the letter. I'm sure ______________ it. (you / find)
4. There was a job advertised in the newspaper recently. At first you were interested, but then you decided not to apply.
   Friend: Have you decided what to do about that job you were interested in?
   You: Yes, ______________ for it. (I / not / apply)
5. You and a friend come home very late. Other people in the house are asleep. Your friend is noisy.
   You: Shh! Don't make so much noise. ______________ everybody up. (you / wake)
6. John has to go to the airport to catch a plane tomorrow morning.
   John: Ann, I need a ride to the airport tomorrow morning.
   Ann: That's no problem. ______________ you. (I / take) What time is your flight?
   John: 10:50.
   Ann: OK, ______________ at about 8:00. (we / leave)
   Later that day, Joe offers John a ride to the airport.
   Joe: John, do you want me to take you to the airport?
   John: No thanks, Joe. ______________ me. (Ann / take)

補充問題 10–13 (pp. 302–304)

UNIT 23

will be -ing と will have + 過去分詞

A

☆ 例文で考えます。現在進行形と未来進行形，未来完了形は，どのように異なりますか？

These people are standing in line to get into the stadium.
(⇒ 今…している)

An hour from now, the stadium will be full.
Everyone **will be watching** the game.
(⇒ …しているところだろう)

Three hours from now, the stadium will be empty.
The game **will have ended**.
Everyone **will have gone** home.
(⇒ …し終えているだろう)

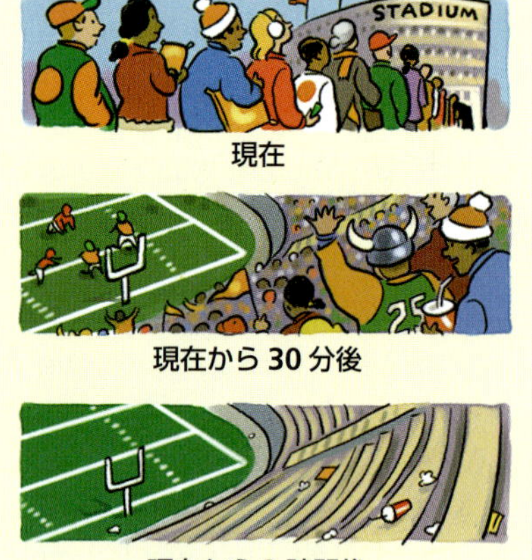

現在

現在から 30 分後

現在から 3 時間後

B

「…しているところだろう」のように，状況から予測できる出来事は I **will be -ing** ... の**未来進行形**で表します。

- I'm leaving on vacation this Saturday. This time next week, I**'ll be lying** on the beach or **swimming** in the ocean.
- You have no chance of getting the job. You**'ll be wasting** your time if you apply for it.

☆ 例文で考えます。will be -ing と will do は，どのように異なりますか？

- Don't call me between 7 and 8. We**'ll be having** dinner.
- Let's wait for Maria to arrive, and then we**'ll have** dinner.

☆ 例文で考えます。未来進行形 (will be -ing) と過去進行形，現在進行形は，どのように異なりますか？

- At 10:00 yesterday, Kelly **was** at the office. She **was working**. (過去進行形)
  It's 10:00 now. She **is** at the office. She **is working**. (現在進行形)
  At 10:00 tomorrow, she **will be** at the office. She **will be working**. (未来進行形)

C

「〜するだろう」のように，**will be -ing** は，未来において始まって完結すると予想できる**動作**を表すことがあります。進行中の動作を表してはいません。

- The government **will be making** a statement about the crisis later today.
- **Will** you **be going** away this summer?
- Later in the program, I**'ll be talking** to the Minister of Education . . .
- Our best player is injured and **won't be playing** in the game on Saturday.

上の例において，**will be -ing** は **(be) going to + 動詞の原形**とほぼ同じ意味で用いられています。

D

「…し終えているだろう」のように，未来の一時点においてそれ以前に終わっていることが予測できる出来事は **will have + 過去分詞**の**未来完了形**で表します。

- Sally always leaves for work at 8:30 in the morning. She won't be at home at 9:00 – she**'ll have gone** to work.
- We're late. The movie **will** already **have started** by the time we get to the theater.

☆ 例文で考えます。未来完了形(will have + 過去分詞)と現在完了形，過去完了形は，どのように異なりますか？

- Ted and Amy **have been** married for 24 years. (現在完了形)
  Next year they **will have been** married for 25 years. (未来完了形)
  When their first child was born, they **had been** married for three years. (過去完了形)

will ➲ Units 20–21　by the time / by then ➲ Unit 117C　未来 ➲ 付録 3

Exercises

23.1 次の文章を読んで，Josh がどのような状況かを確認しなさい。また状況と適合する 1~6 の文に ✓ を付けなさい。a)~d) の少なくとも 1 つには正しい記述が含まれています。

Josh goes to work every day. After breakfast, he leaves home at 8:00 and arrives at work at about 8:45. He starts work immediately and continues until 12:30, when he has lunch (which takes about half an hour). He starts work again at 1:15 and goes home at exactly 4:30. Every day he follows the same routine, and tomorrow will be no exception.

1. 

At 7:45
a) he'll be leaving the house
b) he'll have left the house
c) he'll be at home ✓
d) he'll be having breakfast ✓

2. 

At 8:15
a) he'll be leaving the house
b) he'll have left the house
c) he'll have arrived at work
d) he'll be arriving at work

3. 

At 9:15
a) he'll be working
b) he'll start work
c) he'll have started work
d) he'll be arriving at work

4. **At 12:45**
a) he'll have lunch
b) he'll be having lunch
c) he'll have finished his lunch
d) he'll have started his lunch

5. 

At 4:00
a) he'll have finished work
b) he'll finish work
c) he'll be working
d) he won't have finished work

6. **At 4:45**
a) he'll leave work
b) he'll be leaving work
c) he'll have left work
d) he'll have arrived home

23.2 状況に合うように，(　) 内の語句を will be -ing もしくは will have＋過去分詞の形に変えて文を完成しなさい。

1. Don't call me between 7 and 8. _We'll be having_ (we / have) dinner then.
2. Call me after 8:00. ________ (we / finish) dinner by then.
3. Tomorrow afternoon we're going to play tennis from 3:00 until 4:30. So at 4:00, ________ (we / play) tennis.
4. *A:* Can we meet tomorrow afternoon?
   B: I'm sorry I can't. ________ (I / work).
5. *B has to go to a meeting that begins at 10:00. It will last about an hour.*
   A: Will you be free at 11:30?
   B: Yes, ________ (the meeting / end) by then.
6. Ben is on vacation, and he is spending his money very quickly. If he continues like this, ________ (he / spend) all his money before the end of his vacation.
7. Do you think ________ (you / still / do) the same job 10 years from now?
8. Lisa is from New Zealand. She is traveling around South America right now. So far she has traveled about 1,000 miles. By the end of the trip, ________ (she / travel) more than 3,000 miles.
9. If you need to contact me, ________ (I / stay) at the Bellmore Hotel until Friday.
10. *A:* ________ (you / see) Laura tomorrow?
    B: Yes, probably. Why?
    A: I borrowed this CD from her. Can you give it back to her?

補充問題 10–13 (pp. 302–304)

UNIT 24

when I do / when I've done
when と if (従属節内の時制)

A

☆ イラストを見て考えます。when 節内ではどのような形が用いられていますか？

I'll call you **when I get** home. の文は 2 つの節に分割できます。

主節：I'll call you
when 節 (従属節)：**when I get** home from work

➤ **文全体は tomorrow で示されているように未来の出来事ですが，when 節内では現在時制を用います。when 節内で will は用いません。**

☆ **when 節内では，どのような形が用いられていますか？ 例文から考えなさい。**

- We'll go out **when** it **stops** raining. (× when it will stop)
- **When** you **are** in Los Angeles again, give us a call. (× When you will be)
- 〔子どもに向かって〕What do you want to be **when** you **grow** up? (× will grow)

同様のことが **while** / **before** / **after** / **as soon as** / **until** (= **till**) といった語句で始まる節内にも生じます。

- I'm going to read a lot of books **while I'm** on vacation. (× while I will be)
- I'm going back home on Sunday. **Before** I **go**, I'd like to visit a museum.
- Wait here **until** (= **till**) I **come** back.

B

when / **after** / **until** / **as soon as** といった語句で始まる節内で，**have + 過去分詞**の形の現在完了形を用いることがあります。

- Can I borrow that book **when** you**'ve finished** it?
- Don't say anything while Ben is here. Wait **until** he **has gone**.

従属節内の現在完了形は，主節の出来事より以前に出来事が起こったことを表します。2 つの出来事は同時に生じません。

- **When I've called** Kate, we can have dinner.
  (⇒ 電話が終わってから，夕食を食べよう)

2 つの出来事が同時に生じる場合，従属節内で**現在完了形**は使えません。

- **When** I **call** Kate, I'll ask her about the party. (× When I've called)
  (⇒ 電話して聞いてみよう)

接続詞の持つ意味から出来事の順番が明らかな場合，**単純現在形**と**現在完了形**を同じように用います。

- I'll come **as soon as** I **finish**. = I'll come **as soon as** I**'ve finished**.
- You'll feel better **after** you **have** something to eat. = You'll feel better **after** you**'ve had** something to eat.

C

if で始まる**従属節内**でも，未来の出来事を **if I do** / **if I see** などのような**単純現在形**で表します。

- It's raining hard. We'll get wet **if** we **go** out. (× if we will go)
- I'll be angry **if** it **happens** again. (× if it will happen)
- Hurry up! **If** we **don't hurry**, we'll be late.

D

☆ **例文で考えます。when と if では従属節内の出来事に関して，どのように異なりますか？**

➤ **when 節内では，確実に起きる出来事を述べます。**

- I'm going shopping later. (強い意志) **When** I go shopping, I'll get some cheese.

➤ **if 節内では，起きるかもしれないと思われる出来事を述べます。この場合 when は用いません。**

- I might go shopping later. (おそらく…) **If** I go shopping, I'll get some cheese.
- **If** it is raining tonight, I won't go out. (× When it is raining)
- Don't worry **if** I'm late tonight. (× when I'm late)
- **If** they don't come soon, I'm not going to wait. (× When they don't come)

if ➲ Units 36–38 even if / even when ➲ Unit 109D unless ➲ Unit 112A

Exercises

24.1 未来に関する正しい記述となるように，**will/won't** もしくは単純現在形の（　）内の動詞を組み合わせて文を完成しなさい。

1. I _'ll call_ (call) you when I _get_ (get) home from work.
2. I want to see Jennifer before she __________ (go) out.
3. We're going on a trip tomorrow. I __________ (tell) you all about it when we __________ (come) back.
4. Brian looks very different now. When you __________ (see) him again, you __________ (not / recognize) him.
5. __________ (you / miss) me while I __________ (be) gone?
6. We should do something soon before it __________ (be) too late.
7. I don't want to go without you. I __________ (wait) until you __________ (be) ready.
8. Sue has applied for the job, but she isn't very well qualified for it. I __________ (be) surprised if she __________ (get) it.
9. I'd like to play tennis tomorrow if the weather __________ (be) nice.
10. I'm going out now. If anybody __________ (call) while I __________ (be) out, can you take a message?

24.2 例にならって，2 つの文を 1 つにまとめなさい。

1. You'll be in Los Angeles again. Give us a call.
   Give us a call when _you are in Los Angeles again_ .
2. I'll find a place to live. Then I'll give you my address.
   I __________ when __________ .
3. I'll go shopping. Then I'll come straight home.
   __________ after __________ .
4. It's going to get dark. Let's go home before that.
   __________ before __________ .
5. She must apologize to me first. I won't speak to her until then.
   __________ until __________ .

24.3 状況に合うように，空所に適切な語句を入れて文を完成しなさい。

1. A friend of yours is going on vacation. You want to know what she is going to do. You ask:
   What are you going to do when _you go on vacation_ ?
2. A friend of yours is visiting you. She has to go soon, but you'd like to show her some pictures. You ask:
   Do you have time to look at some pictures before __________ ?
3. You want to sell your car. Jim is interested in buying it, but he hasn't decided yet. You ask:
   Can you let me know as soon as __________ ?
4. A friend of yours is going to visit Hong Kong. You want to know where she is going to stay. You ask:
   Where are you going to stay when __________ ?
5. The traffic is very bad in your town, but they are going to build a new road. You say:
   I think things will be better when they __________ .

24.4 空所に **when** もしくは **if** を入れて文を完成しなさい。

1. Don't worry _if_ I'm late tonight.
2. Chris might call while I'm out tonight. ______ he does, can you take a message?
3. I'm going to Tokyo next week. ______ I'm there, I hope to visit a friend of mine.
4. I think Beth will get the job. I'll be very surprised ______ she doesn't get it.
5. I'm going shopping. ______ you want anything, I can get it for you.
6. I'm going away for a few days. I'll call you ______ I get back.
7. I want you to come to the party, but ______ you don't want to come, that's all right.
8. We can eat at home or, ______ you prefer, we can go to a restaurant.

補充問題 10–13 (pp. 302–304) / 32 (pp. 314–315)

UNIT 25

can, could と (be) able to

A

can＋動詞の原形（can do / can see など）の形は，「…になりうる /…してもよい」のような物事の可能性 / 許可や「…できる」のような人の能力を表します。

- We **can see** the ocean from our hotel window.
- "I don't have a pen." "You **can use** mine."
- **Can** you **speak** any foreign languages?
- I **can come** and help you tomorrow if you want.
- The word "dream" **can be** a noun or a verb.

否定形は **can't**（もしくは **cannot**）を用います。

- I'm afraid I **can't come** to your party on Friday.

同じことを **be able to** を用いて言うこともできますが，**can** の方がより一般的です。

- We **are able to see** the ocean from our hotel window.

can には**現在形** (can) と**過去形** (could) の 2 つの形しかないために，**can** に代わって **be able to** を用いなくてはならない場合があります。

I **can't** sleep.	I **haven't been able to** sleep recently.
Tom **can** come tomorrow.	Tom **might be able to** come tomorrow.
Maria **can** speak French, Spanish, and English.	Applicants for the job **must be able to** speak two foreign languages.

B

could は，以下のような知覚や思考に関わる動詞とよく結び付きます。この場合には **can の過去形**として，「(実際に) …できた」の意味で用います。

see　hear　smell　taste　feel　remember　understand

- We had a nice room in the hotel. We **could see** the ocean.
- As soon as I walked into the room, I **could smell** gas.
- She spoke in a very soft voice, so I **couldn't understand** what she said.

C

could は「(いつも，普通)…できた」のような，人が過去に持っていた一般的な能力や「…してよかった，…することが許されていた」のように過去に許されていたことを表します。

- My grandfather **could speak** five languages.
- We were totally free. We **could do** what we wanted.（⇒ 何をしても許された）

D

☆ could と was able to は，どのように異なりますか？

➤ could は，人が過去に持っていた一般的な能力を表します。ある特定の状況で人が具体的に何かをした場合には，was/were able to もしくは managed to を用います。以下の状況では could は用いられません。

- The fire spread through the building very quickly, but fortunately everybody **was able to escape** / **managed to escape**.（✕ could escape）
- We didn't know where David was, but we **managed to find** / **were able to find** him in the end.（✕ could find）

☆ 以下の例文が表す状況を比較しなさい。

- Jack was an excellent tennis player when he was younger. He **could beat** anybody.（⇒ 誰にも負けないくらい強かった）

⇔ Jack and Ted played tennis yesterday. Ted played very well, but Jack **managed to** / **was able to beat** him.（⇒ 今度だけは勝つことができた）

否定形 couldn't (= **could not**) は，上の例文のいずれの状況でも問題なく使えます。

- My grandfather **couldn't swim**.
- We looked for David everywhere, but we **couldn't find** him.
- Ted played well, but he **couldn't beat** Jack.

could (do) と could have (done) ➲ Unit 25　must ➲ Unit 27　Can/Could you ...? ➲ Unit 35

Exercises

25.1 空所に can もしくは (be) able to を入れて文を完成しなさい。(be) able to しか許されない場合を除いて can を用いること。

1. Eric has traveled a lot. He _can_ speak four languages.
2. I haven't _been able to_ sleep very well recently.
3. Nicole ________ drive, but she doesn't have a car.
4. I used to ________ stand on my head, but I can't do it any more.
5. I can't understand Michael. I've never ________ understand him.
6. I can't see you on Friday, but I ________ meet you on Saturday morning.
7. Ask Catherine about your problem. She might ________ help you.

25.2 ( ) 内に指示されている通りに，自分のことを記述した文を作りなさい。

1. (something you used to be able to do)
   I used to be able to sing well.
2. (something you used to be able to do)
   I used ________
3. (something you would like to be able to do)
   I'd ________
4. (something you have never been able to do)
   I've ________

25.3 以下から適切な動詞を選び，can/can't/could/couldn't の後に続けて文を完成しなさい。

~~come~~ eat hear run sleep wait

1. I'm sorry I _can't come_ to your party next week.
2. When Bob was 16, he ________ 100 meters in 11 seconds.
3. "Are you in a hurry?" "No, I've got plenty of time. I ________."
4. I felt sick yesterday. I ________ anything.
5. Can you speak a little louder? I ________ you very well.
6. "You look tired." "Yes, I ________ last night."

25.4 状況に合うように，was/were able to を用いて文を完成しなさい。

1. *A:* Did everybody escape from the fire?
   B: Yes. Although the fire spread quickly, everybody _was able to escape_.
2. *A:* Did you finish your homework this afternoon?
   B: Yes, nobody was around to disturb me, so I ________.
3. *A:* Did you have any trouble finding Amy's house?
   B: Not really. She'd given us good directions, so we ________.
4. *A:* Did the thief get away?
   B: Yes. No one realized what was happening, and the thief ________.

25.5 could / couldn't / managed to の中から，空所に入れるのに最もふさわしいものを選び文を完成しなさい。

1. My grandfather traveled a lot. He _could_ speak five languages.
2. I looked everywhere for the book, but I _couldn't_ find it.
3. They didn't want to come with us at first, but we _managed to_ persuade them.
4. Laura had hurt her leg and ________ walk very well.
5. Sue wasn't at home when I called, but I ________ contact her at her office.
6. I looked very carefully, and I ________ see someone in the distance.
7. I wanted to buy some tomatoes. The first store I went to didn't have any good ones, but I ________ get some at the next place.
8. My grandmother loved music. She ________ play the piano very well.
9. A girl fell into the river, but fortunately we ________ rescue her.
10. I had forgotten to bring my camera, so I ________ take any photos.

UNIT 26

could（＋ 動詞の原形）と could have（＋ 過去分詞）

A

could にはいくつかの用法があります。**can** の過去形としても使えます。➲Unit 25C

- Listen. I **can hear** something.（現在）
- I listened. I **could hear** something.（過去）

☆ イラストはどのような状況を表していますか？

➤ **could** は **can** の過去形の用法以外に，現在や未来の動作を表します。「…しましょう，…してはどうですか？」のような提案を行う場合，**could** はことに未来の動作を表します。

同様のことが，以下の例文にも見られます。

- *A:* What would you like to do tonight?
  B: We **could go** to the movies.
- *A:* When you go to New York next month, you **could stay** with Candice.
  B: Yes, I guess I **could**.

上の例文中では，いずれも We **can go** to the movies. などのように **can** も使えますが，**could** を用いたほうがより丁寧な提案になります。

B

could は「…だろう」のように現実性が乏しい動作を表します。この場合 can は用いません。

- I'm so tired, I **could sleep** for a week.（✕ I can sleep for a week）

☆ 以下の例文で考えなさい。**can** と **could** は，実現性に関連してどのように異なりますか？

- I **can stay** with Candice when I go to New York.（**現実的**。実現性が高い）
- Maybe I **could stay** with Candice when I go to New York.（不可能ではないが**不確実**）
- This is a wonderful place. I **could stay** here forever.（**非現実的**）

C

could は「…だろう，…かもしれない」のように，現在や未来において起こりうる出来事を表します。この場合，**might** や **may** と同じような意味になります。➲Units 28–29（この場合 can では置き換えられません）

- The story **could be** true, but I don't think it is.（✕ can be true）
- I don't know what time Liz is coming. She **could get** here at any time.

D

「…だろう」の意味の **could** の過去形は，**could have**（＋ 過去分詞）で「…しただろう」を表します。

- I'm so tired, I **could sleep** for a week.（現在）
  I was so tired, I **could have slept** for a week.（過去）
- The situation is bad, but it **could be** worse.（現在）
  The situation was bad, but it **could have been** worse.（過去）

could have（＋ 過去分詞）は，可能性はあったものの実際には起こらなかった出来事を表します。

- Why did you stay at a hotel when you were in New York? You **could have stayed** with Candice.（⇒ 実際には彼女の家に泊まらなかった）
- I didn't know that you wanted to go to the concert. I **could have gotten** you a free ticket.（⇒ 実際にはチケットを取ってあげなかった）
- Dave was lucky. He **could have hurt** himself when he fell, but he's OK.

E

couldn't は「…しないだろう」と，現在において起こりそうにない出来事を表します。

- I **couldn't live** in a big city. I'd hate it.（⇒ 自分にはとてもできそうにもない）
- Everything is fine right now. Things **couldn't be** better.（⇒ 最高だろうね）

「…しないだろう」の意味の **couldn't** の過去形は，**couldn't have**（＋ 過去分詞）で「…しなかっただろう」を表します。

- We had a really good vacation. It **couldn't have been** better.（⇒ 最高だったよ）
- The trip was canceled last week. Paul **couldn't have gone** anyway because he was sick.（⇒ いずれにしても行けなかっただろう）

Exercises

26.1 could と（ ）内の語句を用いて，疑問文に対して「…しましょう」のような提案の文を作りなさい。

1. Where would you like to go on vacation? (to San Diego) *We could go to San Diego.*
2. What should we have for dinner tonight? (fish) We ____
3. When should I call Angela? (now) You ____
4. What should I give Ana for her birthday? (a book) ____
5. When should we go and see Tom? (on Friday) ____

____

26.2 文中の can を could に変えなくてはならないものはどれですか？ 必要に応じて文を書き改めなさい。

1. The story can be true but I don't think it is. *could be true*
2. It's a nice day. We can go for a walk. *OK*（could go も可）
3. I'm so angry I can scream. ____
4. If you're hungry, we can have dinner now. ____
5. It's so nice here. I can stay here all day, but unfortunately I have to go. ____
6. *A:* Where's my bag. Have you seen it?
   B: No, but it can be in the car. ____
7. Peter is a good musician. He plays the flute, and he can also play the piano. ____
8. *A:* I need to borrow a camera.
   B: You can borrow mine. ____
9. The weather is nice now, but it can change later. ____

26.3 空所に could もしくは could have に適切な動詞を続けて入れて，文を完成しなさい。

1. *A:* What should we do tonight?
   B: We *could go* to the movies.
2. *A:* I spent a very boring evening at home yesterday.
   B: Why did you stay at home? You ____ out with us.
3. *A:* There's a job advertised in the paper that I think you are really qualified for.
   B: I guess I ____ for it, but I like my present job.
4. *A:* How was your test? Was it hard?
   B: It wasn't so bad. It ____ worse.
5. *A:* I got very wet walking home in the rain last night.
   B: Why did you walk? You ____ a taxi.
6. *A:* Where should we meet tomorrow?
   B: Well, I ____ to your house if you want.

26.4 couldn't もしくは could't have に続くように，以下から動詞を選び適切な形に変えて文を完成しなさい。

~~be~~ be come find get ~~live~~ wear

1. I *couldn't live* in a big city. I'd hate it.
2. We had a really good vacation. It *couldn't have been* better.
3. I ____ that hat. I'd look silly, and people would laugh at me.
4. We managed to find the restaurant you recommended, but we ____ it without the map that you drew for us.
5. Paul has to get up at 4:00 every morning. I don't know how he does it. I ____ up at that time every day.
6. The staff at the hotel was really nice when we stayed there last summer. They ____ more helpful.
7. *A:* I tried to call you last week. We had a party, and I wanted to invite you.
   B: That's nice of you, but I ____ anyway. I was away all last week.

UNIT 27

must (You must be tired. など)

A

must (not)

☆イラストの状況について考えなさい。must (not) はどのような状況で使われていますか？

➤「…であるに違いない」のように，状況から論理的に判断して何かに十分確信が持てる場合は must を用います。

- You've been traveling all day. You **must be** tired.
  (⇒ Traveling is tiring and you've been traveling all day, so you **must be** tired.)
- "Jim is a hard worker." "Jim? You **must be** joking. He's very lazy."
- I'm sure Sally gave me her phone number. I **must have** it somewhere.

➤「…ではないに違いない」のように，何かではないことに十分確信が持てる場合は must not を用います。

- Their car isn't outside their house. They **must not be** home. (= They **must be** out)
- Brian said he would be here by 9:30. It's 10:00 now, and he's never late. He **must not be coming**.
- They haven't lived here very long. They **must not know** many people.

must (not) は，次のような形で用います。

I/you/he (など)	must (not)	**be** (tired / hungry / home など) **be** (**doing** / **coming** / **joking** など) **do** / **get** / **know** / **have** など

B

must (not) have + 過去分詞

must の過去形は **must (not) have + 過去分詞**で「…だった（ではなかった）に違いない」を表します。

- "We used to live close to the freeway." "Did you? It **must have been** noisy."
- There's nobody at home. They **must have gone** out.
- I've lost one of my gloves. I **must have dropped** it somewhere.
- She walked past me without speaking. She **must not have seen** me.
- Tom walked into a wall. He **must not have been looking** where he was going.

must (not) have + 過去分詞は，次のような形で用います。

I/you/he (など)	must (not)	have	**been** (tired / hungry / noisy など) **been** (**doing** / **coming** / **looking**, など) **gone** / **dropped** / **seen** など

C

can't と must (not)

It can't be true. は「…ではありえない，はずがない」のように，可能性がまったくないことを表します。

- How can you say such a thing? You **can't be** serious!

☆can't と must (not) が用いられる状況は，どのように異なりますか？

- *A:* Joe wants something to eat.
- *B:* But he just had lunch. He **can't be** hungry already.
  (⇒ お昼を食べたばかりなので空腹であるはずがない / 可能性がない)
- *A:* I offered Bill something to eat, but he didn't want anything.
  B: He **must not be** hungry.
  (⇒ きっと空腹ではないと思う。空腹なら何か食べるはず…)

(I can't swim. などの) can't の用法 ➲ Unit 25A, B　(I must go. などの) must の用法 ➲ Unit 30B, C
イギリス英語の用法 ➲ 付録 7

Exercises

27.1 空所に **must** もしくは **must not** を入れて，文を完成しなさい。

1. You've been traveling all day. You *must* be tired.
2. That restaurant ______________ be very good. It's always full of people.
3. That restaurant ______________ be very good. It's always empty.
4. You ______________ be looking forward to going on vacation next week.
5. It rained every day during their vacation, so they ______________ have had a very nice time.
6. You got here very quickly. You ______________ have walked very fast.

27.2 空所に 1 語もしくは 2 語のふさわしい動詞を入れて，文を完成しなさい。

1. I've lost one of my gloves. I must *have dropped* it somewhere.
2. They haven't lived here very long. They must not *know* many people.
3. Ted isn't at work today. He must ______________ sick.
4. Ted wasn't at work last week. He must ______________ sick.
5. Sarah knows a lot about movies. She must ______________ to the movies a lot.
6. Look. James is putting on his hat and coat. He must ______________ out.
7. I left my bike outside last night and now it is gone. Somebody must ______________ it.
8. Sue was in a difficult situation when she lost her job. It must not ______________ easy for her.
9. There is a man walking behind us. He has been walking behind us for the last 20 minutes. He must ______________ us.

27.3 状況に合うように，（　）内の語句と **must have** もしくは **must not have** を用いて文を完成しなさい。

1. The phone rang, but I didn't hear it. (I / asleep) *I must have been asleep.*
2. Julie walked past me without speaking. (she / see / me) *She must not have seen me.*
3. The jacket you bought is very good quality. (it / very expensive)
____
4. I can't find my umbrella. (I / leave / it in the restaurant last night)
____
5. Dave passed the exam without studying for it. (the exam / very difficult)
____
6. She knew everything about our plans. (she / listen / to our conversation)
____
7. Rachel did the opposite of what I asked her to do. (she / understand / what I said)
____
8. When I woke up this morning, the light was on. (I / forget / to turn it off)
____
9. I was awakened in the night by loud music next door. (the neighbors / have / a party)
____

27.4 状況に合うように，**must not** もしくは **can't** を用いて文を完成しなさい。

1. How can you say such a thing? You *can't* be serious!
2. Their car isn't outside their house. They *must not* be home.
3. I just bought a box of cereal yesterday. It ______________ be empty already.
4. The Smiths always go on vacation this time of year, but they are still home. They ______________ be taking a vacation this year.
5. You just started filling out your tax forms 10 minutes ago. You ______________ be finished with them already!
6. Eric is a good friend of Ann's, but he hasn't visited her in the hospital. He ______________ know she's in the hospital.

UNIT 28

may と might 1

A

☆ 例文の状況について考えなさい。may や might は，どのような状況で使われていますか？

あなたは Bob を探しています。はっきりと知っている人はいなかったものの，ヒントはもらえました。

Where's Bob?

He **may be** in his office.（⇒ オフィスにいるかもしれない）

He **might be having** lunch.（⇒ お昼を食べているかもしれない）

Ask Ann. She **might know**.（⇒ 彼なら知っているかもしれない）

➤ 出来事について「…かもしれない，…もありうる」のように可能性がある場合，may や might を用います。

may と **might** の間に大きな違いはありません。

- It **may** be true. = It **might** be true.（⇒ 真実かもしれない）
- She **might** know. = She **may** know.

「…ではないかもしれない」のような出来事が起こらない可能性は **may not**，**might not** で表します。

- It **may not** be true.（⇒ 真実ではないかもしれない）
- She **might not** work here any more.（⇒ ここでは働いていないかもしれない）

may (not)，**might (not)** は，次のような形で用います。

I/you/he（など）	**may** **might**	(**not**)	**be**（true / in his office など） **be**（**doing** / **working** / **having** など） **do** / **know** / **work** / **want** など

B

may have + **過去分詞**や **might have** + **過去分詞**は，「…だったかもしれない」という過去の可能性を表します。

- *A:* I wonder why Kate didn't answer the phone.
  B: She **may have been** asleep.（⇒ 眠かったかもしれない）
- *A:* I can't find my bag anywhere.
  B: You **might have left** it in the store.（⇒ 店に置いてきたかもしれない）
- *A:* I was surprised that Sarah wasn't at the meeting yesterday.
  B: She **might not have known** about it.（⇒ 知らなかったかもしれない）
- *A:* I wonder why David was in such a bad mood yesterday.
  B: He **may not have been feeling** well.（⇒ 気分が良くなったかもしれない）

may (not) have + **過去分詞**，**might (not) have** + **過去分詞**は，次のような形で用います。

I/you/he（など）	**may** **might**	(**not**) **have**	**been**（asleep / at home など） **been**（**doing** / **working** / **feeling** など） **known** / **had** / **wanted** / **left** など

C

could は，**may** や **might** と同様に「…かもしれない，…もありうる」のような可能性を表します。

- It's a strange story, but it **could be** true. (= It may/might be true)
- You **could have left** your bag in the store. (= You may/might have left it there)

否定形 **couldn't** は，**may not** や **might not** とは異なり「…ではありえない，…のはずがない」のように可能性がまったくないことを表します。

- Sarah **couldn't have gotten** my message. Otherwise she would have called me.
  （⇒ 連絡を受け取ったはずがない）
- I wonder why Sarah hasn't called me. I suppose she **might not have gotten** my message.（⇒ 連絡を受け取らなかったかもしれない）

could の用法 ➲ Unit 26　might/may 2 ➲ Unit 29　May I ...? の用法 ➲ Unit 35
if 節内の might の用法 ➲ Units 29B, 36C, 38D　can/could/will/would などの法助動詞の用法 ➲ 付録 4

Exercises

28.1 may と might の 2 通りで文を書き換えなさい。

1. Perhaps Elizabeth is in her office. *She might be in her office.* or *She may be . . .*
2. Perhaps Elizabeth is busy. ____________________
3. Perhaps she is working. ____________________
4. Perhaps she wants to be alone. ____________________
5. Perhaps she was sick yesterday. ____________________
6. Perhaps she went home early. ____________________
7. Perhaps she had to go home early. ____________________
8. Perhaps she was working yesterday. ____________________

may not と might not の 2 通りで文を書き換えなさい。

9. Perhaps she doesn't want to see me. ____________________
10. Perhaps she isn't working today. ____________________
11. Perhaps she wasn't feeling well yesterday. ____________________

28.2 状況に合うように，空所に適切な動詞を入れて文を完成しなさい。

1. "Where's Sam?" "I'm not sure. He might *be having* lunch."
2. "Who is that man with Anna?" "I'm not sure. It might __________ her brother."
3. "Who was the man we saw with Anna yesterday?" "I'm not sure. It may __________ her brother."
4. "What are those people doing by the side of the road?" "I don't know. They might __________ for a bus."
5. "Do you have a stamp?" "No, but ask Sam. He may __________ one."

28.3 状況に合うように，may もしくは might と（ ）内の語句を用いて文を完成しなさい。

1. I can't find Jeff anywhere. I wonder where he is.
   a) (he / go / shopping) *He may have gone shopping.*
   b) (he / play / tennis) *He might be playing tennis.*
2. I'm looking for Tiffany. Do you know where she is?
   a) (she / watch / TV / in her room) ____________________
   b) (she / go / out) ____________________
3. I can't find my umbrella. Have you seen it?
   a) (it / be / in the car) ____________________
   b) (you / leave / in the restaurant last night / it) ____________________
4. Why didn't Dave answer the doorbell? I'm sure he was at home at the time.
   a) (he / not / hear / the doorbell) ____________________
   b) (he / be / in the shower) ____________________

28.4 状況に合うように，might not have ＋過去分詞もしくは couldn't have ＋過去分詞を用いて文を完成しなさい。

1. *A:* Do you think Sarah got the message we left her?
   B: No, she would have contacted us. *She couldn't have gotten it.*
2. *A:* I was surprised Kate wasn't at the meeting. Perhaps she didn't know about it.
   B: That's possible. *She might not have known about it.*
3. *A:* I wonder why they never replied to our letter. Do you think they received it?
   B: Maybe not. They ____________________ .
4. *A:* I wonder how the fire started. Was it an accident?
   B: No, the police say it ____________________ .
5. *A:* Mike says he needs to see you. He tried to find you yesterday.
   B: Well, he ____________________ very hard. I was in my office all day.
6. *A:* The man you spoke to – are you sure he was Chinese?
   B: No, I'm not sure. He ____________________ .

補充問題 16–18 (pp. 305–307)

UNIT 29

may と might 2

A

may や **might** は，「…だろう，…かもしれない」のように未来に起こりうる動作や出来事を表します。

- I haven't decided yet where to go on vacation. I **may go** to Hawaii.
  (⇒ おそらく出かけるでしょう)
- Take an umbrella with you. It **might rain** later. (⇒ おそらく降るでしょう)
- The bus isn't always on time. We **might have** to wait a few minutes.
  (⇒ おそらく待たなければならないでしょう)

may not もしくは **might not** は，「…ではないだろう」のような否定を表します。

- Ann **may not go** out tonight. She isn't feeling well. (⇒ おそらく出かけないでしょう)
- There **might not be** enough time to discuss everything at the meeting.

☆ **will と may/might は，どのように異なりますか？**

- **I'll be** late this evening. (⇒ きっと遅くなるでしょう)
- I **may/might** be late this evening. (⇒ おそらく遅くなるでしょう)

B

may と **might** の間に大きな意味上の違いはありません。

- I **may go** to Hawaii. = I **might go** to Hawaii.
- Lisa **might be** able to help you. = Lisa **may be** able to help you.

事実に反することを仮定する場合 **might** しか用いられません。 この場合 **may** は使えません。

- If I were in Tom's position, I think I **might** look for another job.

実際には「I(私)は Tom の立場になく，別の仕事も探していない」ので，事実に反することを仮定しています。この文中で **may** を用いることはできません。

C

☆ **may/might be -ing は，will be -ing とどのように異なりますか？**

- Don't call me at 8:30. **I'll be watching** the baseball game on TV. (⇒ きっと見ているでしょう)
- Don't call me at 8:30. I **might be watching** (= I **may be watching**) the baseball game on TV. (⇒ おそらく見ているでしょう)

☆ **may/might be -ing は，起こりそうな計画を表します。現在進行形とどのように異なりますか？**

- **I'm going** to Hawaii in July. (⇒ きっと行くことになるでしょう)
- I **may be going** (= I **might be going**) to Hawaii in July. (⇒ おそらく行くことになるでしょう)

実際には，上の **I may/might be going ...** の代わりに **I may/might go ...** を用いても意味的にほとんど変わりません。

D

might as well / may as well

☆ **イラストの状況について考えなさい。might as well と may as well は，どのような状況で用いられていますか？**

Rosa と Maria は，1 時間に 1 本しかないバスに乗りそこねました。この状況は次のように表せます。

What should we do? Should we walk?

We **might as well**. It's a nice day, and I don't want to wait here for an hour.

➤ **We might as well (walk). は「歩くしかない」のように，歩く以外の選択肢が他になく，そうしない理由もない状況を表します。**

might as well の代わりに **may as well** を用いても意味的に違いはありません。

☆ **以下の例文はどのような状況を表しますか？**

- *A:* You'll have to wait two hours to see the doctor.
  B: I **might as well go** home and come back. (⇒ 家に帰って出直すしかない)
- Rents are so high these days, you **may as well buy** a house.
  (⇒ 家賃を払い続けるくらいなら，家を買うのも悪くない)

will be -ing ➲ Unit 23　might/may 1 ➲ Unit 28　May I ...? の用法 ➲ Unit 35
if 節内の might の用法 ➲ Units 36C, 38D

Exercises

29.1 状況に合うように，（　）内の語句と **may** もしくは **might** を用いて文を完成しなさい。

1. Where are you going on vacation? (to Hawaii??)
   I haven't decided yet. *I might go to Hawaii.* ____________
2. What kind of car are you going to buy? (a Toyota??)
   I'm not sure yet. I ____________
3. What are you doing this weekend? (go to the movies??)
   I haven't made up my mind yet. ____________
4. When is Jim coming to see us? (on Saturday??)
   I don't know for sure. ____________
5. Where are you going to hang that picture? (in the dining room??)
   I haven't made up my mind yet. ____________
6. What is Julia going to do when she graduates from high school? (go to college??)
   She's still thinking about it. ____________

29.2 状況に合うように，**might** と以下のいずれかの動詞を組み合わせて文を完成しなさい。

bite　break　need　~~rain~~　slip　wake up

1. Take an umbrella with you when you go out. It *might rain* later.
2. Don't make too much noise. You ____________ the baby.
3. Watch out for that dog. It ____________ you.
4. I don't think we should throw that letter away. We ____________ it later.
5. Be careful. The sidewalk is very icy. You ____________ .
6. I don't want the children to play in this room. They ____________ something.

29.3 状況に合うように，**might be able to** もしくは **might have to** と適切な動詞を組み合わせて文を完成しなさい。

1. I can't help you, but why don't you ask Jane? She *might be able to help* you.
2. I can't meet you tonight, but I ____________ you tomorrow.
3. I'm not working on Saturday, but I ____________ on Sunday.
4. I can come to the meeting, but I ____________ before the end.

29.4 状況に合うように，**might not** を用いて文を完成しなさい。

1. I'm not sure that Ann will come to the party.
   Ann might not come to the party. ____________
2. I'm not sure that I'll go out tonight.
   I ____________
3. You don't know if Sam will like the present you bought for him.
   Sam ____________
4. We don't know if Sue will be able to get together with us tonight.
   ____

29.5 状況に合うように，**might as well** を用いて文を完成しなさい。

1. You and a friend have just missed the bus. The buses run every hour.
   You say: We'll have to wait an hour for the next bus. *We might as well walk.*
2. You have a free ticket for a concert. You're not very excited about the concert, but you decide to go.
   You say: I ____________ to the concert. It's a shame to waste a free ticket.
3. You've just painted your kitchen. You still have a lot of paint, so why not paint the bathroom, too?
   You say: We ____________ . There's plenty of paint left.
4. You and a friend are at home. You're bored. There's a movie on TV starting in a few minutes.
   You say: ____________ . There's nothing else to do.

補充問題 16–18 (pp. 305–307)

UNIT 30

have to と must

A

I **have to do** ... は「…する必要がある，…しなければならない」を表します。

- You can't turn right here. You **have to turn** left.
- I **have to get up** early tomorrow. My flight leaves at 7:30.
- Jason can't meet us tonight. He **has to work** late.
- Last week Nicole broke her arm and **had to go** to the hospital.
- Have you ever **had to go** to the hospital?

do/does/did を用いて，**単純現在形**および**単純過去形**の**疑問文**を作ります。

- What **do** I **have to do** to get a driver's license?
  (× What have I to do?)
- **Does** Kimberly **have to work** tomorrow?
- Why **did** you **have to leave** early?

don't/doesn't/didn't を用いて，**否定文**を作ります。

- I **don't have to get up** early tomorrow.
  (× I haven't to)
- Kimberly **doesn't have to work** on Saturdays.
- We **didn't have to pay** to park the car.

未来の出来事には，次のような形を用います。

I'll have to / I **won't have to** ...
I'm going to have to ...
I **might/may have to** ... (⇒ perhaps I'll have to)

- They can't fix my computer, so **I'll have to buy** a new one.
  (= ... so **I'm going to have to buy** a new one.)
- I **might have to leave** the meeting early. = I **may have to leave** ...

B

must も **have to** と同様に「…する必要がある，…しなければならない」を表します。

- The economic situation is bad. The government **must do** something about it.
  (= The government **has to do** ...)
- If you go to New York, you really **must visit** the Empire State Building.
  (= ... you really **have to** visit ...)

have to の方が **must** より，よく用いられます。

must は，規則や手順を記した文書中で用います。

- Answer all the questions. You **must write** your answers in ink.
- Applications for the job **must be received** by May 18.

C

You **must not do** ... は「…してはいけない，…は許されない」のように禁止を表します。

- Students **must not use** cell phones in class. (⇒ 使ってはいけない)

☆ **must not と don't have to は，どのように意味が異なりますか？**

- You **must keep** this a secret. You **must not tell** anybody.
  (⇒ 誰にもしゃべってはいけない)
- You **don't have to tell** Tim about what happened. I can tell him myself.
  (⇒ わざわざ言うこともないが，言いたければ言ってよい)

D

have to の代わりに **have got to** が使われることがよくあります。2つの形は同じように用います。

- **I've got to work** tomorrow. = I **have to work** tomorrow.
- **He's got to visit** his aunt tonight. = He **has to visit** his aunt tonight.

You must be tired. などのように「…に違いない」の must の用法 ➲ Unit 27

Exercises

30.1 状況に合うように，have to / has to / had to を用いて文を完成しなさい。

1. Jason can't join us tonight. He *has to* work late.
2. Beth left before the end of the meeting. She ______________ go home early.
3. I don't have much time. I ______________ go soon.
4. Kathy may ______________ go out of town on business next week.
5. Eric is usually free on weekends, but sometimes he ______________ work.
6. There was nobody to help me. I ______________ do everything by myself.
7. Julie has ______________ wear glasses since she was a small child.
8. Jeff can't pay his bills. He's going to ______________ sell his car.

30.2 状況に合うように，（　）内の語と have to の適切な形を用いて文を完成しなさい。

1. "I broke my arm last week." "*Did you have to go* (you / go) to the hospital?"
2. "I'm sorry I can't stay very long." "What time ______________ (you / go)?"
3. ______________ (you / wait) long for the bus last night?
4. How old ______________ (you / be) to drive in your country?
5. How does Chris like his new job? ______________ (he / travel) a lot?

30.3 状況に合うように，have to と以下のいずれかの動詞を組み合わせて文を完成しなさい。文は肯定形もしくは否定形のいずれかにすること。

ask　do　~~get up~~　go　make　make　shave　~~show~~

1. I'm not working tomorrow, so I *don't have to get up* early.
2. Steve didn't know how to use the computer, so I *had to show* him.
3. Excuse me for a minute – I ______________ a phone call.
4. I couldn't find the street I wanted. I ______________ somebody for directions.
5. Jack has a beard, so he ______________ .
6. A man was injured in the accident, but he ______________ to the hospital because it wasn't serious.
7. Sue is the vice president of the company. She ______________ important decisions.
8. I'm not so busy. I have a few things to do, but I ______________ them now.

30.4 状況に合うように，might have to，will have to，won't have to のいずれかを選んで文を完成しなさい。

1. They can't fix my computer, so I *'ll have to* buy a new one.
2. I *might have to* leave the party early. My son is going to call me if he needs a ride home.
3. We ______________ take the train downtown instead of driving. It depends on the traffic.
4. Sam ______________ go to jail if he doesn't pay all his old parking tickets.
5. Unfortunately, my father ______________ stay in the hospital another week. The doctor is going to decide tomorrow.
6. If it snows all night, we ______________ go to class tomorrow. It'll be canceled.

30.5 状況に合うように，must not もしくは don't / doesn't have to のいずれかを選んで文を完成しなさい。

1. I don't want anyone to know about this. You *must not* tell anyone.
2. He *doesn't have to* wear a suit to work, but he usually does.
3. I can sleep late tomorrow morning because I ______________ go to work.
4. Whatever you do, you ______________ touch that switch. It's very dangerous.
5. There's an elevator in the building, so we ______________ climb the stairs.
6. You ______________ forget what I told you. It's very important.
7. Lauren ______________ get up early, but she usually does.
8. You ______________ eat or drink on buses. It's not allowed.
9. You ______________ be a good player to enjoy a game of tennis.

補充問題 16–18 (pp. 305–307)

UNIT 31

should

A

You **should do** … は「…すべき，…するのが正しい」のように，アドバイスしたり意見を述べる際に用います。

- You look tired. You **should go** to bed.
- The government **should do** more to reduce crime.
- "**Should** we **invite** Susan to the party?" "Yes, I think we **should**."

should は **I think / I don't think / Do you think …?** などの節の中でよく用います。より丁寧な主張になります。

- **I think** the government **should do** more to reduce crime.
- **I don't think** you **should work** so hard.
- "**Do you think** I **should apply** for this job?" "Yes, **I think** you **should**."

You **shouldn't do** … は「…すべきではない，…するのは正しくない」を表します。

- You **shouldn't believe** everything you read in the newspapers.

should は **must** や **have to** ほど強く主張しません。

- You **should** apologize.（⇒ そうしたほうがよい）
- You **must** apologize. / You **have to** apologize.（⇒ そうするしかない）

B

should は「…でなくてはならない」のように，規則や期待に反している出来事を表します。

- I wonder where Liz is. She **should be** here by now.
  （⇒ もう，ここに来ていなくてはならない）
- The price on this package is wrong. It **should be** $1.29, not $1.59.
- That man on the motorcycle **should be wearing** a helmet.

should は「…するはずだ」のように，出来事を期待する際に用います。

- She's been studying hard for the exam, so she **should pass**.
  （⇒ 合格するはずだ）
- There are plenty of hotels in this city. It **shouldn't be** hard to find a place to stay.（⇒ 難しいはずがない）

C

You **should have done** … の形で，「本当は…すべきだった」を表します。

- You missed a great party last night. You **should have come**. Why didn't you?
  （⇒ 来るべきだった。来ればよかったのに）
- I wonder why they're so late. They **should have been** here an hour ago.

You **shouldn't have done** … の形で，「本当は…するべきではなかった」を表します。

- I feel sick. I **shouldn't have eaten** so much.（⇒ 食べ過ぎるべきではなかった）
- She **shouldn't have been listening** to our conversation. It was private.

should (do) と **should have** (done) は，話題としている時が異なります。

- You look tired. You **should go** to bed now.（**現在**）
- You went to bed very late last night. You **should have gone** to bed earlier.（**過去**）

D

ought to ＋ 動詞の原形

should の代わりに **ought to** を用いることができます。両者の間に意味の違いはありません。

- Do you think I **ought to apply** for this job?
  (= Do you think I **should apply**?)
- That's a terrible thing to say. You **ought to be** ashamed of yourself!
- She's been studying hard for the exam, so she **ought to pass**.

should と had better ➲ Unit 33B

Exercises

31.1 状況に合うように, **should** もしくは **shouldn't** と以下の語句を組み合わせて文を完成しなさい。

~~go away for a few days~~	go to bed so late	look for another job
put some pictures on the walls	take a photo	use her car so much

1. Liz needs a change. *She should go away for a few days.*
2. Your salary is too low. You ______
3. Eric always has trouble getting up. He ______
4. What a beautiful view! You ______
5. Sue drives everywhere. She never walks. She ______
6. Bill's room isn't very interesting. He ______

31.2 状況に合うように, **I think / I don't think 〜 should ...** の文を完成しなさい。

1. Chris and Amy are planning to get married. You think it's a bad idea.
   I don't think they should get married.
2. I have a bad cold but plan to go out tonight. You don't think this is a good idea.
   You say to me: ______
3. Peter needs a job. He's just seen an ad for a job which you think would be ideal for him, but he's not sure whether to apply or not. You say to him: I think
   ______
4. The government wants to raise taxes, but you don't think this is a good idea.
   ______

31.3 状況に合うように, **should (have)** と ( ) 内の動詞を用いて文を完成しなさい。

1. Tracy *should pass* the exam. She's been studying very hard. (pass)
2. You missed a great party last night. *You should have come.* (come)
3. We don't see you enough. You ______ and see us more often. (come)
4. I'm in a difficult position. What do you think I ______ ? (do)
5. I'm sorry that I didn't follow your advice. I ______ what you said. (do)
6. We lost the game, but we ______ . Our team is better than theirs. (win)
7. "Is John here yet?" "Not yet, but he ______ here soon." (be)
8. I mailed the letter three days ago, so it ______ by now. (arrive)

31.4 状況を考えて, **should** もしくは **shouldn't** を用いて文を完成しなさい。文は過去形か現在形のいずれかの形にします。

1. I'm feeling sick. I ate too much. *I shouldn't have eaten so much.*
2. That man on the motorcycle isn't wearing a helmet. That's dangerous.
   He *should be wearing a helmet.*
3. When we got to the restaurant, there were no free tables. We hadn't reserved one.
   We ______
4. The sign says that the store opens every day at 8:30. It is 9:00 now, but the store isn't open yet.
   ______
5. The speed limit is 30 miles an hour, but Kate is driving 50.
   She ______
6. Mai gave me her e-mail address, but I didn't write it down. Now I can't remember it.
   I ______
7. I was driving right behind another car. Suddenly, the driver in front of me stopped, and I drove into the back of his car. It was my fault.
   ______
8. I walked into a wall. I wasn't looking where I was going.
   ______

補充問題 16–18 (pp. 305–307)

UNIT 32

仮定法 (I suggest you do)

A

☆イラストの状況について考えなさい。この状況は，ことばを直接述べる以外にどのような形で表せますか？

➤ イラストの状況は以下のように，**said to** の他に **suggested** を用いて間接的に表すこともできます。

Lisa **said to** Mary, "Why don't you buy some nice clothes?"

＝

Lisa **suggested** that Mary **buy** some nice clothes.

suggest that ... の例文中の **buy** のように**動詞の原形**を用いることを**仮定法** (subjunctive) と呼びます。動詞が**仮定法**になると，I **buy**，he **buy**，she **buy** などのように主語や主節の時制に関係なく**動詞の原形**になります。

I/he/she/it we/you/they	**do/buy/be** など

➤ 名称は「仮定法」ですが，「仮に，もし…ならば」というような仮定の意味はありません。

B

次のような動詞の後で**仮定法**を用います。

demand	insist	propose	recommend	suggest

- I **insisted** he **have** dinner with us.
- The doctor **recommended** that I **rest** for a few days.
- John **demanded** that Lisa **apologize** to him.
- What do you **suggest** I **do**?

It's **essential/imperative/important/necessary/vital** (that) ～ **do**（動詞の原形）のように**仮定法**を用いることがあります。

- **It's essential** that everyone **be** at work by 9:00 tomorrow morning. No exceptions.
- **It's imperative** that the government **do** something about health care.

この**仮定法**の文は，以下のような**不定詞構文**（for ～ to＋動詞の原形）で書き換えられます。

- **It's essential for** everyone **to** be at work by 9:00 tomorrow morning.
- **It's imperative for** the government **to** do something about health care.

C

☆仮定法では次のことに注意します。

➤ **I *not be*，you *not have*，she *not go*** などのように，**not ＋ 動詞の原形で否定形を作ります。**

- The doctor strongly **recommended** that I **not go** to work for two days.
- **It's** very **important** that you **not miss** this appointment with your eye doctor.

➤ 現在，過去，未来といった主節の動詞の時制の影響を受けず，動詞は常に原形となります。

- I insist you **come** with us.
- They insisted I **go** with them.

☆仮定法の **be** について以下の例文で確認しなさい。受動態の構文中によく生じます。➲Unit 60A

- I **insisted** that something **be done** about the problem.
- **It's essential** that this medicine not **be taken** on an empty stomach.
- The airline **recommended** we **be** at the airport two hours before our flight.

D

insist と **suggest** の仮定法の構文は，**-ing**（動名詞）を用いて次のように書き換えられます。

- They **insisted on paying** for dinner. ➲Unit 60A
- It is a beautiful evening, so I **suggest going** for a walk. ➲Unit 51

insist と **suggest** の仮定法の構文は，**不定詞**（to＋動詞の原形）を用いては書き換えられません。

- She **suggested that he buy** some new clothes. (✕ suggested him to buy)
- He **insists on going** with us. (✕ he insists to go)

Exercises

32.1 指定された書き出しで始めて，下の文を上の文と意味的に同じ文にしなさい。

1. "Why don't you buy some new clothes?" said Lisa to Mary.
   Lisa suggested that *Mary buy some new clothes.*
2. "I don't think you should go to work for two days," the doctor said to me.
   The doctor recommended that *I not go to work for two days.*
3. "You really must stay a little longer," she said to me.
   She insisted that ______
4. "Why don't you visit the museum after lunch?" I said to her.
   I suggested that ______
5. "I think it would be a good idea to see a specialist," the doctor said to me.
   The doctor recommended that ______
6. "I think it would be a good idea for you not to lift anything heavy," the specialist said to me.
   The specialist recommended that ______
7. "You have to pay the rent by Friday at the latest," the landlord said to us.
   The landlord demanded that ______
8. "Why don't you go away for a few days?" Josh said to me.
   Josh suggested that ______
9. "I don't think you should give your children snacks right before mealtime," the doctor told me.
   The doctor suggested that ______
10. "Let's have dinner early," Sarah said to us.
    Sarah proposed that ______

32.2 空所に適切な形の動詞を入れて，文を完成しなさい。

1. It's imperative that the government *do* something about health care.
2. I insisted that something *be* done about the problem.
3. Our friends recommended that we ______ our vacation in the mountains.
4. Since Dave hurt Tracy's feelings, I stongly recommended that he ______ to her.
5. The workers at the factory are demanding that their wages ______ raised.
6. Lisa wanted to walk home alone, but we insisted that she ______ for us.
7. The city council has proposed that a new convention center ______ built.
8. What do you suggest I ______ to the party? Something casual?
9. It is essential that every child ______ the opportunity to get a good education.
10. Brad forgot his wife's birthday last year, so it's really important he ______ it this year.
11. It is vital that every runner ______ water during the marathon.

32.3 体を丈夫にしたい Tom に，友人達がさまざまな提案をしています。

それぞれの提案を，指定された書き出しで始めて記述しなさい。

1. Linda suggested that he *try jogging.*
2. Sandra suggested that he ______
3. Bill suggested ______
4. Anna ______

UNIT 33

had better It's time ...

A

had better は I'**d better** / you'**d better** などのように普通，短縮されます。
I'**d better do** ... は「…するほうがよい，望ましい」という意味で，助言に従わないと困ったり，危なくなったりする場合に用います。

- I have to meet Amy in 10 minutes. I'**d better go** now or I'll be late.
- "Do you think I should take an umbrella?" "Yes, you'**d better**. It might rain."
- We'**d better stop** for gas soon. The tank is almost empty.

否定形の「…しないほうがよい」は I'**d better not** (= I had better not) となります。

- "Are you going out tonight?" "I'**d better not**. I've got a lot of work to do."
- You don't look very well. You'**d better not go** to work today.

☆ **had better の形式について注意すべきことは何ですか？**

➤ **話しことばでは普通，I'd better / you'd better などのように短縮されますが，had better が本来の形です。**

- I'**d better** go now = I **had** better go now.

➤ **had そのものは過去時制ですが，had better が意味するのは現在もしくは未来で過去は表しません。**

- I'**d better go** to the bank now / tomorrow.

➤ **I'd better do ... のように better の後にくるのは動詞の原形で，不定詞 (to do) はきません。**

- It might rain. We'**d better take** an umbrella. (× We'd better to take)

B

☆ **had better と should は，どのように異なりますか？**

➤ **had better と should とはやや意味が異なります。had better は，現実に生じている具体的な状況においてのみ用いられます。「誰でも，いつでも…すべき」のように一般的に意見を述べたり助言をする場合には should を用います。**

- It's cold. You'**d better wear** a coat when you go out. (⇒ 今日は寒いのでコートを着たほうがよい)
- You're always at home. You **should go** out more often. (⇒ もっと外出すべき，× had better go)

➤ **had better には「…するほうがよい。さもないと～」のように，助言に従わない場合の危険性がいつも示唆されます。一方，should は単純に「…すべき」と提案します。**

- It's a great movie. You **should** go and see it. (⇒ 見に行くべきだが，行かなくても問題はない)
- The movie starts at 8:30. You'**d better** go now, or you'll be late.

C

It's time . . .

It's time (for ～) **to do** ... は「そろそろ（～が）…すべき時間だ」を表します。

- It's time **to go** home. / It's time for us **to go** home. (⇒ 家に帰る時間だ)

不定詞（to + 動詞の原形）の代わりに，**it's time + 主語 + 動詞**（過去形）の構文も用いられます。以下の例文では，**従属節中に動詞の過去形** (went) が用いられていますが，意味は現在であって過去ではありません。

- It's late. It's time we **went** home.

この構文では従属節中に動詞の現在形を用いることはできません。

- It's 10:00 and he's still in bed. **It's time** he **got** up. (× It's time he gets up)

It's time you **did** ... は「もっと前に…してしまうべきだった，今すぐ…すべきだ」を表します。誰かを批判したり苦情を述べたりする際によく用います。

- **It's time** you **changed** the oil in the car. It hasn't been changed in a long time.
  (⇒ もっと前にオイルを変えるべきだった。今すぐ変えるべきだ)
- The windows are very dirty. I think **it's time** they **were washed**.

It's about time ... では，批判や苦情の気持ちがさらに強まります。

- Jack is a great talker. But **it's about time** he **did** something instead of just talking.
  (⇒ 話ばかりでなく，いいかげん実行すべきだ)

should ➲ Unit 31

Exercises

33.1 状況に合うように，（　）内の語句を用いて had better (not) を含む文を完成しなさい。

1. You're going out for a walk with Tom. It looks as if it might rain. You say to Tom:
   (an umbrella) *We'd better take an umbrella.*
2. Alex has just cut himself. It's a bad cut. You say to him:
   (a bandage) ____________________
3. You and Kate plan to go to a restaurant tonight. It's a popular restaurant. You say to Kate:
   (make a reservation) We ____________________
4. Jill doesn't look very well – not well enough to go to work. You say to her:
   (work) ____________________
5. You received your phone bill four weeks ago, but you haven't paid it yet. If you don't pay soon, you could be in trouble. You say to yourself:
   (pay) ____________________
6. You want to go out, but you're expecting an important phone call. You say to your friend:
   (go out) I ____________________
7. You and Jeff are going to the theater. You've missed the bus, and you don't want to be late. You say to Jeff: (a taxi) ____________________

33.2 had better がふさわしい状況には had better を，そうでない場合には should を空所に入れて文を完成しなさい。

1. I have an appointment in 10 minutes. I *'d better* go now or I'll be late.
2. It's a great movie. You *should* go and see it. You'll really like it.
3. You ________ set your alarm. You'll never wake up on time if you don't.
4. When people are driving, they ________ keep their eyes on the road.
5. I'm glad you came to see us. You ________ come more often.
6. She'll be hurt if we don't invite her to the wedding, so we ________ invite her.
7. These cookies are delicious. You ________ try one.
8. I think everybody ________ learn a foreign language.

33.3 状況に合うように，空所に 1 語もしくは 2 語を入れて文を完成しなさい。

1. a) I need some money. I'd better *go* to the bank.
   b) John is expecting you to call him. You ________ better call him now.
   c) "Should I leave the window open?" "No, you'd better ________ it."
2. a) It's time the government ________ something about the problem.
   b) It's time something ________ about the problem.
   c) I think it's about time you ________ about other people instead of only thinking about yourself.

33.4 状況に合うように，It's time ... で始まる文を完成しなさい。

1. You think the children should be in bed. It's already 11 o'clock.
   It's time the children were in bed.
2. You haven't taken a vacation in ages. You need one now.
   It's time I ____________________
3. You're sitting on a train waiting for it to leave. It should have left five minutes ago.
   ____
4. You enjoy having parties. You haven't had one for a long time.
   ____
5. The company you work for is badly managed. You think some changes should be made.
   ____
6. Andrew has been doing the same job for the last 10 years. He should try something else.
   ____

補充問題 16 (pp. 305–306)

UNIT 34

would

A

would ('d)/wouldn't は「今はそうなっていない」と知りつつ,「…するだろう / …しないだろう」のように現在のことを想像する際に用います。

- It **would be** nice to buy a new car, but we can't afford it.
- **I'd love** to live by the ocean.
- *A:* Should I tell Chris what happened?
  B: No, I **wouldn't say** anything.
  (⇒ 私だったら, 言わない)

would have (done) は「そうではなかった」と知りつつ,「…しただろう / …しなかっただろう」のように過去のことを想像する際に用います。

- They helped us a lot. I don't know what we **would have done** without their help.
- I didn't tell Sam what happened. He **wouldn't have been** pleased. (⇒ 喜ばなかっただろう)

☆ **would (do) と would have (done) とは, どのように異なりますか？**

- I **would call** Sue, but I don't have her number. (⇒ 電話したいのに…, 現在)
  I **would have called** Sue, but I didn't have her number. (⇒ 電話したかったのに…, 過去)
- I'm not going to invite them to the party. They **wouldn't come** anyway.
  I didn't invite them to the party. They **wouldn't have come** anyway.

would は **if** 節を持つ文の主節中でよく使われます。➲Units 36–38

- I **would call** Sue **if** I had her number.
- I **would have called** Sue **if** I'd had her number.

B

☆ **will ('ll) と would ('d) とは, どのように異なりますか？**

- **I'll stay** a little longer. I've got plenty of time. (⇒ もう少しここにいる)
  I'd stay a little longer, but I really have to go now. (⇒ もう, いられない)
- **I'll call** Sue. I've got her number. (⇒ 電話しよう)
  I'd call Sue, but I don't have her number. (⇒ 電話したいのにできない)

従属節中で **would/wouldn't** は **will/won't (will not)** の過去形として用いられます。

現在 (主節)		過去 (従属節)
Tom: **I'll call** you on Sunday.	→	Tom said he**'d call** me on Sunday.
Ann: I promise I **won't be** late.	→	Ann promised that she **wouldn't be** late.
Liz: Darn! The car **won't start**.	→	Liz was annoyed because her car **wouldn't start**.

C

~ wouldn't do … は,「(~が) どうしても…しようとしない」を意味することがあります。

- I tried to warn him, but he **wouldn't listen** to me. (⇒ どうしても聞こうとしない)
- The car **wouldn't start**. (⇒ どうしても動こうとしない)

would は「よく…したものだ」のように, 過去に規則的に行われていた出来事を意味することがあります

- When we were children, we lived by the ocean. In summer, if the weather was nice, we **would** all get up early and go for a swim. (⇒ よく早起きして泳ぎに行った)
- Whenever Richard was angry, he **would** walk out of the room.

この意味の **would** は used to に置き換えられます。➲Unit 17

- Whenever Richard was angry, he **used to walk** out of the room.

will ➲ Units 20–21　Would you …? ➲ Unit 35A　would … if ➲ Units 36–38　wish … would ➲ Unit 39
would like ➲ Units 35E, 56　would prefer / would rather ➲ Unit 57

Exercises

34.1 例にならって自分がしたいこと，したくないことを表す文を完成しなさい。自分のことで答えます。

1. (a place you'd love to live) *I'd love to live by the ocean.*
2. (a job you wouldn't like to do) ______
3. (something you would love to do) ______
4. (something that would be nice to have) ______
5. (a place you'd like to go to) ______

34.2 状況に合うように，**would** に続く動詞を以下から選んで文を完成しなさい。

be be ~~do~~ do enjoy enjoy have pass stop

1. They helped us a lot. I don't know what we *would have done* without their help.
2. You should go and see the movie. You ______ it.
3. It's too bad you couldn't come to the concert yesterday. You ______ it.
4. Do you think I should apply for the job? What ______ you ______ in my position?
5. I was in a hurry when I saw you. Otherwise, I ______ to talk.
6. We took a taxi home last night but got stuck in the traffic. It ______ quicker to walk.
7. Why don't you go and see Claire? She ______ very pleased to see you.
8. Why didn't you take the exam? I'm sure you ______ it.
9. In an ideal world, everybody ______ enough to eat.

34.3 左欄の文の次に続く文を右欄から選び，記号で答えなさい。

1. ~~I'd like to go to Australia one day.~~	a) It wouldn't have been very pleasant.	*c*
2. I wouldn't like to live on a busy street.	b) It would have been fun.	___
3. I'm sorry the trip was canceled.	c) ~~It would be nice.~~	___
4. I'm looking forward to going out tonight.	d) It won't be much fun.	___
5. I'm glad we didn't go out in the rain.	e) It wouldn't be very pleasant.	___
6. I'm not looking forward to the trip.	f) It will be fun.	___

34.4 状況に合うように，**promised** の後に **would** もしくは **wouldn't** を続けた文を完成しなさい。

1. I wonder why Laura is late. *She promised she wouldn't be late.*
2. I wonder why Steve hasn't called. He promised ______
3. Why did you tell Jane what I said? You ______
4. I'm surprised they didn't wait for us. They ______

34.5 状況に合うように，**wouldn't** の後に適切な動詞を続けて文を完成しなさい。

1. I tried to warn him, but he *wouldn't listen* to me.
2. I asked Amanda what had happened, but she ______ me.
3. Paul was very angry about what I'd said and ______ to me for two weeks.
4. Martina insisted on carrying all her luggage. She ______ me help her.

34.6 それぞれの設問はいずれも過去において繰り返し行われた出来事を表します。状況に合うように，**would** の後に続く動詞を以下から選んで文を完成しなさい。

forget help shake share ~~walk~~

1. Whenever Richard was angry, he *would walk* out of the room.
2. We used to live next to railroad tracks. Every time a train went by, the house ______ .
3. George was a very kind man. He ______ always ______ you if you had a problem.
4. Brenda was always very generous. She didn't have much, but she ______ what she had with everyone else.
5. You could never rely on Joe. It didn't matter how many times you reminded him to do something, he ______ always ______ .

補充問題 16–18 (pp. 305–307)

UNIT 35

Can/Could/Would you ...? など（依頼・要求・許可・申し出・勧誘）

A

☆イラストのように，「…してくれますか？，…してください」のような依頼を表す構文にはどのようなものがありますか？

➤ you を主語にした疑問文や if 節中に，can や could を用いた構文

- **Can you** wait a minute, please?（⇒ ちょっと待ってください）
- = **Could you** wait a minute, please?
- Liz, **can you** do me a favor?
- Excuse me, **could you** tell me how to get to the airport?
- I wonder if **you could** help me.

➤ Do you think you could ...? の構文（この場合には，普通 can は用いません）

- **Do you think you could** lend me some money until next week?

➤ you を主語にした疑問文やif 節中に，will や would を用いた構文（can や could の方がより一般的です）

- Liz, **will you** do me a favor?
- **Would you** please be quiet? I'm trying to concentrate.

could や **would** の方が，**can** や **will** よりも丁寧な印象を与えます。

B

☆「…をいただけますか？，…をください」のように，物を要求する構文にはどのようなものがありますか？

➤ Can I have ...?，Could I have ...?，Can I get ...? のように，I を主語にした疑問文

- 〔ギフトショップで〕**Can I have** these postcards, please?（= **Can I get** ...?）
- 〔食事中に〕**Could I have** the salt, please?

➤ May I have ...? の構文

- **May I have** these postcards, please?

C

☆「…してよいですか？，…させてください」のように，許可を求める構文にはどのようなものがありますか？

➤ can, could, may と，主語にした I を含む構文

- 〔電話で〕Hello, **can I** speak to Tom, please?
- "**Could I** use your phone?" "Yes, of course."
- **Do you think I could** borrow your bike?
- "**May I** come in?" "Yes, please do."

may は，より堅苦しい文脈で用いられ，**can** や **could** ほど使われません。

➤ Do you mind if ...?, Is it all right ...?, Is it OK if I ...? の構文

- "**Do you mind if I** use your phone?" "No. Not at all."
  （⇒ …していいですか？ —— いいですよ。答えが否定形となることに注意）
- "**Is it all right if I** come in?" "Yes, of course."

D

☆「…しましょうか？，…します」のように，自ら申し出る構文にはどのようなものがありますか？

➤ Can I ...? や May I ... ? の構文

- "**Can I** get you a cup of coffee?" "Yes, that would be very nice."
- 〔お店で〕"**May I** help you?" "No, thanks. I'm being helped."

may は **can** より，より堅苦しい文脈で用いられます。

E

☆「…しませんか？，…しましょう」のように，何かを提案して勧誘する構文にはどのようなものがありますか？

➤ Would you like ...? の構文（Do you like ...? の構文は用いられません）

- "**Would you like** a cup of coffee?" "Yes, please."（⇒ コーヒーはいかがですか？）
- "**Would you like** to go to the movies with us tonight?" "Yes, I'd love to."

I'd like ... は「…をください，…したい」のように，自分の希望を丁寧に伝えます。

- 〔観光案内所で〕**I'd like** some information about hotels, please.
  （⇒ ホテルについて教えてください）
- 〔お店で〕**I'd like** to try on this jacket, please.

can と could ➲ Units 25–26　mind -ing? ➲ Unit 51　would like ➲ Units 53A, 56B

Exercises

35.1 状況に合うように，can もしくは could で始まる疑問文を完成しなさい。

1. You're carrying a lot of things. You can't open the door yourself. There's a man standing near the door. You say to him:
   Can you open the door, please? or *Could you open the door, please?*
2. You phone Ann, but somebody else answers. Ann isn't there. You want to leave a message for her. You say: __________
3. You're a tourist. You want to go to the post office, but you don't know how to get there. You ask at your hotel: __________
4. You are in a department store. You see some pants you like, and you want to try them on. You say to the salesperson: __________
5. You need a ride home from a party. John drove to the party and lives near you. You say to him: __________

35.2 状況に合うように，（　）内の語句を用いて疑問文を完成しなさい。

1. You want to borrow your friend's camera. What do you say to him?
   (think) *Do you think I could borrow your camera?*
2. You are at a friend's house and you want to use her phone. What do you say?
   (all right) *Is it all right if I use your phone?*
3. You've written a letter in English. Before you send it, you want a friend to check it for you. What do you ask?
   (think) __________
4. You want to leave work early. What do you ask your boss?
   (mind) __________
5. The woman in the next room is playing music. It's very loud. You want her to turn it down. What do you say to her?
   (think) __________
6. You are calling the owner of an apartment that was advertised in the newspaper. You are interested in the apartment and want to see it today. What do you say to the owner?
   (OK) __________
7. You're on a train. The woman next to you has finished reading her newspaper, and you'd like to have a look at it. You ask her.
   (think) __________

35.3 状況に合うように文を完成しなさい。

1. Paul has come to see you. You offer him something to eat.
   You: *Would you like something to eat* ?
   Paul: No, thank you. I've just eaten.
2. You need help replacing the memory card in your camera. You ask Kate.
   You: I don't know how to replace the memory card. __________ ?
   Kate: Sure. It's easy. All you have to do is this.
3. You're on a bus. You have a seat, but an elderly man is standing. You offer him your seat.
   You: __________ ?
   Man: Oh, that's very nice of you. Thank you very much.
4. You're the passenger in a car. Your friend is driving very fast. You ask her to slow down.
   You: You're making me very nervous. __________ ?
   Driver: Oh, I'm sorry. I didn't realize I was going so fast.
5. You've finished your meal in a restaurant and now you want the check. You ask the waiter:
   You: __________ ?
   Waiter: Sure. I'll get it for you now.
6. A friend of yours is interested in one of your books. You invite him to borrow it.
   Friend: This book looks very interesting.
   You: Yes, it's very good. __________ ?

UNIT 36

If I do ...　If I did ...

A

☆ **1) と 2) を比較します。話し手の気持ちの違いは，どのような形の違いとなって現れていますか？**

1) Sue の時計が見つかりません。Sue は，Ann に次のように尋ねます。

Sue: I think I left my watch at your house. Have you seen it?
Ann: No, but I'll look when I get home. **If I find** it, I'll tell you.

➤ **Ann は実際に，自分の家で時計が見つかるかもしれないと考えています。この場合，次の If 構文となります。**

If I find . . . , I'll . . . .

2) Carol は，次のように言いました。

If I found a wallet in the street, I'd take it to the police station.

➤ **Carol は，道で財布を拾うことはないと考えています。つまり，彼女は現実には起こりえない状況を想像しています。この場合，次の If 構文となります。**

If I found . . . , I'd (= **I would**) . . . . (× if I find . . . , I'll . . .)

イラストのように現実には起こりえない状況を想像する場合，**if 節**の中は **if** I **found**，**if** there **was**，**if** we **didn't** などのように**過去時制**となります。形は過去形でも過去の意味はありません。

☆ **太字の部分について，現実にはどうであると考えていますか？**

- What would you do **if** you **won** a million dollars? (⇒ we don't really expect this to happen)
- I don't really want to go to their party, but I probably will go. They'd be hurt **if** I **didn't go**.
- **If** there **was** (= **were**) an election tomorrow, who would you vote for?

if ... was/were について ➲ Unit 37C

B

普通，**if 節**中には **would** は生じません。

- I'd be very frightened **if** somebody **pointed** a gun at me. (× if somebody would point)
- **If** I **didn't** go to their party, they'd be hurt. (× If I wouldn't go)

C

if 節以外の部分（**主節中**）には **would ('d)/wouldn't** が生じます。

- If you got more exercise, you**'d feel** better.
- I'm not tired. If I went to bed now, I **wouldn't sleep**.
- **Would** you **mind** if I used your phone?

would の代わりに **could** や **might** を使うこともあります。

- If you got more exercise, you **might feel** better.（⇒ 気分が良くなるでしょう）
- If it stopped raining, we **could go** out.（⇒ 出かけられるでしょう）

D

現実には起こらないことを想像する文中では，**if** と **when** は置き換えられません。

- They'd be hurt **if** I didn't go to their party. (× when I didn't go)
- What would you do **if** you were bitten by a snake? (× when you were bitten)

would ➲ Units 34, 39　If I knew ... ➲ Unit 37　If I had known ➲ Unit 38

Exercises

36.1 状況に合うように,（　）内の動詞を正しい形にして文を完成しなさい。

1. They would be hurt if *I didn't go* to their party. (not / go)
2. If you got more exercise, you *would feel* better. (feel)
3. If they offered me the job, I think I __________ it. (take)
4. A lot of people would be out of work if the car factory __________ . (close down)
5. If I sold my car, I __________ much money for it. (not / get)
6. 〔エレベーターで〕What would happen if somebody __________ that red button? (press)
7. I'm sure Amy will lend you the money. I'd be very surprised if she __________ . (refuse)
8. Liz gave me this ring. She __________ very upset if I lost it. (be)
9. Dave and Kate are expecting us. They would be very disappointed if we __________ . (not / come)
10. Would Bob mind if I __________ his bike without asking him? (borrow)
11. What would you do if somebody __________ in here with a gun? (walk)
12. I'm sure Sue __________ if you explained the situation to her. (understand)

36.2 What would you do if ...? を用いて,（　）内の状況について友人に尋ねる文を完成しなさい。

1. (imagine – you win a lot of money)
   What would you do if you won a lot of money?
2. (imagine – you lose your passport)
   What __________
3. (imagine – there's a fire in the building)
   ____
4. (imagine – you're in an elevator and it stops between floors)
   ____

36.3 例を参考にして,状況に合うように（　）内の語句を用いた文を完成しなさい。

1. *A:* Should we catch the 10:30 train?
   B: No. (arrive too early) *If we caught the 10:30 train, we'd arrive too early.*
2. *A:* Is Ken going to take the driver's test?
   B: No. (fail) If he __________
3. *A:* Why don't we stay at a hotel?
   B: No. (cost too much) If __________
4. *A:* Is Sally going to apply for the job?
   B: No. (not / get it) If __________
5. *A:* Let's tell them the truth.
   B: No. (not / believe us) If __________
6. *A:* Why don't we invite Bill to the party?
   B: No. (have to invite his friends, too) __________

36.4 自分のことを記述する文を完成しなさい。

1. If you got more exercise, *you'd feel better.*
2. I'd feel very angry if __________
3. If I didn't go to work tomorrow, __________
4. Would you go to the party if __________
5. If you bought a car, __________
6. Would you mind if __________

UNIT 37

If I knew ... I wish I knew ...

A

☆イラストの状況について考えます。Sue は，If I knew の構文でどのようなことを想像していますか？

Sue は Paul に電話をかけたいのですが，電話番号がわからなくてかけられません。Sue は自分のこの状況を次のように記述します。

If I knew his number, I **would call** him.

➤ **Sue は If I knew his number ... のように，knew という過去形を用いています。Sue は，実際には電話番号はわからないものの「わかればなあ…」と想像しています。**

イラストのように現実には起こりえない状況を想像する場合，**if 節**の中は **if** I **knew**，**if** you **were**，**if** we **didn't** などのように**過去時制**となります。形は過去形でも過去の意味はありません。

☆**太字の部分について，現実にはどうであると考えていますか？**

- Tom would read more **if** he **had** more time.（⇒ 実際にはあまり時間がない）
- **If** I **didn't** want to go to the party, I wouldn't go.（⇒ パーティーに行きたい）
- We wouldn't have any money **if** we **didn't** work.（⇒ 実際には働いている）
- **If** you **were** in my position, what would you do?
- It's a shame you can't drive. It would be helpful **if** you **could**.

B

イラストで考えます。I **wish** I **knew**，I **wish** you **were** などのように，**wish** の**従属節**中では動詞の**過去時制**を用います。この時，思ったような状況にないことを「…すればよいのに」と後悔する意味になります。

- **I wish** I **knew** Paul's phone number.
  （⇒ 番号がわかればなあ）
- Do you ever **wish** you **could** fly?
  （⇒「空が飛べればなあ」と思いませんか？）
- It rains a lot here. I **wish** it **didn't** rain so often.
- It's very crowded here. I **wish** there **weren't** so many people.
- I **wish** I **didn't** have to work tomorrow, but unfortunately, I do.

C

If I **was** / **If** I **were**

if や **wish** の節内で主語が単数の場合，**be 動詞**は **was** もしくは **were** となります。**was** の方が，よりくだけた言い方となります。

- **If I was** you, I wouldn't buy that coat. = **If I were** you, . . .
- I'd go out **if it wasn't** so cold. = . . . **if it weren't** so cold.
- **I wish Carol was** here. = **I wish Carol were** here.

D

普通，**if 節**の中や **wish** の**従属節**中では **would** は用いません。

- **If I were** rich, I **would** have a yacht.（✕ If I would be rich）
- **I wish I had** something to read.（✕ I wish I would have）

ただし，I **wish** you **would** listen.（…するとよいのに）のように，活動や変化を願う場合には **wish ... would** を使うことができます。➲ Unit 39D

E

可能（～できる）の意味を持つ **could** は以下のように，**主節**と **if 節**の両方に生じる場合があります。

- You **could** get a better job（⇒ 良い仕事につけるだろう）
  if you **could** use a computer.（⇒ コンピュータが使えれば）

上の例で，**主節**では **would be able to ...** に置き換わり，「…できるだろう」を意味し，**if 節**では **was/were able to ...** に置き換わり，「もし（今）…できるなら」を意味します。

could ➲ Units 25–26　If I do ... と If I did ... ➲ Unit 36
If I had known ... / I wish I had known ... ➲ Unit 38　wish ➲ Unit 39

Exercises

37.1 ( ) 内の動詞を正しい形にして，文を完成しなさい。

1. If I *knew* (know) his phone number, I would call him.
2. I *wouldn't buy* (not / buy) that coat if I were you.
3. I ________________ (help) you if I could, but I'm afraid I can't.
4. We would need a car if we ________________ (live) in the country.
5. If we had the choice, we ________________ (live) in the country.
6. This soup isn't very good. It ________________ (taste) better if it weren't so salty.
7. I wouldn't mind living in Maine if the weather ________________ (be) better.
8. If I were you, I ________________ (not / wait). I ________________ (go) now.
9. You're always tired. If you ________________ (not / go) to bed so late every night, you wouldn't be tired all the time.
10. I think there are too many cars. If there ________________ (not / be) so many cars, there ________________ (not / be) so much pollution.

37.2 現実の状況を踏まえて，それぞれの文を if 節を含む文に書き換えなさい。

1. We don't see you very often because you live so far away.
If you didn't live so far away, we'd see you more often.
2. This book is expensive, so I'm not going to buy it.
I'd ________________ if ________________
3. We don't go out to eat because we can't afford it.
We ________________
4. I can't meet you tomorrow. I have to work late.
If ________________
5. It's raining, so we can't have lunch on the patio.
We ________________
6. I don't want his advice, and that's why I'm not going to ask for it.
If ________________

37.3 状況に合うように，I wish ... で始まる文に書き換えなさい。

1. I don't know many people (and I'm lonely). *I wish I knew more people.*
2. I don't have a cell phone (and I need one). I wish ________________
3. Amanda isn't here (and I need to see her). ________________
4. It's cold (and I hate cold weather). ________________
5. I live in a big city (and I don't like it). ________________
6. I can't go to the party (and I'd like to). ________________
7. I have to work tomorrow (but I'd like to stay in bed).
____
8. I don't know anything about cars (and my car has just broken down).
____
9. I'm not feeling well (and that's not pleasant).
____

37.4 I wish ... で始めて，自分のことを記述する文を作りなさい。

1. (somewhere you'd like to be now – on the beach, in Vietnam, in bed, etc.)
I wish I *were at home in bed now.*
2. (something you'd like to have – a computer, a good job, more friends, etc.)
____
3. (something you'd like to be able to do – sing, speak a language, fly, etc.)
____
4. (something you'd like to be – beautiful, strong, rich, etc.)
____

補充問題 19 (p. 307)

UNIT 38

If I had known ...
I wish I had known ...

A

☆ 枠内の例文の状況について考えます。Liz は，If I had known ... の構文を用いてどのようなことを考えていますか？

先月，Brian は何日か入院していました。Liz はこのことを知らなかったために，お見舞いに行けませんでした。数日前 Liz が Brian に出会った時，Liz は次のように言いました。

If I had known you were in the hospital, **I would have gone** to see you.

➤ **Liz は Brian が入院していたことは知らなかったので，「もし知っていたら…」と考えています。**

事実とは異なる過去の状況を想像する場合，**if 節**の中は if I **had known/been/done** などのように **had＋過去分詞**の**過去完了**となります。

- I didn't see you when you passed me in the street. **If I'd seen you**, of course I would have said hello. (⇒ 君だとわかっていたら…)
- I didn't go out last night. I would have gone out **if** I **hadn't been** so tired. (⇒ 疲れていなかったら…)
- **If** he **had been looking** where he was going, he wouldn't have walked into the wall. (⇒ 進行方向を見ていたら…)
- The view was wonderful. **If I'd had** a camera, I would have taken some pictures. (⇒ カメラを持っていたら…)

☆ **以下の例文ではどのようなことを仮定し，想像していますか？**

- I'm not hungry. **If** I **was** hungry, I would eat something. (⇒ お腹がすいていれば…)〔現在〕
- I wasn't hungry. **If** I **had been** hungry, I would have eaten something. (⇒ お腹がすいていたら…)〔過去〕

B

if 節中では **would** を用いません。**if 節**以外の部分（**主節中**）で用います。

- **If** I **had seen** you, I **would have said** hello. (✕ If I would have seen you)

'd は **would** と **had** の両方の短縮形です。**would** の後には**動詞の原形**，**had** の後には**過去分詞**がきます。

- **If I'd seen** you,　(**I'd** seen = I **had** seen)
  I'd have said hello. (**I'd** have said = I **would** have said)

C

wish を用いて，「残念だが…しなかった」という現実を踏まえて，「…していたらよかったのに」と過去の事実と異なる状況を願う場合には，**I wish ... had 過去分詞**のように**過去完了**を用います。

- I **wish I'd known** that Brian was sick. I would have gone to see him. (⇒ 知っていたらなあ)
- I feel sick. I **wish** I **hadn't eaten** so much cake. (⇒ 食べ過ぎるのではなかった)
- Do you **wish** you **had studied** science instead of languages? (⇒ 科学を勉強していたらと…)

wish の後の**従属節**中では **would have** は用いません。

- The weather was cold on our vacation. I wish it **had been** warmer. (✕ I wish it would have been)

D

☆ **would (do) と would have (done) は，想像する事柄についてどのように異なりますか？**

- If I had gone to the party last night, I **would be** tired now. (⇒ 今頃は疲れているだろう)〔現在〕
- If I had gone to the party last night, I **would have met** lots of people. (⇒ 多くの人に出会えただろう)〔現在〕

would have / **could have** と **might have** では，**might have** の方が可能性は低くなります。

- If the weather hadn't been so bad,
  - we **would have gone** out.
  - we **could have gone** out. (⇒ 出かけられただろう)
  - we **might have gone** out. (⇒ おそらく出かけただろう)

had done ➲ Unit 14　If I do ... と If I did ... ➲ Unit 36　If I knew ... / I wish I knew ➲ Unit 37
wish ➲ Unit 39

Exercises

38.1 (　) 内の動詞を正しい形にして，文を完成しなさい。

1. I didn't know you were in the hospital. If *I'd known* (I / know), *I would have gone* (I / go) to see you.
2. John got to the station in time to catch the train. If ______ (he / miss) the train, ______ (he / be) late for his interview.
3. I'm glad that you reminded me about Rachel's birthday. ______ (I / forget) if ______ (you / not / remind) me.
4. Unfortunately, I didn't have my address book with me when I was on vacation. If ______ (I / have) your address, ______ (I / send) you a postcard.
5. *A:* How was your trip? Did you have a nice time?
   B: It was OK, but ______ (we / enjoy) it more if ______ (the weather / be) nicer.
6. I took a taxi to the hotel, but the traffic was bad. ______ (it / be) quicker if ______ (I / walk).
7. I'm not tired. If ______ (I / be) tired, I'd go home now.
8. I wasn't tired last night. If ______ (I / be) tired, I would have gone home earlier.

38.2 状況に合うように，If ... で始まる文を完成しなさい。

1. I wasn't hungry, so I didn't eat anything.
   If I'd been hungry, I would have eaten something.
2. The accident happened because the road was icy.
   If the road ______
3. I didn't know that Matt had to get up early, so I didn't wake him up.
   If I ______
4. I was able to buy the car only because Jim lent me the money.
   ______
5. Michelle wasn't injured in the crash because she was wearing a seat belt.
   ______
6. You didn't have any breakfast – that's why you're hungry now.
   ______
7. I didn't take a taxi because I didn't have any money.
   ______

38.3 指示された状況において，自分が何をしたかったかを I wish ... で始まる文で記述しなさい。

1. You've eaten too much and now you feel sick. You say:
   I wish I hadn't eaten so much.
2. There was a job advertised in the newspaper. You decided not to apply for it. Now you think that your decision was wrong. You say:
   I wish I ______
3. When you were younger, you didn't learn to play a musical instrument. Now you regret this. You say:
   ______
4. You've painted the door red. Now you think that red was the wrong color. You say:
   ______
5. You are walking in the country. You'd like to take some pictures, but you didn't bring your camera. You say:
   ______
6. You have some unexpected guests. They didn't call to say they were coming. You are very busy and you are not prepared for them. You say (to yourself):
   ______

補充問題 19–21 **(pp. 307–308)**

UNIT 39

wish

A

I wish you luck / **all the best** / **success** / **a happy birthday** などの形で，お祝いしたり幸運を祈ります。

- **I wish you all the best** in the future.（⇒ あなたに幸せが訪れますように）
- I saw Tim before the exam, and **he wished me luck**.（⇒ 彼は私に「がんばれ」と言った）

「～が…するとよい」は，**hope (that) 主語＋動詞**（現在形）もしくは **wish (that) 主語＋動詞**（過去形）で表します。**wish** の**従属節**中には動詞の**現在形**は置けません。

- I **hope** you **get** this letter before you leave town.（○ I **wish** you **got** / × I **wish** you **get**）

☆ **I wish も I hope も，お祝いしたり幸運を祈る時に用います。両者は構文上どのように異なりますか？**

- **I wish** you **a pleasant stay** here.（× I hope you a pleasant stay）
- **I hope** you **have** a pleasant stay here.（× I wish you have）

B

wish は，状況が思わしくなくて「…すればよいのに」と後悔する際にも用います。この場合，**従属節**内の動詞は **knew**，**lived** などのように**過去時制**となります。形は過去でも意味は現在を表します。

- I **wish** I **knew** what to do about the problem.（⇒ どうすればよいかわかればなあ）
- I **wish** you **didn't** have to go so soon.（⇒ すぐに行かなくてもよければなあ）
- Do you **wish** you **lived** near the ocean?（⇒ 海辺で暮らせたらなあ）
- Jack's going on a trip to Mexico soon. I **wish** I **was** going too.（⇒ 一緒に行けたらなあ）

wish の後の**従属節**に **had known**，**had said** などの**過去完了**を置いた構文は，「…していたらよいのに」と過去の出来事を後悔する際に用います。

- I **wish I'd known** about the party. I would have gone if I'd known.（⇒ 知っていたらなあ）
- It was a stupid thing to say. I **wish** I **hadn't said** it.（⇒ 言うんじゃなかった）

類似した他の例 ➲ Units 37, 38

C

I wish I could (do ...). は「…できればよいのに（…できなくて残念）」を表します。

- I'm sorry I have to go. I **wish** I **could stay** longer.（⇒ もっとここにいたいなあ）
- I've met that man before. I **wish** I **could remember** his name.（⇒ 思い出せればなあ）

I wish I could have (done ...). は「…できればよかったのに（…できなかったことが残念）」を表します。

- I hear the party was great. I **wish** I **could have gone**.（⇒ 行きたかったなあ）

D

☆ **イラストの状況について考えます。Jill は，I wish ～ would do の構文でどのようなことを考えていますか？**

今日は一日雨が降り続いています。Jill は雨が嫌いです。この気持ちは次のように表せます。

I wish it **would stop** raining.

すぐにでも雨が止んでほしいのですが，おそらくそうはならないでしょう。Jill もそのことはよくわかっています。

➤ **I wish ～ would do の構文は，これから何か活動が起こり変わってほしいと願う際に用います。普通，話し手はそのようなことは実現しないと考えています。**

I wish ～ would do の構文は「…すればよいのに」のように，現在の状況を好ましくないと考えている際に用います。

- The phone has been ringing for five minutes. **I wish** somebody **would answer** it.
- **I wish** you **would do** something instead of just sitting and doing nothing.

I wish ～ wouldn't do の構文は「…してばかりいて困る」のように，繰り返し行われる行動を批判する際に用います。

- **I wish** you **wouldn't keep interrupting** me.（⇒ 私の邪魔ばかりしている。もう邪魔しないで）

I wish ～ would do の構文で「…すればよいのに」と，願うのは活動や変化であり状態ではありません。

- I **wish** Sarah **would** come.（⇒ 彼女に来てもらいたい）〔活動〕
- ⇔ I **wish** Sarah **was** (= **were**) here now.（⇒ ここにいてもらいたい）〔状態〕/ × I wish Sarah would be）
- I **wish** somebody **would buy** me a car.（⇒ 買ってくれればなあ）〔活動〕
- ⇔ I **wish** I **had** a car.（⇒ 持っていればなあ）〔状態〕/ × I wish I would have）

I wish I knew ➲ Unit 37　I wish I was / I wish I were ➲ Unit 37　I wish I had known ➲ Unit 38

Exercises

39.1 状況に合うように，空所に **wish(ed)** もしくは **hope(d)** を入れて文を完成しなさい。

1. I ___wish___ you a pleasant stay here.
2. Enjoy your vacation. I __________ you have a great time.
3. Good-bye. I __________ you all the best.
4. We said good-bye to each other and __________ each other luck.
5. We're going on a picnic tomorrow, so I __________ the weather is nice.
6. I __________ you luck in your new job. I __________ it works out well for you.

39.2 状況に合うように，**I wish ～ would …** の構文を用いて文を完成しなさい。

1. It's raining. You want to go out, but not in the rain.
   You say: ___I wish it would stop raining.___
2. You're waiting for Jane. She's late and you're getting impatient.
   You say to yourself: I wish __________
3. You're looking for a job – so far without success. Nobody will give you a job.
   You say: I wish somebody __________
4. You can hear a baby crying. It's been crying for a long time and you're trying to study.
   You say: __________

状況に合うように，**I wish ～ wouldn't …** の構文を用いて文を完成しなさい。

5. Your friend drives very fast. You don't like this.
   You say to your friend: I wish you __________
6. Joe leaves the door open all the time. This annoys you.
   You say to Joe: __________
7. A lot of people drop litter in the street. You don't like this.
   You say: I wish people __________

39.3 それぞれの文が文法的に正しいかどうかを考えなさい。正しくない場合には適切な形に変えなさい。

1. I wish Sarah would be here now. ___I wish Sarah were here now.___
2. I wish you would listen to me. __________
3. I wish I would have more free time. __________
4. I wish our house would be a little bigger. __________
5. I wish the weather would change. __________
6. I wish you wouldn't complain all the time. __________
7. I wish everything wouldn't be so expensive. __________

39.4 (　) 内の動詞を適切な形に変えて，文を完成しなさい。

1. It was a stupid thing to say. I wish ___I hadn't said___ it. (I / not / say)
2. I'm fed up with this rain. I wish ___it would stop___ . (it / stop)
3. It's a difficult question. I wish __________ the answer. (I / know)
4. I should have listened to you. I wish __________ your advice. (I / take)
5. You're lucky to be going to Peru. I wish __________ with you. (I / can / come)
6. I have absolutely no energy. I wish __________ so tired. (I / not / be)
7. Aren't they ready yet? I wish __________ up. (they / hurry)
8. It would be nice to stay here longer. I wish __________ to go now. (we / not / have)
9. When we were in Cairo last year, we didn't have time to see all the things we wanted to see. I wish __________ longer. (we / can / stay)
10. It's freezing today. I wish __________ so cold. I hate cold weather. (it / not / be)
11. Joe still doesn't know what he wants to do. I wish __________ . (he / decide)
12. I really didn't enjoy the party. I wish __________ . (we / not / go)

UNIT 40

受動態 1 (is done / was done)

A

☆ イラストを見て考えます。どのような構文でイラストの家は説明されていますか？

This house **was built** in 1935.

➤ **(…) was built の部分は「(…は) 建てられた」の意味を持ち，受動態(passive voice)の動詞と呼びます。「(〜は…を)建てた」という動詞の形は能動態 (active voice) と呼びます。両者は以下のように関係付けられます。**

Somebody **built** this house in 1935. **(能動態)**
主語 / 目的語

This house **was built** in 1935. **(受動態)**
主語

能動態の動詞を持つ文では「〜（主語）は―（目的語）を…した」のように，主語は「何をしたか」を記述します。

- My grandfather was a builder. **He built** this house in 1935. (⇒ 1935 年に彼は家を建てた)
- It's a big company. **It employs** two hundred people.

受動態の動詞を持つ文では「〜（主語）は…された」のように，主語に「何が起こったか」を記述します。

- This house is pretty old. **It was built** in 1935. (⇒ それは 1935 年に建てられた)
- Two hundred people **are employed** by the company.

B

受動態の文では，動作を引き起こした人や物がわからなかったり，述べる必要がないことがよくあります。

- A lot of money **was stolen** in the robbery. (⇒ 大金が盗まれた。誰が盗んだかはわからない)
- **Is** this room **cleaned** every day? (⇒ 誰でもよいが，掃除している人はいますか？)

動作を引き起こした人や物を記述する必要がある場合には，**by 〜**（〜によって）を用いて示します。

- This house was built **by my grandfather**.
- Two hundred people are employed **by the company**.

C

受動態は **be 動詞**（is/was など）**＋過去分詞**（done/cleaned/seen など）で作ります。

(be) done　**(be) cleaned**　**(be) damaged**　**(be) built**　**(be) seen** など

done，seen，known などの不規則変化をする過去分詞 ➲付録 1

☆ **能動態から受動態はどのように作りますか？ 現在時制と過去時制で考えます。**

現在時制（⇒ be 動詞は**現在形**）

能動態：　**clean(s)** / **see(s)** など　　Somebody **cleans** this room every day.

受動態：　**am/is/are** + **cleaned/seen** など　　This room **is cleaned** every day.

- Many accidents **are caused** by careless driving.
- **I'm not** often **invited** to parties.
- How **is** this word **pronounced**?

過去時制（⇒ be 動詞は**過去形**）

能動態：　**cleaned/saw** など　　Somebody **cleaned** this room yesterday.

受動態：　**was/were** + **cleaned/seen** など　　This room **was cleaned** yesterday.

- We **were woken** up by a loud noise during the night.
- "Did you go to the party?"　"No, I **wasn't invited**."
- How much money **was stolen** in the robbery?

➤ **1) 動詞を be 動詞＋過去分詞に変える。be 動詞は現在時制では is/am/are，過去時制では was/were。**
2) 能動態の目的語を受動態の主語の位置に置く。
3) 能動態の主語が重要ではない場合，受動態では省略する。

受動態 2 ➲Unit 41　受動態 3 ➲Unit 42　by ➲Unit 125

Exercises

40.1 状況に合うように以下から適切な動詞を選び，適切な形に変えて文を完成しなさい。

~~cause~~	damage	hold	invite	make
pass	show	surround	translate	write

1. Many accidents *are caused* by dangerous driving.
2. Cheese ______________ from milk.
3. The roof of the building ______________ in a storm a few days ago.
4. You ______________ to the wedding. Why didn't you go?
5. A movie theater is a place where films ______________ .
6. In the United States, elections for president ______________ every four years.
7. Originally the book ______________ in Spanish, and a few years ago it ______________ into English.
8. Although we were driving pretty fast, we ______________ by a lot of other cars.
9. You can't see the house from the road. It ______________ by trees.

40.2 状況に合うように，時制を現在もしくは過去に変えて受動態の疑問文を完成しなさい。

1. Ask about glass. (how / make?) *How is glass made?*
2. Ask about television. (when / invent?) ______________
3. Ask about mountains. (how / form?) ______________
4. Ask about the planet Neptune. (when / discover?) ______________
5. Ask about silver. (what / use for?) ______________

40.3 状況に合うように時制（単純現在形 / 単純過去形）と態（能動態 / 受動態）を適切なものに変え，（ ）内の語句を用いて文を完成しなさい。

1. It's a big factory. Five hundred people *are employed* (employ) there.
2. *Did somebody clean* (somebody / clean) this room yesterday?
3. Water ______________ (cover) most of the Earth's surface.
4. How much of the Earth's surface ______________ (cover) by water?
5. The park gates ______________ (lock) at 6:30 p.m. every evening.
6. The letter ______________ (mail) a week ago, and it ______________ (arrive) yesterday.
7. The boat hit a rock and ______________ (sink) quickly. Fortunately everybody ______________ (rescue).
8. Ron's parents ______________ (die) when he was very young. He and his sister ______________ (bring up) by their grandparents.
9. I was born in Chicago, but I ______________ (grow up) in Houston.
10. While I was on vacation, my camera ______________ (steal) from my hotel room.
11. While I was on vacation, my camera ______________ (disappear) from my hotel room.
12. Why ______________ (Sue / quit) her job? Didn't she like it?
13. Why ______________ (Bill / fire) from his job? What did he do wrong?
14. The company is not independent. It ______________ (own) by a much larger company.
15. I saw an accident last night. Somebody ______________ (call) an ambulance, but nobody ______________ (injure), so the ambulance ______________ (not / need).
16. Where ______________ (these pictures / take)? In Hong Kong? ______________ (you / take) them?

40.4 somebody/they/people などの語句は使わずに，受動態の文を完成しなさい。

1. Somebody cleans the room every day. *The room is cleaned every day.*
2. They canceled all flights because of fog. All ______________
3. People don't use this road much. ______________
4. Somebody accused me of stealing money. I ______________
5. How do people learn languages? How ______________
6. People warned us not to go out alone. ______________

UNIT 41

受動態 2 (be done / been done / being done)

A

☆ 受動態ではwill / can / must /going to / want toなどの後に生じる動詞の原形を，どのように変えますか？

能動態：do/clean/see など（⇒ 動詞の原形）

Somebody **will clean** this room later.

受動態：be + done/cleaned/seen など（⇒ be + 過去分詞）

This room **will be cleaned** later.

➤ do/clean/seeなどの動詞の原形を，be + 過去分詞に変えます。

- The situation is serious. Something must **be done** before it's too late.
- A mystery is something that can't **be explained**.
- The music was very loud and could **be heard** from far away.
- A new supermarket is going to **be built** next year.
- Please go away. I want to **be left** alone.

B

☆ 受動態では should have / might have / would have / seem to have などの後に生じる過去分詞をどのように変えますか？

能動態：done/cleaned/seen など（⇒ 過去分詞）

Somebody **should have cleaned** this room.

受動態：been + done/cleaned/seen など（⇒ been + 過去分詞）

This room **should have been cleaned**.

➤ done/cleaned/seen などの過去分詞を，been + 過去分詞に変えます。

- I haven't received the letter yet. It might **have been sent** to the wrong address.
- If you had locked the car, it wouldn't **have been stolen**.
- There were some problems at first, but they seem to **have been solved**.

C

☆ 受動態では現在完了形の動詞をどのように変えますか？

能動態：have/has + 過去分詞

The room looks nice. Somebody **has cleaned** it.

受動態：have/has been + 過去分詞

The room looks nice. it **has been cleaned**.

➤ have/has + 過去分詞の現在完了形を，have/has been + 過去分詞に変えます。

- Have you heard? The concert **has been canceled**.
- **Have** you ever **been bitten** by a dog?
- "Are you going to the party?" "No, I **haven't been invited**."

☆ 受動態では過去完了形の動詞をどのように変えますか？

能動態：had + 過去分詞

The room looked nice. Somebody **had cleaned** it.

受動態：had been + 過去分詞

The room looks nice. it **had been cleaned**.

➤ had + 過去分詞の過去完了形は，had been + 過去分詞に変えます。

- The vegetables didn't taste very good. They **had been cooked** too long.
- The car was three years old but **hadn't been used** very much.

D

☆ 受動態では現在進行形の動詞をどのように変えますか？

能動態：am/is/are + 現在分詞

Somebody **is cleaning** this room right now.

受動態：am/is/are + being + 過去分詞

This room **is being cleaned** right now.

➤ am/is/are + 現在分詞の現在進行形を，am/is/are + being + 過去分詞に変えます。

- There's somebody walking behind us. I think we **are being followed**.
- 〔お店で〕"Can I help you?" "No, thank you. **I'm being helped**."

☆ 受動態では過去進行形の動詞をどのように変えますか？

能動態：was/were + 現在分詞

Somebody **was cleaning** this room when I arrived.

受動態：was/were + being + 過去分詞

This room **was being cleaned** when I arrived.

➤ was/were + 現在分詞の過去進行形を，was/were + being + 過去分詞に変えます。

- There was somebody walking behind us. We **were being followed**.

受動態 1, 3 ➲ Units 40, 42

Exercises

41.1 それぞれの単語の意味を it can ... もしくは it can't ... を用いて表しなさい。適宜，辞書を参考にしなさい。

If something is

1. washable, *it can be washed.* .
2. unbreakable, it ________ .
3. edible, ________ .
4. unusable, ________ .
5. invisible, ________ .
6. portable, ________ .

41.2 状況に合うように動詞(句)を以下から選び，適切な形に変えて文を完成しなさい。

arrest carry cause ~~do~~ make repair ~~send~~ spend wake up

適宜 might have，should have など，have を用いた形にします。

1. The situation is serious. Something must *be done* before it's too late.
2. I haven't received the letter. It might *have been sent* to the wrong address.
3. A decision will not ________ until the next meeting.
4. Do you think that more money should ________ on education?
5. This road is in very bad condition. It should ________ a long time ago.
6. The injured man couldn't walk and had to ________ .
7. I told the hotel desk clerk I wanted to ________ at 6:30 the next morning.
8. If you hadn't pushed the policeman, you wouldn't ________ .
9. It's not certain how the fire started, but it might ________ by an electrical short circuit.

41.3 somebody や they などの語句は使わずに，受動態の文を完成しなさい。

1. Somebody has cleaned the room. *The room has been cleaned.*
2. Somebody is using the computer right now.
   The computer ________
3. I didn't realize that somebody was recording our conversation.
   I didn't realize that ________
4. When we got to the stadium, we found that they had canceled the game.
   When we got to the stadium, we found that ________
5. They are building a new highway around the city.
   ____
6. They have built a new hospital near the airport.
   ____

41.4 状況に合うように（　）内の語句を用いて，能動態もしくは受動態の文を完成しなさい。

1. There's somebody behind us. (I think / we / follow) *I think we're being followed.*
2. This room looks different. (you / paint / the walls?) *Have you painted the walls?*
3. My car has disappeared. (it / steal!)
   It ________
4. My umbrella has disappeared. (somebody / take)
   Somebody ________
5. When I went into the room, I saw that the table and chairs were not in the same place.
   (the furniture / move) The ________
6. The man next door disappeared six months ago. (he / not / see / since then)
   He ________
7. I wonder how Jane is these days. (I / not / see / for ages)
   I ________
8. I wanted to use a computer at the library last night, but I wasn't able to.
   (the computers / use) All ________
9. Ann can't use her office this week. (it / redecorate)
   It ________
10. The photocopier broke down yesterday, but now it's OK. (it / work / again; it / repair)
    It ________ . It ________
11. A friend of mine was mugged on his way home a few nights ago. (you / ever / mug?)
    ____

補充問題 22–24 **(pp. 308–309)**

UNIT 42

受動態 3

A I was offered ... / we were given ... など：2つの目的語をとる動詞の受動態

give のような動詞は，次のように**二重目的語**をとります。

■ Someone **gave the police *the information*.** (= Someone **gave *the information* to the police.**)

the police：目的語 1（**間接目的語**）　the information：目的語 2（**直接目的語**）

この場合，次のように 2 つの目的語をそれぞれ主語にした **2 通りの受動態**が可能です。

■ **The police** were given ***the information***.
⇔ ***The information*** was given to **the police**.

give 以外に，以下のような動詞が**二重目的語**をとります。

ask　offer　pay　show　teach　tell

2 通りの受動態のうち，**I was offered ... / we were given ...** などのように人を主語とする形の方がよく用いられます。

■ **I was offered *the job***, but I refused it. (⇒ they **offered me *the job***)
■ **You will be given *plenty of time*** to decide. (⇒ we will give **you *plenty of time***)
■ **Have you been shown *the new machine***? (⇒ has anybody shown **you**?)
■ **The men were paid *$200*** to do the work. (⇒ somebody paid **the men *$200***)

B I don't like being ...: -ing 句（動名詞）の受動態

doing / **seeing** などの **-ing 句**（動名詞）は，**being done** / **being seen** のように **being + 過去分詞**で受動態を作ります。

能動態：I don't like **people telling me** what to do.
受動態：I don't like **being told** what to do.

■ I remember **being taken** to the zoo when I was a child.
(⇒ I remember **somebody taking me** to the zoo)
■ Steve hates **being kept** waiting. (⇒ he hates **people keeping him** waiting)
■ We managed to climb over the wall without **being seen**. (⇒ without **anybody seeing us**)

C I was born ...: 普通，過去時制で用いる受動態

I was born ... のような**過去時制**はありますが，× I am born ... のような現在時制はありません。

■ I **was born** in Chicago.
■ Where **were** you **born**? (× Where are you born?)
}**過去**

しかし，以下のように繰り返し行われる出来事を表す場合には，**現在時制**になります。

■ How many babies **are born** every day?(⇒ 毎日，どのくらいの赤ちゃんが生まれていますか？)〔現在〕

D get: 受動態において，be の代わりに用いられることがあります。

■ There was a fight at the game, but nobody **got hurt**. (= nobody **was hurt**)
■ I **don't** often **get invited** to parties. (= **I'm not** often **invited**)
■ I'm surprised Ann **didn't get offered** the job. (= Ann **wasn't offered** the job)

今までなかった出来事が生じたり，何か変化が起きたりする場合にのみ **get** が用いられます。
以下の例においては，**be** は **get** に代えられません。

■ Jill **is liked** by everybody. (× **gets liked**)〔出来事が起こっていない〕
■ He was a mystery man.Very little **was known** about him. (× **got known**)

主にくだけた口語英語において **get** を用います。**be** は状況に関係なく用います。
以下のような表現中で **get + 過去分詞**がよく用いられます。「〜される」のような受け身の意味はありません。

get married, get divorced
get dressed (= **put on** your clothes)
get lost (= **not know** where you are)
get changed (= **change** your clothes)

受動態 1, 2 ➲ Units 40, 41

Exercises

42.1 指定された書き出しで始めて，受動態の文を完成しなさい。

1. They didn't give me the information I needed.
   I *wasn't given the information I needed.*
2. They asked me some difficult questions at the interview.
   I ______
3. Jessica's colleagues gave her a present when she retired.
   Jessica ______
4. Nobody told me about the meeting.
   I wasn't ______
5. How much will they pay you for your work?
   How much will you ______
6. I think they should have offered John the job.
   I think John ______
7. Has anybody shown you what to do?
   Have you ______

42.2 以下から動詞を選び，being に続くよう適切な形に変えて文を完成しなさい。

give hit invite ~~keep~~ pay treat

1. Steve hates *being kept* waiting.
2. We went to the party without ______ .
3. I like giving presents, and I also like ______ them.
4. It's a busy road and I don't like crossing it. I'm afraid of ______ .
5. I'm an adult. I don't like ______ like a child.
6. Few people are prepared to work without ______ .

42.3 以下から 5人の人物を選び，それぞれがいつ生まれたかを述べる文を完成しなさい。(2 人については生れた年が同じです)

Beethoven	**Galileo**	**Elvis Presley**	**1452**	**1869**
John Lennon	**Mahatma Gandhi**	**Leonardo da Vinci**	**1564**	**~~1901~~**
~~Walt Disney~~	**Martin Luther King Jr.**	**William Shakespeare**	**1770**	**1940**
			1929	**1935**

1. *Walt Disney was born in 1901.*
2. ______
3. ______
4. ______
5. ______
6. ______
7. And you? I ______

42.4 以下から動詞を選び，get/got に続くように適切な形に変えて文を完成しなさい。

ask damage ~~hurt~~ pay steal sting stop use

1. There was a fight at the game, but nobody *got hurt* .
2. Ted ______ by a bee while he was sitting in the yard.
3. These tennis courts don't ______ very often. Not many people want to play.
4. I used to have a bicycle, but it ______ a few months ago.
5. Rachel works hard but doesn't ______ very much.
6. Last night I ______ by the police as I was driving home. One of the lights on my car wasn't working.
7. Please pack these things very carefully. I don't want them to ______ .
8. People often want to know what my job is. I often ______ that question.

補充問題 22–24 (pp. 308–309)

UNIT 43

It is said that ... He is said to ... He is supposed to ...

A

☆ 例文の状況について考えなさい。ともに受動態の文ですが，それぞれはどのように結び付きますか？

Henry はかなり高齢です。彼が何歳であるか正確に知る者はいません。このような時，彼が高齢であることを以下の２通りで表せます。

It is said that he is 108 years old.

= He **is said to be** 108 years old.

➤ **he が that 節中から外に出るとともに，動詞が to be に変わります。２つの文は形は異なるものの，ともに People say that he is 108 years old. のように「(はっきりとはしないが) …と言われている」を意味します。**

この構文で用いられる動詞には，以下のようなものがあります：

alleged　believed　considered　expected　known　reported　thought　understood

☆ **＝の左右の文で，太字の部分はどのように対応していますか？　また，to have ＋過去分詞はどのような場合に表れますか？**

- Cathy works very hard.
  It is said that she works 16 hours a day. = She **is said to work** 16 hours a day.
- The police are looking for a missing boy.
  It is believed that the boy is wearing a white sweater and blue jeans. = The boy **is believed to be wearing** a white sweater and blue jeans.
- The strike started three weeks ago.
  It is expected that it will end soon. = The strike **is expected to end** soon.
- A friend of mine has been arrested.
  It is alleged that he hit a police officer. = He **is alleged to have hit** a police officer.
- The two houses belong to the same family.
  It is said that there is a secret tunnel between them. = There **is said to be** a secret tunnel between them.

この構文はニュース報道においてよく用いられます。以下は事故に関する報道です。

- **It is reported that** two people were injured in the explosion. = Two people **are reported to have been injured** in the explosion.

B

(be) supposed to ... : (be) said to ... と同じ意味で，「…と言われている」を表します。

- Let's go and see that movie. It**'s supposed to be** good. (= it **is said to be** good)
- Mark **is supposed to have hit** a police officer, but I don't believe it.

(be) supposed to ... は，これ以外に状況に応じて「…することになっている，…するはずだ」のように意図・調整・期待していたことを表します。

- The plan **is supposed to be** a secret, but everybody seems to know about it.
  (⇒ 計画は誰にも言ってはいけないことになっているのに) 〔意図〕
- What are you doing at work? You**'re supposed to be** on vacation.
  (⇒ 休暇をとっているはずだ) 〔調整〕
- Jane **was supposed to call** me last night, but she didn't.
- Our guests **were supposed to come** at 7:30, but they were late.
- I'd better hurry. **I'm supposed to meet** Chris in 10 minutes.

You**'re not supposed to do ...** は「…してはいけない，…すべきではない」を表します。

- You**'re not supposed to park** your car here. It's private parking only.
- Mr. Bruno is much better after his operation, but he**'s still not supposed to do** any heavy work. (⇒ 重労働はしてはいけない)

Exercises

43.1 それぞれの文を指定された書き出しで始め，下線部の語を用いて別の表現で書き換えなさい。

1. It is expected that the strike will end soon. The strike *is expected to end soon.*
2. It is thought that the prisoner escaped by climbing over a wall.
   The prisoner *is thought to have escaped by climbing over a wall.*
3. It is reported that many people are homeless after the floods.
   Many people ______
4. It is alleged that the man robbed the store of $3,000.
   The man ______
5. It is reported that the building was badly damaged by the fire.
   The building ______
6. a) It is said that the company is losing a lot of money.
   The company ______
   b) It is believed that the company lost a lot of money last year.
   The company ______
   c) It is expected that the company will lose money this year.
   The company ______

43.2 Stan には，以下のようにさまざまな噂があります。

1. Stan speaks 10 languages.
2. He knows a lot of famous people.
3. He is very rich.
4. He has 12 children.
5. He was an actor when he was younger.

Stan

状況に合うように，**supposed to** を用いて **Stan** について記述する文を完成しなさい。

1. *Stan is supposed to speak 10 languages.*
2. He ______
3. ______
4. ______
5. ______

43.3 状況に合うように，**supposed to be** に続く語句を以下から選んで文を完成しなさい。

on a diet **a flower** **my friend** **a joke** ~~**on vacation**~~ **working**

1. What are you doing at work? You *are supposed to be on vacation.*
2. You shouldn't criticize me all the time. You ______
3. I really shouldn't be eating this cake. I ______
4. I'm sorry about what I said. I was trying to be funny. It ______
5. What's this drawing? Is it a tree? Or maybe it ______
6. You shouldn't be reading the paper now. You ______

43.4 状況に合うように，**supposed to** に続く動詞を以下から選んで文を完成しなさい。

arrive **block** **call** ~~**park**~~ **start**

適宜，否定形 **(not supposed to)** を用います。

1. You *'re not supposed to park* here. It's private parking only.
2. We ______ work at 8:15, but we rarely do anything before 8:30.
3. Oh, I ______ Helen, but I completely forgot.
4. This door is a fire exit. You ______ it.
5. My train ______ at 11:30, but it was an hour late.

補充問題 22–24 (pp. 308–309)

UNIT 44

have/get ～ done

A

☆ イラストを見て考えます。Lisa は自分の家の屋根について何をしましたか？

Lisa

Lisa の家の屋根は嵐で壊れてしまいました。昨日，大工さんが来て屋根を修繕しました。この状況は次のような構文で記述できます。

Lisa **had** the roof **repaired** yesterday.

➤ Lisa は屋根を修繕してもらいました。この構文は，Lisa が人に屋根の修繕を依頼したことを意味し，Lisa 自身は屋根を修繕していません。had の目的語である the roof と過去分詞 repaired との間には，the roof was repaired（屋根は修繕された）のような受動態を作る関係があります。

have ～ done（過去分詞）は「～を…してもらう」のように，誰かに自分に代わって何かを依頼する際に用います。

☆ 自分で何かをする場合と誰かに依頼する場合で，構文はどのように異なりますか？

- Lisa **repaired** the roof.（⇒ 自分で修繕した）
  Lisa **had** the roof **repaired**.（⇒ 誰かに修繕してもらった）
- "Did you **paint** your apartment yourself?" "Yes, I like doing things like that."
  "Did you **have** your apartment **painted**?" "No, I painted it myself."

B

この構文では **have＋目的語＋過去分詞**のような語順となります。

have	目的語	過去分詞
Lisa **had**	the roof	**repaired** yesterday.
Where did you **have**	your hair	**cut**?
Our neighbor has just **had**	air conditioning	**installed** in her house.
We are **having**	the house	**painted** this week.
How often do you **have**	your car	**serviced**?
Why don't you **have**	that coat	**cleaned**?
I don't like **having**	my picture	**taken**.

C

get ～ done（過去分詞）

くだけた話しことばでは，**have ～ done** の代わりに **get ～ done** が使われることがあります。

- When are you going to **get the roof repaired**? (= **have** the roof **repaired**)
- I think you should **get your hair cut** really short.

D

以下の例文において，**have/get ～ done**（過去分詞）は「～を…してもらう」のような動作の依頼の意味はありません。

- Eric **had his license taken away** for driving too fast again and again.

= Eric **got his license taken away** for driving . . .

この例文において，Eric は誰かに自分の運転免許証を取り上げるように依頼してはいません。「警察によって，免許証を取り上げられた」を意味します。**have/get ～ done** は「困ったことに～を…される」のように，人や物に対して何らかの好ましくない出来事が起こった場合に用いることがあります。

- James **got** his passport **stolen**.（⇒ パスポートを盗まれた）
- Have you ever **had** your flight **canceled**?（⇒ フライトがキャンセルされたことはありますか？）

Exercises

44.1 イラストを見て，状況を説明している文を選びなさい。

1.

Sarah

a) Sarah is cutting her hair.
b) Sarah is having her hair cut.

2.

Bill

a) Bill is cutting his hair.
b) Bill is having his hair cut.

3.

John

a) John is shining his shoes.
b) John is having his shoes shined.

4.

Sue

a) Sue is taking a picture.
b) Sue is having her picture taken.

44.2 To have ~ done. の構文を用いて，以下から目的語と動詞を選び適切な形に変えて答えを完成しなさい。

~~my car~~ my eyes my jacket my watch

clean repair ~~service~~ test

1. Why did you go to the garage? *To have my car serviced.*
2. Why did you go to the cleaner's? To ______
3. Why did you go to the jeweler's? ______
4. Why did you go to the optician's? ______

44.3 例を参考にして，それぞれの文を書き換えなさい。

1. Lisa didn't repair the roof herself. *She had it repaired.*
2. I didn't cut my hair myself. I ______
3. They didn't paint the house themselves. They ______
4. John didn't build that wall himself. ______
5. I didn't deliver the flowers myself. ______

44.4 状況に合うように（　）内の語句を用い，have ~ done の形で文を完成しなさい。

1. We *are having the house painted* (the house / paint) this week.
2. I lost my key. I'll have to ______ (another key / make).
3. When was the last time you ______ (your hair / cut)?
4. ______ (you / a newspaper / deliver) to your house every day, or do you go out and buy one?
5. *A:* What are those workers doing at your house?
   B: Oh, we ______ (garage / build).
6. You can't see that sign from here? You should ______ (your eyes / check).

同様に get ~ done の形で文を完成しなさい。

7. How often *do you get your car serviced* (your car / service)?
8. This coat is dirty. I should ______ (it / clean).
9. If you want to wear earrings, why don't you ______ (your ears / pierce)?
10. *A:* I heard your computer wasn't working.
    B: That's right, but it's OK now. I ______ (it / repair).

have ~ done の形で，セクション D で解説されている意味を持つ文を（　）内の語句を用いて完成しなさい。

11. Did you hear about Pete? *He had his license taken away* (license / take away).
12. Did I tell you about Jane? She ______ (her purse / steal) last week.
13. Gary was in a fight last night. ______ (his nose / break).

UNIT 45

間接話法 1 (He said that ...)

A

☆ イラストを見て考えます。Tom の言ったことばをどのように人に伝えますか？

➤ Tom が言ったことばを人に伝えるには，2 通りの方法があります。

1) Tom のことばをそのまま繰り返します（直接話法）。
Tom said, **"I'm feeling sick."**

2) Tom のことばを自分の視点から言い換えて伝えます（間接話法）。
Tom said **that he was feeling sick.**

直接話法： Tom said, " I am feeling sick."

間接話法： Tom said that **he was** feeling sick.

書きことばでは，"　"（引用符）で実際に述べたことばをはさみます。

B

間接話法では，Tom **said** that ... や I **told** her that ... などの太字の部分は文の**主動詞**と呼ばれます。**主動詞**は普通，**過去形**になります。また**主動詞**と連動して文の残りの部分（**that 節**）も普通，**過去形**になります。

- Tom **said** that he **was feeling** sick.
- I **told** her that I **didn't have** any money.

以下のように **that** を省略する場合もあります。

- Tom **said that** he was feeling sick. = Tom **said** he was feeling sick.

普通，**直接話法**の "　" 中における**現在形**は**間接話法**の **that 節**中で**過去形**に変わります。

am/is → **was**　　do/does → **did**　　will → **would**
are → **were**　　have/has → **had**　　can → **could**
want/know/go など → **wanted/knew/went** など

☆ 例文の状況について考えます。直接話法から間接話法に変わると，どのように形が変化しますか？

直接話法：Jenny はあなたとの対話で実際に，次のように発言しました。

"My parents **are** fine."
"I'**m** going to learn to drive."
"I **want** to buy a car."
"John **has** quit his job."
"I **can't** come to the party on Friday."
"I **don't** have much free time."
"I'**m** going away for a few days. I'**ll** call you when I **get** back."

Jenny

間接話法：あなたは Jenny との対話の後，Jenny のことばを別の人に次のように伝えます。

- Jenny said that her parents **were** fine.
- She said that she **was** going to learn to drive.
- She said that she **wanted** to buy a car.
- She said that John **had quit** his job.
- She said that she **couldn't** come to the party on Friday.
- She said she **didn't** have much free time.
- She said that she **was** going away for a few days and **would** call me when she **got** back.

C

直接話法中の**単純過去形の動詞**（did/saw/knew など）は，**間接話法**中では，そのまま形を変えずに用いるか，**過去完了形**（had done / had seen / had known など）に変えます。

- **間接話法**：Tom said, "I **woke** up feeling sick, so I **didn't go** to work."
  直接話法：Tom said (that) he **woke** up feeling sick, so he **didn't go** to work.
  = Tom said (that) he **had woken** up feeling sick, so he **hadn't gone** to work.

間接話法 2 ➲ Unit 46　　疑問文の間接話法 ➲ Unit 48B

Exercises

45.1 昨日，あなたは友人の Rob と久しぶりに会いました。あなたとの対話で Rob は次のような発言をしました。

1. I'm living in my own apartment now.
2. My father isn't very well.
3. Amanda and Paul are getting married next month.
4. My sister has had a baby.
5. I don't know what Eric is doing.
6. I saw Nicole at a party in June, and she seemed fine.
7. I haven't seen Diane recently.
8. I'm not enjoying my job very much.
9. You can come and stay at my place if you're ever in Chicago.
10. My car was stolen a few days ago.
11. I want to take a trip, but I can't afford it.
12. I'll tell Amy I saw you.

Rob

Rob が話したことを，あなたがその後出会った別の友人に伝える間接話法の文を完成しなさい。

1. *Rob said that he was living in his own apartment now.*
2. He said that ________
3. He ________
4. ________
5. ________
6. ________
7. ________
8. ________
9. ________
10. ________
11. ________
12. ________

45.2 ある人の発言が以前聞いていたことと逆になっていました。例にならってこの人に対して今の自分の気持ちを述べる文を完成しなさい。

1. *A:* That restaurant is expensive.
   B: It is? *I thought you said it was cheap*.
2. *A:* Sue is coming to the party tonight.
   B: She is? I thought you said she ________.
3. *A:* Ann likes Paul.
   B: She does? Last week you said ________.
4. *A:* I know lots of people.
   B: You do? I thought you said ________.
5. *A:* Pat will be here next week.
   B: She will? But didn't you say ________?
6. *A:* I'm going out tonight.
   B: You are? But you said ________.
7. *A:* I can speak a little French.
   B: You can? But earlier you said ________.
8. *A:* I haven't been to the movies in ages.
   B: You haven't? I thought you said ________.

補充問題 25 (pp. 310–311)

UNIT 46

間接話法 2

A

間接話法では，必ず動詞の時制を変えなければならないというわけではありません。人のことばを伝える際，その状況が今も変わっていない場合には動詞を**過去形**に変える必要はありません。

- **直接話法**：Tom said, "My new job **is** very interesting."
  間接話法：Tom said that his new job **is** very interesting.
  (⇒ His job **is** still interesting.)〔状況は変わっていない〕
- **直接話法**：Ann said, "**I want** to go to South America next year."
  間接話法：Ann told me that **she wants** to go to South America next year.
  (⇒ Ann still wants to go to South America next year.)〔状況は変わっていない〕

同じ状況を，以下のように動詞を**過去形**に変えて表現することもできます。

- Tom said that his new job **was** very interesting.
- Ann told me that she **wanted** to go to South America next year.

現在より前に完結し，現在とは異なる状況を伝える場合には動詞を**過去形**に変えなければなりません。

- Paul left the room suddenly. He said **he had** to go. (× has to go)

B

☆ イラストの表す状況について考えなさい。過去時制を持つ間接話法の文は，どのような意味合いを持ちますか？

数日前にあなたが Sonia と会った時，彼女は Joe について次のように言っていました。

"Joe **is** in the hospital."（**直接話法**）

ところがその直後，ばったり Joe と道で会いました。あなたは Joe に次のように言います。

"I didn't expect to see you, Joe. Sonia said you **were** in the hospital."

➤ **前に聞いていたことと現実とが異なる場合には，動詞を過去形に変えなければなりません。以下のような現在形は用いません。**

× Sonia said you are in the hospital

C

say と tell

「～は…に言った」のように，誰に言ったかを明らかにする場合には **tell** を用います。 ○**TELL … (人)**

- Sonia **told me** that you were in the hospital. (× Sonia said me) (⇒ 目的語（人）を必ず置く)
- What did you **tell the police**? (× say the police)

「～は言った」のように，誰に言ったかを述べる必要がない場合には **say** を用います。 × **SAY** ~~… (人)~~

- Sonia **said** that you were in the hospital. (× Sonia told that . . .) (⇒ 目的語（人）は置かない)
- What did you **say**?

say — to … の形で「～は…に一と言った」を表します。 ○**SAY — (物) to … (人)**

- Ann **said** good-bye **to** me and left. (× Ann said me good-bye) (⇒ 目的語（物）+ to + 人)
- What did you **say to** the police?

D

tell/ask ～ to do …:「～に…してくれるように言う / 頼む」を表します。
間接話法中で**不定詞**（to + 動詞の原形）を用いることがあります。**不定詞**は，ことに動詞 **tell** や **ask** とともに用いられます。

- **直接話法**："**Stay** in bed for a few days," the doctor said to me.
  間接話法：The doctor **told me to** stay in bed for a few days.
- **直接話法**："**Don't shout**," I said to Jim.
  間接話法：I **told** Jim **not to** shout.
- **直接話法**："Please **don't tell** anybody what happened," Jackie said to me.
  間接話法：Jackie **asked me not to tell** anybody what (had) happened.

say を用いて，**～ said (not) to do …**（…するように（…しないように）言った）のように言うこともできます。

- Jackie **said** not **to tell anyone**. (× Jackie said me)

間接話法 1 ➲ Unit 45　疑問文の間接話法 ➲ Unit 48B

Exercises

46.1 Ann はあなたとの対話で，次のような発言をしました。

しかし，その後彼女の発言が前と変わっていました。あなたの気持を述べる文を完成しなさい。

	Ann	あなた
1.	Dave works very hard.	*But you said he was lazy.*
2.	Let's have fish for dinner.	But ______
3.	I'm going to buy a car.	______
4.	Rosa is always short of money.	______
5.	My sister lives in Tokyo.	______
6.	I think Peru is a great place.	______
7.	Let's go out tomorrow night.	______
8.	I've never spoken to Rosa.	______

46.2 say もしくは tell のいずれかを用い，正しい形に変えて文を完成しなさい。

1. Ann *said* good-bye to me and left.
2. ______ us about your vacation. Did you have a good time?
3. Don't just stand there! ______ something!
4. I wonder where Sue is. She ______ she would be here at 8:00.
5. Jack ______ me that he was fed up with his job.
6. The doctor ______ that I should rest for at least a week.
7. Don't ______ anybody what I ______ . It's a secret just between us.
8. "Did she ______ you what happened?" "No, she didn't ______ anything to me."
9. Jason couldn't help me. He ______ me to ask Kate.
10. Gary couldn't help me. He ______ to ask Caroline.

46.3 以下は直接話法の文です。

状況に合うように，上の直接話法の文を適切な形に変えて間接話法の文にしなさい。

1. Bill was taking a long time to get ready, so I told *him to hurry up* .
2. Sarah was driving too fast, so I asked ______ .
3. Sue was nervous about the situation. I told ______ .
4. I couldn't move the piano alone, so I ______ .
5. The customs officer looked at me suspiciously and ______ .
6. The man started asking me personal questions, so I ______ .
7. John was in love with Maria, so he ______ .
8. I didn't want to delay Helen, so I ______ .

補充問題 25 (pp. 310–311)

UNIT 47

疑問文 1

A

複数の**動詞要素**を持つ文では，**第 1 動詞**（最初の動詞要素，助動詞および be 動詞）を**主語**の後に置いて**疑問文**を作ります。最も右側にある**動詞要素**を**主動詞**と呼びます。

主語	+ 第 1 動詞		第 1 動詞	+ 主語
Tom	will	→	will	Tom?
you	have	→	have	you?
The house	was	→	was	the house?

☆ どのような動詞要素がありますか？

- **Will Tom** be here tomorrow?
- **Have you** been working hard?
- When **was the house** built?

第 1	第 2	第 3
will	**be**	なし
have	been	**working**
was	**built**	なし

太字が主動詞。

主語は**第 1 動詞**の後にきます。

- **Is Catherine** working today?（✕ Is working Catherine）〔**第 2 動詞**の後に主語〕

B

I **do** の形を持つ**単純現在形**（➲ Units 2–4, do を主動詞に持つ文）は，**do/does** を用いて**疑問文**を作ります。

you	live	→	**do**	you live?
the film	begins	→	**does**	the film begin?

- **Do** you **live** near here?
- What time **does** the film **begin**?

I **did** の形を持つ**単純過去形**（➲ Units 5–6, 8–9）は，**did** を用いて**疑問文**を作ります。

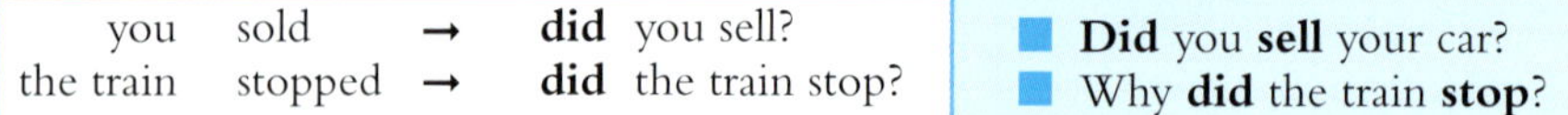

you	sold	→	**did**	you sell?
the train	stopped	→	**did**	the train stop?

- **Did** you **sell** your car?
- Why **did** the train **stop**?

☆ 以下の例文で考えます。who が目的語の場合と主語の場合とで，疑問文の作り方はどのように異なりますか？

➤ **who/what などの疑問詞が文の主語となる場合には，do/does/did を用いずに疑問文を作ります。語順に変化はありません。**

- **Who wants** something to eat?（✕ Who does want）
- **What happened** to you last night?（✕ What did happen）
- **How many people came** to the meeting?（✕ did come）
- **Which bus goes** downtown?（✕ does go）

C

who/what/which/where などの**疑問詞で始まる疑問文**中では，**前置詞**の後に名詞句が現れない場合があります。

- **Who** do you want to speak **to**?
- **Which** job has Ann applied **for**?
- **What** was the weather **like** yesterday?
- **Where** are you **from**?

より堅苦しい文脈では，**前置詞 + whom** の形を用いることがあります。

- **To whom** do you wish to speak?

D

否定疑問文：Isn't it ...? / Didn't you ...? などの形で，「…ではない / なかったのですか？」を表します。

「信じられない」のような驚きの気持ちを表します。

- **Didn't you** hear the doorbell? I rang it three times.

聞き手から**肯定**の返事を期待します。

- "**Haven't we** met somewhere before?"　"Yes, I think we have."

英語では，話し手への同意・不同意にかかわりなく，質問への答えが**肯定文**の場合には **yes**，**否定文**の場合には **no** を用います。

- **Don't you** want to go to the party?
  - **Yes.**（= Yes, I want to go）
  - **No.**（= No, I don't want to go）

Why ...? の**否定疑問文**では，**don't/wasn't** などの要素を主語の後には置きません。

- **Why don't we** go out for a meal tonight?（✕ Why we don't go）
- **Why wasn't Mary** at work yesterday?（✕ Why Mary wasn't）

疑問文 2 ➲ Unit 48　付加疑問文（..., do you? / ..., isn't it? など）➲ Unit 50

Exercises

47.1 Joe の答えが正しく導かれるような疑問文を作りなさい。

1. (where / live?) *Where do you live?* — In Vancouver.
2. (born there?) ______ — No, I was born in Toronto.
3. (married?) ______ — Yes.
4. (how long / married?) ______ — 17 years.
5. (children?) ______ — Yes, two boys.
6. (how old / they?) ______ — 12 and 15.
7. (what / do?) ______ — I'm a journalist.
8. (what / wife / do?) ______ — She's a doctor.

Joe

47.2 例を参考にして，who もしくは what で始まる疑問文を作りなさい。

1. Somebody hit me. — *Who hit you?*
2. I hit somebody. — *Who did you hit?*
3. Somebody paid the bill. — Who ______
4. Something happened. — What ______
5. Diane said something. — ______
6. This book belongs to somebody. — ______
7. Somebody lives in that house. — ______
8. I fell over something. — ______
9. Something fell on the floor. — ______
10. This word means something. — ______
11. I borrowed the money from somebody. — ______
12. I'm worried about something. — ______

47.3 (　) 内の語句を正しい順番に並べ替えて，適切な疑問文を作りなさい。

1. (when / was / built / this house) *When was this house built?*
2. (how / cheese / is / made) ______
3. (when / invented / the computer / was) ______
4. (why / Sue / working / isn't / today) ______
5. (what time / coming / your friends / are) ______
6. (why / was / canceled / the concert) ______
7. (where / your mother / was / born) ______
8. (why / you / to the party / didn't / come) ______
9. (how / the accident / did / happen) ______
10. (why / this machine / doesn't / work) ______

47.4 (　) 内の語句を正しい順番に並べ替えて，適切な否定疑問文を作りなさい。いずれの場合も驚いた気持ちを表します。

1. *A:* We won't see Ann tonight.
   B: Why not? (she / not / come / to the party?) *Isn't she coming to the party?*
2. *A:* I hope we don't see Brian tonight.
   B: Why? (you / not / like / him?) ______
3. *A:* Don't go and see that movie.
   B: Why not? (it / not / good?) ______
4. *A:* I'll have to borrow some money.
   B: Why? (you / not / have / any?) ______

UNIT 48

疑問文 2（間接疑問文）Do you know where ...? / He asked me where ...

A

☆ Do you know where ...? / I don't know why ...? / Could you tell me what ...? などの形がよく用いられます。このように，より大きな文中で where/why/what などの疑問詞が生じる文を間接疑問文と呼びます。間接疑問文では，語順はどのように変わりますか？

直接疑問文：　Where **has Tom** gone?

間接疑問文：**Do you know** where **Tom has** gone?（× Do you know where has Tom gone?）

➤ 間接疑問文中では，主語＋動詞要素の語順となります。

直接疑問文：		間接疑問文：
■ What time **is it**?	⇔	**Do you know** what time **it is**?
■ Who **are those people**?		**I don't know** who **those people are**.
■ Where **can I** find Linda?		**Can you tell me** where **I can** find Linda?
■ How much **will it** cost?		**Do you have any idea** how much **it will** cost?

➤ **I do. / I did.** など，主動詞しか動詞要素を持たない文を間接疑問文にする場合には，**do/does/did** のような語は生じません。

直接疑問文：		間接疑問文：
■ What **time does the movie begin**?	⇔	**Do you know** what time **the movie begins**? (× does the movie begin)
■ What **do you mean**?		**Please explain** what **you mean**.
■ Why **did she leave** early?		**I wonder** why **she left** early.

➤ 疑問詞で始まらない疑問文を間接疑問文にする場合には，**if** や **whether** を疑問詞の位置に置きます。

直接疑問文：		間接疑問文：
■ Did anybody see you?	⇔	Do you know **if** anybody saw you?
		= . . . **whether** anybody saw you?

B

☆ He asked me where ... のように，人が述べたことばを自分の視点から言い換えて伝える間接話法中の疑問文では，直接話法と比べてどのような変化が生じますか？➲ Units 45–46

■ 直接話法：　The police officer said to us, "Where **are you going** ?"

間接話法：　The police officer asked us where **we were going** .

■ 直接話法：　Claire asked, "What time **do the banks close** ?"

間接話法：　Claire wanted to know what time **the banks closed** .

➤ 間接疑問文と同様な語順の変化が生じます。動詞の時制は普通，過去時制となります。➲ Units 45–46

☆ イラストを見て考えます。あなたは就職の面接試験で次のように質問されました。面接官がした質問を友人に間接話法で伝えると，どのようになりますか？

➤ 以下のように間接話法中では，主語 ＋ 動詞要素の語順とし，代名詞を I に変え，動詞を過去時制に変えます。

■ She asked if (= whether) **I was** willing to travel.
■ She wanted to know what **I did** in my spare time.
■ She asked how long **I had** been working at my present job.
■ She asked why **I had** applied for the job. (= ... why **I applied**)
■ She wanted to know if (= whether) **I could** speak another language.
■ She asked if (= whether) **I had** a driver's license.

間接話法 ➲ Units 45–46

Exercises

48.1 例を参考にして，（ ）内の疑問文を間接疑問文にしなさい。

1. (Where has Tom gone?) Do you know *where Tom has gone?*
2. (Where is the post office?) Could you tell me ____
3. (What time is it?) I wonder ____
4. (What does this word mean?) I want to know ____
5. (Has the plane left yet?) Do you know ____
6. (Is Sue going out tonight?) I don't know ____
7. (Where does Carol live?) Do you have any idea ____
8. (Where did I park the car?) I can't remember ____
9. (Is there a bank near here?) Can you tell me ____
10. (What do you want?) Tell me ____
11. (Why didn't Kelly come to the party?) I don't know ____
12. (How much does it cost to park here?) Do you know ____
13. (Who is that woman?) I have no idea ____
14. (Did Ann get my letter?) Do you know ____
15. (How far is it to the airport?) Can you tell me ____

48.2 あなたは電話で Amy と話がしたいのですが，Amy は不在で，知らない人が電話に出ました。この人から，次の 3 点について聞き出す際の対話を完成しなさい。

(1) Where is Amy? (2) When will she be back? (3) Did she go out alone?

A: Do you know where ____ ? (1)
B: Sorry, I have no idea.
A: That's all right. I don't suppose you know ____ . (2)
B: No, I'm afraid I don't.
A: One more thing. Do you happen to know ____ ? (3)
B: I'm sorry. I didn't see her go out. But I'll tell her you called.

48.3 あなたは久しぶりに故郷に戻って来ました。昔の友人の Tony にばったり出会いました。Tony は次から次へと，あなたのことについて質問してきます。

Tony

次に出会った別の友人に，Tony がどのような質問をしたかを間接話法を用いて伝える文を完成しなさい。

1. *He asked me how I was.*
2. He asked me ____
3. He ____
4. ____
5. ____
6. ____
7. ____
8. ____
9. ____

補充問題 25 (pp. 310–311)

UNIT 49

助動詞（have/do/can など） I think so. / I hope so. などを用いて繰り返しを避ける表現

A

以下の例文ではいずれも **2つの動詞要素**があります。

	第1動詞	第2動詞	
I	**have**	**lost**	my keys.
She	**can't**	**come**	to the party.
The hotel	**was**	**built**	ten years ago.
Where	**do** you	**live**?	

上のように**動詞要素**を２つ持つ文における **have/can't/was/do** のような**第１動詞**を**助動詞** (auxiliary verb) と呼びます。この例では，**第２動詞**は最後の**動詞要素**なので，**主動詞**になります。➲Unit 47

助動詞は，会話において**主動詞**以降の文の繰り返しを避けたい時に用います。

- "Have you locked the door?" "Yes, I **have**." (= I have *locked the door*)
- George wasn't working, but Janet **was**. (= Janet was *working*)
- She could lend me the money, but she **won't**. (= she won't *lend me the money*)

I do / I did などの**単純現在形**や**単純過去形**では，**do/does/did** を**助動詞**として用いて繰返しを避けます。➲Unit 47B

- "Do you like onions?" "Yes, I **do**." (= I *like onions*)
- "Does Mark play soccer?" "He **did**, but he **doesn't** any more."

相手の発言を否定する肯定文には**否定形の助動詞**で答え，否定文には**肯定形の助動詞**で答えます。➲Unit 47D

- "You're sitting in my place." "No, **I'm not**." (= I'm not *sitting in your place*)
- "You didn't lock the door before you left." "Yes, I **did**." (= I *locked the door*)

B

You have? / She isn't? / They do? などのように**助動詞**で文を終え，**上昇調**で発音して他人の発言に興味があることを示します。

- "I've just seen David." "**You have**? How is he?"
- "Liz isn't feeling very well today." "**She isn't**? What's wrong with her?"
- "It rained every day during our vacation." "**It did**? What a shame!"
- "Jim and Karen are getting married." "**They are**? Really?"

C

肯定文には **so**, 否定文には **neither** を**助動詞**とともに用いて「〜も…だ」や「〜も…ではない」を表します。

- "I'm tired." "**So am I**." (= I'm tired, too)
- "I never read newspapers." "**Neither do I**." (= I never read newspapers either)
- Sue doesn't have a car, and **neither does Mark**.

so/neither + 助動詞 + 主語の語順となることに注意します。

- I passed the exam, and **so did Paul**. (× so Paul did)

neither の代わりに **not ... either** も用いられます。語順の違いに注意します。

- "I don't have any money." "**Neither** do I." = "I do**n't either**."

D

I think so. / I guess so. / I suppose so. などの形で「そう思う」を表します。

so を目的語の位置に置いて，繰返しを避けて相手に同意する気持ちを表します。

- "Are those people Australian?" "**I think so**." (= I think they are Australian)
- "Will you be home tomorrow morning?" "**I guess so**. (= I guess I'll be home . . .)
- "Do you think Kate has been invited to the party?" "**I suppose so.**"

他に **I hope so.**（そうなってほしい）や **I'm afraid so.**（残念だがそうだろう）といった表現も用いられます。

so を用いた表現の**否定形**は普通，次のようになります。**not** の位置が動詞に応じて異なることに注意します。

I think **so** → **I don't think so**
I hope **so** / I'm afraid **so** / I guess **so** → **I hope not / I'm afraid not / I guess not**
I suppose **so** → **I suppose not**

- "Is that woman French?" "**I think so. / I don't think so.**"
- "Do you think it will rain?" "**I hope so. / I hope not.**" (× I don't hope so)

You have? / She isn't? に関連したイギリス英語の表現 ➲ 付録 7

Exercises

49.1 状況に合うように，適切な助動詞（do/was/could/should など）を空所に入れて文を完成しなさい。必要に応じて否定形（don't/wasn't など）に変えます。

1. I wasn't tired, but my friends *were* .
2. I like hot weather, but Ann ________ .
3. "Is Eric here?" "He ________ five minutes ago, but I think he's gone."
4. Liz said she might call later on tonight, but I don't think she ________ .
5. "Are you and Chris coming to the party?" "I ________ , but Chris ________ ."
6. I don't know whether to apply for the job or not. Do you think I ________ ?
7. "Please don't tell anybody what I said." "Don't worry. I ________ ."
8. "You never listen to me." "Yes, I ________ !"
9. "Can you play a musical instrument?" "No, but I wish I ________ ."
10. "Please help me." "I'm sorry. I ________ if I ________ , but I ________ ."

49.2 あなたはどうしても Alex の言うことに共感できません。例にならって，Alex のことばを否定する文を完成しなさい。

Alex

1. I'm hungry. — *You are? I'm not.*
2. I'm not tired. — *You aren't? I am.*
3. I like baseball. — ________
4. I didn't like the movie. — ________
5. I've never been to South America. — ________
6. I thought the exam was easy. — ________

あなた

49.3 自分の状況を考えて答えます。あなたが Lisa の発言に共感できる場合には，1 の例のように So ... もしくは Neither ... で答えなさい。共感できない場合には，2 の例のように複数の疑問文で答えなさい。

Lisa

1. I feel really tired. — *So do I.*
2. I'm working hard. — *You are? What are you doing?*
3. I watched TV last night. — ________
4. I won't be at home tomorrow. — ________
5. I like to read. I read a lot. — ________
6. I'd like to live somewhere else. — ________
7. I can't go out tonight. — ________

あなた

49.4 あなたは問題の冒頭に記されているように考えています。この状況に合うように，（　）内の動詞を用いて，I think so. / I hope not. などの表現にして対話を完成させなさい。

1. (You don't like rain.)
   A: Is it going to rain? *B:* (hope) *I hope not.*
2. (You're not sure Sarah will get the job she applied for, but her chances look pretty good.)
   A: Do you think Sarah will get the job? *B:* (guess) ________
3. (You're not sure whether Amy is married – probably not.)
   A: Is Amy married? *B:* (think) ________
4. (You need more money quickly.)
   A: Do you think you'll get a raise soon? *B:* (hope) ________
5. (You're a hotel desk clerk. The hotel is full.)
   A: Do you have a room for tonight? *B:* (afraid) ________
6. (You're at a party. You have to leave early.)
   A: Do you have to leave already? *B:* (afraid) ________
7. (You are going to a party. You can't stand John.)
   A: Do you think John will be at the party? *B:* (hope) ________
8. (You're not sure what time the concert is – probably 7:30.)
   A: Is the concert at 7:30? *B:* (think) ________
9. (Ann normally works every day, Monday to Friday. Tomorrow is Wednesday.)
   A: Is Ann working tomorrow? *B:* (suppose) ________

UNIT 50

付加疑問（..., do you? / ..., isn't it? など）

A

☆イラストの状況について考えなさい。どのような形の疑問文が使われていますか？

➤ それぞれの対話はいずれも，**have you?** や **wasn't it?** のように付加疑問と呼ばれる短い疑問文を文の終りに置いています。付加疑問中には，前にくる肯定文や否定文中の助動詞（**have/was/will** など）が現れます。

I **do** や I **did** のような**単純現在形**や**単純過去形**では，**do/does/did** を用いて**付加疑問**を作ります。➲Unit 49

- "Lauren plays the piano, **does**n't she?" "Well, yes, but not very well."
- "You didn't lock the door, **did** you?" "No, I forgot."

B

肯定文には**否定形の付加疑問**が付きます。

肯定文＋否定形の付加疑問	
Maria **will** be here soon,	**won't she?**
There **was** a lot of traffic,	**wasn't there?**
Jim **should** take his medicine,	**shouldn't he?**

否定文には**肯定形の付加疑問**が付きます。

否定文＋肯定形の付加疑問	
Kate **won't** be late,	**will she?**
They **don't** like us,	**do they?**
You **haven't** paid the gas bill,	**have you?**

否定文に**肯定の付加疑問**が付いた文では，**Yes** は相手の発言に**不同意**を，**No** は**同意**を表します。➲Unit 47D

- You're **not** going out today, **are you?** { **Yes.** (= Yes, I am going out) / **No.** (= No, I am not going out)

C

付加疑問が実際に表す意味は，文に与えるイントネーションによって変化します。「…ですよね？ / …ではないですよね？」のように話し手が聞き手に**同意**を求める場合には，**付加疑問**を**下降調**で発音します。

- "It's a nice day, **isn't it**?" "Yes, beautiful."
- "Eric doesn't look too good today, **does he**?" "No, he looks very tired."
- She's very funny. She has a wonderful sense of humor, **doesn't she?**

付加疑問を**上昇調**で発音すると，「…ですか？ /…ではないですか？」のように通常の**疑問文**や**否定疑問文**と同じ意味になります。

- "You haven't seen Lisa today, **have you**?" "No, I haven't."
  (= Have you seen Lisa today by any chance?)

「…はありませんか？ / …を知りませんか？」のように物や情報を尋ねたり，「…していただけませんか？」のように人に何かをしてもらいたい時にも，**否定文＋肯定の付加疑問**の組み合わせを**上昇調**で発音します。

- "You wouldn't have a pen, **would you**?" "Yes, here you are."
- "You couldn't lend me some money, **could you**?" "It depends how much."
- "You don't know where Lauren is, **do you**?" "Sorry, I have no idea."

D

文が **Let's ...** で始まる時，**付加疑問**は **shall we?** となります。

- **Let's** go for a walk, **shall we**?（上昇調）

Do/Listen/Give ... などで始まる**命令文**では，**付加疑問**は **will you?** となります。

- **Listen** to me, **will you**?（上昇調）

I'm ... で始まる時，**付加疑問**は **aren't I?** となります。

- "**I'm** right, **aren't I**?" "Yes, you are."

助動詞（have/do/can など）➲Unit 49

Exercises

50.1 適切な付加疑問を付けて文を完成しなさい。

1.	Tom won't be late, *will he* ?	No, he's never late.
2.	You're tired, *aren't you* ?	Yes, a little.
3.	You've lived here a long time, ________ ?	Yes, 20 years.
4.	You weren't listening, ________ ?	Yes, I was!
5.	Sue doesn't know Ann, ________ ?	No, they've never met.
6.	Jack's on vacation, ________ ?	Yes, he's in Peru.
7.	Mike hasn't called today, ________ ?	No, I don't think so.
8.	You can speak Spanish, ________ ?	Yes, but not fluently.
9.	He won't mind if I use his phone, ________ ?	No, of course he won't.
10.	There are a lot of people here, ________ ?	Yes, more than I expected.
11.	Let's go out tonight, ________ ?	Yes, that would be great.
12.	This isn't very interesting, ________ ?	No, not at all.
13.	I'm too impatient, ________ ?	Yes, you are sometimes.
14.	You wouldn't tell anyone, ________ ?	No, of course not.
15.	Listen to me, ________ ?	OK, I'm listening.
16.	I shouldn't have lost my temper, ________ ?	No, but that's all right.
17.	He'd never met her before, ________ ?	No, that was the first time.

50.2 全体の状況に合うように，（　）内の語句を用いて聞き手から同意を求める付加疑問文を完成しなさい。

1. You look out of the window. The sky is blue and the sun is shining. What do you say to your friend? (beautiful day) *It's a beautiful day, isn't it?*
2. You're with a friend outside a restaurant. You're looking at the prices, which are very high. What do you say? (expensive) It ________
3. You and a colleague have just finished a training course. You really enjoyed it. What do you say to your colleague? (great) The course ________
4. Your friend's hair is much shorter than when you last met. What do you say to her/him? (have / your hair / cut) You ________
5. You and a friend are listening to a woman singing. You like her voice very much. What do you say to your friend? (a good voice)
   She ________
6. You are trying on a jacket in a store. You look in the mirror, and you don't like what you see. What do you say to your friend? (not / look / very good)
   It ________
7. You and a friend are walking over a small wooden bridge. The bridge is very old and some parts are broken. What do you say? (not / very safe)
   This bridge ________

50.3 知らないことを尋ねたり，人に何かをしてもらう付加疑問文を完成しなさい。

1. You need a pen. Maybe Kelly has one. Ask her.
   Kelly, you don't have a pen, do you?
2. The cashier is putting your groceries in a plastic bag, but maybe he could give you a paper bag. Ask him.
   Excuse me, you ________
3. You're looking for Ann. Maybe Kate knows where she is. Ask her.
   Kate, you ________
4. You need a bicycle pump. Maybe Nicole has one. Ask her.
   Nicole, ________
5. You're looking for your keys. Maybe Robert has seen them. Ask him.
   Robert, ________
6. Ann has a car and you need a ride to the station. Maybe she'll take you. Ask her.
   Ann, ________

UNIT 51

動詞 + -ing (enjoy doing / stop doing など)

A

☆ 例文の状況について考えます。動詞の後にどのような形が現れていますか？

- I **enjoy** read**ing**. (× I enjoy to read)
- Would you **mind** clos**ing** the door? (× mind to close)
- Sam **suggested** go**ing** to the movies. (× suggested to go)

➤ **enjoy/mind/suggest といった動詞は，後に -ing をとりますが，to + 動詞の原形（不定詞）はとりません。**

同様に後に **-ing** しかとらない動詞には，次のようなものがあります。

stop	**postpone**	**consider**	**admit**
finish	**avoid**	**imagine**	**deny**
quit	**risk**	**miss**	**recommend**

- Suddenly everybody **stopped** talk**ing**. There was silence.
- I'll do the shopping when I've **finished** clean**ing** the apartment.
- He tried to **avoid** answer**ing** my question.
- Have you ever **considered** go**ing** to live in another country?

-ing の否定形は **not -ing** となります。

- When I'm on vacation, I **enjoy not** hav**ing** to get up early.

B

以下のような**句動詞**も後に **-ing** をとります。

give up (= stop)
put off (= postpone)
go on (= continue)
keep / **keep on** (= do something continuously or repeatedly)

- Paula has **given up** try**ing** to lose weight.
- Jenny doesn't want to retire. She wants to **go on** work**ing**.
- You **keep** interrupt**ing** when I'm talking! = You **keep on** interrupt**ing** . . .

C

以下の動詞は**動詞 + 目的詞 + -ing** の形で，「～が…しているのを一する」を表します。

- I can't **imagine George** rid**ing** a motorcycle.
- "Sorry to **keep you** wait**ing** so long." "That's all right."

この構文の**受動態**は **being + done/seen/kept**（過去分詞）**+ -ing** の形となります。

- I don't **mind being kept** wait**ing**. (⇔ I don't mind **people** keep**ing** me wait**ing**.)
  受動態 **能動態**

D

「～したことを…」のように完了した**過去**の出来事は，**動詞 + having + done/stolen/said**（過去分詞）の形で表します。

- They admitted **having stolen** the money.

過去の出来事について単純に，**動詞 + -ing** の形で表すこともあります。

- They admitted **stealing** the money.
- I now regret **saying** (= **having said**) what I said.

動詞 regret について ➲ Unit 54B

E

本ユニット中に登場する動詞の中には，**-ing** の他に **that** 節を後にとるものもあります。ことに **admit/deny/suggest** のような動詞でよく見られます。

- She **denied that** she had stolen the money. (= She **denied** steal**ing** . . .)
- Sam **suggested that** we go to the movies. (= Sam **suggested** go**ing** . . .)

I suggest you do（仮定法）➲ Unit 32　being done（受動態）➲ Unit 41D　動詞 + to + 動詞の原形 ➲ Unit 52
目的語として to + 動詞の原形と -ing の両方をとる動詞 ➲ Units 53C, 54–56　regret / go on ➲ Unit 54B
go on / keep on ➲ Unit 138A

Exercises

51.1 状況に合うように，以下から動詞を選び適切な形にして文を完成しなさい。

~~answer~~ apply be forget listen pay
lose make read try use write

1. He tried to avoid *answering* my question.
2. Could you please stop ________ so much noise?
3. I enjoy ________ to music.
4. I considered ________ for the job, but in the end I decided against it.
5. Have you finished ________ the newspaper yet?
6. Let's buy a house. I don't want to go on ________ rent every month.
7. I don't mind you ________ the phone as long as you pay for all your calls.
8. My memory is getting worse. I keep ________ things.
9. I've put off ________ the letter so many times. I really have to do it today.
10. What a mean thing to do! Can you imagine anybody ________ so mean?
11. Sarah gave up ________ to find a job in this country and decided to go abroad.
12. If you invest your money in the stock market, you risk ________ it.

51.2 -ing を含む形を用いて，対話の内容をまとめる文を完成しなさい。

1. What should we do? / We could go to the movies.
She suggested *going to the movies*.
2. You were driving too fast. / You're right. Sorry!
She admitted ________.
3. Let's go swimming. / Good idea!
She suggested ________.
4. You broke my DVD player. / No, I didn't!
He denied ________.
5. Can you wait a few minutes? / Sure, no problem.
They didn't mind ________.

51.3 -ing を含む形を用いて，最初の文と同じ意味になるように 2 番目の文を完成しなさい。

1. She doesn't really want to retire.
She wants to go on *working* .
2. It's not a good idea to travel during rush hour.
It's better to avoid ________.
3. Should we leave tomorrow instead of today?
Should we postpone ________ until ________?
4. Could you turn the radio down, please ?
Would you mind ________?
5. Please don't interrupt me all the time.
Would you mind ________?

51.4 -ing を含む形を用いて，自由に文を完成しなさい。

1. She's a very interesting person. I always enjoy *talking to her* .
2. I'm afraid there aren't any chairs. I hope you don't mind ________.
3. It was a beautiful day, so I suggested ________.
4. It was very funny. I couldn't stop ________.
5. My car isn't very reliable. It keeps ________.

UNIT 52

動詞 + to + 動詞の原形 (decide to + 動詞の原形 / forget to + 動詞の原形など)

A

以下のような動詞は **to + 動詞の原形**（不定詞）を後にとります。

offer	**decide**	**hope**	**deserve**	**promise**
agree	**plan**	**manage**	**afford**	**threaten**
refuse	**arrange**	**fail**	**forget**	**learn**

- It was late, so we **decided to take** a taxi home.
- David was in a difficult situation, so I **agreed to help** him.
- How old were you when you **learned to drive**? (= learned **how** to drive)
- Karen **failed to make** a good impression at the job interview.

to + 動詞の原形の否定形は **not to + 動詞の原形**となります。

- We **decided not to go** out because of the weather.
- I **promised not to be** late.

enjoy/think/suggest などの動詞は，後に**不定詞**をとりません。

- I **enjoy** read**ing**. (× enjoy to read)
- Sam **suggested** go**ing** to the movies. (× suggested to go)
- Are you **thinking of** buy**ing** a car? (× thinking to buy)

後に -ing をとる動詞 ➲ Unit 51　動詞 + 前置詞 + -ing 構文 ➲ Unit 60

B

以下の動詞も **to + 動詞の原形**を後にとります。

seem　**appear**　**tend**　**pretend**　**claim**

- They **seem to have** plenty of money.
- I like Dan, but I think he **tends to talk** too much.
- Ann **pretended not to see** me when she passed me on the street.

上の動詞の場合，**to + 動詞の原形**が **to be doing** のように**進行不定詞**や，**to have done** のように**完了不定詞**となることがあります。

- I **pretended to be** read**ing** the newspaper. (= I pretended that I **was** read**ing**)
- You **seem to have lost** weight. (= it seems that you **have lost** weight)
- Joe **seems to be** enjoy**ing** his new job. (= it seems that he **is** enjoy**ing** it)

C

動詞 **dare** は **dare + 動詞の原形**のように，**to** なしで直接，**動詞の原形**を後にとることがあります。

- I wouldn't **dare to tell** him. = I wouldn't **dare tell** him.

dare は普通，**疑問文**や**否定文**で用い，「平気で…するのか？」や「あえて…しない」を表します。

D

以下のような動詞では，**to + 動詞 + 疑問詞**（what/whether/how など）**+ to + 動詞の原形**の形が用いられます。

ask	**decide**	**know**	**remember**	**forget**
learn	**understand**	**wonder**	**explain**	

We **asked**	**how**	**to get**	to the station.
Have you **decided**	**where**	**to go**	for your vacation?
I don't **know**	**whether**	**to apply**	for the job or not.
Do you **understand**	**what**	**to do**?	

show/tell/ask/advise/teach といった動詞では，**動詞 + 目的語 + 疑問詞**（what/whether/how など）**+ to + 動詞の原形**の形も用いられます。

- Can somebody **show me how to change** the film in this camera?
- Ask Jack. He'll **tell you what to do**.

動詞 + -ing ➲ Unit 51　動詞 + 目的語 + to + 動詞の原形 ➲ Unit 53
動詞 + to + 動詞の原形と動詞 + -ing ➲ Units 54–56

Exercises

52.1 to＋動詞の原形を含む形を用いて，対話の内容をまとめる文を完成しなさい。

1. Should we get married? — Yes. — They decided *to get married*.
2. Please help me. — OK. — She agreed ______.
3. Can I carry your bags for you? — No, thanks. I can manage. — He offered ______.
4. Let's meet at 8:00. — OK, fine. — They arranged ______.
5. What's your name? — I'm not going to tell you. — She refused ______.
6. Please don't tell anyone. — I won't. I promise. — She promised ______.

52.2 状況に合うように（　）内の動詞を「to＋動詞の原形もしくは -ing」の形にして文を完成しなさい。動詞＋-ing については適宜 Unit 51 を参照すること。

1. When I'm tired, I enjoy *watching* television. It's relaxing. (watch)
2. It was a nice day, so we decided ______ for a walk. (go)
3. There was a lot of traffic, but we managed ______ to the airport on time. (get)
4. I'm not in a hurry. I don't mind ______ . (wait)
5. They don't have much money. They can't afford ______ out very often. (eat)
6. We've got new computer software in our office. I haven't learned ______ it yet. (use)
7. I wish that dog would stop ______ . It's driving me crazy. (bark)
8. Our neighbor threatened ______ the police if we didn't stop the noise. (call)
9. We were hungry, so I suggested ______ dinner early. (have)
10. We were all afraid to speak. Nobody dared ______ anything. (say)
11. Hurry up! I don't want to risk ______ the train. (miss)
12. I'm still looking for a job, but I hope ______ something soon. (find)

52.3 （　）内の動詞を用いて，それぞれの文を書き換えなさい。

1. You've lost weight. (seem) *You seem to have lost weight.*
2. Tom is worried about something. (appear) Tom appears ______
3. You know a lot of people. (seem) You ______
4. My English is getting better. (seem) ______
5. That car has broken down. (appear) ______
6. David forgets things. (tend) ______
7. They have solved the problem. (claim) ______

52.4 以下から適切な動詞を選んで，what/how/whether＋動詞の構文を完成しなさい。

do ~~**get**~~ **go** **ride** **say** **use**

1. Do you know *how to get* to John's house?
2. Can you show me ______ this washing machine?
3. Would you know ______ if there was a fire in the building?
4. You'll never forget ______ a bicycle once you've learned.
5. I was really astonished. I didn't know ______ .
6. I was invited to the party, but I haven't decided ______ or not.

補充問題 26–28 (pp. 311–313)

UNIT 53

動詞（+ 目的語）+ to + 動詞の原形 (I want you to + 動詞の原形など)

A

以下のような動詞は **to + 動詞の原形**（不定詞）を後にとります。

want	ask	help	expect
beg	would like	would prefer	mean （= …するつもり / ～を…させるつもりである）

この動詞は**動詞 + to + 動詞の原形**と**動詞 + 目的語 + to + 動詞の原形**の 2 つの形をとります。

動詞 + to + 動詞の原形：（主語が）～することを… ⇔ **動詞 + 目的語 + to + 動詞の原形**：（目的語が）～することを…

- We **expected to be** late.
- **Would** you **like to go** now?
- He doesn't **want to know**.

- We expected **Dan to be** late.
- Would you like **me to go** now?
- He doesn't want **anybody to know**.

want の後に **to + 動詞の原形**はきますが，**that 節**はきません。

- Do you **want me to come** with you? (✕ Do you want that I come)

help は，**help（+ 目的語）+ 動詞の原形**のように to を置かない形もとります。

- Can you help me **to move** this table? = Can you help me **move** this table?

B

以下のような動詞は，**動詞 + 目的語 + to + 動詞の原形**の形で用います。

tell	remind	force	encourage	teach	enable
order	warn	invite	persuade	get （（説得や準備をして）～に…してもらう）	

- Can you **remind me to call** Ann tomorrow?
- Who **taught you to drive**?
- I didn't move the piano by myself. I **got somebody to help** me.
- Jim said the switch was dangerous and **warned me not to touch** it.

動詞を**受動態**（I was warned / we were told など）にすると，全体は以下のようになります。

- **I was warned not to touch** the switch.

動詞 **suggest** は後に **that 節**をとり，**動詞 + 目的語 + to + 動詞の原形**の形はとりません。➲Units 51A, 51E

- Jane **suggested that I ask** you for advice. (✕ Jane suggested me to ask)

C

動詞の **advise** と **allow** には，**動詞 + -ing** と**動詞 + 目的語 + to + 動詞の原形**の 2 通りの形が可能です。

動詞 + -ing（目的語なし）

- I wouldn't **advise** stay**ing** in that hotel.
- They don't **allow** park**ing** in front of the building.

動詞 + 目的語 + to + 動詞の原形

- I wouldn't **advise anybody to stay** in that hotel.
- They don't **allow people to park** in front of the building.

それぞれの構文に対応して，以下のように 2 通りの**受動態**が可能です。

- Park**ing isn't allowed** in front of the building.
- You **aren't allowed to park** in front of the building.

D

make と let

動詞の **make** と **let** は，**動詞 + 目的語 + 動詞の原形**（do/open/feel など）の形をとります。いずれも「～（目的語）に…させる」のような**使役**の意味になります。

- I **made him promise** that he wouldn't tell anybody what happened. (✕ to promise)
- Hot weather **makes me feel** tired.（⇒ 自分の意思に関係なく，私を疲れさせる）
- Her parents wouldn't **let her go** out alone.（⇒ 出かけたいと思っている彼女の外出を許す）
- **Let me carry** your bag for you.

make ～ do のように **to** なしで**動詞の原形**を用いますが，**受動態**になると **(be) made to do** のように **to** が現れます。

- We **were made to wait** for two hours. (⇔ They **made us wait** . . .)

能動態　　受動態

suggest ➲ Units 32, 51　tell/ask + 目的語 + to ～ ➲ Unit 46D　動詞 + -ing ➲ Unit 51
動詞 + to + 動詞の原形 ➲ Unit 52　動詞 + to + 動詞の原形と動詞 + -ing ➲ Units 54–56　help ➲ Unit 55C

Exercises

53.1 状況に合うように以下から適切な動詞を選び，**do you want me to ...?** あるいは **would you like me to ...?** の構文中にあてはめて疑問文を完成しなさい。使用する動詞については，自分で適切なものを考えて使用してもかまいません。

~~come~~ lend repeat show shut wait

1. Do you want to go alone, or *do you want me to come with you*?
2. Do you have enough money, or do you want ________________?
3. Should I leave the window open, or would you ________________?
4. Do you know how to use the machine, or would ________________?
5. Did you hear what I said, or do ________________?
6. Can I go now, or do ________________?

53.2 それぞれの対話の内容をまとめる文を完成しなさい。

1. "Lock the door." — "OK." She told *him to lock the door*.
2. "Why don't you stay with us for a few days?" — "That would be nice." They invited her ________________.
3. "Can I use your phone?" — "No!" She wouldn't let ________________.
4. "Be careful." — "Don't worry. I will." She warned ________________.
5. "Can you give me a hand?" — "Sure." He asked ________________.

53.3 左欄の文とほぼ同じ意味になるように，右欄の文を完成しなさい。

1. My father said I could use his car. — My father allowed *me to use his car.*
2. I was surprised that it rained. — I didn't expect ________________
3. Don't stop him from doing what he wants. — Let ________________
4. He looks older when he wears glasses. — Glasses make ________________
5. I think you should know the truth. — I want ________________
6. Don't let me forget to call my sister. — Remind ________________
7. At first I didn't want to apply for the job, but Sarah convinced me. — Sarah persuaded ________________
8. My lawyer said I shouldn't say anything to the police. — My lawyer advised ________________
9. I was told that I shouldn't believe everything he says. — I was warned ________________
10. If you have a car, you are able to get around more easily. — Having a car enables ________________

53.4 状況に合うように，(　) 内の動詞を -ing，不定詞，動詞の原形のいずれかの形に変えて文を完成しなさい。

1. They don't allow people *to park* in front of the building. (park)
2. I've never been to Hong Kong, but I'd like ________________ there. (go)
3. I'm in a difficult position. What do you advise me ________________? (do)
4. The movie was very sad. It made me ________________. (cry)
5. Lauren's parents always encouraged her ________________ hard at school. (study)
6. I wouldn't advise ________________ at that restaurant. The food is terrible. (eat)
7. She said the letter was personal and wouldn't let me ________________ it. (read)
8. We are not allowed ________________ personal phone calls at work. (make)
9. "I don't think Alex likes me." "What makes you ________________ that?" (think)

補充問題 26–28 (pp. 311–313)

UNIT 54

動詞＋-ingと動詞＋to＋動詞の原形 1 (remember/regret ～ など)

A

動詞の中には後に **-ing** を置くものと **to ＋ 動詞の原形**を置くものがあります。

普通，後に -ing がくる動詞：

admit	finish	postpone
avoid	imagine	risk
consider	keep (on)	stop
deny	mind	suggest
enjoy		

➲ Unit 51

普通，後に to ＋ 動詞の原形がくる動詞：

afford	fail	offer
agree	forget	plan
arrange	hope	promise
decide	learn	refuse
deserve	manage	threaten

➲ Unit 52

B

動詞の中には後に **-ing** と **to ＋ 動詞の原形**の両方を置くものの，意味が変わるものがあります。

remember

I remember doing ...（実際に…したことをその後も覚えている / …したことを後から思い出す）

- I know I locked the door. I clearly **remember locking** it.
  （⇒ 鍵をかけたことを思い出した）
- He could **remember driving** along the road just before the accident, but he couldn't remember the accident itself.

I remembered to do ...（…すべきことを思い出したので，実際にした / 忘れずに…した）

- I **remembered to lock** the door, but I forgot to shut the windows.
  （⇒ 思い出して実際に鍵をかけた）
- Please **remember to mail** the letter.
  （⇒ 忘れずにポストに入れて）

regret

I regret doing ...（実際に…したことを，後から申し訳なく思う）

- I now **regret saying** what I said. I shouldn't have said it.
- It began to get cold and he **regretted not wearing** his coat.

I regret to say / to tell you / **to inform** you.（申し訳ありませんが…です）

- 〔正式な手紙で〕We **regret to inform** you that we cannot offer you the job.

go on

go on doing ...（これまで通り…し続ける）

- The president **went on talking** for hours.
- We need to change. We can't **go on living** like this.

go on to do ...（新しく…し始める / 次に…する）

- After discussing the economy, the president then **went on to talk** about foreign policy.

C

以下の動詞は後に **-ing** と **to ＋ 動詞の原形**の両方をとります。意味に違いはありません。

begin　start　continue　bother

- It has **started raining**. = It has **started to rain**.
- Don't **bother locking** the door. = Don't **bother to lock** ...

普通 **-ing** は2つ以上連続させません。連続させる場合には2つ目を **to ＋ 動詞の原形**にします。

- It's start**ing to rain**. (✕ It's starting raining)

動詞＋-ing ➲ Unit 51　動詞＋to＋動詞の原形 ➲ Units 52–53
その他の動詞＋to＋動詞の原形と動詞＋-ingの用法 ➲ Units 55–56

Exercises

54.1 状況に合うように，（ ）内の語を -ing もしくは「to + 動詞の原形」の形に変えて文を完成しなさい。両方の形が可能な場合もあります。

1. They denied _stealing_ the money. (steal)
2. I don't enjoy __________ very much. (drive)
3. I don't want __________ out tonight. I'm too tired. (go)
4. I can't afford __________ out tonight. I don't have enough money. (go)
5. Has it stopped __________ yet? (rain)
6. Our team was really unlucky yesterday. We deserved __________ the game. (win)
7. Why do you keep __________ me questions? Can't you leave me alone? (ask)
8. Please stop __________ me questions! (ask)
9. I refuse __________ any more questions. (answer)
10. One of the boys admitted __________ the window. (break)
11. The boy's father promised __________ for the window to be repaired. (pay)
12. If the company continues __________ money, the factory may be closed. (lose)
13. "Does Sarah know about the meeting?" "No, I forgot __________ her." (tell)
14. The baby began __________ in the middle of the night. (cry)
15. Julie has been sick, but now she's beginning __________ better. (get)
16. I enjoyed __________ you. I hope __________ you again soon. (meet, see)

54.2 Tom には小さい頃，次のような出来事がありました。

1. He was in the hospital when he was four.
2. He cried on his first day of school.
3. He said he wanted to be a doctor
4. He went to Miami when he was eight.
5. Once he fell into a river.
6. Once he was bitten by a dog.

この中で，Tom には 1, 2, 4 についての記憶はあるものの，3, 5, 6 については覚えていません。この状況を He can remember ... もしくは He can't remember ... で始まる文で記述しなさい。

1. _He can remember being in the hospital when he was four._
2. __________
3. __________
4. __________
5. __________
6. __________

54.3 状況に合うような動詞を自分なりに考えて，-ing もしくは「to + 動詞の原形」の形に変えて文を完成しなさい。

1. a) Please remember _to lock_ the door when you go out.
   b) *A:* You lent me some money a few months ago.
      B: I did? Are you sure? I don't remember __________ you any money.
   c) *A:* Did you remember __________ your sister?
      B: Oh no, I completely forgot. I'll call her tomorrow.
   d) When you see Amanda, remember __________ hello for me, OK?
   e) Someone must have taken my bag. I clearly remember __________ it by the window, and now it's gone.
2. a) I believe that what I said was fair. I don't regret __________ it.
   b) I knew they were in trouble, but I regret __________ I did nothing to help them.
3. a) Ben joined the company nine years ago. He became assistant manager after two years, and a few years later he went on __________ manager of the company.
   b) I can't go on __________ here any more. I want a different job.
   c) When I came into the room, Liz was reading a newspaper. She looked up and said hello and then went on __________ her newspaper.

補充問題 26–28 (pp. 311–313)

UNIT 55

動詞＋-ingと動詞＋to＋動詞の原形 2 (try/need/help)

A try to do と try -ing

try to＋動詞の原形は「(がんばって) …しようとする」を意味します。

- I was very tired. I **tried to keep** my eyes open, but I couldn't. (⇒ 実際にはできなかった)
- Please **try to be** quiet when you come home. Everyone will be asleep.

try … には，以下のように「(確認のため試しに) …してみる」の意味もあります。

- These cookies are delicious. You should **try** one. (⇒ 試しに1つ食べてみたら)
- We couldn't find anywhere to stay. We **tried** every hotel in the town, but they were all full. (⇒ 実際に行った)

try が「(試しに) …してみる」の意味を持つ時，後には **-ing** がきます。

- *A:* The photocopier doesn't seem to be working.
  B: **Try pressing** the green button. (⇒ 緑のボタンを押してみてください)

☆「テーブルを動かす」という動作について，どのように異なりますか？

- I **tried to move** the table, but it was too heavy. (⇒ 実際にはできなかった)
- I didn't like the way the furniture was arranged, so I **tried moving** the table to the other side of the room. But it still didn't look right, so I moved it back again.

B need to do / need to be done / need doing

I need to do … は「**私が**…する必要がある」のように，動作を行う**人**を強調します。

I need to do … = it is necessary for me to do …

- I **need to get** more exercise.
- He **needs to work** harder if he wants to make progress.
- I don't **need to come** to the meeting, do I?

~ needs to be done は「**~は**…されなくてはならない」のように，動作を受ける**物**を強調します。

- My cell phone **needs to be charged**.
- Do you think my pants **need to be washed**?

need to be done の代わりに **need doing** を用いることもあります。

- My cell phone **needs charging**.
- Do you think my pants **need washing**?

C help と can't help

help to＋動詞の原形もしくは **help＋動詞の原形**は「…するのを助ける / 協力して…する」を意味します。

- Everybody **helped to clean up** after the party.
- = Everybody **helped clean up** . . .
- Can you **help** me **to move** this table?
- = Can you **help** me move . . .

I can't help doing … は「…しないではいられない / …せざるをえない」を意味します。

- I don't like him, but he has a lot of problems. I **can't help feeling** sorry for him.
- She tried to be serious, but she **couldn't help laughing**.
  (⇒ 笑わずにはいられなかった)
- I'm sorry I'm so nervous. I **can't help it**.
  (⇒ どうしてもあがってしまう)

動詞＋-ing ➲ Unit 51　動詞＋to＋動詞の原形 ➲ Units 52–53
その他の動詞＋to＋動詞の原形と動詞＋-ingの用法 ➲ Units 54, 56

Exercises

55.1 状況に合うように以下から **try** の後に続くものを選び，適切な形に変えて文を完成しなさい。

call his office ~~**change the batteries**~~ **turn it the other way** **take an aspirin**

1. The radio isn't working. I wonder what's wrong with it. — Have you *tried changing the batteries?*
2. I can't open the door. The key won't turn. — Try ______
3. I have a terrible headache. I wish I could get rid of it. — Have you ______
4. I can't reach Fred. He's not at home. What should I do? — Why don't you ______

55.2 それぞれのイラストが表す状況に合うように以下から **need(s)** の後に続くものを選び，適切な形に変えて表しなさい。

~~**clean**~~ **cut** **empty** **paint** **tighten**

1. These pants are dirty. *They need to be cleaned.* OR *They need cleaning.*
2. The room doesn't look very nice. ______
3. The grass is very long. It ______
4. The screws are loose. ______
5. The garbage can is full. ______

55.3 状況に合うように，（ ）内の動詞を正しい形に変えて文を完成しなさい。

1. a) I was very tired. I tried *to keep* (keep) my eyes open, but I couldn't.
   b) I rang the doorbell, but there was no answer. Then I tried ______ (knock) on the door, but there was still no answer.
   c) We tried ______ (put) out the fire, but we were unsuccessful. We had to call the fire department.
   d) Sue needed to borrow some money. She tried ______ (ask) Jerry, but he was short of money, too.
   e) I tried ______ (reach) the shelf, but I wasn't tall enough.
   f) Please don't bother me. I'm trying ______ (concentrate).
2. a) I need a change. I need ______ (go) away for a while.
   b) My grandmother isn't able to look after herself any more. She needs ______ (look) after.
   c) The windows are dirty. They need ______ (wash).
   d) Your hair is getting very long. It needs ______ (cut).
   e) You don't need ______ (iron) that shirt. It doesn't need ______ (iron).
3. a) They were talking very loudly. I couldn't help ______ (overhear) them.
   b) Can you help me ______ (get) dinner ready?
   c) He looks so funny. Whenever I see him, I can't help ______ (smile).
   d) The beautiful weather helped ______ (make) it a wonderful vacation.

UNIT 56

動詞 + -ing と動詞 + to + 動詞の原形 3 (like / would like など)

A

like / love / hate

like/love/hate + -ing / to + 動詞の原形は「…（繰り返される習慣的な動作，一般的な動作）が好き / 大好き / 嫌い」を表します。**-ing** と **to + 動詞の原形**の間に意味的な違いはありません。

- Do you **like** gett**ing** up early? = Do you **like to get** up early?
- Stephanie **hates** fly**ing**. = Stephanie **hates to fly**.
- I **love** meet**ing** people. = I **love to meet** people.
- I don't **like** be**ing** kept waiting. = . . . **like to be** kept waiting.
- I don't **like** friends call**ing** me at work. = . . . friends **to call** me at work.

しかし，以下のような例外があります。

1) 話している時点ですでに存在していたり，過去に存在していた具体的な状況を記述する場合には動詞の後に **-ing** は置けますが，**to + 動詞の原形**は置けません。

- Paul lives in Vancouver now. He **likes** liv**ing** there.（⇒ 今バンクーバーに住んでいて，そのことが好き）
- Do you **like** be**ing** a student?（⇒ 今あなたは学生で，そのことが好きですか？）
- The office I worked at was horrible. I **hated** work**ing** there.（⇒ 前にそこで働いていて，そのことが嫌い）

2) **I like to + 動詞の原形**と **I like -ing** の間に違いが認められる場合があります。

I like -ing … は「…を実際によく行い，楽しんでいる」を表します。

- I **like** clean**ing** the kitchen.（⇒ 台所掃除が好き）

I like to + 動詞の原形は「楽しくない時もあるが…するという考えは好き⇒良いことだ」を表します。

- It's not my favorite job, but I **like to clean** the kitchen as often as possible.（⇒ 台所掃除は良いことだ）

enjoy（…を楽しむ）と **mind**（…を嫌だと思う）の後には **-ing** のみがきます（to + 動詞の原形はきません）。

- I **enjoy** clean**ing** the kitchen. (× I enjoy to clean)
- I **don't mind** clean**ing** the kitchen. (× I don't mind to clean)

B

would like / would love / would hate / would prefer

would like / would love / would hate / would prefer は，限定された状況において「…したい / とても…したい / …したくない / …するほうがよい」を表します。後には普通 **to + 動詞の原形**がきます。

- **I'd like** (= **would like**) to go away for a few days.
- **Would** you **like to come** to dinner on Friday?
- I **wouldn't like to go** on vacation alone.
- **I'd love to meet** your family.
- **Would** you **prefer to have** dinner now or later?

☆ I like と I would like (=I'd like) とは，どのように異なりますか？

- I **like playing** tennis. / I **like to play** tennis.（⇒ 一般的にテニスが好き）
- **I'd like to play** tennis today.（⇒ 今日，テニスをしたい）

Would you mind -ing? は「…してもかまいませんか？」を表し，**mind** の後には常に **-ing** がきます（to + 動詞の原形はきません）。

- **Would** you **mind closing** the door, please?

C

I would like to have done … は「…したかった」のように，何かをしなかったり，できなかったことを後悔していることを意味します。

- It's too bad we didn't see Johnny when we were in Nashville. I **would like to have seen** him again.
- We**'d like to have gone** on vacation, but we didn't have enough money.

would love / would hate / would prefer の後にも，同じように **to have done …** の表現がきて「とても…したかった / …したくなかった（だろう）/ …したほうがよかった（だろう）」を表します。

- Poor Tom! I **would hate to have been** in his position.
- **I'd love to have gone** to the party, but it was impossible.

enjoy/mind ➲ Unit 51 would like ➲ Units 35E, 53A prefer ➲ Unit 57

Exercises

56.1 自分のことについて答えなさい。( ) 内の動作が好きか嫌いかを表す文を，以下の動詞の中から 1 つを選んで記述します。

like / don't like   love   hate   enjoy   don't mind

1. (fly) *I don't like flying.* OR *I don't like to fly.*
2. (play cards) ______
3. (be alone) ______
4. (go to museums) ______
5. (cook) ______

56.2 ( ) 内の語句を用いて文を完成しなさい。その際，状況に合うように動詞の 1 つを -ing もしくは to + 動詞の原形に変えます。-ing と to + 動詞の原形の両方が可能な場合もあります。

1. Paul lives in Vancouver now. It's nice. He likes it.
   (he / like / live / there) *He likes living there.*
2. Jane is a biology teacher. She likes her job.
   (she / like / teach / biology) She ______
3. Joe always carries his camera with him and takes a lot of photographs.
   (he / like / take / photographs) ______
4. I used to work in a supermarket. I didn't like it much.
   (I / not / like / work / there) ______
5. Rachel is studying medicine. She likes it.
   (she / like / study / medicine) ______
6. Dan is famous, but he doesn't like it.
   (he / not / like / be / famous) ______
7. Jennifer is a very cautious person. She doesn't take many risks.
   (she / not / like / take / risks) ______
8. I don't like surprises.
   (I / like / know / things / ahead of time) ______

56.3 状況に合うように空所に入る適切な動詞を自分で考え，-ing もしくは to + 動詞の原形に変えて文を完成しなさい。-ing と to + 動詞の原形の両方が可能な文が 1 つだけあります。

1. It's good to visit other places – I enjoy *traveling* .
2. "Would you like ______ down?" "No, thanks, I'll stand."
3. I'm not quite ready yet. Would you mind ______ a little longer?
4. When I was a child, I hated ______ to bed early.
5. When I have to catch a plane, I'm always worried that I'll miss it. So I like ______ to the airport ahead of time.
6. I enjoy ______ busy. I don't like it when there's nothing to do.
7. I would love ______ to your wedding, but unfortunately I can't.
8. I don't like ______ in this part of town. I want to move somewhere else.
9. Do you have a minute? I'd like ______ to you about something.
10. When there's bad news and good news, I like ______ the bad news first.

56.4 状況に合うように ( ) 内の動詞を **would ... to have (done)** の形にあてはめて，文を完成しなさい。

1. It's too bad I couldn't go to the wedding. (like) *I would like to have gone to the wedding.*
2. It's a shame I didn't see the program. (like) ______
3. I'm glad I didn't lose my watch. (hate) ______
4. It's too bad I didn't meet your parents. (love) ______
5. I'm glad I wasn't alone. (not / like) ______
6. It's a shame I couldn't travel by train. (prefer) ______

UNIT 57

prefer と would rather

A prefer to + 動詞の原形と prefer -ing

prefer の後には **to + 動詞の原形**も **-ing** も置くことができます。いずれも「…するほうがよい」のように，一般的により好きなものを述べる際に用います。

- I don't like cities. I **prefer to live** in the country. = I **prefer living** in the country.

☆「B よりも A がよい / B するよりも A するほうがよい」には，以下の構文を用います。A と B の形の違いに注意します。

	A	B
I prefer	**~**	**to …**
I prefer	**doing ~**	**to doing …**
⇔ I prefer	**to do ~**	**rather than (do) …**

- I **prefer** this coat **to** the coat you were wearing yesterday.
- I **prefer driving to traveling** by train.

⇔

- I **prefer to drive rather than travel** by train.
- Ann **prefers to live** in the country **rather than** in a city. = . . . **rather than live** in a city.

B would prefer (I'd prefer . . .)

would prefer … は，一般的ではなく具体的な状況で「…のほうがよい / …したい」を表します。

- "**Would** you **prefer** tea or coffee?" "Coffee, please."

「…するほうがよい」は **would prefer to do** のように **to + 動詞の原形**を用い，**-ing** は用いません。

- "Should we take the train?" "No, I**'d prefer to drive**." (× I'd prefer driving)
- **I'd prefer to stay** at home tonight **rather than go** to the movies.

C would rather (I'd rather . . .)

would rather (do) も具体的な状況で「…するほうがよい / …したい」を表します。**would prefer (to do)** と意味的な違いはありません。**(do)** の部分は，**do/have/stay** などのように **to** を置かずに直接，**動詞の原形**がきます。

- "Should we take the train?" { "**I'd prefer to drive**." / "**I'd rather drive**." (× to drive) }
- "**Would** you **rather have** tea or coffee?" "Coffee, please."

否定形は **I'd rather not (do …)**（…しないほうがよい / …したくない）となります。

- I'm tired. I**'d rather not go** out tonight, if you don't mind.
- "Do you want to go out tonight?" "**I'd rather not**."

「B するよりも，A するほうがよい」の構文は，**would rather A (do ~) than B (do …)** の形で表します。

- **I'd rather stay** at home tonight **than go** to the movies.

D I'd rather ~ did . . .

I'd rather ~ did … は「~が…するほうがよい / ~に…してもらいたい」を表します。**I'd rather** の後には，**did** のような動詞の**過去形**がきます（do のような動詞の現在形はきません）。

- "I'll fix your car tomorrow, OK?" "**I'd rather** you **did** it today." (⇔ I'd prefer this)
- "Is it OK if Ben stays here?" "**I'd rather** he **came** with us." (× he comes)
- Shall I tell them, or **would** you **rather** they **didn't** know? (× don't know)

この構文では，**I'd rather** の後の動詞は**過去形** (did/came など) になりますが，「(今) …してもらいたい」のように現在の意味を持ちます。

- I'd rather **make** dinner now.

⇔ I'd rather you **made** dinner now. (× I'd rather you make)

I'd rather ~ didn't (do …) は「~が…しないほうがよい / ~に…してもらいたくない」を表します。

- **I'd rather you didn't tell** anyone what I said.
- "Should I tell Stephanie?" "**I'd rather you didn't**."

would prefer ➲ Unit 56B prefer ~ to … ➲ Unit 133D

Exercises

57.1 I prefer ~ to ... の構文を用いて，（　）内の 2 つの事柄についてどちらが好きか，自分の一般的な好みを表す文を完成しなさい。

1. (drive / fly)
   I prefer driving to flying.
2. (tennis / soccer)
   I prefer ________
3. (call people / send e-mails)
   I ________ to ________
4. (go to the movies / watch videos at home)
   ____

上の 3 と 4 で作成した文を I prefer to ~ rather than ... の構文で書き換えなさい。

5. (1) I prefer to drive rather than travel by train.
6. (3) I prefer to ________
7. (4) ________

57.2 以下から適切な語句を選び，I'd prefer ... もしくは I'd rather ... の後に続けて対話を完成しなさい。

eat at home	~~take a taxi~~	**go alone**
wait a few minutes	**listen to some music**	**stand**
go for a swim	~~wait till later~~	**think about it for a while**

1. Should we walk home? (prefer) I'd prefer to take a taxi.
2. Do you want to eat now? (rather) I'd rather wait till later.
3. Would you like to watch TV? (rather) ________
4. Do you want to go to a restaurant? (prefer) ________
5. Let's leave now. (rather) ________
6. What about a game of tennis? (rather) ________
7. I think we should decide now. (prefer) ________
8. Would you like to sit down? (rather) ________
9. Do you want me to come with you? (prefer) ________

上の解答のいくつかと意味が同じになるように，than もしくは rather than を用いて文を完成しなさい。

10. I'd prefer to take a taxi rather than walk home.
11. I'd prefer to go for a swim ________
12. I'd rather eat at home ________
13. I'd prefer to think about it for a while ________
14. I'd rather listen to some music ________

57.3 状況に合うように，would you rather I ... を用いて文を完成しなさい。

1. Are you going to make dinner or would you rather I made it?
2. Are you going to tell Ann what happened or would you rather ________?
3. Are you going to go shopping or ________?
4. Are you going to call Diane or ________?

57.4 状況に合うように，空所に適切な語句を入れて文を完成しなさい。

1. "Should I tell Ann the news?" "No, I'd rather she didn't know."
2. Do you want me to go now, or would you rather I ________ here?
3. Do you want to go out tonight or would you rather ________ at home?
4. This is a private letter addressed to me. I'd rather you ________ read it.
5. I don't really like these shoes. I'd rather they ________ a different color.
6. *A:* Do you mind if I turn on the radio?
   B: I'd rather you ________. I'm trying to study.

UNIT 58

前置詞 (in/for/about など) + -ing

A

前置詞（in/for/about など）の後に動詞を置く場合，その動詞は **-ing** 形になります。

	前置詞	動詞 (-ing)	
Are you interested	**in**	work**ing**	for us?
I'm not very good	**at**	learn**ing**	languages.
Sue must be fed up	**with**	study**ing**.	
What are the advantages	**of**	hav**ing**	a car?
Thanks very much	**for**	invit**ing**	me to your party.
How	**about**	meet**ing**	for lunch tomorrow?
Why don't you go out	**instead of**	sitt**ing**	at home all the time?
Carol went to work	**in spite of**	feel**ing**	sick.

instead of ~ doing ...（～が…する代わりに）や **fed up with ~ doing ...**（～が…することにはうんざりする）などのように，**-ing** の前に**人**を表す名詞句（～）を置く形もよく用いられます。

- I'm fed up with **people** telling me what to do.

B

次のような**前置詞 + -ing** もよく用いられます。

before -ing と after -ing:「～する前に / ～する後に」

- **Before going** out, I called Sarah. (× Before to go out)
- What did you do **after finishing** school?

-ing の代わりに，**Before I went out ...** や **... after you finished school** の形も用いられます。

by -ing:「～することによって」

- The burglars got into the house **by** break**ing** a window and climb**ing** in.
- You can improve your English **by** read**ing** more.
- She made herself sick **by** not eat**ing** properly.
- Many accidents are caused **by** people driv**ing** too fast.

without -ing:「～することなしに」

- We ran 10 miles **without** stopp**ing**.
- It was a stupid thing to say. I said it **without** think**ing**.
- She needs to work **without** people disturb**ing** her. (= . . . **without** be**ing** disturbed.)
- I have enough problems of my own **without** hav**ing** to worry about yours.

C

to + - ing（look forward to doing ... など）

to do / **to see** などのように，**to** は**不定詞**（to + 動詞の原形）を構成する要素です。

- We decided **to go** out.
- Would you like **to meet** for lunch tomorrow?

一方，**in**/**for**/**about**/**from** などと同様に **to** は**前置詞**にもなります。

- We drove from Houston **to Chicago**.
- I prefer tea **to coffee**.
- Are you looking forward **to the weekend**?

前置詞の後に**動詞**を置く場合，その動詞は **-ing** 形になります。

in do**ing**   **about** meet**ing**   **without** stopp**ing**

したがって，**to** が**前置詞**で後に**動詞**を置く場合は **-ing** 形にしなければなりません。

- I prefer driving **to** travel**ing** by train. (× to travel)
- Are you looking forward **to** go**ing** on vacation? (× looking forward to go)

be/get used to -ing ➲ Unit 59   動詞 + 前置詞 + -ing ➲ Unit 60   while/when -ing ➲ Unit 66B
in spite of ➲ Unit 110   前置詞 ➲ Units 118–133

Exercises

58.1 最初の文と同じ意味になるように，2 番目の文を完成しなさい。

1. Why is it useful to have a car?
   What are the advantages of *having a car* ?
2. I don't intend to apply for the job.
   I have no intention of ______ .
3. Karen has a good memory for names.
   Karen is good at ______ .
4. Mark won't pass the exam. He has no chance.
   Mark has no chance of ______ .
5. Did you get into trouble because you were late?
   Did you get into trouble for ______ ?
6. We didn't eat at home. We went to a restaurant instead.
   Instead of ______ .
7. We got into the exhibition. We didn't have to wait in line.
   We got into the exhibition without ______ .
8. Our team played well, but we lost the game.
   Our team lost the game in spite of ______ .

58.2 状況に合うように，by の後に以下から語句を選び適切な形に変えて続け，文を完成しなさい。

borrow too much money ~~**break a window**~~ **drive too fast**
put some pictures on the walls **stand on a chair** **turn a key**

1. The burglars got into the house *by breaking a window* .
2. I was able to reach the top shelf ______ .
3. You start the engine of a car ______ .
4. Kevin got himself into financial trouble ______ .
5. You can put people's lives in danger ______ .
6. We made the room look nicer ______ .

58.3 状況に合うように，空所に適切な 1 語を入れて文を完成しなさい。

1. We ran 10 miles without *stopping* .
2. He left the hotel without ______ his bill.
3. It's a nice morning. How about ______ for a walk?
4. We were able to translate the letter into English without ______ a dictionary.
5. Before ______ to bed, I like to have a hot drink.
6. It was a long trip. I was very tired after ______ on a train for 36 hours.
7. I was annoyed because the decision was made without anybody ______ me.
8. After ______ the same job for 10 years, I felt I needed a change.
9. We got lost because we went straight instead of ______ left.
10. I like these pictures you took. You're good at ______ pictures.

58.4 状況に合うように，質問の答えとなる文を I'm (not) looking forward to で始めて完成しなさい。

1. You are going on vacation next week. How do you feel?
   I'm looking forward to going on vacation.
2. Diane is a good friend of yours and she is coming to visit you soon. So you will see her again soon. How do you feel? I'm ______
3. You are going to the dentist tomorrow. You don't enjoy going to the dentist. How do you feel?
   I'm not ______
4. Carol hates school, but she is graduating next summer. How does she feel?
   ______
5. You've arranged to play tennis tomorrow. You like tennis a lot. How do you feel?
   ______

UNIT 59

be/get used to do ... (I'm used to ...)

A

☆ イラストの状況について考えなさい。get/used to ... は，どのような状況で用いられていますか？

Lisa

➤ **be used to ...** は「…に慣れている」という状態，**get used to ...** は「…に慣れる」という変化を表します。

1) Lisa は東京で暮らしているアメリカ人です。日本はアメリカと異なり左側通行なので，最初はとても困りました。

She **wasn't used to it.**
She **wasn't used to driving** on the left.
(⇒ 彼女は左側通行に慣れていなかった)

2) その後練習を積み，左側通行にも困らなくなりました。

She **got used to driving** on the left.
(⇒ 彼女は左側通行に慣れた)

3) 今は何も問題なくなりました。

She **is used to driving** on the left.
(⇒ 彼女は左側通行に慣れている)

B

I'm used to ... は **used to** の後に**名詞句**や**動名詞** (-ing) **句**を置き，「…に慣れている」を表します。

- Frank lives alone. He doesn't mind this because he has lived alone for 15 years. It is not strange for him. He **is used to it**. He **is used to living** alone.
- I bought some new shoes. They felt strange at first because I **wasn't used to them**.
- Our new apartment is on a very busy street. I expect we'll **get used to the noise**, but for now it's very annoying.
- Diane has a new job. She has to get up much earlier now than before – at 6:30. She finds this difficult, because she **isn't used to getting up** so early.
- Barbara's husband is often away. She doesn't mind. She **is used to him** being away.

C

be/get used の後には，**不定詞**（to + 動詞の原形 : to do / to drive）はきません（**-ing** がきます）。

- She is used **to driving** on the left. (× She is used to drive)

I am use to ... の構文中の **to** は**前置詞**で，**不定詞**の一部ではありません。したがって，**to** の後に動詞を置く場合には**動名詞** (-ing) になります（動詞の原形を置くことはできません）。

- Frank is used **to living** alone. (× Frank is used to live)
- Lisa had to get used **to driving** on the left. (× get used to drive)

D

I am used to doing.（…することに慣れている）と **I used to do.**（以前は…よくした）とを混同しないようにします。

I am used **to** (**doing**) ...:「初めてではないので…しても困らない」

- I **am** used **to the weather** in this country.
- I **am** used **to driving** on the left because I've lived in Japan a long time.

I used **to do** ...:「以前はよく…していたが，今はしていない」
この構文は**過去**の出来事についてのみ用います（現在の出来事は表しません）。このため，**I used to do.**（過去形）に対応する現在形として × I am used to do. のような形はありません。

- I **used to drive** to work every day, but these days I usually ride my bike.
- We **used to live** in a small town, but now we live in Los Angeles.

used to (do) ➲ Unit 17　　to + -ing ➲ Unit 58C

Exercises

59.1 まず，セクションの A でもう一度 Lisa に関する状況を確認しなさい。以下には Lisa と似たような状況が示されています。状況に合うように，**used to** を用いて文を完成しなさい。

1. Juan is Spanish and went to live in Canada. In Spain he usually had dinner late in the evening, but in Canada dinner was at 6:00. This was very early for him, and he found it very strange at first.
   When Juan first went to Canada, he *wasn't used to having* dinner so early, but after a while he ______ it. Now he finds it normal.
   He ______ at 6:00.
2. Julia is a nurse. A year ago she started working nights. At first she found it hard and didn't like it.
   She ______ nights, and it took her a few months to ______ it. Now, after a year, she's pretty happy. She ______ nights.

59.2 状況に合うように，**I'm (not) used to ...** を用いて文を完成しなさい。

1. You live alone. You don't mind this. You have always lived alone.
   Friend: Do you get a little lonely sometimes?
   You: No, *I'm used to living alone.*
2. You sleep on the floor. You don't mind this. You have always slept on the floor.
   Friend: Wouldn't you prefer to sleep in a bed?
   You: No, I ______
3. You have to work long hours in your job. This is not a problem for you. You have always worked long hours.
   Friend: You have to work very long hours in your job, don't you?
   You: Yes, but I don't mind that. I ______
4. You usually go to bed early. Last night you went to bed very late (for you) and as a result, you are very tired this morning.
   Friend: You look tired this morning.
   You: Yes, ______

59.3 状況に合うように，**get/got used to** を用いて文を完成しなさい。

1. Some friends of yours have just moved into an apartment on a busy street. It's very noisy.
   They'll have to *get used to the noise.*
2. Sue moved from a big house to a much smaller one. She found it strange at first.
   She had to ______ in a much smaller house.
3. The children at school got a new teacher. She was different from the teacher before her, but this wasn't a problem for the children. They soon ______
4. Some people you know from the United States are going to live in your country. What will they have to get used to?
   They'll have to ______

59.4 セクションの C と D を参考にして，状況に合うように空所に適切な 1 語を入れて文を完成しなさい。

1. Lisa had to get used to *driving* on the left.
2. We used to *live* in a small town, but now we live in Los Angeles.
3. Tom used to ______ a lot of coffee. Now he prefers tea.
4. I feel very full after that meal. I'm not used to ______ so much.
5. I wouldn't like to share an office. I'm used to ______ my own office.
6. I used to ______ a car, but I sold it a few months ago.
7. When we were children, we used to ______ swimming every day.
8. There used to ______ a movie theater here, but it was torn down a few years ago.
9. I'm the boss here! I'm not used to ______ told what to do.

補充問題 26–28 (pp. 311–313)

UNIT 60

動詞＋前置詞＋-ing (succeed in -ing / accuse ～ of -ing など)

A

さまざまな動詞が，**動詞＋前置詞**（in/for/about など）＋**目的語***の構文を作ります。

動詞＋	前置詞	＋目的語
We **talked**	**about**	the problem.
You should **apologize**	**for**	what you said.

目的語の位置に動詞がくると **-ing** になります。

動詞＋	前置詞	＋-ing（目的語）
We **talked**	**about**	go**ing** to South America.
You should **apologize**	**for**	not tell**ing** the truth.

同様の構文を作る動詞には，次のようなものもあります。

succeed (in)	Have you **succeeded**	**in**	find**ing** a job yet?
insist (on)	They **insisted**	**on**	pay**ing** for dinner.
think (of)	I'm **thinking**	**of**	buy**ing** a house.
dream (of)	I wouldn't **dream**	**of**	ask**ing** them for money.
approve (of)	He doesn't **approve**	**of**	swear**ing**.
decide (against)	We have **decided**	**against**	mov**ing** to Chicago.
feel (like)	Do you **feel**	**like**	go**ing** out tonight?
look forward (to)	I'm **looking forward**	**to**	meet**ing** her.

この構文は **approve of ～ doing …** や **look forward to ～ doing …** のように，**-ing** の前に**人**を表す名詞句を置いた形も可能で「～が…するのを ―」を表します。⊃ Unit 51C

- I don't approve **of people** kill**ing** animals for fun.
- We are all looking forward **to Bob** com**ing** home.

B

以下の動詞は**動詞＋目的語＋前置詞＋-ing** の構文を作ります。

	動詞＋	目的語	＋前置詞	＋-ing（目的語）
congratulate (on)	I **congratulated**	Ann	**on**	gett**ing** a new job.
accuse (of)	They **accused**	us	**of**	tell**ing** lies.
suspect (of)	Nobody **suspected**	the general	**of**	be**ing** a spy.
prevent (from)	What **prevented**	you	**from**	com**ing** to see us?
keep (from)	The noise **keeps**	me	**from**	fall**ing** asleep.
stop (from)	The rain didn't **stop**	us	**from**	enjoy**ing** our vacation.
thank (for)	I forgot to **thank**	them	**for**	help**ing** me.
excuse (for)	**Please excuse**	me	**for**	not return**ing** your call.

以下のように**受動態**を作る動詞もあります。

- We **were accused of** tell**ing** lies.
- The general **was suspected of** be**ing** a spy.

apologize は **apologize to ～ for …** のような構文を作ります。**apologize** の後の **to** は省略できません。

- I apologized **to them** for keeping them waiting. (✕ I apologized them)

* **目的語 (object)**：本書では動詞の後のみならず，前置詞の後の名詞句や動名詞句などについても目的語として言及しています。

 decide to … ⊃ Unit 52A　前置詞＋-ing ⊃ Unit 58　動詞＋前置詞 ⊃ Units 129–133

Exercises

60.1 状況に合うように，空所に適切な 1 語を入れて文を完成しなさい。

1. Our neighbors apologized for ___making___ so much noise.
2. I feel lazy. I don't feel like ____________ any work.
3. I wanted to go out alone, but Joe insisted on ____________ with me.
4. I'm fed up with my job. I'm thinking of ____________ something else.
5. We have decided against ____________ a new car because we can't really afford it.
6. I hope you get in touch with me soon. I'm looking forward to ____________ from you.
7. The weather was extremely bad and this kept us from ____________ out.
8. The man who was arrested is suspected of ____________ a false passport.
9. I think you should apologize to Sue for ____________ so rude to her.
10. Some parents don't approve of their children ____________ a lot of television.
11. I'm sorry I can't come to your party, but thank you very much for ____________ me.

60.2 状況に合うように適切な前置詞を自分なりに考え，その前置詞に続く動詞を以下から選び，正しい形に変えて文を完成しなさい。

carry	**cause**	**escape**	**~~go~~**	**interrupt**
live	**see**	**solve**	**spend**	**walk**

1. Do you feel ___like going___ out tonight?
2. It took us a long time, but we finally succeeded ________________ the problem.
3. I've always dreamed ________________ in a small house by the sea.
4. The driver of the other car accused me ________________ the accident.
5. There's a fence around the lawn to stop people ________________ on the grass.
6. Excuse me ________________ you, but may I ask you something?
7. Where are you thinking ________________ your vacation this year?
8. The guards weren't able to prevent the prisoner ________________ .
9. My bag wasn't very heavy, but Dave insisted ________________ it for me.
10. It's too bad Paul can't come to the party. I was really looking forward ________________ him.

60.3 イラストの人物の発言を記述する文を完成しなさい。

1. You / Kevin: "It was nice of you to help me. Thanks a lot." — Kevin thanked ___me for helping him___ .
2. Ann / Tom: "I'll take you to the station. I insist." — Tom insisted ________________ .
3. You / Dan: "I hear you got married. Congratulations!" — Dan congratulated me ________________ .
4. Sue / Jenny: "It was nice of you to come to see me. Thank you." — Jenny thanked ________________ .
5. You / Kate: "I'm sorry I didn't call earlier." — Kate apologized ________________ .
6. You / Jane: "You're selfish." — Jane accused ________________ .

補充問題 27–28 (pp. 312–313)

UNIT 61

後に -ing を伴うさまざまな表現

A

「…する意義がある / ない」を表す以下の表現で後に動詞がくる場合，**-ing** になります。

There's no point in doing **. . . :**「…する意義がない / …するのは無駄だ」

- **There's no point in** hav**ing** a car if you never use it.
- **There was no point in** wait**ing** any longer, so we left.

しかし実際には,「…を～する意義, 狙い」の意味で **the** point **of** do**ing** ... の形の方がよく用いられます。

- **What's the point of** hav**ing** a car if you never use it?

There's no use / It's no use doing **. . . :**「…する意義がない / …するのは無駄だ」

- There's nothing you can do about the situation, so **there's no use** worry**ing** about it.
- = . . . **it's no use** worry**ing** about it.

It's worth / It's not worth doing **. . . :**「…する意義や価値がある / ない」

- I live only a short walk from here, so **it's not worth** tak**ing** a taxi.
- Our flight was very early in the morning, so **it wasn't worth** go**ing** to bed.

It's worth / **It's not worth** doing **...** の構文で，**-ing** の後にくる目的語を主語にして，a movie is **worth seeing** や a book is **worth reading** などのような形もよく用います。

- What was the movie like? Was it **worth seeing**?
- Thieves broke into the house but didn't take anything. There was nothing **worth stealing**.

B

have trouble -ing, have difficulty -ing / have a problem -ing:「…するのが難しい / …するのに苦労する」

have trouble do**ing ...** のように，**trouble** の後に **-ing** を置いた形がよく用いられます。

- I **had** no **trouble** find**ing** a place to live. (✕ trouble to find)
- Did you **have** any **trouble** gett**ing** a visa?
- People often **have** a lot of **trouble** read**ing** my writing.

同様のことを，have **difficulty** / **a problem** do**ing** ... のような形で表すことがあります。

- I had **difficulty** find**ing** a place to live.
- = I had **a problem** find**ing** a place to live.

C

後に **-ing** を伴う，次のような形もよく用いられます。

spend/waste ～（時間）do**ing ...:**「…して無駄に（～時間を）過ごす」

- He **spent** hours try**ing** to repair the clock.
- I **waste** a lot of time daydream**ing**.

(be) **busy** do**ing ...:**「…するのに / …して忙しい」

- She said she couldn't go with us. She was too **busy** do**ing** other things.

D

go swimming（泳ぎに行く）**/ go fishing**（釣りに行く）など

スポーツを中心に，さまざまな活動について **go -ing**（…しに行く）の形を使います。

go swimm**ing** **go** sail**ing** **go** fish**ing** **go** hik**ing** **go** ski**ing** **go** jogg**ing**

スポーツ以外では **go** shopp**ing**（買い物に行く）や **go** sightsee**ing**（観光に行く）のような形があります。

- How often do you **go** swimm**ing**?
- I'd like to **go** ski**ing**.
- When was the last time you **went** shopp**ing**?
- I've never **gone** sail**ing**.

Exercises

61.1 状況に合うように，There's no point ... で始まる文を完成しなさい。

1. Why have a car if you never use it?
   There's no point in having a car if you never use it.
2. Why work if you don't need money?
   ____
3. Don't try to study if you feel tired.
   ____
4. Why hurry if you've got plenty of time?
   ____

61.2 状況に合うように，空所に適切な語句を入れて対話を完成しなさい。

1.	Should we take a taxi home?	No, it isn't far. It's not worth *taking a taxi* .
2.	If you need help, why don't you ask Dave?	There's no use ________ . He won't be able to do anything.
3.	I don't really want to go out tonight.	Well, stay at home! There's no point ________ ________ if you don't want to.
4.	Should I call Ann now?	No, don't waste your time ________ now. She won't be home.
5.	Are you going to complain about what happened?	No, it's not worth ________ . Nobody will do anything about it.
6.	Do you ever read newspapers?	No, I'm usually too busy ____ care of the kids.
7.	Do you want to keep these old clothes?	No, let's throw them away. They're not worth ________ .

61.3 空所に適切な語句を入れて，状況を説明する文を完成しなさい。

1. I managed to get a visa, but it was difficult.
   I had trouble *getting a visa* .
2. I find it hard to remember people's names.
   I have a problem ____________________ .
3. Sarah managed to get a job without any trouble.
   She had no difficulty ____________________ .
4. It won't be difficult to get a ticket for the game.
   You won't have any trouble ____________________ .
5. Do you think it's difficult to understand him?
   Do you have a problem ____________________ ?

61.4 状況に合うように，空所に適切な 1 語を補って文を完成しなさい。

1. I waste a lot of time *daydreaming* .
2. Every morning I spend about an hour ________ the newspaper.
3. "What's Karen doing?" "She's going away tomorrow, so she's busy ________ ."
4. I think you waste too much time ________ television.
5. There's a beautiful view from that hill. It's worth ________ to the top.
6. There's no use ________ for the job. I know I wouldn't get it.
7. Just stay calm. There's no point in ________ angry.

61.5 状況に合うように，以下から語句を選び適切な形に変えて空所に補い，文を完成しなさい。

go riding ~~**go sailing**~~ **go shopping** **go skiing** **go swimming**

1. Robbie lives by the ocean and he's got a boat, so he often *goes sailing* .
2. It was a very hot day, so we ________ at the pool.
3. There's plenty of snow in the mountains, so we'll be able to ________ .
4. Michelle has two horses. She ________ regularly.
5. "Where's Dan?" "He ________ . There were a few things he needed to buy."

補充問題 27–28 (pp. 312–313)

UNIT 62

to + 動詞の原形, for ... と so that ...（目的を表す表現）

A

to + 動詞の原形は，「…するために（～する）」のように人が**動作をする目的**や**理由**を表します。

- "Why are you going out?"　"**To mail** a letter."（⇒ 手紙を出しに行ってきます）
- A friend of mine called **to invite** me to a party.
- We shouted **to warn** everybody of the danger.

to + 動詞の原形は，「…するために（存在する）」のように何かが**存在する目的**や**理由**を表します。

- This fence is **to keep** people out of the yard.（⇒ この柵は人を庭に入らせないためのもの）
- The president has a team of bodyguards **to protect** him.

B

～(物) + to + 動詞の原形で，「…できる / …するべき ～」を表します。

- It's hard to find **a place to park** downtown.（⇒ 自動車を駐車できる場所）
- Would you like **something to eat**?
- Do you have **much work to do**?（⇒ やらなければならない多くの仕事）
- I get lonely if there's **nobody to talk to**.
- I need **something to open** this bottle **with**.

money/time/chance/opportunity/energy/courage など **+ to + 動詞の原形**で，「…するための —」を表します。

- They gave us **some money to buy** some food.（⇒ 食料を買うためのお金）
- Do you have **much opportunity to practice** your English?
- I need **a few days to think** about your proposal.

C

for . . . と to . . .

ともに「…するために」を表しますが，**for** の後には**名詞句**，**to** の後には**動詞の原形**がきます。

for + 名詞句	**to + 動詞の原形**
I'm going to Spain **for a vacation**.	I'm going to Spain **to learn** Spanish.（× for learn, × for learning）
What would you like **for dinner**?	What would you like **to eat**?
Let's go to the pool **for a swim**.	Let's go to the pool **to have** a swim.

— for ～ to do ... の形で，「～が…するための —」を表します。

- There weren't any chairs **for us to sit on**, so we had to sit on the floor.

「～が…する」のように，動作を行う人を限定せずに「…するために」と物が使われる**一般的な目的**を表す際には，**for + -ing** もしくは **to + 動詞の原形**を用います。

- Do you use this brush **for** wash**ing** the dishes? (= . . . **to wash** the dishes?)（⇒ 皿を洗うために）

What ... for? の形で「…は何のためですか？」のように**目的**を尋ねます。

- **What** is this switch **for**?
- **What** did you do that **for**?

D

so that . . .

so that ...（…は主語と動詞を持つ節）が「…するために」のような**目的**を表すことがあります。

以下のような状況において，ことに **to + 動詞の原形**ではなく **so that ...** を用いて**目的**を表します。

1)「…しないように」のように，**so that ... won't/wouldn't** の形で**否定の目的**を表す場合。

- I hurried **so that** I **wouldn't** be late.（⇒ 遅れないように）
- Leave early **so that** you **won't** (= **don't**) miss the bus.

2)「…できるように」のように，**so that ... can/could** の形で**肯定の目的**を表す場合。

- She's learning English **so that** she **can** study in Canada.（⇒ カナダで勉強できるように）
- We moved to the city **so that** we **could** see our children more often.

Exercises

62.1 A と B から表現を 1 つずつ選び，to を用いて適切な文を完成しなさい。

A	B
1. ~~I shouted~~	I want to keep warm
2. I had to go to the bank	I wanted to report that my car had been stolen
3. I'm saving money	I want to go to Canada
4. I went into the hospital	I had to have an operation
5. I'm wearing two sweaters	I needed to get some money
6. I called the police	~~I wanted to warn people of the danger~~

1. *I shouted to warn people of the danger.*
2. I had to go to the bank ______
3. I ______
4. ______
5. ______
6. ______

62.2 1 語もしくは 2 語で空所にふさわしい形の動詞を入れて，文を完成しなさい。

1. The president has a team of bodyguards *to protect* him.
2. I didn't have enough time ______ the newspaper today.
3. I took a taxi home. I didn't have the energy ______ .
4. "Would you like something ______ ?" "Yes. A cup of coffee, please."
5. We need a bag ______ these things in.
6. There will be a meeting next week ______ the problem.
7. I wish we had enough money ______ another car.
8. I saw Kelly at the party, but we didn't have a chance ______ to each other.
9. I need some new clothes. I don't have anything nice ______ .
10. They've just passed their exams. They're having a party ______ .
11. I can't do all this work alone. I need somebody ______ me.

62.3 状況に合うように，to もしくは for を用いて文を完成しなさい。

1. I'm going to Spain *for* a vacation.
2. You need a lot of experience ______ this job.
3. You need a lot of experience ______ do this job.
4. We'll need more time ______ make a decision.
5. I went to the dentist ______ a check-up.
6. I had to put on my glasses ______ read the letter.
7. Do you have to wear glasses ______ reading?
8. I wish we had a yard ______ the children ______ play in.

62.4 so that を用いて，状況を説明する文を完成しなさい。

1. I hurried. I didn't want to be late.
   I hurried so that I wouldn't be late.
2. I wore warm clothes. I didn't want to be cold.
   I wore ______
3. I left Dave my phone number. I wanted him to be able to contact me.
   I ______
4. We whispered. We didn't want anybody else to hear our conversation.
   ______ nobody ______
5. Please arrive early. We want to be able to start the meeting on time.
   Please ______
6. Jennifer locked the door. She didn't want to be disturbed.
   ______
7. I slowed down. I wanted the car behind me to be able to pass.
   ______

UNIT 63

形容詞＋to＋動詞の原形

A

hard to understand：「理解することが難しい」

☆ 例文について考えます。1) と 2) はどのように異なりますか？

■ Jim doesn't speak very clearly.
1) It is **hard to understand** him.
2) He is **hard to understand**.

➤ 1) と 2) とは同じ意味を表します。1) の目的語 him を主語の it の位置に移動して 2) ができました。したがって，2) で understand の後に him を残すことはできません。

■ He is hard **to understand**. (✕ He is hard to understand him.)

次のような形容詞も上と同様に 1) と 2) の構文が可能です。

easy	**difficult**	**impossible**	**dangerous**	**safe**	**expensive**
cheap	**nice**	**good**	**interesting**	**exciting**	

■ Do you think it is **safe** (for us) **to drink this water**?
(⇒（私たちが）この水を飲んでも安全であると…)
Do you think this water is **safe** (for us) **to drink**? (✕ to drink it)

■ The questions on the exam were very difficult. It was **impossible to answer them**.
The questions on the exam were very difficult. They were **impossible to answer**.
(✕ to answer them)

■ Jill has lots of interesting ideas. It's **interesting to talk** to her.
Jill **is interesting to talk to**. (✕ to talk to her.)

形容詞＋名詞のように，形容詞の後に名詞を置く形もあります。

■ This is a **difficult question** (for me) **to answer**. (⇒（私には）答えにくい質問 / ✕ to answer it)

B

(It's) nice of (you) to . . .：「（～が）…することはよい / 親切にも…してくれた」

nice は **It's nice of ～ to do ...** のような構文を作ります。

■ It was **nice of you to take** me to the airport. Thank you very much.
(⇒ 親切にも…まで迎えに来てくれた)

次のような形容詞も**形容詞＋（of～）＋to＋動詞の原形**の構文を作ります。

careless	**kind**	**mean**	**considerate**	**foolish**	**stupid**	**generous**	**unfair**

■ It's **foolish of Mary to quit** her job when she needs the money.
■ I think it was very **unfair of him to criticize** me. (⇒ 彼が私の悪口を言うなんてあんまりだ)

C

I'm sorry to . . . / I was surprised to . . .：「…して残念に思う / …して驚いた」

形容詞＋to＋動詞の原形で，「…することに対し～」のように **to＋動詞の原形**が表す動作にどのような感情を持って反応したかを表します。

■ I was **sorry to hear** that your father is ill. (⇒ …と聞いて残念でした)

この構文を作る**形容詞**には，さらに次のようなものがあります。

happy	**disappointed**	**glad**	**surprised**	**pleased**	**amazed**	**sad**	**relieved**

■ Was Julia **surprised to see** you?
■ It was a long and tiring trip. We were **glad to get** home.

D

the first (person) **to know / the next** (train) **to arrive**：「最初に知る（人）/ 次に到着する（電車）」

the first/second/third などや，もしくは **the last, the next, the only** などに続けて（**＋名詞**）**＋to＋動詞の原形**を置く構文もあります。

■ If I have any more news, you will be **the first** (person) **to know**. (⇒ まず君に教えるよ)
■ **The next** plane **to arrive** at gate 4 will be Flight 268 from Bogota.
■ Everybody was late except me. I was **the only** one **to arrive** on time.

E

～ is sure/certain/likely/bound to do：「きっと / おそらく…する」 出来事が起こる確実さを表します。

■ Carla is a very good student. She's **bound to pass** the exam. (⇒ きっと合格する)
■ I'm **likely to get** home late tonight. (⇒ おそらく今日は帰りが遅くなる)

afraid/interested/sorry ➲ Unit 64　it（形式主語）➲ Unit 82C　enough/too＋形容詞 ➲ Unit 101

Exercises

63.1 (セクション A) 指定された語句で始めて，同じ意味を表す文を完成しなさい。

1. It's hard to understand him. — He *is hard to understand.*
2. It's easy to use this machine. — This machine is ______
3. It was very difficult to open the window. — The window ______
4. It's impossible to translate some words. — Some words ______
5. It's expensive to maintain a car. — A ______
6. It's not safe to stand on that chair. — That ______

63.2 (セクション A) ( ) 内の形容詞を形容詞＋名詞＋to＋動詞の原形の構文にあてはめて，状況を表す文を完成しなさい。

1. I couldn't answer the question. (difficult) — It was a *difficult question to answer.*
2. Everybody makes that mistake. (easy) — It's an ______
3. I like living in this place. (nice) — It's a ______
4. We enjoyed watching the game. (good) — It was a ______

63.3 (セクション B) 状況に合うように以下から形容詞を選び，it で始まる文を完成しなさい。

careless **inconsiderate** ~~**kind**~~ **nice**

1. Sue has offered to help me. *It's kind of Sue to offer to help me.*
2. You make the same mistake again and again.
   It ______
3. Dan and Jenny invited me to stay with them.
   ______
4. The neighbors make so much noise at night.
   ______

63.4 (セクション C) 状況に合うように以下から語句を選び，適切な形に変えて文を完成しなさい。

sorry / hear **glad / hear** ~~**pleased / get**~~ **surprised / see**

1. We *were pleased to get* your letter last week.
2. I got your message. I ______ that you're doing well.
3. We ______ Paula at the party. We didn't expect her to come.
4. I ______ that your mother isn't well. I hope she gets better soon.

63.5 (セクション D) 状況に合うように，( )内の語句に to＋動詞の原形を続けて文を完成しなさい。

1. Nobody left before me. (the first) I was *the first person to leave.*
2. Everybody else arrived before Paul.
   (the last) Paul was the ______
3. Jenny passed the exam. All the other students failed.
   (the only) Jenny was ______
4. I complained to the restaurant manager about the service. Another customer had already complained.
   (the second) I was ______
5. Neil Armstrong walked on the moon in 1969. Nobody had done this before him.
   (the first) Neil Armstrong was ______

63.6 (セクション E) 状況に合うように，( ) 内の語句と適切な動詞を用いて文を完成しなさい。動詞は適切な形に変えること。

1. Diane is a very good student. She *is bound to pass* the exam. (bound)
2. I'm not surprised you're tired. After such a long trip, you ______ tired. (bound)
3. Toshi has a very bad memory. He ______ what you tell him. (sure)
4. I don't think you need an umbrella. It ______. (not likely)
5. The holiday begins this Friday. There ______ a lot of traffic on the roads. (likely)

UNIT 64

to＋動詞の原形 (afraid to do) と 前置詞＋-ing (afraid of -ing)

A

☆ afraid to＋動詞の原形と afraid of -ing とは，どのように異なりますか？

➤ **I am afraid to do ...** は「危険であったり良くない結果になりそうなので…したくない，不安で…できない」を表します。動作は自分の意志で行い，実際にするかしないかは選択できます。

- This part of town is dangerous. People are **afraid to walk** here at night.
(⇒ この地域は危険なので歩きたくない。実際人々は歩いていない)
- James was **afraid to tell** his parents what happened.
(⇒ James は自分の親には言いたくない。きっと怒ったり心配したりしてしまうから)

➤ **I am afraid of (～) doing.** は「(良くない出来事や事故が) …するかもしれない」を表します。自分の意志で行うことには用いません。

- The sidewalk was icy, so we walked very carefully. We were **afraid of falling**.
(⇒ 転んでしまったかもしれない / × we were afraid to fall)
- I don't like dogs. I'm always **afraid of being bitten**. (× afraid to be bitten)

➤ 両者の関係は，以下のように「ひょっとして～が起きるかもしれないので (be afraid of (～) doing)，自分の意志では…できない (be afraid to do)」のようにまとめられます。

- I was **afraid to go** near the dog because I was **afraid of being** bitten.

B

☆ interested in -ing と interested to＋動詞の原形とは，どのように異なりますか？

➤ **I am interested in -ing ...** は「…することに興味がある，…したい」を表します。

- Let me know if you're **interested in joining** the club. (× to join)
- I tried to sell my car, but nobody was **interested in buying** it. (× to buy)

➤ **I'm interested to＋動詞の原形**は「…して興味を持った，関心した」のように，何かを見聞きして感じたことを表します。例えば，**I was interested to hear it.** は「そのことを聞いて興味を持った」を表します。

- I was **interested to hear** that Tanya quit her job.
- Ask Mike for his opinion. I would be **interested to know** what he thinks.
(⇒ 彼がどう考えているか知りたい)

この構文は **surprised to＋動詞の原形**や **glad to＋動詞の原形**といった構文と同じです。➲Unit 63C

- I was **surprised to hear** that Tanya quit her job.

C

☆ sorry to＋動詞の原形と sorry for/about -ing とは，どのように異なりますか？

➤ **sorry to＋動詞の原形**は「…して残念に思う」を表します。➲Unit 63C

- I was **sorry to hear** that Nicky lost her job. (⇒ …と聞いて残念でした)
- I've enjoyed my stay here. I'll be **sorry to leave**.

何かをした時に，その場で「…してごめんなさい」のように謝る際にも **sorry to＋動詞の原形**を用います。

- I'm **sorry to call** you so late, but I need to ask you something.
(⇒ 夜遅くに電話してごめんなさい)

➤ **sorry for/about -ing** は，過去にしたことに対して「…してごめんなさい」のように謝る際に用います。

- I'm **sorry for** (= **about**) **shouting** at you yesterday. (× sorry to shout)

同じことを，以下のように sorry の後に文 (節) を置いた形でも表せます。

- I'm **sorry I shouted** at you yesterday.

D

構文が異なることに注意します。

I **want to** (do) / **I'd like to** (do) (⇒ …したい)	⇔	I'm **thinking of** (doing) / I **dream of** (doing) (⇒ …したい)
I **failed to** (do) (⇒ …できた)	⇔	I **succeeded in** (doing) (⇒ …できた)
I **allowed** them **to** (do) (⇒ ～に…させる)	⇔	I **stopped**/**prevented** them **from** (doing) (⇒ ～に…させない)

それぞれの構文の例文については ➲Units 52–53, 60

動詞＋前置詞＋-ing ➲Unit 60　形容詞＋前置詞 ➲Units 127–128　sorry about/for ➲Unit 127

Exercises

64.1 状況に合うように，（ ）内の語句を afraid to ＋動詞の原形もしくは afraid of -ing の構文中に用いて文を完成しなさい。

1. The streets are unsafe at night.
   (a lot of people / afraid / go / out) *A lot of people are afraid to go out.*
2. We walked very carefully along the icy path.
   (we / afraid / fall) *We were afraid of falling.*
3. I don't usually carry my passport with me.
   (I / afraid / lose / it) ____________________
4. I thought she would be angry if I told her what had happened.
   (I / afraid / tell / her) ____________________
5. We rushed to the station.
   (we / afraid / miss / our train) ____________________
6. In the middle of the film there was an especially horrifying scene.
   (we / afraid / look) ____________________
7. The vase was very valuable, so I held it carefully.
   (I / afraid / drop / it) ____________________
8. I thought the food on my plate didn't look fresh.
   a) (I / afraid / eat / it) ____________________
   b) (I / afraid / get / sick) ____________________

64.2 状況に合うように以下から適切な語を選び，in -ing もしくは to ＋動詞の原形の構文中に用いて文を完成しなさい。

~~buy~~ get know look read start

1. I'm trying to sell my car, but nobody is interested *in buying* it.
2. Julia is interested ____________ her own business.
3. I was interested ____________ your letter in the newspaper last week.
4. Ben wants to stay single. He's not interested ____________ married.
5. I met Mark a few days ago. You'll be interested ____________ that he's just gotten a job in Buenos Aires.
6. I don't enjoy sightseeing. I'm not interested ____________ at old buildings.

64.3 状況に合うように，（ ）内の語を sorry for/about -ing もしくは sorry to ＋動詞の原形の構文中に用いて文を完成させなさい。

1. I'm *sorry to call* you so late, but I need to ask you something. (call)
2. I was ____________ that you didn't get the job you applied for. (hear)
3. I'm ____________ all those bad things about you. I didn't mean them. (say)
4. I'm ____________ you, but do you have a pen I could borrow? (bother)
5. I'm ____________ the book you lent me. I'll buy you another one. (lose)

64.4 状況に合うように，（ ）内の語句を用いて文を完成しなさい。

1. a) We wanted *to leave* the building. (leave)
   b) We weren't allowed ____________ the building. (leave)
   c) We were prevented ____________ the building. (leave)
2. a) Peter failed ____________ the problem. (solve)
   b) Chris succeeded ____________ the problem. (solve)
3. a) I'm thinking ____________ away next week. (go)
   b) I'm hoping ____________ away next week. (go)
   c) I'd like ____________ away next week. (go)
   d) I'm looking forward ____________ away next week. (go)
4. a) Lisa wanted ____________ me lunch. (buy)
   b) Lisa promised ____________ me lunch. (buy)
   c) Lisa insisted ____________ me lunch. (buy)
   d) Lisa wouldn't dream ____________ me lunch. (buy)

補充問題 27 (p. 312)

UNIT 65

see ～ do と see ～ doing

A

☆ イラストの状況について考えなさい。あなたは Tom が車に近づき，乗り込み，去っていく一部始終を見ていました。この状況はどのような構文で表せますか？

➤ この状況は，I saw ～ do（動詞の原形）...（私は～が…するのを見た）のような構文で表します。

■ I saw Tom **get** into his car and **drive** away.

この構文は以下のように，**単純過去形**の構文 1）と「…を見た」の構文 2）を合わせて作られました。

1) Somebody **did** something + 2) I **saw** this

⇔ I **saw** somebody **do** something

この構文では get/drive/do などのように**動詞の原形**を用い，to get / to drive / to do などのような **to + 動詞の原形**は用いません。

B

☆ イラストの状況について考えなさい。昨日，あなたが自動車を運転していたら，通りがかりに Kate がバス停でバスを待っているのが目に入りました。この状況はどのような構文で表せますか？

➤ この状況は，I saw ～ doing.（私は～が…しているのを見た）のような構文で表します。

■ I saw Kate **waiting** for a bus.

この構文は以下のように，**過去進行形**の構文 1）と「…を見た」の構文 2）を合わせて作られました。

1) Somebody **was doing** something + 2) I **saw** this

⇔ I **saw** somebody **doing** something

この構文では waiting/doing などのように **-ing** を用います。

C

☆ 例文で考えます。see ～ do と see ～ -ing の構文は，どのように異なりますか？

➤ **He did something.**（単純過去形）+ **I saw this.** ⇒ **I saw him do something.**
「わたし」は彼の行動について始めから終りまですべて見ていました。

■ He **fell** off the wall. + I saw this. ⇒ I saw him **fall** off the wall.（⇒彼が壁から落ちたのを見た）

■ The accident **happened**. + Did you see it? ⇒ Did you see the accident **happen**?

➤ **He was doing something.**（過去進行形）+ **I saw this.** ⇒ **I saw him doing something.**
「わたし」は彼が何かをしているのを見ましたが，彼の行動は一部しか見ていません。

■ He **was walking** along the street.
I saw this when I drove past in my car.
} I saw him **walking** along the street.（⇒ 彼が道を歩いているのを見た）

両者の違いが重要ではなく，どちらを用いてもよい場合もあります。

■ I've never seen her **dance**. = I've never seen her **dancing**.

D

see や **hear** をはじめ，次のような動詞でこの構文が用いられます。

■ I didn't **hear** you **come** in. (⇐ You came in. + I didn't hear this.)

■ Liz suddenly **felt** somebody **touch** her on the shoulder.

■ Did you **notice** anyone **go** out?

■ I could **hear** it **raining**. (⇐ It was raining. + I could hear it.)

■ The missing children were last **seen playing** near the river.

■ **Listen to** the birds **singing**!

■ Can you **smell** something **burning**?

■ I **found** Sue in my room **reading** my letters.

Exercises

65.1 状況に合うように，空所に適切な語句を入れて対話を完成しなさい。

1. Did anybody go out?	I don't think so. I didn't see *anybody go out* .
2. Has Sarah arrived yet?	Yes, I think I heard her ________ .
3. How do you know I took the money?	I know because I saw you ________ .
4. Did the doorbell ring?	I don't think so. I didn't hear ________ .
5. Can Tom play the piano?	I've never heard ________ .
6. Did I lock the door when I went out?	Yes, I saw ________ .
7. How did the woman fall?	I don't know. I didn't see ________ .

65.2 あなたとあなたの友達はイラストが表すそれぞれの状況について，吹き出しで示されていることばを発しました。それらの状況を表す文を完成しなさい。

1. *We saw Kate waiting for a bus.*
2. We saw Dave and Helen ________
3. We saw ________ in a restaurant.
4. We heard ________
5. We could ________
6. ________

65.3 状況に合うように以下から語を選び，適切な形に変えて文を完成しなさい。

climb	~~**come**~~	**crawl**	**cry**	**explode**	**ride**
run	**say**	~~**sing**~~	**slam**	**sleep**	**tell**

1. Listen to the birds *singing* !
2. I didn't hear you *come* in.
3. We listened to the old man ________ his story from beginning to end.
4. Listen! Can you hear a baby ________ ?
5. I looked out of the window and saw Dan ________ his bike along the road.
6. I thought I heard somebody ________ "Hi," so I turned around.
7. We watched two men ________ across the yard and ________ through an open window into the house.
8. Everybody heard the bomb ________ . It made a tremendous noise.
9. Oh! I can feel something ________ up my leg! It must be an insect.
10. I heard somebody ________ the door in the middle of the night. It woke me up.
11. When we got home, we found a cat ________ under the kitchen table.

UNIT 66

-ing 句（分詞構文：Feeling tired, I went to bed early.）

A

2つの文が関係し合う場合，どちらか一方を **-ing** で始まる形に変えて1つにまとめられます。

Joe was playing football. He hurt his knee.（⇒ 彼はフットボールをしていた。彼は膝をけがした）

↓

- Joe hurt his knee **playing football**.（⇒ フットボールをしていて，彼は膝をけがした）

You were feeling tired. So you went to bed early.（⇒ あなたは疲れていた。そのため，早めに寝た）

↓

- **Feeling tired**, I went to bed early.（⇒ 私は疲れていたので，早めに寝た）

上の例文で，playing football（フットボールをしている）や feeling tired のような **-ing** を先頭に置いた語句のまとまりを **-ing 句（分詞構文）**と呼びます。Feeling tired, ... の例のように，**-ing 句**が文頭にきた場合，**カンマ（,）**を句の終わりに置きます。

B

2つの事柄が同時に生じる時に **-ing 句**を用います。

- Kate is in the kitchen **making coffee**.
（⇒ 台所にいてコーヒーを入れている）
- A man ran out of the house **shouting**.
（⇒ 家から飛び出しながら叫んでいた）
- Do something! Don't just stand there **doing nothing**!

別の動作を行っている最中にある動作が生じる時，時間的により長い方の動作を **-ing 句**で表します。

- Joe hurt his knee **playing football**.（⇒ サッカーをしている最中に）
- Did you cut yourself **shaving**?（⇒ ひげを剃っている最中に）

同様に while や when の後に **-ing 句**を置いて表すこともあります。

- Jim hurt his knee **while playing** football.
- Be careful **when crossing** the street.（⇒ 通りを渡っている時は）

C

ある動作が別の動作より前に生じた時，最初に起こった動作を **having ＋過去分詞の -ing 句**で表します。

- **Having found** a hotel, we looked for someplace to have dinner.
- **Having finished** her work, she went home.

同じことを **after -ing 句**で表すこともあります。**after** によって時間的な関係が明確になるので，**having ＋過去分詞の -ing 句**にする必要はありません。

- **After finishing** her work, she went home.

2つの短い動作が連続して起こる場合にも，よく **having ＋過去分詞**ではなく**単純形の -ing 句**で最初の動作を表すこともあります。

- **Taking** a key out of his pocket, he opened the door.

D

-ing 句は「…なので」のように，何かをする理由を表します。この場合 **-ing 句**は普通，文頭に置きます。

- **Feeling** tired, I went to bed early.（⇒ 疲れていたので…）
- **Being** unemployed, he doesn't have much money.（⇒ 失業中なので…）
- **Not having** a car, she has trouble getting around.（⇒ 自動車を持っていないので…）
- **Having** already **seen** the movie twice, I didn't want to go again with my friends.
（⇒ すでに2回見たので…）

このように説明や理由を述べる **-ing 句**は，話しことばより書きことばでよく用いられます。

-ing 句と -ed 句（後置修飾）➲ Unit 95

Exercises

66.1 A と B から表現を 1 つずつ選び，-ing 句を用いて適切な文を完成しなさい。

A	B
1. ~~Kate was in the kitchen.~~	She was trying not to make any noise.
2. Diane was sitting in an armchair.	She looked at the sights and took pictures.
3. Sue opened the door carefully.	She said she would be back in an hour.
4. Sarah went out.	She was reading a book.
5. Linda was in London for two years.	~~She was making coffee.~~
6. Mary walked around the town.	She worked as a teacher.

1. *Kate was in the kitchen making coffee.*
2. Diane was sitting ______
3. Sue ______
4. ______
5. ______
6. ______

66.2 状況に合うように，-ing 句を用いて 2 つの文を 1 つにまとめなさい。

1. Joe was playing football. He hurt his knee. *Joe hurt his knee playing football.*
2. I was watching television. I fell asleep.
   I ______
3. The man slipped and fell. He was getting off a bus.
   The man ______
4. I was walking home in the rain. I got very wet.
   I ______
5. Laura was driving to work yesterday. She had an accident.
   ______
6. Two kids got lost. They were hiking in the woods.
   ______

66.3 状況に合うように，Having ... で始まる文を完成しなさい。

1. She finished her work. Then she went home.
   Having finished her work, she went home.
2. We bought our tickets. Then we went into the theater.
   ______
3. They had dinner, and then they continued their trip.
   ______
4. After I'd done the shopping, I stopped for a cup of coffee.
   ______

66.4 セクション D を参考にして，-ing もしくは Not -ing で始まる文を完成しなさい。状況に応じて「Having + 過去分詞」の形にします。

1. I felt tired. So I went to bed early.
   Feeling tired, I went to bed early.
2. I thought they might be hungry. So I offered them something to eat.
   ______
3. Sally is a vegetarian. So she doesn't eat any kind of meat.
   ______
4. I didn't know his e-mail address. So I wasn't able to contact him.
   ______
5. Sarah has traveled a lot. So she knows a lot about other countries.
   ______
6. I wasn't able to speak the local language. So I had trouble communicating.
   ______
7. We had spent nearly all our money. So we couldn't afford to stay in a hotel.
   ______

UNIT 67 可算名詞と不可算名詞 1

A

☆ 名詞には数えられる可算名詞と数えられない不可算名詞とがあります。それぞれはどのように異なりますか？

可算名詞

- I eat a **banana** every day.
- I like **bananas**.

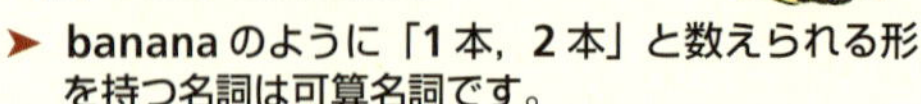

➤ **banana** のように「1本，2本」と数えられる形を持つ名詞は可算名詞です。

可算名詞には**単数形** (banana) と**複数形** (bananas) の **2 つの形**があります。

可算名詞は one banana, two bananas などのように，数を表す語句とともに用いられることがあります。

不可算名詞

- I eat **rice** every day.
- I like **rice**.

➤ rice のように一定の形を持たず普通，袋や茶碗などの容器に入れられている名詞は不可算名詞です。

不可算名詞には **1 つの形** (rice) しかありません。

不可算名詞は数を表す語句とともには用いられません。one rice, two rices などの形はありません。

☆ 例文にはどのような可算名詞と不可算名詞が生じていますか？　左右の例文で比較します。

- Kate was singing **a song**.
- There's **a** nice **beach** near here.
- Do you have **a** $10 **bill**?
- It wasn't your fault. It was **an accident**.
- There are no **batteries** in the radio.
- We don't have enough **cups**.

- Kate was listening to (some) **music**.
- There's **sand** in my shoes.
- Do you have any **money**?
- It wasn't your fault. It was bad **luck**.
- There is no **electricity** in this house.
- We don't have enough **water**.

B

可算名詞

可算名詞の**単数形**の前には**不定冠詞** (a/an) を置きます。

a beach / **a student** / **an umbrella**

単数可算名詞は，**a**/**an**/**the**/**my** などの語句を前に置かずに，単独では用いません。

- I want **a banana**. (✕ I want banana)
- There's been **an accident**. (✕ There's been accident)

複数可算名詞は単独で用います。

- I like **bananas**. (⇒ バナナ全般が好き)
- **Accidents** can be prevented.

不可算名詞

不可算名詞の前には**不定冠詞** (a/an) を置くことはできません。a sand や a rice のような形はありません。**a ... of** を前に置くことがあります。

a bowl of / **a pound of** / **a grain of** rice

不可算名詞は **the**/**my**/**some** などの語句を置かずに，単独で用いることができます。

- I eat **rice** every day.
- There's **blood** on your shirt.
- Can you hear **music**?

C

可算名詞

複数可算名詞の前に **some** や **any** を置き「いくつかの～ /2, 3 の～」を表します。

- We sang **some songs**.
- Did you buy **any apples**?

many や **a few** / **few** は**複数可算名詞**の前に置き，「多くの～」や「2, 3 の～ / ほとんど～はない」を表します。

- We didn't take **many pictures**.
- I have a **few things** to do.

不可算名詞

不可算名詞の前に **some** や **any** を置き「いくらかの～」を表します。

- We listened to **some music**.
- Did you buy **any** apple **juice**?

much や **a little** / **little** は**不可算名詞**の前に置き，「多くの～」や「少しの～ / ほとんど～はない」を表します。

- We didn't do **much shopping**.
- I have a **little work** to do.

可算名詞と不可算名詞 2 ➲ Unit 68　children / the children ➲ Unit 73
many/much/few/little ➲ Unit 85　some と any ➲ Unit 83

Exercises

67.1 a/an を持たないために誤りとなった文を選び，誤りを正しなさい。

1. Joe goes everywhere by bike. He doesn't have car. _a car._
2. Helen was listening to music when I arrived. _OK_
3. We went to very nice restaurant last weekend. ________
4. I brush my teeth with toothpaste. ________
5. I use toothbrush to brush my teeth. ________
6. Can you tell me if there's bank near here? ________
7. My brother works for insurance company in Detroit. ________
8. I don't like violence. ________
9. Can you smell paint? ________
10. When we were in Rome, we stayed in big hotel. ________
11. We need gas. I hope we come to gas station soon. ________
12. I wonder if you can help me. I have problem. ________
13. I like your suggestion. It's very interesting idea. ________
14. John has interview for job tomorrow. ________
15. I like volleyball. It's good game. ________
16. Liz doesn't usually wear jewelry. ________
17. Jane was wearing beautiful necklace. ________

67.2 状況に合うように以下から適切な語を選び，必要に応じて a/an を付けて文を完成しなさい。

~~accident~~ blood coat cookie decision electricity interview key minute ~~music~~ question sugar

1. It wasn't your fault. It was _an accident_.
2. Listen! Can you hear _music_?
3. I couldn't get into the house because I didn't have ________.
4. It's very warm today. Why are you wearing ________?
5. Do you take ________ in your coffee?
6. Are you hungry? Would you like ________ with your coffee?
7. Our lives would be very difficult without ________.
8. "I had ________ for a job yesterday." "You did? How did it go?"
9. The heart pumps ________ through the body.
10. Excuse me, but can I ask you ________?
11. I'm not ready yet. Can you wait ________, please?
12. We can't delay much longer. We have to make ________ soon.

67.3 状況に合うように以下から適切な語を選び，必要に応じて複数形にしたり a/an を付けたりして文を完成しなさい。

air day friend language letter line meat patience people ~~picture~~ space umbrella

1. I had my camera, but I didn't take any _pictures_.
2. There are seven ________ in a week.
3. A vegetarian is a person who doesn't eat ________.
4. Outside the movie theater, there was ________ of people waiting to see the movie.
5. I'm not very good at writing ________.
6. Last night I went out with some ________ of mine.
7. There were very few ________ in town today. The streets were almost empty.
8. I'm going out for a walk. I need some fresh ________.
9. Gary always wants things quickly. He doesn't have much ________.
10. I think it's going to rain. Do you have ________ I could borrow?
11. Do you speak any foreign ________?
12. Our apartment is very small. We don't have much ________.

UNIT 68

可算名詞と不可算名詞 2

A

☆ 可算名詞と不可算名詞の両方の用法を持つ名詞があります。この場合普通，意味が異なります。以下の例文中の可算名詞と不可算名詞は，どのように意味が異なりますか？

可算名詞	不可算名詞
■ Did you hear **a noise** just now? （一回の騒音，ドシンという音）	■ I can't work here. There's too much **noise**. （ものすごい騒音，× many noises）
■ I bought **a paper** to read. （一部の新聞）	■ I need some **paper** to write on. （字を書く材料としての紙）
■ There's **a hair** in my soup! （一本の髪の毛）	■ You've got very long **hair**. （頭のすべての髪の毛，× hairs）
■ You can stay with us. There is **a** spare **room**. （家の中の一部屋）	■ You can't sit here. There isn't any **room**. （空間，隙間）
■ I had some interesting **experiences** while I was traveling. （私に起こったさまざまな出来事）	■ They offered me the job because I had a lot of **experience**. （経験，× experiences）
■ Enjoy your trip. Have a good **time**!	■ I can't wait. I don't have **time**.

coffee/tea/juice/beer などの「飲み物」は普通，**不可算名詞**です。

■ I don't like **coffee** very much.

a cup of coffee や two cups of coffee の意味で **a coffee**, **two coffees** の形を用いることがあります。

■ **Two** coffees and **an orange juice**, please.

B

以下の名詞は普通，**不可算名詞**として用います。

advice	**baggage**	**behavior**	**bread**	**chaos**	**damage**
furniture	**information**	**luck**	**luggage**	**news**	**permission**
progress	**scenery**	**traffic**	**weather**	**work**	

不可算名詞なので **a/an** を前に置くことはできません。

■ I'm going to buy **some bread**. ⇒ . . . **a loaf of bread**. (× a bread)

■ Enjoy your vacation! I hope you have good **weather**. (× a good weather)

複数形にもなりません。

■ Where are you going to put all your **furniture**? (× furnitures)

■ Let me know if you need more **information**. (× informations)

news は **-s** で終わっていますが**不可算名詞**です。**複数形**ではありません。

■ The **news was** very depressing. (× The news were)

travel は一般的に「**旅行**」，**trip** は具体的な体験としての「**旅**」を意味します。意味は似ていますが，**trip** は**可算名詞**，**travel** は**不可算名詞**です。

■ They spend a lot of money on **travel**.

■ We had **a** very good **trip**. (× a good travel)

似たような意味を持ちながら，**可算名詞**と**不可算名詞**では形が異なる名詞には，次のようなものがあります。

可算名詞	不可算名詞
■ I'm looking for **a job**.	■ I'm looking for **work**. (× a work)
■ What **a** beautiful **view**!	■ What beautiful **scenery**!
■ It's **a** nice **day** today.	■ It's nice **weather** today.
■ We had a lot of **bags** and **suitcases**.	■ We had a lot of **baggage/luggage**.
■ **These chairs** are mine.	■ **This furniture** is mine.
■ That's **a** good **suggestion**.	■ That's good **advice**.

可算名詞と不可算名詞 1 ➲ Unit 67

Exercises

68.1 下線部の正しい方を選んで，文を完成しなさい。

1. "Did you hear ~~noise~~ / a noise just now?" "No, I didn't hear anything." (a noise が正しい).
2. a) If you want to know the news, you can read paper / a paper.
   b) I want to print some documents, but the printer is out of paper / papers.
3. a) I thought there was somebody in the house because there was light / a light on inside.
   b) Light / A light comes from the sun.
4. a) I was in a hurry this morning. I didn't have time / a time for breakfast.
   b) "Did you have a good vacation?" "Yes, we had wonderful time / a wonderful time."
5. This is nice room / a nice room. Did you decorate it yourself?
6. Sue was very helpful. She gave us some very useful advice / advices.
7. Did you have nice weather / a nice weather when you were away?
8. We were very unfortunate. We had bad luck / a bad luck.
9. Is it difficult to find a work / job at this time?
10. Our travel / trip from Paris to Istanbul by train was very tiring.
11. When the fire alarm rang, there was total chaos / a total chaos.
12. I had to buy a / some bread because I wanted to make some sandwiches.
13. Bad news don't / doesn't make people happy.
14. Your hair is / Your hairs are too long. You should have it / them cut.
15. The damage / The damages caused by the storm will cost a lot to repair.

68.2 状況に合うように以下から適切な語を選び，必要に応じて複数形にして文を完成しなさい。

advice	**chair**	**experience**	**experience**	**furniture**	**hair**
information	**job**	~~**luggage**~~	**permission**	**progress**	**work**

1. I didn't have much __luggage__ – just two small bags.
2. They'll tell you all you want to know. They'll give you plenty of ________.
3. There is room for everybody to sit down. There are plenty of ________.
4. We have no ________, not even a bed or a table.
5. "What does Alan look like?" "He's got a long beard and very short ________."
6. Carla's English is better than it was. She's made ________.
7. Mike is unemployed. He can't find a ________.
8. Mike is unemployed. He can't find ________.
9. If you want to leave early, you have to ask for ________.
10. I didn't know what to do. So I asked Chris for ________.
11. I don't think Ann will get the job. She doesn't have enough ________.
12. Rita has done many interesting things. She could write a book about her ________.

68.3 セクション B の不可算名詞を用いて，それぞれの状況について尋ねたり説明する文を完成しなさい。

1. Your friends have just arrived at the station. You can't see any suitcases or bags.
   You ask them: Do __you have any luggage__?
2. You go into the tourist office. You want to know about places to see in the city.
   You say: I'd like ________.
3. You are a student. You want your teacher to advise you about which courses to take.
   You say: Can you give me ________?
4. You want to watch the news on TV, but you don't know when it is on.
   You ask your friend: What time ________?
5. You are at the top of a mountain. You can see a very long way. It's beautiful.
   You say: It ________, isn't it?
6. You look out the window. The weather is horrible: cold, wet, and windy.
   You say: What ________!

UNIT 69

可算名詞の前に置く a/an や some の用法

A

☆ 単数可算名詞と複数可算名詞では直前に置く語が異なります。どのような語が置かれますか？

単数	a **dog**	a **child**	the **evening**	this **party**	an **umbrella**
複数	**dogs**	some **children**	the **evenings**	these **parties**	two **umbrellas**

➤ 単数可算名詞の前には a/an が置かれることがあります。

- Good-bye! Have **a** nice **evening**.
- Do you need **an umbrella**?

➤ a/an/the/my/this などの語句を前に置かず，単独で単数可算名詞を用いることはできません。

- She never wears **a** hat. (✕ She never wears hat)
- Be careful of **the** dog. (✕ Be careful of dog)
- What **a** beautiful day!
- I've got **a** headache.

B

物や人の種類や一般的な性質を表す際には，**a/an ... ＋単数可算名詞**を用います。

- That's **a nice table**.（あれは素敵なテーブルです。⇒ あのテーブルは素敵です）

種類や一般的な性質は，**some** や **the** などを前に置かずに**複数可算名詞**を単独で用いても表せます。

- Those are **nice chairs**. (✕ some nice chairs)

以下はいずれも，種類や一般的な性質を表しています。

a/an ... ＋単数可算名詞	**複数可算名詞**
A dog is **an animal**.	Dogs **are animals**.
I'm **an optimist**.	We're **optimists**.
Tim's father is **a doctor**.	Most of my friends are **students**.
Are you **a good driver**?	Are they **good students**?
Jill is **a really nice person**.	Jill's parents are **really nice people**.
What **a pretty dress**!	What **awful shoes**!

~ has a long nose / a nice face / blue eyes / small hands などの形で，人の外見上の特徴を表します。

Jack has **a long nose**. (✕ the long nose)	Jack has **blue eyes**. (✕ the blue eyes)

人の職業も同様に **a/an ... ＋単数可算名詞**で表します。

- Sandra is **a nurse**. (✕ Sandra is nurse)
- Would you like to be **an English teacher**?

C

複数可算名詞は **some** とともによく用います。**some ＋複数可算名詞**には以下の 2 つの用法があります。

1)「いくつかの…」のように数個程度の多くない複数を表します。(= a number of / a few of / a pair of)

- I've seen **some** good **movies** recently. (✕ I've seen good movies)
- **Some friends** of mine are coming to stay this weekend.
- I need **some** new **sunglasses**. (= a new pair of sunglasses，1 つのサングラス)

物について限定せずに全般的に記述する際には**複数可算名詞**を**単独**で用います。**some ＋複数可算名詞**の形は用いません。➲Unit 73

- I love **bananas**. (✕ some bananas)
- My aunt is a writer. She writes **books**. (✕ some books)

some を前に置かずに「いくつかの…」を表すことがあります。**some** を持つ形と意味上の違いはありません。

- There are (**some**) **eggs** in the refrigerator if you're hungry.

2)「…もある」のように，すべてではないことを表します。

- **Some children** learn very quickly.（⇒ 速く学ぶ子どももいるが，すべてではない）
- Tomorrow there will be rain in **some places**, but most of the country will be dry.

可算名詞と不可算名詞 ➲ Units 67–68　a/an と the ➲ Unit 70　some と any ➲ Unit 83

Exercises

69.1 それぞれのものが，どのような種類に属するかを説明する文を完成しなさい。必要に応じて辞書を用いてもかまいません。

1. an ant? _It's an insect._
2. ants and bees? _They're insects._
3. a cauliflower? ________
4. chess? ________
5. a violin, a trumpet, and a flute? ________
6. a skyscraper? ________
7. Earth, Mars, Venus, and Jupiter? ________
8. a tulip? ________
9. the Nile, the Rhine, and the Mississippi? ________
10. a pigeon, an eagle, and a crow? ________

それぞれが，どのような人物かを一般的に説明する文を完成しなさい。

11. Beethoven? _He was a composer._
12. Shakespeare? ________
13. Albert Einstein? ________
14. George Washington, Abraham Lincoln, and John F. Kennedy? ________
15. Marilyn Monroe? ________
16. Elvis Presley and John Lennon? ________
17. Van Gogh, Renoir, and Picasso? ________

69.2 それぞれの人が行うことにふさわしい職業を以下から選び，文を完成しなさい。

chef	**interpreter**	**journalist**	**~~nurse~~**
plumber	**surgeon**	**travel agent**	**waiter**

1. Sarah takes care of patients in the hospital. _She's a nurse._
2. Gary works in a restaurant. He brings the food to the tables. He ________
3. Mary arranges people's trips for them. She ________
4. Kevin works in a hospital. He operates on people. ________
5. Jonathan cooks in a restaurant. ________
6. Jane writes articles for a newspaper. ________
7. Dave installs and repairs water pipes. ________
8. Linda translates what people are saying from one language into another so that they can understand each other. ________

69.3 状況に合うように空所に a/an もしくは some を入れて，文を完成しなさい。何も必要ない場合には – を記入します。

1. I've seen _some_ good films recently.
2. What's wrong with you? Do you have _a_ headache?
3. I know a lot of people. Most of them are _–_ students.
4. When I was ________ child, I used to be very shy.
5. Would you like to be ________ actor?
6. Do you collect ________ stamps?
7. What ________ beautiful garden!
8. ________ birds, for example, the penguin, cannot fly.
9. Do you enjoy going to ________ concerts?
10. I've been walking for three hours. I've got ________ sore feet.
11. I don't feel very well this morning. I've got ________ sore throat.
12. Maria speaks ________ English, but not very much.
13. It's too bad we don't have ________ camera. I'd like to take ________ picture of that house.
14. Those are ________ nice shoes. Where did you get them?
15. I'm going shopping. I want to buy ________ new shoes.
16. You need ________ visa to visit ________ countries, but not all of them.
17. Jane is ________ teacher. Her parents were ________ teachers, too.
18. I don't believe him. He's ________ liar. He's always telling ________ lies.

UNIT 70

a/an と the

A

☆ イラスト見て考えなさい。a/an と the は，どのように使い分けられていますか？

I had **a** sandwich and **an** apple for lunch.
The sandwich wasn't very good, but **the** apple was delicious.
John
Karen

➤ John は，Karen との会話で初めてサンドイッチとリンゴについて話題にしているので，a sandwich や an apple のように言っています。

➤ 最初の文で，John がすでにサンドイッチとリンゴについて話題にしているので，the sandwich や the apple のように言っています。Karen はサンドイッチやリンゴがどれを指しているか（John が昼に食べたサンドイッチとリンゴ）理解しています。

以下の例文においても，**a/an** を付けて初めて導入された事物に，2 回目以降，**the** が付いています。

- **A** man and **a** woman were sitting across from me. **The** man was American, but I think **the** woman was British.
- When we were on vacation, we stayed at **a** hotel. Sometimes we ate at **the** hotel, and sometimes we went to **a** restaurant.

B

具体的な一つの物や一人の人に特定する場合には **the** を，しない場合には **a/an** を用います。

- Tim sat down on **a** chair. (⇒ 部屋の中にある多くの椅子の中の一つ。どれか一つを特定していない)
  Tim sat down on **the** chair **nearest the door**.（⇒「ドアに一番近い椅子」のように特定する）
- Paula is looking for **a** job.（⇒ 具体的にどのような仕事かは特定していない）
  Did Paula get **the** job **she applied for**?（⇒「応募したあの仕事」のように特定する）
- Do you have **a** car?（⇒「私のあの自動車」のように特定する）
  I washed **the** car yesterday.（⇒ 具体的にどの自動車かは特定していない）

C

全体の状況から何を指しているかが話し手にも聞き手にも明らかな場合には **the** を用います。例えば，**the** light / **the** floor / **the** ceiling / **the** door / **the** carpet などでは，いずれも「部屋」の中にあるものを指します。

- Can you turn off **the** light, please?（⇒ この部屋にある「照明」）
- I took a taxi to **the** station.（⇒ その町にある「駅」）
- 〔あるお店で〕I'd like to speak to **the** manager, please.（⇒ この店の「店長」）

同様に (go to) **the bank** / **the post office** のような形もよく用います。

- I have to go to **the bank** and then I'm going to **the post office**.
  （⇒ 話し手の頭の中に思い浮かぶ「銀行」や「郵便局」）

同様に (go to) **the doctor** / **the dentist** / **the hospital** のような形もよく用います。

- Carol isn't very well. She went to **the doctor**.（⇒ Carol がいつも利用する病院の「医師」）
- Two people were taken to **the hospital** after the accident.

☆ 例文で考えなさい。the と a が付いた名詞句は，どのように異なりますか？

- I have to go **the bank** today.（⇒（いつもの）銀行に行かなくてはならない）
  Is there **a bank** near here?（⇒ 近くに（どれでもよいから）銀行はありますか？）
- I don't like going to **the dentist**.
  My sister is **a dentist**.

D

a/an は，once **a week** / three times **a day** / $1.59 **a pound** のように単位を表す名詞の前に「…につき」を表します。

- "How often do you go to the movies?"　"About once **a month**."（⇒ 月に 1 度）
- "How much are those potatoes?"　"A dollar **a pound**."
- Helen works eight hours **a day**, six days **a week**.

a/an ➲ Unit 69　the ➲ Units 71–76

Exercises

70.1 空所に a/an もしくは the を入れて，文を完成しなさい。

1. This morning I bought __a__ newspaper and ________ magazine. ________ newspaper is in my briefcase, but I can't remember where I put ________ magazine.
2. I saw ________ accident this morning. ________ car crashed into ________ tree. ________ driver of ________ car wasn't hurt, but ________ car was badly damaged.
3. There are two cars parked outside: ________ blue one and ________ gray one. ________ blue one belongs to my neighbors; I don't know who ________ owner of ________ gray one is.
4. My friends live in ________ old house in ________ small town. There is ________ beautiful garden behind ________ house. I would like to have ________ garden like that.

70.2 空所に a/an もしくは the を入れて，文を完成しなさい。

1. a) This house is very nice. Does it have __a__ yard?
   b) It's a beautiful day. Let's sit in ________ yard.
   c) I like living in this house, but it's too bad that ________ yard is so small.
2. a) Can you recommend ________ good restaurant?
   b) We had dinner in ________ very nice restaurant.
   c) We had dinner in ________ most expensive restaurant in town.
3. a) She has ________ French name, but in fact she's English, not French.
   b) What's ________ name of that man we met yesterday?
   c) We stayed at a very nice hotel – I can't remember ________ name now.
4. a) There isn't ________ airport near where I live. ________ nearest airport is 70 miles away.
   b) Our flight was delayed. We had to wait at ________ airport for three hours.
   c) Excuse me, please. Can you tell me how to get to ________ airport?
5. a) "Are you going away next week?" "No, ________ week after next."
   b) I'm going away for ________ week in September.
   c) Gary has a part-time job. He works three mornings ________ week.

70.3 必要に応じてそれぞれの文中の名詞に a/an あるいは the を付けて，文を完成しなさい。

1. Would you like apple? __an apple__
2. How often do you go to dentist? ________
3. Could you close door, please? ________
4. I'm sorry. I didn't mean to do that. It was mistake. ________
5. Excuse me, where is bus station, please? ________
6. I have problem. Can you help me? ________
7. I'm just going to post office. I won't be long. ________
8. There were no chairs, so we sat on floor. ________
9. Are you finished with book I lent you? ________
10. My sister has just gotten job at bank in Atlanta. ________
11. We live in small apartment near hospital. ________
12. There's supermarket on corner near my house. ________

70.4 質問に対する自分自身のことに関する答えを，セクション D の once a week / three times a day などの表現を用いて完成しなさい。

1. How often do you go to the movies? __Three or four times a year.__
2. How much does it cost to rent a car in your country? __About $40 a day.__
3. How often do you go to the movies? ________
4. How often do you take a vacation? ________
5. What's the normal speed limit on highways in your country? ________
6. How much sleep do you need? ________
7. How often do you go out at night? ________
8. How much television do you watch (on average)? ________

補充問題 29 (p. 313)

UNIT 71

the の用法 1

A

1つしか存在しないと普通考えられる物には **the** を付けます。

- What is **the** longest river in **the** world?（⇒ 世界一長い川は1つ）
- **The** earth goes around **the** sun, and **the** moon goes around **the** earth.（⇒ 地球は1つ）
- Have you ever crossed **the** equator?
- I'm going away at **the** end of this month.

国の首都（capital）も1つしかないので **the** が付きます。

- Paris is **the** capital of France. (× Paris is capital of . . .)

1つに限定され **the** が与えられた物についても，種類や一般的な特徴を述べる場合には **a/an** を用います。
➲Unit 69B

- **The** sun is **a** star.（⇒ 太陽は星である）
- **The** hotel we stayed at was **a** very nice hotel.（⇒ 滞在したホテルはとてもよかった）

B

sky，**sea**，**ocean**，**ground**，**country**，**environment** のような語には普通 **the** が付きます。

- We looked up at all the stars in **the sky**. (× in sky)
- Would you like to live in **the country**?（⇒ 田舎）
- We must do more to protect **the environment**.（⇒ 環境）

「宇宙」を意味する **space** には **the** が付きません。

- There are millions of stars **in space**.（⇒ 宇宙には，× in the space）
- I tried to park my car, but **the space** was too small.（⇒ 空間，余地）

C

same（同じ～）の前には **the** を置きます。

- Your sweater is **the same** color as mine.（⇒ 私と同じ色，× is same color）
- "Are these keys **the same**?" "No, they're different."

D

(go to) **the movies** / **the theater**（映画，演劇に行く）のように，**the** が付いてもどれであるかをはっきりと指し示さない場合があります。

- I go to **the movies** a lot, but I haven't been to **the theater** in ages.

「映画にはよく行くが，演劇には長いこと行っていない」という意味で，the movies，the theater は実際にある具体的な映画館や劇場を特定していません。

「ラジオ（放送）」は **the radio** のように **the** が付きますが，「テレビ（放送）」は **television** や **TV** のように **the** は付きません。

- I listen to **the radio** a lot. ⇔ I watch **television** a lot.
- We heard the news on **the radio**. ⇔ We watched the news on **TV**.

「テレビ受像機」を意味する場合には，**the television** のように **the** が付きます。

- Can you turn off **the television**, please?

E

breakfast, lunch, dinner

breakfast, **lunch**, **dinner** などの食事の名前には普通 **the** を付けません。

- What did you have for **breakfast**?
- We had **lunch** in a very nice restaurant.
- What time is **dinner**?

食事の名前に形容詞がある場合には **a** が付きます。

- We had **a** very **nice lunch**. (× We had very nice lunch)

F

Gate 10, Room 126 など

名詞＋数の形の前には the を付けません。

- Our plane leaves from **Gate 10**. (× the Gate 10)
- 〔お店で〕Do you have these shoes in **size 9**? (× the size 9)

同様に，以下の場合にも **the** は付きません。

room 126（ホテルの部屋），**page 29**（本のページ），**question 3**（テスト番号），**platform 6**（駅のフォーム）など

Exercises

71.1 必要に応じて空所に a/an を入れて，それぞれの対話を完成しなさい。何も必要ない場合には - を記入すること。

1. *A:* Where did you have _-_ lunch?
   B: We went to _a_ restaurant.
2. *A:* Did you have ________ nice vacation?
   B: Yes, it was ________ best vacation I've ever had.
3. *A:* Where's ________ nearest drugstore?
   B: There's one on ________ next block.
4. *A:* Do you often listen to ________ radio?
   B: No. In fact, I don't have ________ radio.
5. *A:* Would you like to travel in ________ outer space?
   B: Yes, I'd love to go to ________ moon.
6. *A:* Do you go to ________ movies very often?
   B: No, not very often. But I watch a lot of movies on ________ television.
7. *A:* It was ________ nice day yesterday, wasn't it?
   B: Yes, it was beautiful. We went for a walk by ________ ocean.
8. *A:* What did you have for ________ breakfast this morning?
   B: Nothing. I never eat ________ breakfast.
9. *A:* Excuse me, where is ________ Room 225, please?
   B: It's on ________ second floor.
10. *A:* We spent all our money because we stayed at ________ most expensive hotel in town.
    B: Why didn't you stay at ________ cheaper hotel?

71.2 必要に応じて空所に the を入れて，文を完成しなさい。何も必要ない場合には - を記入すること。

1. I haven't been to _the_ movies in ages.
2. I lay down on ________ ground and looked up at ________ sky.
3. Sarah spends most of her free time watching ________ television.
4. ________ television was on, but nobody was watching it.
5. Lisa and I arrived at ________ same time.
6. Have you had ________ dinner yet?
7. You'll find ________ information you need at ________ top of ________ page 15.
8. What's ________ capital city of Canada?

71.3 例にならい状況を把握したうえで，a/an と the を用いて文を完成しなさい。a/an と the の用法については Unit 70 も参照すること。

1. Sun is star. _The sun is a star._
2. Paul lives in small town in country. ________________
3. Moon goes around earth every 27 days. ________________
4. I'm fed up with doing same thing every day. ________________
5. It was very hot day. It was hottest day of year. ________________
6. I don't usually have lunch, but I always eat good breakfast. ________________
7. If you live in foreign country, you should try to learn language. ________________
8. We missed our train because we were waiting on wrong platform. ________________
9. Next train to San Diego leaves from Platform 3. ________________

71.4 状況に合うように以下から適切な語句を選び，必要に応じて the を付けて文を完成しなさい。

breakfast ~~**dinner**~~ **gate** **Gate 21** **movies** **question 8** **ocean**

1. "Are you going out tonight?" "Yes, after _dinner_."
2. There was no wind, so ________________ was very calm.
3. The test wasn't too difficult, but I couldn't answer ________________.
4. "I'm going to ________________ tonight." "Really? What are you going to see?"
5. I didn't have time for ________________ this morning because I was in a hurry.
6. Oh, ________________ is open. I must have forgotten to close it.
7. *(airport announcement)* Flight AB123 to Tokyo is now boarding at ________________.

補充問題 29 (p. 313)

UNIT 72

the の用法 2（school / the school など）

A

☆イラストを見て考えなさい。school と the school は，どのように異なりますか？

Claudia is 10 years old. Every day she goes to **school**. She's at **school** now. **School** begins at 8:30 and ends at 3:00.

➤ Claudia は学校に通う生徒です。Claudia について「学校に通っている」や「(学習のため) 学校にいる」のように，学校本来の目的に関連して考える場合，She goes to *school*. や She is at *school* now. のように無冠詞にします。この場合，特定の学校を意味しません。

Today Claudia's mother wants to speak to her daughter's teacher. So she has gone to **the school** to see her. She's at **the school** now.

➤ Claudia のお母さんは生徒ではありません。「学校」を考えても，学習には関連してきません。この場合は，She has gone to *the school*. や She is at *the school* now. のように the が付きます。the school は「Claudia の学校」のように特定の学校を意味します。

B

prison/jail, **college**, **class**, **church** についても同じように用います。場所を特定せずに本来の目的に関連して，「どの…」のようにと特定せずに全般的に考える場合は **the** を付けません。

- Ken's brother is in **prison** for robbery.（⇒ Ken の兄は刑務所で服役している。どの刑務所かは特定していない）
- When I finish **high school**, I want to go to **college**.
- Mrs. Kelly goes to **church** every Sunday.（⇒ 教会で宗教活動をする）
- I was **in class** for five hours today.（⇒ 学校にいて 5 時間の授業を受けていた）

- Ken went to **the prison** to visit his brother.（⇒ Ken は囚人ではない。「兄のいる刑務所」のように特定できる）
- Dan is a student at **the college** where I used to work.（⇒ 前に働いていた大学）
- Some workmen went to **the church** to repair the roof.（⇒ 屋根の修理なので宗教活動はしない）
- Who is the youngest student in **the class**?（⇒ そのクラスの中で）

これまで述べてきた以外の場所を表す語には，**the hospital**, **the bank**, **the station** などのように，通常の名詞と同様に状況に応じて **the** が付きます。

関連する the の用法 ➲ **Units 70C, 71D**

C

bed, work, home

go to bed / **be in bed** などのように「寝る / 寝転んで」の意味で bed を特定せずに，bed の持つ本来の目的に関連した意味で用いる場合は **the** を付けません。(✕ go to the bed, ✕ be in the bed)

- It's time to go to **bed** now.
- Do you ever have breakfast **in bed**?

⇔ ■ I sat down on **the bed**.（⇒ そのベッドで）

go to work / **be at work** / **start work** / **finish work** などのように「働く，仕事をする」などに関連した意味を持つ場合は **the** を付けません。

- Ann didn't go to **work** yesterday.
- What time do you usually finish **work**?

go home / **come work** / **arrive work** / **get home** / **be** (at) **home** などのように「帰宅する，家にいる」などを表す場合は **the** を付けません。

- It's late. Let's go **home**.
- Will you be (at) **home** tomorrow afternoon?

the のその他の用法 ➲ Units 70–71, 73–76　　in bed / as school などの前置詞の用法 ➲ Units 120–122
home ➲ Unit 123D　　to/in the hospital に関連したイギリス英語の用法 ➲ 付録 7

Exercises

72.1 状況に合うように以下から語句を選び，適切な前置詞（to/at/in など）の後に続けて文を完成しなさい。

bed ~~**college**~~ **home** **prison** **school** **high school** **work**

1. When Julie finishes high school, she wants to study economics *in college* .
2. In Mexico, children from the age of six have to go ________ .
3. Mark didn't go out last night. He stayed ________ .
4. There is a lot of traffic in the morning when everybody is going ________ .
5. Jeff hasn't graduated yet. He is still ________ .
6 Bill never gets up before 9:00. It's 8:30 now, so he is still ________ .
7. If you commit a serious crime, you could be sent ________ .

72.2 状況に合うように（ ）内の語を用いて，文を完成しなさい。必要に応じて the を付けること。

1. (**school**)
   a) Every semester parents are invited to *the school* to meet the teachers.
   b) Why aren't your children in *school* today? Are they sick?
   c) When he was younger, Ted hated ________ .
   d) What time does ________ usually start in your country?
   e) *A:* How do your children get home from ________ ? By bus?
   B: No, they walk. ________ isn't very far away.
   f) What sort of job does Jenny want to do when she finishes ________ ?
   g) There were some people waiting outside ________ to meet their children.
2. (**college**)
   a) In your country, do many people go to ________ ?
   b) The Smiths have four children in ________ at the same time.
   c) This is only a small town, but ________ is one of the best in the country.
3. (**church**)
   a) John's mother is a regular churchgoer. She goes to ________ every Sunday.
   b) John himself doesn't go to ________ .
   c) John went to ________ to take some pictures of the building.
4. (**class**)
   a) The professor isn't in his office at this time. He's in ________ .
   b) The teacher asked ________ to turn off their cell phones.
   c) I'll get a newspaper on my way to ________ this afternoon.
   d) Not even the best student in ________ could answer the question.
5. (**prison**)
   a) In some places people are in ________ because of their political beliefs.
   b) A few days ago, the fire department was called to ________ to put out a fire.
   c) The judge decided to fine the man $500 instead of sending him to ________ .
6. (**home**/**work**/**bed**)
   a) I like to read in ________ before I go to sleep.
   b) It's nice to travel around, but there's no place like ________ !
   c) Should we meet after ________ tomorrow?
   d) If I'm feeling tired, I go to ________ early.
   e) What time do you usually start ________ in the morning?
   f) The economic situation was very bad. Many people were out of ________ .

補充問題 29 (p. 313)

UNIT 73

the の用法 3 (children / the children)

A

物や人を全般的に話題にする場合，**複数可算名詞**や**不可算名詞**に the を付けずに単独で用います。

- I'm afraid of **dogs**. (× the dogs)
  (⇒ 全般的に犬が嫌い。一部の犬に限ったことではない)
- **Doctors** are paid more than **teachers**.
- Do you collect **stamps**?
- **Crime** is a problem in most big cities. (× The crime)
- **Life** has changed a lot in the last 30 years. (× The life)
- Do you like **classical music** / **Chinese food** / **fast cars**?
- My favorite sport is **football**/**skiing**/**hockey**.
- My favorite subject at school was **history**/**physics**/**English**.

most people / **most** books / **most** cars などのように，特定せずに「たいていの…」を表す場合は the は付けません。

- **Most hotels** accept credit cards. (× The most hotels)

B

物や人について具体的に特定する場合には the を付けます。

☆ 例文で考えなさい。the のない形とある形は，どのように異なりますか？

➤ the を付けない：物や人を全般的に話題にする	➤ the を付ける：物や人について具体的に特定する
Children learn from playing. (⇒ 単独の複数可算名詞。子どもというものは…，子ども全般)	We took **the children** to the zoo. (⇒ どの子どもか特定できる。おそらくは「話し手の子ども」)
I couldn't live without **music**.	The movie wasn't very good, but I liked **the music**. (⇒ その映画中の音楽)
All **cars** have wheels.	All **the cars** in this parking lot belong to people who work here.
Sugar isn't very good for you. (⇒ 単独の不可算名詞。砂糖というものは…)	Can you pass **the sugar**, please? (⇒ そのテーブルの上の砂糖)
Do **Americans** drink much tea? (⇒ アメリカ人全般)	Do **the Americans you know** drink tea? (⇒ あなたの知っているアメリカ人。アメリカ人全般を指し示していない)

C

指示しているのが，「物や人全般」なのか「特定された物や人」なのか明確ではない場合があります。修飾要素で限定していても，特定していない場合には the は付きません。

the を付けずに，物や人全般を指し示す	the を付けて，複数の物や人について具体的に特定する
I like working with **people**. (⇒ 人というものは…。人全般)	
I like working with **people who are lively**. (⇒ 元気のよい人たち。すべての人を意味しないが，具体的にどの人々かは特定していない)	I like **the people I work with**. (⇒ 私が一緒に仕事をしている（あの）人たち。どの人々か具体的に特定している)
Do you like **coffee**? (⇒ コーヒー全般)	
Do you like **strong black coffee**? (⇒ 濃いめのブラックコーヒー。具体的にどのコーヒーかは特定していない)	Did you like **the coffee we had after dinner last night**? (⇒ 夕食後に飲んだ（あの）コーヒー)

the のその他の用法 ➲ Units 71–72　　the young / the English などの the + 形容詞用法 ➲ Unit 74

Exercises

73.1 まず，自分が好きであったり嫌いであったりする事柄を以下から 4 つ選びます。

boxing	**cats**	**fast food restaurants**	**football**	~~**hot weather**~~
math	**opera**	**small children**	**rock music**	**zoos**

次に，選んだ事柄について以下の表現で始めて，自分のことを記述する文を完成しなさい。

I like . . . / I don't like . . . **I don't mind . . .**
I love . . . / I hate . . . **I'm interested in . . . / I'm not interested in . . .**

1. *I don't like hot weather very much.*
2. ______
3. ______
4. ______
5. ______

73.2 状況に合うように，以下から適切な語を選んで文を完成しなさい。必要に応じて the を付けること。

~~(the) **basketball**~~	(the) **grass**	(the) **patience**	(the) **people**
(the) **questions**	(the) **meat**	~~(the) **information**~~	(the) **hotels**
(the) **history**	(the) **water**	(the) **spiders**	(the) **lies**

1. My favorite sport is *basketball* .
2. *The information* we were given wasn't correct.
3. Some people are afraid of ______ .
4. A vegetarian is somebody who doesn't eat ______ .
5. The test wasn't very difficult. I answered ______ without any trouble.
6. Do you know ______ who live next door?
7. ______ is the study of the past.
8. George always tells the truth. He never tells ______ .
9. We couldn't find anywhere to stay downtown. All ______ were full.
10. ______ in the pool didn't look very clean, so we didn't go swimming.
11. Don't sit on ______ . It's wet from the rain.
12. You need ______ to teach young children.

73.3 状況に合うように，下線部から適切な語句を選んで文を完成しなさい。

1. I'm afraid of dogs / ~~the dogs~~.（dogs が正しい）
2. Can you pass ~~salt~~ / the salt, please?（the salt が正しい）
3. Apples / The apples are good for you.
4. Look at apples / the apples on that tree! They're very big.
5. Women / The women live longer than men / the men.
6. I don't drink tea / the tea. I don't like it.
7. We had a very good meal. Vegetables / The vegetables were especially good.
8. Life / The life is strange sometimes. Some very strange things happen.
9. I like skiing / the skiing, but I'm not very good at it.
10. Who are people / the people in this photograph?
11. What makes people / the people violent? What causes aggression / the aggression?
12. All books / All the books on the top shelf belong to me.
13. Don't stay in that hotel. It's very noisy and beds / the beds are very uncomfortable.
14. A pacifist is somebody who is against war / the war.
15. First World War / The First World War lasted from 1914 until 1918.
16. I'd like to go to Egypt and see Pyramids / the Pyramids.
17. Someone gave me a book about history / the history of modern art / the modern art.
18. Ron and Brenda got married, but marriage / the marriage didn't last very long.
19. Most people / The most people believe that marriage / the marriage and family life / the family life are the basis of society / the society.

補充問題 29 (p. 313)

UNIT 74

the の用法 4 (the giraffe / the telephone / the piano など, the + 形容詞)

A

☆ 例文で考えなさい。the + 単数可算名詞は何を表しますか？

- **The giraffe** is the tallest of all animals.
- **The bicycle** is an excellent means of transportation.
- When was **the telephone** invented?
- **The dollar** is the currency (= the money) of the United States.

➤ ここで the giraffe は「種族としてのキリン / キリンという動物」を表し，実在する 1 頭のキリンを意味しません。the + 単数可算名詞は，動物の種族や機械の種類を表します。

同様に楽器の前に **the** を置いて，「…という楽器」のように全体を表します。

- Can you play **the** guitar?
- **The** piano is my favorite instrument.

☆ a + 単数可算名詞と the + 単数可算名詞とは，どのように異なりますか？

- I'd like to have **a piano**. ⇔ I can't play **the piano**.
- We saw **a giraffe** at the zoo. ⇔ **The giraffe** is my favorite animal.

➤ どれでもよいから「1つの…」　➤「…という楽器 / 動物」

「種族としてのヒト (the human race)」は，**the** を付けずに **man** のみで表します。

- What do you know about the origins of **man**? (× the man)

B

the + 形容詞：「～である人々」を表します。以下のような表現がよく用いられます。

the young	**the rich**	**the sick**	**the blind**	**the injured**
the old	**the poor**	**the disabled**	**the deaf**	**the dead**
the elderly	**the homeless**	**the unemployed**		

the young は young people（若い人たち），**the rich** は rich people（お金持ち）などを表します。

- Do you think **the rich** should pay higher taxes?
- The government has promised to provide more money to help **the homeless**.

the + 形容詞は常に**複数**の人々を表します。1 人の人について a young や the injured のような表現は用いません。1 人の人については **a** young **person** や **the** injured **woman** などのように表現します。**複数**の人々について，**the poor** や **the young** のような表現はありますが，× the poors や × the youngs のように複数の s を付けた表現はありません。

C

the + 国籍を表す語

the French / **the English** / **the Spanish** などのように，語尾が **-ch** か **-sh** で終わる国籍を表す形容詞の前に **the** を置き「～の人々，～国人」のように，ある国に属する国民全体を表します。

- **The French** are famous for their food.（⇒ フランス人は作る料理で…）

the French / **the English** などは**複数**を表します。1 人の人について a French / an English などの表現は用いず，**a Frenchman** / **an Englishwoman** などの表現を用います。

the Chinese / **the Sudanese** / **the Japanese** などのように，語尾が **-ese** で終わる国籍を表す形容詞についても **the** を前に置き「～の人々，～国人」を表します。

- **The Chinese** invented printing.

この場合には，**a** Japan**ese** / **a** Sudan**ese**（スーダン人）/ **a** Vietnam**ese**（ベトナム人）のような単数形を持ちます。

同様に **the Swiss**（= the people of Switzerland, スイス人）は単数形 **a Swiss** を持ちます。

その他の国籍を表す語の場合，通常の可算名詞と同様に **a/an** を前に置く**単数形**と **-s** で終わる**複数形**を持ちます。

an Italian → Italians　　**a Mexican → Mexicans**　　**a Thai → Thais**

Italians などのように **-s** で終わる**複数形**を持つ場合，単独で用いられる**複数可算名詞**が「～の人々，～国人」を表すので，**the** Italians のように **the** を置いた形は特定の人々を指し，人々全般は表しません。➲ Unit 73

a/an と the の使い分け ➲ Unit 70　　the の用法 ➲ Units 71–73　　the の付く固有名詞，付かない固有名詞 ➲ Units 75–76

Exercises

74.1 以下の 1～4 から語を選び，the を前に置いて質問に対する適切な答えを作りなさい。適宜，辞書を参照しなさい。

1. *Animals*		2. *Birds*		3. *Inventions*		4. *Currencies*	
tiger	elephant	eagle	penguin	telephone	wheel	dollar	peso
rabbit	cheetah	swan	owl	telescope	laser	euro	rupee
giraffe	kangaroo	parrot	robin	helicopter	typewriter	ruble	yen

1. a) Which of the animals is the tallest? *the giraffe*
   b) Which animal can run the fastest? ______
   c) Which of these animals is found in Australia? ______
2. a) Which of these birds has a long neck? ______
   b) Which of these birds cannot fly? ______
   c) Which bird flies at night? ______
3. a) Which of these inventions is the oldest? ______
   b) Which one is the most recent? ______
   c) Which one was especially important for astronomy? ______
4. a) What is the currency of India? ______
   b) What is the currency of Canada? ______
   c) And the currency of your country? ______

74.2 空所に the もしくは a を入れて，文を完成しなさい。

1. When was *the* telephone invented?
2. Can you play ______ musical instrument?
3. Jill plays ______ violin in an orchestra.
4. There was ______ piano in the corner of the room.
5. Can you play ______ piano?
6. Our society is based on ______ family.
7. Michael comes from ______ large family.
8. ______ computer has changed the way we live.

74.3 以下から適切な語を選び，the の後に置いて文を完成しなさい。

injured poor rich sick unemployed ~~young~~

1. *The young* have the future in their hands.
2. Ambulances arrived at the scene of the accident and took ______ to the hospital.
3. Life is all right if you have a job, but things are not so easy for ______ .
4. Julia has been a nurse all her life. She has spent her life caring for ______ .
5. In England, there is an old story about a man called Robin Hood. It is said that he took money from ______ and gave the money to ______ .

74.4 それぞれの国の人について，単数形と複数形を記入しなさい。

	1人（a/an を前に置く）	全般的に「～国人」(複数)
1. Canada	*a Canadian*	*Canadians*
2. Germany		
3. France		
4. Russia		
5. China		
6. Brazil		
7. Japan		

UNIT 75

the の付く固有名詞，付かない固有名詞 1

A

人名(Ann, Ann Taylor など)には **the** を付けません。同様に，以下のように地名にも普通 **the** は付けません。

大陸	Africa (× the Africa), Asia, South America
国，州など	France (× the France), Japan, Brazil, Texas
島	Sicily, Bermuda, Vancouver Island, Cuba
都市，町など	Cairo, New York, Bangkok
山	Everest, Kilimanjaro, Fuji

一方，**Republic**（共和国），**Kingdom**（王国），**States**（州）を含む国名には **the** が付きます。

the Czech **Republic**　　**the** United **Kingdom** (the UK)
the Dominican **Republic**　　**the** United **States** of America (the USA)

☆ **the** に関して，同じ国名でもどのように異なりますか？

■ We visited **Canada** and **the United States**.

B

Mr./Mrs./Captain/Doctor など＋人名の形では **the** を付けません。

Mr. Johnson / **Doctor** Johnson / **Captain** Johnson / **President** Johnson など (× the . . .)
Uncle Robert / **Saint** Catherine / **Princess** Anne など (× the . . .)

☆ **the** に関して，**doctor** はどのように異なりますか？

■ We called **the doctor**.
We called **Doctor** Johnson. (× the Doctor Johnson)

mount/lake＋地名の形でも，同様に **the** は付けません。

Mount Everest　**Mount** McKinley　**Lake** Superior　**Lake** Victoria (× the . . .)

■ They live near **the lake**. (⇒ その湖の近く)
They live near **Lake Superior**. (⇒ スペリオル湖。the は付きません)

C

大洋，海，川，湾，運河の名前には **the** が付きます。

the Atlantic（大洋）	**the** Gulf of Mexico	**the** Amazon
the Indian Ocean	**the** Channel（イギリス海峡：「英仏海峡」とも呼ばれる）	**the** Nile
the Caribbean（海）		**the** Panama Canal

砂漠の名前にも **the** が付きます。

the Sahara (Desert)　**the** Gobi Desert

D

「～家の人々」を表す**人名の複数形**や，**複数形**で終わる**地名**には **the** が付きます。

人	**the** Mitchell**s**（ミッチェル家の人々），**the** Johnson**s**
国	**the** Netherland**s**, **the** Philippine**s**, **the** United State**s**
諸島	**the** Bahama**s**, **the** Canarie**s**, **the** Hawaiian Island**s**
山脈	**the** Rocky Mountain**s** / **the** Rockie**s**, **the** Ande**s**, **the** Alp**s**

■ The highest mountain in **the Andes** is **Mount Aconcagua**. (⇒ アンデス山脈，アコンカグア山)

E

☆ **the** に関してどのように異なりますか？

the north (of Mexico)　⇔　**northern** Mexico (⇒ the は付きません)
the southeast (of Canada)　⇔　**southeastern** Canada

➤ **north**（北）や **southeast**（南東）のような方角を表す名詞には **the** が付きますが，**northern**（北の），**southeastern**（南東の）のような形容詞には **the** は付きません。

■ Sweden is in **northern Europe**; Spain is in **the south**.

同様に，**the** Middle East（中東），**the** Far East（極東）も方角を表す名詞なので **the** が付きます。

一方，地域名や国名中に生じた **north/south** などの方角を表す名詞には **the** が付きません。

North America　**South Africa**　**southeast Texas**

地図上では，固有名詞に付けられた **the** は普通，表記されません。

the の付く固有名詞，付かない固有名詞 2 ➲ Unit 76

Exercises

75.1 必要に応じて空所に the を入れて，文を完成しなさい。何も必要ない場合には – を記入すること。

1. Who is _–_ Doctor Johnson?
2. I was sick, so I went to see ________ doctor.
3. The most powerful person in ________ United States is ________ president.
4. ________ President Kennedy was assassinated in 1963.
5. Do you know ________ Wilsons? They're a very nice couple.
6. Do you know ________ Professor Brown's phone number?

75.2 必要に応じてそれぞれの文中の名詞句に the を付けて，文を完成しなさい。

1. Everest was first climbed in 1953. _OK_
2. Sapporo is in north of Japan. _in the north of Japan_
3. Africa is much larger than Europe. ________
4. Last year I visited Mexico and United States. ________
5. South of India is warmer than north. ________
6. Portugal is in western Europe. ________
7. France and Britain are separated by Channel. ________
8. Jim has traveled a lot in Middle East. ________
9. Chicago is on Lake Michigan. ________
10. Next year we're going skiing in Swiss Alps. ________
11. UK consists of Great Britain and Northern Ireland. ________
12. Seychelles are a group of islands in Indian Ocean. ________
13. The highest mountain in Africa is Kilimanjaro. ________
14. Hudson River flows into Atlantic Ocean. ________

75.3 地名や国名などに関するそれぞれの質問の答えを以下から選び，the が必要な場合には適宜 the を入れた形を記入しなさい。英語で記述された地図を参照すること。

Continents	*Countries*	*Oceans and seas*	*Mountains*	*Rivers and canals*	
Africa	Canada	~~Atlantic Ocean~~	Alps	Amazon	Suez Canal
Asia	Denmark	Indian Ocean	Andes	Danube	Thames
Australia	Indonesia	Pacific Ocean	Himalayas	Mississippi	Volga
Europe	Sweden	Black Sea	Rockies	Nile	
North America	Thailand	Mediterranean	Urals	Panama Canal	
South America	United States	Red Sea		Rhine	

1. What do you have to cross to travel from Europe to America? _the Atlantic Ocean_
2. Where is Argentina? ________
3. What is the longest river in Africa? ________
4. Of which country is Stockholm the capital? ________
5. Of which country is Washington, D.C., the capital? ________
6. What is the name of the mountain range in the west of North America? ________
7. What is the name of the sea between Africa and Europe? ________
8. What is the smallest continent in the world? ________
9. What is the name of the ocean between North America and Asia? ________
10. What is the name of the ocean between Africa and Australia? ________
11. Which river flows through London? ________
12. Which river flows through Memphis and New Orleans? ________
13. Of which country is Bangkok the capital? ________
14. What joins the Atlantic and Pacific Oceans? ________
15. What is the longest river in South America? ________

UNIT 76

the の付く固有名詞，付かない固有名詞 2

A

the の付かない固有名詞

street（通り）/ road（道路）/ square（広場）/ park（公園）などの固有名詞には，普通 **the** は付きません。

Union **Street** （× the . . .）　Fifth **Avenue**　Central **Park**
Wilshire **Boulevard**　**Broadway**　Times **Square**

空港，駅，大学のように重要な公共の建築物や施設の名前は，以下のように2語からなる場合がよくあります。

Kennedy Airport　**Cambridge University**

上の例では，最初の語は Kennedy のような人名や Cambridge のような地名を表します。このような場合には普通 **the** を置きません。同様な構造を持ち **the** を付けない固有名詞には，次のようなものがあります：

Penn Station （× the . . .）　**Boston University**　**Carnegie Hall**
Lincoln Center　**Buckingham Palace**

☆ **同じ地名でも，the に関してどのように異なりますか？**

Buckingham Palace （× the . . .） ⇔ **the Royal Palace**

（Royal は形容詞で，Buckinghan のような地名ではないことに注意）

B

上のセクション **A** 以外の建築物や施設の名前には，普通 **the** が付きます。

ホテル / レストラン	**the** Sheraton **Hotel**, **the** Delhi **Restaurant**, **the** Holiday **Inn**（⇒ ホテル）
演劇場 / 映画館	**the** Shubert **Theater**, **the** Cineplex **Odeon**（⇒ 映画館）
美術館 / ギャラリー	**the** Guggenheim **Museum**, **the** National **Gallery**
その他の建築物 / 橋	**the** Empire State **Building**, **the** White **House**, **the** Brooklyn **Bridge**

施設の種類を表す名詞はよく省略されます。

the Sheraton (Hotel)　**the Palace** (Theater)　**the Guggenheim** (Museum)

the ＋ **名詞**だけで表される固有名詞もあります。

the Acropolis　**the Kremlin**　**the Pentagon**

C

of を含む固有名詞は普通 **the** が付きます。

the Bank of England　**the** Museum of Modern Art
the Great Wall of China　**the** Tower of London

☆ **いずれも大学名を表しますが，どのような場合に the が付きますか？**

the University of Michigan ⇔ **Michigan State University**（⇒ the が付きません）

D

店，レストラン，ホテル，銀行などは，創設者の名前を持つことがよくあります。創設者の名前は -'s や -s で終わり，前に **the** を置きません。

Joe's Diner　**McDonald's**　**Macy's**（⇒ デパート）

教会名は St. ～のように表され，聖人の名前を持つことがよくあります。この場合にも **the** は付きません。

St. John's Church （× the St. John's Church）　**St. Patrick's Cathedral**

E

新聞や組織の名前には，普通 **the** が付きます。

新聞	**the** Washington Post, **the** Financial Times, **the** Tribune
組織	**the** European Union, **the** BBC, **the** Red Cross

企業や航空会社の名前には，普通 **the** が付きません。

Fiat （× the Fiat）　**Sony**　**Delta Air Lines**
Coca-Cola　**Apple Computer**　**Cambridge University Press**

the の付く固有名詞，付かない固有名詞 1 ➲ Unit 75

Exercises

76.1 地図を見て質問に答えます。地図上に示された場所や通りの名前を記述して，答えの文を完成しなさい（必要に応じて the を用いること）。地図上では普通，固有名詞に与えられる the は表記されません。

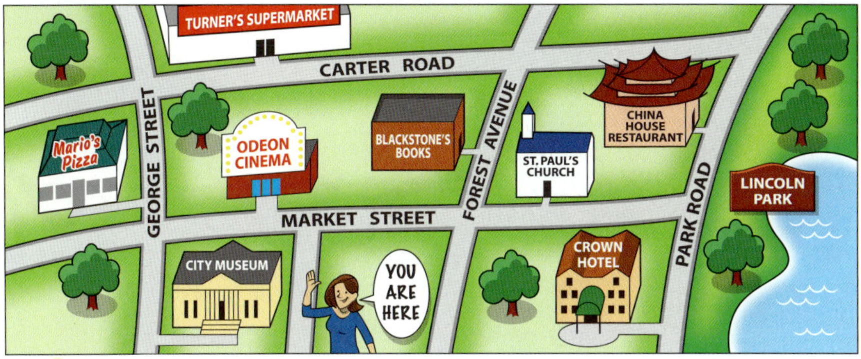

1. Is there a movie theater near here? — Yes, _the Odeon on Market Street_ .
2. Is there a supermarket near here? — Yes, ______ on ______ .
3. Is there a hotel near here? — Yes, ______ on ______ .
4. Is there a church near here? — Yes, ______ .
5. Is there a museum near here? — Yes, ______ .
6. Is there a bookstore near here? — Yes, ______ .
7. Is there a park near here? — Yes, ______ at the end of ______ .
8. Is there a restaurant near here? — There are two. ______ or ______ .

76.2 以下のそれぞれの固有名詞がどこにあるかを表す文を完成しなさい。必要に応じて the を付けること。

Acropolis **Broadway** **Buckingham Palace** **Eiffel Tower**
Kremlin **White House** **Taj Mahal** ~~**Times Square**~~

1. _Times Square_ is in New York.
2. ______ is in Paris.
3. ______ is in Agra, India.
4. ______ is in Washington, D.C.
5. ______ is in Moscow.
6. ______ is in New York.
7. ______ is in Athens.
8. ______ is in London.

76.3 下線部には the のある形とない形が示されています。正しい方を選んで文を完成しなさい。

1. Have you ever been to ~~British Museum~~ / the British Museum?（the British Museum が正しい）
2. The biggest park in New York is Central Park / the Central Park.
3. My favorite park in London is St. James's Park / the St. James's Park.
4. Ramada Inn / The Ramada Inn is on Main Street / the Main Street.
5. We flew to Mexico City from O'Hare Airport / the O'Hare Airport.
6. Frank is a student at McGill University / the McGill University.
7. If you're looking for a department store, I would recommend Harrison's / the Harrison's.
8. If you're looking for a place to have lunch, I would recommend Ship Inn / the Ship Inn.
9. Statue of Liberty / The Statue of Liberty is at the entrance to New York Harbor / the New York Harbor.
10. You should go to Science Museum / the Science Museum. It's very interesting.
11. John works for IBM / the IBM now. He used to work for General Electric / the General Electric.
12. "Which movie theater are you going to tonight?" "Classic / The Classic."
13. I'd like to go to China and see Great Wall / the Great Wall.
14. "Which newspaper do you want?" "Washington Post / The Washington Post."
15. This book is published by Cambridge University Press / the Cambridge University Press.

補充問題 29 (p. 313)

UNIT 77

単数か複数か注意すべき名詞

A

☆イラストで確認します。対になる部分を持ち，１つの物でありながら複数形で表す名詞には何がありますか？

物としては１つでも複数形で表されるので，**複数名詞に対応する動詞**の形を用います。

- My **pants are** too long. (× my pants is)

このような名詞について **a pair of** ＋**名詞複数形**で表すこともあります。

- **Those are** nice **jeans**. = That**'s a** nice **pair** of jeans. (× a nice jeans)
- I need **some** new **glasses**. = I need **a** new **pair of** glasses.

B

以下のように「～学」や「～術」などの意味を持つ **-ics** で終わる名詞は，**-s** で終わっていても**単数名詞に対応する動詞**の形を用います。

economics　**electronics**　**gymnastics**　**mathematics**　**physics**　**politics**

- **Gymnastics** is my favorite sport. (× Gymnastics are)

news も**単数名詞**として扱います。➲Unit 68B

- What time **is the news** on television? (× are the news)

以下のような **-s** で終わる名詞は，**単数**としても**複数**としても扱います。

means	**a means** of transportation	**many means** of transportation
series	**a** television **series**	**two** television **series**
species	**a species** of bird	**200 species** of birds

C

police は形は単数形でも，**複数名詞に対応する動詞**の形を用います。

- The **police are** investigating the murder, but **haven't** arrested anyone yet. (× The police is . . . hasn't)

１人の警察官は，**a police officer** / **a policeman** / **a policewoman** のように表します。(× a police)

D

person の複数形として persons はあまり用いず，代わりに **people** を用います(people は複数として扱います)。

- He's **a** nice **person**. ⇔ They are nice **people**. (× nice persons)
- **Many people don't** have enough to eat. (× Many people doesn't)

E

合計金額，期間，距離などは**単数**として扱い，**単数名詞に対応する動詞**の形を用います。

- **Twenty thousand dollars** (＝it) **was** stolen in the robbery. (× were stolen)
- **Three years** (＝it) **is** a long time to be without a job. (× Three years are)
- **Six miles is** a long way to walk every day.

the の付く固有名詞，付かない固有名詞 ➲Units 75–76

Exercises

77.1 セクションAとBの中の単語を空所に入れて，文を完成しなさい。必要に応じてaもしくはsomeを前に置くこと。

1. My eyesight isn't very good. I need __glasses__ .
2. __A species__ is a group of animals or plants that have the same characteristics.
3. Soccer players don't wear pants when they play. They wear ____________ .
4. The bicycle is ____________ of transportation.
5. The bicycle and the car are ____________ of transportation.
6. I want to cut this piece of material. I need ____________ .
7. A friend of mine is writing ____________ of articles for the local newspaper.
8. There are a lot of American TV ____________ shown throughout the world.
9. While we were out walking, we saw 25 different ____________ of birds.

77.2 それぞれの3つの単語が表す学問名などを空所に記入しなさい。名称の書き出しは与えられたものを使用すること。

1. calculate	algebra	equation	m athematics
2. government	election	senator	p ____________
3. finance	trade	employment	e ____________
4. light	heat	gravity	ph ____________
5. exercises	somersault	parallel bars	gy ____________
6. computer	silicon chip	video games	el ____________

77.3 下線部には単数名詞と複数名詞に対応する形が示されています。正しい方を選んで文を完成しなさい。

1. Gymnastics is / ~~are~~ my favorite sport. (isが正しい)
2. The pants you bought for me doesn't / don't fit me.
3. The police want / wants to interview two men about the robbery last week.
4. Physics was / were my best subject at school.
5. Can I borrow your scissors? Mine isn't / aren't sharp enough.
6. Fortunately the news wasn't / weren't as bad as we expected.
7. Three days isn't / aren't long enough for a good vacation.
8. I can't find my binoculars. Do you know where it is / they are?
9. It's a nice place to visit. The people is / are very friendly.
10. Does / Do the police know how the accident happened?
11. I don't like very hot weather. Ninety degrees is / are too hot for me.

77.4 それぞれの文について誤りのある部分を○で囲み，正しい形に書き直しなさい。

1. (Three years are) a long time to be without a job. __Three years is a long time__
2. The news is very depressing these days. __OK__
3. Susan was wearing a black jeans. ____________
4. I like Matt and Jill. They're very nice persons. ____________
5. I need more than ten dollars. Ten dollars isn't enough. ____________
6. I'm going to buy a new pajama. ____________
7. There was a police directing traffic on the street. ____________
8. What are the police going to do? ____________
9. This scissors isn't very sharp. ____________
10. Do you think two days are enough to see all the sights of Toronto? ____________
11. Many people has heard about the problem. ____________

UNIT 78

名詞＋名詞で作られる名詞 (a tennis ball / a headache など)

A

名詞＋名詞のように２つの名詞を並べて，１つの物や人を表します。

a **tennis ball** a **bank manager** a **car accident**
income tax the **water temperature**

この形では最初の名詞が形容詞的な働きをして，どのような物や人であるかを具体的に表します。

☆＝に注目し，それぞれがどのような物や人であるかを考えなさい。

a **tennis ball** = a **ball** used to play **tennis**（⇒テニスボール）
a **car accident** = an **accident** that happens while driving a **car**
income tax = **tax** that you pay on your **income**
the **water temperature** = the **temperature** of the **water**
a **Boston doctor** = a **doctor** from **Boston**
my **life story** = the **story** of my **life**

☆それぞれはどのような物や人ですか？

a **television** camera a **television** program a **television** studio a **television** producer

➤いずれも **television**（テレビ）に関係しますが，それぞれは異なる物や人を表します。

language **problems** marriage **problems** health **problems** work **problems**

➤それぞれは性質が異なるものの，本質的には **problem**（問題）です。

☆＝に注目し，それぞれがどのように異なるかを考えなさい。

garden vegetables（= **vegetables** that are grown in a garden，庭で栽培される野菜）
a **vegetable garden**（= a **garden** where vegetables are grown，野菜が栽培される庭）

最初の名詞が -ing で終わる場合があります。この場合 **-ing** は「〜するための…」のように次の名詞を説明します。

a **frying** pan a **sleeping** bag（⇒眠るための袋，寝袋） a **swimming** pool a **dining** room

３つ以上の名詞がまとまって１つの物や人を表す場合もあります。

- I waited at the **hotel reception desk**.
- We watched the **World Swimming Championships** on television.
- Everyone is talking about the **government corruption scandal**.

B

このように２つの名詞がまとまって１つの名詞になる場合，**1語**で表記される場合もあれば，**2語**で表記される場合もあります。

a **headache** **toothpaste** a **weekend** **pea soup** a **road sign**

表記を１語で行うのか，２語で行うのかはっきりとした決まりはありません。よくわからない場合には２語で表記します。

C

☆（ ）内の記述に注目し，それぞれがどのように異なるかを考えなさい。

a **sugar bowl**（⇒ボウルには何も入っていなくてもよい） ⇔ a **bowl of sugar**（⇒ボウルには砂糖が入っている）
a **toolbox**（⇒箱には何も入っていなくてもよい） ⇔ a **box of tools**（⇒箱には道具が詰まっている）

D

名詞＋名詞の形で，形容詞的な働きをする**最初の名詞**は，形の上では普通，**単数形**になります。しかし，多くの場合**複数**の意味を表します。例えば，a **book**store（書店）は複数の本（books）を売る店であり，an **apple** tree は複数のりんご（apples）がなる木を表します。

☆＝や×に注目し，名詞＋名詞の最初の名詞の形と意味がどのようになっているかを考えなさい。最初の名詞は「数詞-(ハイフン）名詞」の形で表されています。

a three-**hour** trip（= a trip that takes three **hours**）
a 10-**dollar** bill（× dollars）
a four-**week** course（× weeks）
two 14-**year**-old girls（× years）
a six-**page** letter（× pages）
a two-**story** house（× stories）

☆それぞれの形と意味を確認しなさい。

- It was **a** three-**hour** trip. ⇔ The trip took three **hours**.

-'s と of ... ➲ Unit 79 a week's vacation / three weeks' vacation など ➲ Unit 79E

Exercises

78.1 それぞれの物や人を定義する文を完成しなさい。「名詞 + 名詞」の形を用いること。

1. A ticket for a concert is *a concert ticket*.
2. Problems concerning health are *health problems*.
3. A magazine about computers is ______.
4. Pictures taken on your vacation are your ______.
5. Chocolate made with milk is ______.
6. Somebody whose job is to inspect factories is ______.
7. A horse that runs in races is ______.
8. A race for horses is ______.
9. A lawyer in Los Angeles is ______.
10. The results of your exams are your ______.
11. The carpet in the dining room is ______.
12. A scandal involving an oil company is ______.
13. A building with five stories is ______.
14. A plan to improve traffic is ______.
15. A course that lasts five days is ______.
16. A question that has two parts is ______.
17. A girl who is seven years old is ______.

78.2 それぞれの説明は何を表していますか？ 以下から 2 つの名詞を選んで「名詞 + 名詞」の形で答えなさい。

~~accident~~	belt	card	credit	editor	forecast	newspaper
number	~~car~~	room	seat	shop	weather	window

1. This can be caused by bad driving. *a car accident*
2. If you're staying at a hotel, you need to remember this. your ______
3. You should wear this when you're in a car. a ______
4. You can often use this to pay for things instead of cash. a ______
5. If you want to know if it's going to rain, you can read or listen to this. the ______
6. This person is a top journalist. a ______
7. You might stop to look in this when you're walking along a street. a ______

78.3 状況に合うように以下から適切な語句を選び，必要に応じて単数形 (day/page など) もしくは複数形 (days/pages など) にして文を完成しなさい。

15 minute(s)	six mile(s)	five day(s)	~~10 page(s)~~
six mile(s)	two hour(s)	five course(s)	500 year(s)
60 minute(s)	20 dollar(s)	two year(s)	~~450 page(s)~~

1. It's quite a long book. There are *450 pages*.
2. A few days ago I received a *10-page* letter from Julia.
3. I didn't have any change. I only had a ______ bill.
4. At work in the morning I usually have a ______ break for coffee.
5. There are ______ in an hour.
6. It's only a ______ flight from New York to Montreal.
7. It was a very big meal. There were ______.
8. Mary has just started a new job. She's got a ______ contract.
9. The oldest building in the city is the ______ castle.
10. I work ______ a week. Saturday and Sunday are free.
11. We went for a long walk in the country. We walked ______.
12. We went for a ______ walk in the country.

UNIT 79

-'s (your sister's name) と of ... (the name of the book)

A

「… の ～」のような所属や所有の意味は，**-'s**（アポストロフィ s）もしくは **of ...** で表されます。
-'s は普通，人や動物を表す名詞に付きます。

- **Tom's** computer isn't working. (× the computer of Tom)
- How old are **Chris's** children? (× the children of Chris)
- What's (= What is) **your sister's** name?
- What's **Tom's sister's** name?
- Be careful. Don't step on **the cat's** tail.

-'s の後の名詞が省略される場合もあります。

- This isn't my book. It's **my sister's**. (= my sister's book)

人に対して，常に **-'s** を使うわけではありません。例えば次のような例では **of ...** を用います。

- What was the name **of the man who called you**?（the man who called you（あなたに電話をかけてきた人）のような関係詞節には -'s が付きません）

-'s は，次のような状況でも用います。

a woman's hat（⇒ a hat for a woman, 女性向けの帽子），**a boy's name**（⇒ a name for a boy, 男の子向けの帽子），**a bird's egg**（⇒ an egg laid by a bird，鳥が産んだ卵）

B

単数名詞には **-'s** を付けます。

my **sister's** room（⇒ 妹もしくは姉の 1 人の部屋）　**Mr. Carter's** house（⇒ カーター氏 1 人の家）

sisters, friends などのように **-s** で終わる複数名詞には，単語の終わりに**アポストロフィ（ ' ）**のみを付けます。

my sisters' room（⇒ 2 人以上の姉妹の部屋）
the Carters' house（⇒ カーター夫妻の家 / カーター家の家）

men, women, children, people のように **-s** で終わらない複数名詞には **-'s** を付けます。

the men's changing room　a **children's** book (= a book for children)

以下のような場合には，2 語以上で構成される名詞でも **-'s** が付きます。

Jack and Karen's wedding　**Mr. and Mrs. Carter's** house

C

物や抽象的な考えなどには普通，～ **of the book** / ～ **of the restaurant** のように **of ...** を用います。**-'s** は用いません。

the door **of the garage** (× the garage's door)
the name **of the book**　the owner **of the restaurant**

-'s や **of ...** の代わりに**名詞＋名詞**の形をとる場合もあります。➲Unit 78

the **garage door**　the **restaurant owner**

the beginning/end/middle of ...，**the top/bottom of ...**，**the front/back/side of ...** などもよく用いられます。

the beginning of the month (× the month's beginning)
the top of the hill　**the back of** the car

D

組織や集団には普通，**-'s** と **of ...** のいずれの形も使えます。

the government's decision = the decision **of the government**
the company's success = the success **of the company**

人や動物ではありませんが，場所を表す名詞に **-'s** を付けることがあります。

the city's streets　**the world's** population　**Brazil's** largest city

E

人や動物ではありませんが，**yesterday** / **next week** など，時を表す表現に **-'s** を付けることがあります。

- Do you still have **yesterday's** newspaper?
- **Next week's** meeting has been canceled.

この他，**today's/tomorrow's/tonights's/Monday's** などのような表現もよく用いられます。
期間を表す表現にも **-'s**（-s で終わる複数形にはアポストロフィのみ（ ' ））を付けることがあります。

- I've got **a week's** vacation starting on Monday.
- Sally needs **eight hours'** sleep a night.
- Brenda got to work 15 minutes late but lost **an hour's** pay.

the garage door のような「名詞＋名詞」の形 ➲ Unit 78　a three-hour trip, a 10-dollar bill ➲ Unit 78D

Exercises

79.1 それぞれの下線部が of ... の形ではなく，-'s や -' の形を用いたほうがより自然になるものを選び，適切な形に変えなさい。

1. Who is the owner of this restaurant? _OK_
2. Where are the children of Chris? _Chris's children_
3. Is this the umbrella of your friend? ______
4. Write your name at the top of the page. ______
5. I've never met the daughter of Charles. ______
6. Have you met the son of Mary and Dan? ______
7. We don't know the cause of the problem. ______
8. Do we still have the newspaper of yesterday? ______
9. What's the name of this street? ______
10. What is the cost of a new computer? ______
11. The friends of your children are here. ______
12. The garden of our neighbors is very nice. ______
13. I work on the ground floor of the building. ______
14. The hair of Bill is very long. ______
15. I couldn't go to the party of Catherine. ______
16. What's the name of the woman who lives next door? ______
17. Have you seen the car of the parents of Mike? ______
18. What's the meaning of this expression? ______
19. Do you agree with the economic policy of the government? ______

79.2 's を用いて書き直しなさい。

1. a hat for a woman _a woman's hat_
2. a name for a boy ______
3. clothes for children ______
4. a school for girls ______
5. a nest for a bird ______
6. a magazine for women ______

79.3 下線部の語を文頭に置いて，文全体を書き直しなさい。

1. The meeting tomorrow has been canceled.
   Tomorrow's meeting has been canceled.
2. The storm last week caused a lot of damage.
   Last ______
3. The only movie theater in the town has closed down.
   The ______
4. The weather in Chicago is very changeable.
   ______
5. Tourism is the main industry in the region.
   ______

79.4 (　) 内の語を用いて，状況を説明する文を完成しなさい。

1. I bought groceries at the supermarket last night. They will last us for a week.
   So I bought _a week's groceries_ last night. (groceries)
2. Kim got a new car. It cost the same as her salary for a year.
   So Kim's new car cost her ______ . (salary)
3. Jim lost his job. His company gave him extra money equal to his pay for four weeks.
   So Jim got ______ when he lost his job. (pay)
4. Last night I went to bed at midnight and woke up at 5 a.m. After that I couldn't sleep.
   So I only had ______ . (sleep)
5. I haven't been able to rest all day. I haven't rested for even a minute.
   So I haven't had ______ all day. (rest)

UNIT 80

myself/yourself/themselves などの再帰代名詞

A

☆ イラストを見て考えなさい。自己紹介をしている Steve の動作はどのように記述できますか？

➤ 以下のように **himself** を用いて記述します。

Steve **introduced himself** to the other guests.

主語と目的語が同一の人を表す場合，**myself/yourself/himself** などの**再帰代名詞**を用います。

Steve 主語 introduced **himself** 目的語

再帰代名詞には，次のようなものがあります。

単数	my**self**	your**self**（あなた自身）	him**self**/her**self**/it**self**
複数	our**selves**	your**selves**（あなたたち自身）	them**selves**

- I don't want you to pay for me. **I**'ll pay for **myself**. (× I'll pay for me)
- Julia had a great vacation. **She** really enjoyed **herself**.
- 〔1人の人に向かって〕Do **you** talk to **yourself** sometimes?
- 〔複数の人に向かって〕If **you** want more to eat, help **yourselves**.

☆ 以下の動詞 blame（〜を非難する）の構文で，非難する人とされる人は，どのように異なりますか？

- It's not our fault. **You** can't blame **us**.
- It's our own fault. **We** should blame **ourselves**.

B

動詞 **feel/relax/concentrate/meet** は，**myself** のような**再帰代名詞**を目的語にしません。

- I **feel** nervous. I can't **relax**.
- You have to try and **concentrate**. (× concentrate yourself)
- What time should we **meet**? (× meet ourselves, × meet us)

動詞 **wash/shave/dress** は，普通 **myself** のような**再帰代名詞**を目的語にしません。

- He got up, **washed**, **shaved**, and **dressed**. (× washed himself など)

「着替える」の意味では **dress** 以外に，**get dressed** のような表現もよく用います。(He **got dressed**.)

C

☆ イラストで考えます。-selves と each other は，どのように異なりますか？

- Kate and Joe stood in front of the mirror and looked at **themselves**.
  (⇒ それぞれをそれぞれの鏡で見た)
- Kate looked at Joe; Joe looked at Kate. They looked at **each other**. (⇒ お互いに見つめあった)

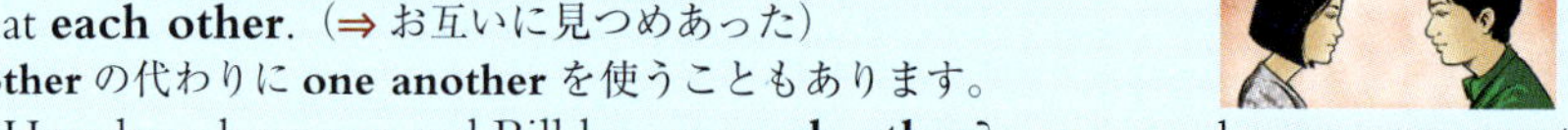

each other の代わりに **one another** を使うこともあります。

- How long have you and Bill known **each other**? = . . . known **one another**?
- Sue and Ann don't like **each other**. = . . . don't like **one another**.
- Do you and Sarah live near **each other**? = . . . near **one another**?

D

主語と目的語が同一ではない場合にも，**myself/yourself** などの**再帰代名詞**を用いることがあります。

- "Who repaired your bicycle for you?" "**I** repaired it **myself**."

I repaired it **myself**. は「他ならぬ私が修理した」の意味で，**myself** は **I** を強調します。

☆ それぞれの再帰代名詞は何を強調していますか？

- I'm not going to do your work for you. **You** can do it **yourself**. (⇒ 私ではなくあなたが)
- **Let's** paint the house **ourselves**. It will be much cheaper.
- The **movie itself** wasn't very good, but I loved the music.
- I don't think Sue will get the job. **Sue herself** doesn't think she'll get it.
  (= **Sue** doesn't think she'll get it **herself**. Sue 自身も考えていない)

get dressed / get married など get を用いた用法 ➲ Unit 42D　　by myself / by yourself など ➲ Unit 81D

Exercises

80.1 状況に合うように，以下から動詞を選び適切な形に変え，myself/yourself などの再帰代名詞を後に置いて文を完成しなさい。

blame　burn　enjoy　express　hurt　~~introduce~~　put

1. Steve *introduced himself* to the other guests at the party.
2. Bill fell down some steps, but fortunately he didn't ______ badly.
3. It isn't Sue's fault. She really shouldn't ______.
4. Please try and understand how I feel. ______ in my position.
5. The children had a great time at the beach. They really ______.
6. Be careful! That pan is very hot. Don't ______.
7. Sometimes I can't say exactly what I mean. I wish I could ______ better.

80.2 状況に合うように，myself/yourself/ourselves などの再帰代名詞と me/you/us などの代名詞の目的格の中から適切なものを選び，空所に入れて文を完成しなさい。

1. Julia had a great vacation. She enjoyed *herself*.
2. It's not my fault. You can't blame ______.
3. What I did was really bad. I'm ashamed of ______.
4. We've got a problem. I hope you can help ______.
5. "Can I have another cookie?" "Of course. Help ______!"
6. I want you to meet Sarah. I'll introduce ______ to her.
7. Don't worry about Tom and me. We can take care of ______.
8. I gave them a key to our house so that they could let ______ in.
9. I didn't want anybody to see the letters, so I burned ______.

80.3 状況に合うように，以下から動詞を選び適切な形に変え，myself/yourself などの再帰代名詞を必要に応じて後に置いて文を完成しなさい。

concentrate　defend　dry　~~feel~~　meet　relax

1. I was sick yesterday, but I *feel* much better today.
2. She climbed out of the swimming pool and ______ with a towel.
3. I tried to study, but I couldn't ______.
4. If somebody attacks you, you need to be able to ______.
5. I'm going out with Chris tonight. We're ______ at 7:30.
6. You're always rushing around. Why don't you sit down and ______?

80.4 状況に合うように，-selves の形の再帰代名詞もしくは each other のいずれかを空所に入れて文を完成しなさい。

1. How long have you and Bill known *each other*?
2. If people work too hard, they can make ______ sick.
3. I need you and you need me. We need ______.
4. In the U.S., friends often give ______ presents at Christmas.
5. Some people are very selfish. They think only of ______.
6. Tracy and I don't see ______ very often these days.
7. We couldn't get back into the house. We had locked ______ out.
8. They've had an argument. They're not speaking to ______ at the moment.
9. We'd never met before, so we introduced ______ to ______.

80.5 状況に合うように，myself/yourself/itself などの再帰代名詞を含む表現を用いて，質問に対する答えを完成しなさい。

1. Who repaired the bicycle for you? — Nobody. I *repaired it myself.*
2. Who cuts Brian's hair for him? — Nobody. He cuts ______
3. Do you want me to mail that letter for you? — No, I'll ______
4. Who told you that Linda was getting married? — Linda ______
5. Can you call John for me? — Why can't you ______?

UNIT 81

a friend of **mine** **my own** house **by myself**

A

a friend of mine / a friend of Tom's など

a friend **of mine/yours/his/hers/ours/theirs** は「…の友達」を意味します。

- I'm going to a wedding on Saturday. **A friend of mine** is getting married. (✕ a friend of me)
- We took a trip with **some friends of ours**. (✕ some friends of us)
- Michael had an argument with **a neighbor of his**.
- It was **a good idea of yours** to go to the movies.

my sister や **Tom** などの名詞には，**a friend of my sister's/Tom's** などのように **-'s** を付けた形を用います。

- That woman over there is **a friend of my sister's**.
- It was **a good idea of Tom's** to go to the movies.

B

my own . . . / your own . . . など

own は以下のように，直前に **my/your/his** などの所有格代名詞を置いて用います：

my own house　**your own** car　**her own** room
(✕ an own house, ✕ an own car など)

my/your/his/her/its/our/their + own + 名詞は，「…自身の～」のように，名詞が「私 / あなた / 彼」などの所有物で，他人と共有したり借りたものではないことを表します。

- I don't want to share a room with anybody. I want **my own room**.
- Vicky and George would like to have **their own house**.
- It's a shame that the apartment doesn't have **its own parking space**.
- It's **my own fault** that I don't have any money. I buy too many things I don't need.
- Why do you want to borrow my car? Why don't you use **your own**? (= your own car)

動詞 + my/your など + own + 名詞の形で，「自分で自分の～を…する」のように人に頼らず自分で何かをすることを表します。

- Bill usually cuts **his own hair**. (⇒ 床屋には行かずに，自分で自分の髪の毛を切る)
- I'd like to have a garden so that I could grow **my own vegetables**. (⇒ 店で買うのではなく，自分で栽培する)

Bill usually cuts **his own hair**.

C

on my own / on your own など

「他人に頼らず，独立して，一人で」を表します。(= independently)

- My children are living **on their own**. (⇒ 親元を離れ，独立して生計を立てている)
- I traveled around Japan **on my own**. (⇒ ツアー旅行ではなく，一人旅で)
- Are you raising your children **on your own**? (⇒ 一人で，離婚した配偶者に頼らずに)

D

by myself / by yourself など

「一人ぼっちで，他人を伴わずに」を表します。(= alone, without other people)

- I like living **by myself**. (⇒ 一人で暮らすのが好き)
- "Did you go to Hawaii **by yourself**?" "No, with a friend."
- Jack was sitting **by himself** in a corner of the café.
- Student drivers are not allowed to drive **by themselves**.

myself/yourself/themselves など ➲ Unit 80

Exercises

81.1 セクションAの **a friend of mine** などの形を用いて下線部の表現を書き換え，同じ意味を表す文を完成しなさい。

1. I am meeting one of my friends tonight. *I'm meeting a friend of mine tonight.*
2. We met one of your relatives. We met a ____________
3. Jason borrowed one of my books. Jason ____________
4. Ann invited some of her friends to her place. Ann ____________
5. We had dinner with one of our neighbors. ____________
6. I took a trip with two of my friends. ____________
7. Is that man one of your friends? ____________
8. I met one of Amy's friends at the party. ____________

81.2 状況に合うように以下から適切な語を選び，**my own / your own** などの後に続けて文を完成しなさい。

~~bedroom~~ **business** **opinions** **private beach** **words**

1. I share a kitchen and bathroom, but I have *my own bedroom* .
2. Gary doesn't think the same as me. He's got ____________ .
3. Julia is fed up with working for other people. She wants to start ____________ .
4. We stayed at a luxury hotel on the ocean. The hotel had ____________ .
5. On the test we had to read a story, and then write it in ____________ .

81.3 状況に合うように，**my own / your own** などの語句を用いて文を完成しなさい。

1. Why do you want to borrow my car?
   Why don't you use your own car?
2. How can you blame me? It's not my fault.
   It's ____________ .
3. She's always using my ideas.
   Why can't she use ____________ ?
4. Please don't worry about my problems.
   You've got ____________ .
5. I can't make his decisions for him.
   He has to make ____________ .

81.4 状況に合うように以下から適切な動詞を選び，**my own / your own** などの語句の前に置いて文を完成しなさい。

bake ~~cut~~ **make** **write**

1. Bill never goes to the barber. He *cuts his own hair* .
2. Mary doesn't buy many clothes. She usually ____________ .
3. We don't often buy bread. We usually ____________ .
4. Paul is a singer. He sings songs written by other people, but he also ____________
   ____________ .

81.5 状況に合うように，**on my own / by myself** などの語句を用いて文を完成しなさい。

1. Did you go to Hawaii by *yourself* ?
2. I'm glad I live with other people. I wouldn't like to live on ____________ .
3. The box was too heavy for me to lift by ____________ .
4. "Who was Tom with when you saw him?" "Nobody. He was by ____________ ."
5. I think my brother is too young to make that decision on ____________ .
6. I don't think she knows many people. When I see her, she is always by ____________ .
7. My sister graduated from college and is living on ____________ .
8. Do you like working with other people, or do you prefer working by ____________ ?
9. We had no help decorating the apartment. We did it completely on ____________ .
10. I went out with Sally because she didn't want to go out by ____________ .

UNIT 82

There ... と It ...

A

there と it

☆ レストランは，上の対話の中でどのように記述されていますか？

➤「(あなたは知らないかもしれないが) ～がある」のように，何かの存在を始めて話題にする場合は thereを用います。

- **There's** a new restaurant on Main Street. (× A new restaurant is on Main Street)
- I'm sorry I'm late. **There was** a lot of traffic. (× It was a lot of traffic)
- Things are more expensive now. **There has been** a big increase in the cost of living.

➤「それ，そこ」のように，すでに話題となっている物・場所・事実・状況を具体的に指示する場合は itを用います。（「それ，そこ」と何かを指示しない itの用法については，以下のセクション Cの例も参照のこと）

- We went to the new restaurant. **It**'s very good. (**It** = the restaurant)
- I wasn't expecting them to come. **It** was a complete surprise. (**It** = that they came)

there は存在（ある / ない）を表し，**it** は前出の名詞句を指し示します。

- I don't like this town. **There**'s nothing to do here. **It**'s a boring place.
  (⇒ 何もすることが**ない**ので，**そこ**は退屈)

there は「そこへ / そこで / そこに」のように前出の名詞句に関連して方向や場所を表すこともあります。

- The new restaurant is very good. I went **there** (= to the restaurant) last night.
- When we got to the party, there were already a lot of people **there** (= at the party).

B

there will be ～（～があるだろう），**there must be ～**（～があるに違いない），**there might be ～**（～があるかもしれない），**there used to be ～**（かつて～があった）などの形もよく用いられます。

- **Will there be** many people at the party?（⇒ たくさん来るでしょうか？）
- "**Is there** a flight to Miami tonight?" "**There might be**. I'll check."
- If people drove more carefully, **there wouldn't be** so many accidents.

there must have been ～（～があったに違いない），**there should have been ～**（～すべきだった，すればよかった）などの形もよく用いられます。

- There was music playing. **There must have been** somebody at home.

ここでも **there** は「～がある / ない」のように何かを新しく話題にするのに対し，**it** は前出の名詞句を指し示します。

- They live on a busy street. **There must be** a lot of noise from the traffic. (⇒ ～**があるに違いない**)
  They live on a busy main street. **It must be** very noisy. (⇒ **それは**～に違いない)
- **There used to be** a movie theater on Main Street, but it closed a few years ago.
  That building is now a supermarket. **It used to be** a movie theater.

there is sure/certain/likely/bound to be ～は「必ず～がある」を表します。

- **There is bound** (= sure) **to be** a flight to Miami tonight.

C

it は，以下のように文末の**不定詞**の代わりに用いられることがあります（**形式主語**としての **it**）。「それ」と指示しません。

- **It**'s dangerous to **walk in the street**. (**It** = to walk in the street)

To walk in the street is dangerous. のように，**不定詞**を主語とする形はあまり使いません。普通は **it** で文を始め，**不定詞**を文末に置きます。**it** は**不定詞**のほか，**that** 節や**動名詞**の代わりに用いられることもあります。

- **It** didn't take us long **to get here**. (**It** = to get here)
- **It**'s too bad (**that**) **Sandra can't come to the party**. (**It** = (that) Sandra can't ...)
- Let's go. **It**'s not worth **waiting any longer**. (**It** = waiting any longer)

it は，距離・時間・天候などを話題にする場合にも用います。「それ」と指示しません。

- How far is **it** from here to the airport?
- What day is **it** today?
- **It**'s been a long time since I saw you.
- **It** was windy. (⇔ **There** was **a cold wind**.)

It's worth ... / It's no use ... / There's no point ... ➲Unit 61A　There is + -ing 句 / -ed 句 ➲Unit 95

Exercises

82.1 状況に合うように，there is/was もしくは it is/was のいずれかを空所に入れて文を完成しなさい。必要に応じて疑問形（Is there ...? / Is it ...? など）や否定形（isn't/wasn't）の形にすること。

1. I'm sorry I'm late. _There was_ a lot of traffic.
2. What's the new restaurant like? _Is it_ good?
3. " ________ a bookstore near here?" "Yes, ________ one on Hill Street."
4. When we got to the movie theater, ________ a line outside. ________ a very long line, so we decided not to wait.
5. I couldn't see anything. ________ completely dark.
6. ________ trouble at the basketball game last night. They had to call the police.
7. How far ________ from Hong Kong to Taipei?
8. ________ Keith's birthday yesterday. We had a party.
9. ________ too windy to play tennis today. Let's play tomorrow instead.
10. I wanted to visit the museum, but ________ enough time.
11. " ________ time to leave?" "Yes, ________ almost midnight."
12. A few days ago ________ a storm. ________ a lot of damage.
13. ________ a beautiful day yesterday. We went on a picnic.
14. ________ anything on television, so I turned it off.
15. ________ an accident on Main Street, but ________ very serious.

82.2 例にならって，there で始まる文に書き換えなさい。

1. The roads were busy today. _There was a lot of traffic._
2. This soup is very salty. There ________ in the soup.
3. The box was empty. ________ in the box.
4. The movie was very violent. ________
5. The shopping mall was very crowded. ________ ________
6. I like this town – it's lively. ________

82.3 状況に合うように以下から適切な語句を選び，there will be / there would be などの形に変えて文を完成しなさい。

will **might** ~~**would**~~ **wouldn't** **should** **used to** **(be) going to**

1. If people drove more carefully, _there would be_ fewer accidents.
2. "Do we have any eggs?" "I'm not sure. ________ some in the fridge."
3. I think everything will be OK. I don't think ________ any problems.
4. Look at the sky. ________ a storm.
5. "Is there a school in this town?" "Not now. ________ one, but it closed."
6. People drive too fast on this road. I think ________ a speed limit.
7. If people weren't aggressive, ________ any wars.

82.4 それぞれの文について誤りのある部分を○で囲み，it もしくは there を用いて正しい形に書き直しなさい。

1. They live on a busy street. (It must be) a lot of noise. _There must be a lot of noise._
2. Last winter it was very cold, and it was a lot of snow. ________
3. It used to be a church here, but it was torn down. ________
4. Why was she so unfriendly? It must have been a reason. ________
5. It's a long way from my house to the nearest store. ________
6. *A:* Where can we park the car?
   B: Don't worry. It's sure to be a parking lot somewhere. ________
7. After the lecture, it will be an opportunity to ask questions. ________
8. I like the place where I live, but it would be nicer to live by the ocean. ________
9. I was told that it would be somebody to meet me at the airport, but it wasn't anybody. ________
10. The situation is still the same. It has been no change. ________
11. I don't know who'll win, but it's sure to be a good game. ________

UNIT 83

some と any

A

普通 **some**（および somebody/someone/something）は**肯定文**で用い，**any**（および anybody など）は**否定文**で用います。

some	any
■ We bought **some** flowers.	■ We did**n't** buy **any** flowers.
■ He's busy. He's got **some** work to do.	■ He's lazy. He **never** does **any** work.
■ There's **somebody** at the door.	■ There is**n't** **anybody** at the door.
■ I'm hungry. I want **something** to eat.	■ I'm not hungry. I do**n't** want **anything** to eat.

以下のような例文では not, never, no などが現れていないものの，意味的に否定を含むので **any** を用います。

■ She went out **without any** money. (⇒ She did**n't** take **any** money with her.)
■ He **refused** to eat **anything**. (⇒ He did**n't** eat **anything**.)
■ **Hardly anybody** passed the examination. (⇒ Almost **nobody** passed.)

B

疑問文中では **some** も **any** も生じます。**some** が疑問文中で使われると下の ⇒ で示したように，話し手は「～がいる / いるように思う」と人や物が実際に存在していることを知っていたり，存在すると考えています。

■ Are you waiting for **somebody**?（⇒ 待っている人がいるのですね？）

疑問文中の **some** は，「～を…しますか？」のように聞き手に勧めたり，「～してくれますか？」のようにお願いしたりする場合にも用います。

■ Would you like **something** to eat?（⇒ 何か召し上がりますか？）
■ Can I have **some** sugar, please?（⇒ お砂糖をいただけますか？）

しかし普通，疑問文中では **any** を用います。この場合，物や人が存在するかどうかはわかっていません。

■ "Do you have **any** luggage?"　"No, I don't."
■ I can't find my bag. Has **anybody** seen it?

C

if 節中では普通 **any** を用います。

■ **If** there are **any** letters for me, can you send them on?
■ **If anyone** has any questions, I'll be glad to answer them.
■ Let me know **if** you need **anything**.

以下の文では **if** は生じていませんが，意味的に「もしも～」の意味を持つので **any** が生じています。

■ I'm sorry for **any** trouble I've caused. (= if I have caused any trouble)
■ **Anyone** who wants to take the exam should tell me by Friday. (= if there is anyone)

D

any は**肯定文**中で「どのような～でも問題ない」を表します。

■ You can take **any** bus. They all go downtown.（⇒ どのようなバスに乗ろうとかまわない）
■ "Sing a song."　"Which song should I sing?"　"**Any** song. I don't care."（⇒ 歌なら何でもよい）
■ Come and see me **anytime** you want.
■ "Let's go out somewhere."　"Where should we go?"　"**Anywhere**. It doesn't matter."
■ We left the door unlocked. **Anybody** could have come in.

something には **anything** のような「何でもよい」の意味はありません。

■ *A:* I'm hungry. I want **something** to eat.（⇒ 何か食べたい）
B: What would you like?
A: I don't care. **Anything**.（⇒ 食べられるものがあれば，何でもよい）

E

somebody/someone/anybody/anyone は**単数**として扱います。

■ **Someone** is here to see you.

しかし以下のように，これらの語を **they/them/their** のような**複数**を表す代名詞で受けることがあります。

■ **Someone** has forgotten **their** umbrella. (= his or her umbrella)
■ If **anybody** wants to leave early, **they** can.　(= he or she can)

not ... any ➲ Unit 84　some of / any of ... ➲ Unit 86　hardly any ➲ Unit 99C

Exercises

83.1 空所に some もしくは any を入れて，文を完成しなさい。

1. We didn't buy ___any___ flowers.
2. I'm going out tonight with ______________ friends of mine.
3. *A:* Have you seen ______________ good movies recently?
   B: No, I haven't been to the movies in ages.
4. I didn't have ______________ money, so I had to borrow ______________ .
5. Can I have ______________ milk in my coffee, please?
6. I was too tired to do ______________ work.
7. You can cash these traveler's checks at ______________ bank.
8. Can you give me ______________ information about places of interest in the area?
9. With the special tourist bus pass, you can travel on ______________ bus you like.
10. If there are ______________ words you don't understand, use a dictionary.

83.2 some- または any- に body/one/thing/where のいずれかを組み合わせて語を作り，空所に入れて文を完成しなさい。

1. I was too surprised to say ___anything___ .
2. There's ______________ at the door. Can you go and see who it is?
3. Does ______________ mind if I open the window?
4. I wasn't feeling hungry, so I didn't eat ______________ .
5. You must be hungry. Would you like ______________ to eat?
6. Quick, let's go! There's ______________ coming and I don't want ______________ to see us.
7. Sarah was upset about ______________ and refused to talk to ______________ .
8. This machine is very easy to use. ______________ can learn to use it very quickly.
9. There was hardly ______________ on the beach. It was almost deserted.
10. "Do you live ______________ near Jim?" "No, he lives in another part of town."
11. *A:* Where do you want to go on vacation?
    B: Let's go ______________ warm and sunny.
12. They stay at home all the time. They never seem to go ______________ .
13. I'm going out now. If ______________ calls while I'm out, tell them I'll be back at 11:30.
14. Why are you looking under the bed? Did you lose ______________ ?
15. ______________ who saw the accident should contact the police.
16. "Can I ask you ______________ ?" "Sure. What do you want to ask?"
17. Sue is very secretive. She never tells ______________ . （2語で）

83.3 空所に any ＋名詞もしくは anybody/anyone/anything/anywhere のいずれかを入れて，質問への答えを完成しなさい。

1. Which bus do I have to catch? — ___Any bus.___ They all go downtown.
2. Which day should I come? — It doesn't matter. ______________ .
3. What do you want to eat? — ______________ . I don't care. Whatever you have.
4. Where should I sit? — It's up to you. You can sit ______________ you like.
5. What kind of job are you looking for? — ______________ . It doesn't matter.
6. What time should I call tomorrow? — ______________ . I'll be home all day.
7. Who should I invite to the party? — I don't care. ______________ you like.
8. Which newspaper should I buy? — ______________ . Whatever they have at the store.

UNIT 84

no/none/any　nothing/nobody など

A

no と none

no＋名詞は，**not a** 〜もしくは **not any** 〜と同じ意味で「1 つも〜ない / まったく〜ない」を表します。

- We had to walk home because there was **no bus**.（⇒ 1 台もなかった）
- Sue will have **no difficulty** finding a job.（⇒ まったく難しくないだろう）
- There were **no stores** open.（⇒ 店がまったくなかった）

no＋名詞は，以下のように文頭に置くことがあります：

- **No reason** was given for the change of plan.

none は，後に名詞を置かずに単独で用います。

- "How much money do you have?"　"**None**." (= no money)
- All the tickets have been sold. There are **none** left. (= no tickets left)

あるいは **none of** の形で用います。

- This money is all yours. **None of it** is mine.

none of＋複数可算名詞の後では，動詞は単数名詞に対応する形にも複数名詞に対応する形にもなります。複数名詞に対応する形がより一般的です。

- None of the stores **were** (= **was**) open.

B

nothing, nobody / no one, nowhere

これらの否定的な語は文頭に置くことができます。また，疑問文の答えとして単独で用いることができます。

- **Nobody** (= **No one**) came to visit me while I was in the hospital.
- "What happened?"　"**Nothing**."
- "Where are you going?"　"**Nowhere**. I'm staying here."

動詞の後に置くこともできます。ことに **be** や **have** などを動詞に持つ場合には普通，後に置かれます。

- The house is empty. There**'s no one** living there.
- We **had nothing** to eat.

nothing/nobody のような語は，**not＋anything/anybody** のような形と同じ意味になります。

- I didn't say **anything**. (= I said **nothing**.)
- Jane didn't tell **anybody** about her plans. (= Jane told **nobody** . . .)
- They don't have **anywhere** to live. (= They have **nowhere** to live.)

nothing/nobody のような否定を含む語がある時，同じ文中で **isn't, didn't** のような動詞の否定形は使えません。

- I **said** nothing. (✕ I didn't say nothing)
- Nobody **tells** me anything. (✕ Nobody doesn't tell me)

C

any/anything/anybody のような語は，同じ文中に **not** がない場合「どちら / どれ / 誰でも…ない」を表します。➲ Unit 83D

☆ 以下の例文の組において，no と any，nothing と anything はどのように異なりますか？

- There was **no** bus, so we walked home.
  You can take **any** bus. They all go downtown.（⇒ どのバスでも）
- "What do you want to eat?"　"**Nothing**. I'm not hungry."
  I'm so hungry I could eat **anything**.（⇒ 何を食べようとも）
- The exam was extremely difficult. **Nobody** passed.（⇒ 合格者はいなかった。全員不合格）
  The exam was very easy. **Anybody** could have passed.（⇒ どのような人でも）

D

nobody や **no one** の後では，**they/them/their** などの複数を表す代名詞で受ける場合があります。➲ Unit 83E

- **Nobody** called, did **they**? (= did he or she)
- **No one** did what I asked **them** to do. (= him or her)
- **Nobody** in the class did **their** homework. (= his or her homework)

some と any ➲ Unit 83　none of ... ➲ Unit 86　any bigger / no better など ➲ Unit 103B

Exercises

84.1 空所に no/none/any のいずれかを入れて，文を完成しなさい。

1. It was a holiday, so there were ___no___ stores open.
2. I don't have ___any___ money. Can you lend me some?
3. We had to walk home because there were __________ taxis.
4. We had to walk home because there weren't __________ taxis.
5. "How many eggs do we have?" " __________ . Should I go and get some?"
6. We took a few pictures, but __________ of them were very good.
7. What a stupid thing to do! __________ intelligent person would do something like that.
8. I'll try to answer __________ questions you ask me.
9. I couldn't answer __________ of the questions they asked me.
10. We canceled the party because __________ of the people we invited were able to come.
11. I tried to call Chris, but there was __________ answer.

84.2 none / nobody / no one / nothing / nowhere のいずれかを用いて，質問への答えを作りなさい。

1. What did you do? ___Nothing.___
2. Who were you talking to? __________
3. How much luggage do you have? __________
4. Where are you going? __________
5. How many mistakes did you make? __________
6. How much did you pay? __________

次に any/anybody/anything/anywhere を用いて，上の 1～6 の答えを文の形に書き直しなさい。

7. (1) ___I didn't do anything.___
8. (2) I __________
9. (3) __________
10. (4) __________
11. (5) __________
12. (6) __________

84.3 no- または any- に body/one/thing/where のいずれかを組み合わせて語を作り，空所に入れて文を完成しなさい。

1. I don't want ___anything___ to drink. I'm not thirsty.
2. The bus was completely empty. There was __________ on it.
3. "Where did you go for vacation?" " __________ . I stayed home."
4. I went to the mall, but I didn't buy __________ .
5. *A:* What did you buy?
   B: __________ . I couldn't find __________ I wanted.
6. The town is still the same as it was years ago. __________ has changed.
7. Have you seen my watch? I can't find it __________ .
8. There was complete silence in the room. __________ said __________ .

84.4 下線部の正しい方を選んで，文を完成しなさい。

1. She didn't tell ~~nobody~~ / anybody about her plans.（anybody が正しい）
2. The accident looked serious, but fortunately nobody / anybody was injured.
3. I looked out the window, but I couldn't see no one / anyone.
4. My job is very easy. Nobody / Anybody could do it.
5. "What's in that box?" "Nothing / Anything. It's empty."
6. The situation is uncertain. Nothing / Anything could happen.
7. I don't know nothing / anything about economics.

補充問題 30 (pp. 313–314)

UNIT 85

much, many, little, few, a lot, plenty

A

much と **little** は不可算名詞の前に置きます。

much time **much luck** **little energy** **little money**

many と **few** は複数可算名詞の前に置きます。

many friends **many people** **few cars** **few countries**

B

a lot of / **lots of** / **plenty of** は不可算名詞の前にも，複数可算名詞の前にも置きます。

a lot of luck **lots of time** **plenty of money**
a lot of friends **lots of people** **plenty of ideas**

plenty of の plenty は，「有り余るほどの～」のように量が不足することなく十分である様子を意味します。

- There's no need to hurry. We've got **plenty of time**.

C

much は普通，否定文や疑問文で用います。肯定文ではあまり用いません。この傾向はことに，話しことばにおいて見られます。

☆ 否定文から肯定文になるのに伴い，「たくさんの」を表すことばは，どのように変化していますか？

- We did**n't** spend **much** money.
- ⇔ We spent **a lot of** money. (× We spent much money)
- Do you see David **much**?
- ⇔ I see David **a lot**. (× I see David much)

many, **a lot of**, **lots of** には，このような制約はありません。肯定文，否定文，疑問文のいずれでも使えます。

- **Many** people drive too fast. = **A lot of** / **Lots of** people drive too fast.
- Do you know **many** people? = Do you know **a lot of** / **lots of** people?
- There aren't **many** tourists here. = There aren't **a lot of** tourists here.

year, **week**, **day** といった語は，**many years** / **many weeks** / **many days** のように **many** と結び付き，**a lot of** とは結び付きません。

- We've lived here for **many years**. (× a lot of years)

D

little や **few** のように前に **a** の付かない形は，「ほとんど～ない」のように**否定**の意味を持ちます。

- Gary is very busy with his job. He has **little time** for other things.
  (⇒ 必要な量だけ時間がない，…する時間はほとんどない)
- Vicky doesn't like living in Paris. She has **few** friends there.
  (⇒ 必要な数だけ友達がいない，友達はほとんどいない)

似たような意味で **very little** や **very few** のように，**very** を前に置いた形もよく用いられます。

- Gary has **very little** time for other things.
- Vicky has **very few** friends in Paris.

E

a little や **a few** のように **a** が付くと，「少ないが，十分～がある」のように**肯定**の意味を持ちます。

a little: 「いくらか / 少ない量」(= some, a small amount)

- Let's go and get something to drink. We have **a little** time before the train leaves.
  (⇒ ちょっと何かを飲むには十分な時間)
- "Do you speak English?" "**A little**." (⇒ 簡単に話をする程度の英語)

a few: 「いくつか / 少ない数」(= some, a small number)

- I enjoy my life here. I have **a few** friends, and we get together pretty often.
  (⇒ 多いとは言えないが，楽しむには十分な数の友達)
- "When was the last time you saw Claire?" "**A few** days ago." (⇒ 数日前に)

little と **a little**，**few** と **a few** の間には，いずれも「ほとんど～ない」と「少ないが，十分～ある」の違いがあります。

- He spoke **little** English, so it was difficult to communicate with him. (⇒ ほとんど話さなかった)
- He spoke **a little** English, so we were able to communicate with him. (⇒ 少しは話した)
- She's lucky. She has **few** problems. (⇒ ほとんど問題はない)
- Things are not going so well for her. She has **a few** problems. (⇒ 2, 3 問題がある)

似たような意味で **only a little** や **only a few** のように，**only** を前に置いた形もよく用いられます。

- Hurry! We have **only a little** time. (× only little time)
- The town was very small. There were **only a few** streets. (× only few streets)

可算名詞と不可算名詞 ➲ Units 67–68

Exercises

85.1 それぞれの文中で，much ではなく many や a lot (of) を用いたほうが正しかったり，より自然になるものを○で囲み，適切な形に書き換えなさい。

1. We didn't spend much money. — OK
2. Sue drinks much tea. — a lot of tea
3. Joe always puts much salt on his food. ______
4. We'll have to hurry. We don't have much time. ______
5. It cost much to fix the car. ______
6. Did it cost much to fix the car? ______
7. I don't know much people in this town. ______
8. I use the phone much at work. ______
9. There wasn't much traffic this morning. ______
10. You need much money to travel around the world. ______

85.2 状況に合うように以下から適切な語句を選び，plenty (of) の後に続けて文を完成しなさい。

hotels money room things to see ~~time~~ to learn

1. There's no need to hurry. There's plenty of time.
2. He doesn't have any financial problems. He has ______
3. Come and sit with us. There's ______
4. She knows a lot, but she still has ______
5. It's an interesting town to visit. There ______
6. I'm sure we'll find somewhere to stay. ______

85.3 状況に合うように much/many/few/little の中から適切なものを選び，空所に入れて文を完成しなさい。

1. He isn't very popular. He has very few friends.
2. Ann is very busy these days. She has ______ free time.
3. Did you take ______ pictures when you were on vacation?
4. I'm not very busy today. I don't have ______ to do.
5. This is a very modern city. There are ______ old buildings.
6. The weather has been very dry recently. We've had very ______ rain.
7. "Do you know Boston?" "No, I haven't been there for ______ years."

85.4 必要に応じて，下線部の語句に a を付け加えなさい。

1. She's lucky. She has few problems. — OK
2. Things are not going so well for her. She has few problems. — a few problems
3. Can you lend me few dollars? ______
4. There was little traffic, so the trip didn't take very long. ______
5. I can't give you a decision yet. I need little time to think. ______
6. It was a surprise that he won the match. Few people expected him to win. ______
7. I don't know much Spanish – only few words. ______
8. I wonder how Sam is. I haven't seen him for few months. ______

85.5 状況に合うように little / a little / few / a few の中から適切なものを選び，空所に入れて文を完成しなさい。

1. Gary is very busy with his job. He has little time for other things.
2. Listen carefully. I'm going to give you ______ advice.
3. Do you mind if I ask you ______ questions?
4. It's not a very interesting place to visit, so ______ tourists come here.
5. I don't think Jill would be a good teacher. She has ______ patience.
6. "Would you like cream in your coffee?" "Yes, please, ______."
7. This is a very boring place to live. There's ______ to do.
8. "Have you ever been to Paris?" "Yes, I've been there ______ times."

UNIT 86

all / all of　most / most of　no / none of など

A

all　some　any　most　much/many　little/few　no

上の語は **some food** / **few books** のように名詞の前に直接置きます。具体的な事物を特定していません。

- **All cars** have wheels.（⇒ すべての自動車に…）
- **Some cars** can go faster than others.
- 〔看板で〕**NO CARS**.（自動車進入禁止）
- **Many people** drive too fast.
- I don't go out very often. I stay home **most days**.

NO
CARS

上の例では，all of cars や some of people などのように **of** を後に置いた形にはできません。（**of** を置く形についてはセクション**B**を参照）

- **Some people** learn languages more easily than others.
  (× Some of people)

「たいていの～」を表す **most** には **the** が付きません。

- **Most tourists** don't visit this part of town. (× The most tourists)

B

all　some　any　most　much/many　little/few　half　none

上の語が **some of** / **most of** のように **of** を伴う場合，**of** の後には **the/this/that/these/those/my** など* を前に置き，何を指しているか特定できる**名詞句**がきます。例えば **some of the people** や **some of those people** のような形は可能ですが，some of people のような **the** を持たない形にはできません。

- **Some of the people** I work with are not very friendly.
- **None of this money** is mine.
- Have you read **any of these books**?
- I was sick yesterday. I spent **most of the day** in bed.

all や **half** の後には，**of** なしで何を指しているか特定できる**名詞句**を置くこともできます。

- **All my friends** live in Los Angeles.　=　All **of** my friends . . .
- **Half this money** is mine.　=　Half **of** this money . . .

☆ **名詞句が何を指しているか具体的に特定しない場合とする場合では，どのように異なりますか？**

- **All flowers** are beautiful.（⇒「花はすべて…」のように花全般を指す）
  All (of) **the flowers in this garden** are beautiful.（⇒「この庭の花はすべて…」のように特定）
- **Most problems** have a solution.（⇒「たいていの問題には…」のように特定しない）
  We were able to solve **most of the problems we had**.（⇒「その問題の多くは…」のように特定）

C

of / **some of** / **none of** などの後に **it/us/you/them** などの**目的格の代名詞**を置き，**all of us** / **all of you** / **half of it** / **half of them** のような形を用いることがあります。

- "How many of these people do you know?"　"**None of them**. / **A few of them**."
- Do **any of you** want to come to a party tonight?
- "Do you like this music?"　"**Some of it**. Not **all of it**."

この形では，**it/us/you/them** などの代名詞の前の **of** は省略できません。

- **All of us** were late. (× All us)
- I haven't finished the book yet. I've only read **half of it**. (× half it)

D

some/most/none のような語は，後に名詞を置かず**単独**で用いることができます。

- Some cars have four doors and **some** have two.
- A few of the shops were open, but **most** (of them) were closed.
- Half this money is mine, and **half** (of it) is yours. (× the half)

* このような語全体をまとめて「限定詞」(determiner) と呼びます。

some と any ➲ Unit 83　no と none ➲ Unit 84　much/many/little/few ➲ Unit 85
all ➲ Units 88, 107C　all of whom / most of which など ➲ Unit 94B

Exercises

86.1 必要に応じて空所に of を入れて，文を完成しなさい。必要がない場合には - を記入すること。

1. All ___-___ cars have wheels.
2. None ___of___ this money is mine.
3. Some ________ movies are very violent.
4. Some ________ the movies I've seen recently have been very violent.
5. Jim has lived in Houston all ________ his life.
6. Many ________ people watch too much TV.
7. Are any ________ those letters for me?
8. Kate has lived in Miami most ________ her life.
9. Jim thinks all ________ museums are boring.
10. Most ________ days I get up before 7:00.

86.2 状況に合うように以下から適切な語句を選び，必要に応じて some of / most of のように of を付け加えて文を完成しなさい。

accidents	**large cities**	**my dinner**	**my teammates**
birds	**her friends**	**my spare time**	**the population**
~~**cars**~~	**her opinions**	**the buildings**	~~**these books**~~

1. I haven't read many ___of these books___ .
2. All ___cars___ have wheels.
3. I spend much ____________________ gardening.
4. Many ____________________ are caused by bad driving.
5. It's an old town. Many ____________________ are over 400 years old.
6. When she got married, she kept it a secret. She didn't tell any ____________________ .
7. Not many people live in the north of the country. Most ____________________ live in the south.
8. Not all ____________________ can fly. For example, the penguin can't fly.
9. Our team played badly and lost the game. None ____________________ played well.
10. Julia and I have very different ideas. I don't agree with many ____________________ .
11. New York, like most ____________________ , has a traffic problem.
12. I had no appetite. I could only eat half ____________________ .

86.3 状況に合うように，自分で空所に合う語句を考えて文を完成しなさい。

1. The building was damaged in the explosion. All ___the windows___ were broken.
2. We had a very lazy vacation. We spent most of ____________________ on the beach.
3. I went to the movies by myself. None of ____________________ wanted to come.
4. The test was difficult. I could only answer half ____________________ .
5. Some of ____________________ you took at the wedding were very good.
6. *A:* Have you spent all ____________________ I gave you?
   B: No, there's still some left.

86.4 状況に合うように，all of / some of / none of に it/them/us を続けて all of it / some of them / none of us などのような形にし，空所に入れて文を完成しなさい。

1. These books are all Jane's. ___None of them___ belong to me.
2. "How many of these books have you read?" "____________________ . Every one."
3. We all got wet in the rain because ____________________ had an umbrella.
4. Some of this money is yours, and ____________________ is mine.
5. I asked some people for directions, but ____________________ was able to help me.
6. She made up the whole story from beginning to end. ____________________ was true.
7. Not all the tourists in the group were Spanish. ____________________ were French.
8. I watched most of the movie, but not ____________________ .

UNIT 87

both / both of　neither / neither of either / either of

A

both/neither/either

both/neither/either は 2 つの物について，**both** books，**neither** book，**either** book のように後に名詞を置いて用います。

☆ 食事に出かけたい素敵なレストランが 2 つあります。このレストランについて次のように記述できます。

- **Both restaurants** are very good.（⇒ レストランは両方とも…，× The both restaurants）
- **Neither restaurant** is expensive.（⇒ どちらのレストランも…ない）
- We can go to **either restaurant**. I don't care.
（⇒ どちらのレストランでも問題ない）

B

both of . . . / neither of . . . / either of . . .

both of / neither of / either of の後には，**the/these/my/Tom's** などを前に置いた何を指しているか特定できる名詞句がきます。**both of the restaurant** は可能ですが，both of restaurants のような **the** を持たない形にはできません。

- **Both of these** restaurants are very good.
- **Neither of the** restaurants we went to was (= were) expensive.
- I haven't been to **either of those** restaurants.（⇒ どちらのレストランにも行ったことがない）

both の後には，**of** なしで何を指しているか特定できる名詞句を置くこともできます。

- **Both my parents** are from Michigan.　=　Both **of** my parents . . .

both of / neither of / either of などの後に，**us/you/them** のような目的格の代名詞を置くことがあります。

- 〔2 人に話しかけて〕Can **either of you** speak Spanish?
- I asked two people the way to the station, but **neither of them** knew.

us/you/them のような目的格の代名詞の前では **both of** を置きます。**of** は省略できません。

- **Both of us** were very tired.（× Both us were . . .）

neither of ... の後に生じた動詞は，単数名詞に対応する形にも複数名詞に対応する形にもなります。

- Neither of the children **wants** (= **want**) to go to bed.

C

both/neither/either のような語は，後に名詞を置かず単独で用いることができます。

- I couldn't decide which of the two shirts to buy. I liked **both**.
(= I liked **both** of them.)
- "Is your friend British or American?"　"**Neither**. She's Australian."
- "Do you want tea or coffee?"　"**Either**. It doesn't matter."

D

both/neither/either の後には，以下のように **and/nor/or** をはさむように名詞句を 2 つ置くことがあります。

both ～ and . . . （～も…も）	**Both** Ann **and** Tom were late. I was **both** tired **and** hungry when I got home.
neither ～ nor . . . （～も…も ― ない）	**Neither** Liz **nor** Robin came to the party. She said she would contact me, but she **neither** wrote **nor** called.
either ～ or . . . （～か…か）	I'm not sure where he's from. He's **either** Spanish **or** Italian. **Either** you apologize, **or** I'll never speak to you again.

E

☆ either/neither/both は 2 つの事物，any/none/all は 3 つ以上の事物に関して用います。両者の違いを以下の例文で確認しなさい。

There are **two** good hotels here. You could stay at **either** of them.	There are **many** good hotels here. You could stay at **any** of them.
We tried **two** hotels. **Neither** of them had any rooms. **Both** of them were full.	We tried **a lot of** hotels. **None** of them had any rooms. **All** of them were full.

neither do I / I don't either ➲ Unit 49C　　both of whom / neither of which ➲ Unit 94B
both ➲ Unit 107C

Exercises

87.1 状況に合うように both/neither/either の中から適切なものを選び，文を完成しなさい。

1. "Do you want tea or coffee?" "*Either.* It really doesn't matter."
2. "What's the date today – the 18th or the 19th?" "____________ . It's the 20th."
3. *A:* Where did you go for vacation – Florida or Puerto Rico?
   B: We went to ____________ . A week in Florida and a week in Puerto Rico.
4. "When should I call you, morning or afternoon?" "____________ . I'll be home all day."
5. "Where's Kate? Is she at work or at home?" "____________ . She's out of town."

87.2 空所に both/neither/either のいずれかを入れて，文を完成しなさい。必要に応じて of を付け加えること。

1. *Both* my parents are from California.
2. To get downtown, you can take the city streets or you can take the freeway. You can go ____________ way.
3. I tried to call George twice, but ____________ times he was out.
4. ____________ Tom's parents is American. His father is Polish, and his mother is Italian.
5. I saw an accident this morning. One car drove into the back of another. Fortunately ____________ driver was injured, but ____________ cars were badly damaged.
6. I have two sisters and a brother. My brother is working, but ____________ my sisters are still in school.

87.3 空所に both/neither/either に of us/them を続けて入れて，文を完成しなさい。

1. I asked two people the way to the airport, but *neither of them* could help me.
2. I was invited to two parties last week, but I couldn't go to ____________ .
3. There were two windows in the room. It was very warm, so I opened ____________ .
4. Sarah and I play tennis together regularly, but ____________ can play very well.
5. I tried two bookstores for the book I wanted, but ____________ had it.

87.4 状況に合うように both ～ and ... / neither ～ nor ... / either ～ or ... の形を使って，文を書き換えなさい。

1. Chris was late. So was Pat. *Both Chris and Pat were late.*
2. He didn't write and he didn't call. *He neither wrote nor called.*
3. Joe is on vacation and so is Sam. ____________
4. Joe doesn't have a car. Sam doesn't have one either. ____________
5. Brian doesn't watch TV, and he doesn't read newspapers. ____________
6. It was a boring movie. It was long, too.
   The movie ____________
7. Is that man's name Richard? Or is it Robert? It's one or the other.
   That man's name ____________
8. I don't have time to go on vacation. And I don't have the money.
   I have ____________
9. We can leave today, or we can leave tomorrow – whichever you prefer.
   We ____________

87.5 空所に neither/either/none/any のいずれかを入れて，文を完成しなさい。

1. We tried a lot of hotels, but *none* of them had any rooms.
2. I took two books with me on vacation, but I didn't read ____________ of them.
3. I took five books with me on vacation, but I didn't read ____________ of them.
4. There are a few stores on the next block, but ____________ of them sells newspapers.
5. You can call me at ____________ time during the evening. I'm always at home.
6. I can meet you next Monday or Friday. Would ____________ of those days be convenient for you?
7. John and I couldn't get into the house because ____________ of us had a key.

UNIT 88

all, every と whole

A

☆ all と everybody/everyone は，どのように異なりますか？

ともに「どの人も，すべての人」の意味を持ちますが，**everybody/everyone** の代わりに **all** を用いることはできません。

- **Everybody** enjoyed the party. (× All enjoyed)

all は **all of us/you/them** のような形で用います。一方，**everybody** に of は付きません。

- **All of us** enjoyed the party. (× Everybody of us)

B

☆ all と everything は，どのように異なりますか？

all と **everything** は同じように使うことができます。以下ではともに「…するすべて」を表します。

- I'll do **all I can** to help. = I'll do **everything I can** to help.

all は **all I can** / **all you need** のような形で用いますが，単独では用いません。**everything** は単独で用います。

- He thinks he knows **everything**. (× he knows all)
- Our vacation was a disaster. **Everything** went wrong. (× All went wrong)

all は **all about** ～のような形でも用います。

- He knows **all about** computers.

all は後に節を置き「…した唯一の物」を意味します。**everything** にこの用法はありません。

- **All** I've eaten today is a sandwich.（⇒ 今日食べた唯一の物は～ / 今日は～しか食べていない）

C

every/everybody/everyone/everything は単数扱いします。動詞も単数可算名詞に対応した形で受けます。

- **Every seat** in the theater **was** taken.
- **Everyone has** arrived. (× have arrived)

しかし **everybody/everyone** については，**they/them/their** のような複数の代名詞で受けることがあります。

- **Everybody** said **they** enjoyed **themselves**. (= he or she enjoyed himself or herself)

D

☆ whole と all は，どのように異なりますか？

whole は「全部の～，～全体」を意味し，後に単数可算名詞を置きます。

- Did you read **the whole book**?（⇒ その本の一部ではなく全部）
- Lila has lived **her whole life** in Chile.
- I was so hungry, I ate **a whole package** of cookies.（⇒ 1 箱全部）

whole の前には **the/my/her** などがきます。**all** には前にくる語はありません。

- **the whole** way / **all the** way　　**her whole** life / **all her** life

whole の後に普通，不可算名詞は置きません。不可算名詞の前には **all** を置きます。

- I've spent **all the money** you gave me. (× the whole money)

E

every/all/whole は，後に**時を表す語句**を置いてよく用います。

every day / **every Monday** / **every 10 minutes** / **every three weeks** などのように，**every＋時を表す表現**を用いて「～ごとに，毎～」といった出来事が起きる割合や頻度を表します。

- When we were on vacation, we went to the beach **every day**. (× all days)
- The bus service is very good. There's a bus **every 10 minutes**.
- We don't see each other very often – about **every six months**.

all day / **the whole day** は「朝から晩までずっと」を意味します。all the day, all the week のように **the** の付く形は用いません。

- We spent **all day** / **the whole day** at the beach.
- Dan was very quiet. He didn't say a word **all night** / **the whole night**.

all the time は「常に，絶え間なく」を表し，**every time ...** は「…する度ごとに」を表します。

- They never go out. They are at home **all the time**.（⇒ いつも家にいる）
- **Every time** I see you, you look different.（⇒ 会う度にあなたは…）

可算名詞と不可算名詞 ⊃ Units 67–68　all / all of ⊃ Unit 86　each と every ⊃ Unit 89
every one ⊃ Unit 89D　all に関連した語順 ⊃ Unit 107C

Exercises

88.1 空所に all, everything, everybody（あるいは everyone）を入れて，文を完成しなさい。

1. It was a good party. _Everyone_ enjoyed it.
2. _All_ I've eaten today is a sandwich.
3. ______ has their faults. Nobody is perfect.
4. Nothing has changed. ______ is the same as it was.
5. Kate told me ______ about her new job. It sounds very interesting.
6. Can ______ write their name on a piece of paper, please?
7. Why are you always thinking about money? Money isn't ______ .
8. I didn't have much money with me. ______ I had was 10 dollars.
9. When the fire alarm rang, ______ left the building immediately.
10. Sue didn't say where she was going. ______ she said was that she was going away.
11. We have completely different opinions. I disagree with ______ she says.
12. We all did well on the exam. ______ in our class passed.
13. We all did well on the exam. ______ of us passed.
14. Why are you so lazy? Why do you expect me to do ______ for you?

88.2 whole を用いて，状況を説明する文を完成しなさい。

1. I read the book from beginning to end.
   I read the whole book.
2. Everyone on the team played well.
   The ______
3. Paul opened a box of chocolates. When he finished eating, there were no chocolates left in the box. He ate ______
4. The police came to the house. They were looking for something. They searched everywhere, every room. They ______
5. Everyone in Dave and Jane's family plays tennis. Dave and Jane play, and so do all their children. The ______
6. Ann worked from early in the morning until late at night.
   ______
7. Jack and Lisa spent a week at the beach on vacation. It rained from the beginning of the week to the end. It ______

whole の代わりに all を用いて，上の 6 および 7 の答えを書き換えなさい。

8. (6) Ann ______
9. (7) ______

88.3 状況に合うように以下の語句を every に続けて空所に入れ，文を完成しなさい。

five minutes ~~**10 minutes**~~ **four hours** **six months** **four years**

1. The bus service is very good. There's a bus _every 10 minutes._
2. Tom is sick. He has some medicine. He has to take it ______
3. The Olympic Games take place ______
4. We live near a busy airport. A plane flies over our house ______
5. It's a good idea to have a check-up with the dentist ______

88.4 下線部の正しい方を選んで，文を完成しなさい。

1. I spent ~~the whole money~~ / all the money you gave me.（all the moneyが正解）
2. Sue works every day / all days except Sunday.
3. I'm tired. I've been working hard all the day / all day.
4. It was a terrible fire. Whole building / The whole building was destroyed.
5. I've been trying to call her, but every time / all the time I call, the line is busy.
6. I don't like the weather here. It rains every time / all the time.
7. When I was on vacation, all my luggage / my whole luggage was stolen.

補充問題 30 (pp. 313–314)

UNIT 89

each と every

A

each と every は似たような意味を持ち，どちらでも同じように用いられる場合があります。

- **Each** time (= **Every** time) I see you, you look different.
- There's a ceiling fan in **each** room (= **every** room) of the house.

☆ 図を見て考えます。each と every は，どのように異なりますか？

➤ each は，事物をばらばらに 1 つずつとらえます。

- Study **each sentence** carefully.
  (⇒ 文を 1つずつ…)

each = X+X+X+X

少数の事物については every より each を用います。

- There were four books on the table. **Each book** was a different color.
- 〔トランプで〕At the beginning of the game, **each player** has three cards.

➤ every は，複数ある事物を 1 つの集合として考える場合に用います。意味的には all に似ています。

- **Every sentence** must have a verb.
  (⇒ 全般的にとらえて，すべての文には)

every = (XXXXXXXXXXXXXXXXXXXXXXXXXXXXXXXXXX)

多数の事物については each より every を用います。

- Kate loves reading. She has read **every book** in the library. (= all the books)
- I would like to visit **every country** in the world. (= all the countries)

each は 2 つの事物に対して用いられますが，every は用いられません。

- In a baseball game, **each team** has nine players. (✕ every team)

every は物が生じる頻度を述べる際に用いられますが，each は用いられません。

- "How often do you use your computer?" "**Every day.**" (✕ Each day)
- There's a bus **every 10 minutes**. (✕ each 10 minutes)

B

☆ 形の上で each と every は，どのように異なりますか？

each の後には普通，名詞を置きます。

each book　　**each student**

each は，単独で用いることができます。

- None of the rooms was the same. **Each** (= each room) was different.

each one のような形も用います。

- **Each one** was different.

each of + the ~ / these ~ / them のように，**of** の後に特定できる名詞句や代名詞を置いた形も用います

- Read **each of these** sentences carefully.
- **Each of the** books is a different color.
- **Each of them** is a different color.

every の後には普通，名詞を置きます。

every book　　**every student**

every は，後に名詞を置かず単独で用いることができません。

- *A:* Have you read all these books?
  B: Yes, **every one**.

of を後に置く場合には **every one of** のような形にします。every of のような形はありません。

- I've read **every one of those** books. (✕ every of those books)
- I've read **every one of them**.

C

単独で用いる **each** は，文中にも文尾にも置くことができます。

- The students were **each** given a book. (⇒ 生徒 1人ひとりに…)
- These oranges cost 75 cents **each**.

D

everyone と every one

1 語で書き表す **everyone** は人についてのみ用います。**everybody** と同じように使われます。

2 語で書き表す **every one** は人にも物にも用います。**each one** と似た使われ方をします。➲ セクション B

- **Everyone** enjoyed the party. (= **Everybody** . . .)
- Sarah is invited to lots of parties and she goes to **every one**. (= to **every party**)

each other ➲ Unit 80C　　all と every ➲ Unit 88

Exercises

89.1 空所に each もしくは every を入れて，イラストの状況を説明する文を完成しなさい。

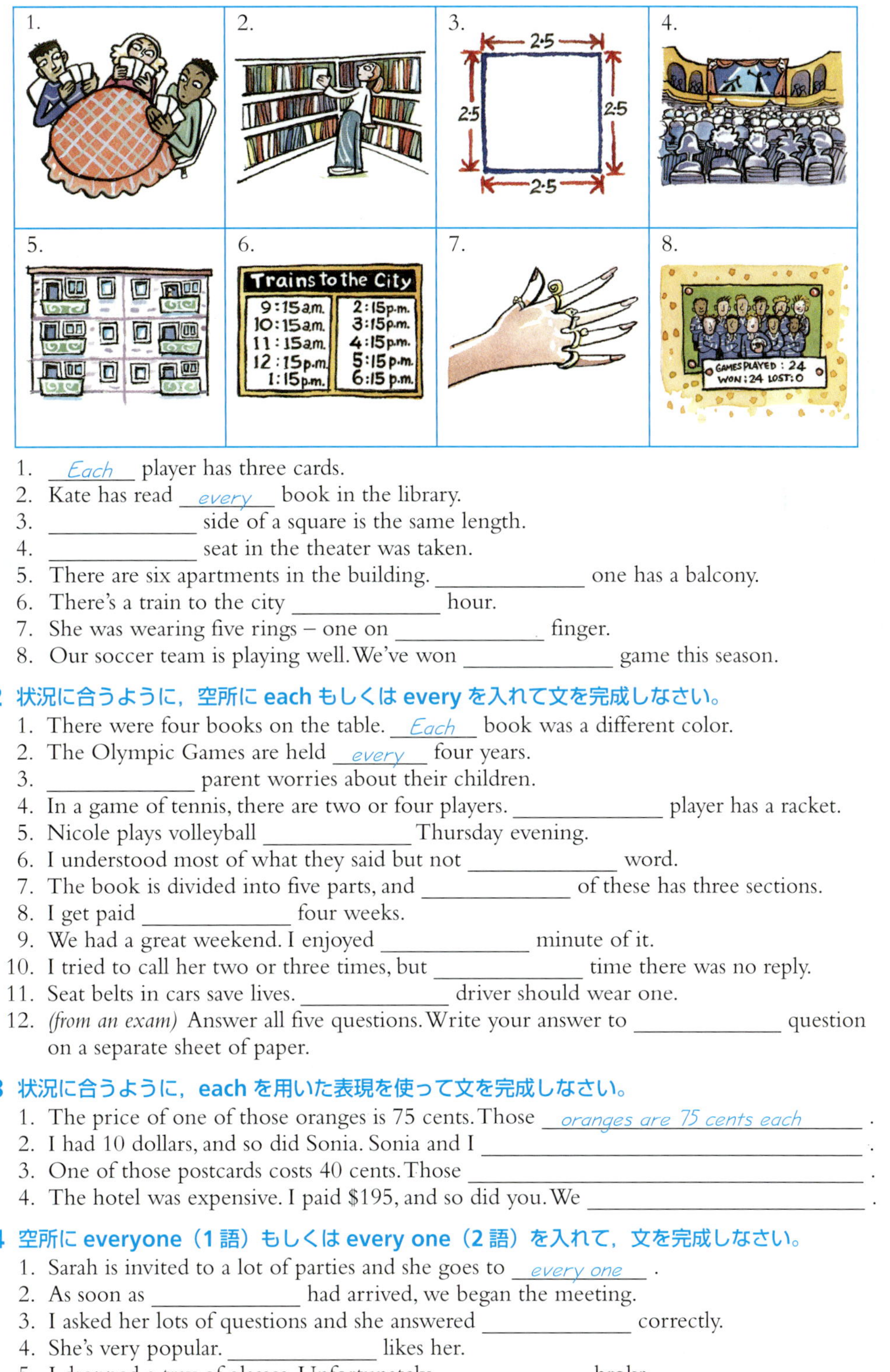

1. *Each* player has three cards.
2. Kate has read *every* book in the library.
3. ______ side of a square is the same length.
4. ______ seat in the theater was taken.
5. There are six apartments in the building. ______ one has a balcony.
6. There's a train to the city ______ hour.
7. She was wearing five rings – one on ______ finger.
8. Our soccer team is playing well. We've won ______ game this season.

89.2 状況に合うように，空所に each もしくは every を入れて文を完成しなさい。

1. There were four books on the table. *Each* book was a different color.
2. The Olympic Games are held *every* four years.
3. ______ parent worries about their children.
4. In a game of tennis, there are two or four players. ______ player has a racket.
5. Nicole plays volleyball ______ Thursday evening.
6. I understood most of what they said but not ______ word.
7. The book is divided into five parts, and ______ of these has three sections.
8. I get paid ______ four weeks.
9. We had a great weekend. I enjoyed ______ minute of it.
10. I tried to call her two or three times, but ______ time there was no reply.
11. Seat belts in cars save lives. ______ driver should wear one.
12. *(from an exam)* Answer all five questions. Write your answer to ______ question on a separate sheet of paper.

89.3 状況に合うように，each を用いた表現を使って文を完成しなさい。

1. The price of one of those oranges is 75 cents. Those *oranges are 75 cents each* .
2. I had 10 dollars, and so did Sonia. Sonia and I ______ .
3. One of those postcards costs 40 cents. Those ______ .
4. The hotel was expensive. I paid $195, and so did you. We ______ .

89.4 空所に everyone（1 語）もしくは every one（2 語）を入れて，文を完成しなさい。

1. Sarah is invited to a lot of parties and she goes to *every one* .
2. As soon as ______ had arrived, we began the meeting.
3. I asked her lots of questions and she answered ______ correctly.
4. She's very popular. ______ likes her.
5. I dropped a tray of glasses. Unfortunately, ______ broke.

UNIT 90

関係詞節 1：主格の who/that/which を持った関係詞節

A

☆ 例文から考えます。関係詞節はどのような働きをしますか？

The woman **who lives next door** is a doctor. (⇒ 隣に住んでいる女性は…)

関係詞節

➤ 文の一部で複数の語を持ち，主語と動詞を持つまとまりを節と呼びます。関係詞節は，話し手がどの人や物について話題としているかを示したり，人や物の種類や性質を説明する節です。

- The woman **who lives next door** ... (⇒ 隣に住んでいる女性：どの女性を指しているか説明)
- People **who live in the country** ... (⇒ その国に住んでいる人々：人々の種類を説明)

人について話題にする場合，関係詞節を **who** で始めます。

the woman – she lives next door – is a doctor
↓ 主格の she を **who** に変える
⇒ The woman **who lives next door** is a doctor.

we know a lot of people – they live in the country
↓ 主格の they を **who** に変える
⇒ We know a lot of people **who live in the country**.

- An architect is someone **who designs buildings**.
- What was the name of the person **who called you**?
- Anyone **who wants to apply for the job** must do so by Friday.

人について話題にする場合，**who** の代わりに **that** を用いることもできます。**which** は使いません。

- The woman **that lives next door** is a doctor. (✕ the woman **which**)

that ではなく **who** しか使えない場合もあります。➲ Unit 93

B

物について話題にする場合，関係詞節を **that** もしくは **which** で始めます。この場合 **who** は使いません。

where is the cheese? – it was in the refrigerator
↓ 主格の it を **that/which** に変える
⇒ Where is the cheese { **that** / **which** } **was in the refrigerator?**

- I don't like stories **that have unhappy endings**. (= stories **which** have ...)
- Barbara works for a company **that makes furniture**. (= a company **which** makes furniture)
- The machine **that broke down** is working again now. (= The machine **which** broke down)

that の方が **which** よりよく用いられます。しかし，**which** しか使えない場合もあります。➲ Unit 93

C

what ... は「…すること，物」を表します。**what** は **that** と異なり，左側に説明される名詞句を持ちません。

- **What** happened was my fault. (⇒ **起こったこと**はすべて…)
- Everything **that happened** was my fault. (✕ Everything what happened)
- The machine **that broke down** is now working again. (✕ The machine what broke down)

D

主格の代名詞から作られた**関係詞節**は **who/that/which** で始め，he/she/they/it などでは始めません。

- I've never spoken to the woman **who lives** next door. (✕ the woman she lives)

he/she/they/it などで始まる関係詞節 ➲ Unit 91B

関係詞節 2–5 ➲ Units 91–94

Exercises

90.1 以下から適切な動詞表現を選び，who の後に続けて（　）内の語句を説明する文を完成しなさい。

he/she { steals from a store / ~~designs buildings~~ / doesn't believe in God / is not brave }

he/she { buys something from a store / pays rent to live in a room or apartment / breaks into a house to steal things / expects the worst to happen }

1. (an architect) *An architect is someone who designs buildings.*
2. (a burglar) A burglar is someone ______
3. (a customer) ______
4. (a shoplifter) ______
5. (a coward) ______
6. (an atheist) ______
7. (a pessimist) ______
8. (a tenant) ______

90.2 who/that/which のいずれかを用いて，2 つの文を 1 つにまとめなさい。

1. A girl was injured in the accident. She is now in the hospital.
   The girl who was injured in the accident is now in the hospital.
2. A waitress served us. She was impolite and impatient.
   The ______
3. A building was destroyed in the fire. It has now been rebuilt.
   The ______
4. Some people were arrested. They have now been released.
   The ______
5. A bus goes to the airport. It runs every half hour.
   The ______

90.3 状況に合うように以下から適切なものを選び，関係詞節に変えて空所に入れ，文を完成しなさい。

he invented the telephone	~~it makes furniture~~
she runs away from home	it gives you the meanings of words
they stole my car	it can support life
they were on the wall	it cannot be explained

1. Barbara works for a company *that makes furniture* .
2. The book is about a girl ______ .
3. What happened to the pictures ______ ?
4. A mystery is something ______ .
5. The police have caught the men ______ .
6. A dictionary is a book ______ .
7. Alexander Bell was the man ______ .
8. It seems that Earth is the only planet ______ .

90.4 それぞれの文について誤りのある部分を○で囲み，正しい形に書き直しなさい。

1. I don't like (stories who have) unhappy endings. *stories that have*
2. What was the name of the person who called you? *OK*
3. Where's the nearest shop who sells newspapers? ______
4. The driver which caused the accident was fined $500. ______
5. Do you know the person that took these photographs? ______
6. We live in a world what is changing all the time. ______
7. Dan said some things about me that were not true. ______
8. What was the name of the horse it won the race? ______

UNIT 91

関係詞節 2：目的格の who/that/which を持った関係詞節と省略

A

☆ Unit 90 の例文をもう一度考えます。who/that/which は，関係詞節中でどのような働きをしていますか？

- The woman **who lives next door** is a doctor. (= The woman **that** lives . . .)
  The woman lives next door. ➤ **who (⇒ the woman) は主語。**
- Where is the cheese **that was in the refrigerator**? (= the cheese **which** was . . .)
  The cheese was in the refrigerator. ➤ **that (⇒ the cheese) は主語。**

who/that/which が**関係詞節**中で**主語**となる場合には省略できません。以下は正しい文ではありません。

- × The woman lives next door is a doctor.
- × Where is the cheese was in the refrigerator.

B

☆ もとになった文で考えます。who/that/which は，関係詞節中でどのような働きをしていますか？

- The woman **who I wanted to see** was away on vacation.
  I wanted to see **the woman**. ➤ **who（⇒ the woman）は目的語で，I が主語。**
- Have you found the keys **that** you lost?
  You lost the keys. ➤ **that (⇒ the keys) は目的語で，youが主語。**

who/that/which が**関係詞節**中で**目的語**となる場合には省略できます。以下は正しい文になります。

- The **woman I wanted to see** was away. = The woman **who** I wanted to see . . .
- Have you found **the keys you lost**? = . . . the keys **that** you lost?
- **The dress Ann bought** doesn't fit her very well. = The dress **that** Ann bought . . .
- Is there **anything I can do**? = . . . anything **that** I can do?

このような**関係詞節**中では，**動詞**の後に**目的語**を置くことはできません。

the keys you lost (× the keys you lost them)
the dress Ann bought (× the dress Ann bought it)

C

☆ 前置詞（in/to/for など）が関係詞節の終りに生じています。もとの形を考えます。

Tom is talking **to** a woman – do you know her?
⇒ Do you know the woman (who/that) **Tom is talking to**?

I slept **in** a bed last night – it wasn't very comfortable
⇒ The bed (that/which) **I slept in last night** wasn't very comfortable.

➤ **前置詞の後にあった名詞句を先行詞にして関係詞節を作ります。その結果，関係詞節中では前置詞の後から名詞句がなくなります。who/that/which は主語ではないので，省略できます。**

- Are these the books **you were looking for**? = . . . the books **that/which** you were . . .
- The woman **he fell in love with** left him after a month. = The woman **who/that** he . . .
- The man **I was sitting next to on the plane** talked all the time.
  = The man **who/that** I was sitting next to . . .

このような**関係詞節**中では，**前置詞**の後に**名詞句**を置くことはできません。

the books you were looking for (× the books you were looking for them)

D

左側に説明される名詞句を持つ以下のような**関係詞節**では **what** は使えません。➲ Unit 90C

- Everything **(that) they said** was true. (× Everything what they said)
- I gave her all the money **(that) I had**. (× all the money what I had)

what ... は「…すること，物」を表します。

- Did you hear **what they said**? (= the things that they said)

関係詞節 1 ➲ Unit 90　関係詞節 3–5 ➲ Units 92–94　whom ➲ Unit 92B

Exercises

91.1 それぞれの文中で **who** や **that** が必要となる部分を○で囲み，正しい形に書き直しなさい。

1. The woman lives next door is a doctor — *The woman who lives next door*
2. Have you found the keys you lost? — *OK*
3. The people we met last night were very nice. ______
4. The people work in the office are very nice. ______
5. The people I work with are very nice. ______
6. What have you done with the money I gave you? ______
7. What happened to the money was on the table? ______
8. What's the worst film you've ever seen? ______
9. What's the best thing it has ever happened to you? ______

91.2 関係詞節を用いて，状況を説明する文を完成しなさい。

1. Your friend lost some keys. You want to know if he has found them. You say:
   Have you found the keys *you lost* ?
2. A friend is wearing a dress. You like it. You tell her:
   I like the dress ______ .
3. A friend is going to see a movie. You want to know the name of the movie. You say:
   What's the name of the movie ______ ?
4. You wanted to visit a museum. It was closed when you got there. You tell a friend:
   The museum ______ was closed when we got there.
5. You invited some people to your party. Some of them couldn't come. You tell someone:
   Some of the people ______ couldn't come.
6. Your friend had to do some work. You want to know if she has finished. You say:
   Have you finished the work ______ ?
7. You rented a car. It broke down after a few miles. You tell a friend:
   The car ______ broke down after a few miles.
8. You stayed at a hotel. Tom had recommended it to you. You tell a friend:
   We stayed at a hotel ______ .

91.3 状況に合うように以下から適切なものを選び，前置詞を含んだ関係詞節に変えて空所に入れ，文を完成しなさい。

we went to a party last night	you can rely on Brian	we were invited to a wedding
I work with some people	I applied for a job	you told me about a hotel
~~you were looking for some books~~	I saw you with a man	

1. Are these the books *you were looking for* ?
2. Unfortunately we couldn't go to the wedding ______ .
3. I enjoy my job. I like the people ______ .
4. What's the name of that hotel ______ .
5. The party ______ wasn't very much fun.
6. I didn't get the job ______ .
7. Brian is a good person to know. He's somebody ______ .
8. Who was that man ______ in the restaurant?

91.4 状況に合うように空所に **that** もしくは **what** を入れて，文を完成しなさい。何も必要ない場合には - を記入します。

1. I gave her all the money *-* I had.（all the money **that** I had も正解）
2. Did you hear *what* they said?
3. They give their children everything ______ they want.
4. Tell me ______ you want, and I'll try to get it for you.
5. Why do you blame me for everything ______ goes wrong?
6. I won't be able to do much, but I'll do ______ I can.
7. I won't be able to do much, but I'll do the best ______ I can.
8. I don't agree with ______ you've just said.
9. I don't trust him. I don't believe anything ______ he says.

UNIT 92

関係詞節 3：whose/whom/where で始まる関係詞節

A

whose

his/her/their を **whose** に変えて**関係詞節**を作ります。

we saw some people – their car had broken down

We saw some people **whose car had broken down**.

☆ 普通 whose は人に関連して用います。もとの文ではどのような代名詞でしたか？

- A widow is a woman **whose husband is dead**. (⇒ **her** husband is dead)
- What's the name of the man **whose car you borrowed**? (⇒ you borrowed **his** car)
- I met someone **whose brother I went to school with**. (⇒ I went to school with **his/her** brother)

☆ who と whose は，どのように異なりますか？ もとの文の代名詞から確認します。

- I met a man **who** knows you. (⇒ **he** knows you)
- I met a man **whose sister** knows you. (⇒ **his sister** knows you)

B

whom

動詞の目的語は **who** を用いて**関係詞節**を作ります（➲Unit 91B）が，**who** の代わりに **whom** を用いることもできます。

- The woman **whom I wanted to see** was away on vacation. (I wanted to see **her**)

to whom / from whom / with whom のように，**前置詞**を前に置いて **whom** を用いる形もあります。

- The people **with whom I work** are very nice. (I work **with them**)

話しことばではあまり **whom** は用いません。**who** や **that** の方がよく用いられます。➲Unit 91

- The woman **I wanted to see** . . . = The woman **who/that** I wanted to see . . .
- The people **I work with** . . . = The people **who/that** I work with . . .

C

where

where を用いて，**場所**について説明する**関係詞節**を作ります。

the restaurant – we had dinner there – it was near the airport

⇒ The restaurant **where we had dinner** was near the airport.

- I recently went back to **the town where I grew up**. (= . . . the town I grew up in = . . . the town **that** I grew up in ➲Unit 91)
- I would like to live in **a place where there is plenty of sunshine.**

D

「…する日 / 年 / 時」は **that** を用いて以下のように表します。**that** はよく省略されます。

the day / the year / the timeなど { something happens / = **that** something happens }

- Do you remember **the day** (**that**) **we went to the zoo?**
- **The last time** (**that**) **I saw her**, she looked fine.
- I haven't seen them since **the year** (**that**) **they got married.**

E

「…する理由」は **that** や **why** を用いて以下のように表します。**that/why** はよく省略されます。

the reason { something happens / = **that/why** something happens }

- **The reason I'm calling you** is to ask your advice. (= The reason **that** I'm calling / The reason **why** I'm calling)

関係詞節 1–2 ➲Units 90–91 関係詞節 4–5 ➲Units 93–94 whom ➲Unit 94

Exercises

92.1 あなたはパーティーで次の人たちに会いました。

パーティーの翌日，友達にパーティーで会った人について説明する文を **who** もしくは **whose** を用いて完成しなさい。

1. I met somebody _whose mother writes detective stories_ .
2. I met a man ______ .
3. I met a woman ______ .
4. I met somebody ______ .
5. I met a couple ______ .
6. I met somebody ______ .

92.2 where を用いて状況を説明する文を完成しなさい。

1. You grew up in a small town. You went back there recently. You tell someone this.
   I recently went back to the small town _where I grew up_ .
2. You want to buy some postcards. You ask a friend where you can do this.
   Is there someplace near here ______ ?
3. You work in a factory. The factory is going to close down next month. You tell a friend:
   The factory ______ is going to close down next month.
4. Sue is staying at a hotel. You want to know the name of the hotel. You ask a friend:
   Do you know the name of the hotel ______ ?
5. You play baseball in a park on Sundays. You show a friend the park. You say:
   This is the park ______ on Sundays.

92.3 状況に合うように who/whom/whose/where から適切なものを選び，空所に入れて文を完成しなさい。

1. What's the name of the man _whose_ car you borrowed?
2. A cemetery is a place ______ people are buried.
3. A pacifist is a person ______ believes that all wars are wrong.
4. An orphan is a child ______ parents are dead.
5. What was the name of the person to ______ you spoke on the phone?
6. The place ______ we spent our vacation was really beautiful.
7. This school is only for children ______ first language is not English.
8. The woman with ______ he fell in love left him after a month.

92.4 セクション D と E を参考にして，自分のことを記述する文を完成しなさい。

1. I'll always remember the day _I first met you_ .
2. I'll never forget the time ______ .
3. The reason ______ was that I didn't know your address.
4. Unfortunately I wasn't at home the evening ______ .
5. The reason ______ is that they don't need one.
6. ______ was the year ______ .

UNIT 93

関係詞節 4：情報を追加する継続用法としての関係詞節 (1)

A

☆ 関係詞節には文字で書いた際，直前にカンマ（,）が置かれないもの（制限用法）と置かれるもの（継続用法）との 2 種類があります。それぞれはどのように異なりますか？

制限用法

- The woman who lives next door is a doctor.
- Barbara works for a company that makes furniture.
- We stayed at the hotel (that) you recommended.

➤ 制限用法の関係詞節は，話し手がどの人や物について話題としているかを示したり，人や物の種類や性質を説明します。

The woman **who lives next door**
（⇒ さまざまな女性の中で，どの女性かを説明）

A company **that makes furniture**
（⇒ 会社は会社でも，どのような種類の会社かを説明）

The hotel (**that**) **you recommended**
（⇒ どのホテルかを説明）

制限用法は直前にカンマ（,）を置かずに表記します。

- People who come from Texas love football.

継続用法

- My brother Jim, who lives in Houston, is a doctor.
- Brad told me about his new job, which he's enjoying a lot.
- We stayed at the Grand Hotel, which a friend of ours recommended.

継続用法の関係詞節では，聞き手と話し手の双方が my brother Jim, Brad's new job, the Grand Hotel のように，すでにどの人や物について話題にしているか知っています。

➤ 継続用法の関係詞節は，話題となっている具体的な人や物についてさらに情報を追加します。

継続用法は直前にカンマを置いて表記します。

- My English teacher, who comes from Texas, loves computers.

B

☆ 制限用法でも継続用法でも，ともに人に対しては who，物に対しては which を用います。しかし，実際にはいくつかの点で用法が異なります。どのように異なりますか？

制限用法

that を who や which の代わりに使います。

- Do you know anyone **who/that** speaks French and Italian?
- Barbara works for a company **which/that** makes furniture.

目的語となった who/which/that は省略できます。 ➲ Unit 91

- We stayed at the hotel (which/that) you recommended.
- This morning I met somebody (who/that) I hadn't seen for ages.

whom はあまり用いません。➲ Unit 92B

継続用法

..., that は使えません。

- John, **who** (✕ that) speaks French and Italian, works as a tour guide.
- Brad told me about his new job, **which** (✕ that) he's enjoying a lot.

..., who/which は省略できません。

- We stayed at the Grand Hotel, **which** a friend of ours recommended.
- This morning I met Chris, **who** I hadn't seen for ages.

目的語となった人については whom を用いることができます。

- This morning I met Chris, **whom** I hadn't seen for ages.

whose と **where** は，制限用法でも継続用法でも用いることができます。

- We met some people **whose** car had broken down.
- What's the name of the place **where** you spent your vacation?
- Amy, **whose** car had broken down, was in a very bad mood.
- Mrs. Bond is spending a few weeks in Sweden, **where** her daughter lives.

制限用法の関係詞節 ➲ Units 90–92　継続用法の関係詞節 ➲ Unit 94

Exercises

93.1 **who(m)/whose/which/where の中から適切なものを選び，（　）内の文を継続用法の関係詞節にして 1 つの文にしなさい。**

1. Ann is very friendly. (She lives next door.)
   Ann, who lives next door, is very friendly.
2. We stayed at the Grand Hotel. (A friend of ours had recommended it.)
   We stayed at the Grand Hotel, which a friend of ours had recommended.
3. We often go to visit our friends in New York. (It is not very far away.)
   ______
4. I went to see the doctor. (He told me to rest for a few days.)
   ______
5. John is one of my closest friends. (I have known him for a very long time.)
   John, ______
6. Sheila is away from home a lot. (Her job involves a lot of travel.)
   ______
7. The new stadium will be opened next month. (It can hold 90,000 people.)
   ______
8. Alaska is the largest state in the United States. (My brother lives there.)
   ______
9. A friend of mine helped me to get a job. (His father is the manager of a company.)
   ______

93.2 **制限用法もしくは継続用法の関係詞節を用いて，状況を説明する文を完成しなさい。**

1. There's a woman living next door to me. She's a doctor.
   The woman *who lives next door to me is a doctor.*
2. I have a brother named Jim. He lives in Houston. He's a doctor.
   My brother Jim, *who lives in Houston, is a doctor.*
3. There was a strike at the car factory. It began 10 days ago. It is now over.
   The strike at the car factory ______
4. I was looking for a book this morning. I've found it now.
   I've found ______
5. London was once the largest city in the world, but the population is now decreasing.
   The population of London, ______
6. A job was advertised. A lot of people applied for it. Few of them had the necessary qualifications. Few of ______
7. Amanda has a son. She showed me a picture of him. He's a police officer.
   Amanda showed me ______

93.3 **それぞれの文について誤りのある部分を◯で囲み，正しい形に書き換えなさい（必要に応じてカンマを前に置くこと）。**

1. Brad told me about his new job that he's enjoying a lot.
   Brad told me about his new job, which he's enjoying a lot.
2. My office that is on the second floor is very small.
   ______
3. The office I'm using these days is very small.
   ______
4. Ben's father that used to be a teacher now works for a TV company.
   ______
5. The doctor that examined me couldn't find anything wrong.
   ______
6. The sun that is one of millions of stars in the universe provides us with heat and light.
   ______

UNIT 94

関係詞節 5：情報を追加する継続用法としての関係詞節 (2)

A ..., 前置詞 + whom/which

..., to whom / ..., with whom / ..., about which / ..., without which のように，カンマ (,) に続けて，人に対しては前置詞 + **whom**，物に対しては前置詞 + **which** の形を用いて継続用法の関係詞節を作ります。

- Mr. Carter, **to whom** I spoke at the meeting, is very interested in our plan.
- Fortunately we had a map, **without which** we would have gotten lost.

普通，話しことばでは前置詞 + **whom/which** の形よりも，関係詞節中の動詞の後に前置詞だけを残した形を用います。この場合，人に対しては関係詞節の先頭に **whom** ではなく **who** を置きます。

- This is my friend from Canada, **who** I was telling you **about**. (× **whom** I was . . .)
- Yesterday we visited the City Museum, **which** I'd never been **to** before.

B ..., all of / most of など + whom/which

前置詞の後の目的格の代名詞を **whom** に変えて，継続用法の関係詞節を作ります。

Mary has three brothers. All of them are married.（2 つの文）

⇒ Mary has three brothers, **all of whom** are married.（1 つの文）

They asked me a lot of questions. I couldn't answer most of them .（2 つの文）

⇒ They asked me a lot of questions, **most of which** I couldn't answer.（1 つの文）

同様に以下の前置詞で終わる語句も，継続用法の関係詞節を作ります。

..., none of / neither of / any of / either of **..., some of / many of / much of /** (a) **few of** **..., both of / half of / each of / one of / two of** など	**+ whom**（人に対して） **+ which**（物に対して）

- Tom tried on three jackets, **none of which** fit him.
- Two men, **neither of whom** I had ever seen before, came into the office.
- They have three cars, **two of which** they rarely use.
- Sue has a lot of friends, **many of whom** she went to school with.

..., the cause of which / ..., the name of which などのような継続用法もよく用いられます。

- The building was destroyed in a fire, **the cause of which** was never established.
- We stayed at a beautiful hotel, **the name of which** I can't remember now.

C ..., which

☆ 例文で考えます。継続用法の which は何を指していますか？

⇒ Joe got the job. This surprised everybody.（2 つの文）

⇒ Joe got the job, **which** surprised everybody.（1 つの文）

関係詞節

➤ 例文中の継続用法の which は，Joe got the job. という直前の文全体を指しています。このような場合には，カンマに続けて which を用います。左側に説明される名詞を持つので，what は使えません。

- Sarah couldn't meet us, **which** was a shame. (× what was a shame)
- The weather was good, **which** we hadn't expected. (× what we hadn't expected)

what の用法 ➲ Units 90C, 91D

all of / most of など ➲ Unit 86　both of など ➲ Unit 87　関係詞節 1–4 ➲ Units 90–93

Exercises

94.1 「..., 前置詞 + whom/which」の形を用いて，より正式な形の関係詞節に書き換えなさい。

1. Yesterday we visited the City Museum, which I'd never been to before.
   Yesterday we visited the City Museum, *to which I'd never been before* .
2. My brother showed us his new car, which he's very proud of.
   My brother showed us his new car, ______________________________ .
3. This is a picture of our friends Chris and Sam, who we went on vacation with.
   This is a picture of our friends Chris and Sam, ______________________________ .
4. The wedding, which only members of the family were invited to, took place on Friday.
   The wedding, ______________________________ ,
   took place on Friday.

94.2 最初の文の情報を用いて，「..., all of / ..., most of や the ... of + whom/which」のような形を使って 2 番目の文を完成しなさい。

1. All of Mary's brothers are married.
   Mary has three brothers, *all of whom are married* .
2. Most of the information we were given was useless.
   We were given a lot of information, ______________________________ .
3. Jane has received neither of the letters I sent her.
   I sent Jane two letters, ______________________________ .
4. None of the ten people who applied for the job was suitable.
   Ten people applied for the job, ______________________________ .
5. Kate hardly ever uses one of her computers.
   Kate has got two computers, ______________________________ .
6. Mike gave half of the $50,000 he won to his parents.
   Mike won $50,000, ______________________________ .
7. Both of Julia's sisters are teachers.
   Julia has two sisters, ______________________________ .
8. I went to a party – I knew only a few of the people there.
   There were a lot of people at the party, ______________________________ .
9. The sides of the road we drove along were lined with trees.
   We drove along the road, the ______________________________ .
10. The aim of the company's new business plan is to save money.
    The company has a new business plan, ______________________________ .

94.3 左右から 1 つずつ文を選び，状況に合うように継続用法の関係詞節を含む文を作りなさい。

1. ~~Laura couldn't come to the party.~~	This was very nice of her.
2. Jane doesn't have a phone.	This means we can't take our trip tomorrow.
3. Neil has passed his exams.	This makes it difficult to contact her.
4. Our flight was delayed.	This makes it difficult to sleep sometimes.
5. Kate offered to let me stay at her house.	~~This was a shame.~~
6. The street I live on is very noisy at night.	This is good news.
7. Our car has broken down.	This meant we had to wait three hours at the airport.

1. Laura couldn't come to the party, *which was a shame.*
2. Jane ______________________________
3. ______________________________
4. ______________________________
5. ______________________________
6. ______________________________
7. ______________________________

UNIT 95

-ing 句と -ed 句 (the woman **talking to Tom**, the boy **injured in the accident**)

A

☆ 句は複数の語を持ち節（文）を構成する要素です（節について ➲ Unit 90）。例文中の -ing や -ed で始まる句は何を表しますか？ イラストを見て考えます。

Do you know the woman **talking to Tom**?
-ing 句
(⇒ Tom と話をしている～)

The boy **injured in the accident** was taken to the hospital.
-ed 句
(⇒ 事故でけがをした～)

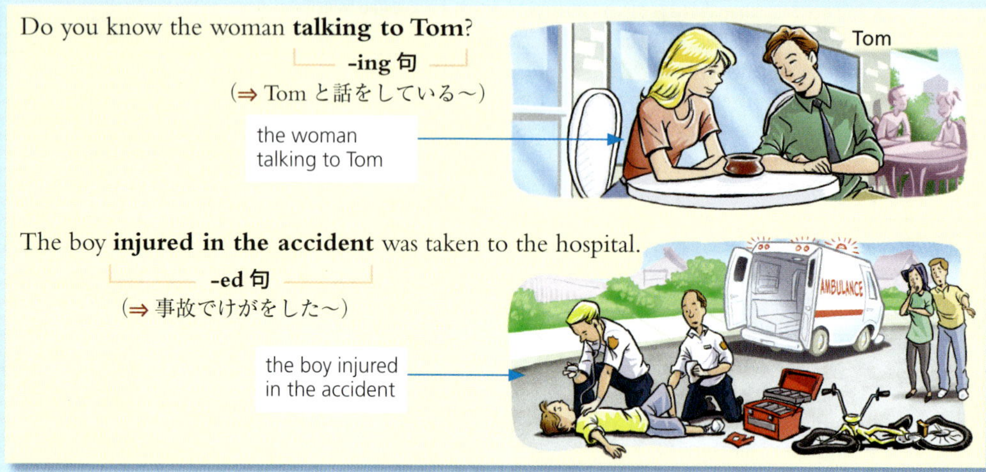

B

-ing 句は，「～の時に，…している～（人 / 物）」のように**能動的な意味**を持ち，関係詞節同様に左側に説明される名詞句を持ちます。

- Do you know the woman **talking to Sam**?（⇒「今，Sam と話をしている」女性）
- Police **investigating the crime** are looking for three men.（⇒「今，その犯罪を捜査している」警察）
- Who were those people **waiting outside**?（⇒「あの時，外で待っていた」人たち）
- I was awakened by a bell **ringing**.（⇒「その時，鳴っていた」ベル）

-ing 句は，ある時点で成立していた**一時的な動作**のみならず，常に成立している**状態**を表すこともあります。

- The road **connecting the two towns** is very narrow.（⇒「2 つの町をつなぐ」道路）
- I have a large bedroom **overlooking the garden**.（⇒「庭を見下ろす」部屋）
- Can you think of the name of a flower **beginning with "t"**?（⇒「t で始まる」名前の花）

C

-ed 句は「…された～（人 / 物）」のように**受動的な意味**を持ちます。

- The boy **injured in the accident** was taken to the hospital.（⇒「事故でけがをした」少年）
- George showed me some pictures **painted by his father**（⇒「彼の父によって描かれた」絵）

injured や **painted** のような動詞の **-ed 形**は**過去分詞**と呼ばれます。**stolen/made/written** などのように，多くの**過去分詞**が語尾に -ed を持たず**不規則変化**します。

- The police never found the money **stolen in the robbery**.
- Most of the goods **made in this factory** are exported.

以下の例において **left** は「使われていない，残った」の意味を持つ**過去分詞**です。

- We've eaten almost all the chocolates. There are only a few **left**.

D

-ing 句と -ed 句を **there is /there was** などの句の後に置いた形がよく用いられます。

- **There were** some children **swimming** in the river.
- **Is there** anybody **waiting**?
- **There was** a big red car **parked** outside the house.

see/hear ～ doing ... ➲ Unit 65　-ing 句（分詞構文）➲ Unit 66　There (is) ➲ Unit 82
made/stolen などの不規則変化をする過去分詞 ➲ 付録 1

Exercises

95.1 2 つの文を -ing 句を用いて 1 つにまとめ，状況を説明する文を完成しなさい。

1. A bell was ringing. I was awakened by it.
   I was awakened by *a bell ringing* .
2. A man was sitting next to me on the plane. I didn't talk much to him.
   I didn't talk much to the __________ .
3. A taxi was taking us to the airport. It broke down.
   The __________ broke down.
4. There's a path at the end of this street. The path leads to the river.
   At the end of the street there's a __________ .
5. A factory has just opened in town. It employs 500 people.
   A __________ has just opened in town.
6. The company sent me a brochure. It contained the information I needed.
   The company sent me __________ .

95.2 2 つの文を -ed 句を用いて 1 つにまとめ，状況を説明する文を完成しなさい。

1. A boy was injured in the accident. He was taken to the hospital.
   The boy *injured in the accident* was taken to the hospital.
2. A gate was damaged in the storm. It has now been repaired.
   The gate __________ has now been repaired.
3. A number of suggestions were made at the meeting. Most of them were not very practical.
   Most of the __________ were not very practical.
4. Some paintings were stolen from the museum. They haven't been found yet.
   The __________ haven't been found yet.
5. A man was arrested by the police. What was his name?
   What was the name of __________ ?

95.3 状況に合うように，以下から動詞を選び適切な形に変えて空所に入れ，文を完成しなさい。

blow drive ~~invite~~ live name offer read ~~ring~~ sell sit

1. I was awakened by a bell *ringing* .
2. Some of the people *invited* to the party can't come.
3. Life must be very unpleasant for people __________ near busy airports.
4. A few days after the interview, I received a letter __________ me the job.
5. Somebody __________ Jack phoned while you were out.
6. There was a tree __________ down in the storm last night.
7. The waiting room was empty except for a young man __________ by the window __________ a magazine.
8. Look! The man __________ the red car almost hit the person __________ newspapers on the street corner.

95.4 (　) 内の語句を There is / There was などの後に続け，適切な形に変えて文を完成しなさい。

1. That house is empty. (nobody / live / in it) *There's nobody living in it.*
2. The accident wasn't serious. (nobody / injure) *There was nobody injured.*
3. I can hear footsteps. (somebody / come)
   There __________
4. The train was full. (a lot of people / travel)
   ____
5. We were the only guests at the hotel. (nobody else / stay there)
   ____
6. The piece of paper was blank. (nothing / write / on it)
   ____
7. The school offers English courses in the evening. (a new course / begin / next Monday)
   ____

UNIT 96

-ing や -ed の語尾を持つ形容詞 (boring/bored など)

A

☆ イラストを見て考えます。boring と bored は，どのように異なりますか？

Jane は長い間ずっと同じ仕事をしています。くる日もくる日も同じことの繰り返しです。今の仕事に興味を持てず，今と違うことがしたいと考えています。この時，彼女の仕事と彼女自身について以下のように記述できます。

Jane's job is **boring**.
Jane is **bored** (with her job).

➤ 物や人が退屈であることを boring，人が退屈していることを bored で表します。

以下の例文が示すように，**bored** と **boring** の間には「人が **bored**（退屈する）のは物や人が **boring**（退屈である）であるから / 物や人が **boring** であるので人が **bored**」のような関係があります。

- Jane is **bored** because her job is **boring**.
- Jane's job is **boring**, so Jane is **bored**. (× Jane is boring)

「人が **boring**」というのは，「その人によって周りの人が **bored** となる」を意味します。

- George always talks about the same things. He's really **boring**.

B

☆ 例文で考えます。-ing で終わる形容詞と -ed で終わる形容詞とは，どのように異なりますか？

-ing

- My job is { **boring**. / **interesting**. / **tiring**. / **satisfying**. / **depressing**. など }

➤ -ing で終わる形容詞は，仕事がどのようなものであるかを説明します。

-ed

- I'm **bored** with my job.
- I'm not **interested** in my job any more.
- I get very **tired** doing my job.
- I'm not **satisfied** with my job.
- My job makes me **depressed**. など

➤ -ed で終わる形容詞は，仕事について人がどのように感じたかを説明します。

☆ 左右を比べて考えます。-ing で終わる形容詞と -ed で終わる形容詞とは，どのように異なりますか？

interesting
- Julia thinks politics is **interesting**.
- Did you meet anyone **interesting** at the party?

interested
- Julia is **interested** in politics. (× interesting in politics)
- Are you **interested** in buying a car? I'm trying to sell mine.

surprising
- It was **surprising** that he passed the exam.

surprised
- Everybody was **surprised** that he passed the exam.

disappointing
- The movie was **disappointing**. We expected it to be much better.

disappointed
- We were **disappointed** with the movie. We expected it to be much better.

shocking
- The news was **shocking**.

shocked
- I was **shocked** when I heard the news.

Exercises

96.1 ( ) 内の語を -ing もしくは -ed を語尾に持つ形容詞にして，状況を説明する文を完成しなさい。

1. The movie wasn't as good as we had expected. (disappoint-)
   a) The movie was _disappointing_ .
   b) We were _disappointed_ with the movie.
2. Diana teaches young children. It's a very hard job, but she enjoys it. (exhaust-)
   a) She enjoys her job, but it's often ________ .
   b) At the end of a day's work, she is often ________ .
3. It's been raining all day. I hate this weather. (depress-)
   a) This weather is ________ .
   b) This weather makes me ________ .
   c) It's silly to get ________ because of the weather.
4. Claire is going to Mexico next month. She has never been there before. (excit-)
   a) It will be an ________ experience for her.
   b) Going to new places is always ________ .
   c) She is really ________ about going to Mexico.

96.2 下線部の正しい方を選んで，文を完成しなさい。

1. I was ~~disappointing~~ / disappointed with the movie. I had expected it to be better.
   (disappointed が正しい)
2. Are you interesting / interested in tennis?
3. The tennis match was very exciting / excited. I had a great time.
4. It's sometimes embarrassing / embarrassed when you have to ask people for money.
5. Do you get embarrassing / embarrassed easily?
6. I never expected to get the job. I was really amazing / amazed when it was offered to me.
7. She has learned really fast. She has made astonishing / astonished progress.
8. I didn't find the situation funny. I was not amusing / amused.
9. It was a really terrifying / terrified experience. Everybody was very shocking / shocked.
10. Why do you always look so boring / bored? Is your life really so boring / bored?
11. He's one of the most boring / bored people I've ever met. He never stops talking and he never says anything interesting / interested.

96.3 状況に合うように以下から適切な語を選び，空所に入れて文を完成しなさい。

amusing/amused	**annoying/annoyed**	**boring/bored**
confusing/confused	**disgusting/disgusted**	**exciting/excited**
exhausting/exhausted	**interesting/interested**	~~**surprising**~~ **/surprised**

1. He works very hard. It's not _surprising_ that he's always tired.
2. I don't have anything to do. I'm ________ .
3. The teacher's explanation was ________ . Most of the students didn't understand it.
4. The kitchen hadn't been cleaned in ages. It was really ________ .
5. I seldom go to art galleries. I'm not particularly ________ in art.
6. You don't have to get ________ just because I'm a few minutes late.
7. The lecture was ________ . I fell asleep.
8. I've been working very hard all day and now I'm ________ .
9. I'm starting a new job next week. I'm very ________ about it.
10. Tom is very good at telling funny stories. He can be very ________ .
11. Liz is a very ________ person. She knows a lot, she's traveled a lot, and she's done lots of different things.

UNIT 97

形容詞の語順 (a nice new house), 動詞の後にくる形容詞 (you look tired)

A

☆ 1つの名詞の前に複数の形容詞がくる場合があります。その際，語順はどのように決まりますか？

- My brother lives in a **nice new** house.
- There was a **beautiful large round wooden** table in the kitchen.

new/large/round/wooden などの形容詞は「**事実を表す形容詞**」と呼ばれます。**事実を表す形容詞**は，年齢，大きさ，色などの事実についての情報をもたらします。

一方，**nice/beautiful** などの形容詞は「**意見を表す形容詞**」と呼ばれます。**意見を表す形容詞**は，物や人について，人がどのように考えているかを表します。

➤「意見を表す形容詞」は普通，「事実を表す形容詞」よりも前にきます。

冠詞	意見を表す形容詞	事実を表す形容詞	名詞
a	**nice**	**long**	summer vacation
an	**interesting**	**young**	man
	delicious	**hot**	vegetable soup
a	**beautiful**	**large round wooden**	table

B

☆ 2つ以上の事実を表す形容詞が名詞の前にくる場合，以下のような順番で配置します。例文の形容詞はどのような順番で現れていますか？ 番号で確認します。

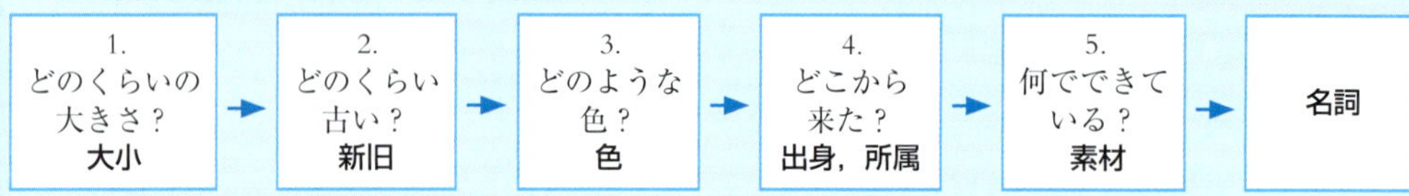

a **tall young** man (1 → 2)
big blue eyes (1 → 3)
a **small black plastic** bag (1 → 3 → 5)
a **large wooden** table (1 → 5)
an **old Russian** song (2 → 4)
an **old white cotton** shirt (2 → 3 → 5)

普通，**大きさや長さを表す形容詞**（big/small/tall/short/long など）は，**形や広さを表す形容詞**（round/fat/thin/slim/wide など）よりも前にきます。

a **large round** table　a **tall thin** girl　a **long narrow** street

2つ以上の**色を表す形容詞**を並べる際には **and** を用います。

a **black and white** dress　a **red, white, and green** flag

しかし**色以外の形容詞＋色**の場合には，普通 **and** は用いません。

a **long black** dress (✕ a long and black dress)

C

be/get/become/seem のような**動詞**の後に**形容詞**がくることがあります。

- **Be careful**!
- I'm **tired** and I'm **getting hungry**.
- As the movie went on, it **became** more and more **boring**.
- Your friend **seems** very **nice**.

どのように人や物が見えたり (look)，感じたり (feel)，聞こえたり (sound)，味がしたり (taste)，臭いや香りがしたり (smell) を表す際には，**形容詞を動詞の後に**置きます。このような動詞を**知覚動詞**と呼びます。

- You **look tired**. / I **feel tired**. / She **sounds tired**.
- The dinner **smells good**.
- This milk **tastes** a little **strange**.

一方，どのように人が動作を行ったのかを表す際には**副詞を動詞**の後に置きます。➲ Units 98–99

- Drive **carefully**! (✕ Drive careful)
- Susan plays the piano very **well**. (✕ plays . . . very good)

D

the first two days / the next few weeks / the last 10 minutes などのように，**数を表す語**はより**名詞**の近くに置きます。

- I didn't enjoy the **first two** days of the course. (✕ the two first days)
- They'll be away for the **next few** weeks. (✕ the few next weeks)

副詞 ➲ Units 98–99　比較級（cheaper など）➲ Units 102–104　最上級（cheapest など）➲ Unit 105

Exercises

97.1 (　) 内の形容詞を正しい位置に入れなさい（必要に応じて and を補うこと）。

1. a beautiful table (wooden / round) *a beautiful round wooden table*
2. an unusual ring (gold) ______
3. an old house (beautiful) ______
4. black gloves (leather) ______
5. an Italian film (old) ______
6. a long face (thin) ______
7. big clouds (black) ______
8. a sunny day (lovely) ______
9. an ugly dress (yellow) ______
10. a wide avenue (long) ______
11. a red car (old / little) ______
12. a new sweater (green / nice) ______
13. a metal box (black / small) ______
14. a big cat (fat / black) ______
15. a little country inn (old / charming) ______
16. long hair (black / beautiful) ______
17. an old painting (interesting / French) ______
18. an enormous umbrella (red / yellow) ______

97.2 状況に合うように左右から動詞と形容詞を 1 つずつ選び，適切な形に変えて空所に入れ，文を完成しなさい。

feel	look	~~seem~~
smell	sound	taste

awful	fine	interesting
nice	~~upset~~	wet

1. Helen *seemed upset* this morning. Do you know what was wrong?
2. I can't eat this. I just tried it and it ______ .
3. I was sick yesterday, but I ______ today.
4. What beautiful flowers! They ______ , too.
5. You ______ . Have you been out in the rain?
6. Jim was telling me about his new job. It ______ – much better than his old job.

97.3 状況に合うように (　) 内からより適切な語を選び，空所に入れて文を完成しなさい。

1. This milk tastes *strange* . (strange / strangely)
2. I always feel ______ when the sun is shining. (happy / happily)
3. The children were playing ______ in the yard. (happy / happily)
4. The man became ______ when the manager of the restaurant asked him to leave. (violent / violently)
5. You look ______ ! Are you all right? (terrible / terribly)
6. There's no point in doing a job if you don't do it ______ . (proper / properly)
7. The soup tastes ______ . (good / well)
8. Hurry up! You're always so ______ . (slow / slowly)

97.4 the first ... / the next ... / the last ... を用いて，左の語句の状況を書き換えなさい。

1. the first day and the second day of the course *the first two days of the course*
2. next week and the week after *the next two weeks*
3. yesterday and the day before yesterday ______
4. the first week and the second week of May ______
5. tomorrow and a few days after that ______
6. questions 1, 2, and 3 on the exam ______
7. next year and the year after ______
8. the last day of our vacation and the two days before that ______

補充問題 31 (p. 314)

UNIT 98

形容詞と副詞 1 (quick/quickly)

A

☆ 例文で考えます。太字体の語は何と呼ばれ，どのような形の上での特徴がありますか？

- Our vacation was too short – the time passed very **quickly**.
- Two people were **seriously** injured in the accident.

➤ quickly や seriously などの語は副詞と呼ばれ，多くは形容詞に -ly の語尾を付けて作られます。

形容詞：	quick	serious	careful	quiet	heavy	bad
副詞：	quickly	seriously	carefully	quietly	heavily	badly

語尾 -ly に関連してつづり方で注意すべきこと ➲ 付録 6 **副詞**の中には **-ly** で終わらないものもあります。
また，以下のように **-ly** で終わる**形容詞**もあります。

friendly **lively** **elderly** **lonely** **silly** **lovely**

B

☆ 形容詞と副詞は，どのように異なりますか？

➤ quick/careful などの形容詞は，名詞を修飾して，人や物がどのようであるかを説明します。

- Tom is a **careful driver**. (✕ a carefully driver)
- We didn't go out because of the **heavy rain**.

➤ quickly/carefully などの副詞は，動詞を修飾して，どのように人が行動したり出来事が起きるかを説明します。

- Tom **drove carefully** along the narrow road. (✕ drove careful)
- We didn't go out because it was **raining heavily**. (✕ raining heavy)

☆ 形容詞と副詞は，普通どのような位置に生じますか？

形容詞は名詞の前

- She speaks **perfect English**.
  形容詞 + 名詞

副詞は動詞の後

- She **speaks** English **perfectly**.
  動詞 + 名詞 + 副詞

be/look/feel/sound などの動詞の後にくる形容詞もあります。➲ Units 97C

☆ いずれも動詞の後にきますが，形容詞と副詞では，どのように異なりますか？

形容詞（名詞を説明）

- Please **be quiet**. (⇒〔あなたが〕静かに)
- I was disappointed that my exam results **were** so **bad**.
- Why do you always **look** so **serious**?
- I **feel happy**.

副詞（動詞を説明）

- Please **speak quietly**. (⇒ 静かに話す)
- I was unhappy that I **did** so **badly** on the exam. (✕ did so bad)
- Why do you never **take** me **seriously**?
- The children were **playing happily**.

C

副詞は**動詞**の後以外に，**形容詞**や他の**副詞**の前に置くこともあります。

reasonably cheap （副詞 + 形容詞）
terribly sorry （副詞 + 形容詞）
incredibly quickly （副詞 + 副詞）

- It's a **reasonably cheap** restaurant, and the food is **extremely good**.
- I'm **terribly sorry**. I didn't mean to push you. (✕ terrible sorry)
- Maria learns languages **incredibly quickly**.
- The test was **surprisingly easy**.

副詞は injured/organized/written などのような**過去分詞**の前にも置きます。

- Two people were **seriously injured** in the accident. (✕ serious injured)
- The conference was very **badly organized**.

be/look/feel などの動詞の後にくる形容詞 ➲ Unit 97C　　形容詞と副詞 2 ➲ Unit 99

Exercises

98.1 状況に合うように，空所に副詞を入れて文を完成しなさい（それぞれ指定された文字で始めること）。

1. We didn't go out because it was raining he*avily*.
2. Our team lost the game because we played very ba________.
3. I had little trouble finding a place to live. I found an apartment quite ea________.
4. We had to wait for a long time, but we didn't complain. We waited pat________.
5. Nobody knew Steve was coming to see us. He arrived unex________.
6. Mike stays in shape by playing tennis reg________.
7. I don't speak French very well, but I can understand per________ if people speak sl________ and cl________.

98.2 状況に合うように（　）内からより適切な語を選び，空所に入れて文を完成しなさい。

1. Two people were *seriously* injured in the accident. (serious / seriously)
2. The driver of the car had *serious* injuries. (serious / seriously)
3. I think you behaved very ________. (selfish / selfishly)
4. Kelly is ________ upset about losing her job. (terrible / terribly)
5. There was a ________ change in the weather. (sudden / suddenly)
6. Everybody at the party was ________ dressed. (colorful / colorfully)
7. Linda likes wearing ________ clothes. (colorful / colorfully)
8. Liz fell and hurt herself really ________. (bad / badly)
9. These pants are already coming apart. They're ________ made. (bad / badly)
10. Don't go up that ladder. It doesn't look ________. (safe / safely)

98.3 状況に合うように以下から適切な語を選び，空所に入れて文を完成しなさい。空所には **careful** のような形容詞，もしくは **carefully** のような副詞のいずれかが入ります。

careful(ly)	**complete(ly)**	**continuous(ly)**	**financial(ly)**	**fluent(ly)**
happy / happily	**nervous(ly)**	**perfect(ly)**	~~**quick(ly)**~~	**special(ly)**

1. Our vacation was too short. The time passed very *quickly*.
2. Tom doesn't take risks when he's driving. He's always ________.
3. Sue works ________. She never seems to stop.
4. Amy and Eric are very ________ married.
5. Nicole's English is very ________ although she makes a lot of mistakes.
6. I cooked this meal ________ for you, so I hope you like it.
7. Everything was very quiet. There was ________ silence.
8. I tried on the shoes and they fit me ________.
9. Do you usually feel ________ before exams?
10. I'd like to buy a car, but it's ________ impossible for me at this time.

98.4 状況に合うように左右から適切な語を 1 つずつ選び，空所に入れて文を完成しなさい。

absolutely	**badly**	**completely**
~~**reasonably**~~	**seriously**	**slightly**
unnecessarily	**unusually**	

changed	~~**cheap**~~	**damaged**
enormous	**ill**	**long**
planned	**quiet**	

1. I thought the restaurant would be expensive, but it was *reasonably cheap*.
2. Steve's mother is ________ in the hospital.
3. What a big house! It's ________.
4. It wasn't a serious accident. The car was only ________.
5. The children are normally very lively, but they're ________ today.
6. When I returned home after 20 years, everything had ________.
7. The movie was ________. It could have been much shorter.
8. A lot went wrong during our vacation because it was ________.

補充問題 31 (p. 314)

UNIT 99

形容詞と副詞 2 (well/fast/late, hard/hardly)

A

good/well

「良い」を表す**形容詞**は **good** ですが，「よく，上手に」を表す**副詞**は **well** になります。

- Your English is **good**. ⇔ You **speak** English **well**.
- Susan is a **good** pianist. ⇔ Susan **plays** the piano **well**.

dressed/known などの**過去分詞**の前には **well** を置きます（good は置きません）。➲ Unit 98C

well dressed　**well known**　**well educated**　**well paid**

- Gary's father is a **well known** writer.

well には，**副詞**以外に「元気である，健康である」という**形容詞**としての用法があります。

- "How are you today?" "I'm very **well**, thanks."

B

fast/hard/late

同じ形で，**形容詞**にも**副詞**にも用いられるものがあります。

形容詞

- Jack is a **very fast runner**.
- Kate is a **hard worker**.
- I was **late**.

副詞

- Jack can **run** very **fast**.
- Kate **works hard**. (× works hardly)
- I **got up late** this morning.

late は「遅い（形容詞）/ 遅く（副詞）」を意味しますが，**lately** は **recently** 同様「最近」を意味する**副詞**です。

- Have you seen Tom **lately**?

C

hardly

hardly は「ほとんど…ない」を意味する**副詞**です（否定的な意味を持つことに注意）。

- Sarah wasn't very friendly at the party. She **hardly** spoke to me.
（⇒ ほとんど，まったくと言ってよいほど話さなかった）
- We've only met once or twice. We **hardly** know each other.

hard は「一生懸命に」を意味する**副詞**です（hardly との意味の違いに注意）。

- He tried **hard** to find a job, but he had no luck.（⇒ 一生懸命，探そうとした）
- I'm not surprised he didn't find a job. He **hardly** tried to find one.（⇒ ほとんど探そうとしなかった）

hardly の後には **any/anybody/anyone/anything/anywhere** といった語がよくきます。

- *A:* How much money have we got?
B: **Hardly any**.（⇒ ほとんど持っていません）
- These two cameras are very similar. There's **hardly any** difference between them.
- The results of the test were very bad. **Hardly anybody** in our class passed.（⇒ ほとんど誰も合格しなかった）

hardly は **any-** の直前に置く以外に，**動詞**をはさんで置くことも可能です。

- She said **hardly anything**. = She **hardly** said **anything**.
- We've got **hardly any** money. = We've **hardly** got any **money**.

I can hardly do ... は「難しくてほとんど…できない」を意味します。

- Your writing is terrible. I **can hardly** read it.
（⇒ 難しくてほとんど読めない）
- My leg was hurting me. I **could hardly** walk.

hardly ever は「めったに…ない」を意味します。

- I'm nearly always at home at night. I **hardly ever** go out.

hardly は「間違いなく…ではない，…ないのは当然だ」を意味することがあります。

- It's **hardly surprising** that you're tired. You haven't slept for three days.（⇒ 疲れていても驚くべきことではない，疲れて当然）
- The situation is serious, but it's **hardly a crisis**.
（⇒ 危機的状況ではないことは確か，危機的状況ではない）

you look tired のように動詞の後にくる形容詞 ➲ Unit 97C　形容詞と副詞 1 ➲ Unit 98

Exercises

99.1 状況に合うように空所に good もしくは well を入れて，文を完成しなさい。

1. I play tennis but I'm not very _good_ .
2. Your test results were very ______ .
3. You did ______ on the test.
4. The weather was ______ while we were on vacation.
5. I didn't sleep ______ last night.
6. Jason speaks Spanish very ______ .
7. Jason's Spanish is very ______ .
8. Our new business isn't doing very ______ at the moment.
9. I like your jacket. It looks ______ on you.
10. I've met her a few times, but I don't know her ______ .

99.2 状況に合うように well の後に続く語を以下から選び，空所に入れて文を完成しなさい。

~~behaved~~ **dressed** **informed** **known** **maintained** **paid** **written**

1. The children were very good. They were _well behaved_ .
2. I'm surprised you haven't heard of her. She is quite ______ .
3. Our neighbors' yard is neat and clean. It is very ______ .
4. I enjoyed the book you lent me. It's a great story, and it's very ______ .
5. Tania knows a lot about many things. She is very ______ .
6. Mark always wears nice clothes. He is always ______ .
7. Jane has a lot of responsibility in her job, but she isn't very ______ .

99.3 下線部の語について誤りがある場合には，正しい形を記入しなさい。

1. I'm tired because I've been working hard. _OK_
2. I tried hard to remember her name, but I couldn't. ______
3. This coat is practically unused. I've hardly worn it. ______
4. Judy is a good tennis player. She hits the ball hardly. ______
5. Don't walk so fast! I can't keep up with you. ______
6. I had plenty of time, so I was walking slow. ______

99.4 状況に合うように hardly の後に続く語を以下から選び，空所に入れて文を完成しなさい。

change **hear** ~~know~~ **recognize** **say** **sleep** **speak**

1. Scott and Amy have only met once before. They _hardly know_ each other.
2. You're speaking very quietly. I can ______ you.
3. I'm very tired this morning. I ______ last night.
4. We were so shocked when we heard the news, we could ______ .
5. Kate was very quiet this evening. She ______ a word.
6. You look the same now as you looked 15 years ago. You've ______ .
7. I met Dave a few days ago. I hadn't seen him for a long time and he looks very different now. I ______ him.

99.5 hardly の後に any/anybody/anything/anywhere/ever の中から選んだ 1 語を続け，空所に入れて文を完成しなさい。

1. I'll have to go shopping. There's _hardly anything_ to eat.
2. It was a very warm day. There was ______ wind.
3. "Do you know much about computers?" "No, ______ ."
4. The hotel was almost empty. There was ______ staying there.
5. I listen to the radio a lot, but I ______ watch television.
6. Our new boss is not very popular. ______ likes her.
7. It was very crowded in the room. There was ______ to sit.
8. We used to be good friends, but we ______ see each other now.
9. It was nice driving this morning. There was ______ traffic.
10. I hate this town. There's ______ to do and ______ to go.

補充問題 31 (p. 314)

UNIT 100

so と such

A

☆ so と such は，語順の上でどのように異なりますか？

➤ **so は形容詞と副詞の直前に置きます。**

so stupid　**so quick**
so nice　**so quickly**

- I didn't like the book. The story was **so stupid**.
- I like Liz and Joe. They are **so nice**.

➤ **such は名詞句の前に置きます。**

such a story　**such people**

形容詞の付いた**名詞**には so ではなく **such** を用います。

such a stupid **story**　**such** nice **people**

- I didn't like the book. It was **such** a stupid **story**. (✕ a so stupid story)
- I like Liz and Joe. They are **such nice people**. (✕ so nice people)

such + (a/an) + 形容詞 + 名詞という語順に注意。

such a big **dog** (✕ a such big dog)

B

so も such も「とても～」のように，修飾する**形容詞**（so の場合には副詞も）の意味を強調します。

- It's a beautiful day, isn't it? It's **so warm**. (⇒ とても寒い)
- It's difficult to understand him because he talks **so quietly**.

「とても～なので…」は **so + 形容詞 + that ...** で表します。

- The book was **so good that** I couldn't put it down.
- I was **so tired that** I fell asleep in the armchair.

that はよく省略されます。

- I was **so tired** I fell asleep.

- It was a great holiday. We had **such a good time**. (⇒ とても楽しい時間を)

「とても～なので…」は **such + (a/an) + 形容詞 + 名詞 + that ...** で表します。

- It was **such a good book that** I couldn't put it down.
- It was **such nice weather that** we spent the whole day on the beach.

that はよく省略されます。

- It was **such nice weather** we spent . . .

C

so も such も「このように，それほど」を表します。

- Somebody told me the house was built 100 years ago. I didn't realize it was **so old**. (⇒ それほど古いとは…)
- I'm tired because I got up at six. I don't usually get up **so early**.
- I expected the weather to be cooler. I'm surprised it is **so warm**.

- I didn't realize it was **such an old house**.
- You know it's not true. How can you say **such a thing**?

no such ～は「そのような～はない」を表します。

- You won't find the word 'blid' in the dictionary. There's **no such word**. (⇒ そんなことばはない)

D

☆ 似たような意味を so と such を用いて，どのように表しますか？

とても長く

so long

- I haven't seen her for **so long** I've forgotten what she looks like.

such a long time

- I haven't seen her for **such a long time**. (✕ so long time)

とても遠く

so far

- I didn't know it was **so far**.

such a long way

- I didn't know it was **such a long way**.

たくさん

so much, so many

- I'm sorry I'm late – there was **so much** traffic.

such a lot (of)

- I'm sorry I'm late – there was **such a lot** of traffic.

not so ... as ➲ Unit 104A　such as ➲ Unit 114B

Exercises

100.1 状況に合うように空所に so, such, such a のいずれかを入れて，文を完成しなさい。

1. It's difficult to understand him because he speaks ___so___ quietly.
2. I like Liz and Joe. They're ___such___ nice people.
3. It was a great vacation. We had ___such a___ good time.
4. I was surprised that he looked __________ good after his recent illness.
5. Everything is __________ expensive these days, isn't it?
6. The weather is beautiful, isn't it? I didn't expect it to be __________ nice day.
7. I have to go. I didn't realize it was __________ late.
8. He always looks good. He wears __________ nice clothes.
9. It was __________ boring movie that I fell asleep while I was watching it.
10. I couldn't believe the news. It was __________ shock.
11. I think she works too hard. She looks __________ tired all the time.
12. The food at the hotel was __________ awful. I've never eaten __________ awful food.
13. They've got __________ much money that they don't know what to do with it.
14. I didn't realize you lived __________ long way from downtown.
15. The party was really great. It was __________ shame you couldn't come.

100.2 左右から文を 1 つずつ選び，so もしくは such を用いて 1 つの文にしなさい。

1. ~~She worked hard.~~	You could hear it from miles away.
2. ~~It was a beautiful day.~~	You would think it was her native language.
3. I was tired.	We spent the whole day indoors.
4. We had a good time on vacation.	~~She made herself sick.~~
5. She speaks English well.	I couldn't keep my eyes open.
6. I've got a lot to do.	I didn't eat anything else for the rest of the day.
7. The music was loud.	~~We decided to go to the beach.~~
8. I had a big breakfast.	I didn't know what to say.
9. It was terrible weather.	I don't know where to begin.
10. I was surprised.	We didn't want to come home.

1. *She worked so hard (that) she made herself sick.*
2. *It was such a beautiful day (that) we decided to go to the beach.*
3. I was ____________________
4. ____________________
5. ____________________
6. ____________________
7. ____________________
8. ____________________
9. ____________________
10. ____________________

100.3 状況に合う文を自分なりに考えて完成しなさい。

1. a) We enjoyed our vacation. It was so ___relaxing___.
   b) We enjoyed our vacation. We had such ___a good time___.
2. a) I like Catherine. She's so __________.
   b) I like Catherine. She's such __________.
3. a) I like New York. It's so __________.
   b) I like New York. It's such __________.
4. a) I wouldn't like to be a teacher. It's so __________.
   b) I wouldn't like to be a teacher. It's such __________.
5. a) It's great to see you again! I haven't seen you for so __________.
   b) It's great to see you again! I haven't seen you for such __________.

UNIT 101

enough と too

A

enough は形容詞や副詞の後に置きます。

- I can't run very far. I'm not **fit enough**. (× enough fit)
- Let's go. We've waited **long enough**.
- Is Joe going to apply for the job? Is he **experienced enough**?

too ～は「～し過ぎ」, **not ～ enough** は「十分に～ない」を表します。

- You never stop working. You work **too hard**.
  (⇒ 必要以上に働いている，働き過ぎ)
- You're lazy. You do**n't** work **hard enough**.
  (⇒ 必要な量に達していない，十分働いていない)

B

enough は名詞の前に置きます。

- I can't run very far. I don't have **enough energy**. (× energy enough)
- Is Joe going to apply for the job? Does he have **enough experience**?
- We've got **enough money**. We don't need any more.
- Some of us had to sit on the floor because there weren't **enough chairs**.

enough は **be** 動詞の後には置きません。

- We didn't have **enough time**. (× the time wasn't enough)
- There is **enough money**. (× the money is enough)

enough を，後に名詞を置かずに単独で用いることがあります。

- We don't need any more money. We've got **enough**.

☆ **enough は不可算名詞，複数可算名詞のいずれの前にも置くことができます。too much/many と，どう異なりますか？** ➲ Unit 67C

- There's **too much** furniture in this room. There's not **enough space**.
- There were **too many people** and not **enough chairs**.

C

「人 / 物にとって十分～だ / ～過ぎる」は **enough/too ～ for 人 / 物**の形で表します。

- We don't have **enough** money **for a vacation**.
- Is Joe experienced **enough for the job**?
- This shirt is **too** big **for me**. I need a smaller size.

「... するには十分～だ / ～過ぎて…できない」は **enough/too ～ to + 動詞の原形**のように不定詞を用いた形で表します。この時，for -ing のような -ing は使えません。

- We don't have **enough money to go** on vacation. (× for going)
- Is Joe **experienced enough to do** the job?
- They're **too young to get** married. / They're not **old enough to get** married.
- Let's take a taxi. It's **too far to walk** home from here.
- The bridge is just **wide enough** for two cars **to pass** each other

D

☆ **「～過ぎて…できない」を表す以下の構文で，動詞の後の目的語はどのように異なりますか？**

a) The food was very hot. We couldn't eat **it**.
b) The food was so hot that we couldn't eat **it**.
c) The food was **too** hot **to eat**. (⇒ it なし)

➤ **a（2 つの文）と b（so ～ that ...）では動詞の後に目的語が必要ですが，c（不定詞構文）では置けません。**

- These boxes are **too heavy to carry**.
  (× too heavy to carry them)
- The wallet was **too big to put** in my pocket.
  (× too big to put it)
- This chair isn't **strong enough to stand** on.
  (× strong enough to stand on it)

to + 動詞の原形と for ...（目的を表す表現） ➲ Unit 62
形容詞 + to + 動詞の原形（difficult to understand など） ➲ Unit 63

Exercises

101.1 状況に合うように enough の前後に置く語を以下から選び，空所に入れて文を完成しなさい。

big ~~chairs~~ **cups** ~~fit~~ **milk** **money**
qualified **room** **time** **warm** **well**

1. I can't run very far. I'm not _fit enough_ .
2. Some of us had to sit on the floor because there weren't _enough chairs_ .
3. I'd like to buy a car, but I don't have ______ right now.
4. Do you have ______ in your coffee, or would you like some more?
5. Are you ______ ? Or should I turn up the heat?
6. It's only a small car. There isn't ______ for all of us.
7. Steve didn't feel ______ to go to work this morning.
8. I enjoyed my trip to Paris, but there wasn't ______ to do everything I wanted.
9. Do you think I am ______ to apply for the job?
10. Try this jacket on and see if it's ______ for you.
11. There weren't ______ for everybody to have coffee at the same time.

101.2 状況に合うように，質問に対する答えの文を（　）内の語と too もしくは enough と組み合わせて完成しなさい。

	Question		Answer
1.	Are they going to get married?	(old)	No, they're not _old enough to get married_ .
2.	I need to talk to you about something.	(busy)	Well, I'm afraid I'm ______ to you now.
3.	Let's go to the movies.	(late)	No, it's ______ to the movies.
4.	Why don't we sit outside?	(warm)	It's not ______ outside.
5.	Would you like to be a politician?	(shy)	No, I'm ______ a politician.
6.	Would you like to be a teacher?	(patience)	No, I don't have ______ a teacher.
7.	Did you hear what he was saying?	(far away)	No, we were ______ what he was saying.
8.	Can he read a newspaper in English?	(English)	No, he doesn't know ______ a newspaper.

101.3 too もしくは enough を用いた不定詞構文を用いて，2 つの文を 1 つにまとめなさい。

1. We couldn't carry the boxes. They were too heavy.
   The boxes were too heavy to carry.
2. I can't drink this coffee. It's too hot.
   This coffee is ______
3. Nobody could move the piano. It was too heavy.
   The piano ______
4. Don't eat these apples. They're not ripe enough.
   These apples ______
5. I can't explain the situation. It is too complicated.
   The situation ______
6. We couldn't climb over the wall. It was too high.
   The wall ______
7. Three people can't sit on this sofa. It isn't big enough.
   This sofa ______
8. You can't see some things without a microscope. They are too small.
   Some ______

UNIT 102

比較 1 (cheaper, more expensive など)

A

☆ 枠内の会話の例文で考えます。どのような形の語が使われていますか？

Should I drive or take the train?
You should drive. It's **cheaper**.
Don't take the train. It's **more expensive**.

➤ cheaper（より安い）や more expensive（より高い）のような形を比較級と呼びます。

比較級の後に **than** を続けて，2つの事物を比べることができます。

- It's **cheaper** to go by car **than** by train.
- Going by train is **more expensive than** going by car.

B

比較級は，形容詞や副詞の語尾に **-er** を付けて作る場合と，語の前に **more** を置いて作る場合とがあります。

1音節からなる**短い語**では **-er** を付けます。

cheap → cheap**er** **fast** → fast**er**
large → larg**er** **thin** → thinn**er**

語尾が **-y** で終わる **2音節語**には **-er** を付けます。

luck**y** → luck**ier** earl**y** → earl**ier**
eas**y** → eas**ier** prett**y** → prett**ier**

語尾 -er に関してつづり方で注意すべきこと ➲付録 6

2音節以上の**長い語**では **more** を置きます。

more serious **more often**
more expensive **more comfortable**

語尾が **-y** で終わる**副詞**には **more** を付けます。

more slowly **more seriously**
more quietly **more carefully**

☆ 副詞の語尾に -er を付けた比較級と more を置いた比較級を，左右の例文で比較して確認します。

- You're **older** than me.
- The test was pretty easy – **easier** than I expected.
- Can you walk a little **faster**?
- I'd like to have a **bigger** car.
- Last night I went to bed **earlier** than usual.

- You're **more patient** than me.
- The test was pretty difficult – **more difficult** than I expected.
- Can you walk a little **more slowly**?
- I'd like to have a **more reliable** car.
- I don't play tennis much these days. I used to play **more often**.

以下のような **2音節**の**形容詞**は，**-er** と **more** の2通りで比較級が作られます。

clever **narrow** **quiet** **shallow** **simple**

- It's too noisy here. Can we go somewhere **quieter** / **more quiet**?

C

形容詞の中には，比較級をセクション **B** の操作によって**規則的に作れない**ものがあります。

good/well → **better**

- The yard looks **better** since you cleaned it up.
- I know him **well** – probably **better** than anybody else knows him.

bad/badly → **worse**:

- "How is your headache? Better?" "No, it's **worse**."
- He did very badly on the test – **worse** than expected.

far → **farther** (= **further**):

- "It's a long walk from here to the park – **farther** than I thought. (= **further** than)

futher には「さらに，他の」の意味があります（father にはこの意味はありません）。

- Let me know if you hear any **further** news. (⇒ any more news)

比較 2–3 ➲ Units 103–104 最上級（cheapest / most expensive など）➲ Unit 105

Exercises

102.1 状況に合うように空所に適切な比較級の語句を入れて，文を完成しなさい。

1. It's too noisy here. Can we go somewhere *quieter* ?
2. This coffee is very weak. I like it a little ________ .
3. The hotel was surprisingly big. I expected it to be ________ .
4. The hotel was surprisingly cheap. I expected it to be ________ .
5. The weather is too cold here. I'd like to live somewhere ________ .
6. My job is kind of boring sometimes. I'd like to do something ________ .
7. It's too bad you live so far away. I wish you lived ________ .
8. I was surprised how easy it was to use the computer. I thought it would be ________ .
9. Your work isn't very good. I'm sure you can do ________ .
10. Don't worry. The situation isn't so bad. It could be ________ .
11. I was surprised we got here so quickly. I expected the trip to take ________ .
12. You're talking very loudly. Can you speak a little ________ ?
13. You hardly ever call me. Why don't you call me ________ ?
14. You're standing too close to the camera. Can you move a little ________ away?
15. You were a little depressed yesterday, but you look ________ today.

102.2 状況に合うように，以下から語を選び適切な比較級に変えて空所に入れ，文を完成しなさい。

big	**crowded**	~~**early**~~	**easily**	**high**	**important**
interested	**peaceful**	~~**reliable**~~	**serious**	**simple**	**thin**

1. I was feeling tired last night, so I went to bed *earlier than* usual.
2. I'd like to have a *more reliable* car. Mine keeps breaking down.
3. Unfortunately, her illness was ________ we thought at first.
4. You look ________ . Have you lost weight?
5. I want a ________ apartment. We don't have enough space here.
6. He doesn't study very hard. He's ________ in having a good time.
7. Health and happiness are ________ money.
8. The instructions were very complicated. They could have been ________ .
9. There were a lot of people on the bus. It was ________ usual.
10. I like living in the country. It's ________ living in a city.
11. You'll find your way around the city ________ if you have a good map.
12. In some parts of the country, prices are ________ in others.

102.3 それぞれの状況を説明する文を，比較級を用いて完成しなさい。

1. Yesterday the temperature was 6 degrees. Today it is only 3 degrees.
   It's *colder today than it was yesterday* .
2. The trip takes four hours by car and five hours by train.
   It takes ________ .
3. Dave and I went for a run. I ran five miles. Dave stopped after three.
   I ran ________ .
4. Chris and Joe both did badly on the test. Chris got a C, but Joe only got a C–.
   Joe did ________ .
5. I expected my friends to arrive at about 4:00. In fact they arrived at 2:30.
   My friends ________ .
6. You can go by bus or by train. The buses run every 30 minutes. The trains run every hour.
   The buses ________ .
7. We were very busy at work today. We're not usually so busy.
   We ________ .

UNIT 103

比較 2 (much better / any better / better and better / the sooner the better)

A

比較級の前には以下のような語句をよく置きます。

much **a lot** **far** (= a lot) **a bit** **a little** **slightly** (= a little)

- Let's drive. It's **much cheaper**. (= **a lot cheaper**)
- "How do you feel?" "**Much better**, thanks."
- Don't go by train. It's **a lot more expensive**. (= **much more expensive**)
- Could you speak **a bit more slowly**? (= **a little more slowly**)
- This bag is **slightly heavier** than the other one.
- Her illness was **far more serious** than we thought at first.
(= **much more serious** / **a lot more serious**)

B

any longer / **no bigger** などのように，**any** と **no** を比較級の前に置くことがあります。

- I've waited long enough. I'm not waiting **any longer**. (⇒ もうこれ以上は待てない)
- We expected their house to be very big, but it's **no bigger** than ours.
= . . . it is**n't any bigger** than ours. (⇒ ～よりまったく大きくない，～と同じような大きさ)
- How do you feel now? Do you feel **any better**? (⇒ 少しは気分がよくなりましたか？)
- This hotel is better than the other one, and it's **no more expensive**.
(⇒ ～よりまったく高くない，～と同じ値段)

C

better and better / more and more など

比較級 + **and** + 比較級の形で，「ますます～」のように変化が継続して起こることを表します。

- Your English is improving. It's getting **better and better**. (⇒ どんどんうまくなっている)
- The city is growing fast. It's getting **bigger and bigger**.
- Cathy got **more and more bored** in her job. In the end, she quit.
- These days **more and more** people are learning English.

D

the sooner the better

the + 比較級 + **the better** の形で，「より～であるほうがよい，できるだけ～」を意味します。

- "What time should we leave?" "**The sooner the better**." (⇒早ければ早いほど，できるだけ早く)
- *A:* What sort of box do you want? A big one?
B: Yes, **the bigger the better**. (⇒ 大きければ大きいほど，できるだけ大きく)
- When you're traveling, **the less luggage** you have **the better**.

the + 比較級 ～ **the** + 比較級 **...** の形で，「～すればするほど…」のように2つの出来事が関連して起きることを意味します。

- **The warmer** the weather, **the better** I feel. (⇒ 暖かくなるほど気分がよくなる)
- **The sooner** we leave, **the earlier** we will arrive.
- **The younger** you are, **the easier** it is to learn.
- **The more expensive** the hotel, **the better** the service.
- **The more electricity** you use, **the higher** your bill will be.
- **The more** I thought about the plan, **the less** I liked it.

E

older と **elder**

old の比較級は **elder** です。

- David looks **older** than he really is.

家族の一員について，「より年長な」は **older** もしくは **elder** で表します。**older** は **my/your** など + **elder** + **sister/brother/daughter/son** のような形で用います。

- **My elder sister** is a TV producer. (= My **older** sister . . .)

elder は，**my elder sister** のように名詞の前に置いて用います。動詞の後には置きません。

- My sister is **older** than me. (✕ elder than me)

any/no ➲ Unit 84 比較 1, 3 ➲ Units 102, 104 eldest ➲ Unit 105D even + 比較級 ➲ Unit 109C

Exercises

103.1 状況に合うように (　) 内の語句の前に much / a little などを置いて，文を完成しなさい（必要に応じて than を加えること)。

1. Her illness was ___much more serious than___ we thought at first. (much / serious)
2. This bag is too small. I need something ______________________ . (much / big)
3. I'm afraid the problem is ______________________ it seems. (much / complicated)
4. It was very hot yesterday. Today it's ______________________ . (a little / cool)
5. I enjoyed our visit to the museum. It was ______________________ I expected. (far / interesting)
6. You're driving too fast. Can you drive ______________________ ? (a little / slowly)
7. It's ______________________ to learn a foreign language in a country where it is spoken. (a lot / easy)
8. I thought she was younger than me, but in fact she's ______________________ . (slightly / old)

103.2 状況に合うように「any/no + 比較級」の形を用いて，文を完成しなさい（必要に応じて than を加えること)。

1. I've waited long enough. I'm not waiting ___any longer___ .
2. I'm sorry I'm a little late, but I couldn't get here ______________________ .
3. This store isn't expensive. The prices are ______________________ anywhere else.
4. I need to stop for a rest. I can't walk ______________________ .
5. The traffic isn't particularly bad today. It's ______________________ usual.

103.3 セクション C を参考にして，「比較級 + and + 比較級」の形を用いて文を完成しなさい。

1. Cathy got ___more and more bored___ in her job. In the end she quit. (bored)
2. That hole in your sweater is getting ______________________ . (big)
3. My bags seemed to get ______________________ as I carried them. (heavy)
4. As I waited for my interview, I became ______________________ . (nervous)
5. As the day went on, the weather got ______________________ . (bad)
6. Health care is becoming ______________________ . (expensive)
7. Since Anna went to Canada, her English has gotten ______________________ . (good)
8. As the conversation went on, Paul became ______________________ . (talkative)

103.4 セクション D の構文を用いて，(　) 内の語を適切な形にして文を完成しなさい。

1. I like warm weather.
   The warmer the weather, ___the better I feel___ . (feel)
2. I didn't really like him when we first met.
   But the more I got to know him, ______________________ . (like)
3. If you're in business, you want to make a profit.
   The more goods you sell, ______________________ . (profit)
4. It's hard to concentrate when you're tired.
   The more tired you are, ______________________ . (hard)
5. Kate had to wait a very long time.
   The longer she waited, ______________________ . (impatient / become)

103.5 下線部の older と elder の正しい方を選んで，文を完成しなさい（両方正しい場合もあります)。

1. My ✓older / ✓elder sister is a TV producer. (older も elder も正しい)
2. I'm surprised Diane is only 25. I thought she was older / elder.
3. Jane's younger sister is still in school. Her older / elder sister is a nurse.
4. Martin is older / elder than his brother.

UNIT 104

比較 3 (as ～ as ... / than)

A

☆ イラストで考えます。どのような構文が使われていますか？

Sarah Eric David

Sara，Eric，David はいずれもお金持ちです。Sara には 2,000 万ドル，Eric には 1,500 万ドル，David には 1,000 万ドルの貯金があります。
このことは，次のように記述できます。

Eric is rich.
He is **richer than** David.
But he is**n't as rich as** Sarah.
(⇒ Sarah is **richer than** he is)

➤「…ほど～ではない」のように 2 つの事物を比べる際に，not as ～ (as ...) の構文を用います。この構文は，比較級を用いた書き換えが可能です。

☆ 以下の not as ～ (as ...) の構文の意味を，比較級の構文への書き換えから考えます。

- Richard is**n't as old as** he looks.
  (⇒ 見かけほど老けていない，he looks **older than** he is: 実際より老けて見える)
- The shopping mall was**n't as crowded as** usual.
  (⇒ いつもほど混んでいなかった，it is usually **more crowded**: いつもの方が混んでいる)
- Jenny did**n't** do **as well** on the test **as** she had hoped.
  (⇒ she had hoped to do **better**)
- The weather is better today. It's **not as cold**. (⇒ yesterday was **colder**)
- I do**n't** know **as many** people **as** you do. (⇒ you know **more** people)
- *A:* How much did it cost? Fifty dollars?
  B: No, **not as much as** that. (⇒ less than fifty dollars)

not so ～ (as ...) のように，**as** の代わりに **so** を用いた形もよく使います。

- It's not warm, but it is**n't so** cold **as** yesterday. (⇒ it is**n't as** cold **as** . . .)

less ～ than ... は，**not as ～ (as ...)** と同様に「…ほど～ではない」の意味で用いられます。

- I spent **less money than** you. (⇒ I did**n't** spend **as** much money **as** you)
- The shopping mall was **less crowded than** usual. (⇒ it was**n't as** crowded **as** usual)
- Ted talks **less than** his brother. (⇒ he does**n't** talk **as** much **as** his brother does)

B

肯定文と疑問文では not のない **as ～ as ...** を使います。**so ～ (as ...)** は否定文中にのみ生じます。

- I'm sorry I'm late. I got here **as fast as** I could.
- There's plenty of food. You can have **as much as** you want.
- Let's walk. It's **just as quick as** taking the bus.
- Can you send me the money **as soon as possible**, please?

twice as ～ as ..., three times as ～ as ... のような形で，「…の 2 倍～である / 3 倍～である」を表します。

- Gas is **twice as expensive as** it was a few years ago.
- Their house is about **three times as big as** ours.

C

the same as ～は「～と同じ」を表します。the same like ～のように，like を用いた形はありません。

- Ann's salary is **the same as** mine. = Ann gets **the same** salary **as** me.
- David is **the same** age **as** James.
- "What would you like to drink?" "I'll have **the same as** you."

D

than の後では **than me** のように**目的格**にするか，**than I am** のように**主語＋動詞**の形にします。than I のように，主格の代名詞だけを残すことはあまりありません。

- You're taller **than I am**. = You're taller **than me**.
  (You're taller than I. とはあまり言いません)
- He's not as clever **as she is**. = He's not as clever **as her**.
- They have more money **than we do**. = They have more money **than us**.
- I can't run as fast as **he can**. = I can't run as fast **as him**.

比較 1–2 ➲ Units 102–103 as long as ➲ Unit 112B as と like ➲ Unit 114

Exercises

104.1 状況に合うように as ～ as ... の形を用いて，文を完成しなさい。

1. I'm pretty tall, but you are taller. I'm not *as tall as you* .
2. My salary is high, but yours is higher.
   My salary isn't ______ .
3. You know a little about cars, but I know more.
   You don't ______ .
4. It's still cold, but it was colder yesterday.
   It isn't ______ .
5. I still feel tired, but I felt a lot more tired yesterday.
   I don't ______ .
6. Our neighbors have lived here quite a while, but we've lived here longer.
   Our neighbors haven't ______ .
7. I was a little nervous before the interview, but usually I'm a lot more nervous.
   I wasn't ______ .

104.2 同じ意味を表す文を完成しなさい。

1. Jack is younger than he looks. Jack isn't *as old as he looks* .
2. I didn't spend as much money as you. You *spent more money than me* .
3. The station was closer than I thought. The station wasn't ______ .
4. The meal didn't cost as much as I expected. The meal cost ______ .
5. I go out less than I used to. I don't ______ .
6. Karen's hair isn't as long as it used to be. Karen used to ______ .
7. I know them better than you do. You don't ______ .
8. There are fewer people at this meeting than at the last one.
   There aren't ______ .

104.3 状況に合うように以下から適切な語を選び，as ～ as の形を用いて文を完成しなさい。

bad	**comfortable**	~~**fast**~~	**long**	**often**
quietly	**well qualified**	**well**	**soon**	

1. I'm sorry I'm late. I got here *as fast as* I could.
2. It was a difficult question. I answered it ______ I could.
3. "How long can I stay with you?" "You can stay ______ you like."
4. I need the information quickly, so let me know ______ possible.
5. I like to stay in shape, so I go swimming ______ I can.
6. I didn't want to wake anybody, so I came in ______ I could.

以下の問題では just as ～ as の形を用いて，文を完成しなさい。

7. I'm going to sleep on the floor. It's ______ the bed.
8. Why did he get the job rather than me? I'm ______ him.
9. At first I thought he was nice, but really he's ______ everybody else.

104.4 状況に合うように the same as ～を用いて，文を書き換えなさい。

1. David and James are both 22 years old. David *is the same age as James* .
2. You and I both have dark brown hair. Your hair ______ .
3. I arrived at 10:25 and so did you. I ______ .
4. My birthday is April 5. Tom's birthday is April 5, too. My ______ .

104.5 状況に合うように than ... もしくは as ... を用いて，文を書き換えなさい。

1. I can't reach as high as you. You are taller *than me* .
2. He doesn't know much. I know more ______ .
3. I don't work especially hard. Most people work as hard ______ .
4. We were very surprised. Nobody was more surprised ______ .
5. She's not a very good player. I'm a better player ______ .
6. They've been very lucky. I wish we were as lucky ______ .

UNIT 105

最上級 (the longest / the most enjoyable など)

A

☆ 枠内の例文で考えます。どのような形の形容詞が用いられていますか？

What is the **longest river** in the world?
What was **the most enjoyable** vacation you've ever taken?

➤ 以上の例文中の longest（最も長い）や most enjoyable（最も楽しい）を最上級と呼びます。

B

最上級は，**形容詞**や**副詞**の語尾に **-est** を付けて作る場合と，**語の前**に **most** を置いて作る場合とがあります。比較級の場合と同様に，**1 音節語**は語尾に **-est** を付けて作り，**2 音節以上の語**では **most** を単語の前に置いて作ります。➲ Unit 102

long → long**est** **hot** → hott**est** **easy** → easi**est** **hard** → hard**est**
⇔ **most** famous **most** boring **most** difficult **most** expensive

最上級を**規則的に作れない形容詞**もあります。

good → **best** bad → **worst** far → **farthest/furthest**

語尾 -est に関してつづり方で注意すべきこと ➲ 付録 6

C

the longest / **the most famous** などのように普通，最上級の前には **the** を置きます。

- Yesterday was **the hottest** day of the year.
- The film was really boring. It was **the most boring** film I've ever seen.
- She is a really nice person – one of **the nicest** people I know.
- Why does he always come to see me at **the worst** possible time?

☆ 最上級の文を比較級を用いて書き換えると，どうなりますか？

- This hotel is **the cheapest** in town.（最上級）

⇔ This hotel is **cheaper** than all the others in town.（比較級）

- He's **the most patient** person I've ever met.

⇔ He's much **more patient** than I am.

D

oldest と **eldest**

old の最上級は **oldest** です。

- That church is **the oldest** building in the town. (✕ the eldest)

家族について「最も年長である」は **oldest**，もしくは **eldest** で表します。➲ Unit 103

- **My eldest son** is 13 years old. (= My **oldest** son)
- Are you **the eldest** in your family? (= the **oldest**)

E

場所に関連して「最も～」のような**最上級**を用いた**比較**を行う場合は，**in** を**場所**の**前**に置きます。

- What's the longest river **in the world**? (✕ of the world)
- We had a nice room. It was one of the best **in the hotel**. (✕ of the hotel)

in の**後**には，場所以外に，クラスや会社のような組織や集団を表す**名詞句**がくる場合もあります。

- Who is the youngest student **in the class**? (✕ of the class)

時間に関連して**最上級**を用いた**比較**を行う場合は **of** を用います。

- What was the happiest day **of your life**?
- Yesterday was the hottest day **of the year**.

F

最上級の後には，**I have done.** の形の**現在完了形**がよくきます。➲ Unit 7B

- What's **the most important** decision you**'ve** ever **had** to make?
- That was **the best** vacation **I've taken** for a long time.
  (⇒ 今までの長い期間の中で一番の休暇，ひさしぶりの素晴らしい休暇)

比較級 (cheaper / more expensive など) ➲ Units 102–104 elder ➲ Unit 103E

Exercises

105.1 状況に合うように最上級と of もしくは in の前置詞を用いて，文を完成しなさい。

1. It's a very good room. It *is the best room in* the hotel.
2. It's a very cheap restaurant. It's ________________ town.
3. It was a very happy day. It was ________________ my life.
4. She's a very intelligent student. She ________________ the class.
5. It's a very valuable painting. It ________________ the gallery.
6. Spring is a very busy time for me. It ________________ the year.

以下の問題では「one of + 最上級 ... + 前置詞」の形を用いて，文を完成しなさい。

7. It's a very good room. It *is one of the best rooms in* the hotel.
8. He's a very rich man. He's one ________________ the world.
9. It's a very old house. It ________________ the city.
10. It's a very good college. It ________________ the state.
11. It was a very bad experience. It ________________ my life.
12. He's a very dangerous criminal. He ________________ the country.

105.2 状況に合うように（ ）内の語を適切な最上級もしくは比較級にして，文を完成しなさい。

1. We stayed at *the cheapest* hotel in town. (cheap)
2. Our hotel was *cheaper* than all the others in town. (cheap)
3. The United States is very large, but Canada is ________________ . (large)
4. What's ________________ country in the world? (small)
5. I wasn't feeling well yesterday, but I feel a little ________________ today. (good)
6. It was an awful day. It was ________________ day of my life. (bad)
7. What is ________________ sport in your country? (popular)
8. Everest is ________________ mountain in the world. It is ________________ than any other mountain. (high)
9. We had a great vacation. It was one of ________________ vacations we've ever taken. (enjoyable)
10. I prefer this chair to the other one. It's ________________ . (comfortable)
11. What's ________________ way to get to the station? (quick)
12. Sue and Kevin have three daughters. ________________ is 14 years old. (old)

105.3 状況に合うように（ ）内の語句を適切な「最上級 ... + ever」の形にして，発言を完成しなさい。

1. You've just been to the movies. The movie was extremely boring. You tell your friend: (boring / movie / see) That's *the most boring movie I've ever seen* .
2. Your friend has just told you a joke, which you think is very funny. You say: (funny / joke / hear) That's ________________ .
3. You're drinking coffee with a friend. It's really good coffee. You say: (good / coffee / taste) This ________________ .
4. You are talking to a friend about Mary. Mary is very generous. You tell your friend about her: (generous / person / meet) She ________________ .
5. You have just run 10 miles. You've never run farther than this. You say to your friend: (far / run) That ________________ .
6. You decided to quit your job. Now you think this was a bad mistake. You say to your friend: (bad / mistake / make) It ________________ .
7. Your friend meets a lot of people, some of them famous. You ask your friend: (famous / person / meet?) Who ________________ ?

UNIT 106

語順 1：「動詞＋目的語」と「場所＋時」の語順

A

動詞＋目的語

動詞と目的語は普通，**動詞＋目的語**のような語順で現れます。他の語句が動詞と目的語の間に入ることはありません。

	動詞＋	目的語	
I	**like**	**my job**	very much. (✕ I like very much my job)
Did you	**see**	**your friends**	yesterday?
Ann often	**plays**	**tennis**.	

☆ それぞれの例文で，「動詞＋目的語」の語順が守られていることを確認します。

- Do you **eat** **meat** every day? (✕ Do you eat every day meat?)
- Everybody **enjoyed** **the party** very much. (✕ enjoyed very much the party)
- Our guide **spoke** **English** fluently. (✕ spoke fluently English)
- I lost all my money, and I also **lost** **my passport** . (✕ I lost also my passport)
- At the end of the block, you'll **see** **a supermarket** on your left.
(✕ see on your left a supermarket)

B

場所＋時

「どこ？」の答えとなる**場所**を表す表現は普通，**動詞の直後**にきます。

go home　**live in a city**　**walk to work** など

動詞が目的語を持つ場合，**場所を表す表現は動詞＋目的語の直後**にきます。

take somebody home　**meet a friend on the street**

「いつ？ / どのくらいの頻度で？ / どのくらいの期間で？」の答えとなる**時**を表す表現は普通，**場所の直後**にきます。

	場所　＋	時
Tom walks	**to work**	**every morning**. (✕ every morning to work)
Sam has been	**in Canada**	**since April**.
We arrived	**at the airport**	**early**.

☆ それぞれの例文で，「場所＋時」の語順が守られていることを確認します。

- I'm going **to Paris** **on Monday** . (✕ I'm going on Monday to Paris)
- They have lived **in the same house** **for a long time** .
- Don't be late. Make sure you're **here** **by 8:00** .
- Sarah gave me a ride **home** **after the party** .
- You really shouldn't go **to bed** **so late** .

時を表す表現は**文頭**に置くこともできます。

- **On Monday** I'm going to Paris.
- **Every morning** Tom walks to work.

always/never/often のような**時**を表す表現は，文頭や文末ではなく**文中**で**動詞**と結び付いて現れます。

➲ Unit 107

疑問文の語順 ➲ Units 47–48　形容詞の語順 ➲ Unit 97　語順 2 ➲ Unit 107

Exercises

106.1 それぞれの文について誤りのある語順の部分を○で囲み，正しい形に書き直しなさい。

1. Everybody enjoyed the party very much. _OK_
2. Tom walks every morning to work. _Tom walks to work every morning._
3. Jim doesn't like very much basketball. ______
4. I drink three or four cups of coffee every morning. ______
5. I ate quickly my breakfast and went out. ______
6. Are you going to invite to the party a lot of people? ______
7. I called Tom immediately after hearing the news. ______
8. Did you go late to bed last night? ______
9. Did you learn a lot of things at school today? ______
10. I met on my way home a friend of mine. ______

106.2 (　) 内の語句を適切な順番に並べ替えて，文を完成しなさい。

1. (the party / very much / everybody enjoyed) _Everybody enjoyed the party very much._
2. (we won / easily / the game) ______
3. (quietly / the door / I closed) ______
4. (Diane / quite well / speaks / Chinese) ______
5. (Tim / all the time / TV / watches) ______
6. (again / please don't ask / that question) ______
7. (golf / every weekend / does Ken play?) ______
8. (some money / I borrowed / from a friend of mine) ______

106.3 (　) 内の語句を適切な順番に並べ替えて,文を完成しなさい(それぞれ指定された語句で始めること)。

1. (for a long time / have lived / in the same house)
   They _have lived in the same house for a long time_.
2. (to the supermarket / every Friday / go)
   I ______.
3. (home / did you come / so late)
   Why ______?
4. (her children / takes / every day / to school)
   Sarah ______.
5. (been / recently / to the movies)
   I haven't ______.
6. (at the top of the page / your name / write)
   Please ______.
7. (her name / after a few minutes / remembered)
   I ______.
8. (around the town / all morning / walked)
   We ______.
9. (on Saturday night / didn't see you / at the party)
   I ______.
10. (some interesting books / found / in the library)
    We ______.
11. (her umbrella / last night / in a restaurant / left)
    Jackie ______.
12. (across from the park / a new hotel / are building)
    They ______.

UNIT 107

語順 2：動詞と結び付く副詞の語順

A

☆ 例文で考えます。副詞は文のどこに生じていますか？

- Helen **always drives** to work.
- We were feeling very tired, and we **were also** hungry.
- The concert **will probably be** canceled.

➤ always/also/probably などの副詞は，文頭や文末ではなく文中で動詞と結び付いて現れます。

B

文中に生じる**副詞**は，以下のような原則に基づいて位置が決まります（例外が多いことに注意）。

1) 以下の表中の **drives** や **fell** のように**動詞要素**が 1 つしかない場合，普通，**副詞は動詞の前**に置きます。

	副詞	動詞	
Helen	**always**	**drives**	to work.
I	**almost**	**fell**	as I was going down the stairs.

- I cleaned the house and **also cooked** dinner. (× cooked also)
- Lucy **hardly ever watches** television and **rarely reads** newspapers.
- "Should I give you my address?" "No, I **already have** it."

have to の場合も，**always/also/probably** などの副詞は前に置かれます。➲ 以下 (3)

- Joe never calls me. I **always have to** call him. (× I have always to call)

2) **am/is/are/was/were** などの **be 動詞**の場合，**副詞は後**に置かれます。

- We were feeling very tired, and we **were also** hungry.
- Why are you always late? You**'re never** on time.
- The traffic **isn't usually** as bad as it was this morning.

3) 以下の表中の **doesn't eat**，**are going**，**will be** のように**動詞要素**が複数ある場合，**副詞は最初の動詞要素**（第 1 動詞 ➲ Unit 47A）の後に置かれます。

	第 1 動詞	副詞	第 2 動詞	
I	**can**	**never**	**remember**	her name.
Claire	**doesn't**	**often**	**eat**	meat.
	Are you	**definitely**	**going**	to the party tomorrow?
The concert	**will**	**probably**	**be**	canceled.

- You **have always been** very kind to me.
- Jack can't cook. He **can't even boil** an egg.
- **Do** you **still work** for the same company?
- The house **was only built** a year ago, and it**'s already falling** down.

probably は，動詞全体を構成する**動詞要素**の数に関係なく，**not/isn't/won't/can't** のような**否定を表す語の前**に置きます。

- I **probably won't** see you. = I will **probably not** see you. (× I won't probably)

C

☆ 例文で考えます。副詞の all と both は文のどこに生じていますか？

- We **all felt** sick after we ate. (⇒ 動詞全体が1語から成り立っているが動詞の前。× we felt all sick)
- My parents **are both** teachers. (⇒ be動詞の後。× my parents both are teachers)
- Sarah and Jane **have both applied** for the job. (⇒ 第 1動詞の後)
- We **are all going** out tonight. (⇒ 第 1動詞の後)

D

語句の繰り返しを避けるために，**is/will/did** のような**第 1 動詞**を**文末**に置く場合があります。➲ Unit 49

このような場合，**always/never** といった**副詞**の位置がセクション **B** の原則と異なることに注意します。

- He always says he won't be late, but he **always is**. (= he **is always** late)
- I've never done it, and I **never will**. (= I **will never** do it)

always/never のような**副詞**は**第 1 動詞の前**に置きます。

語順 1 ➲ Unit 106

Exercises

107.1 下線部の語について適切な位置にあるかを確認し，正しくない場合には訂正しなさい。

1. Helen drives always to work. _Helen always drives to work._
2. I cleaned the house and also cooked dinner. _OK_
3. I take usually a shower in the morning ______
4. We soon found the solution to the problem. ______
5. Steve gets hardly ever angry. ______
6. I did some shopping, and I went also to the bank. ______
7. Jane has always to hurry in the morning. ______
8. We all were tired, so we all fell asleep. ______
9. She always says she'll call me, but she never does. ______

107.2 ( ) 内の語を文中の正しい位置に入れて，全体を書き換えなさい。

1. Claire doesn't eat meat. (often) _Claire doesn't often eat meat._
2. a) We were on vacation in Spain. (all) ______
   b) We were staying at the same hotel. (all) ______
   c) We enjoyed ourselves. (all) ______
3. Catherine is very generous. (always) ______
4. I don't have to work on Saturdays. (usually) ______
5. Do you watch TV in the evenings? (always) ______
6. Josh is studying Spanish, and he is studying Japanese. (also)
   Josh is studying Spanish, and he ______
7. a) The new hotel is very expensive. (probably) ______
   b) It costs a lot to stay there. (probably) ______
8. a) I can help you. (probably) ______
   b) I can't help you. (probably) ______

107.3 ( ) 内の語句を適切な順番に並べ替えて，文を完成しなさい。

1. I _can never remember_ her name. (remember / never / can)
2. I ______ sugar in my coffee. (take / usually)
3. I ______ hungry when I get home from work. (am / usually)
4. *A:* Where's Joe?
   B: He ______ home early. (gone / has / probably)
5. Mark and Diane ______ in Texas. (both / were / born)
6. Liz is a good pianist. She ______ very well. (sing / also / can)
7. Our cat ______ under the bed. (often / sleeps)
8. They live on the same street as me, but I ______ to them. (never / have / spoken)
9. We ______ a long time for the bus. (have / always / to wait)
10. My eyesight isn't very good. I ______ with glasses. (read / can / only)
11. I ______ early tomorrow. (probably / leaving / will / be)
12. I'm afraid I ______ able to come to the party. (probably / be / won't)
13. It's hard to contact Sue. Her cell phone ______ on when I call her. (is / hardly ever)
14. We ______ in the same place. We haven't moved. (still / are / living)
15. If we hadn't taken the same train, we ______ each other. (never / met / would / have)
16. *A:* Are you tired?
    B: Yes, I ______ at this time of day. (am / always)

UNIT 108

still, yet と already anymore / any longer / no longer

A

still:「まだ～」のように状況や活動が**継続中**で，変化したり停止したりしていないことを表します。

- It's 10:00 and Joe is **still** in bed.
- When I went to bed, Chris was **still** working.
- Do you **still** want to go to the party, or have you changed your mind?

still は普通，文中で**動詞**と結び付いて現れます。➲ Unit 107

B

anymore / any longer / no longer

not ～ anymore や **not ～ any longer** は「もはや～ない」のように，状況が**変化**したことを表します。**anymore** と **any longer** は**文末**に置きます。

- Lucy doesn't work here **anymore** (= **any longer**). She left last month.
  (× Lucy doesn't still work here.)
- We used to be good friends, but we are**n't anymore** (= **any longer**).

not ～ any longer の代わりに **no longer** を用いることがあります。**no longer** は**文中**に置きます。

- Lucy **no longer** works here.

意味が異なるので，no longer を no more で置き換えることはできません。

- We are **no longer** friends. (× We are no more friends.)

☆ **例文で確認します。still と not ～ anymore は，どのように異なりますか？**

- Sally **still** works here, but Ann does**n't** work here **anymore**.
  (⇒ Sallyはまだ働いているが〔継続〕，Annはもう働いていない〔変化〕)

C

yet：**疑問文**と**否定文**においてのみ用いられます。**疑問文**では「もう / 今までに～しましたか？」を，**否定文**では「まだ / 今までに～していない」を表します。何か変化が起きることを期待している際に用います。

yet は普通，**文末**に置きます。

- It's 10:00 and Joe **isn't** here **yet**. (⇒ まだここにいない。「もう来てもよい」と期待)
- **Have** you **met** your new neighbors **yet**? (⇒「もう会いましたか？」と期待)
- "Where are you going for vacation?" "We **don't** know **yet**."

yet は，**Have you met ... yet?** のような**現在完了**の文中でよく生じます。➲ Unit 8D

☆ **例文で確認します。yet と still は，どのように異なりますか？ yet には変化への期待があります。**

- Mike lost his job six months ago and **is still** unemployed. (⇒ まだ，失業している)
  Mike lost his job six months ago and **hasn't found** another job **yet**. (⇒ まだ，見つからない)
- **Is** it **still** raining? (⇒ まだ，降っていますか？)
  Has it **stopped** raining **yet**? (⇒ もう，止みましたか？)

still は否定文中でも生じます。**否定**を表す**語**の**直前**に置きます。

- She said she would be here an hour ago, and she **still** has**n't** come.

上の文は she hasn't come yet の文と似ていますが，**still ～ not** の構文の方が，驚きやいらだちなどのより強い気持ちを表します。

- I wrote to him last week. He has**n't** replied **yet**. (⇒「もうすぐ返事をくれる」という期待)
- I wrote to him months ago and he **still** has**n't** replied. (⇒「もっと早く返事をすべきだ」という非難)

D

already：「すでに～」のように予想していたより物事が早く起こったことを表します。

already は普通，文頭や文末ではなく**文中**で生じます。➲ Unit 107

- "What time is Sue leaving?" "She has **already** left." (= sooner than you expected)
- Should I tell Joe what happened, or does he **already** know?
- I've just had lunch, and I'm **already** hungry.

現在完了形 + already/yet ➲ Unit 8D　語順 2 ➲ Unit 107

Exercises

108.1 Paul が数年前に言ったことと今言っていることから，( ) 内の事柄について変化したかを考えます。still もしくは anymore を用いて，Paul の現在の状況を記述する文を完成しなさい。

I travel a lot.
I work in a store.
I write poems.
I want to be a teacher.
I'm interested in politics.
I'm single.
I go fishing a lot.
Paul a few years ago
I travel a lot.
I work in a hospital.
I gave up writing poems.
I want to be a teacher.
I'm not interested in politics.
I'm single.
I haven't been fishing in years.
Paul now

1. (travel) *He still travels a lot.*
2. (store) *He doesn't work in a store anymore.*
3. (poems) He ______
4. (teacher) ______
5. (politics) ______
6. (single) ______
7. (fishing) ______
8. (beard) ______

以下では no longer を用いて記述しなさい。

9. *He no longer works in a store.*
10. ______
11. ______
12. ______

108.2 それぞれの still を含む文について，以下から適切な動詞を選び not ～ yet と組み合わせて，ほぼ同じような意味を表す文を完成しなさい。

decide **find** **finish** **leave** ~~**stop**~~ **take off** **wake up**

1. It's still raining. *It hasn't stopped raining yet* .
2. Gary is still here. He ______ .
3. They're still repairing the road. They ______ .
4. The children are still asleep. ______ .
5. Is Ann still looking for a place to live? ______ ?
6. I'm still wondering what to do. ______ .
7. The plane is still waiting on the runway. ______ .

108.3 例にならい状況を把握したうえで，下線部を still，yet，already，anymore の中から適切なものを選んで書き換えなさい。

1. Mike lost his job a year ago, and he is unemployed. *he is still unemployed*
2. Should I tell Joe what happened, or does he know? *does he already know*
3. I'm hungry. Is dinner ready? *Is dinner ready yet*
4. I was hungry earlier, but I'm not hungry. *I'm not hungry anymore*
5. Can we wait a few minutes? I don't want to go out. ______
6. Jenny used to work at the airport, but she doesn't work there. ______
7. I used to live in Tokyo. I have a lot of friends there. ______
8. "Let me introduce you to Jim." "You don't have to. We've met." ______
9. Do you live in the same place, or have you moved? ______
10. Would you like to eat with us, or have you eaten? ______
11. "Where's John?" "He's not here. He'll be here soon." ______
12. Tim said he'd be here at 8:30. It's 9:00 now, and he isn't here. ______
13. Do you want to join the club, or are you a member? ______
14. It happened a long time ago, but I can remember it very clearly. ______
15. I've put on weight. These pants don't fit me. ______
16. "Have you finished with the paper?" "No, I'm reading it." ______

UNIT 109

even

A

☆ イラストを見て考えます。普通ではないことは何ですか？ そのことを英語でどう記述しますか？

Tina はテレビが大好きで，バスルームにも置いています。
このことは，次のように記述できます。

She has a TV set in every room of the house – **even** the bathroom.

➤「～でさえ」のように普通ではなく，驚いてしまう場合に even を用います。バスルームにテレビを置くことに驚いています。

☆ 以下の例文で，普通ではないことは何ですか？

- These pictures are really awful. **Even I** could take better pictures than these.
  (⇒ ひどい写真だ。私だってもっとうまい写真が撮れるだろう)
- He always wears a coat – **even in hot weather**.
- Nobody would help her – **not even her best friend**.
- = **Not even** her best friend would help her.

B

even はまれに動詞と結び付いて，文中で用いられることがあります。➲ Unit 107

- Sue has traveled all over the world. She has **even** been to the Antarctic.
  (⇒ 驚くなかれ，南極にも行ったことがある。そのくらい世界中を飛び回っている)
- They are very rich. They **even** have their own private jet.

not even ～は「～さえない」という驚きを表します。

- I can't cook. I ca**n't even** boil an egg. (⇒ ゆで卵くらい誰にでもできる。それすら作れない)
- They weren't very friendly to us. They did**n't even** say hello.
- Jenny is in great shape. She's just run five miles, and she's **not even** out of breath.

C

even + 比較級は，「もっと～」のように比較級を強調して強い驚きを表します。

- I got up very early, but Jack got up **even earlier**. (⇒ Jack はもっと早く起きた)
- I knew I didn't have much money, but I have **even less** than I thought.
- We were surprised to get a letter from her. We were **even more surprised** when she came to see us a few days later.

D

even though / even when / even if は，「たとえ～でも / ～の時でさえ / たとえ～だとしても」を表し，後に主語＋動詞を置きます。

- **Even though she can't** drive, she bought a car.
  (she can't = 主語＋動詞)
- He never shouts, **even when he's** angry.
- I'll probably see you tomorrow. But **even if I don't see** you tomorrow, I'm sure we'll see each other before the weekend.

though, when, if のない even だけの形で，後に主語＋動詞を置くことはできません。

- **Even though she can't** drive, she bought a car. (× Even she can't drive)
- I can't reach the shelf **even if I stand** on a chair. (× even I stand)

☆ 例文で考えます。even if と if は，どのように異なりますか？

- We're going to the beach tomorrow. It doesn't matter what the weather is like.
  We're going **even if** it's raining. (⇒ たとえ雨が降っても～)
- We want to go to the beach tomorrow, but we won't go **if** it's raining. (⇒ 雨が降ったら～)

if と when ➲ Unit 24D　　though / even though ➲ Unit 110E

Exercises

109.1 Julie と Sarah，Amanda は 3 人で旅行に出かけました。それぞれについての情報を読んで，even もしくは not even を用いて状況を説明する文を完成しなさい。

Julie	Sarah 	Amanda 
is usually happy is usually on time likes getting up early is very interested in art	doesn't really like art is usually miserable usually hates hotels doesn't have a camera	is almost always late is a good photographer loves staying at hotels isn't good at getting up early

1. They stayed at a hotel. Everybody liked it, *even Sarah* .
2. They arranged to meet. They all arrived on time, ________ .
3. They went to an art gallery. Nobody enjoyed it, ________ .
4. Yesterday they had to get up early. They all managed to do this, ________ .
5. They were together yesterday. They were all in a good mood, ________ .
6. None of them took any pictures, ________ .

109.2 状況に合うように（　）内の語句を even とともに用いて，文を完成しなさい。

1. Sue has been all over the world. (the Antarctic) *She has even been to the Antarctic.*
2. We painted the whole room. (the floor) We ________
3. Rachel has met lots of famous people. (the president)
   She ________
4. You could hear the noise from a long way away. (from two blocks away)
   You ________

以下の問題では not even ～ の形を用いて，文を完成しなさい。

5. They didn't say anything to us. (hello) *They didn't even say hello.*
6. I can't remember anything about her. (her name)
   I ________
7. There isn't anything to do in this town. (a movie theater)
   ____
8. He didn't tell anybody where he was going. (his wife)
   ____
9. I don't know anyone on my street. (the people next door)
   ____

109.3 状況に合うように「even + 比較級」の形を用いて，文を完成しなさい。

1. It was very hot yesterday, but today it's *even hotter* .
2. The church is 200 years old, but the house next to it is ________ .
3. That's a very good idea, but I've got an ________ one.
4. The first question was very difficult to answer. The second one was ________ .
5. I did very badly on the test, but most of my friends did ________ .
6. Neither of us was hungry. I ate very little, and my friend ate ________ .

109.4 状況に合うように if，even，even if，even though のいずれかを用いて，文を完成しなさい。

1. *Even though* she can't drive, she bought a car.
2. The bus leaves in five minutes, but we can still catch it ________ we run.
3. The bus leaves in two minutes. We won't catch it now ________ we run.
4. His Spanish isn't very good – ________ after three years in Mexico.
5. His Spanish isn't very good ________ he's lived in Mexico for three years.
6. ________ with the heat on, it was very cold in the house.
7. I couldn't sleep ________ I was very tired.
8. I won't forgive them for what they did ________ they apologize.
9. ________ I hadn't eaten anything for 24 hours, I wasn't hungry.

補充問題 32 (pp. 314–315)

UNIT 110

although / though / even though / in spite of / despite

A

☆イラストを見て考えます。普通ではないことは何ですか？ そのことを英語でどう記述しますか？

昨年，Paul と Joanne はビーチで休暇を過ごしました。雨がひどく降りましたが，2人は楽しく過ごしました。このことは，次のように記述できます。

Although it rained a lot, they had a good time.
(⇒ It rained a lot, *but* they . . .)

= **In spite of** / **Despite** } **the rain**, they had a good time.

➤「雨にもかかわらず楽しんだ」は，**although + 主語 + 動詞**や **in spite of / despite + 名詞句**の形を用いて表します。

B

although は「～であるにもかかわらず」を表し，後に**主語 + 動詞**を置きます。

- **Although it rained** a lot, we enjoyed our vacation.
- I didn't get the job **although I was** well qualified.

☆例文で考えます。although と because は，どのように異なりますか？

- We went out **although** it was raining.（⇒ 雨が降っていたが～）
- We didn't go out **because** it was raining.（⇒ 雨が降っていたので～）

C

in spite of ～は「～にもかかわらず」を表し，後に**名詞句**，**this**，**that**，**what で始まる関係詞節**，**-ing**（動名詞）などを置きます。

- **In spite of the rain**, we enjoyed our vacation.
- I didn't get the job **in spite of being** well qualified.
- She wasn't feeling well, but **in spite of this** she went to work.
- **In spite of what** I said yesterday, I still love you.

despite ～も **in spite of ～**と同様「～にもかかわらず」を表します。despite of のような of の付いた形はありません。

- She felt sick, but **despite this** she went to work. (✕ despite of this)

in spite of the fact (that) 主語 + 動詞や **despite the fact (that) 主語 + 動詞**の形で，「～が … する / ～である事実にもかかわらず」を表します。

- I didn't get the job { **in spite of the fact** (that) / **despite the fact** (that) } I was extremely qualified.

☆例文で考えます。in spite of と because of は，どのように異なりますか？

- We went out **in spite of the rain**.（⇒ ... despite the rain，雨にもかかわらず）
- We didn't go out **because of the rain**.（⇒ 雨のために～）

D

☆although の後には主語 + 動詞がきますが，in spite of / despite の後にはこないことを例文で確認します。

- **Although the traffic was** bad, / **In spite of the traffic**, } we arrived on time. (✕ In spite of the traffic was bad)
- I couldn't sleep { **although I was** very tired. / **despite being** very tired. } (✕ despite I was tired)

E

although の代わりに **though** を用いることがあります。ともに「～ではあるが」を表します。

- I didn't get the job **though** I had all the necessary qualifications.

話しことばでは **though** を**文末**に置き，前にある文を受け「～ではあるのだけれど」の意味で用いることがあります。

- The house isn't very nice. I like the garden, **though**.（⇒ 庭は気に入っているんだけどね）
- I see them every day. I've never spoken to them, **though**.
  (⇒ 一度も話をしたことはないんだけど)

even though は **although** と同様「～ではあるが」を表しますが，**although** よりも強い意味を持ちます。though を置かない even だけの形はありません。

- **Even though** I was really tired, I couldn't sleep. (✕ Even I was really tired . . .)

even ➲ Unit 109

Exercises

110.1 状況に合うように以下から文を選び，although の後に続けて空所に入れ，文を完成しなさい。

I didn't speak the language	~~he has a very important job~~
I had never seen her before	we don't like them very much
it was pretty cold	the heat was on
I'd met her twice before	we've known each other a long time

1. *Although he has a very important job* , he isn't particularly well paid.
2. ________________ , I recognized her from a photograph.
3. She wasn't wearing a coat ________________ .
4. We thought we'd better invite them to the party ________________ .
5. ________________ , I managed to make myself understood.
6. ________________ , the room wasn't warm.
7. I didn't recognize her ________________ .
8. We're not very good friends ________________ .

110.2 状況に合うように although / in spite of / because / because of から適切なものを選び，空所に入れて文を完成しなさい。

1. *Although* it rained a lot, we enjoyed our vacation.
2. a) ________ all our careful plans, a lot of things went wrong.
   b) ________ we had planned everything carefully, a lot of things went wrong.
3. a) I went home early ________ I wasn't feeling well.
   b) I went to work the next day ________ I was still feeling sick.
4. a) She only accepted the job ________ the salary, which was very high.
   b) She accepted the job ________ the salary, which was rather low.
5. a) I managed to get to sleep ________ there was a lot of noise.
   b) I couldn't get to sleep ________ the noise.

以下の問題では，空所に入る文を自分なりに考えて記入しなさい。

6. a) He passed the exam although ________________ .
   b) He passed the exam because ________________ .
7. a) I didn't eat anything although ________________ .
   b) I didn't eat anything in spite of ________________ .

110.3 (　) 内の語句を用いて，2 つの文を 1 つにまとめなさい。

1. I couldn't sleep. I was very tired. (despite)
   I couldn't sleep despite being very tired.
2. They have very little money. They are happy. (in spite of)
   ____
3. My foot was injured. I managed to walk to the nearest town. (although)
   ____
4. I enjoyed the movie. The story was silly. (in spite of)
   ____
5. We live on the same street. We hardly ever see each other. (despite)
   ____
6. I got very wet in the rain. I was only out for five minutes. (even though)
   ____

110.4 状況に合うように (　) 内の語句を用いて，文末に though のある文を完成しなさい。

1. The house isn't very nice. (like / yard) *I like the yard, though.*
2. It's warm today. (very windy) ________________
3. We didn't like the food. (ate) ________________
4. Liz is very nice. (don't like / husband) I ________________

補充問題 32 (pp. 314–315)

UNIT 111 in case

A

☆ イラストを見て考えます。イラストの人物は何を心配していますか？そのことを英語でどう記述しますか？

パンクに備えてスペアタイヤを用意しておくとよいでしょう。このことは，次のように記述できます。

Your car should have a spare tire **in case** you have a flat tire.

➤ in case + 主語 + 動詞は，主語 + 動詞が肯定の場合は「～するかもしれないので…する」，否定の場合は「～ないといけないので…する」のように動作を行う理由を表します。

☆ 例文はどのような理由を表していますか？

- I'll leave my cell phone on **in case Jane calls**.（⇒ Jane が電話するかもしれないので）
- I'll draw a map for you **in case you can't find our house**.（⇒ 家がわからなくなるといけないので）
- I'll remind them about the meeting **in case they've forgotten**.（⇒ 忘れてしまっているかもしれないので）

「万一～するといけないので」のように，**in case** よりも出来事が起きる可能性が少ない場合には **just in case** を用います。

- I don't think it will rain, but I'll take an umbrella **just in case**. (= **just in case** it rains)

未来の出来事を表す場合でも，**in case** の後の動詞中に will を用いてはいけません。**現在時制**を用います。

➲ Unit 24

- I'll leave my phone on **in case** Jane **calls**. (✕ in case Jane will call)

B

in case ～と **if** ～（もし～であるならば）との意味の違いに注意します。**in case** ～は，「後で～するかもしれないので，今…する / しない」のように，人が今，動作をしたりしなかったりする**理由**を述べます。

☆ 例文で考えます。in case と if は，どのように異なりますか？

in case

- We'll buy some more food **in case** Tom comes.
（⇒ おそらく Tom が来る。来る来ないに関係なく，今，食べ物をもっと買っておこう。そうしておけば，もし彼が来たとしても食べ物がある）
- I'll give you my phone number **in case** you need to contact me.
- You should register your bike **in case** it is stolen.

if

- We'll buy some more food **if** Tom comes.
（⇒ おおそらく Tom が来る。もし彼が来れば，もっと食べ物を買う。しかしもし来なければ，食べ物は買わない）
- You can call me at the hotel **if** you need to contact me.
- You should inform the police **if** your bike is stolen.

C

「～するかもしれなかったので…した」のような**過去の出来事の理由**は，**in case** + **過去時制**で表します。

- I left my phone on **in case Jane called**.
（⇒ Jane が電話をかけてくる可能性があったので，伝言を残しておいた）
- I drew a map for Sarah **in case** she **couldn't** find the house.
- We rang the doorbell again **in case** they **hadn't** heard it the first time.

D

☆ in case of ～と in case + 主語 + 動詞とは，どのように異なりますか？

in case of ～は「もし～になった時には，～の場合は」を表し，看板や掲示などの**書きことば**で用いられ，後に**名詞句**がきます。

- **In case of fire**, please leave the building as quickly as possible.（⇒ 火事になった場合には）
- **In case of emergency**, call this number.（⇒ 緊急時には）

if ➲ Units 24, 36–38

Exercises

111.1 Barbara はハイキングに出かけようとしています。持っていくべき物を以下から選びなさい。

~~**some chocolate**~~ **a map** **a raincoat** **a camera** **some water**

その項目を選んだ理由を，以下から選びます。

it's possible she'll get lost perhaps she'll be thirsty she might want to take some pictures	~~she might get hungry~~ maybe it will rain

in case を用いて，Barbara にその項目を選んだ理由を説明しなさい。

1. *Take some chocolate with you in case you get hungry.*
2. Take __________
3. __________
4. __________
5. __________

111.2 状況に合うように．自分の発言を **in case** を用いて完成しなさい。

1. It's possible that Mary will need to contact you, so you give her your phone number.
   You say: Here's my phone number *in case you need to contact me* .
2. A friend of yours is going away for a long time. Maybe you won't see her again before she goes, so you decide to say good-bye now.
   You say: I'll say good-bye now __________ .
3. You are shopping in a supermarket with a friend. You think you have everything you need, but perhaps you've forgotten something. Your friend has the list. You ask her to check it.
   You say: Can you __________ ?
4. You are giving a friend some advice about using a computer. You think he should back up (= *copy*) his files because the computer might crash (and he would lose all his data).
   You say: You should back up __________ .

111.3 状況を説明する文を **in case** を用いて完成しなさい。

1. There was a possibility that Jane would call. So I left my phone switched on.
   I left *my phone on in case Jane called* .
2. Mike thought that he might forget the name of the book. So he wrote it down.
   He wrote down __________ .
3. I thought my parents might be worried about me. So I called them.
   I called __________ .
4. I sent an e-mail to Liz, but I didn't get an answer. So I sent another e-mail because I thought that maybe she hadn't gotten the first one.
   I sent __________ .
5. I met some people when I was on vacation in France. They said they might come to New York one day. I live in New York, so I gave them my address.
   I gave __________ .

111.4 状況に合うように，空所に **in case** もしくは **if** を入れて文を完成しなさい。

1. I'll draw a map for you *in case* you can't find our house.
2. You should tell the police *if* you have any information about the crime.
3. I hope you'll come to Chicago sometime. ______ you come, you can stay with us.
4. This letter is for Susan. Can you give it to her ______ you see her?
5. Write your name and address on your bag ______ you lose it.
6. Go to the Lost and Found office ______ you lose your bag.
7. The burglar alarm will ring ______ somebody tries to break into the house.
8. You should lock your bike to something ______ somebody tries to steal it.
9. I was advised to get insurance ______ I needed medical treatment while I was abroad.

補充問題 32 **(pp. 314–315)**

UNIT 112

unless as long as provided/providing

A unless

☆イラストを見て考えます。Oasis Clubを利用するにはどうしますか？ そのことを英語でどう記述しますか？

Oasis Club を利用するには会員になる必要があります。このことは，次のように記述できます。

You can't go in **unless you are a member**.

この文は，以下のように２通りで書き換えられます。

You can't go in *except if* you are a member.
(⇒ メンバーである場合を除いて入れない)

= You can go in *only if* you are a member.
(⇒ メンバーである場合のみ入れる)

➤ **unless ～は「もし～でなければ」を表します。**

☆例文で考えます。unless はどのような条件を表していますか？

- I'll see you tomorrow **unless I have to work late**. (⇒ 残業にならなければ～)
- There are no buses to the beach. **Unless you have a car**, it's difficult to get there.
(⇒ 自動車を持っていなければ～)
- "Should I tell Liz what happened?" "**Not unless she asks you**."
(⇒ 彼女が聞いてこなければ言わない。彼女が聞いてきたら言う)
- Sally hates to complain. She wouldn't complain about something **unless it was really bad**. (⇒ よほどひどいことがない限り～)
- We can take a taxi to the restaurant – **unless you'd prefer to walk**.
(⇒ どうしても歩きたいというのでなければ～)

unless ～は **if ... not** ～で書き換えられます。

- **Unless we leave now**, we'll be late. = **If we don't leave now**, we'll . . .

B as long as など

as long as = **so long as**
provided (**that**) = **providing** (**that**)
｝いずれも「もし～ならば」や「～する限り」のような条件を表します。

☆例文で考えます。どのような条件を表していますか？

- You can borrow my car { **as long as** / **so long as** } you promise not to drive too fast.
(⇒ 車は貸してあげます。ですがスピードを出し過ぎないと約束してください。これが条件です)
- Traveling by car is convenient { **provided** (**that**) / **providing** (**that**) } you have somewhere to park.
(⇒ 駐車する場所があれば)
- { **Providing** (**that**) / **Provided** (**that**) } the room is clean, I don't care which hotel we stay at.
(⇒ 部屋が清潔であることが条件です。ほかは気にしません)

C

未来の出来事を話題にする場合でも **unless** / **as long as** / **so long as** / **provided** / **providing** の後の動詞中に will を用いません。現在時制にします。➲ Unit 24A

- I'm not going out **unless** it **stops** raining. (× unless it will stop)
- **Providing** the weather is good, we're going on a picnic.
(× providing the weather will be good)

if ➲ Units 24, 36–38

Exercises

112.1 unless を用いて文を書き換えなさい。

1. You need to try a little harder, or you won't pass the exam.
   You won't pass the exam unless you try a little harder.
2. Listen carefully, or you won't know what to do.
   You won't know what to do ______
3. She has to apologize to me, or I'll never speak to her again.
   ______
4. You have to speak very slowly, or he won't be able to understand you.
   ______
5. Business has got to improve soon, or the company will have to close.
   ______

112.2 unless を用いて文を書き換えなさい。

1. The club isn't open to everyone. You are allowed in only if you're a member.
   You aren't allowed in the club unless you're a member.
2. I don't want to go to the party alone. I'm going only if you go, too.
   I'm not going ______
3. Don't worry about the dog. It will attack you only if you move suddenly.
   The dog ______
4. Ben isn't very talkative. He'll speak to you only if you ask him something.
   Ben ______
5. The doctor will see you only if it's an emergency.
   The doctor ______

112.3 下線部の正しい方を選んで，文を完成しなさい。

1. You can borrow my car ~~unless~~ / as long as you promise not to drive too fast.
   (as long as が正しい)
2. I'm playing tennis tomorrow unless / providing it rains.
3. I'm playing tennis tomorrow unless / providing it doesn't rain.
4. I don't mind if you come home late unless / as long as you come in quietly.
5. I'm going now unless / provided you want me to stay.
6. I don't watch TV unless / as long as I've got nothing else to do.
7. Children are allowed to use the swimming pool unless / provided they are with an adult.
8. Unless / Provided they are with an adult, children are not allowed to use the swimming pool.
9. We can sit here in the corner unless / as long as you'd rather sit over there by the window.
10. *A:* Our vacation cost a lot of money.
    B: Did it? Well, that doesn't matter unless / as long as you had a good time.

112.4 自分のことを記述する文を完成しなさい。

1. We'll be late unless *we take a taxi* ______.
2. I like hot weather as long as ______.
3. It takes Kate about 20 minutes to drive to work provided ______.
4. I don't mind walking home as long as ______.
5. I like to walk to work in the morning unless ______.
6. We can meet tomorrow unless ______.
7. You can borrow the money providing ______.
8. You won't achieve anything unless ______.

UNIT 113

as（～と同時に，～なので）

A

as . . . = at the same time ...（…と同時に / …すると）

as は**接続詞**で後に**主語＋動詞**を置き，イラストのように２つの出来事が同時に起きていることを表します。

- We all waved good-bye to Liz **as** she drove away.
  （⇒ 私たちが手を振るのと同時に Liz は車を走らせた）
- I watched her **as** she opened the letter.
- **As** I walked along the street, I looked in the store windows.
- Can you turn off the light **as** you go out, please?

Bye!

Liz

「…しようとしたところで」のように，**過去進行形**で表す動作を行っていた最中に別の何かが起こった時にも **as ...** を用います。

- Jill slipped **as she was getting off** the bus.
- We met Paul **as we were leaving** the hotel.
  （⇒ ホテルを出ようとしたところで…）

過去進行形（was getting / were going など）➲Unit 6

just as ... は「ちょうど…した時に」を表します。

- **Just as** I sat down, the phone rang.（⇒ ちょうど座ったら，…）
- I had to leave **just as** the conversation was getting interesting.

as ... は「…するにつれて」のように，**２つの出来事**がかなり長い期間に同時進行する場合にも用います。

- **As** the day went on, the weather got worse.
- I began to enjoy the job more **as** I got used to it.

the day went on

the weather got worse

（⇒ その日時間が経つにつれて，天気は崩れた）

☆ 例文で考えます。as と when は似ていますが，when ... は出来事が連続して生じることを表します。

➤ as は，２つの出来事が同時に起きる際にのみ用います。

- **As we walked home**, we talked about what we would have for dinner.
  （⇒ 歩いて家に帰りながら…）

➤ when は，ある出来事が起こってから別の出来事が起きる場合に用います。

- **When we got home**, we started cooking dinner.
  （⇒ 家に帰ってから…）

B

as . . . = because ...（…なので）**理由**を表します。

- **As it was a national holiday** last Thursday, all the banks were closed.
  (= because it was a national holiday)
- The thief was difficult to identify **as he was wearing a mask** during the robbery.

since ... も同様に「…なので」と**理由**を表します。

- **Since it was a national holiday** last Thursday, all the banks were closed.
- The thief was difficult to identify **since he was wearing a mask** during the robbery.

☆ 例文で考えます。as と when は似ていますが，when は理由を表しません。

- I couldn't contact David **as he was on a business trip**, and he doesn't have a cell phone.（⇒ 出張中だったので…）
- **As they lived near us**, we used to see them pretty often.
  （⇒ 近所に暮らしていたので…）

- David's passport was stolen **when he was on a business trip**.
  （⇒ 出張中に…）
- **When they lived near us**, we used to see them pretty often.
  （⇒ 近所に暮らしていた時…）

as ～ as ... ➲ Unit 104　like と as ➲ Unit 114　as if ➲ Unit 115

Exercises

113.1 セクション A を参考にして，左右から文を 1 つずつ選び，as ...（…するのと同時に）を用いて 1 つの文にしなさい。

1. ~~we all waved good-bye to Liz~~	we were driving along the road
2. we all smiled	I was taking a hot dish out of the oven
3. I burned myself	~~she drove away~~
4. the crowd cheered	we posed for the photograph
5. a dog ran out in front of the car	the two teams ran onto the field

1. *We all waved good-bye to Liz as she drove away.*
2. ______
3. ______
4. ______
5. ______

113.2 それぞれの文中の as ... の意味を選びなさい。

	because ...	at the same time ...
1. **As** they live near me, I see them fairly often.	✔	______
2. Jill slipped **as** she was getting off the bus.	______	✔
3. **As** I was tired, I went to bed early.	______	______
4. Unfortunately, **as** I was parking the car, I hit the car behind me.	______	______
5. **As** we climbed the hill, we got more and more tired.	______	______
6. We decided to go out to eat **as** we had no food at home.	______	______
7. **As** we don't use the car very often, we've decided to sell it.	______	______

例にならって as ... が because ...（…なので）を意味する文を上から選んで，since を用いて書き換えなさい。

8. *Since they live near me, I see them pretty often.*
9. ______
10. ______
11. ______

113.3 それぞれの文から as ではなく when を用いなければならない部分を○で囲み，正しい形に書き直しなさい。

1. Maria got married (as she was 22). *when she was 22*
2. As the day went on, the weather got worse. *OK*
3. He dropped the glass as he was taking it out of the cabinet. ______
4. My camera was stolen as I was asleep on the beach. ______
5. As I finished high school, I went into the army. ______
6. The train slowed down as it approached the station. ______
7. I used to live near the ocean as I was a child. ______

113.4 自分のことを記述する文を完成しなさい。

1. I saw you as ______
2. It started to rain just as ______
3. As I didn't have enough money for a taxi, ______
4. Just as I took the photograph, ______

UNIT 114

like と as

A

like ～は「～のような」や「～と同じ」を表します。この用法では **like** は as に置き換えられません。

- What a beautiful house! It's **like a palace**. (× as a palace)
- "What does Sandra do?" "She's a teacher, **like me**." (× as me)
- Be careful! The floor has been polished. It's **like walking on ice**. (× as walking)
- It's raining again. I hate weather **like this**. (× as this)

ここでの **like** は**前置詞**で，後には a palace のような**名詞句**，me，this のような**代名詞**，walking ... のような **-ing**（動名詞）がきます。

like ～（人 / 物）-ing の形で「～（人 / 物）が…するような / に」を表します。

- "What's that noise?" "It sounds **like a baby** cry**ing**." (⇒ 赤ん坊が泣くような…)

B

like ～は，「例えば～のような」を表すことがあります。

- Some sports, **like** race-car driving, can be dangerous.

such as ～も「例えば～のような」を表します。

- Some sports, **such as** race-car driving, can be dangerous.

C

as ... は「…するのと同じように / …と同じ状態で」を表します。**as** は**接続詞**で後には**主語＋動詞**がきます。

- I didn't move anything. I left everything **as it was**. (⇒ 私がやって見せたように…)
- You should have done it **as I showed you**. (⇒ 元と同じ状態で…)

くだけた**話しことば**では，**as** の代わりに **like** を用いることがあります。この場合，**like** は**接続詞**で後には**主語＋動詞**がきます。

- I left everything **like it was**.

like には**接続詞**と**前置詞**の用法があります。**as** に**前置詞**の用法はないので，後に名詞句はきません。

- You should have done it **as I showed you**. (= **like** I showed you)
- You should have done it **like this**. (× **as** this)

as usual / **as always** は「いつもと同じように」を表します。

- You're late **as usual**.
- **As always**, Nick was the first to complain.

D

do の後にきた **as＋主語＋動詞**は，**what** で置き換えられ「…すること / …のように」を表します。

- You can do **as you like**. (⇒ do what you like, あなたが好きなことを / 好きなようにする)
- They did **as they promised**. (⇒ did what they promised, 約束したことを / 約束通したようにした)

as you know / **as I said** / **as she expected** / **as I thought** のような形もよく用います。それぞれ「あなたも知っているように / 私が言ったように / 彼女が予想したように / 私が考えたように」を表し，**直前**や**直後**の**文全体**を修飾します。

- **As you know**, it's Emma's birthday next week. (⇒ あなたもすでにご存知のように…)
- Ann failed her driving test, **as she expected**. (⇒ 彼女が前から予想していたように…)

like I said（私が言ったように）のように，内部に **say** のある言い方を除いて上の **as** の代わりに like は使えません。

- **As I said** yesterday, I'm sure we can solve the problem. = **Like I said** yesterday . . .

E

☆ **枠内の例文で考えます。as にも前置詞として，後に名詞句を置く用法があります。like とどのように異なりますか？**

- Brenda Casey is the manager of a company. **As the manager**, she has to make many important decisions. (⇒ マネージャーとして…)
- Mary Stone is the assistant manager. **Like the manager** (Brenda Casey), she also has to make important decisions. (⇒ まるでマネージャーのように…)

➤ **前置詞としての as ～は，「～として，～の形で」のような意味で用います。like ～にはこの意味はありません。**

- A few years ago I worked **as a taxi driver**. (× like a taxi driver)
- We don't have a car, so we use the garage **as a workshop**.
- Many words, for example "work" and "rain," can be used **as verbs or nouns**.
- New York is all right **as a place to visit**, but I wouldn't like to live there.
- The news of the tragedy came **as a great shock**.

as ～ as ... ➲ Unit 104　as（～と同時に，～なので）➲ Unit 113　as if ➲ Unit 115

Exercises

114.1 それぞれの文から as ではなく like を用いなければならない部分を○で囲み，正しい形に書き直しなさい。

1. It's raining again. I hate weather as this. _weather like this_
2. Ann failed her driving test, as she expected. _OK_
3. Do you think Carol looks as her mother? ______
4. Tim gets on my nerves. I can't stand people as him. ______
5. Why didn't you do it as I told you to do it? ______
6. Brian is a student, as most of his friends. ______
7. You never listen. Talking to you is as talking to the wall. ______
8. As I said yesterday, I'm thinking of changing my job. ______
9. Tom's idea seemed to be a good one, so we did as he suggested. ______
10. I'll call you tomorrow as usual, OK? ______
11. Suddenly there was a terrible noise. It was as a bomb exploding. ______
12. She's a very good swimmer. She swims as a fish. ______

114.2 状況に合うように，以下の語句を like もしくは as に続けて空所に入れて，文を完成しなさい。

a beginner	**blocks of ice**	~~**a palace**~~	**a birthday present**
a child	**a church**	**winter**	**a tour guide**

1. This house is beautiful. It's _like a palace_.
2. My feet are really cold. They're ______.
3. I've been playing tennis for years, but I still play ______.
4. Margaret once had a part-time job ______.
5. I wonder what that building with the tower is. It looks ______.
6. My brother gave me this watch ______ a long time ago.
7. It's very cold for the middle of summer. It's ______.
8. He's 22 years old, but he sometimes behaves ______.

114.3 状況に合うように，空所に like もしくは as を入れて文を完成しなさい。どちらも入れることができる場合もあります。

1. We heard a noise _like_ a baby crying.
2. Your English is very fluent. I wish I could speak ______ you.
3. Don't take my advice if you don't want to. You can do ______ you like.
4. You waste too much time doing things ______ sitting in cafés all day.
5. I wish I had a car ______ yours.
6. You don't need to change your clothes. You can go out ______ you are.
7. My neighbor's house is full of lots of interesting things. It's ______ a museum.
8. We saw Kevin last night. He was very cheerful, ______ always.
9. Sally has been working ______ a waitress for the last two months.
10. While we were on vacation, we spent most of our time doing active things ______ sailing, water skiing, and swimming.
11. You're different from the other people I know. I don't know anyone ______ you.
12. We don't need all the bedrooms in the house, so we use one of them ______ a study.
13. The news that Sue and Gary were getting married came ______ a complete surprise to me.
14. ______ her father, Catherine has a very good voice.
15. At the moment I've got a temporary job in a bookstore. It's OK ______ a temporary job, but I wouldn't like to do it permanently.
16. ______ you can imagine, we were very tired after such a long trip.
17. This tea is awful. It tastes ______ water.
18. I think I preferred this room ______ it was, before we decorated it.

UNIT 115

like / as if / as though

A

like は **look/sound/feel + like ...** の構文中では**接続詞**として後に**主語 + 動詞**を置き，「(〜は) …のように見える / 聞こえる / 感じる」を表します。

- That house **looks like** it's going to fall down. (⇒ 今にも崩れそうに見える)
- Helen **sounded like** she had a cold, didn't she?
- I've just come back from vacation, but I feel very tired. I don't **feel like** I just had a vacation.

like の代わりに **as if** や **as though** を使うこともできます。

- That house looks **as if** it's going to fall down.
- I don't feel **as though** I just had a vacation.

話しことばでは **like** の方が，**as if** や **as though** よりよく用いられます。

☆ **look の後には何がきますか？**

- You look **tired**. (look + 形容詞)
- You look { **like** / **as if** } **you didn't sleep** last night.

(look (like / as if) + 主語 + 動詞)

☆ **この家をどのように記述しますか？**

B

It looks like / **It sounds like** + **主語** + **動詞**は，「…しているように見える / 聞こえる」を表します。

- Sandra is very late, isn't she? **It looks like** she isn't coming.
- We took an umbrella because **it looked like** it was going to rain. (⇒ 雨が降りそうだ)
- Do you hear that music next door? **It sounds like** they are having a party. (⇒ パーティーでもしているみたいだ)

like は **as if** もしくは **as though** で置き換えられます。

- It looks **as if** she isn't coming.
- It looks **as though** she isn't coming.

C

動詞 + **like** / **as if** / **as though ...** は「…しているかのように〜する」と，どのように動作が行われるかを説明します。

- He **ran like** he was running for his life. (⇒ 命を賭けるかのように / 死に物狂いで，走った)
- After the interruption, the speaker **went on talking as if** nothing had happened.
- When I told them my plan, they **looked at me as though** I was crazy.

D

as if の後では**現在**のことを話題にしていながら，**動詞**を**過去時制**にすることがあります。

- I don't like Tim. He talks **as if** he **knew** everything.

上の文は，「(今) 何でも知っているかのように話をしている」を表し，過去を意味しません。実際に「何でも知っている」はずはなく，現実と異なることを話題にしています。このような場合，**as if he knew** のように**過去時制**を用います。動詞の **wish** (…であればなあ) の後でも同じことが生じます。➲ Unit 37

☆ **as if ... の形から，どのような現実が考えられますか？**

- She's always asking me to do things for her – **as if I didn't** have enough to do already. (⇒ 実際のところ，私にはすべきことが十分ある)
- Gary's only 40. Why do you talk about him **as if he was** an old man? (⇒ 実際のところ，老人ではない)

現実と異なることを**過去時制**を用いて表す時，was ではなく **were** を用いることがあります。

- Why do you talk about him **as if he were** (= **was**) an old man?
- They treat me **as if I were** (= **was**) their own son. (⇒ 実際のところ，息子ではない)

If I was/were ➲ Unit 37C　look/sound など + 形容詞 ➲ Unit 97C　like と as ➲ Unit 114

Exercises

115.1 ( ) 内の語句を look/sound/feel + like ... の構文中で用いて，状況に合う自分の発言を完成しなさい。

1. You meet Bill. He has a black eye and some bandages on his face. (be / a fight)
   You say to him:
   You look like you've been in a fight.
2. Christine comes into the room. She looks absolutely terrified. (see / a ghost)
   You say to her: What's the matter? You __________
3. Joe is on vacation. He's talking to you on the phone and sounds very happy. (enjoy / yourself)
   You say to him: You __________
4. You have just run a mile. You are absolutely exhausted. (run / a marathon)
   You say to a friend: I __________

115.2 以下から適切なものを選び，It looks like ... / It sounds like ... の構文にあてはめて状況を説明する文を完成しなさい。

you should see a doctor	there's been an accident	they are having an argument
it's going to rain	~~she isn't coming~~	we'll have to walk

1. Sandra said she would be here an hour ago.
   You say: *It looks like she isn't coming.*
2. The sky is full of black clouds.
   You say: It __________
3. You hear two people shouting at each other next door.
   You say: __________
4. You see an ambulance, some police officers, and two damaged cars at the side of the road.
   You say: __________
5. You and a friend have just missed the last bus home.
   You say: __________
6. Dave isn't feeling well. He tells you all about it.
   You say: __________

115.3 以下から適切な語句を選び，as if ... の構文中で用いて状況を説明する文を完成しなさい（動詞の時制は適切な形に変えること）。

she / enjoy / it	I / go / be sick	not / eat / for a week
~~he / need / a good rest~~	she / hurt / her leg	he / mean / what he / say
I / not / exist	she / not / want / come	

1. Mark looks very tired. He looks *as if he needs a good rest*.
2. I don't think Paul was joking. He looked __________.
3. What's the matter with Liz? She's walking __________.
4. Peter was extremely hungry and ate his dinner very quickly.
   He ate __________.
5. Carol had a bored expression on her face during the concert.
   She didn't look __________.
6. I've just eaten too many chocolates. Now I don't feel well.
   I feel __________.
7. I called Liz and invited her to the party, but she wasn't very enthusiastic about it.
   She sounded __________.
8. I went into the office, but nobody spoke to me or looked at me.
   Everybody ignored me __________.

115.4 as if を含む文を完成しなさい（動詞の時制についてはセクション D を参考にすること）。

1. Brian is a terrible driver. He drives *as if he were* the only driver on the road.
2. I'm 20 years old, so please don't talk to me __________ I __________ a child.
3. Steve has never met Maria, but he talks about her __________ his best friend.
4. It was a long time ago that we first met, but I remember it __________ yesterday.

UNIT 116

for, during と while

A

for と during

for + 継続期間は「～の間」のように，どのくらいの間出来事が継続するかを表します。

for **two hours**（2 時間）　for **a week**（1 週間）　for **ages**（長い間）

- We watched television **for two hours** last night.
- Diane is going away **for a week** in September.
- Where have you been? I've been waiting **for ages**.
- Are you going away **for the weekend**?

during + 名詞句は「～の間に」を表しますが，期間ではなくいつ出来事が起こったかを表します。

during **the movie**（映画の間に）　during **our vacation**（休暇の間に）　during **the night**（夜の間に）

- I fell asleep **during the movie**.
- We met some really nice people **during our vacation**.
- The ground is wet. It must have rained **during the night**.

the morning / the afternoon / the summer のような**時**を表す**語句**の前には，**during** と同じように **in** を置くことがあります。

- It must have rained **in the night**. (= **during** the night)
- I'll call you sometime **during the afternoon**. (= **in the** afternoon)

during を**継続期間**を表す**語**の**前**に置いて，出来事がどのくらい継続するかを表すことはできません（**for** を用います）。

- It rained **for** three days without stopping. (× during three days)

☆ **例文で考えます。during と for は，どのように異なりますか？**

- I fell asleep **during the movie**. I was asleep **for half an hour**.
  (⇒ 映画の間に，1 時間半寝てしまった)

B

during と while

☆ **例文で考えます。during と while はともに「～の間に」を表しますが，どのように異なりますか？**

➤ **during は名詞句の前に置きます。**

- I fell asleep **during the movie**.
  （the movie = 名詞句）
- We met a lot of interesting people **during our vacation**. (⇒ 休暇の間に)
- Robert suddenly began to feel sick **during the exam**.

➤ **while は主語 + 動詞の前に置き，節を作ります。**

- I fell asleep **while I was watching TV**.
  （I = 主語，was watching = 動詞：主語 + 動詞）
- We met a lot of interesting people **while we were on vacation**. (⇒ 休暇の間に)
- Robert suddenly began to feel sick **while he was taking the exam**.

☆ **while の作る節を以下の例で確認します。**

- We saw Claire **while we were waiting** for the bus.
- **While you were** out, there was a phone call for you.
- Chris read a book **while I watched** TV.

while節の内部では，未来の出来事でも will を用いずに**現在形**で記述します。

- I'll be in Toronto next week. I hope to see Tom **while I'm** there.
  (× while I will be there)
- What are you going to do **while** you **are** waiting? (× while you will be waiting)

Unit 24 も参照のこと。

for と since ➲ Unit 12A　while + -ing ➲ Unit 66B

Exercises

116.1 状況に合うように，空所に **for** もしくは **during** を入れて文を完成しなさい。

1. It rained *for* three days without stopping.
2. I fell asleep *during* the movie.
3. I went to the theater last night. I met Sue ______ the intermission.
4. Matt hasn't lived in the United States all his life. He lived in Brazil ______ four years.
5. Production at the factory was seriously affected ______ the strike.
6. I felt really sick last week. I could hardly eat anything ______ three days.
7. I waited for you ______ half an hour and decided that you weren't coming.
8. Sarah was very angry with me. She didn't speak to me ______ a week.
9. We usually go out on weekends, but we don't often go out ______ the week.
10. Jack started a new job a few weeks ago. Before that he was out of work ______ six months.
11. I need a change. I think I'll go away ______ a few days.
12. The president gave a long speech. She spoke ______ two hours.
13. We were hungry when we arrived. We hadn't had anything to eat ______ the trip.
14. We were hungry when we arrived. We hadn't had anything to eat ______ eight hours.

116.2 状況に合うように，空所に **during** もしくは **while** を入れて文を完成しなさい。

1. We met a lot of interesting people *while* we were on vacation.
2. We met a lot of interesting people *during* our vacation.
3. I met Mike ______ I was shopping.
4. ______ I was on vacation, I didn't read any newspapers or watch TV.
5. ______ our stay in Paris, we visited a lot of museums and galleries.
6. The phone rang three times ______ we were having dinner.
7. The phone rang three times ______ the night.
8. I had been away for many years. ______ that time, many things had changed.
9. What did they say about me ______ I was out of the room?
10. I went out for dinner last night. Unfortunately, I began to feel sick ______ the meal and had to go home.
11. Please don't interrupt me ______ I'm speaking.
12. There were many interruptions ______ the president's speech.
13. Can you set the table ______ I get dinner ready?
14. We were hungry when we arrived. We hadn't had anything to eat ______ we were traveling.

116.3 状況に合うように，自分のことを記述する文を完成しなさい。

1. I fell asleep while *I was watching television.*
2. I fell asleep during *the movie.*
3. I hurt my arm while ______
4. Can you wait here while ______
5. Most of the students looked bored during ______
6. I was asked a lot of questions during ______
7. Don't open the car door while ______
8. The lights suddenly went out while ______
9. It started to rain during ______
10. It started to rain while ______

補充問題 33 (p. 315)

UNIT 117 by と until　by the time ...

A

by + 時を表す語句で，「～までに」のように動作が起きる期間を表します。

- I sent the letter to them today, so they should receive it **by Monday**.
  (⇒ 月曜日までに，月曜日を過ぎることなく)
- We'd better hurry. We have to be home **by 5:00**.
  (⇒ 5 時までに，5 時を過ぎることなく)
- Where's Sue? She should be here **by now**.
  (⇒ 今よりも前に，もう)

This milk should be sold **by August 14.**
(⇒ 8月14日が販売期限)

B

until (= **till**) + 時を表す語句で，「～まで」のように状況が継続する期間を表します。

- "Shall we go now?" "No, let's wait **until** (= **till**) it stops raining." (⇒ 雨がやむまで待ち続ける)
- I couldn't get up this morning. { I stayed in bed **until** half past ten. / I didn't get up **until** half past ten. }

☆ 例文で考えます。until と by は，どのように異なりますか？

until	by
➤ ある時点まで状況が継続する。	➤ ある時点までに出来事が起きる。
■ Fred **will be away until** Monday. (⇒ 戻ってくるのは月曜日)	■ Fred **will be back by** Monday. (⇒ 月曜日，もしくはそれ以前に戻ってくる)
■ **I'll be working until** 11:30. (⇒ 11:30 に仕事を終える)	■ **I'll have finished my work by** 11:30. (⇒ 遅くても 11:30 には仕事を終える)

C

以下の例で **by the time** + **主語** + **動詞**（現在形）は，未来の一時点までの期間を表します。未来のことが**現在形**で表されます。

- It's too late to go to the bank now. **By the time we get there**, it will be closed.
  (⇒ 今から後，銀行に到着するまでの間に…)
- 〔絵はがきで〕Our vacation ends tomorrow. So **by the time you receive this postcard**, I'll be back home.
  (⇒ 休暇が終わる明日以降，このはがきが届くまでの間に…)
- Hurry up! **By the time we get to the theater**, the play will already have started.

以下の例で **by the time** + **主語** + **動詞**（過去形）は，過去の一時点までの期間を表します。

- Karen's car broke down on the way to the party last night. **By the time she arrived**, most of the other guests had left.
  (⇒ 昨晩，自動車が故障してパーティーになかなか到着できなかった。この到着するまでの間に…)
- I had a lot of work to do last night. I was very tired **by the time I finished**.
  (⇒ 昨晩，山ほどの仕事があった。仕事はなかなか終わらなかった。この仕事が完了するまでの間に…)
- We went to the theater last night. It took us a long time to find a place to park. **By the time we got to the theater**, the play had already started.

by then や **by that time** は「その時までに」のように，すでに述べられている出来事が起きた時までの期間を表します。

- Karen finally arrived at the party at midnight, but **by then** (= **by that time**), most of the guests had left.
  (⇒ パーティーにようやく到着する頃には夜中になっていた。その時までに…)

will be -ing と will have 過去分詞 ➲ Unit 23　　by のその他の用法 ➲ Units 40B, 58B, 125

Exercises

117.1 by を用いて文を書き換えなさい。

1. We have to be home no later than 5:00.
   We have to be home by 5:00.
2. I have to be at the airport no later than 8:30.
   I have to be at the airport ______
3. Let me know no later than Saturday whether you can come to the party.
   Let me know ______
4. Please make sure that you're here no later than 2:00.
   Please make sure that ______
5. If we leave now, we should arrive no later than lunchtime.
   If we leave now, ______

117.2 状況に合うように，空所に by もしくは until を入れて文を完成しなさい。

1. Fred is out of town. He'll be away until Monday.
2. Sorry, but I have to go. I have to be home ______ 5:00.
3. I've been offered a job. I haven't decided yet whether to accept it or not.
   I have to decide ______ Friday.
4. I think I'll wait ______ Thursday before making a decision.
5. It's too late to go shopping. The stores are open only ______ 5:30 today.
   They'll be closed ______ now.
6. I'd better pay the phone bill. It has to be paid ______ tomorrow.
7. Don't pay the bill today. Wait ______ tomorrow.
8. *A:* Have you finished redecorating your house?
   B: Not yet. We hope to finish ______ the end of the week.
9. *A:* I'm going out now. I'll be back at about 10:30. Will you still be here?
   B: I don't think so. I'll probably have left ______ then.
10. I'm moving into my new apartment next week. I'm staying with a friend
    ______ then.
11. I've got a lot of work to do. ______ the time I finish, it will be time to go to bed.
12. If you want to take the exam, you have to register ______ April 3.

117.3 状況に合うように，by もしくは until を用いて自分の考えを記述する文を完成しなさい。

1. Fred is out of town at the moment. He'll be away until Monday.
2. Fred is out of town at the moment. He'll be back by Monday.
3. I'm going out. I won't be very long. Wait here ______.
4. I'm going out to buy a few things. It's 4:30 now. I won't be long. I'll be back ______.
5. If you want to apply for the job, your application must be received ______.
6. Last night I watched TV ______.

117.4 状況を説明する文を By the time ... で始めて完成しなさい。

1. I was invited to a party, but I got there much later than I intended.
   By the time I got to the party, most of the other guests had left.
2. I wanted to catch a train, but it took me longer than expected to get to the station.
   ______, my train had already left.
3. I intended to go shopping after finishing work. But I finished much later than expected.
   ______, it was too late to go shopping.
4. I saw two men who looked as if they were trying to steal a car. I called the police, but it was some time before they arrived.
   ______, the two men had disappeared.
5. We climbed a mountain, and it took us a very long time to get to the top. There wasn't much time to enjoy the view.
   ______, we had to come down again.

補充問題 33 (p. 315)

UNIT 118

at/on/in（時を表す前置詞）

A

☆ at, on, in は，時を表す語句の前に置き「～に」を意味する前置詞ですが，それぞれどのような「時」を表していますか？

■ They arrived **at 5:00**.
■ They arrived **on Friday**.
■ They arrived **in October**. / They arrived **in 1968**.

➤ at は，1 日の中での時刻や主な時間帯とともに用います。
at 5:00　**at 11:45**　**at midnight**　**at lunchtime**　**at sunset** など

➤ on は，週の曜日 / 日付 / 特別の名称が与えられた日などとともに用います。
on Friday / on Fridays　**on May 16, 1999**　**on Christmas Day**　**on my birthday**
on the weekend, **on weekends**

➤ in は，月 / 年 / 季節などのより長い期間とともに用います。
in October　**in 1988**　**in the 18th century**　**in the past**
in (the) winter　**in the 1990s**　**in the Middle Ages**　**in the future**

B

at は，ことに以下のような時を表す表現中に現れます。

at night
at Christmas
at this time / at the moment
at the same time

■ I don't like going out **at night**.
■ Do you give each other presents **at Christmas**?
■ Mr. Brown is busy **at this time / at the moment**.
■ Liz and I arrived **at the same time**.

C

morning/afternoon/evening などの時間帯の前には **in** を置きます。曜日で指定される場合には **on** を置きます

in the morning(s) ⇔ **on Friday morning(s)**
in the afternoon(s)　**on Sunday afternoon(s)**
in the evening(s)　**on Monday evening(s)** など

■ I'll see you **in the morning**.
■ Do you work **in the evenings**?
■ I'll see you **on Friday morning**.
■ Do you work **on Saturday evenings**?

D

時を表す語句の前に **last/next/this/every** が置かれている場合には，at/on/in の前置詞は置きません。

■ I'll see you **next Friday**. (× on next Friday)
■ They got married **last March**.

さらに**話しことば**では，曜日や日付の前の **on** をよく省略します。

■ I'll see you **on Friday**. = I'll see you **Friday**.
■ She works **on Saturday** mornings. = She works **Saturday** mornings.
■ They got married **on March 12**. = They got married **March 12**.

E

in a few minutes や **in six months** のような **in** + **期間**を表す表現は，「～後に」のように**未来の一時点**を表します。

■ The train will be leaving **in a few minutes**.（⇒ 今から数分後に）
■ Andy has left town. He'll be back **in a week**.（⇒ 今から 1 週間後に）
■ She'll be here **in a moment**.（⇒ 今からすぐ後に，間もなく）

in six month's time や **in a week's time** などの形も，同じように「～後に」を表します。

■ They're getting married **in six months' time**. = ...**in six months**.

in + **期間**の形で「～かかって，～後に」のように，**動作**に要した**時間**を表すことがあります。

■ I learned to drive **in four weeks**.（⇒ 運転を覚えるのに 4 週間かかった）

on/in time, at/in the end ➲ Unit 119　in/at/on（場所を表す前置詞）➲ Units 120–122
in/at/on（その他の用法）➲ Unit 124　イギリス英語の用法 ➲ 付録 7

Exercises

118.1 状況に合うように at, on, in の後に続く語句を以下から選び，空所に入れて文を完成しなさい。

the evening	**about 20 minutes**	~~**1492**~~	**the same**
the moment	**July 21, 1969**	**the 1920s**	**time**
Saturdays	**the Middle Ages**	**11 seconds**	**night**

1. Columbus made his first voyage from Europe to America _in 1492_ .
2. If the sky is clear, you can see the stars ________ .
3. After working hard during the day, I like to relax ________ .
4. Neil Armstrong was the first man to walk on the moon ________ .
5. It's difficult to listen if everyone is speaking ________ .
6. Jazz became popular in the United States ________ .
7. I'm just going out to the store. I'll be back ________ .
8. *(on the phone)* "Can I speak to Dan?" "I'm sorry, but he's not here ________ ."
9. Many of Europe's great cathedrals were built ________ .
10. Bob is a very fast runner. He can run 100 meters ________ .
11. Liz works from Monday to Friday. Sometimes she also works ________ .

118.2 状況に合うように at, on, in から適切な語を選び，空所に入れて文を完成しなさい。

1. Mozart was born in Salzburg _in_ 1756.
2. "Have you seen Kate recently?" "Yes, I saw her ____ Tuesday."
3. The price of electricity is going up ____ October.
4. ____ weekends, we often go for long walks in the country.
5. I've been invited to a wedding ____ February 14.
6. Henry is 63. He'll be retiring from his job ____ two years.
7. I'm busy right now, but I'll be with you ____ a moment.
8. Jenny's brother is an engineer, but he doesn't have a job ____ the moment.
9. There are usually a lot of parties ____ New Year's Eve.
10. I don't like driving ____ night.
11. My car is being repaired. It will be ready ____ two hours.
12. The telephone and the doorbell rang ____ the same time.
13. Mary and David always go out for dinner ____ their wedding anniversary.
14. It was a short book and easy to read. I read it ____ a day.
15. ____ Saturday night I went to bed ____ midnight.
16. We traveled overnight to Paris and arrived ____ 5:00 ____ the morning.
17. The course begins ____ January 7 and ends sometime ____ April.
18. I might not be at home ____ Tuesday morning, but I'll be there ____ the afternoon.

118.3 a) と b) の正しい方を選びなさい。両方が問題なく使える場合には「両方正しい」と記入します。

	a)	b)	
1.	a) I'll see you on Friday.	b) I'll see you Friday.	両方正しい
2.	a) I'll see you on next Friday.	b) I'll see you next Friday.	b
3.	a) Paul got married in April.	b) Paul got married April.	____
4.	a) They never go out on Sunday evenings.	b) They never go out Sunday evenings.	____
5.	a) We usually take a short vacation on Christmas.	b) We usually take a short vacation at Christmas.	____
6.	a) What are you doing the weekend?	b) What are you doing on the weekend?	____
7.	a) Will you be here on Tuesday?	b) Will you be here Tuesday?	____
8.	a) We were sick at the same time.	b) We were sick in the same time.	____
9.	a) Sue got married at May 18, 2002.	b) Sue got married on May 18, 2002.	____
10.	a) He finished school last June.	b) He finished school in last June.	____

補充問題 33 (p. 315)

UNIT 119

on time と in time
at the end と in the end

A

☆ on time と in time は，どのように異なりますか？

➤ on time は「時間通りに，遅れずに」を表します。出来事は計画された時刻通りに起きています。

- The 11:45 train left **on time**.（⇒ 定刻通り 11:45 に出発した）
- "I'll meet you at 7:30." "OK, but please be **on time**."（⇒ 遅れずに，7:30 には来てください）
- The conference was well organized. Everything began and ended **on time**.

on time の反意語は **late**（遅れて）です。

- Be **on time**. Don't be **late**.

➤ in time は in time for ～ / to do ～の形で，「～に / ～するのに，間に合うように」を表します。

- Will you be home **in time for dinner**?（⇒ 夕食に間に合うように）
- I've sent Jill a birthday present. I hope it arrives **in time** (for her birthday).（⇒ 彼女の誕生日，もしくはそれ以前に）
- I'm in a hurry. I want to be home **in time to see** the game on television.（⇒ 試合をテレビで見られるように）

on time の反意語は **too late**（遅すぎる）です。

- I got home **too late** to see the game on television.

just in time は「ぎりぎりで間に合う，ほとんど遅れてしまいそうになる」を表します。

- We got to the station **just in time** for our train.
- A child ran into the street in front of the car – I managed to stop **just in time**.

B

☆ at the end と in the end は，どのように異なりますか？

➤ at the end of ～は「～の終わりに」のように，何かの終了時を指定します。

at the end of the month **at the end of January** **at the end of the game**
at the end of the movie **at the end of the course** **at the end of the concert**

- I'm going away **at the end of January** / **at the end of the month**.
- **At the end of the concert**, there was great applause.
- The players shook hands **at the end of the game**.

in the end of ～のような形はありません（× in the end of January, × in the end of the concert）。

at the end (of ～) の反意語は **at the beginning (of ～)**（～の初めに）です（of ～は省略されることがあります）。

- I'm going away **at the beginning of January**. (× in the beginning)

➤ in the end は「最後には，ついに」を表します。状況が最終的にどのようになったかを述べる際に用います。

- We had a lot of problems with our car. We sold it **in the end**.（⇒ 最後には売れた）
- He got angrier and angrier. **In the end** he just walked out of the room.
- Alan couldn't decide where to go on vacation. He didn't go anywhere **in the end**. (× at the end)

in the end の反意語は **at first**（最初は）です。

- **At first** we didn't get along very well, but **in the end** we became good friends.

at/on/in（時を表す前置詞）➲ Unit 118

Exercises

119.1 空所に on time もしくは in time を入れて，文を完成しなさい。

1. The bus was late this morning, but it's usually *on time* .
2. The movie was supposed to start at 8:30, but it didn't begin ________ .
3. I like to get up ________ to have a big breakfast before going to work.
4. We want to start the meeting ________ , so please don't be late.
5. I just washed this shirt. I want to wear it tonight, so I hope it will dry ________ .
6. The train service isn't very good. The trains are seldom ________ .
7. I nearly missed my flight this morning. I got to the airport just ________ .
8. I almost forgot that it was Joe's birthday. Fortunately I remembered ________ .
9. Why aren't you ever ________ ? You always keep everybody waiting.

119.2 状況に合うように ( ) 内の語句と just in time を用い，適切な形に変えて文を完成しなさい。

1. A child ran into the street in front of your car. You saw the child at the last moment.
   (manage / stop) *I managed to stop just in time.*
2. You were walking home. Just after you got home, it started to rain very heavily.
   (get / home) I ________
3. Tim was going to sit on the chair you had just painted. You said, "Don't sit on that chair!" so he didn't. (stop / him) I ________
4. You and a friend went to the movies. You were late, and you thought you would miss the beginning of the film. But the film began just as you sat down in the theater.
   (get / theater / beginning of the film)
   We ________

119.3 状況に合うように，以下から適切な語句を選び at the end と組み合わせて文を完成しなさい。

the course ~~**the game**~~ **the interview** **the month** **the race**

1. The players shook hands *at the end of the game* .
2. I usually get paid ________ .
3. The students had a party ________ .
4. Two of the runners collapsed ________ .
5. To my surprise, I was offered the job ________ .

119.4 状況に合うように ( ) 内の語句と in the end を組み合わせ，適切な形に変えて文を完成しなさい。

1. We had a lot of problems with our car.
   (sell) *In the end we sold it.*
2. Judy got more and more fed up with her job.
   (resign) ________
3. I tried to learn German, but I found it too difficult.
   (give up) ________
4. We couldn't decide whether to go to the party or not.
   (not / go) ________

119.5 空所に at もしくは in を入れて，文を完成しなさい。

1. I'm going away *at* the end of the month.
2. It took me a long time to find a job. ________ the end I got a job in a hotel.
3. Are you going away ________ the beginning of August or ________ the end?
4. I couldn't decide what to buy Laura for her birthday. I didn't buy her anything ________ the end.
5. We waited ages for a taxi. We gave up ________ the end and walked home.
6. I'll be moving to a new address ________ the end of September.
7. We had a few problems at first, but ________ the end everything was OK.
8. I'm going away ________ the end of this week.
9. *A:* I didn't know what to do.
   B: Yes, you were in a difficult position. What did you do ________ the end?

UNIT 120

in/at/on（場所を表す前置詞）1

A

☆イラストで考えます。in はどのような場所に関連した状態を表しますか？

in a room
in a building
in a box

in a garden
in a town/city
in a country

in a pool
in an ocean
in a river

- There's somebody **in the room** / **in the building** / **in the garden**.
- What do you have **in your hand** / **in your mouth**?
- When we were **in Chile**, we spent a few days **in Santiago**.
- I have a friend who lives **in a small village in the mountains**.
- There were some people swimming **in the pool** / **in the ocean** / **in the river**.

➤ in ～ :「～の中に」
壁のある空間や境界に囲まれた平面の中や，水の中に浸かっている状態。

B

☆イラストで考えます。at はどのような場所に関連した状態を表しますか？

at the bus stop

at the door

at the intersection

at the front desk

- Do you know that man standing **at the bus stop** / **at the door** / **at the window**?
- Turn left **at the traffic light** / **at the church** / **at the intersection**.
- We have to get off the bus **at the next stop**.
- When you leave the hotel, please leave your key **at the front desk**.

➤ at ～ :「～に」
点でとらえられる場所の近くまで到達した状態。

C

☆イラストと例文で考えます。on はどのような場所に関連した状態を表しますか？

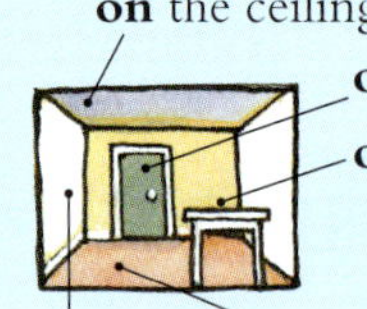

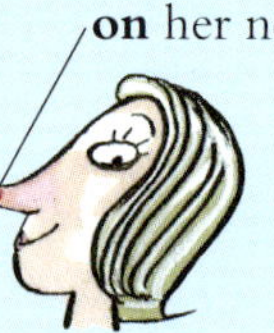

on a page

on an island

- I sat **on the floor** / **on the ground** / **on the grass** / **on the beach** / **on a chair**.
- There's a dirty mark **on the wall** / **on the ceiling** / **on your nose** / **on your shirt**.
- Have you seen the notice **on the bulletin board** / **on the door**?
- You'll find the listings of TV programs **on page 7** (of the newspaper).
- The hotel is **on a small island** in the middle of the lake.

➤ on ～ :「～の上に」
平面に接触している状態。

D

☆例文で考えます。in と at は，どのように異なりますか？

- There were a lot of people **in the store**. It was very crowded.（⇒ 店の中に）
  Go along this road, then turn left **at the store**.（⇒ 店のあるところで）
- I'll meet you **in the hotel lobby**.
  I'll meet you **at the entrance to the hotel**.

☆例文とイラストで考えます。in と on は，どのように異なりますか？

- There is some water **in the bottle**.（⇒ びんの中に）
  There is a label **on the bottle**.（⇒ びんの表面に）

☆例文で考えます。at と on は，どのように異なりますか？

- There is somebody **at the door**. Should I go and see who it is?（⇒ ドアのところに）
  There is a sign **on the door**. It says "Do not disturb."（⇒ ドアの表面に）

in/at/on（場所を表す前置詞）2–3 ➲ Units 121–122

Exercises

120.1 状況に合うように in, at, on から適切な前置詞を 1 つ選び，（　）内の語句の前に置いてイラストに関する質問の答えとなる文を完成しなさい。

1. Where's the label? *On the bottle.*
2. Where's the butterfly? ______
3. Where is the car waiting? ______
4. a) Where's the sign? ______
   b) Where's the key? ______
5. Where are the shelves? ______
6. Where's the Eiffel Tower? ______
7. a) Where's the man standing? ______
   b) Where's the telephone? ______
8. Where are the children playing? ______

120.2 状況に合うように in, at, on のいずれかの前置詞の後に続く語句を以下から選び，空所に入れて文を完成しなさい。

the window	**your coffee**	**the mountains**	**that tree**
my guitar	**~~the river~~**	**the island**	**the next gas station**

1. Look at those people swimming *in the river* .
2. One of the strings ______ is broken.
3. There's something wrong with the car. We'd better stop ______ .
4. Would you like sugar ______ ?
5. The leaves ______ are a beautiful color.
6. Last year we had a wonderful ski trip ______ .
7. There's nobody living ______ . It's uninhabited.
8. He spends most of the day sitting ______ and looking outside.

120.3 空所に in, at, on のいずれかを入れて，文を完成しなさい。

1. There was a long line of people *at* the bus stop.
2. Nicole was wearing a silver ring ______ her little finger.
3. There was an accident ______ the intersection this morning.
4. I wasn't sure whether I had come to the right office. There was no name ______ the door.
5. There are some beautiful trees ______ the park.
6. You'll find the sports results ______ the back page of the newspaper.
7. I wouldn't like an office job. I couldn't spend the whole day sitting ______ a desk.
8. My brother lives ______ a small town ______ eastern Tennessee.
9. The man the police are looking for has a scar ______ his right cheek.
10. The headquarters of the company are ______ Tokyo.
11. I like that picture hanging ______ the wall ______ the kitchen.
12. If you come here by bus, get off ______ the stop after the traffic light.

補充問題 34 (pp. 315–316)

UNIT 121 in/at/on（場所を表す前置詞）2

A

☆ 以下はよく用いられる in ～の表現です。どのような語句と in は結び付きますか？

in a row
（⇒（横）1 列になって）

in a line / in a row **in bed**
in the sky / in the world **in the country / in the countryside**
in an office / in a department **in a photograph / in a picture**
in a book / in a (news)paper / in a magazine / in a letter

- When I go to the movies, I like to sit **in the front row**.
- I just started working **in the sales department**.
- Who is the woman **in that photo**?
- Have you seen this picture **in today's paper**?

in the front / in the back (of ～) で,「(～の) 前方 / 後方で」を表します。of の後には，自動車，建物，劇場，人の集団などがきます。

in the front（⇒ 前方で）
in the back（⇒ 後方で）

- I was sitting **in the back** (of the car) when we crashed.
- Let's sit **in the front** (of the movie theater).
- John was standing **in the back** of the crowd.

B

☆ 以下はよく用いられる on ～の表現です。どのような語句と on は結び付きますか？

on the left / on the right **on the left-hand side / right-hand side**
on the ground floor / on the first floor / on the second floor など
on a map / on a menu / on a list
on a farm / on a ranch

- In Britain they drive **on the left**. (= . . . **on the left-hand side**.)
- Our apartment is **on the second floor** of the building.
- Here's a shopping list. Don't buy anything that's not **on the list**.
- Have you ever worked **on a farm**? It's a lot like working **on a ranch**.

on a river / on a street / on a road / on the coast のように，川，道路，沿岸線など，地図上で線として表される物に接する場合にも **on** を用います。「～に面して」を表します。

- Washington, D.C., is **on the East Coast** of the United States, **on the Potomac River**.
- I live **on Main Street**. My brother lives **on Elm**. (= on Elm Street)

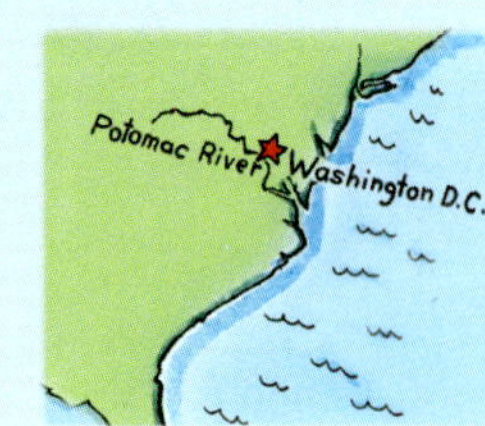

on the way (to ～) は「(～へ行く) 途中で」を表します。

- We stopped at a small town **on the way** to Atlanta.

on the front / on the back (of ～) で「(～の) 表 / 裏に」を表します。**of** の後には，手紙，1 枚の紙，写真などがきます。

- I wrote the date **on the back** of the photo.

C

at the top / at the bottom / at the end (of ～) は「(～の) 一番上に / 一番下に / 一番奥に」を表します。

- Write your name **at the top of the page**.
- Jane's house is **at the other end of the street**.
（⇒ 通りの突き当たりに）

at the top (of the page)（⇒ ページ上部に）
at the bottom (of the page)（⇒ ページ下部に）

D

☆ イラストで確認します。それぞれどのような場所を表しますか？

- The television is **in the corner** of the room.
（⇒ 部屋の隅で）

at the corner (= **on the corner** of a street)（⇒ 通りの角で）

- There is a mailbox **at/on the corner** of the street.

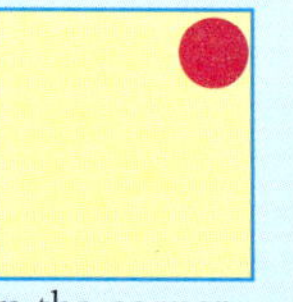
in the corner（⇒ 境界で区切られた区域内の隅に）

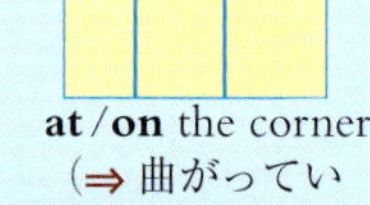
at / on the corner（⇒ 曲がっている地点で）

in the world ➲ Unit 105 in/at/on（場所を表す前置詞）1, 3 ➲ Units 120, 122 イギリス英語の用法 ➲ 付録 7

Exercises

121.1 状況に合うように，in, at, on から適切な前置詞を 1 つ選び（　）内の語句の前に置いて，イラストに関する質問の答えの文を完成しなさい。

1. Sue (sales department)	2. (second floor)	3. (corner)	4. (corner)	5. (top / stairs)
6. (back / car)	7. (front) Liz	8. (left)	9. Gary (back row)	10. Kate (farm)

1. Where does Sue work? *In the sales department.*
2. Sue lives in this building. Where's her apartment exactly? ______
3. Where is the woman standing? ______
4. Where is the man standing? ______
5. Where's the cat? ______
6. Where's the dog? ______
7. Liz is in this group of people. Where is she? ______
8. Where's the post office? ______
9. Gary is at the movies. Where is he sitting? ______
10. Where does Kate work? ______

121.2 in, at, on のいずれかの前置詞の後ろに続く語句を以下から選び，空所に入れて文を完成しなさい。

the West Coast **the world** **the back of the class** **~~the sky~~**
the front row **the right** **the back of this card** **the way to work**

1. It was a lovely day. There wasn't a cloud *in the sky*.
2. In most countries people drive ______.
3. What is the tallest building ______?
4. I usually buy a newspaper ______ in the morning.
5. San Francisco is ______ of the United States.
6. We went to the theater last night. We had seats ______.
7. I couldn't hear the teacher. She spoke quietly and I was sitting ______.
8. I don't have your address. Could you write it ______?

121.3 空所に in, at, on のいずれかの前置詞を入れて，文を完成しなさい。

1. Write your name *at* the top of the page.
2. Is your sister ______ this photo? I don't recognize her.
3. I didn't feel very well when I woke up, so I stayed ______ bed.
4. We normally use the front entrance to the building, but there's another one ______ the back.
5. Is there anything interesting ______ the paper today?
6. There was a list of names, but my name wasn't ______ the list.
7. ______ the end of the block, there is a small store. You'll see it ______ the corner.
8. I love to look up at the stars ______ the sky at night.
9. When I'm a passenger in a car, I prefer to sit ______ the front.
10. It's a very small town. You probably won't find it ______ your map.
11. Joe works ______ the furniture department of a large store.
12. Paris is ______ the Seine River.
13. I don't like cities. I'd rather live ______ the country.
14. My office is ______ the top floor. It's ______ the left as you come out of the elevator.

補充問題 34 (pp. 315–316)

UNIT 122

in/at/on（場所を表す前置詞）3

A

at home / in the hospital など「**人を収容する施設**」に関する**前置詞**

「家にいる / 仕事をしている」は **at home / at work** のように **at** を用います。

■ I'll be **at work** until 5:30, but I'll be **at home** all evening.

「家にいる」は **be/stay home** のように **at** を省くことがあります。

■ You can stop by anytime. I'll **be home** all evening.

「入院している」は **in the hospital**,「服役している」は **in prison/jail** のように **in** を用います。➲Unit 72B

■ Ann's mother is **in the hospital**.

school や **college** には **at** も **in** も可能です。「(生徒や学生として) 学校 / 大学にいる」は **at school/college** のように **at** を用います。

■ Kim is not living at home. She's away **at college**. (⇒ 実家を離れて大学にいる)

「〜を学んでいる」のように,学校でしていることを話題にする場合は **in school/college** のように **in** を用います。

■ Amy works at a bank and her brother is **in medical school**. (⇒ 医大で医学を学んでいる)

B

at a party / at a concert など「**イベント**」に関する**前置詞**

パーティーや会議などの「イベント」に関しては, **at a party / at a conference** のように **at** を用います。

■ Were there many people **at the party / at the meeting / at the wedding**?

■ I saw Steve **at a tennis match / at a concert** on Saturday.

C

「**建物**」に関して用いられる **in** と **at**

「建物」に関しては **in** も **at** も用いることができます。「レストランで食事する」は eat **in a restaurant** と eat **at a restaurant**,「スーパーで…を買う」は buy ... **in a supermarket** と buy ... **at a supermarket** のように2通りが可能です。コンサート, 映画, パーティー, 会議などの「イベント」が開催される建物には, 普通 **at** を用います。

■ We went to a concert **at Lincoln Center**. (⇒ コンサートはリンカーンセンターで開催された)

■ The meeting took place **at the company's headquarters** in New York.

駅や空港に関しては **at the station / at the airport** のように **at** を用います。

■ Don't meet me **at the station**. I can get a taxi.

個人の家に関しては **at** を用います（個人名の後に -'s（アポストロフィ s）がくることに注意)。

■ I was **at Sue's house** last night. = I was **at Sue's** last night.

同様に病院や美容院についても, **at the doctor's**, **at the hairdresser's** のように **at** を用います。

「〜の中に / で」の意味で空間としての建物を話題にする場合には **in** を用い, at は用いません。

■ We had dinner **at the hotel**. (⇒〔接客施設としての〕ホテルで)

⇔ All the rooms **in the hotel** have air conditioning. (⇒ ホテルの中にある, × at the hotel)

■ I was **at Sue's (house)** last night. (⇒ Sue の家にいた)

⇔ It's always cold **in Sue's house**. The heating doesn't work very well.
(⇒ Sue の家の中は, × at Sue's house)

D

「**町や都市**」に関して用いられる **in** と **at**

「町, 都市, 村」に関しては, 普通 **in** を用います。

■ Sam's parents live **in St. Louis**. (× at St. Louis)

■ The Louvre is a famous art museum **in Paris**. (× at Paris)

しかし, 移動中の通過点として,「駅や空港, 町や都市」を話題にする場合には **at** と **in** の両方が可能です。

■ Does this train stop **at** (= **in**) **Denver**? (= at the Denver station)

■ We stopped **at** (= **in**) **a** small **town** on the way to Denver.

E

「**乗り物**」に関して用いられる **at** と **in**

「バス, 電車, 飛行機, 船」については **on a bus / on a train / on a plane / on a ship** のように **on** を用います。一方,「自動車, タクシー」については **in a car / in a taxi** のように **in** を用います。

■ **The bus** was very full. There were too many people **on it**.

■ Mary arrived **in a taxi**.

「自転車, オートバイ, 馬」に関して,「〜に乗って」は **on a bike (= bicycle) / on a motorcycle / on a horse** のように **on** を用います。

■ Jane passed me **on her bike**.

at school / in prison など ➲Unit 72　in/at/on（場所を表す前置詞）1–2 ➲Units 120–121
to/at/in/into ➲Unit 123　by car / by bike など ➲Unit 125B

Exercises

122.1 状況に合うように，in, at, on から適切な前置詞を1つ選び（　）内の語句の前に置いて，イラストに関して記述する文を完成しなさい。

1. (the airport)	2. Dave (a train)	3. Karen (a conference)	4. Martin (the hospital)
5. Judy (the hairdresser's)	6. Gary (his bike)	7. (New York)	8. (the Ford Theater)

1. You can rent a car *at the airport* .
2. Dave is ______ .
3. Karen is ______ .
4. Martin is ______ .
5. Judy is ______ .
6. I saw Gary ______ .
7. We spent a few days ______ .
8. We went to a show ______ .

122.2 in, at, on のいずれかの前置詞の後に続く語句を以下から選び，空所に入れて文を完成しなさい。

the plane **the hospital** **a taxi** ~~**the station**~~ **the party**
the gym **school** **prison** **the airport**

1. My train arrives at 11:30. Can you meet me *at the station* ?
2. We walked to the restaurant, but we went home ______ .
3. Did you have a good time ______ ? I heard it was a lot of fun.
4. I enjoyed the flight, but the food ______ wasn't very good.
5. *A:* What does your sister do? Does she have a job?
   B: No, she's only 16. She's still ______ .
6. I play basketball ______ on Friday evenings.
7. A friend of mine was injured in an accident a few days ago. She's still ______ .
8. Our flight was delayed. We had to wait ______ for four hours.
9. Some people are ______ for crimes that they did not commit.

122.3 空所に in, at, on のいずれかの前置詞を入れて，文を完成しなさい。

1. We went to a concert *at* Lincoln Center.
2. It was a very slow train. It stopped ______ every station.
3. My parents live ______ a suburb of Chicago.
4. I haven't seen Kate for some time. I last saw her ______ David's wedding.
5. We stayed ______ a very nice hotel when we were ______ Amsterdam.
6. There were 50 rooms ______ the hotel.
7. I don't know where my umbrella is. Maybe I left it ______ the bus.
8. I wasn't home when you called. I was ______ my sister's house.
9. There must be somebody ______ the house. The lights are on.
10. The exhibition ______ the Museum of Modern Art closed on Saturday.
11. Should we go ______ your car or mine?
12. What are you doing ______ home? I expected you to be ______ work.
13. "Did you like the movie?" "Yes, but it was too hot ______ the theater."
14. Paul lives ______ Boston. He's a student ______ Boston University.

補充問題 34 (pp. 315–316)

UNIT 123

to/at/in/into

A

前置詞 **to** は **go/come/travel + to + 場所 / イベント**の形で，「～へ」のような目標への移動を表します。

go to China	**go to** bed	**come to** my house
go back to Italy	**go to** the bank	**be taken to** the hospital
return to Boston	**go to** a concert	**be sent to** prison
welcome 人 **to** ～		**drive to** the airport

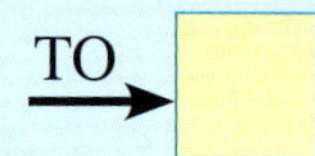

- When are your friends **going back to** Italy? (✕ going back in Italy)
- Three people were injured in the accident and **taken to** the hospital.
- **Welcome to** our country! (✕ Welcome in)

同様に **a trip to** / **a visit to** / **on my way to** ～のような形もよく用いられます。「～への旅 / 訪問 / ～に行く途中」を意味します。

- Did you enjoy **your trip to** Paris / **your visit to** the zoo?

☆ **例文で考えます。移動を表す to と場所を表す in/at は，どのように異なりますか？（in/at には動きがありません）**

- They are **going to** France. ⇔ They **live in** France.
- Can you **come to** the party? ⇔ I'll see **you at** the party.

B

been to

～ has been to … は「～は…に行ってきた，行ったことがある」を表します。

- I've **been to Italy** four times, but I've never **been to Rome**.
- Amanda has never **been to a hockey game** in her life.

C

get と arrive

get to ～は「～に到着する，着く」を表します。

- What time did they **get to London** / **get to work** / **get to the party** / **get to the hotel**?

しかし同じ「～に到着する」の意味でも，動詞 **arrive** の場合には **arrive in** ～, **arrive at** ～のような形をとり，後に to は置きません。「町や国」を目的地とする場合には **in** を用います。

- They **arrived in Rio de Janeiro** / **in Brazil** a week ago.

「建物のある場所やイベント」には **at** を用います。

- When did they **arrive at the hotel** / **at the airport** / **at the party**?

D

home

go home / **come home** / **get home** / **arrive home** / **on the way home** のように，「家へ…」の意味で動詞と組み合わせ，前置詞なしで **home** を用います。

目標への移動を表しますが，to home のような形はありません。

- I'm tired. Let's **go home** now. (✕ go to home)
- I met Linda **on my way home**. (✕ my way to home)

E

into

前置詞 **into** は **go/get + into** ～のような形で，「～の中へ」のように目標の内部への移動を表します。

- I opened the door, **went into** the room, and sat down.
- A bird **flew into** the kitchen through the window.

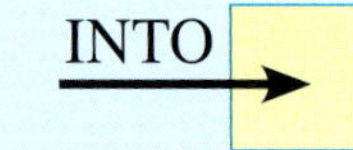

go/get/put のような動詞の場合には，**in** を **into** の代わりに用いることもあります。

- She **got in** the car and drove away. (= She **got into** the car . . .)
- I read the letter and **put it** back **in the envelope**.

into ～の反意語は **out of** ～（～外へ）です。場所の中から外への移動を表します。

- She **got out of** the car and **went into** a shop.

バス，電車，飛行機などの乗り物に関して，「～に乗る / ～から降りる」は **get on/off** ～を用います。into や out of は用いません。

- She **got on the bus** and I never saw her again.

been to ➲ Unit 7　**in/at/on**（場所を表す前置詞）1–3 ➲ Units 120–122　**at home** ➲ Unit 122A
into と in ➲ Unit 135A

Exercises

123.1 空所に to, at, in, into のいずれかの前置詞を入れて，文を完成しなさい。不要な場合は – を記入すること。

1. Three people were taken _to_ the hospital after the accident.
2. I met Kate on my way _–_ home.（前置詞は不要）
3. We left our luggage ________ the hotel and went to find something to eat.
4. Should we take a taxi ________ the station, or should we walk?
5. I have to go ________ the bank today to change some money.
6. The Mississippi River flows ________ the Gulf of Mexico.
7. "Do you have your camera?" "No, I left it ________ home."
8. Have you ever been ________ China?
9. I had lost my key, but I managed to climb ________ the house through a window.
10. We got stuck in a traffic jam on our way ________ the airport.
11. We had lunch ________ the airport while we were waiting for our plane.
12. Welcome ________ the hotel. We hope you enjoy your stay here.
13. I got a flat tire, so I turned ________ a parking lot to change it.
14. Did you enjoy your visit ________ the zoo?
15. I'm tired. As soon as I get ________ home, I'm going ________ bed.
16. Marcel is French. He has just returned ________ France after two years ________ Brazil.
17. Carl was born ______ Chicago, but his family moved ______ New York when he was three. He still lives ________ New York.

123.2 自分のことで考えます。以下の場所に行ったことはありますか？ 行ったことがある場合，何度行きましたか？ 場所を 3 つ選び，been to を用いて文を完成しなさい。

Australia Hong Kong Mexico Paris Thailand Tokyo Washington, D.C.

1. （解答例） _I've never been to Australia. / I've been to Thailand once._
2. ________________________________
3. ________________________________
4. ________________________________

123.3 空所に to, at, in のいずれかの前置詞を入れて，文を完成しなさい。不要な場合は – を記入すること。

1. What time does this bus get _to_ Vancouver?
2. What time does this bus arrive ________ Vancouver?
3. What time did you get ________ home last night?
4. What time do you usually arrive ________ work in the morning?
5. When we got ________ the theater, there was a long line outside.
6. I arrived ________ home feeling very tired.

123.4 状況に合うように，got の後に into, out of, on, off のいずれかと適切な語句を続けて文を完成しなさい。

1. You were walking home. A friend passed you in her car. She saw you, stopped, and offered you a ride. She opened the door. What did you do? _I got into the car._
2. You were waiting for the bus. At last your bus came. The doors opened. What did you do then? I ________________________________
3. You drove home in your car. You stopped outside your house and parked the car. What did you do then? ________________________________
4. You were traveling by train to Chicago. When the train got to Chicago, what did you do? ________________________________
5. You needed a taxi. After a few minutes a taxi stopped for you. You opened the door. What did you do then? ________________________________
6. You were traveling by air. At the end of your flight, your plane landed at the airport and stopped. The doors were opened. You took your bag and stood up. What did you do then? ________________________________

補充問題 34 (pp. 315–316)

UNIT 124

in/at/on（その他の用法）

A よく用いられる in を含む表現

in the rain / **in the sun** / **in the shade** / **in the dark** / **in bad weather** のように，雨，日光，影，暗闇，悪天候などに包み込まれる様子を表します。

- We sat **in the shade**. It was too hot to sit **in the sun**.（⇒ 日なたに座る）
- Don't go out **in the rain**. Wait until it stops.

(write) **in ink** / **in pen** / **in pencil** など，どのような道具で書くのかを説明します。

- When you take the exam, you're not allowed to write **in pencil**.（⇒ 鉛筆で字を書く）

(write) **in words** / **in numbers** / **in capital letters** など，どのような文字やことばで書くのかを説明します。

- Please write your name **in capital letters**.（⇒ 大文字で字を書く）
- Write the story **in your own words**.（⇒ 他人ではなく自分のことばで書く）

(be/fall) **in love** (**with** ～)：「(～に) 恋をする」

- Have you ever been **in love with** anybody?

in (my) **opinion, ...**：「(～の) 意見としては…」 文頭に置く。

- **In my opinion**, the movie wasn't very good.

B よく用いられる at を含む表現

at the age of ～ / **at** ～ **miles an hour** / **at** ～ **degrees** など，数を表す語句とともに **at** を用いて，「～の年齢で / 時速～マイルで / ～度の角度で」などを表します。

- Tracy left school **at 16**. = ... **at the age of 16**.（⇒ 16 歳で）
- The train was traveling **at 120 miles an hour**.
- Water boils **at 100 degrees Celsius**.（⇒ 100℃で）

☆ 機内放送でよく聞きます。

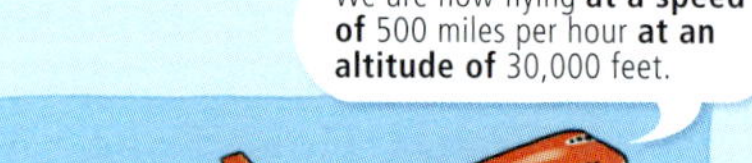

We are now flying at a speed of 500 miles per hour at an altitude of 30,000 feet.

C よく用いられる on を含む表現

(be/go) **on vacation** / **on business** / **on a trip** / **on a tour** / **on a cruise** など，自宅を離れて行う活動を表す語句と一緒に **on** を用いて，「～をしている / ～に出かける」を表します。

- I'm going **on vacation** next week.
- Emma's away **on business** at this time.
- One day I'd like to go **on a world tour**.

「～に休暇に出かける」は **to** を用いて，go to ～ **for vacation** のような形を用いることもあります。

- Steve has gone to France **for vacation**.

D on を含むその他の表現

on television / **on the radio:**「テレビで / ラジオで」 the の用法 ➲ Unit 71D

- I didn't watch the news **on television**, but I heard it **on the radio**.

on the phone/telephone:「電話で」

- I've never met her, but I've spoken to her **on the phone** a few times.

(be/go) **on strike:**「ストライキ中で / ストライキに突入する」

- There are no trains today. The railroad workers are **on strike**.

(be/go) **on a diet:**「ダイエット中で / ダイエットを始める」

- I've put on a lot of weight. I'll have to go **on a diet**.

(be) **on fire:**「燃えている，火事になって」

- Look! That car is **on fire**.

on the whole:「全体としては」

- Sometimes I have problems at work, but **on the whole** I enjoy my job.

on purpose:「わざと」

- I'm sorry. I didn't mean to annoy you. I didn't do it **on purpose**.

at/on/in（時を表す前置詞）➲ Unit 118　in/at/on（場所を表す前置詞）1–3 ➲ Units 120–122

Exercises

124.1 状況に合うように前置詞 in の後に続く語句を以下から選び，空所に入れて文を完成しなさい。

capital letters **cold weather** **love** **my opinion**
pencil ~~**the rain**~~ **the shade**

1. Don't go out _in the rain_ . Wait until it stops.
2. Matt likes to keep warm, so he doesn't go out much ______________ .
3. If you write ______________ and make a mistake, you can erase it and correct it.
4. They fell ______________ almost immediately and were married a few weeks later.
5. Please write your address clearly, preferably ______________ .
6. It's too hot in the sun. I'm going to sit ______________ .
7. Ann thought the restaurant was OK, but ______________ it wasn't very good.

124.2 状況に合うように前置詞 on の後に続く語句を以下から選び，空所に入れて文を完成しなさい。

business ~~**fire**~~ **purpose** **television** **vacation**
a diet **the phone** **strike** **a tour** **the whole**

1. Look! That car is _on fire_ ! Somebody call the fire department.
2. Workers at the factory have gone ______________ for better pay and conditions.
3. Soon after we arrived, we were taken ______________ of the city.
4. I feel lazy tonight. Is there anything worth watching ______________ ?
5. I'm sorry. It was an accident. I didn't do it ______________ .
6. Richard has put on a lot of weight recently. I think he should go ______________ .
7. Jane's job involves a lot of traveling. She is out of town a lot ______________ .
8. *A:* I'm going ______________ next week.
   B: Where are you going? Somewhere nice?
9. *A:* Is Sarah here?
   B: Yes, but she's ______________ at the moment. She won't be long.
10. *A:* How did your exams go?
    B: Well, there were some difficult questions, but ______________ they were OK.

124.3 空所に on，in，at，for のいずれかの前置詞を入れて，文を完成しなさい。

1. Water boils _at_ 100 degrees Celsius.
2. When I was 14, I went ________ a trip to Mexico organized by my school.
3. There was panic when people realized that the building was ________ fire.
4. Julia's grandmother died recently ________ the age of 79.
5. Can you turn the light on, please? I don't want to sit ________ the dark.
6. We didn't go ________ vacation last year. We stayed at home.
7. I'm going to Miami ________ a short vacation next month.
8. I won't be here next week. I'll be ________ vacation.
9. Technology has developed ________ great speed.
10. Allan got married ________ 17, which is really young to get married.
11. I heard an interesting program ________ the radio this morning.
12. ________ my opinion, violent films should not be shown ________ television.
13. I wouldn't want to go ________ a cruise. I think I'd get bored.
14. I can't eat a lot. I'm supposed to be ________ a diet.
15. I wouldn't want his job. He spends most of his time talking ________ the phone.
16. The earth travels around the sun ________ a speed of 67,000 miles an hour.
17. "Did you enjoy your vacation?" "Not every minute, but ________ the whole, yes."
18. When you write a check, you have to write the amount ________ words and figures.

補充問題 34 (pp. 315–316)

UNIT 125

by

A

by ～は「～によって」のように，どのような方法，手段，道具を用いて活動を行うかを表します。

send something **by mail** contact somebody **by phone** / **by e-mail** / **by fax**
do something **by hand** pay **by check** / **by credit card**

- Can I pay **by credit card**?
- You can contact me **by phone**, **by fax**, or **by e-mail**.

「現金で支払う」は **pay cash** や **pay in cash** のような形を用います。by cash のような用法はありません。
by mistake（誤って）や **by accident** / **by chance**（偶然に）のような表現もよく用いられます。

- We hadn't arranged to meet. We met **by chance**.

「わざと～をする」は do ～ **on purpose** のように **on** を用います。

- I didn't do it **on purpose**. It was an accident.

by chance，**by check** などのように，**by の後**に the や a/an を置かずに直接，**名詞**を置きます。by the chance, by a check のような形はありません。

B

by＋**乗り物**は「～によって」のように，どのように移動するかといった**交通手段**を表します。

by car / **by train** / **by plane** / **by boat** / **by ship** / **by bus** / **by bike** など
by road（トラックで，陸路で）/ **by rail**（鉄道で）/ **by air**（飛行機で）/ **by sea**（船で）/
by subway（地下鉄で）

- Joanne usually goes to work **by bus**.
- Do you prefer to travel **by plane** or **by train**?

「歩いて，徒歩で」は **on foot** のように **on** を用います。

- Did you come here **by car** or **on foot**?

by の後には a/the/my などの付かない**名詞**がきます。my car / the train / a taxi などの名詞句はきません。「自分の車で」や「その電車で」といった手段をより限定する場合には，以下のように by 以外の**前置詞**がきます。

by car ⇔ **in my** car （× by my car）
by train ⇔ **on the** train （× by the train）

a/the/my などで修飾された自動車やタクシーを手段とする場合には，**in** を用います。

- They didn't come **in their car**. They came **in a taxi**.

a/the/my などで修飾された自転車や電車，バスなどの交通機関を手段とする場合には，**on** を用います。

- We came **on the 6:45 train**.

C

— is done（**by ～**）のような受動態で，誰が動作を行ったかを **by ～**（～によって）で表します。

- Have you ever been bitten **by a dog**?
- The program was watched **by millions of people**.

with ～は「～を用いて」のような手段を表します。**by ～**のように誰が動作を行ったかは表しません。

- The door must have been opened **with a key**. (× by a key)
（⇒ 鍵でドアが開けられた，誰かが鍵でドアを開けた）
- The door must have been opened **by somebody** with a key.

a play **by Shakespeare** / a painting **by Rembrandt** / a novel **by Tolstoy** のような「～ **by 作者**」の形をよく使います。

- Have you read anything **by** Ernest Hemingway?

D

by ～は「～の隣に，そばに」を表すことがあります。

- Come and sit **by me**. (= beside me)
- "Where's the light switch?" "**By the door**."

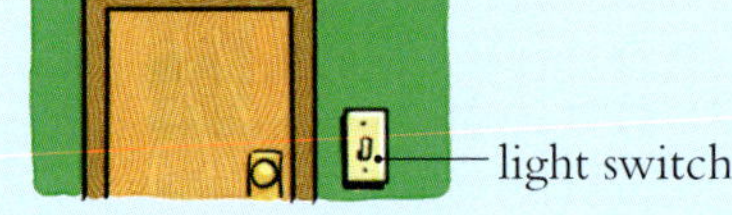

E

by ～は数量を表す語句を伴って，「～だけ，～分」のように２つの物の間の**差**を表すことがあります。

- Claire's salary has just gone up **from** $3,000 a month **to** $3,300. So it has increased **by $300** / **by 10 percent**.
- Carl and Mike ran a 100-meter race. Carl won **by** about **three meters**. （⇒ 約３メートル差で）

New Salary — $3,300/month
salary increased **by $300**
Old Salary — $3,000/month

☆ **by が表す差を確認します。**

受動態の中の by ➲ Unit 40B　by + -ing ➲ Unit 58B　by myself ➲ Unit 81D　時を表す by ➲ Unit 117

Exercises

125.1 状況に合うように前置詞 by の後に続く語句を以下から選び，空所に入れて文を完成しなさい。

~~chance~~ **credit card** **hand** **mistake** **satellite**

1. We hadn't arranged to meet. We met _by chance_ .
2. I didn't mean to take your umbrella. I took it ______ .
3. Don't put the sweater in the washing machine. It has to be washed ______ .
4. I don't need cash. I can pay the bill ______ .
5. The two cities were connected ______ for a television program.

125.2 空所に by, in, on のいずれかの前置詞を入れて，文を完成しなさい。

1. Joanne usually goes to work _by_ bus.
2. I saw Jane this morning. She was ______ the bus.
3. How did you get here? Did you come ______ train?
4. I decided not to go ______ car. I went ______ my bike instead.
5. I didn't feel like walking home, so I came home ______ a taxi.
6. Sorry we're late. We missed the bus, so we had to come ______ foot.
7. How long does it take to cross the Atlantic ______ ship?

125.3 例を参考にして，歌，絵画，映画，本などを解説する文を 3 つ作りなさい。

1. _War and Peace is a book by Tolstoy._
2. _Romeo and Juliet is a play by Shakespeare._
3. ______
4. ______
5. ______

125.4 空所に by, in, on, with のいずれかの前置詞を入れて，文を完成しなさい。

1. Have you ever been bitten _by_ a dog?
2. The plane was badly damaged ______ lightning.
3. We managed to put the fire out ______ a fire extinguisher.
4. Who is that man standing ______ the window?
5. These photos were taken ______ a friend of mine.
6. I don't mind going ______ car, but I don't want to go ______ your car.
7. There was a small table ______ the bed ______ a lamp and a clock ______ it.

125.5 それぞれの文について誤りのある部分を○で囲み，正しい形に書き直しなさい。

1. Did you come here (by Kate's car) or yours? _in Kate's car_
2. I don't like traveling on bus. ______
3. These photographs were taken by a very good camera. ______
4. I know this music is from Beethoven, but I can't remember what it's called. ______
5. I couldn't pay by cash – I didn't have any money on me. ______
6. We lost the game only because of a mistake of one of our players. ______

125.6 状況に合うように，by ～を含む語句を用いて文を完成しなさい。

1. Claire's salary was $2,000 a month. Now it is $2,200.
   Her salary _has increased by $200 a month._
2. My daily newspaper used to cost a dollar. Starting today, it will cost $1.25.
   The price has gone up ______
3. There was an election. Helen won. She got 25 votes and Norman got 23.
   Helen won ______
4. I went to Kate's house to see her, but she had gone out five minutes before I arrived.
   I missed ______

補充問題 34 (pp. 315–316)

UNIT 126

名詞＋前置詞（reason for, cause of など，前置詞とよく結び付く名詞）

A

名詞＋for ～

a **check FOR ～**（金額）**:**「～の小切手」

■ They sent me **a check for** $200.（⇒ 額面200ドルの小切手）

a **demand** / a **need FOR ～:**「～の需要／必要性」

■ The company closed down because there wasn't enough **demand for** its product.

■ There's no excuse for behavior like that. There's no **need for** it.（⇒ まったくいらない）

a **reason FOR ～:**「～の理由」

■ The train was late, but nobody knew the **reason for** the delay.（× reason of）

B

名詞＋of ～

an **advantage** / a **disadvantage OF ～:**「～の長所／短所」

■ The **advantage of living alone** is that you can do what you like.

there is/are ... 構文中では，**there is** an advantage **to/in** doing ～（～することに長所がある）のように **to** もしくは **in** を用います。

■ **There are** many advantages **to** living alone.（= . . . **in** living alone)

a **cause OF ～:**「～の原因」

■ The **cause of** the explosion is unknown.

a **photo** / a **picture** / a **map** / a **plan** / a **drawing OF ～:**「～の写真／絵画／地図／計画／絵」

■ Rachel showed me some **photos of** her family.

■ I had a **map of** the town, so I was able to find my way around.

C

名詞＋in ～

an **increase** / a **decrease** / a **rise** / a **drop IN ～**（価格・量など）**:**「～の増加／減少／上昇／下降」

■ There has been an **increase in** the number of traffic accidents recently.

■ Last year was a bad one for the company. There was a big **drop in** sales.

D

名詞＋to ～ / toward ～

damage TO ～:「～への損害」

■ The accident was my fault, so I had to pay for the **damage to** the other car.

an **invitation TO ～**（パーティー，結婚式など）**:**「～への招待」

■ Did you get an **invitation to** the party?

a **solution TO** (a problem) / a **key TO** (a door) / an **answer TO** (a question) / a **reply TO** (a letter) / a **reaction TO ～:**「～に対する解決／鍵／答え／返事／反応」のような形もよく用います。

■ I hope we find a **solution to** the problem.（× a solution of the problem)

■ I was surprised at her **reaction to** my suggestion.

an **attitude TOWARD ～:**「～に対する態度」

■ His **attitude toward** his job is very negative.

E

名詞＋with ～ / between ～

a **relationship** / a **connection** / **contact WITH ～:**「～との関係，つながり」

■ Do you have a good **relationship with** your parents?

■ The police want to question a man in **connection with** the robbery.

～（前置詞の後の名詞句）が2つの物や人の場合には，a **relationship** / a **connection** / **contact** / a **difference between** ～のように **between** を用います。

■ The police believe that there is no **connection between** the two crimes.

■ There are some **differences between** British and American English.

Exercises

126.1 例にならって，「名詞＋前置詞」の形で文を書き換えなさい。

1. What caused the explosion?
   What was the cause *of the explosion* ?
2. We're trying to solve the problem.
   We're trying to find a solution ____________ .
3. Sue gets along well with her brother.
   Sue has a good relationship ____________ .
4. The cost of living has gone up a lot.
   There has been a big increase ____________ .
5. I don't know how to answer your question.
   I can't think of an answer ____________ .
6. I don't think that a new road is necessary.
   I don't think there is any need ____________ .
7. I think that working at home has many advantages.
   I think that there are many advantages ____________ .
8. The number of people without jobs fell last month.
   Last month there was a drop ____________ .
9. Nobody wants to buy shoes like these any more.
   There is no demand ____________ .
10. In what way is your job different from mine?
    What is the difference ____________ ?

126.2 状況に合うように，以下から名詞を選び適切な前置詞と組み合わせ，空所に入れて文を完成しなさい。

cause connection contact damage invitation
key ~~map~~ pictures reason reply

1. On the wall there were some pictures and a *map of* the world.
2. Thank you for the ____________ your party next week.
3. Since she left home two years ago, Sofia has had little ____________ her family.
4. I can't open this door. Do you have a ____________ the other door?
5. The ____________ the fire at the hotel last night is still unknown.
6. I e-mailed Jim last week, but I still haven't received a ____________ my message.
7. The two companies are completely independent. There is no ____________ them.
8. Jane showed me some old ____________ the city the way it looked 100 years ago.
9. Carol has decided to quit her job. I don't know her ____________ doing this.
10. It wasn't a bad accident. The ____________ the car wasn't serious.

126.3 空所に適切な前置詞を入れて，文を完成しなさい。

1. There are some differences *between* British and American English.
2. Money isn't the solution ________ every problem.
3. There has been an increase ________ the amount of traffic using this road.
4. When I opened the envelope, I was delighted to find a check ________ $500.
5. The advantage ________ having a car is that you don't have to rely on public transportation.
6. There are many advantages ________ being able to speak a foreign language.
7. Everything can be explained. There's a reason ________ everything.
8. When Paul left home, his attitude ________ his parents seemed to change.
9. Ben and I used to be good friends, but I don't have much contact ________ him now.
10. There has been a sharp rise ________ property values in the past few years.
11. What was Ann's reaction ________ the news?
12. If I give you the camera, can you take a picture ________ me?
13. The company has rejected the workers' demands ________ an increase ________ pay.
14. What was the answer ________ question 3 on the test?
15. The fact that Jane was offered a job has no connection ________ the fact that she is a friend of the managing director.

補充問題 34 (pp. 315–316)

UNIT 127

形容詞 + 前置詞 1

A

it was ~（**形容詞**）**of** you to + 動詞の原形:「~にも…する，…することは~」のように行動を評価します。

主語を it にして，形容詞には **nice/kind/good/generous/polite/stupid/silly** などがきます。

- Thank you. It was very **kind of** you to help me.（⇒ ご親切にも助けていただいて…）
- It is **stupid of** me to go out without a coat in such cold weather.

主語が it ではなく人の場合には，人 + (be) + **形容詞** + **TO** + 人のように **to** を用います。➲セクション B

- They have always been very **nice to** me.（× with me）
- Why were you so **unfriendly to** Lucy?

B

形容詞 + about/with/at ~: 人が持つ感情を表します。形容詞と前置詞の後の語句に注意します。

furious/angry/mad/upset ABOUT ~:「~に憤慨する，激怒する，動揺する」

- Max is really **angry about** what his brother said.（⇒ 弟が言ったことに腹を立てている）

mad	**AT**		激怒する」
upset	**WITH**	**~ FOR doing . . . :**「~が…したことに	動揺する」
furious/angry	**AT / WITH**		怒る」

- My parents are **mad at** me **for** disobeying them.
- Are you **upset with** me **for** being late?（⇒ 私が遅れたことに怒っているの？）
- Pat's **furious with** me **for** telling her secret.（= **furious at** me）

excited/worried/upset/nervous/happy ABOUT doing:「…（状況）について~となる」

- Are you **excited about** going away next week?
- Lisa is **upset about** not being invited to the party.（⇒ 招かれなかったことに腹を立てている）

delighted/pleased/satisfied/happy/disappointed WITH ~:「~（受け取った物 / 結果）について~となる」

- I was very **pleased with** the present you gave me.
- Were you **happy with** your exam results?（⇒ 試験の結果に満足していますか？）

C

形容詞 + at/by/with ~: 人が持つ感情を表します。形容詞によって前置詞が決まります。

surprised/shocked/amazed/astonished AT/BY ~:「~に驚く」

- Everybody was **surprised at** (= **by**) the news.
- I hope you weren't **shocked by** (= **at**) what I said.

impressed WITH/BY ~:「~に感動する，感心する」

- I'm very **impressed with** (= **by**) her English. It's very good.

fed up/bored WITH ~:「~に飽きる，うんざりする」

- I don't enjoy my job any more. I'm **fed up with** it. / I'm **bored with** it.

D

be/feel sorry about/for ~:「（人）が~について申し訳ない / 気の毒に思う」のように感情を表します。

sorry ABOUT ~: about の後には，その場の状況や起こった出来事がきます。

- I'm **sorry about** the mess. I'll clean it up later.（⇒ 散らかしてごめんなさい〔状況〕）
- We're all **sorry about** Julie losing her job.（⇒ Julie の失業を残念に思います〔出来事〕）

sorry FOR/ABOUT ~: about の後には人のした行為がきます。

- Alex is very **sorry for** what he said.（= **sorry about** what he said）
- I'm **sorry for** shouting at you yesterday.（= **sorry about** shouting）

I'm **sorry I (did ...)** のように，前置詞のない構文もよく用いられます。

- I'm **sorry I shouted** at you yesterday.

feel/be sorry FOR ~: for の後には良くない状況にある人がきます。

- I **feel sorry for** Matt. He's had a lot of bad luck.（× I feel sorry about Matt）

前置詞 + -ing ➲ Unit 58　　形容詞 + to ➲ Unit 63　　sorry to ... / sorry for ... ➲ Unit 64C
形容詞 + 前置詞 2 ➲Unit 128

Exercises

127.1 状況に合うように ( ) 内の語句を用いて，会話の答えの文を完成しなさい。

1. I went out in the cold without a coat. — (silly) *That was silly of you.*
2. Sue offered to drive me to the airport. — (nice) That was ______ her.
3. I needed money and Tom gave me some. — (generous) That ______
4. They didn't invite us to their party. — (not very nice) That ______
5. Can I help you with your luggage? — (very kind) ______ you.
6. Kevin didn't thank me for the present. — (not very polite) ______
7. They've had an argument and now they refuse to speak to each other. — (a little childish) ______

127.2 状況に合うように，以下から形容詞を選び適切な前置詞を後ろに置き，空所に入れて文を完成しなさい。

astonished bored ~~excited~~ impressed kind nervous sorry upset

1. Are you *excited about* going away next week?
2. Thank you for all your help. You've been very ______ me.
3. I wouldn't want to be in her position. I feel ______ her.
4. I'm really ______ taking my driver's test. I hope I don't fail.
5. Why do you always get so ______ things that don't matter?
6. I wasn't very ______ the service at the restaurant. We had to wait ages before our food arrived.
7. Ben isn't very happy at college. He says he's ______ the classes he's taking.
8. I had never seen so many people before. I was ______ the crowds.

127.3 適切な前置詞を空所に入れて，文を完成しなさい。

1. I was delighted *with* the present you gave me.
2. It was very nice ______ you to do my shopping for me. Thank you very much.
3. Why are you always so rude ______ your parents? Can't you be nice ______ them?
4. It was careless ______ you to leave the door unlocked when you went out.
5. They didn't reply to our letter, which wasn't very polite ______ them.
6. We always have the same food every day. I'm fed up ______ it.
7. I can't understand people who are cruel ______ animals.
8. We enjoyed our vacation, but we were a little disappointed ______ the hotel.
9. I was surprised ______ the way he behaved. It was completely out of character.
10. I've been trying to learn Spanish, but I'm not very satisfied ______ my progress.
11. Linda doesn't look very well. I'm worried ______ her.
12. Are you angry ______ what happened?
13. I'm sorry ______ what I did. I hope you're not mad ______ me.
14. The people next door are furious ______ us ______ making so much noise last night.
15. Jill starts her new job next week. She's quite excited ______ it.
16. I'm sorry ______ the smell of paint in this room. I'm redecorating it.
17. I was shocked ______ what I saw. I'd never seen anything like it before.
18. The man we interviewed for the job was intelligent, but we weren't very impressed ______ his appearance.
19. Are you still upset ______ what I said to you yesterday?
20. He said he was sorry ______ the situation, but there was nothing he could do.
21. I felt sorry ______ the children when we went on vacation. It rained every day and they had to spend most of the time indoors.

補充問題 35 (p. 316)

UNIT 128

形容詞＋前置詞 2

A 形容詞 + of ~ (1)

afraid/frightened/terrified/scared OF ~: 「~を恐れる / ~にぎょっとする / ~にぞっとする / ~を怖がる」

■ "Are you **afraid of** spiders?" "Yes, I'm **terrified of** them."

fond/proud/ashamed/jealous/envious OF ~: 「~を好む / 自慢する / 恥じる / ねたむ / うらやむ」

■ Why are you always so **jealous of** other people?

suspicious/critical/tolerant OF ~: 「~を疑う / ~に口やかましいく / ~に寛大な」

■ He didn't trust me. He was **suspicious of** my intentions.

B 形容詞 + of ~ (2)

aware/conscious OF ~: 「~に気づく，~がわかる」

■ "Did you know he was married?" "No, I wasn't **aware of** that."

capable/incapable OF ~: 「~ができる / できない」

■ I'm sure you are **capable of** passing the exam.

full/short OF ~: 「~でいっぱい / ~が不足している」

■ The letter I wrote was **full of** mistakes. (× full with)

■ I'm a little **short of** money. Can you lend me some?

typical OF ~: 「~に特有な，~によくある」

■ He's late again. It's **typical of** him to keep everybody waiting.

tired/sick OF ~: 「~に飽きる，うんざりする」

■ Come on, let's go! I'm **tired of** waiting. (= I've had enough of waiting.)

certain/sure OF = ABOUT ~: 「きっと~，~を確信する」

■ I think she's arriving tonight, but I'm not **sure of** that. = . . . sure **about** that.

C 形容詞 + at/to/from/in/on/with/for

good/bad/excellent/better/hopeless AT ~: 「~が上手 / 下手 / より上手 / ことにすぐれる / 見込みがない」

■ I'm not very **good at** repairing things. (× good in repairing things)

married/engaged TO ~: 「~と結婚している / 婚約している」

■ Linda is **married to** an American. (× married with，この意味で with は使えません)

しかし，Linda is married **with** three children. で「結婚して 3 人の子どもがいる」を表します。

similar TO ~: 「~と似ている」

■ Your writing is **similar to** mine.

different FROM / different THAN ~: 「~と異なる」

■ The film was **different from** what I'd expected. (= **different than** what I'd expected.)

interested IN ~: 「~に興味がある」

■ Are you **interested in** art?

dependent ON ~ / independent OF ~: 「~に頼っている / ~から独立している」

■ I don't want to be **dependent on** anybody.

crowded WITH ~: 「~で混雑している」

■ The streets were **crowded with** tourists. (⇔ **full of** tourists，full の後には of)

famous FOR ~: 「~で有名な」

■ The Italian city of Florence is **famous for** its art treasures.

responsible FOR ~: 「~に責任がある」

■ Who was **responsible for** all that noise last night?

前置詞 + -ing ➲ Unit 58　afraid of/to ➲ Unit 64A　形容詞＋前置詞 2 ➲Unit 127
different に関連したイギリス英語の用法 ➲ 付録 7

Exercises

128.1 同じ意味を表すように，右側の文を完成しなさい。

1. There were lots of tourists in the streets. The streets were crowded _with tourists_ .
2. There was a lot of furniture in the room. The room was full ________ .
3. Who made this mess? Who is responsible ________ ?
4. We don't have enough time. We're a little short ________ .
5. I'm not a very good tennis player. I'm not very good ________ .
6. Catherine's husband is Russian. Catherine is married ________ .
7. I don't trust Robert. I'm suspicious ________ .
8. My problem is not the same as yours. My problem is different ________ .

128.2 状況に合うように，以下から形容詞を選び適切な前置詞を後に置いて，文を完成しなさい。

afraid different interested proud responsible similar ~~sure~~

1. I think she's arriving tonight, but I'm not _sure of_ that.
2. Your camera is ________ mine, but it isn't exactly the same.
3. Don't worry. I'll take care of you. There's nothing to be ________ .
4. I never watch the news on television. I'm not ________ the news.
5. The editor is the person who is ________ what appears in a newspaper.
6. Sarah loves gardening. She's very ________ her garden and loves showing it to visitors.
7. I was surprised when I met Lisa for the first time. She was ________ what I expected.

128.3 空所に適切な前置詞を入れて，文を完成しなさい。

1. The letter I wrote was full _of_ mistakes.
2. My hometown is not an especially interesting place. It's not famous ________ anything.
3. Kate is very fond ________ her younger brother.
4. I don't like climbing ladders. I'm scared ________ heights.
5. You look bored. You don't seem interested ________ what I'm saying.
6. Did you know that Liz is engaged ________ a friend of mine?
7. I'm not ashamed ________ what I did. In fact I'm quite proud ________ it.
8. Mark has no money of his own. He's totally dependent ________ his parents.
9. These days everybody is aware ________ the dangers of smoking.
10. The station platform was crowded ________ people waiting for the train.
11. Sue is much more successful than I am. Sometimes I feel a little jealous ________ her.
12. I'm tired ________ doing the same thing every day. I need a change.
13. Do you know anyone who might be interested ________ buying an old car?
14. We've got plenty to eat. The fridge is full ________ food.
15. She is a very honest person. I don't think she is capable ________ telling a lie.
16. Helen works hard and she's extremely good ________ her job.
17. I'm not surprised he changed his mind at the last minute. That's typical ________ him.
18. The woman Sam is married ________ runs a software business.
19. We're short _____ staff in our office at the moment. We need more people to do the work.

128.4 自分のことについて，( ) 内の事柄が上手かどうかを記述する文を完成しなさい。

good pretty good not very good hopeless

1. (repairing things) _I'm not very good at repairing things._
2. (telling jokes) ________
3. (mathematics) ________
4. (remembering names) ________

補充問題 35 (p. 316)

UNIT 129

動詞＋前置詞 1：to と at

A

動詞 + to

talk/speak TO ~:「～に話しかける，～と話をする」 with も可能ですが to ほど使われません。
- Who was that man you were **talking to**?

listen TO ~:「～を聞く」
- We spent the evening **listening to** music. (✕ listening music)

apologize TO ~ (for ...) **:**「(…について) ～に謝る」
- They **apologized to me** for what happened. (✕ They apologized me)

explain . . . TO ~:「～を…に説明する」
- Can you **explain** this word **to me**? (✕ explain me this word)

that や**疑問詞**で始まる節には **explain/describe (to ~)** + that/what/how/why ... の形を用います。
- I **explained to them** why I was worried. (✕ I explained them. to は省略できません)
- Let me **describe to you** what I saw. (✕ Let me describe you)

B

以下の動詞では後に直接，**目的語**がきます（to は置きません）。

call/phone/telephone ~:「～に電話する，～と電話で話をする」
- Did you **call your father** yesterday? (✕ call to your father)

answer ~:「～に答える」
- He refused to **answer my question**. (✕ answer to my question)

ask ~:「～に尋ねる」
- Can I **ask you** a question? (✕ ask to you)

thank ~ (for ...) **:**「～に（…を）感謝する」
- He **thanked me** for helping him. (✕ He thanked to me)

C

動詞 + at

look/stare/glance AT ~:「～を見る / 見つめる / ちらりと見る」

have a look / take a look AT ~:「～を見る」
- Why are you **looking at** me like that?

laugh AT ~:「～を笑う」
- I look stupid with this haircut. Everybody will **laugh at** me.

aim/point ~ AT . . . :「～を…に向ける」

shoot/fire (a gun) **AT ~:**「～に向かって（銃を）発砲する」
- Don't **point** that knife **at** me. It's dangerous.
- We saw someone with a gun **shooting at** birds, but he didn't hit any.

D

以下の動詞では後に **at** も **to** もきますが，at と to で意味が異なります。

shout AT ~:「(怒って) ～をどなる」
- He got very angry and started **shouting at** me.

shout TO ~:「(聞こえるように) ～に大声で話す」
- He **shouted to** me from the other side of the street.

throw ~ AT . . . :「(…にぶつけようとして) ～を…に目がけて投げる」
- Somebody **threw** an egg **at** the politician.

throw ~ TO . . . :「(…がつかまえられるように) ～を…に目がけて投げる」
- Lisa shouted "Catch!" and **threw** the keys **to** me from the window.

動詞 + 前置詞 2–4 ➲ Units 130–131　ask for ➲ Unit 130C　apologize for / thank ~ for ... ➲ Unit 132B
動詞 + to の形を作るその他の動詞 ➲ Unit 133D

Exercises

129.1 自分が（ ）内に記述されているように何かが理解できない時，相手に説明を求める文を記述します。**Can you explain ...?** の形で始めなさい。

1. (I don't understand this word.)
   Can you explain this word to me?
2. (I don't understand what you mean.)
   Can you explain to me what you mean?
3. (I don't understand this question.)
   Can you explain ______
4. (I don't understand the problem.)
   Can ______
5. (I don't understand how this machine works.)
   ______
6. (I don't understand what I have to do.)
   ______

129.2 必要に応じて空所に **to** を入れなさい（必要ない場合には – を記入すること）。

1. I know who she is, but I've never spoken *to* her.
2. Why didn't you answer *–* my letter?
3. I like to listen ______ the radio while I'm having breakfast.
4. We'd better call ______ the restaurant to reserve a table.
5. "Did Mike apologize ______ you?" "Yes, he said he was very sorry."
6. I explained ______ everybody the reasons for my decision.
7. I thanked ______ everybody for all the help they had given me.
8. Ask me what you like, and I'll try and answer ______ your questions.
9. Mike described ______ me exactly what happened.
10. Karen won't be able to help you, so there's no point in asking ______ her.

129.3 状況に合うように以下から動詞を選び，「動詞 ＋ 前置詞」の形にし，空所に入れて文を完成しなさい。

~~**explain**~~ **glance** ~~**laugh**~~ **listen** **point** **speak** **throw** **throw**

1. I look stupid with this haircut. Everybody will *laugh at* me.
2. I don't understand this. Can you *explain* it *to* me?
3. Sue and Kevin had an argument and now they're not ______ each other.
4. Be careful with those scissors! Don't ______ them ______ me!
5. I ______ my watch to see what time it was.
6. Please ______ me! I've got something important to tell you.
7. Don't ______ stones ______ the birds! It's cruel.
8. If you don't want that sandwich, ______ it ______ the birds. They'll eat it.

129.4 状況に合うように空所に **to** もしくは **at** を入れて，文を完成しなさい。

1. Lisa shouted, "Catch!" and threw the keys *to* me from the window.
2. Look ______ these flowers. Aren't they pretty?
3. Please don't shout ______ me! Try to calm down.
4. I saw Sue as I was riding along the road. I shouted ______ her, but she didn't hear me.
5. Don't listen ______ what he says. He doesn't know what he's talking about.
6. What's so funny? What are you laughing ______ ?
7. Do you think I could have a look ______ your magazine, please?
8. I'm a little lonely. I need somebody to talk ______ .
9. She was so angry she threw a book ______ the wall.
10. The woman sitting opposite me on the train kept staring ______ me.
11. Can I speak ______ you a moment? There's something I want to ask you.

補充問題 36 (p. 316)

UNIT 130

動詞 + 前置詞 2：about/for/of/after

A 動詞 + about

talk/read/know ABOUT ～：「～について話す / 読む / 知る」
tell ～ ABOUT ～：「…について～に話す」
- We **talked about** a lot of things at the meeting.

have a discussion ABOUT ～，discuss ～：「～について討論する」
動詞 **discuss** は直後に**目的語**を置き，後に about ～は置きません。(✕ discuss about ～)
- We **had a discussion about** what we should do.
- We **discussed** a lot of things at the meeting. (✕ discussed about)

do ～ ABOUT . . . :「…について～をする」 悪い状況が改善されるよう対策を講じる。
- If you're worried about the problem, you should **do** something **about** it. (⇒ 何とかすべき)

B care about, care for と take care of

care ABOUT ～：「～を気づかう，気にする」
- He's very selfish. He doesn't **care about** other people.

疑問詞で始まる節には about を置かずに，**care + what/where/how ...** の形を用います。
- You can do what you like. I don't **care what** you do.

care FOR ～：大きく次の 2 つの意味があります：
1)（普通，疑問文や否定文で）～を好む，～が好き
- Would you **care for** a cup of coffee? (= Would you like . . . ?)
- I don't **care for** very hot weather. (= I don't like . . .)

2) ～の世話をする，介護する（人の安全と健康を確保する）
- Alan is 85 and lives alone. He needs somebody to **care for** him.

take care OF ～：「～の世話をする，介護する」に加え，「責任を持って～をする，～を引き受ける」の意味を持ちます。
- John gave up his job to **take care of** his elderly parents.
- I'll **take care of** all the travel arrangements – you don't need to do anything.

C 動詞 + for

ask (～) FOR . . . :「(～（人）に）…を（与えるように）求める」
- I wrote to the company **asking** them **for** more information about the job.

しかし「～に…を尋ねる」の意味では，I asked him the way to ... や She asked me my name. のように for は用いません。

apply (TO) ～ FOR . . . :「(～（人，会社，学校など）に）…（職や仕事）を求めて申請する，応募する」
- I think you'd be good at this job. Why don't you **apply for** it?

wait FOR ～：「～を待つ」
- Don't **wait for** me. I'll join you later.
- I'm not going out yet. I'm **waiting for** the rain to stop.

search (～) FOR . . . :「…を見つけようと（～（人，場所，カバンなど））を探す」
- I've **searched** the house **for** my keys, but I still can't find them.

leave (～) FOR . . . :「(～（ある場所）から）…（別の場所）へ出発する」
- I haven't seen her since she **left** (home) **for** the office this morning. (✕ left to the office)

D look for と look after

look FOR ～：「～を探す」
- I've lost my keys. Can you help me **look for** them?

look AFTER ～：「～の世話をする」
- Alan is 85 and lives alone. He needs somebody to **look after** him. (✕ look for)
- You can borrow this book if you promise to **look after** it.

think/hear などの動詞 + about/of ➲ Unit 131　　動詞 + for の形を作るその他の動詞 ➲ Unit 132B

Exercises

130.1 必要に応じて空所に適切な前置詞を入れなさい（必要ない場合には - を記入すること）。

1. I'm not going out yet. I'm waiting _for_ the rain to stop.
2. I couldn't find the street I was looking for, so I stopped someone to ask ______ directions.
3. I've applied ________ a job at the factory. I don't know if I'll get it.
4. I've applied ________ three colleges. I hope one of them accepts me.
5. I've searched everywhere ________ John, but I haven't been able to find him.
6. I don't want to talk ________ what happened last night. Let's forget it.
7. I don't want to discuss ________ what happened last night. Let's forget it.
8. We had an interesting discussion ________ the problem, but we didn't reach a decision.
9. We discussed ________ the problem, but we didn't reach a decision.
10. I don't want to go out yet. I'm waiting ________ the mail to arrive.
11. Ken and Sonia are touring Italy. They're in Rome right now, but tomorrow they leave ________ Venice.
12. The roof of the house is in very bad condition. I think we ought to do something _____ it.
13. We waited ________ Steve for half an hour, but he never came.
14. Tomorrow morning I have to catch a plane. I'm leaving my house _____ the airport at 7:30.

130.2 状況に合うように以下から動詞を選び，「動詞＋前置詞」の形にし，空所に入れて文を完成しなさい。

apply ask do leave look ~~search~~ talk wait

1. Police are _searching for_ the man who escaped from prison.
2. We're still ______________________ a reply to our letter. We haven't heard anything yet.
3. I think Ben likes his job, but he doesn't ______________________ it much.
4. When I'd finished my meal, I ______________ the waiter ________ the check.
5. Cathy is unemployed. She has ______________________ several jobs, but she hasn't had any luck.
6. If something is wrong, why don't you ______________ something ________ it?
7. Linda's car is very old, but it's in excellent condition. She __________________ it very well.
8. Diane is from Boston, but now she lives in Paris. She ____________ Boston ________ Paris when she was 19.

130.3 状況に合うように，care の後に適切な前置詞を入れなさい（入らない場合は - を記入すること）。

1. He's very selfish. He doesn't care _about_ other people.
2. Are you hungry? Would you care ________ something to eat?
3. She doesn't care ________ the exam. She doesn't care whether she passes or fails.
4. Please let me borrow your camera. I promise I'll take good care ________ it.
5. "Do you like this coat?" "Not really. I don't care ________ the color."
6. Don't worry about the shopping. I'll take care ________ that.
7. I want to have a nice vacation. I don't care ________ the cost.
8. I want to have a nice vacation. I don't care ________ how much it costs.

130.4 状況に合うようにlook forもしくはlook afterを適切な形に変え，空所に入れて文を完成しなさい。

1. I _looked for_ my keys, but I couldn't find them anywhere.
2. Kate is ______________________ a job. I hope she finds one soon.
3. Who ______________________ you when you were sick?
4. I'm ______________________ Elizabeth. Have you seen her?
5. The parking lot was full, so we had to ______________________ somewhere else to park.
6. A babysitter is somebody who ______________________ other people's children.

補充問題 36 (p. 316)

UNIT 131

動詞＋前置詞 3：about と of

A

dream ABOUT ～：「(寝ていて) ～の夢を見る」

- I **dreamed about** you last night.

dream OF / ABOUT being . . . / doing . . . :「…となること / …をすることを夢見る，想像する」

- Do you **dream of/about** being rich and famous?

(I) **wouldn't dream OF** doing . . . :「決して…しない」

- "Don't tell anyone what I said." "No, I **wouldn't dream of** it." (⇒ 決して言いません)

B

hear ABOUT ～：「～について聞く (～について噂で聞いている)」

- Did you **hear about** what happened at the club on Saturday night?

hear OF ～：「～について聞く (人や物が今どうしているか知っている)」

- "Who is Tom Hart?" "I have no idea. I've never **heard of** him." (× heard from him)

hear FROM ～：「～手紙，電話，伝言をもらう」

- "Have you **heard from** Jane recently?" "Yes, she called a few days ago."

C

think ABOUT と think OF

think ABOUT ～：「～について考える」 精神を集中した持続的な活動。➲Unit 4B

- I've **thought about** what you said, and I've decided to take your advice.
- "Will you lend me the money?" "I'll **think about** it."

think OF ～：「～を思いつく，思い出す (考えが浮かんでくる)」

- He told me his name, but I can't **think of** it now. (× think about it)
- That's a good idea. Why didn't I **think of** that? (× think about that)

think ～ of . . . は「…をどう思う？」と質問したり，「…は～だと思う」のように意見を述べる際にも用います。

- "What did you **think of** the film?" "I didn't **think** much **of** it."
  (⇒ どう思う？――たいしたことない)

実際には **think of** と **think about** とは大きな違いはなく，どちらを用いてもよい場合があります。

- When I'm alone, I often **think of** (= **about**) you.

think of/about doing は，「これから…しようと考えている」のように未来に起こりうる活動を表します。

- My sister is **thinking of** (= **about**) going to Canada. (⇒ カナダに行こうと考えている)

D

remind ～ ABOUT . . .：「～に…を忘れるなと言う」 他人によって，忘れそうになったことを思い出す。

- I'm glad you **reminded** me **about** the meeting. I had completely forgotten about it.

remind ～ OF . . .：「～に…を思い出させる，連想させる (自ら記憶を思い返して)」

- This house **reminds** me **of** the one I lived in when I was a child.
- Look at this picture of Richard. Who does he **remind** you **of**?

E

complain (**TO ～**) **ABOUT . . .：**「(～に) …について不満を言う」

- We **complained to** the manager of the restaurant **about** the food.

complain OF ～：「～ (痛み，病気など) があると言う」

- We called the doctor because George was **complaining of** a pain in his stomach.

F

warn ～ ABOUT . . .：「～に…(今存在している，不正，危険，異常性)に注意するように言う，警告する」

- I knew he was a strange person. I had been **warned about** him. (× warned of him)
- Vicky **warned** me **about** the traffic. She said it would be bad.

warn ～ ABOUT/OF . . .：「～に…(今後起こりうる，不正，危険，異常性)に注意するように言う，警告する」

- Scientists have **warned** us **about/of** the effects of global warming.

remind/warn ～ to＋動詞の原形 ➲ Unit 53B

Exercises

131.1 空所に適切な前置詞を入れて，文を完成しなさい。

1. Did you hear __about__ what happened at the party on Saturday?
2. "I had a strange dream last night." "Did you? What did you dream ________ ?"
3. Our neighbors complained ________ us ________ the noise we made last night.
4. Kevin was complaining ________ pains in his chest, so he went to the doctor.
5. I love this music. It reminds me ________ a warm day in spring.
6. He loves his job. He thinks ________ his job all the time, he dreams ________ it, he talks ________ it, and I'm sick of hearing ________ it.
7. I tried to remember the name of the book, but I couldn't think ________ it.
8. Jackie warned me ________ the water. She said it wasn't safe to drink.
9. We warned our children ________ the dangers of playing in the street.

131.2 状況に合うように以下から適切な動詞を選び，「動詞 + 前置詞」の形にして空所に入れ，文を完成しなさい。

complain dream hear remind remind ~~think~~ think warn

1. That's a good idea. Why didn't I __think of__ that?
2. Bill is never satisfied. He is always ____________________ something.
3. I can't make a decision yet. I need time to ____________________ your proposal.
4. Before you go into the house, I should ______________ you ________ the dog. He is very aggressive sometimes, so be careful.
5. She's not a well-known singer. Not many people have ____________________ her.
6. *A*: You wouldn't leave without telling me, would you?
   B: Of course not. I wouldn't ____________________ it.
7. I would have forgotten my appointment if Jane hadn't ______________ me ________ it.
8. Do you see that man over there? Does he __________ you ________ anybody you know?

131.3 状況に合うように，hear もしくは heard の後に適切な前置詞（about/of/from）を続けて文を完成しなさい。

1. I've never __heard of__ Tom Hart. Who is he?
2. "Did you ____________________ the accident last night?" "Yes, Vicky told me."
3. Jill used to call quite often, but I haven't ____________________ her for a long time now.
4. *A*: Have you ____________________ a writer called William Hudson?
   B: No, I don't think so. What sort of writer is he?
5. Thank you for your letter. It was good to ____________________ you again.
6. "Do you want to ____________________ our vacation?" "Not now. Tell me later."
7. I live in a small town in Texas. You've probably never ____________________ it.

131.4 状況に合うように，空所に think about もしくは think of を入れて文を完成しなさい。about と of がともに可能な場合もあります，また，think は適切な形（think/thinking/thought）に変えること。

1. You look serious. What are you __thinking about__ ?
2. I like to have time to make decisions. I like to ____________________ things carefully.
3. I don't know what to get Sarah for her birthday. Can you ____________________ anything?
4. *A*: I've finished reading the book you lent me.
   B: You have? What did you ____________________ it? Did you like it?
5. We're ____________________ going out for dinner tonight. Would you like to come?
6. I don't really want to go out with Tom tonight. I'll have to ________________ an excuse.
7. When I was offered the job, I didn't accept immediately. I went away and ____________________ it for a while. In the end I decided to take the job.
8. I don't ______________ much ____________ this coffee. It's like water.
9. Carol is very homesick. She's always ____________________ her family back home.

補充問題 36 (p. 316)

UNIT 132

動詞＋前置詞 4：of/for/from/on

A 動詞 + of

accuse/suspect ~ OF . . . :「～は…であると非難する / 疑う」
- Sue **accused** me **of** being selfish.
- Some students were **suspected of** cheating on the exam.

approve/disapprove OF . . . :「～を良く思う，…に同意する / …を良くないと思う，…に反対する」
- His parents don't **approve of** what he does, but they can't stop him.

die OF (= **FROM**) **~ :**「～(病気)で死ぬ」
- "What did he **die of**?" "A heart attack."

consist OF ~ :「～から成り立つ」
- We had an enormous meal. It **consisted of** seven courses.

B 動詞 + for

pay (~) **FOR . . . :**「(～に) …の代金を支払う」
- I didn't have enough money to **pay for** the meal. (× pay the meal)

しかし，**a bill**（請求書），**a fine**（罰金），**tax**（税金），**rent**（家賃），**a sum of money**（一定額のお金）などについては for は付きません。
- I didn't have enough money to **pay the rent**.

thank/forgive ~ FOR . . . :「～に…について感謝する / 許す」
- I'll never **forgive** them **for** what they did.

apologize (to ~) **FOR . . . :**「(～に) …について謝る」
- When I realized I was wrong, I **apologized** (to them) **for** my mistake.

blame ~ FOR . . . :「…は～のせいであると非難する」

~ (be) **to blame . . . :**「…は～のせいである」
- Everybody **blamed** me **for** the accident. (⇒ 事故は私のせいだと責めた)
- Everybody said that I was **to blame for** the accident. (⇒ 事故は私のせいであると言った)

blame ~ ON . . . :「～は…のせいであると非難する」
- Everybody **blamed** the accident **on** me. (⇒ 事故は私のせいだと責めた)

C 動詞 + from

suffer FROM ~ :「～（病気など）で苦しむ，～にかかる」
- The number of people **suffering from** heart disease has increased.

protect ~ FROM (= **AGAINST**) **. . . :**「…から～を守る」
- Sun block **protects** the skin **from** the sun. (= . . . **against** the sun.)

D 動詞 + on

depend/rely ON ~ :「～で決まる，～に頼る」
- "What time will you be home?" "I don't know. It **depends on** the traffic."
- You can **rely on** Jill. She always keeps her promises.

疑問詞で始まる節には on を置かずに，**depend + when/where/how ...** の形を用いることもあります。
- "Are you going to buy it?" "It **depends how** much it is." (= It depends **on** how much)

live ON ~ :「～（お金，食べ物など）で生活する」
- Michael's salary is very low. It isn't enough to **live on**. (⇒ とても暮らせない)

congratulate / compliment ~ ON . . . :「～の…を祝う / ほめる」
- I **congratulated** her **on** being admitted to law school.

動詞＋前置詞＋-ing ➲ Unit 60　動詞＋for の形を作るその他の動詞 ➲ Unit 130
動詞＋on の形を作るその他の動詞 ➲ Unit 133E

Exercises

132.1 最初の文と同じ意味を表すように 2 番目の文を書き換えなさい。

1. Sue said I was selfish.
   Sue accused me *of being selfish* ________.
2. The misunderstanding was my fault, so I apologized.
   I apologized ________.
3. Jane won the tournament, so I congratulated her.
   I congratulated Jane ________.
4. He has enemies, but he has a bodyguard to protect him.
   He has a bodyguard to protect him ________.
5. There are nine players on a baseball team.
   A baseball team consists ________.
6. Sandra eats only bread and eggs.
   She lives ________.

132.2 for もしくは on で始まる語句を空所に入れて，文を完成しなさい。すべての文に blame があることに注意します。

1. Liz said that what happened was Joe's fault.
   Liz blamed Joe *for what happened* ________.
2. You always say everything is my fault.
   You always blame me ________.
3. Do you think the economic crisis is the fault of the government?
   Do you blame the government ________?
4. I think the increase in violent crime is the fault of television.
   I blame the increase in violent crime ________.

3，4 の文を blame for を用いて書き換えなさい。

5. (3.) Do you think the government ________?
6. (4.) I think that ________.

132.3 状況に合うように以下から適切な動詞を選び，「動詞 + 前置詞」の形にして空所に入れ，文を完成しなさい。

accuse apologize ~~approve~~ congratulate depend live pay

1. His parents don't *approve of* what he does, but they can't stop him.
2. When you went to the theater with Paul, who ________ the tickets?
3. It's a terrible feeling when you are ________ something you didn't do.
4. *A*: Are you going to the beach tomorrow?
   B: I hope so. It ________ the weather.
5. Things are very cheap there. You can ________ very little money.
6. When I saw David, I ________ him ________ passing his driving test.
7. You were very rude to Liz. Don't you think you should ________ her?

132.4 空所に適切な前置詞を入れて，文を完成しなさい（必要ない場合には – を記入すること）。

1. Some students were suspected *of* cheating on the exam.
2. Sally is often sick. She suffers ________ very bad headaches.
3. You know that you can rely ________ me if you ever need any help.
4. It is terrible that some people are dying ________ hunger while others eat too much.
5. Are you going to apologize ________ what you did?
6. The accident was my fault, so I had to pay ________ the repairs.
7. I didn't have enough money to pay ________ the bill.
8. I complimented her ________ her English. She spoke very fluently, and her pronunciation was excellent.
9. She doesn't have a job. She depends ________ her parents for money.
10. I don't know whether I'll go out tonight. It depends ________ how I feel.
11. They wore warm clothes to protect themselves ________ the cold.
12. Cake consists mainly ________ sugar, flour, and butter.

補充問題 36 (p. 316)

UNIT 133

動詞＋前置詞 5：in/into/with/to/on

A 動詞＋in

believe IN ～：「～（の存在や正当性）を信じる」

■ Do you **believe in** God?（⇒ 神様がいると思いますか？）

■ I **believe in** saying what I think.（⇒ 思った通りのことを言うべきだと思う）

しかし,「～（物）が真であると思う」や「～（人）が事実通りのことを述べていると思う」の意味で「～を信じる」と述べる時，**believe** ～のように前置詞を置かずに直接，目的語を動詞の後に置きます。

■ The story can't be true. I don't **believe it**.（⇒ そんな話は信じない，× believe in it）

specialize IN ～：「～を専門にする」

■ Helen is a lawyer. She **specializes in** corporate law.

succeed IN ～：「～に成功する，～がうまくいく」

■ I hope you **succeed in** finding the job you want.

B 動詞＋into

break INTO ～：「（泥棒などが）～に押し入る」

■ Our house was **broken into** a few days ago, but nothing was stolen.

crash/drive/bump/run INTO ～：「（物がつぶれる大きな音を立てて）～に衝突する /（乗り物が）～に衝突する /（ドシンと音を立てて）～に衝突する / ～とはち合わせする，偶然出会う」

■ He lost control of the car and **crashed into** a wall.

divide/cut/split ～ INTO . . .（2つ以上の部分）**：**「～を…（の部分）に分ける / 切る / 割る」

■ The book is **divided into** three parts.

translate ～ FROM A **INTO** B**:**「～（書籍，文章，会話など）を言語 A から言語 B に翻訳する」

■ Ernest Hemingway's books have been **translated into** many languages.

C 動詞＋with

collide WITH . . . :「…と衝突する」

■ There was an accident this morning. A bus **collided with** a car.

fill ～ WITH . . . :「～を…で満たす」 ⇔ full of ～ ➲ Unit 128B

■ Take this pot and **fill** it **with** water.

provide/supply ～ WITH . . . :「～に…を与える，供給する」

■ The school **provides** all its students **with** books.

D 動詞＋to

happen TO ～：「～に起きる，発生する」

■ What **happened to** that gold watch you used to have?
（⇒ 前にしていた金時計はどうなりましたか？）

invite ～ TO . . . :「～を…（パーティーや結婚式など）に招待する」

■ They only **invited** a few people **to** their wedding.

prefer ～ TO . . . :「…よりも～の方を好む」

■ I **prefer** tea **to** coffee.

E 動詞＋on

concentrate ON ～：「～に集中する」

■ Don't look out the window. **Concentrate on** your work.

insist ON ～：「～を主張する」

■ I wanted to go alone, but some friends of mine **insisted on** coming with me.

spend (～) ON . . . :「…に（～の金額の）お金を使う」

■ How much do you **spend on** food each week?

動詞＋前置詞＋-ing ➲ Unit 60　　動詞＋to の形を作るその他の動詞 ➲ Unit 129
動詞＋on の形を作るその他の動詞 ➲ Unit 132D

Exercises

133.1 2 つの文が同じ意味を表すように 2 番目の文を書き換えなさい。

1. There was a collision between a bus and a car.
   A bus collided _with a car_ .
2. I don't mind big cities, but I prefer small towns.
   I prefer ________ .
3. I got all the information I needed from Jane.
   Jane provided me ________ .
4. This morning I bought a pair of shoes, which cost $70.
   This morning I spent ________ .

133.2 状況に合うように以下から適切な動詞を選び,「動詞 + 前置詞」の形にして空所に入れ, 文を完成しなさい。

believe concentrate divide drive fill happen ~~insist~~ invite succeed

1. I wanted to go alone, but Sue _insisted on_ coming with me.
2. I haven't seen Mike for ages. I wonder what has ________ him.
3. We've been ________ the party, but unfortunately we can't go.
4. It's a very large house. It's ________ four apartments.
5. I don't ________ ghosts. I think people only imagine that they see them.
6. Steve gave me an empty bucket and told me to ________ it ________ water.
7. I was driving along when the car in front of me stopped suddenly. Unfortunately I couldn't stop in time and ________ the back of it.
8. Don't try and do two things together. ________ one thing at a time.
9. It wasn't easy, but in the end we ________ finding a solution to the problem.

133.3 空所に適切な前置詞を入れて文を完成しなさい（必要がない場合には – を記入すること）。

1. The school provides all its students _with_ books.
2. A strange thing happened ________ me a few days ago.
3. Mark decided to give up sports so that he could concentrate ________ his studies.
4. I don't believe ________ working very hard. It's not worth it.
5. My present job isn't wonderful, but I prefer it ________ what I did before.
6. I hope you succeed ________ getting what you want.
7. As I was coming out of the room, I collided ________ somebody who was coming in.
8. There was an awful noise as the car crashed ________ a tree.
9. Patrick is a photographer. He specializes ________ sports photography.
10. Do you spend much money ________ clothes?
11. The country is divided ________ six regions.
12. I prefer traveling by train ________ driving. It's much more pleasant.
13. I was amazed when Joe walked into the room. I couldn't believe ________ it.
14. Somebody broke ________ my car and stole the radio.
15. I was very cold, but Tom insisted ________ keeping the window open.
16. Some words are difficult to translate ________ one language ________ another.
17. What happened ________ the money I lent you? What did you spend it ________ ?
18. The teacher decided to split the class ________ four groups.
19. I filled the tank, but unfortunately I filled it ________ the wrong kind of gas.

133.4 前置詞を用いて, 自分のことを記述する文を完成しなさい。

1. I wanted to go out alone, but my friend insisted _on coming with me_ .
2. I spend a lot of money ________ .
6. I saw the accident. The car crashed ________ .
4. Chris prefers basketball ________ .
5. Shakespeare's plays have been translated ________ .

UNIT 134

句動詞 1：「句動詞」とは何か？

A

☆ 句動詞とは何ですか？

動詞の後に以下のような語を置き，全体を **1 つの動詞**のように用いることがあります。

in	on	up	away	around	about	over	by
out	off	down	back	through	along	forward	

➤ このようにして作られた **look out / get on / take off / run away** などを「**句動詞**」(**phrasal verb**)と呼びます。

以下のように，**on/off/out** などの語は動き方や移動を表し，**句動詞**全体の意味がある程度予測できます。

get on（乗る） ■ The bus was full. We couldn't **get on**.
drive off（車で出て行く） ■ A woman got into the car and **drove off**.
come back（帰る） ■ Sally is leaving tomorrow and **coming back** on Saturday.
turn around（振り返る） ■ When I touched him on the shoulder, he **turned around**.

しかし，以下のように，**on/off/out** などの 2 番目の要素から全体の意味が予測できない場合もよくあります。

break down（故障する） ■ Sorry I'm late. The car **broke down**.
take off（離陸する） ■ It was my first flight. I was nervous as the plane **took off**.
run out（使い切る） ■ We don't have any more milk. We **ran out**.
get along（やっていく） ■ My brother and I **get along** well.（⇒ 仲がよい）
get by（何とかする） ■ My French isn't very good, but it's enough to **get by**.

その他の句動詞 ➲ Units 135-142

B

句動詞の後に**前置詞**がくることもあります。

句動詞	前置詞	
run away	**from**（～から逃げる）	■ Why did you **run away from** me?
keep up	**with**（～について行く）	■ You're walking too fast. I can't **keep up with** you.
look up	**at**（～を見上げる）	■ We **looked up at** the plane as it flew above us.
look forward	**to**（～を楽しみに待つ）	■ Are you **looking forward to** the weekend?
get along	**with**（～とうまくやる）	■ Do you **get along with** your boss?

C

句動詞は目的語をとることがあります。普通，目的語が生じる位置は，**句動詞全体の直後**と**動詞の直後**の 2 つの可能性があります。

I **turned on** the light. = I **turned** the light **on**.
目的語 目的語

代名詞が目的語となる場合，目的語は**動詞の直後**にのみ生じます。

I **turned** it **on**.（× I turned on it）

☆ **代名詞以外の名詞句と代名詞では，目的語の生じる位置はどのように異なりますか？**

■ Could you { **fill out** this form? / **fill** this form **out**? }

⇒ They gave me a form and told me to **fill it out**.（× fill out it）

■ Don't { **throw away** this postcard. / **throw** this postcard **away**. }

⇒ I want to keep this postcard, so don't **throw it away**.（× throw away it）

■ I'm going to { **take off** my shoes. / **take** my shoes **off**. }

⇒ These shoes are uncomfortable. I'm going to **take them off**.（× take off them）

■ Don't { **wake up** the baby. / **wake** the baby **up**. }

⇒ The baby is asleep. Don't **wake her up**.（× wake up her）

句動詞 2–9 ➲ Units 135–142 イギリス英語の用法 ➲ 付録 7

Exercises

134.1 以下の A と B の語を 1 つずつ選び，適宜組み合わせ空所に入れて文を完成しなさい。同じ語を複数回用いてもかまいません，ただし，動詞は適切な形に変えること。

A **fly get go look sit run** B **away by down on out around up**

1. The bus was full. We couldn't _get on_ .
2. I've been standing for the last two hours. I'm going to ________ for a bit.
3. A cat tried to catch the bird, but the bird ________ just in time.
4. We were trapped in the building. We couldn't ________ .
5. "Did you get fish at the store?" "I couldn't. They had ________ ."
6. "Do you speak German?" "Not very well, but I can ________ ."
7. The cost of living is higher now. Prices have ________ a lot.
8. I thought there was somebody behind me, but when I ________ , there was nobody there.

134.2 以下の A と B の語を 1 つずつ選び，適宜組み合わせ空所に入れて文を完成しなさい。同じ語を複数回用いてもかまいません。

A **along away back forward in up** B **at through to with**

1. You're walking too fast. I can't keep _up with_ you.
2. My vacation is nearly over. Next week I'll be ________ work.
3. We went ________ the top floor of the building to admire the view.
4. Are you looking ________ the party next week?
5. There was a bank robbery last week. The robbers got ________ $50,000.
6. I love to look ________ the stars in the sky at night.
7. I was sitting in the kitchen when suddenly a bird flew ________ the open window.
8. "Why did Sally quit her job?" "She didn't get ________ her co-workers."

134.3 状況に合うように，以下から句動詞を選び **it/them/me** と組み合わせ，空所に入れて文を完成しなさい。

~~fill out~~ get out give back turn on take off wake up

1. They gave me a form and told me to _fill it out_ .
2. I'm going to bed now. Can you ________ at 6:30?
3. I've got something in my eye and I can't ________ .
4. I don't like it when people borrow things and don't ________ .
5. I want to use the heater. How do I ________ ?
6. My shoes are dirty. I'd better ________ before going into the house.

134.4 空所に名詞句もしくは代名詞と（ ）内の語を入れて，自分の考えとして記述する文を完成しなさい。

1. Don't throw _away this newspaper_ . I want to read it. (away)
2. "Do you want this postcard?" "No, you can throw _it away_ ." (away)
3. I borrowed these books from the library. I have to take ________ tomorrow. (back)
4. We can turn ________ . Nobody is watching it. (off)
5. *A*: How did the vase get broken?
   B: Unfortunately, I knocked ________ while I was cleaning. (over)
6. Shh! My mother is asleep. I don't want to wake ________ . (up)
7. It's pretty cold. You should put ________ if you're going out. (on)
8. It was only a small fire. I was able to put ________ easily. (out)
9. I took ________ because they were uncomfortable and my feet were hurting. (off)
10. It's a little dark in this room. Should I turn ________ ? (on)

補充問題 37–41 (pp. 317–318)

UNIT 135

句動詞 2：in/out

A

☆ 句動詞において，in を持つ場合と out を持つ場合とでは，どのように異なりますか？

➤ **in:** 部屋，建物，自動車などの中に入る

- How did the thieves **get in**?
- Here's a key, so you can **let yourself in**.
- Sally walked up to the edge of the pool and **dived in**.（⇒ 水の中に飛び込んだ）
- I've got a new apartment. I'm **moving in** on Friday.
- As soon as I got to the airport, I **checked in**.

この他 **go in**, **come in**, **walk in**, **break in** などのような形も用いられます。

in は句動詞を構成しますが，**into** は構成しません。**into** は前置詞として後に名詞句がきます。

- I'm moving **in** next week.
- I'm moving **into my new apartment** on Friday.

➤ **out:** 部屋，建物，自動車などの中から出る

- He just stood up and **walked out**.
- I had no key, so I was **locked out**.
- She swam up and down the pool, and then **climbed out**.
- Tim opened the window and **looked out**.
- 〔ホテルで〕What time do we have to **check out**?

この他 **go out**, **get out**, **move out**, **let ～ out** などのような形も用いられます。

out of は句動詞を構成しません。**out of** は前置詞として後に名詞句がきます。

- He walked **out**.
- He walked **out of the room**.

B

動詞 + **in** の形を作るその他の句動詞

drop in :「ちょっと立ち寄る」

- I **dropped in** to see Chris on my way home.

join in :「（すでに始まっている活動に）参加する」

- We're playing a game. Why don't you **join in**?

plug in ～ :「～（電化製品）をコンセントに入れる」

- The fridge isn't working because you haven't **plugged** it **in**.

hand in / turn in ～ :「～（書かれた，課題，レポート，申込用紙など）を（教員や上司に）提出する」

- Your report is due this week. Please **hand** it **in** by Friday at 3 p.m.

fit in :「集団にうまくなじんでいる，とけ込んでいる」

- Some children have trouble **fitting in** at a new school.

C

動詞 + **out** の形を作るその他の句動詞

eat out :「自宅ではなくレストランで食事する，外食する」

- There wasn't anything to eat at home, so we decided to **eat out**.

drop out of ～ :「～（大学，学校，授業，レース）を途中でやめる」

- Gary went to college but **dropped out** after a year.

get out of ～ :「～（準備したり，約束したこと）から手を引く，逃れる」

- I promised I'd go to the wedding. I don't want to go, but I can't **get out** of it now.

cut ～out (of . . .) :「（新聞や雑誌などから）～を切り抜く」

- There was a beautiful picture in the magazine, so I **cut** it **out** and kept it.

leave ～out :「～を省く，とり除く」

- In the sentence "She said that she was sick," you can **leave out** the word "that."

fill out ～ :「～（書式やアンケートなど）に記入する」

- I have to **fill out** this application by the end of the week.

句動詞 1（句動詞とは何か？）➲Unit 134　　動詞 + out の形のその他の句動詞 ➲Unit 136

Exercises

135.1 空所に適切な動詞を正しい形に変えて入れ，文を完成しなさい。

1. Here's a key so that you can *let* yourself in.
2. Liz doesn't like cooking, so she ________ out a lot.
3. Eva isn't living in this apartment anymore. She ________ out a few weeks ago.
4. If you're in our part of town, you should ________ in and see us.
5. When I ________ in at the airport, I was told my flight was delayed.
6. There were some advertisements in the paper that I wanted to keep, so I ________ them out.
7. I wanted to iron some clothes, but there was nowhere to ________ the iron in.
8. Everyone else at the party was dressed up. In my jeans, I didn't ________ in.
9. Throw this away. I don't have time to ________ out useless questionnaires.
10. Sue is going to ________ in her essay a week early in order to be free next weekend.
11. Soup isn't very tasty if you ________ out the salt.
12. Paul started taking a Spanish class, but he ________ out after a few weeks.

135.2 空所に in, into, out, out of の中から適切なものを入れて，文を完成しなさい。

1. I've got a new apartment. I'm moving *in* on Friday.
2. We checked ______ the hotel as soon as we arrived.
3. As soon as we arrived at the hotel, we checked ______ .
4. The car stopped and the driver got ______ .
5. Thieves broke ______ the house while we were away.
6. Why did Sarah drop ______ college? Did she fail her exams?

135.3 状況に合うように，空所に「動詞 + in もしくは out (of)」の形の句動詞を入れて文を完成しなさい。

1. Sally walked to the edge of the pool, *dived in* , and swam to the other end.
2. Not all the runners finished the race. Three of them ____________ .
3. I went to see Joe and Sue in their new house. They ____________ last week.
4. I've told you everything you need to know. I don't think I've ____________ anything.
5. Some people in the crowd started singing. Then a few more people ____________ , and soon everybody was singing.
6. We go to restaurants a lot. We like ____________ .
7. Sam is still new at the job, but his co-workers already like him. Everyone agrees that he ____________ well.
8. I ____________ to see Laura a few days ago. She was fine.
9. *A*: Can we meet tomorrow morning at 10:00?
   B: Probably. I'm supposed to go to another meeting, but I think I can ____________ it.

135.4 状況に合うように，空所に ( ) 内の動詞を用いた句動詞を入れ，適切な形に変えて文を完成しなさい。

1. *A*: The fridge isn't working.
   B: That's because you haven't *plugged it in* . (plug)
2. *A*: What do I have to do with these forms?
   B: ____________ and send them to this address. (fill)
3. *A*: Your book report is better than mine, but you got a lower grade.
   B: That's because I ____________ late. (hand)
4. *A*: Don't you usually put nuts in these cookies?
   B: This time I ____________ because Jill is allergic to them. (leave)
5. *A*: Have you been to that new club on Bridge Street?
   B: We wanted to go there a few nights ago, but the doorman wouldn't ____________ because we weren't members. (let)

補充問題 37–41 (pp. 317–318)

UNIT 136

句動詞 3：out

A

out :「燃えていない，輝いていない」

go out（消える） ■ Suddenly all the lights in the building **went out**.
put out ~（~（火，煙草，電灯）を消す） ■ We managed to **put** the fire **out**.
turn out ~（~（電灯）をつける） ■ I **turned** the lights **out** before leaving.
blow out ~（~（ろうそく）を吹き消す） ■ We don't need the candle. You can **blow** it **out**.

B work out

work out:「運動する，トレーニングする」
■ Rachel **works out** at the gym three times a week.

work out:「良い結果となる，うまくいく」
■ Good luck for the future. I hope everything **works out** well for you.
■ *A:* Why did James leave the company?
B: Things didn't **work out**.（⇒ 仕事がうまくいかなかった）

work out ~ :「~（問題，困難など）を解決する」
■ The family has been having some problems, but I'm sure they'll **work** things **out**.

work out ~ :「~（計画，合意，契約など）を苦労して作る」
■ The two sides in the conflict are trying to **work out** a peace plan.

C 動詞 + out の形を作るその他の句動詞

carry out ~ :「~（命令，実験，調査，研究，計画など）を実行する」
■ Soldiers are expected to **carry out** orders.
■ An investigation into the accident will be **carried out** as soon as possible.

figure out ~ :「~を理解する」
■ Can you help me **figure out** why my answer to this math problem is wrong?
■ Why did Erica do that? I can't **figure** her **out**.

find out + that/what/when ~（節）/ **find out about ~**（名詞句）**:**「~について情報を得る，知る」
■ The police never **found out** who committed the murder.
■ I just **found out** that it's Helen's birthday today.
■ I went online to **find out about** hotels in the town.

hand/give ~ out :「一人ずつ~を配る，与える」
■ At the end of the lecture, the speaker **handed out** information sheets to the audience.

point ~ out (to . . .) :「…に~を指摘する，注意を向けさせる」
■ As we drove through the city, our guide **pointed out** all the sights.
■ I didn't realize I'd made a mistake until somebody **pointed** it **out to** me.

run out (of ~) :「~を使い切る」 ➲Unit 134A
■ We **ran out of** gas on the freeway.（⇒ ガソリンを使い切った）

turn out to be ~ / **turn out ~**（good, nice などの形容詞）/ **turn out** that ~（節）**:**「~とわかる，~になる」
■ Nobody believed Paul at first, but he **turned out** to be right.
（⇒ 最後には Paul が正しいことが明らかになった）
■ The weather wasn't so good in the morning, but it **turned out** nice later.
■ I thought they knew each other, but it **turned out** that they'd never met.

try out ~ :「~（機械，システム，新しいアイディアなど）が問題ないかテストする，確認する」
■ The company is **trying out** a new computer system at the moment.

句動詞 1（句動詞とは何か？）➲Unit 134　動詞 + out の形のその他の句動詞 ➲Unit 135

Exercises

136.1 以下から，それぞれの句動詞の後に置くことができる語句を選びなさい。

a candle　a campfire　~~a light~~　a problem　a mistake　a new product　an order

1. turn out *a light*
2. point out ______
3. blow out ______
4. carry out ______
5. put out ______
6. try out ______
7. work out ______

136.2 状況に合うように空所に「動詞 + out」の形の句動詞を入れて，文を完成しなさい。

1. The company is *trying out* a new computer system at the moment.
2. Steve is in shape. He plays a lot of sports and ______ regularly.
3. The road will be closed for two days next week while repairs are ______ .
4. We didn't manage to discuss everything at the meeting. We ______ of time.
5. My father helped me ______ a plan to save money.
6. I called the station to ______ what time the train arrived.
7. The new drug will be ______ on a small group of patients.
8. I thought the two books were the same until a friend of mine ______ the difference.
9. They got married a few years ago, but it didn't ______ , and they separated.
10. There was a power outage and all the lights ______ .
11. We thought she was American at first, but she ______ to be Swedish.
12. I haven't been able to ______ how the water is getting into the house.
13. I haven't applied for the job yet. I want to ______ more about the company first.
14. It took the fire department two hours to ______ the fire.

136.3 空所に「動詞 + out」の形の句動詞を入れて，イラストの状況を説明する文を完成しなさい。

1. The lights have *gone out* .
2. The man with a beard is ______ ______ leaflets.
3. The weather has ______ ______ .
4. Sally and Kim are ______ ______ at the gym.
5. Joe has ______ of water.
6. Lisa is trying to ______ how to ______ .

136.4 状況に合うように空所に「動詞 + out」の形の句動詞を入れて，対話を完成しなさい。

1. *A:* Do we still need the candle?
   B: No, you can *blow it out* .
2. *A:* This recipe looks interesting.
   B: Yes, let's ______ .
3. *A:* Jason is strange. I'm not sure I like him.
   B: I agree. I can't ______ .
4. *A:* You realize that tomorrow's a holiday, don't you?
   B: No, I completely forgot. Thanks for ______ to me.

補充問題 37–41 (pp. 317–318)

UNIT 137

句動詞 4：on/off (1)

A

on と off： 電灯や機械に関連して「電源が入っている / いない」を表します。

the light **is on**（電灯がついている）/ **put** the light **on**（電灯をつける）/ **leave** the light **on**（電灯をつけたままにする）/ **turn** the light **on/off**（電灯をつける / 消す）/ **shut** the light **off**（電灯を消す）

- Should I **leave** the lights **on** or **turn** them **off**?
- "**Is** the heat **on**?" "No, I **shut** it **off**."
- Who **left** the computer **on**?

put on some music / a CD / a DVD：「音楽 / CD / DVD をかける」

- "What's this CD like?" "It's great. Should I **put** it **on**?"

B

on と off： 出来事に関連して「起きた / 起きなかった」を表します。

go on：「起きる，生じる」

- What's all that noise? What's **going on**?（⇒ 何が起きているんだ？）

call ~ off：「～を中止する，キャンセルする」

- The open air concert had to be **called off** because of the weather.

put ~ off / put off doing ~：「～を延期する」

- The wedding has been **put off** until January.
- We can't **put off** making a decision. We have to decide now.

C

on と off： 衣服や装身具，体重などに関連して「付ける / 脱ぐ」を表します。

put on ~：「～（衣服，眼鏡，化粧，シートベルトなど）を着る，付ける」

- My hands were cold, so I **put** my gloves **on**.

put on weight：「太る」を表します。

- I've **put on** five pounds in the last month.

try on ~：「～（衣服）を試着する」

- I **tried on** a jacket in the store, but it didn't fit me very well.

have ~ on：「～（衣服，宝石，香水など）を着る，付ける」

- I like the perfume you **had on** yesterday.

take off ~：「～（衣服，眼鏡など）を脱ぐ，外す」

- It was warm, so I **took off** my jacket.

D

off： 人や場所などに関連して「遠ざかる / 離れる」を表します。

be off (to ~)：「（～へ）出かける，外出する」

- Tomorrow **I'm off** to Paris / **I'm off** to the store.
  （⇒ パリに行きます / 買い物に行きます）

walk off（立ち去る）/ **run off**（走り去る）/ **drive off**（自動車で走り去る）/ **ride off**（自動車，自転車，馬で走り去る）/ **go off**（立ち去る）は，**walk away**，**run away** などのように **away** を用いた形と似た意味を表します。

- Diane got on her bike and **rode off**.
- Mark left home at the age of 18 and **went off** to Canada.

take off：「（飛行機が）離陸する」

- After a long delay the plane finally **took off**.

see ~ off：「～を（空港や駅まで）見送る」

- Helen was going away. We went to the station with her to **see her off**.

句動詞 1（句動詞とは何か？）➲ Unit 134　動詞＋on/off の形のその他の句動詞 ➲ Unit 138

Exercises

137.1 状況に合うように，**put on** の後に続く名詞句を以下から選んで文を完成しなさい。

~~a CD~~ **the heat** **the light** **a DVD** **the radio**

1. I wanted to listen to some music, so I *put a CD on* .
2. It was getting cold, so I ______ .
3. I wanted to hear the news, so I ______ .
4. It was getting dark, so I ______ .
5. I wanted to watch a movie, so I ______ .

137.2 状況に合うように，空所に「動詞 + **on**」もしくは「動詞 + **off**」の形を入れて文を完成しなさい。

1. It was warm, so I *took off* my jacket.
2. What are all these people doing? What's ______ ?
3. The weather was too bad for the plane to ______ , so the flight was delayed.
4. I didn't want to be disturbed, so I ______ my cell phone.
5. Rachel got into her car and ______ at high speed.
6. Tim has ______ weight since I last saw him. He used to be quite thin.
7. The clothes Bill ______ weren't warm enough so he borrowed my jacket.
8. Don't ______ until tomorrow what you can do today.
9. There was going to be a strike by bus drivers, but now they have been offered more money and the strike has been ______ .
10. Are you cold? Should I get you a sweater to ______ ?
11. When I go away, I prefer to be alone at the station or airport. I don't like it when people come to ______ me ______ .

137.3 イラストの状況を説明する文を完成しなさい。

1. Her hands were cold, so she *put her gloves on* .
2. The plane ______ at 10:55.
3. Maria ______ , but it was too big for her.
4. The game ______ because of the weather.
5. Mark's parents went to the airport to ______ .
6. He took his sunglasses out of his pocket and ______ .

UNIT 138

句動詞 5 : on/off (2)

A 動詞 + on :「～し続ける」のような動作の継続を表します。

drive on / walk on / play on :「運転し続ける / 歩き続ける / 演奏，再生，上演し続ける」
- Should we stop at this gas station or should we **drive on** to the next one?

go on :「続く」
- The party **went on** until 4 o'clock in the morning.

go on doing ～ **:**「～し続ける」
- We can't **go on** spending money like this. We'll have nothing left soon.

go on with ～ :「～し続ける」の意味で，同じように用いられます。
- Don't let me disturb you. Please **go on with** what you were doing.

keep on doing ～ **:**「～し続ける，繰り返し～する」
- He **keeps on** criticizing me. I'm really tired of it!

drag on :「長引く，必要以上に時間をかける」
- Let's make a decision now. I don't want this problem to **drag on**.

B 動詞 + on の形を作るその他の句動詞

hold on / hang on :「待つ」
- 〔電話で〕**Hold on** a minute. I'll see if Max is home. (⇒ 電話を切らないで待つ)

move on :「新しく活動を始める，話題を変える」
- 〔講義で〕That's enough about the political situation. Let's **move on** to the economy.

take on ～ :「～(仕事，追加の仕事，責任など) を引き受けて十分に行う」
- When Sally was sick, a friend **took on** her work at the office.

C 動詞 + off

doze off / drop off / nod off :「(うっかり) うたた寝する，居眠りする」
- The lecture wasn't very interesting. In fact, I **dozed off** in the middle of it.

drop ～ off :「～を降ろす，置いて行く」
- Sue **drops** her children **off** at school before she goes to work every morning.

go off :「爆発する」
- A bomb **went off** in a hotel downtown, but fortunately nobody was hurt.

以下の例のように **alarm** (警報，アラーム) を主語にして，「鳴る」(= ring) を表すこともあります。
- Did you hear the alarm **go off**?

lay ～ off :「(十分な仕事がないために，会社の事情で) ～を解雇する」
- My brother was **laid off** two months ago and still hasn't found another job.

rip ～ off :「～をだます，あざむく〔くだけた表現〕」
- Did you really pay $2,000 for that painting? I think you were **ripped off**.
  (⇒ 払い過ぎ，だまされた)

show off :「(能力や知識を) 誇示する，見せびらかす」
- Look at that boy on the bike riding with no hands. He's just **showing off**.

tell ～ off :「(良くないことをしたので) ～をしかりつける」
- Claire's mother **told** her **off** for wearing dirty shoes in the house.

go on ➲ Unit 51B　句動詞 1 (句動詞とは何か？) ➲ Unit 134
動詞 + on/off の形のその他の句動詞 ➲ Unit 137

Exercises

138.1 下線部の語句を「動詞 + on」もしくは「動詞 + off」の形の句動詞に書き換えなさい。

1. Did you hear the bomb <u>explode</u>?
   Did you hear the bomb _go off_ ?
2. The meeting <u>continued</u> longer than I expected.
   The meeting ____________ longer than I expected.
3. We didn't stop to rest. We <u>continued walking</u>.
   We didn't stop to rest. We ____________ .
4. I <u>fell asleep</u> while I was watching TV.
   I ____________ while I was watching TV.
5. Gary doesn't want to retire. He wants to <u>continue working</u>.
   Gary doesn't want to retire. He wants to ____________ working.
6. The fire alarm <u>rang</u> in the middle of the night.
   The fire alarm ____________ in the middle of the night.
7. Martin <u>calls me continuously</u>. It's very annoying.
   Martin ____________ . It's very annoying.

138.2 状況に合うように，空所に「動詞 + on」もしくは「動詞 + off」の形の句動詞を入れて文を完成しなさい。

1. We can't _go on_ spending money like this. We'll have nothing left soon.
2. I was standing by the car when suddenly the alarm ____________ .
3. I ____________ my clothes at the laundry and then I went shopping.
4. *A:* Michael seems very busy at the office these days.
   B: Yes, he has ____________ too much extra work, I think.
5. Bill paid too much for the car he bought. I think he was ____________ .
6. As time ____________ , I feel less and less upset about what happened.
7. I was very tired at work today. I nearly ____________ at my desk a couple of times.
8. Ben was ____________ by his boss for being late for work repeatedly.
9. If business doesn't improve, my company may have to ____________ some employees.
10. There was a very loud noise. It sounded like a bomb ____________ .
11. I ____________ making the same mistake. It's very frustrating.
12. Please ____________ with what you were saying. I'm sorry I interrupted you.
13. Peter is always trying to impress people. He's always ____________ .
14. "Are you ready to go yet?" "Almost. Can you ____________ just a while longer?"

138.3 状況に合うように以下から適切な動詞を選び，後に on もしくは off を付けた句動詞にして文を完成しなさい。必要に応じて語を追加してもかまいません。

drag go go ~~hold~~ lay move rip tell

1. *A:*〔電話で〕May I speak to Mrs. Jones?
   B: _Hold on_ a second. I'll get her for you.
2. *A:* Are you still working on that project? I can't believe it isn't finished.
   B: I know. I'm fed up with it. It's really ____________ .
3. *A:* We took a taxi to the airport. It cost forty dollars.
   B: Forty dollars! Normally it costs about twenty dollars. You ____________ .
4. *A:* Why were you late for work this morning?
   B: I overslept. My alarm clock didn't ____________ .
5. *A:* Have we discussed this point enough?
   B: I think so. Let's ____________ to the next point on our agenda.
6. *A:* There won't be any more interruptions. I've turned off my phone.
   B: Good. Let's ____________ what we were doing.
7. *A:* Some children at the next table in the restaurant were behaving very badly.
   B: Why didn't their parents ____________ ?
8. *A:* Why did Paul quit his job?
   B: He didn't quit. He was ____________ .

補充問題 37–41 (pp. 317–318)

UNIT 139

句動詞 6：up/down

A

句動詞中の up と down：それぞれ上と下の方向の意味を動詞に付け加えます。

put ~ up (on . . .)：「(…の上に) ～を貼る」
- I **put** some pictures **up** on the wall.

pick ~ up：「～を拾い上げる」
- There was a letter on the floor. I **picked** it **up** and looked at it.

stand up：「立ち上がる」
- Alan **stood up** and walked out.

turn ~ up：「～を上げる，上に向ける」
- I can't hear the TV. Can you **turn** it **up** a little?

take ~ down (from . . .)：「(…から) ～を下ろす」
- I didn't like the picture, so I **took** it **down**.

put ~ down：「～を置く」
- I stopped writing and **put down** my pen.

sit down / bend down / lie down：
「座る / 腰を曲げる / 横になる」
- I **bent down** to tie my shoes.

turn ~ down：「～を下げる，弱める」
- The oven is too hot. **Turn** it **down** to 325 degrees.

B

tear down, cut down など：downは立っているものを倒す意味を動詞に加えます。

tear down ~：「～(建物) を解体する」
cut down ~：「～(木) を切り倒す」
blow ~ down：「～を吹き倒す」
- Some old houses were **torn down** to make room for the new shopping mall.
- *A:* Why did you **cut down** the tree in your yard?
  B: I didn't. It was **blown down** in the storm last week.

burn down：「火事で倒壊する，全焼する」
- They were able to put out the fire before the house **burned down**.

C

down：downは動詞に少しずつ大きさが小さくなったり，持っている**量が減る**意味を加えます。

slow down：「スピードを落とす」
- You're driving too fast. **Slow down**.

calm (~) down：「落ち着く，～を落ち着かせる」
- **Calm down**. There's no point in getting mad.

cut down (on ~)：「(～を食べたり，飲んだり，したりする回数を) 減らす」
- I'm trying to **cut down on** coffee. I drink too much of it.

D

動詞 + down の形を作るその他の句動詞

break down：「(機械，自動車が) 故障する」
- The car **broke down** and I had to call for help.

会議や話し合いなどについて，「決裂する，物別れになる」を表すこともあります。
- Talks between the two groups **broke down** without a solution being reached.
  (⇒ 話し合いは物別れになった)

close down：「商売を中止する，閉店する，廃業する」
- There used to be a shop on this street; it **closed down** a few years ago.

let ~ down：「(期待通りのことをしなかったため) ～を失望させる」
- You can always rely on Pete. He'll never **let** you **down**.

turn ~ down：「～(応募，申請，提案) を断る，取り下げる」
- I applied for several jobs, but I was **turned down** for all of them.
- Rachel was offered the job, but she decided to **turn** it **down**.

write ~ down：「(後から情報が必要になるかもしれないので) ～を紙に書き留める」
- I can't remember Tim's address. I **wrote** it **down**, but I can't find it.

句動詞 1（句動詞とは何か？）➲ Unit 134　　動詞 + up の形のその他の句動詞 ➲ Units 140–141

Exercises

139.1 状況に合うように以下から適切な動詞を選び，後に **up** もしくは **down** を付けた句動詞にして文を完成しなさい。

calm　let　put　~~take~~　turn　turn

1. I don't like this picture on the wall. I'm going to *take it down* .
2. The music is too loud. Can you ______________________________ ?
3. David was very angry. I tried to ______________________________ .
4. I've bought some new curtains. Can you help me ______________________________ ?
5. I promised I would help Anna. I don't want to ______________________________ .
6. I was offered the job, but I decided I didn't want it. So I ______________________________ .

139.2 空所に「動詞 + **up**」もしくは「動詞 + **down**」の形の句動詞を入れて，イラストの状況を説明する文を完成しなさい（必要に応じて語を追加すること）。

1. There used to be a tree in front of the house, but we *cut it down* .
2. There used to be some shelves on the wall, but I ______________________ .
3. The ceiling was so low, he couldn't ______________________ straight.
4. She couldn't hear the radio very well, so she ______________________ .
5. While they were waiting for the bus, they ______________________ on the ground.
6. A lot of trees ______________________ in the storm last week.
7. Sarah gave me her phone number. I ______________________ on a piece of paper.
8. Liz dropped her keys, so she ______________________ and ______________________ .

139.3 状況に合うように，「動詞 + **down**」の形の句動詞を空所に入れて文を完成しなさい（動詞は適切な形に変えること）。

1. I stopped writing and *put down* my pen.
2. I was really upset. It took me a long time to ______________________ .
3. The train ______________________ as it approached the station.
4. Sarah applied for medical school, but she ______________________ .
5. Our car is very reliable. It has never ______________________ .
6. I need to spend less money. I'm going to ______________ on things I don't really need.
7. I didn't play very well. I felt that I had ______________ the other players on the team.
8. The shop ______________________ because it was losing money.
9. This is a very ugly building. Many people would like it to ______________________ .
10. I don't understand why you ______________________ the chance to work abroad for a year. It would have been a great experience.
11. Unfortunately, the house ______________________ before the fire department got there, but no one was hurt.
12. The strike is going to continue. Talks between the two sides have ______________________ without agreement.

補充問題 37–41 (pp. 317–318)

UNIT 140

句動詞 7: up (1)

A

go up / come up / walk up (to ~) :「(~に) 近づく」
- A man **came up to** me in the street and asked me for money.

catch up (with ~) :「前を行く人より速く動いて(~に) 追いつく」
- I'm not ready to go yet. You go on and I'll **catch up with** you.

keep up (with ~) :「速度やレベルを保って(~に) ついて行く」
- You're walking too fast. I can't **keep up** (**with** you).
- You're doing well. **Keep** it **up**!

B

set up ~ :「~(組織，会社，事業，システム，ホームページなど) を立ち上げる，セットアップする」
- The government has **set up** a committee to investigate the problem.

take up ~ :「~(趣味，スポーツ，活動など) を始める」
- Laura **took up** photography a few years ago. She takes really good pictures.

C

grow up :「成長する」
- Sara was born in Mexico but **grew up** in the United States.

bring up ~ :「~(子ども) を育てる，世話をする」
- Her parents died when she was a child, so she was **brought up** by her grandparents.

D

back up

back ~ up :「~(人) を支援する，助ける」
- Will you **back** me **up** if I tell the police what happened?
(⇒ 私が嘘をついていないと言ってください)

back up ~ :「~(コンピュータのファイル)をバックアップする，コピーを作成する」
- You've spent a long time on that document; you'd better **back up** your files.

back up ~ :「~(自動車)をバックで動かす，後退させる」
- I couldn't turn around in the narrow street. I had to **back** the car **up** for a block.

交通が「渋滞する，動かなくなる」を表すこともあります。
- Cars are **backed up** for a mile at the entrance to the stadium.

E

end up ~ / end up doing ~ :「最後は~で終わる，結局~になる」
- There was a fight in the street and three men **ended up** in the hospital.
(⇒ 最後には，3 人の男が病院送りとなった)
- I couldn't find a hotel and **ended up** sleeping on a bench at the station.
(⇒ 最後には，駅のベンチで寝ていた)

give up:「あきらめる」/ **give ~ up:**「~をやめる，放棄する」
- Don't **give up**. Keep trying!
- Ted failed his driving test at age 80, so he had to **give up** driving. (⇒ 運転をやめる)

make up ~ :「~を構成する」/ be **made up of ~ :**「~から成り立つ，~で作られる」
- Children under 16 **make up** half the population of the city.
(⇒ 人口の半分が 16 歳以下の子ども)
- Air is **made up** mainly **of** nitrogen and oxygen. (⇒ 窒素と酸素でできている)

take up ~ :「~(空間，時間) を使う，占める」
- Most of the space in the room was **taken up** by a large table.

turn up / show up :「到着する，現れる」
- We arranged to meet Dave last night, but he didn't **turn up**.

use ~ up :「~を何も残らないように使い切る」
- I'm going to make some soup. I want to **use up** the vegetables I have.

句動詞 1 (句動詞とは何か?) ➲Unit 134　動詞 + up の形のその他の句動詞 ➲Units 139, 141

Exercises

140.1 空所にセクション A の中の動詞を含む 3 語からなる語句を入れて，イラストの状況を説明する文を完成しなさい。

1. A man __came up to__ me in the street and asked me the way to the station.
2. Sue ____________________ the front door of the house and rang the doorbell.
3. Tom was a long way behind the other runners, but he managed to ____________________ them.
4. Tanya was running too fast for Paul. He couldn't ____________________ her.

140.2 状況に合うように以下から適切な動詞を選び，後に up を付けた句動詞にして文を完成しなさい。

back ~~**end**~~ **end** **give** **give** **grow** **make** **take** **take** **turn** **use**

1. I couldn't find a hotel and __ended up__ sleeping on a bench at the station.
2. I'm feeling very tired now. I've ____________________ all my energy.
3. I hadn't ____________________ my files and my computer crashed. I lost everything I was working on.
4. People often ask children what they want to be when they ____________________ .
5. We invited Tim to the party, but he didn't ____________________ .
6. Two years ago Mark ____________________ his studies to be a professional basketball player.
7. *A:* Do you play any sports?
   B: Not right now, but I'm thinking of ____________________ tennis.
8. You don't have enough determination. You ____________________ too easily.
9. Karen traveled a lot for a few years and ____________________ in Canada, where she still lives.
10. I do a lot of gardening. It ____________________ most of my free time.
11. There are two universities in the city, and students ____________________ 20 percent of the population.

140.3 状況に合うように以下から適切な動詞を選び，後に up を付けた句動詞にして文を完成しなさい（必要に応じてその他の語を追加すること）。

back **back** **bring** ~~**catch**~~ ~~**give**~~ **go** **keep** **keep** **make** **set**

1. Sue was on the volleyball team, but she got injured and had to __give it up__ .
2. I'm not ready yet. You go on and I'll __catch up with__ you.
3. Helen has her own Web site. A friend of hers helped her to ____________________ .
4. Steven is having problems at school. He can't ____________________ the rest of the class.
5. Although I ____________________ in the country, I have always preferred cities.
6. Our team started the game well, but we couldn't ____________________ , and in the end we lost.
7. Traffic has been ____________________ on this road for an hour. Is there another way to go?
8. I saw Mike at the party, so I ____________________ him and said hello.
9. When I was on my trip, I joined a tour group. The group ____________________ two Americans, three Germans, five Italians, and myself.
10. "I agree with your solution and will give you my support." "Thanks for ____________________ ."

補充問題 37–41 (pp. 317–318)

UNIT 141

句動詞 8：up (2)

A

bring up ～：「～（話題，提案，問題）を言い出す，持ち出す」
- I don't want to hear any more about this issue. Please don't **bring** it **up** again.

come up：「話題に上がる，会話や会議で取り上げられる」
- Some interesting issues **came up** in our discussion yesterday.

come up with ～：「～(アイディア，提案）を思いつく，考え出す」
- Sarah is very creative. She's always **coming up with** new ideas.

make ～ up：「～をでっち上げる，真実ではないものを作り上げる」
- What Kevin told you about himself wasn't true. He **made** it all **up**.

B

cheer up：「元気になる，気持が高まる」/ **cheer ～ up：**「～を励ます，元気づける」
- You look so sad! **Cheer up**!
- Helen is depressed these days. What can we do to **cheer her up**?

save up for ～ / to do . . . :「～を買うために」/「…するために，お金を貯める」
- Dan is **saving up** for a trip around the world.

clear up：「天気が晴れる，明るくなる」
- It was raining when I got up, but it **cleared up** during the morning.

C

blow up：「爆発する」/ **blow ～ up：**「～を爆弾などで吹き飛ばす，破壊する」
- The engine caught fire and **blew up**.
- The bridge was **blown up** during the war.

tear ～ up：「～をびりびりに裂く，ずたずたに引き裂く」
- I didn't read the letter. I just **tore** it **up** and threw it away.

beat ～ up：「～をめった打ちにする，～を何度もなぐりひどいけがを負わせる」
- A friend of mine was attacked and **beaten up** a few days ago. He was badly hurt and had to go to the hospital.

D

break up / split up (with ～)**：**「(～と）別れる，離婚する」
- I'm surprised to hear that Sue and Paul have **split up**. They seemed very happy together the last time I saw them.

clean ～ up：「～をきれいにする，片づける，整頓する」
- Look at this mess! Who is going to **clean** it **up**?

fix up ～：「～（建物，部屋，自動車など）を修理する，元通りにする」
- I love how you've **fixed up** this room. It looks so much nicer.

look ～ up in a . . . **：**「～（語句）を…（辞書，百科事典など）で引く，探す」
- If you don't know the meaning of a word, you can **look** it **up** in a dictionary.

put up with ～：「～に耐える，我慢する」
- We live on a busy road, so we have to **put up with** a lot of noise from the traffic.

hold up ～：「～（人，計画，移動）を止める，妨げる，遅らせる」
- Don't wait for me. I don't want to **hold** you **up**.
- Plans to build a new factory have been **held up** because of the company's financial problems.

mix up ～ / get ～ mixed up：「～（人，物）を混同する，間違える」
- The two brothers look very similar. Many people **mix** them **up**.
(= . . . **get** them **mixed up**, ⇒ 兄と弟を間違える）

句動詞 1（句動詞とは何か？）➲Unit 134　動詞＋up の形のその他の句動詞 ➲Units 139–140

Exercises

141.1 左欄の 1〜7 の文の後にくる語句を，右欄の A〜G の中から 1 つ選びなさい。

1. I'm going to tear up	A a new camera	1. *F*
2. Jane came up with	B a lot of bad weather	2. ______
3. Paul is always making up	C the two medicines	3. ______
4. Be careful not to mix up	D an interesting suggestion	4. ______
5. I don't think you should bring up	E excuses	5. ______
6. I'm saving up for	F ~~the letter~~	6. ______
7. We had to put up with	G that subject	7. ______

141.2 空所に 2〜3 語からなる語句を入れて，イラストの状況を説明する文を完成しなさい。

1.

The weather was horrible this morning, but it's *cleared up* now.

2.

Linda was late because she was ______________________ by the traffic.

3.

They bought an old house and ______________ ___________ . It's really nice now.

4.

Pete was really depressed. We took him out for dinner to ______________________ .

141.3 空所に「動詞 + up」の句動詞を入れて，文を完成しなさい（必要に応じてその他の語を追加すること）。

1. I love how you've *fixed up* this room. It looks so much nicer.
2. The ship ______________________ and sank. The cause of the explosion was never discovered.
3. Two men have been arrested after a man was ______________________ outside a restaurant last night. The injured man was taken to the hospital.
4. "Is Robert still going out with Tina?" "No, they've ______________________ ."
5. An interesting question ______________________ in class today.
6. The weather is terrible this morning, isn't it? I hope it ______________________ later.
7. I wanted to call Chris, but I dialed Laura's number by mistake. I got their phone numbers ______________________ .

141.4 空所に「動詞 + up」の句動詞を入れて，文を完成しなさい（必要に応じてその他の語を追加すること）。

1. Don't wait for me. I don't want to *hold you up* .
2. I don't know what this word means. I'll have to ______________________ .
3. There's nothing we can do about the problem. We'll just have to ______________________ it.
4. "Was that story true?" "No, I ______________________ ."
5. I think we should follow Tom's suggestion. Nobody has ______________________ a better plan.
6. I hate this photo of me. I'm going to ______________________ .
7. I'm trying to spend less money these days. I'm ______________________ a trip to Australia.
8. After the party, my place was a mess. Some friends helped me ______________________ .

補充問題 37–41 (pp. 317–318)

UNIT 142

句動詞 9：away/back

A

☆ away と back は，どのように異なりますか？

away

➤ 自分の家から離れて

- We're **going away** on a trip today.

➤ 場所・人・物から離れて

- The woman got into her car and **drove away**.
- I tried to take a picture of the bird, but it **flew away**.
- I dropped the ticket and it **blew away** in the wind.
- The police searched the house and **took away** a computer.

その他，**walk away**（歩き去る），**run away**（走り去る），**look away**（目をそらす）のような句動詞もよく用いられます。

back

➤ 自分の家に帰る

- We'll **be back** in three weeks.

➤ 場所・人・物に戻る

- *A:* I'm going out now.
  B: What time will you **be back**?
- After eating at a restaurant, we **walked back** to our hotel.
- I've still got Jane's keys. I forgot to **give** them **back** to her.
- When you're finished with that book, can you **put** it **back** on the shelf?

その他，**go back**（戻る），**come back**（帰る），**get back**（回復する），**take ~ back**（~を戻す）のような句動詞もよく用いられます。

B

動詞 + away の形を作るその他の句動詞

get away：「逃げる，難しい状況を解決せずに放置する」

- We tried to catch the thief, but he managed to **get away**.

get away with ~：「良くないことをしながら罰を受けないままでいる，受けずに逃げる」

- I parked in a no-parking zone, but I **got away with** it.

keep away (from ~)：「（~から）離れる，遠ざかる」

- **Keep away from** the edge of the pool. You might fall in.

give ~ away：「もはや必要なくなったので~を無料で与える，寄贈する」

- "Did you sell your old computer?" "No, I **gave** it **away**."

put ~ away：「収納すべき場所へと目につかないように片づける，しまう」

- When the children had finished playing with their toys, they **put** them **away**.

throw ~ away：「ごみとして~を捨てる」

- I kept the letter, but I **threw away** the envelope.

C

動詞 + back の形を作るその他の句動詞

wave back：「手を振り返す」/ **smile back**：「ほほえみ返す」/ **shout back**：「どなり返す」/ **write back**：「返事を書く」/ **hit ~ back**：「~をなぐり返す」

- I waved to her and she **waved back**.

call/phone (~) back：「（~に）電話を返す，折り返し電話する」

- I can't talk to you now. I'll **call** you **back** in 10 minutes.

get back to ~：「~に電話や電子メールなどで返事をする」

- I sent him an e-mail, but he never **got back to** me.

look back (on ~)：「（過去に起こった~を）思い返す，振り返る」

- My first job was at a travel agency. I didn't like it very much at the time but, **looking back on** it, I learned a lot, and it was a very useful experience.

pay back ~：「~（お金）を返す」/ **pay ~ back**：「~（人）にお金を返す」

- If you borrow money, you have to **pay** it **back**.
- Thanks for lending me the money. I'll **pay** you **back** next week.

句動詞 1（句動詞とは何か？）➲ Unit 134

Exercises

142.1 状況に合うように，空所に適切な動詞を正しい形に変えて入れ，文を完成しなさい。

1. The woman got into her car and *drove* away.
2. Here's the money you need. ______________ me back when you can.
3. Don't ______________ that box away. It could be useful.
4. Jane doesn't do anything at work. I don't know how she ______________ away with it.
5. I'm going out now. I'll ______________ back at about 10:30.
6. You should think more about the future; don't ______________ back all the time.
7. Gary is very generous. He won some money in the lottery and ______________ it all away.
8. I'll ______________ back to you as soon as I have the information you need.

142.2 状況に合うように，空所に「動詞 + away」の句動詞を入れて文を完成しなさい。

1. I was away all day yesterday. I *got back* very late.
2. I haven't seen our neighbors for a while. I think they must ______________ .
3. "I'm going out now." "OK. What time will you ______________ ?"
4. A man was trying to break into a car. When he saw me, he ______________ .
5. I smiled at him, but he didn't ______________ .
6. If you cheat on the exam, you might ______________ with it. But you might get caught.
7. Be careful! That's an electric fence. ______________ from it.

142.3 空所に適切な語句を入れて，イラストの状況を説明する文を完成しなさい。

1. She waved to him, and he *waved back* .	2. It was windy. I dropped a $20 bill and it ______________ .	3. Sue — Sue opened the letter, read it, and ______________ in the envelope.
4. He tried to talk to her, but she just ______________ .	5. Ellie / Ben — Ellie threw the ball to Ben, and he ______________ .	6. His shoes were worn out, so he ______________ .

142.4 状況に合うように，（　）内の動詞を用いて「動詞 + away」の句動詞を作り，空所に入れて文を完成しなさい。

1. *A:* Do you still have my keys?
   B: No. Don't you remember? I *gave them back* to you yesterday. (give)
2. *A:* Do you want this magazine?
   B: No, I'm finished with it. You can ______________ . (throw)
3. *A:* How are your new jeans? Do they fit you OK?
   B: No, I'm going to ______________ to the shop. (take)
4. *A:* Here's the money you asked me to lend you.
   B: Thanks. I'll ______________ as soon as I can. (pay)
5. *A:* What happened to all the books you used to have?
   B: I didn't want them any more, so I ______________ . (give)
6. *A:* Did you call Sarah?
   B: She wasn't there. I left a message asking her to ______________ . (call)

補充問題 37-41 (pp. 317-318)

付録 1

規則動詞と不規則動詞

➤ 動詞の過去形と過去分詞形は，どのように作りますか？

1.1 規則動詞

語尾に **-ed** を付けて，単純過去形と過去分詞形のできる動詞を規則動詞と呼びます。

原形	clean	finish	use	paint	stop	carry
単純過去形 過去分詞形	cleaned	finished	used	painted	stopped	carried

-ed を付けて規則変化する動詞を作る際のつづり方の規則 ➲ 付録 6

I cleaned / they finished / she carried などの単純過去形 ➲ Unit 5

過去完了形は，完了時制と受動態の構文で用います。

完了時制 (**have**/**has**/**had** cleaned):

- I **have cleaned** the windows.（現在完了形 ➲ Units 7–9）
- They were still working. They **hadn't finished**.（過去完了形 ➲ Unit 14）

受動態 (**is** clean**ed** / **was** clean**ed** など):

- He **was carried** out of the room.（単純過去形）
- This gate has just **been painted**.（現在完了形）

➲ Units 40–42

1.2 不規則動詞

I saw/ I have seen の **saw**（単純過去形）や **seen**（過去分詞形）のように，語尾に **-ed** を付けて単純過去形と過去分詞形を作ることのできない動詞を不規則動詞と呼びます。不規則動詞は次のように分類できます。

・**A-A-A: hit-hit-hit** のように，原形，単純過去形，過去分詞形の **3** つの形が同じになる。

- Don't **hit** me.（原形）
- Somebody **hit** me as I came into the room.（単純過去形）
- I've never **hit** anybody in my life.（過去分詞形—現在完了形）
- George was **hit** on the head by a stone.（過去分詞形—受動態）

・**A-B-B: tell-told-told** のように，原形とは異なるものの単純過去形と過去分詞形が同じ形になる。

- Can you **tell** me what to do?（原形）
- She **told** me to come back the next day.（単純過去形）
- Have you **told** anybody about your new job?（過去分詞形—現在完了形）
- I was **told** to come back the next day.（過去分詞形—受動態）

・**A-B-C: wake-woke-woken** のように，原形，単純過去形，過去分詞形ですべて形が異なる。

- I'll **wake** you up.（原形）
- I **woke** up in the middle of the night.（単純過去形）
- The baby has **woken** up.（過去分詞形—現在完了形）
- I was **woken** up by a loud noise.（過去分詞形—受動態）

1.3 不規則動詞変化表：表以外の動詞で不規則変化するものはありません。表にない動詞は規則変化します。

原形	単純過去形	過去分詞形
be	was/were	been
beat	beat	beaten
become	became	become
begin	began	begun
bend	bent	bent
bet	bet	bet
bite	bit	bitten

原形	単純過去形	過去分詞形
blow	blew	blown
break	broke	broken
bring	brought	brought
broadcast	broadcast	broadcast
build	built	built
burst	burst	burst
buy	bought	bought

原形	単純過去形	過去分詞形
catch	caught	caught
choose	chose	chosen
come	came	come
cost	cost	cost
creep	crept	crept
cut	cut	cut
deal	dealt	dealt
dig	dug	dug
do	did	done
draw	drew	drawn
drink	drank	drunk
drive	drove	driven
eat	ate	eaten
fall	fell	fallen
feed	fed	fed
feel	felt	felt
fight	fought	fought
find	found	found
fit	fit	fit
flee	fled	fled
fly	flew	flown
forbid	forbade	forbidden
forget	forgot	forgotten
forgive	forgave	forgiven
freeze	froze	frozen
get	got	gotten
give	gave	given
go	went	gone
grow	grew	grown
hang	hung	hung
have	had	had
hear	heard	heard
hide	hid	hidden
hit	hit	hit
hold	held	held
hurt	hurt	hurt
keep	kept	kept
kneel	knelt	knelt
know	knew	known
lay	laid	laid
lead	led	led
leave	left	left
lend	lent	lent
let	let	let
lie	lay	lain
light	lit/lighted	lit/lighted
lose	lost	lost
make	made	made
mean	meant	meant
meet	met	met
pay	paid	paid
put	put	put

原形	単純過去形	過去分詞形
quit	quit	quit
read	read [red]*	read [red]*
ride	rode	ridden
ring	rang	rung
rise	rose	risen
run	ran	run
say	said	said
see	saw	seen
seek	sought	sought
sell	sold	sold
send	sent	sent
set	set	set
sew	sewed	sewn/sewed
shake	shook	shaken
shine	shone/shined	shone/shined
shoot	shot	shot
show	showed	shown/showed
shrink	shrank	shrunk
shut	shut	shut
sing	sang	sung
sink	sank	sunk
sit	sat	sat
sleep	slept	slept
slide	slid	slid
speak	spoke	spoken
spend	spent	spent
spit	spit/spat	spit/spat
split	split	split
spread	spread	spread
spring	sprang	sprung
stand	stood	stood
steal	stole	stolen
stick	stuck	stuck
sting	stung	stung
stink	stank	stunk
strike	struck	struck
swear	swore	sworn
sweep	swept	swept
swim	swam	swum
swing	swung	swung
take	took	taken
teach	taught	taught
tear	tore	torn
tell	told	told
think	thought	thought
throw	threw	thrown
understand	understood	understood
wake	woke	woken
wear	wore	worn
weep	wept	wept
win	won	won
write	wrote	written

* 発音記号

付録 2
現在時制と過去時制

☆ 現在時制と過去時制には，どのような動詞の形がありますか？

	単純形	進行形
現在形	I **do** 単純現在形 ➲ Units 2–4 ■ Ann often **plays** tennis. ■ I **work** in a bank, but **I don't enjoy** it much. ■ **Do** you **like** parties? ■ It **doesn't rain** so much in summer.	I **am doing** 現在進行形 ➲ Units 1, 3–4 ■ "Where's Ann?" "She**'s playing** tennis." ■ Please don't disturb me now. **I'm working**. ■ Hello. **Are** you **enjoying** the party? ■ It isn't **raining** right now.
現在完了形	I **have done** 単純現在完了形 ➲ Units 7–9, 11–13 ■ Ann **has played** tennis many times. ■ Where's Tom? **Have** you **seen** him this morning? ■ How long **have** you and Chris **known** each other? ■ *A:* Is it still raining? *B:* No, it **has stopped**. ■ I'm hungry. I **haven't eaten** anything since breakfast.	I **have been doing** 現在完了進行形 ➲ Units 10–13 ■ Ann is tired. She **has been playing** tennis. ■ You're out of breath. **Have** you **been running**? ■ How long **have** you **been studying** English? ■ It's still raining. It **has been raining** all day. ■ I **haven't been feeling** well recently. Maybe I should go to the doctor.
過去形	I **did** 単純過去形 ➲ Units 5–6, 8–9 ■ Ann **played** tennis yesterday afternoon. ■ **I lost** my key a few days ago. ■ There was a movie on TV last night, but we **didn't watch** it. ■ What **did** you **do** when you finished work yesterday?	I **was doing** 過去進行形 ➲ Unit 6 ■ I saw Ann at the park yesterday. She **was playing** tennis. ■ I dropped my key when I **was trying** to open the door. ■ The television was on, but we **weren't watching** it. ■ What **were** you **doing at** this time yesterday?
過去完了形	I **had done** 過去完了形 ➲ Unit 14 ■ It wasn't her first game of tennis. She **had played** many times before. ■ They couldn't get into the house because they **had lost** the key. ■ The house was dirty because I **hadn't cleaned** it for weeks.	I **had been doing** 過去完了進行形 ➲ Unit 15 ■ Ann was tired last night because she **had been playing** tennis in the afternoon. ■ George decided to go to the doctor because he **hadn't been feeling** well.

受動態 ➲ Units 40–42

付録 3
未来

☆ 未来を表す動詞の形には，どのようなものがありますか？ それぞれはどのように異なりますか？

3.1 未来を表す動詞の形

■ **I'm leaving tomorrow.**	現在進行形	➲ Unit 18A
■ My train **leaves** at 9:30.	単純現在形	➲ Unit 18B
■ **I'm going to leave** tomorrow.	**(be) going to**	➲ Units 19, 22
■ **I'll leave** tomorrow.	**will**	➲ Units 20–22
■ **I'll be leaving** tomorrow.	未来進行形	➲ Unit 23
■ **I'll have left** by this time tomorrow.	未来完了形	➲ Unit 23
■ I hope to see you before I **leave** tomorrow.	単純現在形	➲ Unit 24

3.2 さまざまな未来の動作と動詞の形

現在進行形：すでに計画し準備した未来の動作。

- ■ **I'm leaving** tomorrow. I've got my plane ticket.（⇒ 出発することを計画して準備した）
- ■ "When **are** they **getting** married?" "On July 24."

単純現在形：交通機関の時刻表や映画のプログラムなどのように，予定が組まれている未来の動作。

- ■ My train **leaves** at 11:30.（⇒ 時刻表上の情報）
- ■ What time **does** the movie **start**?

(be) going to + 動詞の原形：「…するつもり」のように，すでに決心している未来の動作。

- ■ I've decided not to stay here any longer. **I'm going to leave** tomorrow.
  (= I'm leaving tomorrow. この意味は現在進行形でも表せます。➲Unit 19B)
- ■ "Your shoes are dirty." "Yes, I know. **I'm going to clean** them."

will ('ll)：話している時点で，「私は…する，…しよう」と決めたり同意した未来の動作。

- ■ *A:* I don't want you to stay here any longer.
  B: OK. **I'll leave** tomorrow.（⇒ Bは話している時に「出ていく」と決心した）
- ■ That bag looks heavy. **I'll help** you with it.
- ■ I **won't tell** anybody what happened. I promise. (**won't = will not**)

3.3 未来の出来事や状況を表す動詞の形

will do ... / will be ...：「…するだろう / …となるだろう」のように，未来の出来事や状況を予測します。

- ■ I don't think John is happy at work. I think he**'ll leave** soon.
- ■ This time next year **I'll be** in Japan. Where **will** you **be**?

(be) going to + 動詞の原形：現在の状況から考えられる未来の出来事を表します。

- ■ Look at those black clouds. It**'s going to rain**.（⇒ 今，見える雲から雨が降ると予測できる）

3.4 未来進行形と未来完了形

will be -ing：「…しているところだろう」のように，未来に進行していると予測できる動作。

- ■ This time next week I'll be on vacation. **I'll be lying** on a beach or **swimming** in the ocean.

will be -ing：「…する」のように，自然に未来に始まり完結する動作を表すことがあります。➲Unit 23C

- ■ What time **will** you **be leaving** tomorrow?

will have 過去分詞：未来の1時点までに完了していることが予測できる動作。

- ■ I won't be here this time tomorrow. **I'll have** already **left**.

3.5 when/if/while/before などの節の内部では，未来の動作や出来事を現在形で表します。➲Unit 24

- ■ I hope to see you **before** I **leave** tomorrow. (× before I will leave)
- ■ **When** you **are** in New York again, come and see us. (× When you will be)
- ■ **If** we **don't hurry**, we'll be late.

付録 4
法助動詞（can/could/will/would など）

ここでは法助動詞が作る形と大まかな意味を確認します。それぞれの法助動詞に関するより詳しい解説については，Units 25–35 を参照してください。

4.1 以下の法助動詞は，どのような活動を表しますか？

can **could**	■ I **can go** out tonight.（⇒ …することに何ら問題がない） ■ I **can't go** out tonight. ■ I **could go** out tonight, but I don't feel like it. ■ I **couldn't go** out last night.（= I wasn't able）
can = **may**	■ **Can** / **May** } I **go** out tonight?（⇒ …することを許してくれますか？）
will/won't **would**	■ I think **I'll go** out tonight. ■ I promise I **won't go** out. ■ I **would go** out tonight, but I have too much to do. ■ I promised I **wouldn't go** out.
should/shall	■ **Should** we **go** out tonight?（= **Shall** we . . .） （⇒ …するのがよいと思いますか？〔疑問文〕）
should = **ought to**	■ I { **should** / **ought to** } **go** out tonight.（⇒ …するのがよいでしょう）

could/would/should + have + 過去分詞は，どのような出来事を表しますか？

could **would** **should**	■ I **could have gone** out last night, but I decided to stay at home. ■ I **would have gone** out last night, but I had too much to do. ■ I **should have gone** out last night. I'm sorry I didn't.

4.2 will/would/may などの法助動詞は，出来事が起こる可能性や確実性を表します。

will **would**	■ "What time **will** she **be** here?"　"She**'ll be** here soon." ■ She **would be** here now, but she's been delayed.
should = **ought to**	■ She { **should** / **ought to** } **be** here soon.（⇒ 間もなくここに来るはずだ）
may = **might** = **could**	■ She { **may** / **might** / **could** } **be** here now. I'm not sure.（⇒ ここにいるかもしれない）
must **can't**	■ She **must be** here. I saw her come in. ■ She **must not be** here. I've looked everywhere for her. ■ She **can't be** here. I know for sure she is away on vacation.

would/should/might/could など + have + 過去分詞は，どのような出来事を表しますか？

will **would**	■ She **will have arrived** by now.（⇒ 今頃は到着しただろう） ■ She **would have arrived** earlier, but she was delayed.
should	■ I wonder where she is. She **should have arrived** by now.
may = **might** = **could**	■ She { **may** / **might** / **could** } **have arrived**. I'm not sure.（⇒ 到着したかもしれない）
must **couldn't**	■ She **must have arrived** by now.（⇒ 到着したに違いない） ■ She **couldn't have arrived** yet. It's much too early. （⇒ 到着したことはありえない）

付録 5
短縮形（I'm/you've/didn't など）

5.1 英語の**話しことば**では，普通 I am / you have / did not などの形の代わりに，**I'm/you've/didn't** などの**短縮形**（縮約形）を用います。このような短縮形は，友人への手紙や連絡などのくだけた**書きことば**でも用いますが，学校に提出する小論文や仕事上の報告書などでは短縮形ではない形を用います。

短縮形では以下のように，省略した文字を**アポストロフィ(')**で表記します:

I'm = I am　you've = you have　didn't = did not

5.2 主な短縮形

'm = am	I**'m**						
's = is / has		he**'s**	she**'s**	it**'s**			
're = are					you**'re**	we**'re**	they**'re**
've = have	I**'ve**				you**'ve**	we**'ve**	they**'ve**
'll = will	I**'ll**	he**'ll**	she**'ll**		you**'ll**	we**'ll**	they**'ll**
'd = would / had	I**'d**	he**'d**	she**'d**		you**'d**	we**'d**	they**'d**

's = is/has

- She**'s** sick. (= She **is** sick.)
- She**'s** gone away. (= She **has** gone)

ただし，**'s** の形をしていても let**'s** は let **us** の短縮形です。

- Let**'s** go now. (= Let **us** go)

'd = would/had

- I**'d** see a doctor if I were you. (= I **would** see)
- I**'d** never seen her before. (= I **had** never seen)

's や **'d** のような**短縮形**を，**who/what** のような疑問詞や **that/there/here** のような語と組み合わせてよく用います。ことに **'s** をよく用います。

who**'s**　what**'s**　where**'s**　how**'s**　that**'s**　there**'s**　here**'s**　who**'ll**　there**'ll**　who**'d**

- Who**'s** that woman over there? (= who **is**)
- What**'s** happened? (= what **has**)
- Do you think there**'ll** be many people at the party? (= there **will**)

名詞の後でも**短縮形**（ことに **'s**）を使うことがあります。

- Catherine**'s** going out tonight. (= Catherine **is**)
- My best friend**'s** just gotten married. (= My best friend **has**)

文の終わりに置かれた動詞には**強勢**が与えられ，強く発音されます。この位置では 'm/'s/'re/'ve/'ll/'d のような**短縮形**は用いません。

- "Are you tired?"　"Yes, I **am**." (× Yes, I'm.)
- Do you know where she **is**? (× Do you know where she's?)

5.3 否定（not）の意味を持つ短縮形

isn't	(= is not)	**don't**	(= do not)	**haven't**	(= have not)
aren't	(= are not)	**doesn't**	(= does not)	**hasn't**	(= has not)
wasn't	(= was not)	**didn't**	(= did not)	**hadn't**	(= had not)
weren't	(= were not)				
can't	(= cannot)	**couldn't**	(= could not)		
won't	(= will not)	**wouldn't**	(= would not)		
		shouldn't	(= should not)		

is と **are** の**否定の短縮形**には，以下の 2 通りが可能です。

he **isn't** / she **isn't** / it **isn't**　=　he**'s not** / she**'s not** / it**'s not**

you **aren't** / we **aren't** / they **aren't**　=　you**'re not** / we**'re not** / they**'re not**

付録 6
つづり

6.1 名詞，動詞，形容詞は，次のような語尾を持ちます。

名詞 ＋ -s/-es（複数形）	book**s**	idea**s**	match**es**
動詞 ＋ -s/-es（he/she/it が主語）	work**s**	enjoy**s**	wash**es**
動詞 ＋ -ing	work**ing**	enjoy**ing**	wash**ing**
動詞 ＋ -ed	work**ed**	enjoy**ed**	wash**ed**
形容詞 ＋ -er（比較級）	cheap**er**	quick**er**	bright**er**
形容詞 ＋ -est（最上級）	cheap**est**	quick**est**	bright**est**
形容詞 ＋ -ly（副詞）	cheap**ly**	quick**ly**	bright**ly**

名詞と動詞には -s と -es の 2 つの語尾があります。普通は -s の語尾を持ちますが，-es となる場合については **6.2**，もともとの語につづり上の変化が生じる場合については **6.3** 以降を参照してください。

6.2 -es の語尾を持つ名詞と動詞

-s, -ss, -sh, -ch, -x でつづられる語尾を持つ語は -es の語尾を持ちます。

bu**s**/bus**es**　　mi**ss**/miss**es**　　wa**sh**/wash**es**

mat**ch**/match**es**　　sear**ch**/search**es**　　bo**x**/box**es**

-o の語尾を持つ以下の語も -es の語尾を持ちます。語尾が -o で終わっていても photo—photos, piano—pianos のように変化する場合もあります。

potat**o**/potato**es**　　tomat**o**/tomat**oes**

do/do**es**　　go/go**es**

6.3 -y の語尾を持つ語 (baby, carry, easy など)

語が，子音字* + y（-by，-ry，-sy，-vy など）の語尾を持つ時

・**-s:** y を i に変えて -es を付けます。

bab**y**/bab**ies**　　stor**y**/stor**ies**　　countr**y**/countr**ies**　　secretar**y**/secretar**ies**
hurr**y**/hurr**ies**　　stud**y**/stud**ies**　　appl**y**/appl**ies**　　tr**y**/tr**ies**

・**-ed:** y を i に変えて -ed を付けます。

hurr**y**/hurr**ied**　　stud**y**/stud**ied**　　appl**y**/appl**ied**　　tr**y**/tr**ied**

・**-er, -est:** y を i に変えて -er, -est を付けます。

eas**y**/eas**ier**/eas**iest**　　heav**y**/heav**ier**/heav**iest**　　luck**y**/luck**ier**/luck**iest**

・**-ly:** y を i に変えて -ly を付けます。

eas**y**/eas**ily**　　heav**y**/heav**ily**　　temporar**y**/temporar**ily**

-y の語尾を持っていても -ing を付ける場合には，つづりを変えずに y をそのまま残します。

hurry**ing**　　study**ing**　　apply**ing**　　try**ing**

語が，母音字* + y（-ay, -ey. -oy, uy）の語尾の場合も y をそのまま残します。

pla**y**/pla**ys**/pla**yed**　　monk**ey**/monk**eys**　　enj**oy**/enj**oys**/enj**oyed**　　b**uy**/b**uys**

day—daily はこの例外です。また，pay—paid, lay—laid, say—said のような不規則変化動詞もこの規則には従いません。

6.4 -ie の語尾を持つ動詞 (die, lie, tie)

-ie の語尾を持つ動詞に -ing を付ける場合，-ie を y に変えて -ing を付けます。

die/d**ying**　　**lie**/l**ying**　　**tie**/t**ying**

*アルファベットの中で，a e i o u を母音字，それ以外の文字を子音字と呼びます。

6.5 -e の語尾を持つ語（hope, dance, wide など）

-e の語尾を持つ動詞

-e を取って -ing を付けます。

hop**e**/hop**ing**　smil**e**/smil**ing**　danc**e**/danc**ing**　confus**e**/confus**ing**

be—being は，この規則の例外です。また，-ee で終わる動詞も see—seeing，agree—agreeing のように，元の語につづりの変化は起こりません。

規則動詞を過去形にする場合には，-e を取って -ed を付けます。

hop**e**/hop**ed**　smil**e**/smil**ed**　danc**e**/danc**ed**　confus**e**/confus**ed**

-e の語尾を持つ形容詞と副詞

-e を取って -er, -est を付けて比較級，最上級にします。

wid**e**/wid**er**/wid**est**　lat**e**/lat**er**/lat**est**　larg**e**/larg**er**/larg**est**

-e の語尾を持つ形容詞は，語尾の -e を省略せずに -ly を付けて副詞にします。

polit**e**/polit**ely**　extrem**e**/extrem**ely**　absolut**e**/absolut**ely**

simple，terrible のように -le の語尾を持つ形容詞は，語尾の -e を取って -ply，-bly のような形の副詞にします。

sim**ple**/sim**ply**　terri**ble**/terri**bly**　reasona**ble**/reasona**bly**

6.6 語尾の子音字の 2 重化（stop — stopping — stopped, wet — wetter — wettest など）

以下のように，母音字 + 子音字の語尾を持つ語があります。

st**op**　pl**an**　r**ub**　b**ig**　w**et**　th**in**　pref**er**　regr**et**

このような語に -ing，-ed，-er，-est などの語尾を付ける場合，-p → -pp，-n → -nn のように語尾の子音字を重ねてつづります。

sto**p**	p → **pp**	sto**pp**ing	sto**pp**ed	bi**g**	g → **gg**	bi**gg**er	bi**gg**est
pla**n**	n → **nn**	pla**nn**ing	pla**nn**ed	we**t**	t → **tt**	we**tt**er	we**tt**est
ru**b**	b → **bb**	ru**bb**ing	ru**bb**ed	thi**n**	n → **nn**	thi**nn**er	thi**nn**est

prefer，begin などのように，語が 2 つ以上の音節を持ち，かつ，最終音節に強勢が置かれる場合，語尾の子音字を重ねてつづります。

preFER / prefe**rr**ing / prefe**rr**ed　perMIT / permi**tt**ing / permi**tt**ed
reGRET / regre**tt**ing / regre**tt**ed　beGIN / begi**nn**ing

最終音節に強勢が置かれない場合，語尾の子音字は重ねてつづりません。

VISit / visi**t**ing / visi**t**ed　deVELop / develo**p**ing / develo**p**ed
HAPpen / happe**n**ing / happe**n**ed　reMEMber / remembe**r**ing / remembe**r**ed

語尾の子音字の 2 重化に関するイギリス英語のつづり方 ➲ 付録 7

語尾の子音字の 2 重化に関連して，以下の事柄にも注意します。

・語が -rt，-lp，-ng などの 2 つの子音字で終わる場合，子音字の 2 重化は生じません。

sta**rt** / sta**rt**ing / sta**rt**ed　he**lp** / he**lp**ing / he**lp**ed　lo**ng** / lo**ng**er / lo**ng**est

・語が -oil，-eed などのように語尾の子音字の前に 2 つの母音字がある場合，子音字の 2 重化は生じません。

b**oil** / b**oil**ing / b**oil**ed　n**eed** / n**eed**ing / n**eed**ed　expl**ain** / expl**ain**ing / expl**ain**ed
ch**eap** / ch**eap**er / ch**eap**est　l**oud** / l**oud**er / l**oud**est　qu**iet** / qu**iet**er / qu**iet**est

・語尾の子音字が y や w の場合，母音として発音されるため子音字の 2 重化は生じません。

sta**y** / sta**y**ing / sta**y**ed　gro**w** / gro**w**ing　ne**w** / ne**w**er / ne**w**est

付録 7

アメリカ英語とイギリス英語

本書が記述するアメリカ英語（厳密には北アメリカ英語）とイギリス英語には，いくつかの文法上の違いがあります。

Unit	北アメリカ英語	イギリス英語
8A–C	今までなかったり，最近起きた出来事は，**単純過去形**と**現在完了形**の両方で記述できます。 ■ I **lost** my keys. **Did** you **see** them? = **I've lost** my keys. **Have** you **seen** them? ■ Sally isn't here. { She **went** out. / She**'s gone** out. **just**, **already**, **yet** は**単純過去形**の文にも，**現在完了形**の文にも生じます。 ■ I'm not hungry. { I **just had** lunch. / **I've just had** lunch. ■ *A:* What time is Mark leaving? *B:* { He **already left**. / He **has already left**. ■ **Did** you **finish** your work **yet**? = **Have** you **finished** your work **yet**?	今までなかったり，最近起きた出来事は，ふつう**現在完了形**で記述します。 ■ **I've lost** my keys. **Have** you **seen** them? ■ Sally isn't here. She**'s gone** out. **just**, **already**, **yet** は，ふつう**現在完了形**の文に生じます。 ■ I'm not hungry. **I've just had** lunch. ■ *A:* What time is Mark leaving? *B:* He **has already left**. ■ **Have** you **finished** your work **yet**?
27	**「…ないに違いない」**のように，何かではないことに十分確信が持てる場合に **must not** を用います。 ■ Their car isn't outside their house. They **must not** be at home. ■ She walked past me without speaking. She **must not** have seen me.	must not ではなく，**can't**（…ではあり得ない）を用います。 ■ Their car isn't outside their house. They **can't** be at home. ■ She walked past me without speaking. She **can't** have seen me.
32	**demand** や **insist** などを主動詞に持つ文の従属節中で，動詞を原形にする**仮定法**を用います。 ■ I **insisted** he **have** dinner with us.	従属節中で助動詞 **should** を用いたり，**単純現在形**や**単純過去形**を使います。 ■ I **insisted** that he **should have** dinner with us. = I **insisted** that he **had** dinner with us.
49B	**You have?** / **She isn't?** などのように**助動詞**で文を終え，相手のことばに興味があることを示します。 ■ *A:* Liz isn't feeling very well today. *B:* **She isn't?** What's wrong with her?	**Have you?** / **Isn't she?** などのように**助動詞**と**主語**を入れ替えます。 ■ *A:* Liz isn't feeling very well today. *B:* **Isn't she?** What's wrong with her?
70C, 122A	to/in **the hospital** のように **the** を付けます。 ■ Two people were taken to **the hospital** after the accident.	to/in **hospital** のように **the** は付けません。 ■ Two people were taken to **hospital** after the accident.
118A	**on the weekend** / **on weekends** ■ Will you be here **on the weekend**?	**at the weekend** / **at weekends** ■ Will you be here **at the weekend**?
121A	**in** the front / **in** the back ■ Let's sit **in** the front (of the movie theater).	**at** the front / **at** the back ■ Let's sit **at** the front (of the cinema).

Unit	北アメリカ英語	イギリス英語
128	**different from / different than** ■ It was **different from/than** what I'd expected.	**different from / different to** ■ It was **different from/to** what I'd expected.
134A	**動詞 + around** は句動詞を作りますが，動詞 + round のような句動詞は，普通用いません。 ■ He turned **around**.	**動詞 + around** も**動詞 + round** も句動詞として用います。 ■ He turned **round**. = He turned **around**.
134A–B	**get along** (**with** ～) ■ Do you **get along with** your boss?	**get on / get along** (**with** ～) ■ Do you **get on with** your boss? = . . . **get along with** your boss?
134C, 135C	**fill out**（書類など） ■ Could you **fill out** this form?	**fill in / fill out**（書類など） ■ Could you **fill in** this form? = . . . **fill out** this form?
139B	**tear down**（建物） ■ Some old houses were **torn down** to make room for a new shopping mall.	**knock down**（建物） ■ Some old houses were **knocked down** to make room for a new shopping mall.
141D	**fix up**（家など） ■ That old house looks great now that it has been **fixed up**.	**do up**（家など） ■ That old house looks great now that it has been **done up**.

付録	北アメリカ英語	イギリス英語
1.3	以下の動詞は，北アメリカ英語では**規則変化**します。 **burn** → burned **dream** → dreamed **lean** → leaned **learn** → learned **smell** → smelled **spell** → spelled **spill** → spilled **spoil** → spoiled **get**の過去分詞は**gotten**になります。 ■ Your English has **gotten** much better.（⇒ ずっとよくなった） **have got**は**have**と同じ「～を持つ」の意味で用います。この時gottenは用いられません。 ■ **I've got** two brothers. (= I have two brothers.)	以下の動詞は，イギリス英語では**規則変化**も**不規則変化**もします。 **burn** → burned/burnt **dream** → dreamed/dreamt **lean** → leaned/leant **learn** → learned/learnt **smell** → smelled/smelt **spell** → spelled/spelt **spill** → spilled/spilt **spoil** → spoiled/spoilt **get**の過去分詞は**got**になります。 ■ Your English has **got** much better. 北アメリカ英語同様，**have**と同じ「～を持つ」の意味で**have got**を用います。 ■ **I've got** two brothers.
6.6	以下の動詞では，語尾の**子音字の 2 重化**は起こりません。 travel → traveling, traveled cancel → canceling, canceled	語尾の**子音字の 2 重化**が起こります。 travel → travelling, travelled cancel → cancelling, cancelled

補充問題

補充問題では，主に次の文法項目を学習します：

Exercise 1	現在形と過去形	Units 1–6, 付録 2
Exercises 2–4	現在形と過去形	Units 1–13, 付録 2
Exercises 5–8	現在形と過去形	Units 1–15, 107, 付録 2
Exercise 9	過去進行形と used to ＋ 動詞の原形	Units 6, 17
Exercises 10–13	未来	Units 18–24, 付録 3
Exercises 14–15	過去形，現在形，未来形	Units 1–24
Exercises 16–18	法助動詞（can/must/would など）	Units 25–34, 付録 4
Exercises 19–21	if（条件）	Units 24, 36–38
Exercises 22–24	受動態	Units 40–43
Exercise 25	間接話法	Units 45–46, 48
Exercises 26–28	動名詞（-ing）と不定詞（to ＋ 動詞の原形）	Units 51–64
Exercise 29	a/an と the	Units 67–76
Exercise 30	代名詞と限定詞	Units 80–89
Exercise 31	形容詞と副詞	Units 96–105
Exercise 32	接続詞	Units 24, 36, 109–115
Exercise 33	時を表す前置詞	Units 13, 116–119
Exercise 34	場所を表す前置詞，その他の前置詞	Units 120–125
Exercise 35	名詞 / 形容詞 ＋ 前置詞	Units 126–128
Exercise 36	動詞 ＋ 前置詞	Units 129–133
Exercises 37–41	句動詞	Units 134–142

現在形と過去形 Units 1–6, 付録 2

1 （ ）内の語句を用いて文を完成しなさい。状況に合うように動詞は単純現在形（I do），現在進行形（I am doing），単純過去形（I did），過去進行形（I was doing）のいずれかの形にします。

1. We can go out now. It _isn't raining_ (not / rain) anymore.
2. Catherine _was waiting_ (wait) for me when I _arrived_ (arrive).
3. I __________ (get) hungry. Let's go and have something to eat.
4. What __________ (you / do) in your spare time? Do you have any hobbies?
5. The weather was horrible when we __________ (arrive). It was cold and it __________ (rain) hard.
6. Louise usually __________ (call) me on Fridays, but she __________ (not / call) last Friday.
7. *A:* The last time I saw you, you __________ (think) of moving to a new apartment.
   B: That's right, but in the end I __________ (decide) to stay where I was.
8. Why __________ (you / look) at me like that? What's the matter?
9. It's usually dry here at this time of the year. It __________ (not / rain) much.
10. The phone __________ (ring) three times while we __________ (have) dinner last night.
11. Linda was busy when we __________ (go) to see her yesterday. She __________ (study) for an exam. We __________ (not / want) to bother her, so we __________ (not / stay) very long.
12. When I __________ (tell) Tom the news, he __________ (not / believe) me at first. He __________ (think) that I __________ (joke).

現在形と過去形　Units 1–13, 付録 2

2 下線部の正しい方を選んで，文を完成しなさい。

1. Everything is going well. We ~~didn't have~~ / haven't had any problems so far.（haven't had が正しい）
2. Lisa didn't go / hasn't gone to work yesterday. She wasn't feeling well.
3. Look! That man over there wears / is wearing the same sweater as you.
4. I went / have been to New Zealand last year.
5. I didn't hear / haven't heard from Ann in the last few days. I wonder why.
6. I wonder why Jim is / is being so nice to me today. He isn't usually like that.
7. Jane had a book open in front of her, but she didn't read / wasn't reading it.
8. I wasn't very busy. I didn't have / wasn't having much to do.
9. It begins / It's beginning to get dark. Should I turn on the light?
10. After finishing high school, Tim got / has got a job in a factory.
11. When Sue heard the news, she wasn't / hasn't been very pleased.
12. This is a nice restaurant, isn't it? Is this the first time you are / you've been here?
13. I need a new job. I'm doing / I've been doing the same job for too long.
14. "Anna has gone out." "She has? What time did she go / has she gone?"
15. "You look tired." "Yes, I've played / I've been playing basketball."
16. Where are you coming / do you come from? Are you Australian?
17. I'd like to see Tina again. It's been a long time since I saw her / that I didn't see her.
18. Robert and Maria have been married since 20 years / for 20 years.

3 状況に合うように空所に適切な形の動詞を用いた語句を入れて，対話中の **A** の質問の文を完成しなさい。

1. *A:* I'm looking for Paul. ___Have you seen___ him?
   B: Yes, he was here a minute ago.
2. *A:* Why ___did you go___ to bed so early last night?
   B: Because I was very tired.
3. *A:* Where ____________________ ?
   B: To the post office. I want to mail these letters. I'll be back in a few minutes.
4. *A:* ____________________ television every night?
   B: No, only if there's something special on.
5. *A:* Your house is very beautiful. How long ____________________ here?
   B: Almost 10 years.
6. *A:* How was your vacation? ____________________ a nice time?
   B: Yes, thanks. It was great.
7. *A:* ____________________ Julie recently?
   B: Yes, we had lunch together a few days ago.
8. *A:* Can you describe the woman you saw? What ____________________ ?
   B: A red sweater and black jeans.
9. *A:* I'm sorry to keep you waiting. ____________________ long?
   B: No, only about 10 minutes.
10. *A:* How long ____________________ you to get to work in the morning?
    B: Usually about 45 minutes. It depends on the traffic.
11. *A:* ____________________ a horse before?
    B: No, this is the first time.
12. *A:* ____________________ to Mexico?
    B: No, never, but I went to Costa Rica a few years ago.

4 状況に合うように自分で空所に合う語句を考えて入れ，会話中の B の答えの文を完成しなさい。

1. *A:* What's the new restaurant like? Is it good?
   B: I have no idea. ___I've never been___ there.
2. *A:* How well do you know Bill?
   B: Very well. We ________________ since we were children.
3. *A:* Did you enjoy your vacation?
   B: Yes, it was fantastic. It's the best vacation ________________ .
4. *A:* Is David still here?
   B: No, I'm afraid he isn't. ________________ about 10 minutes ago.
5. *A:* I like your suit. I haven't seen it before.
   B: It's new. It's the first time ________________ .
6. *A:* How did you cut your knee?
   B: I slipped and fell while ________________ tennis.
7. *A:* Do you ever go swimming?
   B: Not these days. I haven't ________________ a long time.
8. *A:* How often do you go to the movies?
   B: Hardly ever. It's been almost a year ________________ to the movies.
9. *A:* I've bought some new shoes. Do you like them?
   B: Yes, they're very nice. Where ________________ them?

現在形と過去形

Units 1–15, 107, 付録 2

5 (　) 内の語句を用いて文を完成しなさい。状況に合うように動詞は単純過去形 (I did)，過去進行形 (I was doing)，過去完了形 (I had done)，過去完了進行形 (I had been doing) のいずれかの形にします。

1.

Sarah

STATION

5:00

PLATFORM 1 ⇨

5:05

PLATFORM 1 ⇨

Yesterday afternoon Sarah ___went___ (go) to the station to meet Paul. When she ________________ (get) there, Paul ________________ (already / wait) for her. His train ________________ (arrive) early.

2.

Bill

zzzzz

Hello.

When I got home, Bill ________________ (lie) on the sofa. The television was on, but he ________________ (not / watch) it. He ________________ (fall) asleep and ________________ (snore) loudly. I ________________ (turn) the television off and just then he ________________ (wake) up.

3.

Last night I ______________________ (just / go) to bed and ______________________ (read) a book when suddenly I ______________________ (hear) a noise. I ______________________ (get) up to see what it was, but I ______________________ (not / see) anything, so I ______________________ (go) back to bed.

4.

Lisa had to go to Tokyo last week, but she almost ______________________ (miss) the plane. She ______________________ (stand) in line at the check-in counter when she suddenly ______________________ (realize) that she ______________________ (leave) her passport at home. Fortunately she lives near the airport, so she ______________________ (have) time to take a taxi home to get it. She ______________________ (get) back to the airport just in time for her flight.

5.

I ______________________ (meet) Peter and Lucy yesterday as I ______________________ (walk) through the park. They ______________________ (be) to the Sports Center where they ______________________ (play) tennis. They ______________________ (go) to a café and ______________________ (invite) me to join them, but I ______________________ (arrange) to meet another friend and ______________________ (not / have) time.

6 （ ）内の語句を用いて文を完成しなさい。状況に合うように動詞は現在完了形（**I have done**），現在完了進行形（**I have been doing**），過去完了形（**I had done**），過去完了進行形（**I had been doing**）のいずれかの形にします。

1. Amanda is sitting on the ground. She's out of breath.
   (she / run) *She has been running.*
2. Where's my bag? I left it under this chair.
   (somebody / take / it) ______________________
3. We were all surprised when Jenny and Andy got married last year.
   (they / only / know / each other / a few weeks)
   ____
4. It's still raining. I wish it would stop.
   (it / rain / all day) ______________________
5. Suddenly I woke up. I was confused and didn't know where I was.
   (I / dream) ______________________

6. I wasn't hungry at lunchtime, so I didn't have anything to eat.
   (I / have / a big breakfast) ______________________________
7. Every year Robert and Tina spend a few days at the same hotel in Hawaii.
   (they / go / there for years) ______________________________
8. I've got a headache.
   (I / have / it / since I got up) ______________________________
9. Next week Gary is going to run in a marathon.
   (he / train / very hard for it) ______________________________

7 （ ）内の語句を用いて文を完成しなさい。状況に合うように動詞は適切な形にします。

Julia and Kevin are old friends. They meet by chance at the train station.

Julia: Hello, Kevin. (1) ______________ (I / not / see) you in ages. How are you?
Kevin: I'm fine. How about you? (2) ______________ (you / look) good.
Julia: Thanks. So, (3) ______________ (you / go) somewhere or (4) ______________ (you / meet) somebody?
Kevin: (5) ______________ (I / go) to New York for a business meeting.
Julia: Oh. (6) ______________ (you / travel / a lot) on business?
Kevin: Fairly often, yes. And you? Where (7) ______________ (you / go)?
Julia: Nowhere. (8) ______________ (I / meet) a friend. Unfortunately, her train (9) ______________ (be) delayed – (10) ______________ (I / wait) here for nearly an hour.
Kevin: How are your children?
Julia: They're all fine, thanks. The youngest (11) ______________ (just / start) school.
Kevin: How (12) ______________ (she / do)? (13) ______________ (she / like) it?
Julia: Yes, (14) ______________ (she / think) it's great.
Kevin: (15) ______________ (you / work) these days? The last time I (16) ______________ (speak) to you, (17) ______________ (you / work) in a travel agency.
Julia: That's right. Unfortunately, the company (18) ______________ (go) out of business a couple of months after (19) ______________ (I / start) work there, so (20) ______________ (I / lose) my job.
Kevin: And (21) ______________ (you / not / have) a job since then?
Julia: Not a permanent job. (22) ______________ (I / have) a few temporary jobs. By the way, (23) ______________ (you / see) Joe recently?
Kevin: Joe? He's in Canada.
Julia: Really? How long (24) ______________ (he / be) in Canada?
Kevin: About a year now. (25) ______________ (I / see) him a few days before (26) ______________ (he / leave). (27) ______________ (he / be) unemployed for months, so (28) ______________ (he / decide) to try his luck somewhere else. (29) ______________ (he / really / look forward) to going.
Julia: So, what (30) ______________ (he / do) there?
Kevin: I have no idea. (31) ______________ (I / not / hear) from him since (32) ______________ (he / leave). Anyway, I have to go – my train is here. It was really nice to see you again.
Julia: You, too. Bye. Have a good trip.
Kevin: Thanks. Bye.

8 (　) 内の語句を用いて文を完成しなさい。状況に合うように動詞は適切な形にします。

1. Who ______________________ (invent) the bicycle?
2. "Do you still have that class on Wednesdays?" "No, ______________________ (it / end)."
3. I was the last to leave the office last night. Everybody else ______________________ (go) home when I ______________________ (leave).
4. What ______________________ (you / do) last weekend? ______________________ (you / go) away?
5. I like your car. How long ______________________ (you / have) it?
6. It's a shame the trip was canceled. I ______________________ (look) forward to it.
7. Jane is an experienced teacher. ______________________ (she / teach) for 15 years.
8. ______________________ (I / buy) a new jacket last week, but ______________________ (I / not / wear) it yet.
9. A few days ago ______________ (I / see) a man at a party whose face ______________ (be) very familiar. At first I couldn't think where ______________________ (I / see) him before. Then suddenly ______________________ (I / remember) who ______________________ (he / be).
10. ______________________ (you / hear) of Agatha Christie? ______________________ (she / be) a writer who ______________________ (die) in 1976. ______________________ (she / write) more than 70 detective novels. ______________________ (you / read) any of them?
11. *A:* What ______________________ (this word / mean)?
    B: I have no idea. ______________________ (I / never / see) it before. Look it up in the dictionary.
12. *A:* ______________________ (you / get) to the theater in time for the play last night?
    B: No, we were late. By the time we got there, ______________________ (it / already / begin).
13. I went to Sarah's room and ______________________ (knock) on the door, but there ______________________ (be) no answer. Either ______________________ (she / go) out or ______________________ (she / not / want) to see anyone.
14. Patrick asked me how to use the photocopier. ______________________ (he / never / use) it before, so ______________________ (he / not / know) what to do.
15. Liz ______________________ (go) for a swim after work yesterday. ______________________ (she / need) some exercise because ______________________ (she / sit) in an office all day in front of a computer.

過去進行形と used to + 動詞の原形　Units 6, 17

9 状況に合うように，(　) 内の動詞を過去進行形もしくは「used to + 動詞の原形」の形に変えて文を完成しなさい。

1. I haven't been to the movies in ages now. We *used to go* a lot. (go)
2. Ann didn't see me wave to her. She *was looking* in the other direction. (look)
3. I ______________________ a lot, but I don't use my car very much these days. (drive)
4. I asked the taxi driver to slow down. She ______________________ too fast. (drive)
5. Rosemary and Jonathan met for the first time when they ______________________ at the same bank. (work)
6. When I was a child, I ______________________ a lot of bad dreams. (have)
7. I wonder what Joe is doing these days. He ______________________ in Spain when I last heard from him. (live)
8. "Where were you yesterday afternoon?" "I ______________________ volleyball." (play)
9. "Do you play any sports?" "Not these days, but I ______________________ volleyball." (play)
10. George looked very nice at the party. He ______________________ a very stylish suit. (wear)

10 状況に合うように，（　）内の語句を用いて文を完成しなさい。動詞は現在進行形 (I am doing)，(be)going to，will (I'll) のいずれかの形にします。

1. You have made all your vacation plans. Your destination is Jamaica.
   Friend: Have you decided where you're going on vacation yet?
   You: I am going to Jamaica. (I / go)
2. You have made an appointment with the dentist for Friday morning.
   Friend: Do you want to get together on Friday morning?
   You: I can't on Friday. ________ (I / go)
3. You and some friends are planning a vacation in Mexico. You have decided to rent a car, but you haven't arranged this yet.
   Friend: How do you plan to travel around Mexico? By bus?
   You: No, ________ (we / rent)
4. Your friend has two young children. She wants to go out tomorrow night. You offer to take care of the children.
   Friend: I want to go out tomorrow night, but I don't have a babysitter.
   You: That's no problem. ________ (I / take care of)
5. You have already arranged to have lunch with Sue tomorrow.
   Friend: Are you free at lunchtime tomorrow?
   You: No, ________ (have lunch)
6. You are in a restaurant. You and your friend are looking at the menu. Maybe your friend has decided what to have. You ask her/him.
   You: What ________ ? (you / have)
   Friend: I don't know. I can't make up my mind.
7. You and a friend are reading. It's getting dark, and your friend is having trouble reading. You decide to turn on the light.
   Friend: It's getting dark, isn't it? It's difficult to read.
   You: Yes. ________ (I / turn on)
8. You and a friend are reading. It's getting dark and you decide to turn on the light. You stand up and walk toward the light switch.
   Friend: What are you doing?
   You: ________ (I / turn on)

11 （　）内の語句を用いて文を完成しなさい。状況に合うように動詞は現在時制（単純現在形，現在進行形），will (I'll)，shall/should のいずれかの形にします。

Conversation 1 *(in the morning)*

Jenny: (1) Are you doing (you / do) anything tomorrow night, Helen?
Helen: No, why?
Jenny: Well, do you feel like going to the movies? *Strangers on a Plane* is playing. I want to see it, but I don't want to go alone.
Helen: OK, (2) ________ (I / go) with you. What time (3) ________ (we / meet)?
Jenny: Well, the movie (4) ________ (start) at 8:45, so (5) ________ (I / meet) you at about 8:30 outside the theater, OK?
Helen: Fine. (6) ________ (I / see) Tina later on tonight. (7) ________ (I / ask) her if she wants to come, too?
Jenny: Yes, why don't you? (8) ________ (I / see) you tomorrow then. Bye.

Conversation 2 *(later the same day)*

Helen: Jenny and I (9) ______________________ (go) to the movies tomorrow night to see *Strangers on a Plane.* Why don't you come with us?

Tina: I'd love to come. What time (10) ______________________ (the movie / start)?

Helen: 8:45.

Tina: (11) ______________________ (you / meet) outside the theater?

Helen: Yes, at 8:30. Is that OK for you?

Tina: Yes, (12) ______________________ (I / be) there at 8:30.

12 ( ) 内の語句を用いて文を完成しなさい。状況に合うように動詞は適切な形にします。複数の形が可能な場合もあります。

1. *A has decided to learn a language.*
   A: I've decided to try and learn a foreign language.
   B: You have? Which language (1) *are you going to learn* (you / learn)?
   A: Spanish.
   B: (2) ______________________ (you / take) a class?
   A: Yes, (3) ______________________ (it / start) next week.
   B: That's great. I'm sure (4) ______________________ (you / enjoy) it.
   A: I hope so. But I think (5) ______________________ (it / be) a lot of work.

2. *A wants to know about B's vacation plans.*
   A: I hear (1) ______________________ (you / go) on vacation soon.
   B: That's right. (2) ______________________ (we / go) to Brazil.
   A: I hope (3) ______________________ (you / have) a nice time.
   B: Thanks. (4) ______________________ (I / send) you a postcard and (5) ______________________ (I / get) in touch with you when (6) ______________________ (I / get) back.

3. *A invites B to a party.*
   A: (1) ______________________ (I / have) a party next Saturday. Can you come?
   B: On Saturday? I'm not sure. Some friends of mine (2) ______________________ (come) to stay with me next week, but I think (3) ______________________ (they / leave) by Saturday. But if (4) ______________________ (they / be) still here, (5) ______________________ (I / not / be) able to come to the party.
   A: OK. Well, tell me as soon as (6) ______________________ (you / know).
   B: All right. (7) ______________________ (I / call) you during the week.

4. *A and B are two secret agents arranging a meeting. They are talking on the phone.*
   A: Well, what time (1) ______________________ (we / meet)?
   B: Come to the café by the station at 4:00. (2) ______________________ (I / wait) for you when (3) ______________________ (you / arrive). (4) ______________________ (I / sit) by the window and (5) ______________________ (I / wear) a bright green sweater.
   A: OK. (6) ______________________ (Agent 307 / come), too?
   B: No, she can't come.
   A: Oh. (7) ______________________ (I / bring) the documents?
   B: Yes. (8) ______________________ (I / explain) everything when (9) ______________________ (I / see) you. And don't be late.
   A: OK. (10) ______________________ (I / try) to be on time.

13 (　) 内の語句を用いて文を完成しなさい。状況に合うように動詞は以下のいずれかの形にします。

現在進行形 (**I am doing**)	**will ('ll) / won't**
単純過去形 (**I do**)	**will be doing**
(be) going to (I'm going to do)	**should / shall**

1. I'm a little hungry. I think ______________ (I / have) something to eat.
2. Why are you putting on your coat? ______________ (you / go) somewhere?
3. What time ______________ (I / call) you tonight? About 7:30?
4. Look! That plane is flying toward the airport. ______________ (it / land).
5. We have to do something soon before ______________ (it / be) too late.
6. I'm sorry you've decided to leave the company. ______________ (I / miss) you when ______________ (you / go).
7. ______________ (I / give) you my address? If ______________ (I / give) you my address, ______________ (you / send) me a postcard?
8. Are you still watching that TV program? What time ______________ (it / end)?
9. ______________ (I / go) to Chicago next weekend for a wedding. My sister ______________ (get) married.
10. I'm not ready yet. ______________ (I / tell) you when ______________ (I / be) ready. I promise ______________ (I / not / be) very long.
11. *A:* Where are you going?
    B: To the hairdresser. ______________ (I / have) my hair cut.
12. She was very rude to me. I refuse to speak to her again until ______________ (she / apologize).
13. I wonder where ______________ (we / live) 10 years from now?
14. What do you plan to do when ______________ (you / finish) college?

過去形，現在形，未来形　Units 1–24

14 状況に合うように空所に適切な語句を入れて，対話中の B の文を完成しなさい。

1. *A:* How did the accident happen?
   B: I __was going__ too fast and couldn't stop in time.
2. *A:* Is that a new camera?
   B: No, I ______________ it a long time.
3. *A:* Is that a new computer?
   B: Yes, I ______________ it a few weeks ago.
4. *A:* I can't talk to you right now. You can see I'm very busy.
   B: OK. I ______________ back in about half an hour.
5. *A:* This is a nice restaurant. Do you come here often?
   B: No, it's the first time I ______________ here.
6. *A:* Do you play any sports?
   B: No, I ______________ tennis, but I gave it up.
7. *A:* I'm sorry I'm late.
   B: That's OK. I ______________ long.
8. *A:* When you went to Russia last year, was it your first visit?
   B: No, I ______________ there twice before.
9. *A:* Do you have any plans for the weekend?
   B: Yes, I ______________ to a party on Saturday night.
10. *A:* Do you know what Steve's doing these days?
    B: No, I ______________ him in ages.
11. *A:* Will you still be here by the time I get back?
    B: No, I ______________ by then.

15 右の地図を見て考えます。**Robert** は北アメリカを旅行しています。カナダの **Winnipeg** にいる友人に電子メールを書きました。状況に合うように（ ）内の動詞を適切な形に変えて空所に入れ，メールを完成しなさい。

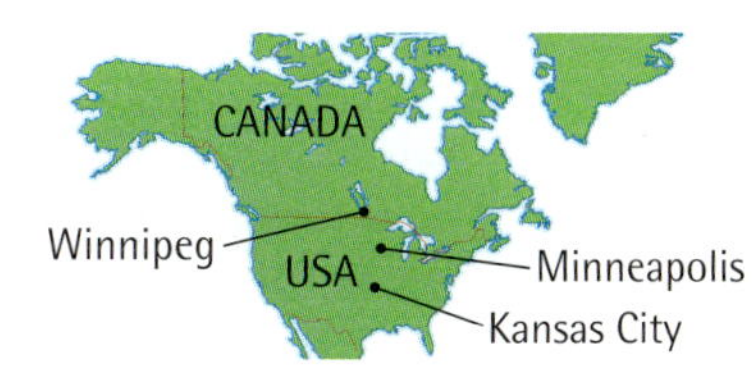

North American travels

To: Chris

Subject: North American travels

Hi

(1) *I've just arrived* (I / just / arrive) in Minneapolis. (2) ________ (I / travel) for more than a month now, and (3) ________ (I / begin) to think about coming home. Everything (4) ________ (I / see) so far (5) ________ (be) really interesting, and (6) ________ (I / meet) some really kind people.

(7) ________ (I / leave) Kansas City a week ago. (8) ________ (I / stay) there with Emily, the aunt of a friend from college. She was really helpful and hospitable and although (9) ________ (I / plan) to stay only a couple of days, (10) ________ (I / end up) staying more than a week.

(11) ________ (I / enjoy) the trip from Kansas City to here. (12) ________ (I / take) the Greyhound bus and (13) ________ (meet) some really interesting people – everybody was really friendly.

So now I'm here, and (14) ________ (I / stay) here for a few days before (15) ________ (I / continue) up to Canada. I'm not sure exactly when (16) ________ (I / get) to Winnipeg – it depends what happens while (17) ________ (I / be) here. But (18) ________ (I / let) you know as soon as (19) ________ (I / know) myself.

(20) ________ (I / stay) with a family here – they're friends of some people I know at home. Tomorrow (21) ________ (we / visit) some people they know who (22) ________ (build) a house on a lake. It isn't finished yet, but (23) ________ (it / be) interesting to see what it's like.

Anyway, that's all for now. (24) ________ (I / be) in touch again soon.

Robert

法助動詞（can/must/would など）　Units 25–34, 付録 4

16 状況に合うように，A～C の中から適切な語句を選び記号で答えなさい。2 つの選択肢が可能な場合もあります。

1. "What time will you be home tonight?" "I'm not sure. I *A or B* late." （AとBがともに正しい）
   A may be　**B** might be　**C** can be
2. I can't find the theater tickets. They ________ out of my pocket.
   A must have fallen　**B** should have fallen　**C** had to fall
3. Somebody ran in front of the car as I was driving. Fortunately, I ________ just in time.
   A could stop　**B** could have stopped　**C** managed to stop
4. We've got plenty of time. We ________ yet.
   A must not leave　**B** couldn't leave　**C** don't have to leave
5. I ________ out but I didn't feel like it, so I stayed at home.
   A could go　**B** could have gone　**C** must have gone

6. I'm sorry I ______________ to your party last week.
A couldn't come **B** couldn't have come **C** wasn't able to come
7. "What do you think of my theory?" "I'm not sure. You ______________ right."
A could be **B** must be **C** might be
8. I couldn't wait for you any longer. I ______________ , and so I went.
A must go **B** must have gone **C** had to go
9. "Do you know where Liz is?" "No. I suppose she ______________ shopping."
A should have gone **B** may have gone **C** could have gone
10. At first they didn't believe me when I told them what had happened, but in the end I ______________ them that I was telling the truth.
A was able to convince **B** managed to convince **C** could convince
11. I promised I'd call Gary tonight. I ______________ .
A can't forget **B** must not forget **C** don't have to forget
12. Why did you leave without me? You ______________ for me.
A must have waited **B** had to wait **C** should have waited
13. Lisa called and suggested ______________ lunch together.
A we have **B** having **C** to have
14. You look nice in that jacket, but you hardly ever wear it. ______________ it more often.
A You'd better wear **B** You should wear **C** You ought to wear
15. Should I buy a car? What's your advice? What ______________ ?
A will you do **B** would you do **C** should you do

17 状況に合うように，（ ）内の語句を用いて文を作りなさい。動詞は適切な形にすること。

1. Don't call them now. (they might / have / lunch)
They might be having lunch.
2. I ate too much. Now I feel sick. (I shouldn't / eat / so much)
I shouldn't have eaten so much.
3. I wonder why Tom didn't call me. (he must / forget)
____
4. Why did you go home so late? (you shouldn't / leave / so late)
____
5. You signed the contract. (it can't / change / now)
____
6. Why weren't you here earlier? (you could / get / here earlier)
____
7. "What's Linda doing?" "I'm not sure." (she may / watch / television)
____
8. Laura was standing outside the movie theater. (she must / wait / for somebody)
____
9. He was in prison at the time that the crime was committed. (he couldn't / do / it)
____
10. Why didn't you ask me to help you? (I would / help / you)
____
11. I'm surprised you weren't told that the road was dangerous. (you should / warn / about it)
____
12. Gary was in a strange mood yesterday. (he might not / feel / very well)
____

18 **can/could/might/must/should/would と（　）内の動詞を用いて，対話中の B の文を完成しなさい。状況によっては「must have / should have + 過去分詞」のような形や，can't/couldn't などの否定形にします。**

1. *A:* I'm hungry.
   B: But you just had lunch. You __can't be__ hungry already. (be)
2. *A:* I haven't seen our neighbors in ages.
   B: Neither have I. They __must have gone__ away. (go)
3. *A:* What's the weather like? Is it raining?
   B: Not right now, but it ______________________ later. (rain)
4. *A:* Where's Julia?
   B: I'm not sure. She ______________________ to the bank. (go)
5. *A:* I didn't see you at Michael's party last week.
   B: No, I had to work that night, so I ______________________ (go)
6. *A:* I saw you at Michael's party last week.
   B: No, you ______________________ me. I didn't go to Michael's party. (see)
7. *A:* What time will we get to Sue's house?
   B: Well, it's about a two-hour drive, so if we leave at 3:00, we ______________________ there by 5:00. (get)
8. *A:* When was the last time you saw Bill?
   B: Years ago. I ______________________ him if I saw him now. (recognize)
9. *A:* Did you hear the explosion?
   B: What explosion?
   A: There was a loud explosion about an hour ago. You ______________________ it. (hear)
10. *A:* We weren't sure which way to go. In the end we turned right.
    B: You went the wrong way. You ______________________ left. (turn)

---

if（条件）　Units 24, 36–38

19 **状況に合うように，（　）内の動詞を適切な形にして文を完成しなさい。**

1. If you __found__ a wallet in the street, what would you do with it? (find)
2. I have to hurry. My friend will be upset if I __'m not__ on time. (not / be)
3. I didn't realize that Gary was in the hospital. If I __had known__ he was in the hospital, I would have gone to visit him. (know)
4. If the phone ________________, can you answer it? (ring)
5. I can't decide what to do. What would you do if you ________________ in my position? (be)
6. *A:* What should we do tomorrow?
   B: Well, if it ________________ a nice day, we can go to the beach. (be)
7. *A:* Let's go to the beach.
   B: No, it's too cold. If it ________________ warmer, I wouldn't mind going. (be)
8. *A:* Did you go to the beach yesterday?
   B: No, it was too cold. If it ________________ warmer, we might have gone. (be)
9. If you ________________ enough money to go anywhere in the world, where would you go? (have)
10. I'm glad we had a map. I'm sure we would have gotten lost if we ________________ one. (not / have)
11. The accident was your fault. If you ________________ more carefully, it wouldn't have happened. (drive)
12. *A:* Why do you read newspapers?
    B: Well, if I ________________ newspapers, I wouldn't know what was happening in the world. (not / read)

20 例にならい，状況を説明する文を完成しなさい。

1. Liz is tired all the time. She shouldn't go to bed so late.
   If ___Liz didn't go to bed so late, she wouldn't be tired all the time.___
2. It's getting late. I don't think Sarah will come to see us now.
   I'd be surprised if Sarah ______
3. I'm sorry I disturbed you. I didn't know you were busy.
   If I'd known you were busy, I ______
4. I don't want them to be upset, so I've decided not to tell them what happened.
   They'd ______ if ______
5. The dog attacked you, but only because you frightened it.
   If ______
6. Unfortunately, I didn't have an umbrella, so I got very wet in the rain.
   I ______
7. Martin failed his driver's test last week. He was very nervous and that's why he failed.
   If Martin ______

21 状況に合うような文を自由に完成しなさい。

1. I'd go out tonight if ______ .
2. I'd have gone out last night if ______ .
3. If you hadn't reminded me, ______ .
4. We wouldn't have been late if ______ .
5. If I'd been able to get tickets, ______ .
6. Who would you call if ______ ?
7. Cities would be nicer places if ______ .
8. If there were no television, ______ .

受動態 Units 40–43

22 状況に合うように，（ ）内の動詞を用いて受動態の文を完成しなさい。

1. There's somebody behind us. I think we ___are being followed___ (follow).
2. A mystery is something that ___can't be explained___ (can't / explain).
3. We didn't play baseball yesterday. The game ______ (cancel).
4. The television ______ (repair). It's working again now.
5. In the middle of town there is a church, which ______ (restore) at this time. The work is almost finished.
6. The tower is the oldest part of the church. It ______ (believe) to be more than 100 years old.
7. If I didn't do my job right, I ______ (would / fire).
8. *A:* I left a newspaper on the desk last night and it isn't there now.
   B: It ______ (might / throw) away.
9. I learned to swim when I was very young. I ______ (teach) by my mother.
10. After ______ (arrest), I was taken to the police station.
11. "______ (you / ever / arrest)?" "No, never."
12. *(TV news report)* Two people ______ (report) to ______ (injure) in an explosion at a factory in Miami early this morning.

23 状況に合うように，（　）内の動詞を能動態もしくは受動態の形にして文を完成しなさい。

1. This house is very old. It __was built__ (build) over 100 years ago.
2. My grandfather was a builder. He __built__ (build) this house many years ago.
3. "Is your car still for sale?" "No, I ________________ (sell) it."
4. *A:* Is the house at the end of the street still for sale?
   B: No, it ________________ (sell).
5. Sometimes mistakes ________________ (make). It's inevitable.
6. I wouldn't leave your car unlocked. It ________________ (might / steal).
7. My bag has disappeared. It ________________ (must / steal).
8. I can't find my hat. Somebody ________________ (must / take) it by mistake.
9. It's a serious problem. I don't know how it ________________ (can / solve).
10. We didn't leave early enough. We ________________ (should / leave) earlier.
11. Nearly every time I travel by plane, my flight ________________ (delay).
12. A new bridge ________________ (build) across the river. Work started last year and the bridge ________________ (expect) to open next year.

24 （　）内の語を適切な形にして，以下の新聞記事を完成しなさい。

1.

Fire at City Hall

City Hall (1) __was damaged__ (damage) in a fire last night. The fire, which (2) ________________ (discover) at about 9:00 p.m., spread very quickly. Nobody (3) ________________ (injure), but two people had to (4) ________________ (rescue) from an upstairs room. A large number of documents (5) ________________ (believe / destroy). It (6) ________________ (not / know) how the fire started.

2.

Convenience Store Robbery

A convenience store clerk (1) ________________ (force) to hand over $500 after (2) ________________ (threaten) by a man with a gun. The man escaped in a car, which (3) ________________ (steal) earlier in the day. The car (4) ________________ (later / find) in a parking lot, where it (5) ________________ (abandon) by the thief. A man (6) ________________ (arrest) in connection with the robbery and (7) ________________ (still / question) by the police.

3.

Road Delays

Repair work started yesterday on Route 22. The road (1) ________________ (resurface), and there will be long delays. Drivers (2) ________________ (ask) to use an alternate route if possible. The work (3) ________________ (expect) to last two weeks. Next Sunday the road (4) ________________ (close), and traffic (5) ________________ (reroute)

4.

Accident

A woman (1) ________________ (take) to the hospital after her car collided with a truck on the freeway yesterday. She (2) ________________ (allow) to go home later that day after treatment. The road (3) ________________ (block) for an hour after the accident, and traffic had to (4) ________________ (reroute). A police investigator said afterward: "The woman was lucky. She could (5) ________________ (kill)."

間接話法

Units 45–46,48

25 イラストの状況を説明する間接話法の文を完成しなさい。

1.

A woman called at lunchtime yesterday and asked *if she could speak to Paul*. I told __________ and __________. I asked __________, but she said __________ later. But she never did.

2.

I went to New York recently, but my trip didn't begin well. I had reserved a hotel room, but when I got to the hotel, they told __________ no __________. When I asked __________, they said __________, but __________. There was nothing I could do. I just had to look for somewhere else to stay.

3.

After getting off the plane, we had to stand in line for an hour to get through immigration. Finally it was our turn. The immigration official asked us __________, and we told __________. Then he wanted to know __________ and __________. He seemed satisfied with our answers, checked our passports, and wished us a pleasant stay.

4.

A: What time is Sue arriving this afternoon?

B: About three. She said __________.

A: Aren't you going to meet her?

B: No, she said __________. She said __________.

5.

What's your job?
How much do you make?
Mind your own business!
You

A few days ago a man called from a marketing company and started asking me questions.
He wanted to know ____________________ and asked ____________________.
I don't like people calling and asking questions like that, so I told ____________________
____________________ and I put the phone down.

6.

now
Louise Sarah

earlier
I'll be at the restaurant at 7:30.
Call me if there's any problem.
I know where the restaurant is.
Paul

Louise and Sarah are in a restaurant waiting for Paul.
Louise: I wonder where Paul is. He said ____________________.
Sarah: Maybe he got lost.
Louise: I don't think so. He said ____________________.
And I told ____________________.

7.

I'm not hungry.
I don't like bananas, so don't buy any.
Jane Joe

Joe: Is there anything to eat?
Jane: You just said ____________________.
Joe: Well, I am now. I'd love a banana.
Jane: A banana? But you said ____________________.
You told ____________________.

動名詞（-ing）と不定詞（to + 動詞の原形）　Units 51–64

26 状況に合うように，（　）内の動詞を適切な形に変えて文を完成しなさい。

1. How old were you when you learned __to drive__? (drive)
2. I don't mind __walking__ home, but I'd rather __take__ a taxi. (walk / take)
3. I can't make a decision. I keep ____________________ my mind. (change)
4. He had made his decision and refused ____________________ his mind. (change)
5. Why did you change your decision? What made you ____________________ your mind? (change)
6. It was a really good vacation. I really enjoyed ____________________ by the ocean again. (be)
7. Did I really tell you I was unhappy? I don't remember ____________________ that. (say)
8. "Remember ____________________ Tom tomorrow." "OK. I won't forget." (call)
9. The water here is not very good. I'd avoid ____________________ it if I were you. (drink)
10. I pretended ____________________ interested in the conversation, but it was really very boring. (be)
11. I got up and looked out the window ____________________ what the weather was like. (see)
12. I have a friend who claims ____________________ able to speak five languages. (be)
13. I like ____________________ carefully about things before ____________________ a decision. (think / make)

14. I had an apartment downtown but I didn't like ______________ there, so I decided ______________ . (live / move)
15. Steve used ______________ a hockey player. He had to stop ______________ because of an injury. (be / play)
16. After ______________ by the police, the man admitted ______________ the car but denied ______________ 100 miles an hour. (stop / steal / drive)
17. *A:* How do you make this machine ______________ ? (work)
    B: I'm not sure. Try ______________ that button and see what happens. (press)

27 ( ) 内の語句を用いて文を完成しなさい。動詞は適切な形にすること。

1. I can't find the tickets. (I / seem / lose / them)
   I seem to have lost them.
2. I don't have far to go. (it / not / worth / take / a taxi)
   It's not worth taking a taxi.
3. The game was getting boring. (we / stop / watch / after a while)
   ____
4. Tim isn't very reliable. (he / tend / forget / things)
   ____
5. I've got a lot of luggage. (you / mind / help / me?)
   ____
6. There's nobody at home. (everybody / seem / go out)
   ____
7. We don't like our apartment. (we / think / move)
   ____
8. The vase was very valuable. (I / afraid / touch / it)
   ____
9. Bill never carries money with him. (he / afraid / robbed)
   ____
10. I wouldn't go to see that movie. (it / not / worth / see)
    ____
11. I'm very tired after that long walk. (I / not / used / walk / so far)
    ____
12. Sue is on vacation. I received a postcard from her yesterday. (she / seem / enjoy / herself)
    ____
13. Dave had lots of vacation pictures. (he / insist / show / them to me)
    ____
14. I don't want to do the shopping. (I'd rather / somebody else / do / it)
    ____

28 1番目の文と似たような意味を表す文を完成しなさい。

1. I was surprised I passed the exam.
   I didn't expect *to pass the exam* .
2. Did you manage to solve the problem?
   Did you succeed *in solving the problem* ?
3. I don't read newspapers anymore.
   I've given up ______________ .
4. I'd prefer not to go out tonight.
   I'd rather ______________ .
5. He can't walk very well.
   He has trouble ______________ .
6. Should I call you tonight?
   Do you want ______________ ?
7. Nobody saw me come in.
   I came in without ______________ .

8. They said I was a liar.
   I was accused ____ .
9. It will be good to see them again.
   I'm looking forward ____ .
10. What do you think I should do?
   What do you advise me ____ ?
11. It's too bad I couldn't go out with you.
   I'd like ____ .
12. I'm sorry that I didn't take your advice.
   I regret ____ .

a/an と the

Units 67–76

29 状況に合うように，空所に a もしくは an 入れて文を完成しなさい。いずれも必要ではない場合には – を記入します。

1. I don't usually like staying at __–__ hotels, but last summer we spent a few days at __a__ very nice hotel at __the__ beach.
2. _____ tennis is my favorite sport. I play once or twice _____ week if I can, but I'm not _____ very good player.
3. I won't be home for _____ dinner this evening. I'm meeting some friends after _____ work, and we're going to _____ movies.
4. _____ unemployment is increasing, and it's very difficult for _____ people to find _____ work.
5. There was _____ accident as I was going _____ home last night. Two people were taken to _____ hospital. I think _____ most accidents are caused by _____ people driving too fast.
6. Carol is _____ economist. She used to work in _____ investment department of _____ Lloyds Bank. Now she works for _____ American bank in _____ United States.
7. *A:* What's _____ name of _____ hotel where you're staying?
   B: _____ Royal. It's on _____ West Street in _____ suburbs. It's near _____ airport.
8. I have two brothers. _____ older one is training to be _____ pilot with _____ Western Airlines. _____ younger one is still in _____ high school. When he finishes _____ school, he wants to go to _____ college to study _____ engineering.

代名詞と限定詞

Units 80–89

30 状況に合うように，A〜C の中から適切な語句を選び記号で答えなさい。2 つの選択肢が可能な場合もあります。

1. I don't remember __A__ about the accident.（A が正しい）
   A anything **B** something **C** nothing
2. Chris and I have known ______________ for quite a long time.
   A us **B** each other **C** ourselves
3. "How often do the buses run?" "______________ 20 minutes."
   A All **B** Each **C** Every
4. I shouted for help, but ______________ came.
   A nobody **B** no one **C** anybody
5. Last night we went out with some friends of ______________ .
   A us **B** our **C** ours
6. It didn't take us a long time to get here. ______________ traffic.
   A It wasn't much **B** There wasn't much **C** It wasn't a lot
7. Can I have ______________ milk in my coffee, please?
   A a little **B** any **C** some
8. Sometimes I find it difficult to ______________ .
   A concentrate **B** concentrate me **C** concentrate myself

9. There's ______________ on at the movies that I want to see, so there's no point in going.
   A something **B** anything **C** nothing
10. I drink ______________ water every day.
   A much **B** a lot of **C** lots of
11. ______________ in the mall are open on Sunday.
   A Most of stores **B** Most of the stores **C** The most of the stores
12. There were about 20 people in the photo. I didn't recognize ______________ of them.
   A any **B** none **C** either
13. I've been waiting ______________ for Sarah to call.
   A all morning **B** the whole morning **C** all the morning
14. I can't afford to buy anything in this store. ______________ so expensive.
   A All is **B** Everything is **C** All are

形容詞と副詞 Units 96–105

31 それぞれの文について誤りのある部分を○で囲み，正しい形に書き直しなさい。

1. The building was (total destroyed) in the fire. *totally destroyed*
2. I didn't like the book. It was such a stupid story. *OK*
3. The city is very polluted. It's the more polluted place I've ever been to. ______________
4. I was disappointing that I didn't get the job. I was well qualified and the interview went well. ______________
5. Could you walk a little more slowly? ______________
6. Joe works hardly, but he doesn't get paid very much. ______________
7. The company's offices are in a modern large building. ______________
8. Dan is a very fast runner. I wish I could run as fast as him. ______________
9. I missed the three last days of the course because I was sick. ______________
10. You don't look happy. What's the matter? ______________
11. The weather has been unusual cold for this time of year. ______________
12. The water in the pool was too dirty to swim in it. ______________
13. I got impatient because we had to wait so long time. ______________
14. Is this box big enough, or do you need a bigger one? ______________
15. This morning I got up more early than usual. ______________

接続詞 Units 24, 36, 109–115

32 下線部の正しい方を選んで，文を完成しなさい。

1. I'll try to be on time, but don't worry if / ~~when~~ I'm late.（ifが正しい）
2. Don't throw that bag away. If / When you don't want it, I'll take it.
3. Please go to the reception desk if / when you arrive at the hotel.
4. We've arranged to play tennis tomorrow, but we won't play if / when it's raining.
5. Jennifer is in her final year at school. She still doesn't know what she's going to do if / when she graduates.
6. What would you do if / when you lost your keys?
7. I hope I'll be able to come to the party, but I'll let you know if / unless I can't.
8. I don't want to be disturbed, so don't call me if / unless it's something important.
9. Please sign the contract if / unless you're happy with the conditions.
10. I like traveling by ship as long as / unless the sea is not rough.
11. You might not remember the name of the hotel, so write it down if / in case you forget it.
12. It's not cold now, but take your coat with you if / in case it gets cold later.
13. Take your coat with you, and then you can put it on if / in case it gets cold later.

14. They always have the television on, even if / if nobody is watching it.
15. Even / Although we played very well, we lost the game.
16. Despite / Although we've known each other a long time, we're not especially close friends.
17. "When did you graduate from high school?" "As / When I was 18."
18. I think Ann will be very pleased as / when she hears the news.

時を表す前置詞

Units 13, 116–119

33 以下から適切な語を選び，空所に入れて文を完成しなさい。

at on in during for since by until

1. Jack is out of town. He'll be back *in* a week.
2. We're having a party ________ Saturday. Can you come?
3. I've got an interview next week. It's ________ 9:30 ________ Tuesday morning.
4. Sue isn't usually here ________ weekends. She goes away.
5. The train service is very good. The trains are nearly always ________ time.
6. It was a confusing situation. Many things were happening ________ the same time.
7. I couldn't decide whether or not to buy the sweater. ________ the end I decided not to.
8. The road is busy all the time, even ________ night.
9. I met a lot of nice people ________ my stay in New York.
10. I saw Helen ________ Friday, but I haven't seen her ________ then.
11. Brian has been doing the same job ________ five years.
12. Lisa's birthday is ________ the end of March. I'm not sure exactly which day it is.
13. We have some friends staying with us ________ the moment. They're staying ________ Friday.
14. If you're interested in applying for the job, your application must be received ________ Friday.
15. I'm just going out. I won't be long – I'll be back ________ 10 minutes.

場所を表す前置詞，その他の前置詞

Units 120–125

34 状況に合うように，空所に適切な前置詞を入れて文を完成しなさい。

1. I'd love to be able to visit every country ________ the world.
2. Jessica White is my favorite author. Have you read anything ________ her?
3. "Is there a bank near here?" "Yes, there's one ________ the end of this block."
4. Tim is out of town at the moment. He's ________ vacation.
5. We live ________ the country, a long way from the nearest town.
6. I've got a stain ________ my jacket. I'll have to have it cleaned.
7. We went ________ a party ________ Linda's house on Saturday.
8. Boston is ________ the East Coast of the United States.
9. Look at the leaves ________ that tree. They're a beautiful color.
10. "Have you ever been ________ Tokyo?" "No, I've never been ________ Japan."
11. Mozart died ________ Vienna in 1791 ________ the age of 35.
12. "Are you ________ this photograph?" "Yes, that's me, ________ the left."
13. We went ________ the theater last night. We had seats ________ the front row.
14. "Where's the light switch?" "It's ________ the wall ________ the door."
15. It was late when we arrived ________ the hotel.
16. I couldn't decide what to eat. There was nothing ________ the menu that I liked.
17. We live ________ a high rise. Our apartment is ________ the fifteenth floor.
18. *A:* What did you think of the movie?
    B: Some parts were a little stupid, but ________ the whole I enjoyed it.
19. "When you paid the hotel bill, did you pay cash?" "No, I paid ________ credit card."
20. "How did you get here? ________ the bus?" "No, ________ car."
21. *A:* I wonder what's ________ TV tonight. Do you have a newspaper?
    B: Yes, the TV listings are ________ the back page.

22. Helen works for a telecommunications company. She works ________ the customer service department.
23. Anna spent two years working ________ Chicago before returning ________ Italy.
24. "Did you enjoy your trip ________ the beach?" "Yes, it was great."
25. Next summer we're going ________ a trip to Canada.

名詞 / 形容詞 + 前置詞 Units 126–128

35 状況に合うように，空所に適切な前置詞を入れて文を完成しなさい。

1. The plan has been changed, but nobody seems to know the reason ________ this.
2. Don't ask me to decide. I'm not very good ________ making decisions.
3. Some people say that Sue is unfriendly, but she's always very nice ________ me.
4. What do you think is the best solution ________ the problem?
5. There has been a big increase ________ the price of land recently.
6. He lives a rather lonely life. He doesn't have much contact ________ other people.
7. Paul is a wonderful photographer. He likes taking pictures ________ people.
8. Michael got married ________ a woman he met when he was in college.
9. He's very brave. He's not afraid ________ anything.
10. I'm surprised ________ the amount of traffic today. I didn't think it would be so heavy.
11. Thank you for lending me the guidebook. It was full ________ useful information.
12. Please come in and sit down. I'm sorry ________ the mess.

動詞 + 前置詞 Units 129–133

36 状況に合うように，空所に適切な前置詞を入れて文を完成しなさい。必要ない場合には – を記入します。

1. She works very hard. You can't accuse her ________ being lazy.
2. Who's going to look ________ your children while you're at work?
3. The problem is becoming serious. We have to discuss ________ it.
4. The problem is becoming serious. We have to do something ________ it.
5. I prefer this chair ________ the other one. It's more comfortable.
6. I have to call ________ the office to tell them I won't be at work today.
7. The river divides the city ________ two parts.
8. "What do you think ________ your new boss?" "She's all right, I guess."
9. Can somebody please explain ________ me what I have to do?
10. I said hello to her, but she didn't answer ________ me.
11. "Do you like staying at hotels?" "It depends ________ the hotel."
12. "Have you ever been to Borla?" "No, I've never heard ________ it. What is it?"
13. You remind me ________ somebody I knew a long time ago. You look just like her.
14. This is wonderful news! I can't believe ________ it.
15. George is not an idealist – he believes ________ being practical.
16. What's so funny? What are you laughing ________ ?
17. What have you done with all the money you had? What did you spend it ________ ?
18. If Kevin asks ________ you ________ money, don't give him any.
19. I apologized ________ Sarah ________ keeping her waiting so long.
20. Lisa was very helpful. I thanked ________ her ________ everything she'd done.

句動詞

37 Aの文への受け答えとなる文をBから選び記号で答えなさい。

A

1. ~~I'd like to apply for a license.~~
2. I'm too warm with my coat on.
3. This jacket looks nice.
4. My phone number is 555-9320.
5. I don't think my car will fit in that space.
6. I'm glad we have a plan.
7. How did you find the mistake?
8. I'm not sure whether to accept their offer or not.
9. I don't know how to put this toy together.
10. It's a subject he doesn't like to talk about.
11. I don't know what this word means.

B

a. I can back up and give you more room.
b. Let me try. I'm sure I can figure it out.
c. Kate pointed it out.
d. ~~Sure, just fill out this form.~~
e. Yes, why don't you try it on?
f. OK, I won't bring it up.
g. Just a minute. I'll write it down.
h. Why don't you take it off then?
i. You can look it up.
j. I think you should turn it down.
k. Yes, now let's work out the details.

1. d　2. ____　3. ____　4. ____　5. ____　6. ____
7. ____　8. ____　9. ____　10. ____　11. ____

38 状況に合うように，A～Dの中から適切な語句を選び記号で答えなさい。

1. Nobody believed Paul at first but he B to be right.（Bが正しい）
   A came out　**B** turned out　**C** worked out　**D** carried out
2. Here's some good news. It will ________ .
   A turn you up　**B** put you up　**C** blow you up　**D** cheer you up
3. I was annoyed with the way the children were behaving, so I ________ .
   A told them up　**B** told them off　**C** told them out　**D** told them over
4. The club committee is ________ of the president, the secretary, and seven other members.
   A set up　**B** made up　**C** set out　**D** made out
5. When you are finished with those board games, please ________ ?
   A put them away　**B** put them out　**C** turn them off　**D** turn them away
6. We moved the table to another room. It ________ too much space here.
   A took in　**B** took up　**C** took off　**D** took over
7. Barbara started taking classes in college, but she ________ after six months.
   A went out　**B** fell out　**C** turned out　**D** dropped out
8. You can't predict everything. Often things don't ________ the way you expect.
   A make out　**B** break out　**C** work out　**D** get out
9. Why are all these people here? What's ________ ?
   A going off　**B** getting off　**C** going on　**D** getting on
10. It's a very busy airport. There are planes ________ or landing every few minutes.
    A going up　**B** taking off　**C** getting up　**D** driving off
11. The traffic was moving slowly because a bus had ________ and was blocking the road.
    A broken down　**B** fallen down　**C** fallen over　**D** broken up
12. Pat feels different from other kids at her school. She doesn't think she ________ .
    A hands in　**B** turns in　**C** drops in　**D** fits in

39 状況に合うように空所に2語を入れて，文を完成しなさい。

1. Keep away from the edge of the pool. You might fall in.
2. I didn't notice that the two pictures were different until Liz pointed it ________ me.
3. I asked Dan if he had any suggestions about what we should do, but he didn't come ________ anything.
4. I'm glad Sarah is coming to the party. I'm really looking ________ seeing her again.
5. Things are changing all the time. It's difficult to keep ________ all these changes.
6. I don't want to run ________ food for the party. Are you sure we have enough?
7. Don't let me interrupt you. Go ________ your work.

8. I'd love to go to your party, but I promised to go see my grandparents this weekend, and I can't get ________________ it. They'd be disappointed if I didn't go.
9. I've had enough of being treated like this. I'm not going to put ________________ it anymore.
10. I didn't enjoy the trip very much at the time, but when I look ________________ it now, I realize it was a good experience and I'm glad I went on it.
11. The wedding was supposed to be a secret, so how did you find ________________ it? Did Jenny tell you?
12. There is a very nice atmosphere in the office where I work. Everybody gets ________________ everybody else.

40 空所に（ ）内の語句と同じ意味を持つ句動詞を入れて，文を完成しなさい。

1. The football game had to be __called off__ because of the weather. (canceled)
2. The story Kate told wasn't true. She __made it up__ . (invented it)
3. A bomb ________________ near the station, but no one was injured. (exploded)
4. George finally ________________ nearly an hour late. (arrived)
5. Here's an application form. Can you ________________ and sign it, please? (complete it)
6. A number of buildings are going to be ________________ to make way for the new road. (demolished)
7. Since my father became ill, my older brother has ________________ more responsibilities in the family. (accepted)
8. Be positive! You must never ________________ ! (stop trying)
9. I was very tired and ________________ in front of the television. (fell asleep)
10. After eight years together, they've decided to ________________ . (separate)
11. The noise is terrible. I can't ________________ any longer. (tolerate it)
12. We don't have a lot of money, but we have enough to ________________ . (manage)
13. I'm sorry I'm late. The meeting ________________ longer than I expected. (continued)
14. We need to make a decision today. We can't ________________ any longer. (delay it)

41 状況に合うように空所に 1 語を入れて，文を完成しなさい。

1. You're driving too fast. Please __slow__ down.
2. It was only a small fire, and I managed to ________________ it out with a bucket of water.
3. The house is empty at the present time, but the new tenants are ________________ in next week.
4. I've ________________ on weight. My clothes don't fit any more.
5. Their house is really nice now. They've ________________ it up really well.
6. I was talking to the woman sitting next to me on the plane, and it ________________ out that she works for the same company as my brother.
7. "Do you know what happened?" "Not yet, but I'm going to ________________ out."
8. There's no need to get angry. ________________ down!
9. Come and see us more often. You can ________________ in any time you like.
10. Sarah has just called to say that she'll be late. She's been ________________ up.
11. You've written my name wrong. It's Martin, not Marin – you ________________ out the T.
12. My mom wants me to take her downtown and ________________ her off at city hall this morning.
13. We had a really interesting discussion, but Jane didn't ________________ in. She just listened.
14. Jonathan is in good shape. He ________________ out at the gym every day.
15. Jenny said she would help me move, but she never came. I can't believe that she ________________ me down.
16. We are still discussing the contract. There are a few things we need to ________________ out.
17. My alarm clock ________________ off in the middle of the night and ________________ me up.

診断テスト

「診断テスト」は, 自分の学習上の弱点を知るためのものです。この「診断テスト」で正しく解答できなかったユニットが自分の学習すべきユニットとなります。それぞれの問題は，本書の目次（pp. iii-vi）にある複数のユニットをまとめる青太字体の見出しと同じ,「現在形と過去形」や「冠詞と名詞」などの見出しでまとめられています。

それぞれの問題文中の空所に入れるのに最もふさわしい語句を選択肢の中から選び，記号で答えてください。選択肢の数は 2～5 の範囲内で変化します。問題によっては複数の選択肢が正解となる場合もあります。

それぞれの問題について，正解できなかったり，正解してもなぜその答えになるかはっきりとわからない場合には，問題の右に示したユニットを学習します。そのユニットを学習すれば，何が，なぜ正解になるのかがわかります。複数のユニットが指示されている場合には，最初に示されたユニットで正解がわかります。

「診断テスト」の正解は p. 362 で確認してください。

正解がわからない場合には，このユニットを学習します。

現在形と過去形

1.1 At first I didn't like my job, but __________ to enjoy it now. **1, 3**
A I'm beginning **B** I begin

1.2 I don't understand this sentence. What __________ ? **2, 4, 7**
A does mean this word **B** does this word mean **C** means this word

1.3 Robert __________ away two or three times a year. **2, 3, 107**
A is going usually **B** is usually going **C** usually goes **D** goes usually

1.4 How __________ now? Better than before? **4**
A you are feeling **B** do you feel **C** are you feeling

1.5 It was a boring weekend. __________ anything. **5**
A I didn't **B** I don't do **C** I didn't do

1.6 Matt __________ while we were having dinner. **6, 9**
A called **B** was calling **C** has called

現在完了形と過去形

2.1 Everything is going well. We __________ any problems so far. **7**
A didn't have **B** don't have **C** haven't had

2.2 Sarah has lost her passport again. It's the second time this __________ . **7**
A has happened **B** happens **C** happened **D** is happening

2.3 "Are you hungry?" "No, __________ lunch." **8**
A I just had **B** I just have **C** I've just had

2.4 It __________ raining for a while, but now it's raining again. **8**
A stopped **B** has stopped **C** was stopped

2.5 My mother __________ in Chile. **8, 14**
A grew up **B** has grown up **C** had grown up

2.6 __________ a lot of candy when you were a child? **9**
A Have you eaten **B** Had you eaten **C** Did you eat

2.7 John __________ in New York for 10 years. Now he lives in Los Angeles. **9, 12**
A lived **B** has lived **C** has been living

2.8 You're out of breath. __________ ? **10**
A Are you running? **B** Have you run? **C** Have you been running?

2.9 Where's the book I gave you? What __________ with it? **11**
A have you done **B** have you been doing **C** are you doing

正解がわからない場合には，このユニットを学習します。

2.10 *A:* ________________ each other for a long time? 12, 11
B: Yes, since we were in high school.
A Do you know **B** Have you known **C** Have you been knowing

2.11 Kelly has been working here ________________ . 13
A for six months **B** since six months **C** six months ago

2.12 It's been two years ________________ Joe. 13
A that I don't see **B** that I haven't seen **C** since I didn't see
D since I saw

2.13 The man sitting next to me on the plane was very nervous. He ________________ before. 14
A hasn't flown **B** didn't fly **C** hadn't flown **D** wasn't flying

2.14 Stephanie was sitting in an armchair resting. She was tired because ________________ very hard. 15
A she was working **B** she's been working **C** she'd been working

2.15 ________________ a car when they were living in Miami? 16, 9
A Do they have **B** Were they having **C** Have they had
D Did they have

2.16 I ________________ tennis a lot, but I don't play very often now. 17
A was playing **B** was used to play **C** used to play

未来

3.1 I'm tired. ________________ to bed now. Good night. 18
A I go **B** I'm going

3.2 ________________ tomorrow, so we can go out somewhere. 18, 20
A I'm not working **B** I don't work **C** I won't work

3.3 That bag looks heavy. ________________ you with it. 20
A I'm helping **B** I help **C** I'll help

3.4 I think the weather ________________ be nice this afternoon. 22, 21
A will **B** shall **C** is going to

3.5 "Ann is in the hospital." "Yes, I know. ________________ her tonight." 22, 19
A I visit **B** I'm going to visit **C** I'll visit

3.6 We're late. The movie ________________ by the time we get to the theater. 23
A will already start **B** will be already started **C** will already have started

3.7 Don't worry ________________ late tonight. 24
A if I'm **B** when I'm **C** when I'll be **D** if I'll be

法助動詞

4.1 The fire spread through the building very quickly, but fortunately everybody ________________ . 25
A was able to escape **B** managed to escape **C** could escape

4.2 I'm so tired I ________________ for a week. 26
A can sleep **B** could sleep **C** could have slept

4.3 The story ________________ be true, but I don't think it is. 26, 28
A might **B** can **C** could **D** may

4.4 Why did you stay at a hotel when you were in Paris? You _______ with Julia. 26
A can stay **B** could stay **C** could have stayed

4.5 "I've lost one of my gloves." "You ________ it somewhere." 27
A must drop **B** must have dropped **C** must be dropping
D must have been dropping

4.6 *A:* I was surprised that Sarah wasn't at the meeting yesterday. 28
B: She ________ about it.
A might not know **B** may not know
C might not have known **D** may not have known

4.7 What was the problem? Why ________ leave early? 30
A had you to **B** did you have to **C** must you **D** you had to

4.8 You missed a great party last night. You ________ . Why didn't you? 31
A must have come **B** should have come **C** ought to come
D had to come

4.9 Lisa ________ some new clothes. 32
A suggested that Mary buy **B** suggested that Mary buys
C suggested Mary to buy

4.10 You're always at home. You ________ out more often. 33
A should go **B** had better go **C** had better to go

4.11 It's late. It's time ________ home. 33
A we go **B** we must go **C** we should go **D** we went

4.12 ________ a little longer, but I really have to go now. 34
A I'd stay **B** I'll stay **C** I can stay **D** I'd have stayed

if と wish

5.1 I'm not tired enough to go to bed. If I ________ to bed now, 36
I wouldn't sleep.
A go **B** went **C** had gone **D** would go

5.2 If I were rich, ________ a yacht. 37
A I'll have **B** I can have **C** I'd have **D** I had

5.3 I wish I ________ have to work tomorrow, but unfortunately I do. 37, 39
A don't **B** didn't **C** wouldn't **D** won't

5.4 The view was wonderful. If ________ a camera with me, I would 38
have taken some photos.
A I had **B** I would have **C** I would have had **D** I'd had

5.5 The weather is horrible. I wish it ________ raining. 39
A would stop **B** stopped **C** stops **D** will stop

受動態

6.1 We ________ by a loud noise during the night. 40
A woke up **B** are woken up **C** were woken up **D** were waking up

6.2 A new supermarket is going to ________ next year. 41
A build **B** be built **C** be building **D** building

6.3 There's somebody walking behind us. I think ________ . 41
A we are following **B** we are being following
C we are followed **D** we are being followed

6.4 "Where ________ ?" "In Los Angeles." 42
A were you born **B** are you born **C** have you been born
D did you born

6.5 There was a fight at the game, but nobody ______________ . **42**
A was hurt **B** got hurt **C** hurt

6.6 Jane ______________ to call me last night, but she didn't. **43**
A supposed **B** is supposed **C** was supposed

6.7 Where ______________ ? Which hairdresser did you go to? **44**
A did you cut your hair **B** have you cut your hair
C did you have cut your hair **D** did you have your hair cut

間接話法

7.1 Paul left the room suddenly. He said he ______________ to go. **46, 45**
A had **B** has **C** have

7.2 Hi, Joe. I didn't expect to see you today. Sonia said you ______________ in the hospital. **46, 45**
A are **B** were **C** was **D** should be

7.3 Ann ______________ and left. **46**
A said good-bye to me **B** said me good-bye **C** told me good-bye

疑問文と繰り返しを避ける助動詞

8.1 "What time ______________ ?" "At 8:30." **47**
A begins the film **B** does begin the film **C** does the film begin

8.2 "Do you know where ______________ ?" "No, he didn't say." **48**
A Tom has gone **B** has Tom gone **C** has gone Tom

8.3 The police officer stopped us and asked us where ______________ . **48**
A were we going **B** are we going **C** we are going **D** we were going

8.4 "Do you think it will rain?" "______________" **49**
A I hope not. **B** I don't hope. **C** I don't hope so.

8.5 "You don't know where Lauren is, ______________ ?" "Sorry, I have no idea." **50**
A don't you **B** do you **C** is she **D** are you

動名詞（-ing）と不定詞（to + 動詞の原形）

9.1 Suddenly everybody stopped ______________ . There was silence. **51**
A talking **B** talk **C** to talk **D** that they talked

9.2 I have to go now. I promised ______________ late. **52, 34**
A not being **B** not to be **C** to not be **D** I wouldn't be

9.3 Do you want ______________ with you, or do you want to go alone? **53**
A me coming **B** me to come **C** that I come **D** that I will come

9.4 I know I locked the door. I clearly remember ______________ it. **54**
A locking **B** to lock **C** to have locked

9.5 She tried to be serious, but she couldn't help ______________ . **55**
A laughing **B** to laugh **C** that she laughed **D** laugh

9.6 Paul lives in Vancouver now. He likes ______________ there. **56**
A living **B** to live

9.7 It's not my favorite job, but I like ______________ the kitchen as often as possible. **56**
A cleaning **B** clean **C** to clean **D** that I clean

9.8 I'm tired. I'd rather ______________ out tonight, if you don't mind. **57**
A not going **B** not to go **C** don't go **D** not go

正解がわからない場合には，このユニットを学習します。

9.9 "Should I stay here?" "I'd rather ________ with us." 57
A you come **B** you to come **C** you came **D** you would come

9.10 Are you looking forward ________ on vacation? 58, 60
A going **B** to go **C** to going **D** that you go

9.11 When Lisa went to Japan, she had to get used ________ on the left. 59
A driving **B** to driving **C** to drive

9.12 I'm thinking ________ a house. Do you think that's a good idea? 60, 64
A to buy **B** of to buy **C** of buying

9.13 I had no ________ a place to live. In fact it was surprisingly easy. 61
A difficulty to find **B** difficulty finding
C trouble to find **D** trouble finding

9.14 A friend of mine called ________ me to a party. 62
A for invite **B** to invite **C** for inviting **D** for to invite

9.15 Jim doesn't speak very clearly. ________ 63
A It is hard to understand him. **B** He is hard to understand.
C He is hard to understand him.

9.16 The sidewalk was icy, so we walked very carefully. We were afraid ________ . 64
A of falling **B** from falling **C** to fall **D** to falling

9.17 I didn't hear you ________ in. You must have been very quiet. 65
A come **B** to come **C** came

9.18 ________ a hotel, we looked for somewhere to have dinner. 66
A Finding **B** After finding **C** Having found **D** We found

冠詞と名詞

10.1 It wasn't your fault. It was ________ . 67
A accident **B** an accident **C** some accident

10.2 Where are you going to put all your ________ ? 68
A furniture **B** furnitures

10.3 "Where are you going?" "I'm going to buy ________ ." 68
A a bread **B** some bread **C** a loaf of bread

10.4 Sandra is ________ . She works at a large hospital. 69, 70
A nurse **B** a nurse **C** the nurse

10.5 Helen works six days ________ week. 70
A in **B** for **C** a **D** the

10.6 There are millions of stars in ________ . 71
A space **B** a space **C** the space

10.7 Every day ________ starts at 9:00 and ends at 3:00. 72
A school **B** a school **C** the school

10.8 ________ a problem in most big cities. 73
A Crime is **B** The crime is **C** The crimes are

10.9 When ________ invented? 74
A was telephone **B** were telephones
C were the telephones **D** was the telephone

10.10 Have you been to ________ ? 75
A Canada or United States B the Canada or the United States
C Canada or the United States D the Canada or United States

10.11 On our first day in Moscow, we visited ________ . 76
A Kremlin B a Kremlin C the Kremlin

10.12 What time ________ on television? 77, 68
A is the news B are the news C is news D is the new

10.13 It took us quite a long time to get here. It was ________ trip. 78
A three hour B a three-hours C a three-hour

10.14 This isn't my book. It's ________ . 79
A my sister B my sister's C from my sister
D of my sister E of my sister's

代名詞と限定詞

11.1 What time should we ________ tomorrow? 80
A meet B meet us C meet ourselves

11.2 I'm going to a wedding on Saturday. ________ is getting married. 81
A A friend of me B A friend of mine C One my friends

11.3 They live on a busy street. ________ a lot of noise from the traffic. 82
A It must be B It must have C There must have D There must be

11.4 He's lazy. He never does ________ work. 83
A some B any C no

11.5 *A:* What would you like to eat? 83
B: I don't care. ________ – whatever you have.
A Something B Anything C Nothing

11.6 We couldn't buy anything because ________ of the stores were open. 84
A all B no one C none D nothing

11.7 We went shopping and spent ________ money. 85
A a lot of B much C lots of D many

11.8 ________ don't visit this part of the town. 86
A The most tourists B Most of tourists C Most tourists

11.9 I asked two people the way to the station, but ________ of them could help me. 87
A none B either C both D neither

11.10 ________ enjoyed the party. It was great. 88
A Everybody B All C All of us D Everybody of us

11.11 The bus service is excellent. There's a bus ________ 10 minutes. 88, 89
A each B every C all

関係詞節

12.1 I don't like stories ________ have unhappy endings. 90
A that B they C which D who

12.2 I didn't believe them at first, but in fact everything ________ was true. 91
A they said B that they said C what they said

12.3 What's the name of the man ________________ ? 92
A you borrowed his car **B** which car you borrowed
C whose car you borrowed **D** his car you borrowed

12.4 Brad told me about his new job, ________________ very much. 93
A that he's enjoying **B** which he's enjoying **C** he's enjoying
D he's enjoying it

12.5 Sarah couldn't meet us, ________________ was a shame. 94
A that **B** it **C** what **D** which

12.6 George showed me some pictures ________________ by his father. 95, 90
A painting **B** painted **C** that were painted **D** they were painted

形容詞と副詞

13.1 Jane doesn't enjoy her job anymore. She's ________________ because every day she does exactly the same thing. 96
A boring **B** bored

13.2 Lisa was carrying a ________________ bag. 97
A black small plastic **B** small and black plastic
C small black plastic **D** plastic small black

13.3 Maria's English is excellent. She speaks ________________ . 98
A perfectly English **B** English perfectly
C perfect English **D** English perfect

13.4 He ________________ to find a job, but he had no luck. 99
A tried hard **B** tried hardly **C** hardly tried

13.5 I haven't seen her for ________________ , I've forgotten what she looks like. 100
A so long **B** so long time **C** a such long time **D** such a long time

13.6 We haven't got ________________ on vacation at the moment. 101
A money enough to go **B** enough money to go
C money enough for going **D** enough money for going

13.7 The test was fairly easy – ________________ I expected. 102
A more easy that **B** more easy than **C** easier than **D** easier as

13.8 The more electricity you use, ________________ . 103
A your bill will be higher **B** will be higher your bill
C the higher your bill will be **D** higher your bill will be

13.9 Patrick is a fast runner. I can't run as fast as ________________ . 104
A he **B** him **C** he can

13.10 The film was really boring. It was ________________ I've ever seen. 105
A most boring film **B** the more boring film
C the film more boring **D** the most boring film

13.11 Ben likes walking. ________________ 106
A Every morning he walks to work. **B** He walks to work every morning.
C He walks every morning to work. **D** He every morning walks to work.

13.12 Joe never calls me. ________________ 107
A Always I have to call him. **B** I always have to call him.
C I have always to call him. **D** I have to call always him.

13.13 Lucy ________________ . She left last month. 108
A still doesn't work here **B** doesn't still work here
C no more works here **D** doesn't work here anymore

13.14 ________________ she can't drive, she has bought a car. 109, 110
A Even **B** Even when **C** Even if **D** Even though

接続詞と前置詞

14.1 I couldn't sleep ________________ very tired. 110
A although I was **B** despite I was **C** despite of being
D in spite of being

14.2 You should register your bike ________________ stolen. 111
A in case it will be **B** if it will be **C** in case it is **D** if it is

14.3 The club is for members only. You ________________ you're a member. 112
A can't go in if **B** can go in only if **C** can't go in unless
D can go in unless

14.4 ________________ the day went on, the weather got worse. 113
A When **B** As **C** While **D** Since

14.5 "What's that noise?" "It sounds ________________ a baby crying." 114, 115
A as **B** like **C** as if **D** as though

14.6 They are very kind to me. They treat me ________________ their own son. 115
A like I'm **B** as if I'm **C** as if I was **D** as if I were

14.7 I'll be in Toronto next week. I hope to see Tom ________________ there. 116
A while I'll be **B** while I'm **C** during my visit **D** during I'm

14.8 Fred is away at the moment. I don't know exactly when he's coming back, 117
but I'm sure he'll be back ________________ Monday.
A by **B** until

前置詞

15.1 Good-bye! I'll see you ________________ . 118
A at Friday morning **B** on Friday morning
C in Friday morning **D** Friday morning

15.2 I'm going away ________________ the end of January. 119
A at **B** on **C** in

15.3 When we were in Chile, we spent a few days ________________ Santiago. 120, 122
A at **B** to **C** in

15.4 Our apartment is ________________ the second floor of the building. 121
A at **B** on **C** in **D** to

15.5 I saw Steve ________________ a concert on Saturday. 122
A at **B** on **C** in **D** to

15.6 When did they ________________ the hotel? 123
A arrive to **B** arrive at **C** arrive in **D** get to **E** get in

15.7 I'm going ________________ vacation next week. I'll be away for two weeks. 124
A at **B** on **C** in **D** for

15.8 We came ________________ 6:45 train, which arrived at 8:30. 125
A in the **B** on the **C** by the **D** by

15.9 *A:* Have you read anything ________________ Ernest Hemingway? **125**
B: No, what sort of books did he write?
A of **B** from **C** by

15.10 The accident was my fault, so I had to pay for the damage ______________ the other car. **126**
A of **B** for **C** to **D** on **E** at

15.11 I like them very much. They have always been very nice _____________ me. **127**
A of **B** for **C** to **D** with

15.12 I'm not very good ________________ fixing things. **128**
A at **B** for **C** in **D** about

15.13 I don't understand this sentence. Can you ________________ ? **129**
A explain to me this word **B** explain me this word
C explain this word to me

15.14 If you're worried about the problem, you should do something ________________ it. **130**
A for **B** about **C** against **D** with

15.15 "Who is Tom Hart?" "I have no idea. I've never heard ____________ him." **131**
A about **B** from **C** after **D** of

15.16 *A:* What time will you be home? **132**
B: I don't know. It depends ________________ the traffic.
A of **B** for **C** from **D** on

15.17 I prefer tea ________________ coffee. **133, 57**
A to **B** than **C** against **D** over

句動詞

16.1 These shoes are uncomfortable. I'm going to ________________ . **134**
A take off **B** take them off **C** take off them

16.2 We're playing a game. Why don't you ________________ ? **135**
A join in **B** come in **C** get in **D** break in

16.3 Nobody believed Paul at first, but he ________________ to be right. **136**
A worked out **B** came out **C** found out **D** turned out

16.4 We can't ________________ making a decision. We have to decide now. **137**
A put away **B** put over **C** put off **D** put out

16.5 The party ________________ until 4:00 in the morning. **138**
A went by **B** went to **C** went on **D** went off

16.6 You can always rely on Pete. He'll never ________________ . **139**
A put you up **B** let you down **C** take you over **D** see you off

16.7 Children under 16 ________________ half the population of the city. **140**
A make up **B** put up **C** take up **D** bring up

16.8 I'm surprised to hear that Sue and Paul have ________________ . They seemed very happy together the last time I saw them. **141**
A broken up **B** ended up **C** finished up **D** split up

16.9 I parked in a no-parking zone, but I ________________ it. **142**
A came up with **B** got away with **C** made off with **D** got along with

Exercises 解答

本書の Exercises（練習問題）の中には，自由に自分の考えを述べるものもあります。その場合でも解答例が与えられていますが，できれば英語の母国語話者や，先生や友人に確認してもらいましょう。なお解答中にある *or* や /，（ ）は入れ換え可能を示します。

UNIT 1

1.1
2. 'm looking (am looking)
3. 's getting (is getting)
4. 're staying (are staying)
5. is losing
6. 's starting (is starting)
7. 're making (are making)
   'm trying (am trying)
8. 's happening (is happening)

1.2
3. 'm not listening (am not listening)
4. 's having (is having)
5. 'm not eating (am not eating)
6. 's studying (is studying)
7. aren't speaking / 're not speaking (are not speaking)
8. 'm getting (am getting)
9. isn't working / 's not working (is not working)

1.3
1. What's he studying
   Is he enjoying
   he's learning
2. is your new job going
   it's getting
   he isn't enjoying / he's not enjoying
   he's beginning

1.4
2. is changing
3. 's getting (is getting)
4. is rising
5. is beginning

UNIT 2

2.1
2. drink
3. opens
4. causes
5. live
6. take
7. connects

2.2
2. do the banks close
3. don't watch (do not watch)
4. does Ricardo come
5. do you do
6. takes . . . does it take
7. does this word mean
8. doesn't exercise (does not exercise)

2.3
3. rises
4. make
5. don't eat
6. doesn't believe
7. translates
8. don't tell
9. flows

2.4
2. Does . . . play tennis?
3. Which newspaper do you read?
4. What does your brother do?
5. How often do you go to the movies?
6. Where do your grandparents live?

2.5
2. I promise
3. I insist
4. I apologize
5. I recommend

UNIT 3

3.1
3. is trying
4. are they talking
5. *OK*
6. It's getting (It is getting)
7. *OK*
8. I'm coming (I am coming)
9. is it going
10. He always gets
11. *OK*

3.2
3. 's waiting (is waiting)
4. Are you listening
5. Do you listen
6. flows
7. 's flowing (is flowing)
8. grow . . . aren't growing / 're not growing (are not growing)
9. 's improving (is improving)
10. 's staying (is staying) . . . stays
11. 'm starting (am starting)
12. 'm learning (am learning) . . .
    's teaching (is teaching)
13. finish . . . 'm working (am working)
14. live . . . do your parents live
15. 's looking (is looking) . . . 's staying (is staying)
16. does your brother do . . . isn't working / 's not working (is not working)
17. enjoy . . . 'm not enjoying (am not enjoying)

3.3
2. 's always breaking down.
3. 'm always making the same mistake. / . . . that mistake.
4. You're always forgetting your glasses.

UNIT 4

4.1
2. Do you believe
3. *OK*
4. It tastes
5. I think

4.2
2. What are you doing? I'm thinking.
3. Who does this umbrella belongto?
4. Dinner smells good.
5. Is anybody sitting there?
6. These gloves don't fit me.

4.3
2. 'm using
3. need
4. does he want
5. is he looking
6. believes
7. don't remember *or* can't remember
8. 'm thinking
9. think . . . don't use
10. consists

4.4
2. is being
3. 's
4. are you being
5. Is he

UNIT 5

5.1
2. had
3. walked to work
4. took her (about) half an hour
5. She started work
6. She didn't have / She didn't eat (She did not have/eat)
7. She finished work
8. She was . . . she got
9. She cooked
10. She didn't go
11. She went to bed
12. She slept

5.2
2. taught
3. sold
4. fell . . . hurt
5. threw . . . caught
6. spent . . . bought . . . cost

5.3

2. did you travel / did you go
3. did it take (you) / were you there
4. did you stay
5. How was the weather?
6. Did you go to / Did you see / Did you visit

5.4

3. didn't disturb
4. left
5. didn't sleep
6. flew
7. didn't cost
8. didn't have
9. were

UNIT 6

6.1

解答例

3. I was working.
4. I was in bed asleep. / I was sleeping.
5. I was getting ready to go out.
6. I was watching TV at home.

6.2

解答例

2. was taking a shower
3. were driving to work
4. was reading the paper
5. was watching it

6.3

1. didn't see ... was looking
2. met ... were going ... was going ... talked ... were waiting *or* waited
3. was riding ... stepped ... was going ... managed ... didn't hit

6.4

2. were you doing
3. Did you go
4. were you driving ... happened
5. took ... wasn't looking
6. didn't know
7. saw ... was trying
8. was walking ... heard ... was following ... started
9. wanted
10. dropped ... was doing ... didn't break

UNIT 7

7.1

2. ... you ever been to Mexico?
3. Have you ever run [in] a marathon?
4. Have you ever spoken to a famous person?
5. ... the most beautiful place you've ever visited? (... you have ever visited?)

7.2

2. haven't seen (have not seen)
3. I haven't eaten (I have not eaten ...)
4. I haven't played (I have not played)
5. I've had / I have had
6. I've never read (I have never)
7. I've never been / I haven't been
8. 's been (has been)
9. I've never tried / I have never tried
10. it's broken down / it has broken down
11. I've never seen / I have never seen

7.3

2. haven't read one / haven't read a newspaper
3. it hasn't made a profit
4. she hasn't worked hard this semester
5. it hasn't snowed [a lot] this winter
6. haven't won many/any games this season

7.4

2. you played tennis before?
   time I've played tennis.
3. Have you ridden a horse before? / Have you been on a horse before?
   No, this is the first time I've ridden a horse. / ... I've been on a horse.
4. Have you been in Los Angeles before?
   No, this is the first time I've been in Los Angeles.

UNIT 8

8.1

2. has changed
3. forgot
4. went
5. had
6. 've lost / have lost

8.2

3. 両方正しい
4. a.
5. b.
6. 両方正しい
7. 両方正しい
8. 両方正しい
9. b.
10. a.

8.3

2. he just went out *or* he's just gone out
3. I didn't finish yet. *or* I haven't finished yet.
4. I already did it. *or* I've already done it.
5. Did you find a place to live yet? *or* Have you found a place to live yet?
6. I didn't decide yet. *or* I haven't decided yet.
7. she just came back *or* she's just come back
8. already invited me *or* has already invited me

UNIT 9

9.1

3. *OK*
4. I bought
5. Where were you
6. graduated
7. *OK*
8. *OK*
9. *OK*
10. was this book

9.2

2. has been cold recently.
3. was cold last week.
4. didn't read a newspaper yesterday.
5. haven't read a newspaper today.
6. has made a lot of money this year.
7. She didn't make so much last year.
8. Have you taken a vacation recently?

9.3

2. got ... was ... went
3. Did you eat ... We've been
4. weren't (were not)
5. worked
6. 's lived (has lived)
7. Did you go ... was ... was
8. died ... never met
9. 've never met (have never met)
10. haven't seen ... he had to
11. have you lived / have you been living ... did you live ... did you live

9.4

Example answers:

2. I haven't bought anything today.
3. I didn't watch TV yesterday.
4. I went out with some friends last night.
5. I haven't been to the movies recently. / I haven't gone to ...
6. I've read a lot of books recently.

UNIT 10

10.1

2. 's been watching television (has been watching)
3. 've been playing tennis (have been playing)
4. 's been running (has been running) / has been jogging

10.2

2. Have you been waiting long?
3. What have you been doing?
4. How long have you been working there?
5. How long have you been selling computers?

10.3

2. 've been waiting (have been waiting)
3. 've been studying Spanish (have been studying Spanish)
4. She's been working there (She has been working there)
5. They've been going there (They have been going there)

10.4

2. I've been looking (I have been looking)
3. are you looking
4. She's been teaching (She has been teaching)
5. I've been thinking (I have been thinking)
6. she's working (she is working)
7. she's been working (she has been working)

UNIT 11

11.1

2. She's been traveling for three months. / She has been traveling . . .
   She's visited six countries so far. / She has visited . . .
3. He's won the national championships four times. / He has won . . .
   He's been playing tennis since he was 10. / He has been playing . . .
4. They've made five movies since they finished college. / They have made . . .
   They've been making movies since they finished college. / They have been making . . .

11.2

2. Have you been waiting long?
3. Have you caught any fish?
4. How many people have you invited?
5. How long have you been teaching?
6. How many books have you written?
   How long have you been writing books?
7. How long have you been saving?
   How much money have you saved?

11.3

2. Somebody's broken / Somebody has broken
3. Have you been working
4. Have you ever worked
5. 's gone / has gone
6. He's appeared / He has appeared
7. I haven't been waiting
8. it's stopped / it has stopped
9. I've lost / I have lost . . . Have you seen
10. I've been reading / I have been reading . . . I haven't finished
11. I've read / I have read

UNIT 12

12.1

3. have been married
4. *OK*
5. It's been raining / It has been raining
6. have you been living
7. has been working
8. *OK*
9. I haven't drunk
10. have you had

12.2

2. How long have you been teaching English? / How long have you taught . . .
3. How long have you known Carol?
4. How long has your brother been in Costa Rica?
5. How long have you had that car?
6. How long has Scott been working at the airport? / How long has Scott worked . . .
7. How long have you been taking guitar lessons?
8. Have you always lived in Chicago?

12.3

3. 's been / has been
4. 've been waiting / have been waiting
5. 've known / have known
6. haven't played
7. 's been watching / has been watching
8. haven't watched
9. 've had / have had
10. hasn't been
11. 've been feeling / have been feeling *or* 've felt / have felt
12. 's lived / has lived *or* 's been living / has been living
13. haven't been
14. 've always wanted / have always wanted

UNIT 13

13.1

2. since
3. for
4. for
5. since
6. for / in
7. since
8. since
9. for

13.2

2. How long has Kate been studying Japanese?
   When did Kate start studying Japanese?
3. How long have you known Jeff?
   When did you first meet Jeff? / When did you and Jeff first meet?
4. How long have Rebecca and David been married?
   When did Rebecca and David get married?

13.3

3. been sick since
4. been sick for
5. married a year ago
6. had a headache since
7. to France three weeks ago.
8. been working in a hotel for six months. / I've worked in a hotel for six months.

13.4

2. No, I haven't seen Laura/her for/in about a month.
3. No, I haven't been to the movies for/in a long time.
4. No, I haven't eaten out for (*or* in) ages. / No, I haven't been to a restaurant in ages.
6. been about a month since I (last) saw Laura/her.
7. it's been a long time since I (last) went to the movies.
8. No, it's been ages since I (last) ate out. *or* . . . since I went to a restaurant.

UNIT 14

14.1

2. It had changed a lot.
3. She'd made plans to do something else. (She had made plans . . .)
4. The movie had already begun.
5. I hadn't seen him in five years.
6. She'd just had breakfast. (She had just had . . .)

14.2
2. 'd never seen her before. (had never seen . . .)
3. 'd never played (tennis) before. (had never played . . .)
4. 'd never been there before. (had never been . . .)

14.3
1. called the police
2. there was . . . had gone
3. He'd just . . . come back from (He had just come back from)
   He looked
4. got a phone call . . . was
   'd sent her (had sent her)
   'd never answered them (had never answered them)

14.4
2. went
3. had gone
4. broke
5. saw . . . had broken . . . stopped

UNIT 15

15.1
2. They'd been playing soccer. (They had been playing . . .)
3. I'd been looking forward to it. (I had been looking forward . . .)
4. She'd been dreaming. (She had been dreaming.)
5. He'd been watching a DVD. (He had been watching . . .)

15.2
2. 'd been waiting . . . [suddenly] realized that I was in . . . *or* . . . that I had come to . . .
3. closed down, . . . had been working . . .
4. had been playing for about 10 minutes . . . a man in the audience started shouting.
5. 解答例
   'd been driving along the road for about 10 minutes . . . the car behind me started honking its horn.

15.3
3. was walking
4. 'd been running (had been running)
5. were eating
6. 'd been eating (had been eating)
7. was looking
8. was waiting . . . 'd been waiting (had been waiting)
9. 'd had (had had)
10. 'd been traveling (had been traveling)

UNIT 16

16.1
3. I don't have a ladder. / I haven't got a ladder.
4. didn't have enough time.
5. He didn't have a map.
6. She doesn't have any money.
7. I don't have enough energy.
8. They didn't have a camera.

16.2
2. Do you have / Have you got
3. Did you have
4. Do you have / Have you got
5. Do you have / Have you got
6. did you have
7. Did you have

16.3
解答例
2. I don't have a bike (now).
   I had a bike (10 years ago).
3. I have a cell phone / I've got a cell phone (now).
   I didn't have a cell phone (10 years ago).
4. I don't have a dog (now).
   I didn't have a dog (10 years ago).
5. I have a guitar / I've got a guitar (now).
   I had a guitar (10 years ago).
6. I don't have long hair (now).
   I didn't have long hair (10 years ago).
7. I have a driver's license / I've got a driver's license (now).
   I didn't have a driver's license (10 years ago).

16.4
2. have a talk
3. had a party
4. have a look
5. 's having a nice time (is having . . .)
6. had a dream
7. Did you have trouble
8. had a baby
9. were having dinner
10. Did you have a good flight?

UNIT 17

17.1
2. used to have/ride
3. used to live
4. used to eat/like/love
5. used to be
6. used to take [me]
7. used to be
8. did you use to go

17.2
3.–6.
He used to go to bed early.
He didn't use to go out every night.
He used to run three miles every morning.
He didn't use to spend much money. / . . . a lot of money.

17.3
2.–10.
used to have lots of friends, . . . she doesn't see many people these days.
used to be very lazy, . . . she works very hard these days.
didn't use to like cheese, . . . she eats lots of cheese now.
used to be a hotel desk clerk, . . . she works in a bookstore now.
used to play the piano, . . . she hasn't played the piano for years.
never used to read newspapers, . . . she reads a newspaper every day now.
didn't use to drink tea, . . . she likes it now.
used to have a dog, . . . it died two years ago.
used to go to a lot of parties, . . . she hasn't been to a party for ages.

UNIT 18

18.1
2. How long are you staying?
3. When are you leaving?
4. Are you going alone?
5. Are you traveling by car?
6. Where are you staying?

18.2
2. 'm working late. / 'm working till 9:00.
3. I'm going to the theater.
4. I'm meeting Julia.

18.3
解答例
2. 'm working tomorrow morning.
3. I'm not doing anything tomorrow night.
4. I'm playing football next Sunday.
5. I'm going to a party this evening.

18.4
3. 're having / are having
4. opens
5. 'm not going / am not going . . . 'm staying / am staying
6. Are you doing
7. 're going / are going . . . starts
8. 'm leaving / am leaving
9. 're meeting / are meeting
10. does this train get
11. 'm going / am going . . . Are you coming
12. does it end
13. 'm not using / am not using
14. 's coming / is coming . . . 's flying / is flying . . . arrives

UNIT 19

19.1

2. What are you going to wear?
3. Where are you going to put it?
4. Who are you going to invite?

19.2

2. I'm going to take it back.
3. I'm not going to take it.
4. I'm going to call her tonight.
5. I'm going to complain.

19.3

2. 's going to be late. (is going to be late.)
3. boat is going to sink.
4. 're going to run out of gas. (are going to . . .)

19.4

2. was going to buy
3. were going to play
4. was going to call
5. was going to quit
6. were going to have

UNIT 20

20.1

2. I'll turn / I'll put
3. I'll go
4. I'll do
5. I'll show / I'll teach
6. I'll have
7. I'll send
8. I'll give / I'll bring
9. I'll stay / I'll wait

20.2

2. I'll go to bed.
3. I'll walk.
4. I'll play tennis (today).
5. I don't think I'll go swimming.

20.3

3. I'll meet
4. I'll lend
5. I'm having
6. I won't forget
7. does your plane leave
8. won't tell
9. Are you doing
10. Will you come

20.4

2. shall I give/buy/get
3. I'll do / I will do
4. shall we go?
5. I won't tell
6. I'll try

UNIT 21

21.1

2. I'm going
3. will get
4. is coming
5. we are going
6. It won't hurt

21.2

2. 'll look / will look
3. 'll like / will like
4. 'll get / will get
5. will live
6. 'll meet / will meet
7. 'll come / will come
8. will take

21.3

2. won't
3. 'll / will
4. won't
5. 'll / will
6. 'll / will
7. won't
8. 'll / will

21.4

解答例

2. I'll be in bed.
3. I'll be at work.
4. I'll probably be at home.
5. I don't know where I'll be this time next year.

21.5

2. think it will rain?
3. think it will end?
4. do you think it will cost?
5. you think they'll get married? / . . . they will get married?
6. do you think you'll be back? / . . . you will be back?
7. do you think will happen?

UNIT 22

22.1

2. I'll lend
3. I'll get
4. I'm going to wash
5. are you going to paint
6. I'm going to buy
7. I'll show
8. I'll do
9. it's going to fall
10. He's going to take . . . he's going to start

22.2

2. I'm going to take . . . I'll join
3. you'll find
4. I'm not going to apply
5. You'll wake
6. I'll take . . . we'll leave . . . Ann is going to take

UNIT 23

23.1

2. b
3. a, c
4. b, d
5. c, d
6. c

23.2

2. We'll have finished
3. we'll be playing
4. I'll be working
5. the meeting will have ended
6. he'll have spent
7. you'll still be doing
8. she'll have traveled
9. I'll be staying
10. Will you be seeing

UNIT 24

24.1

2. goes
3. 'll tell / will tell . . . come
4. see . . . won't recognize / will not recognize
5. Will you be . . . 'm/am
6. 's/is
7. 'll wait / will wait . . . 're/are
8. 'll be / will be . . . gets
9. is
10. calls . . . 'm/am

24.2

2. I'll give you my address . . . I find somewhere to live. *or* . . . I've found somewhere to live.
3. I'll come straight home . . . I do the shopping. *or* . . . I've done the shopping.
4. Let's go home . . . it gets dark.
5. I won't speak to her . . . she apologizes. *or* . . . she has apologized.

24.3

2. you go / you leave
3. you decide *or* you've decided / you have decided
4. you're in Hong Kong / you are in Hong Kong
5. finish the new road / 've finished the new road / have finished the new road *or* build the new road / 've built the new road / have built the new road

24.4

2. If
3. When
4. if
5. If
6. when
7. if
8. if

UNIT 25

25.1

3. can
4. be able to
5. been able to
6. can
7. be able to

25.2

解答例

2. I used to be able to run fast.
3. I'd like to be able to play the piano.
4. I've never been able to get up early.

25.3

2. could run
3. can wait
4. couldn't eat
5. can't hear
6. couldn't sleep

25.4

2. was able to finish it
3. were able to find it
4. was able to get away

25.5

4. couldn't
5. managed to
6. could
7. managed to
8. could
9. managed to
10. couldn't

UNIT 26

26.1

2. could have fish.
3. could call (her) now.
4. You could give her a book.
5. We could go on Friday.

26.2

3. I could scream.
4. *OK* – could have も可
5. I could stay here all day
6. it could be in the car (may/might も可)
7. *OK*
8. *OK* – could borrow も可
9. it could change later (may/might も可)

26.3

2. could have come/gone
3. could apply
4. could have been
5. could have taken
6. could come

26.4

3. couldn't wear
4. couldn't have found
5. couldn't get
6. couldn't have been
7. couldn't have come/gone

UNIT 27

27.1

2. must
3. must not
4. must
5. must not
6. must

27.2

3. be
4. have been
5. go
6. be going
7. have taken / have stolen / have moved
8. have been
9. be following

27.3

3. It must have been very expensive.
4. I must have left it in the restaurant last night.
5. The exam must not have been very difficult.
6. She must have listened to our conversation.
7. She must not have understood what I said.
8. I must have forgotten to turn it off.
9. The neighbors must have been having a party.

27.4

3. can't
4. must not
5. can't
6. must not

UNIT 28

28.1

2. She might/may be busy.
3. She might/may be working.
4. She might/may want to be alone.
5. She might/may have been sick yesterday.
6. She might/may have gone home early.
7. She might/may have had to go home early.
8. She might/may have been working yesterday.
9. She might/may not want to see me.
10. She might/may not be working today.
11. She might/may not have been feeling well yesterday.

28.2

2. be
3. have been
4. be waiting
5. have

28.3

2. a) She might be watching TV in her room.
   b) She might have gone out.
3. a) It might be in the car.
   b) You might have left it in the restaurant last night.
4. a) He might not have heard the doorbell.
   b) He might have been in the shower.

〔might の代わりに may を用いても可〕

28.4

3. might not have received it
4. couldn't have been an accident
5. couldn't have tried
6. might not have been Chinese

UNIT 29

29.1

2. I might/may buy a Toyota.
3. I might/may go to the movies.
4. He might/may come on Saturday.
5. I might/may hang it in the dining room.
6. She might/may go to college.

29.2

2. might wake up
3. might bite
4. might need
5. might slip
6. might break

〔might の代わりに may を用いても可〕

29.3

2. might be able to meet/see
3. might have to work
4. might have to go/leave

〔might の代わりに may を用いても可〕

29.4

2. might not go out tonight.
3. might not like the present you bought him.
4. Sue might not be able to get together with us tonight.

〔might の代わりに may を用いても可〕

29.5

2. might as well go to the concert.
3. might as well paint the bathroom.
4. We might as well watch the movie.

〔might の代わりに may を用いても可〕

UNIT 30

30.1

2. had to
3. have to
4. have to
5. has to
6. had to
7. had to
8. have to

30.2
2. do you have to go
3. Did you have to wait
4. do you have to be
5. Does he have to travel

30.3
3. have to make
4. had to ask
5. doesn't have to shave
6. didn't have to go
7. has to make
8. don't have to do

30.4
3. might have to
4. will have to
5. might have to
6. won't have to

30.5
3. don't have to
4. must not
5. don't have to
6. must not
7. doesn't have to
8. must not
9. don't have to

UNIT 31

31.1
2. should look for another job.
3. shouldn't go to bed so late.
4. should take a photo.
5. shouldn't use her car so much.
6. should put some pictures on the walls.

31.2
2. I don't think you should go out tonight.
3. you should apply for the job.
4. I don't think the government should raise taxes.

31.3
3. should come
4. should do
5. should have done
6. should have won
7. should be
8. should have arrived

31.4
3. should have reserved a table.
4. The store should be open by now. *or* The store should have opened by now.
5. shouldn't be driving so fast. / 50 miles an hour. *or* should be driving 30 miles an hour.
6. should have written it down
7. I shouldn't have been driving right behind another car.
8. I should have looked where I was going. *or* I should have been looking . . .

UNIT 32

32.1
3. I stay a little longer.
4. she visit the museum after lunch.
5. I see a specialist.
6. I not lift anything heavy.
7. we pay the rent by Friday.
8. I go away for a few days.
9. I not give my children snacks before mealtime.
10. we have dinner early.

32.2
3. spend / take
4. apologize
5. be
6. wait
7. be
8. wear
9. have / be given
10. remember / not forget
11. drink / have

32.3
2. walk to work in the morning.
3. that he eat more fruit and vegetables.
4. suggested that he take vitamins.

UNIT 33

33.1
2. You'd better put a bandage on it. (You had better put . . .)
3. 'd better make a reservation. (We had better make a reservation . . .)
4. You'd better not go to work (You had better not go . . .)
5. I'd better pay the phone bill (soon). (I had better pay . . .)
6. I'd better not go out (yet). (I had better not go out . . .)
7. We'd better take/get a taxi. (We had better take . . .)

33.2
3. 'd better (had better)
4. should
5. should
6. 'd better (had better)
7. should
8. should

33.3
1. b) 'd (had)
   c) close/shut
2. a) did
   b) was done
   c) thought

33.4
2. took / had a vacation
3. It's time the train left.
4. It's time I/we had a party.
5. It's time some changes were made.
6. It's time he tried something else.

UNIT 34

34.1
解答例
2. I wouldn't like to be a teacher.
3. I'd love to learn to fly a plane. (I would love to learn . . .)
4. It would be nice to have a big garden.
5. I'd like to go to Mexico. (I would like to go . . .)

34.2
2. 'd enjoy (would enjoy)
3. would have enjoyed
4. would . . . do
5. would have stopped
6. would have been
7. 'd be (would be)
8. would have passed
9. would have

34.3
2. e
3. b
4. f
5. a
6. d

34.4
2. he'd call. (. . . he would call)
3. promised you wouldn't tell her.
4. promised they'd wait (for us).

34.5
2. wouldn't tell
3. wouldn't speak / talk
4. wouldn't let

34.6
2. would shake
3. would . . . help
4. would share
5. would . . . forget

UNIT 35

35.1
2. Can/Could I leave a message (for her)? *or* Can/Could you give her a message?
3. Can/Could you tell me how to get to the post office? *or* . . . the way to the post office? *or* . . . where the post office is?
4. Can/Could I try on these pants? *or* Can/Could I try these [pants] on?
5. Can/Could you give me a ride home? *or* Can/Could I [please] have a ride home?

35.2
3. Do you think you could check this letter (for me)? / . . . check my letter?
4. Do you mind if I leave work early?
5. Do you think you could turn the music down? / . . . turn it down?

6. Is it OK if I come and see the apartment today?
7. Do you think I could have a look at your newspaper?

35.3

2. Can/Could/Would you show me? *or* Do you think you could show me? *or* . . . do it for me?
3. Would you like to sit down? *or* Would you like a seat? *or* Can I offer you a seat?
4. Can/Could/Would you slow down? *or* Do you think you could . . . ?
5. Can/Could/May I/we have the check, please? *or* Do you think I/we could have . . . ? *or* Can I get . . .
6. Would you like to borrow it?

UNIT 36

36.1

3. 'd take (would take)
4. closed down
5. wouldn't get
6. pressed
7. refused
8. 'd be (would be)
9. didn't come
10. borrowed
11. walked
12. would understand

36.2

2. would you do if you lost your passport?
3. What would you do if there was/were a fire in the building?
4. What would you do if you were in an elevator and it stopped between floors?

36.3

2. took his driving test, he'd fail (it). / . . . he would fail (it).
3. we stayed at a hotel, it would cost too much.
4. she applied for the job, she wouldn't get it.
5. we told them the truth, they wouldn't believe us.
6. If we invited Bill, we'd have to invite his friends, too. (. . . we would have to . . .)

36.4

解答例

2. somebody broke into my house.
3. I'd have a much nicer day than usual.
4. you were invited?
5. you'd save a lot of time.
6. I didn't go out with you this evening?

UNIT 37

37.1

3. 'd help (would help)
4. lived
5. 'd live (would live)
6. would taste
7. were/was
8. wouldn't wait . . . 'd go (would go)
9. didn't go
10. weren't . . . wouldn't be

37.2

2. buy it . . . it weren't/wasn't so expensive. (I would buy it) *or* . . . if it were/was cheaper.
3. 'd go out to eat more often if we could afford it. (We would go out . . .)
4. I didn't have to work late, I could meet you tomorrow. *or* . . . I'd meet (I would meet . . .) *or* . . . I'd be able to meet . . .
5. could have lunch on the patio if it weren't raining / wasn't raining.
6. I wanted his advice, I'd ask for it (I would ask for it.)

37.3

2. I had a cell phone.
3. I wish Amanda was/were here.
4. I wish it weren't/wasn't so cold.
5. I wish I didn't live in a big city.
6. I wish I could go to the party.
7. I wish I didn't have to work tomorrow.
8. I wish I knew something about cars.
9. I wish I was feeling / were feeling better.

37.4

解答例

2. I wish I had a big garden.
3. I wish I could tell jokes. *or* . . . I wish I was/were able to . . .
4. I wish I was/were taller.

UNIT 38

38.1

2. he'd missed (he had missed) . . . , he would have been.
3. I would have forgotten . . . you hadn't reminded
4. I'd had (I had had) . . . I would have sent
5. we would have enjoyed . . . the weather had been
6. It would have been . . . I had walked
7. I was / I were
8. I'd been (I had been)

38.2

2. hadn't been icy, the accident wouldn't have happened.
3. had known [that Matt had to get up early], I would have woken him up.
4. If Jim hadn't lent me the money, I wouldn't have been able to buy the car. *or* . . . I couldn't have bought the car.
5. If Michelle hadn't been wearing a seat belt, she would have been injured [in the crash].
6. If you had had (some) breakfast, you wouldn't be hungry now.
7. If I had had (some) money, I would have taken a taxi.

38.3

2. 'd applied (I wish I had applied) for the job.
3. I wish I'd learned to play a musical instrument [when I was younger]. (I wish I had learned . . .)
4. I wish I hadn't painted it red. *or* . . . the door red.
5. I wish I'd brought my camera. (I wish I had brought . . .)
6. I wish they'd called first [to say they were coming]. (I wish they had called) *or* I wish I'd known they were coming. (I wish I had known)

UNIT 39

39.1

2. hope
3. wish
4. wished
5. hope
6. wish . . . hope

39.2

2. Jane/she would come. *or* . . . would hurry up.
3. would give me a job.
4. I wish the/that baby would stop crying.
5. wouldn't drive so fast.
6. I wish you wouldn't leave the door open [all the time].
7. wouldn't drop litter in the street.

39.3

2. *OK*
3. I wish I had more free time.
4. I wish our house was/were a little bigger.
5. *OK*
6. *OK*
7. I wish everything wasn't/weren't so expensive.

39.4
3. I knew
4. I'd taken (I had taken)
5. I could come
6. I wasn't / I weren't
7. they'd hurry (they would hurry)
8. we didn't have
9. we could have stayed *or* we had been able to stay
10. it wasn't/weren't
11. he'd decide (he would decide)
12. we hadn't gone

UNIT 40

40.1
2. is made
3. was damaged
4. were invited
5. are shown
6. are held
7. was written . . . was translated
8. were passed
9. is surrounded

40.2
2. When was television invented?
3. How are mountains formed?
4. When was Neptune discovered?
5. What is silver used for?

40.3
3. covers
4. is covered
5. are locked
6. was mailed . . . arrived
7. sank . . . was rescued
8. died . . . were brought up
9. grew up
10. was stolen
11. disappeared
12. did Sue quit
13. was Bill fired
14. is owned
15. called . . . was injured . . . wasn't needed
16. were these picture taken . . . Did you take

40.4
2. flights were canceled because of fog.
3. This road isn't used much.
4. was accused of stealing money.
5. are languages learned?
6. We were warned not to go out alone.

UNIT 41

41.1
2. can't be broken
3. it can be eaten
4. it can't be used
5. it can't be seen
6. it can be carried

41.2
3. be made
4. be spent
5. have been repaired
6. be carried
7. be woken up
8. have been arrested
9. have been caused

41.3
2. is being used right now.
3. our conversation was being recorded.
4. the game had been canceled.
5. A new highway is being built around the city.
6. A new hospital has been built near the airport.

41.4
3. was stolen! *or* It has been stolen! (It's been)
4. took it! *or* Somebody has taken it!
5. furniture had been moved.
6. hasn't been seen since then.
7. haven't seen her for ages.
8. the computers were being used.
9. 's being redecorated.
10. 's working again. (is working . . .) . . . It's been repaired. (It has been repaired)
11. Have you ever been mugged?

UNIT 42

42.1
2. was asked some difficult questions at the interview.
3. was given a present by her colleagues when she retired.
4. told about the meeting.
5. be paid for your work?
6. should have been offered the job.
7. been shown what to do?

42.2
2. being invited
3. being given
4. being hit
5. being treated
6. being paid

42.3
2.–6.

Beethoven was born in 1770.
John Lennon was born in 1940.
Galileo was born in 1564.
Mahatma Gandhi was born in 1869.
Martin Luther King Jr. was born in 1929.
Elvis Presley was born in 1935.
Leonardo da Vinci was born in 1452.
William Shakespeare was born in 1564.
was born in . . .

42.4
2. got stung
3. get used
4. got stolen
5. get paid
6. got stopped
7. get damaged
8. get asked

UNIT 43

43.1
3. are reported to be homeless after the floods.
4. is alleged to have robbed the store of $3,000.
5. is reported to have been badly damaged by the fire.
6. a) is said to be losing a lot of money
   b) is believed to have lost a lot of money last year.
   c) is expected to lose money this year

43.2
2. is supposed to know a lot of famous people. (He's supposed . . .)
3. He is supposed to be very rich.
4. He is supposed to have 12 children
5. He is supposed to have been an actor when he was younger.

43.3
2. You're supposed to be my friend.
3. I'm supposed to be on a diet. (I am supposed . . .)
4. It was supposed to be a joke.
5. Or maybe it's supposed to be a flower. (it is supposed . . .)
6. You're supposed to be working. (You are supposed . . .)

43.4
2. 're supposed to start (We are supposed . . .)
3. was supposed to call
4. aren't / 're not supposed to block (are not supposed . . .)
5. was supposed to arrive

UNIT 44

44.1
1. b
2. a
3. a
4. b

44.2
2. have my jacket cleaned.
3. To have my watch repaired.
4. To have my eyes tested.

44.3
2. had it cut.
3. had it painted.
4. He had it built.
5. I had them delivered.

44.4

2. have another key made.
3. had your hair cut
4. Do you have a newspaper delivered
5. 're having a garage built
6. have your eyes checked
8. get it cleaned
9. get your ears pierced
10. got it repaired *or* 've gotten it repaired
12. had her purse stolen
13. had his nose broken

UNIT 45

45.1

2. his father wasn't very well.
3. said [that] Amanda and Paul were getting married next month.
4. He said [that] his sister had had a baby.
5. He said [that] he didn't know what Eric was doing.
6. He said [that] he'd seen Nicole at a party in June and she'd seemed fine / he had seen . . . she had seemed fine *or* He said [that] he saw Nicole . . . and she seemed . . .
7. He said [that] he hadn't seen Diane recently.
8. He said [that] he wasn't enjoying his job very much.
9. He said [that] I could come and stay at his place if I was ever in Chicago.
10. He said [that] his car had been stolen a few days ago. *or* . . . his car was stolen a few days ago.
11. He said [that] he wanted to take a trip, but [he] couldn't afford it.
12. He said [that] he'd tell Amy he'd seen me. / . . . he would tell . . . he had seen *or* . . . he saw me.

45.2

解答例

2. wasn't coming / . . . was going somewhere else / . . . was staying at home
3. she didn't like him
4. you didn't know anybody / you didn't know many people
5. she wouldn't be here / she would be away / she was going away
6. you were staying at home / you weren't going out
7. you couldn't speak (any) French / were fluent in French
8. you went to the movies last week / you had gone to the movies last week

UNIT 46

46.1

2. you said you didn't like fish.
3. But you said you couldn't drive.
4. But you said she had a very well-paid job.
5. But you said you didn't have any brothers or sisters.
6. But you said you'd never been to Peru. (you had never been)
7. But you said you were working tomorrow night.
8. But you said she was a friend of yours.

46.2

2. Tell
3. Say
4. said
5. told
6. said
7. tell . . . said
8. tell . . . say
9. told
10. said

46.3

2. her to slow down
3. her not to worry
4. asked Tom to give me a hand *or* . . . to help me
5. asked me to open my bag
6. told him to mind his own business
7. asked her to marry him
8. told her not to wait [for me] if I was late

UNIT 47

47.1

2. Were you born there?
3. Are you married?
4. How long have you been married?
5. Do you have (any) children? *or* Have you got (any) children?
6. How old are they?
7. What do you do?
8. What does your wife do?

47.2

3. paid the bill?
4. happened?
5. What did she/Diane say?
6. Who does it/this book belong to?
7. Who lives in that house? / Who lives there?
8. What did you fall over?
9. What fell on the floor?
10. What does it/this word mean?
11. Who did you borrow it/the money from?
12. What are you worried about?

47.3

2. How is cheese made?
3. When was the computer invented?
4. Why isn't Sue working today?
5. What time are your friends coming?
6. Why was the concert canceled?
7. Where was your mother born?
8. Why didn't you come to the party?
9. How did the accident happen?
10. Why doesn't this machine work?

47.4

2. Don't you like him?
3. Isn't it good?
4. Don't you have any?

UNIT 48

48.1

2. where the post office is?
3. what time it is.
4. what this word means.
5. if/whether the plane has left?
6. if/whether Sue is going out tonight.
7. where Carol lives?
8. where I parked the car.
9. if/whether there is a bank near here?
10. what you want.
11. why Kelly didn't come to the party.
12. how much it costs to park here?
13. who that woman is.
14. if/whether Ann got my letter?
15. how far it is to the airport?

48.2

1. Amy is?
2. when she'll be back. (. . . she will be back)
3. if/whether she went out alone?

48.3

2. where I'd been. (. . . where I had been)
3. asked me how long I'd been back. (. . . how long I had been back)
4. He asked me what I was doing now.
5. He asked me why I'd come back. (. . . why I had come back) *or* . . . why I came back.
6. He asked me where I was living.
7. He asked me if/whether I was glad to be back.
8. He asked me if/whether I planned to stay for a while.
9. He asked me if/whether I could lend him some money.

UNIT 49

49.1

2. doesn't
3. was
4. will
5. am . . . isn't *or* 'm not . . . is
6. should
7. won't
8. do
9. could
10. would . . . could . . . can't

49.2

3. You do? I don't.
4. You didn't? I did.
5. You haven't? I have.
6. You did? I didn't.

49.3

解答例

3. So did I. *or* You did? What did you watch?
4. Neither will I. *or* You won't? Where will you be?
5. So do I. *or* You do? What kind of books do you like?
6. So would I. *or* You would? Where would you like to live?
7. Neither can I. *or* You can't? Why not?

49.4

2. I guess so.
3. I don't think so.
4. I hope so.
5. I'm afraid not.
6. I'm afraid so.
7. I hope not.
8. I think so.
9. I suppose so.

UNIT 50

50.1

3. haven't you
4. were you
5. does she
6. isn't he
7. has he
8. can't you
9. will he
10. aren't there
11. shall we
12. is it
13. aren't I
14. would you
15. will you
16. should I
17. had he

50.2

2. 's (very) expensive, isn't it?
3. was great, wasn't it?
4. 've had your hair cut, haven't you? *or* You had your hair cut, didn't you?
5. has a good voice, doesn't she? *or* She's got / She has got . . . doesn't / . . .doesn't she?
6. doesn't look very good, does it?
7. isn't very safe, is it?

50.3

2. don't give me a paper bag, do you? *or* couldn't give me a paper bag, could you?
3. don't know where Ann is, do you? *or* . . . you haven't seen Ann, have you?
4. you haven't got a bicycle pump, have you? *or* . . . you don't have a bicycle pump, do you?
5. you haven't seen my keys, have you? *or* you didn't see my keys, did you?
6. you couldn't take me to the station, could you? *or* . . . you couldn't give me a ride to the station, could you?

UNIT 51

51.1

2. making
3. listening
4. applying
5. reading
6. paying
7. using
8. forgetting
9. writing
10. being
11. trying
12. losing

51.2

2. driving too fast *or* having driven too fast
3. going swimming *or* going for a swim
4. breaking the/her DVD player *or* having broken the/her DVD
5. waiting a few minutes

51.3

2. traveling during rush hour
3. leaving . . . tomorrow
4. turning the radio down
5. not interrupting me all the time

51.4

解答例

2. standing
3. having a picnic
4. laughing
5. breaking down

UNIT 52

52.1

2. to help him
3. to carry her bags (for her)
4. to meet at 8:00
5. to tell him her name / to give him her name
6. not to tell anyone

52.2

2. to go
3. to get
4. waiting
5. to eat
6. how to use
7. barking
8. to call
9. having
10. to say / say
11. missing
12. to find

52.3

2. to be worried about something.
3. seem to know a lot of people.
4. My English seems to be getting better.
5. That car appears to have broken down.
6. David tends to forget things.
7. They claim to have solved the problem.

52.4

2. how to use
3. what to do
4. how to ride
5. what to say / what to do
6. whether to go

UNIT 53

53.1

2. me to lend you some
3. like me to shut it
4. you like me to show you (how)
5. you want me to repeat it
6. you want me to wait (stay)

53.2

2. to stay with them
3. him use her phone
4. her to be careful
5. her to give him a hand

53.3

2. it to rain.
3. him do what he wants.
4. him look older.
5. you to know the truth.
6. me to call my sister.
7. me to apply for the job.
8. advised me not to say anything to the police.
9. not to believe everything he says.
10. you to get around more easily.

53.4

2. to go
3. to do
4. cry
5. to study
6. eating
7. read
8. to make
9. think

UNIT 54

54.1

2. driving
3. to go
4. to go
5. raining
6. to win
7. asking
8. asking
9. to answer
10. breaking
11. to pay
12. losing *or* to lose
13. to tell
14. crying *or* to cry
15. to get
16. meeting . . . to see

54.2

2. He can remember crying on his first day of school.
3. He can't remember wanting to be a doctor.
4. He can remember going to Miami when he was eight.
5. He can't remember falling into a river.
6. He can't remember being bitten by a dog.

54.3

1. b) lending
   c) to call
   d) to say
   e) leaving/putting
2. a) saying
   b) to say
3. a) to become
   b) working
   c) reading

UNIT 55

55.1

2. turning it the other way.
3. tried taking an aspirin?
4. try calling his office?

55.2

2. It needs painting. / needs to be painted.
3. It needs cutting. / needs to be cut.
4. They need tightening. / need to be tightened.
5. It needs emptying. / to be emptied.

55.3

1. b) knocking
   c) to put
   d) asking
   e) to reach
   f) to concentrate
2. a) to go
   b) looking
   c) washing / to be washed
   d) cutting / to be cut
   e) iron . . . ironing / to be ironed
3. a) overhearing
   b) get *or* to get
   c) smiling
   d) make *or* to make

UNIT 56

56.1

解答例

2. I don't mind playing cards.
3. I don't like being alone. *or* . . . to be alone.
4. I enjoy going to museums.
5. I love cooking. *or* I love to cook.

56.2

2. likes teaching biology.
3. He likes taking photographs. *or* He likes to take photographs.
4. I didn't like working there.
5. She likes studying medicine.
6. He doesn't like being famous.
7. She doesn't like taking risks. *or* She doesn't like to take risks.
8. I like to know things ahead of time.

56.3

2. to sit
3. waiting
4. going *or* to go
5. to get
6. being
7. to come / to go
8. living
9. to talk
10. to hear / hearing / to be told

56.4

2. I would like / I'd like to have seen the program.
3. I would hate / I'd hate to have lost my watch.
4. I would love / I'd love to have met your parents.
5. I wouldn't like to have been alone.
6. I would prefer / I'd prefer to have traveled by train. *or* I would have preferred to travel . . .

UNIT 57

57.1

解答例

2. tennis to soccer.
3. prefer calling people . . . sending e-mails.
4. I prefer going to the movies to watching videos at home.
6. call people rather than send e-mails.
7. I prefer to go to the movies rather than watch videos at home.

57.2

3. I'd rather listen to some music.
4. I'd prefer to eat at home.
5. I'd rather wait a few minutes.
6. I'd rather go for a swim.
7. I'd prefer to think about it for a while.
8. I'd rather stand.
9. I'd prefer to go alone.
11. rather than play tennis.
12. than go to a restaurant.
13. rather than decide now.
14. than watch TV.

57.3

2. I told her
3. would you rather I did it
4. would you rather I called her

57.4

2. stayed/remained/waited
3. stay
4. didn't
5. were
6. didn't

UNIT 58

58.1

2. applying for the job
3. remembering names
4. passing the exam
5. being late
6. eating at home, we went to a restaurant
7. having to wait in line *or* waiting in line
8. playing well

58.2

2. by standing on a chair
3. by turning a key
4. by borrowing too much money
5. by driving too fast
6. by putting some pictures on the walls

58.3

2. paying
3. going
4. using
5. going
6. being/traveling/sitting
7. asking/telling/consulting
8. doing/having
9. turning/going
10. taking

58.4

2. looking forward to seeing her/Diane.
3. looking forward to going to the dentist (tomorrow).
4. She's looking forward to graduating (next summer).
5. I'm looking forward to playing tennis (tomorrow).

UNIT 59

59.1

1. When Juan first went to Canada, he **wasn't used to having** dinner so early, but after a while he **got used to** it. Now he finds it normal. He is **used to eating** / **is used to having dinner** at 6:00.
2. She **wasn't used to working** nights and it took her a few months to **get used to** it. Now, after a year, she's pretty happy. She **is used to working** nights.

59.2

2. 'm used to sleeping on the floor.
3. 'm used to working long hours.
4. I'm not used to going to bed so late.

59.3

2. get used to living in a much smaller house.
3. got used to her. / . . . to the/their new teacher.
4. 解答例
   They'll have to get used to the weather. / . . . to the food. / . . . to speaking a foreign language.

59.4

3. drink
4. eating
5. having
6. have
7. go
8. be
9. being

UNIT 60

60.1

2. doing
3. coming/going
4. doing/trying
5. buying/getting
6. hearing
7. going
8. having/using
9. being
10. watching
11. inviting/asking

60.2

2. in solving
3. of living
4. of causing
5. (from) walking
6. for interrupting
7. of spending
8. from escaping
9. on carrying
10. to seeing

60.3

2. on driving Ann to the station / . . . on taking Ann . . .
3. on getting married
4. Sue for coming to see her
5. (to me) for not calling earlier
6. me of being selfish

UNIT 61

61.1

2. There's no point in working if you don't need money.
3. There's no point in trying to study if you feel tired.
4. There's no point in hurrying if you've got plenty of time.

61.2

2. asking Dave
3. in going out
4. calling her
5. complaining (about what happened)
6. taking
7. keeping

61.3

2. remembering people's names
3. getting a job
4. getting a ticket for the game
5. understanding him

61.4

2. reading
3. packing / getting ready
4. watching
5. going/climbing/walking
6. applying
7. getting / being

61.5

2. went swimming
3. go skiing
4. goes riding
5. 's gone shopping / went shopping

UNIT 62

62.1

2. to get some money.
3. 'm saving money to go to Canada.
4. I went into the hospital to have an operation.
5. I'm wearing two sweaters to keep warm.
6. I called the police to report that my car had been stolen.

62.2

2. to read
3. to walk
4. to drink
5. to put / to carry
6. to discuss / to talk about
7. to buy / to get
8. to talk / to speak
9. to wear / to put on
10. to celebrate
11. to help

62.3

2. for
3. to
4. to
5. for
6. to
7. for
8. for . . . to

62.4

2. warm clothes so that I wouldn't be cold.
3. left Dave my phone number so that he could contact me. / . . . would be able to contact me.
4. We whispered so that . . . else would hear our conversation. / . . . so that nobody could hear . . ./ would be able to hear . . .
5. arrive early so that we can start the meeting on time. / . . . so that we'll be able to start . . .
6. Jennifer locked the door so that she wouldn't be disturbed.
7. I slowed down so that the car behind me could pass. / . . . would pass.

UNIT 63

63.1

2. easy to use.
3. was very difficult to open.
4. are impossible to translate.
5. car is expensive to maintain.
6. chair isn't safe to stand on.

63.2

2. easy mistake to make.
3. nice place to live. *or* . . . nice place to live in.
4. good game to watch.

63.3

2. 's careless of you to make the same mistake again and again.
3. It was nice of them to invite me (to stay with them). / It was nice of Dan and Jenny to . . .
4. It's inconsiderate of them to make so much noise (at night). / It's inconsiderate of the neighbors to . . .

63.4

2. am glad to hear *or* was glad to hear
3. were surprised to see
4. 'm/am sorry to hear *or* was sorry to hear

63.5
2. Paul was the last (person) to arrive.
3. Jenny was the only student to pass (the exam). / . . . the only one to pass (the exam).
4. I was the second customer/person to complain.
5. Neil Armstrong was the first person/man to walk on the moon.

63.6
2. 're/are bound to be
3. 's/is sure to forget
4. 's/is not likely to rain *or* isn't likely to rain
5. 's/is likely to be

UNIT 64

64.1
3. I'm afraid of losing it.
4. I was afraid to tell her.
5. We were afraid of missing our train.
6. We were afraid to look.
7. I was afraid of dropping it.
8. a) I was afraid to eat it.
   b) I was afraid of getting sick.

64.2
2. in starting
3. to read
4. in getting
5. to know
6. in looking

64.3
2. sorry to hear
3. sorry for saying / sorry about saying
4. sorry to bother
5. sorry for losing / sorry about losing

64.4
1. b) to leave
   c) from leaving
2. a) to solve
   b) in solving
3. a) of/about going
   b) to go
   c) to go
   d) to going
4. a) to buy
   b) to buy
   c) on buying
   d) of buying

UNIT 65

65.1
2. arrive
3. take it / do it
4. it ring
5. him play / him playing
6. you lock it / you do it
7. her fall

65.2
2. playing tennis.
3. Claire eating.
4. Bill playing his guitar.
5. smell the dinner burning.
6. We saw Linda jogging/running.

65.3
3. tell
4. crying
5. riding
6. say
7. run . . . climb
8. explode
9. crawling
10. slam
11. sleeping

UNIT 66

66.1
2. in an armchair reading a book.
3. opened the door carefully trying not to make any noise.
4. Sarah went out saying she would be back in an hour.
5. Linda was in London for two years working as a teacher.
6. Mary walked around the town looking at the sights and taking pictures.

66.2
2. fell asleep watching television.
3. slipped and fell getting off a bus.
4. got very wet walking home in the rain.
5. Laura had an accident driving to work yesterday.
6. Two kids got lost hiking in the woods.

66.3
2. Having bought our tickets, we went into the theater.
3. Having had dinner, they continued their trip.
4. Having done the shopping, I stopped for a cup of coffee.

66.4
2. Thinking they might be hungry, I offered them something to eat.
3. Being a vegetarian, Sally doesn't eat any kind of meat.
4. Not knowing his e-mail address, I wasn't able to contact him.
5. Having traveled a lot, Sarah knows a lot about other countries.
6. Not being able to speak the local language, I had trouble communicating.
7. Having spent nearly all our money, we couldn't afford to stay at a hotel.

UNIT 67

67.1
3. We went to **a** very nice restaurant . . .
4. *OK*
5. I use **a** toothbrush . . .
6. . . . if there's **a** bank near here?
7. . . . for **an** insurance company
8. *OK*
9. *OK*
10. . . . we stayed in **a** big hotel.
11. . . . I hope we come to **a** gas station soon.
12. . . . I have **a** problem.
13. . . . It's **a** very interesting idea.
14. John has **an** interview for **a** job tomorrow.
15. . . . It's **a** good game.
16. *OK*
17. Jane was wearing **a** beautiful necklace.

67.2
3. a key
4. a coat
5. sugar
6. a cookie
7. electricity
8. an interview
9. blood
10. a question
11. a minute
12. a decision

67.3
2. days
3. meat
4. a line
5. letters
6. friends
7. people
8. air
9. patience
10. an umbrella
11. languages
12. space

UNIT 68

68.1
2. a) a paper
   b) paper
3. a) a light
   b) Light
4. a) time
   b) a wonderful time
5. a nice room
6. advice
7. nice weather
8. bad luck
9. job
10. trip
11. total chaos
12. some
13. doesn't
14. Your hair is . . . it
15. The damage

68.2

2. information
3. chairs
4. furniture
5. hair
6. progress
7. job
8. work
9. permission
10. advice
11. experience
12. experiences

68.3

2. some information about places to see in the city
3. some advice about which courses to take / . . . courses I can take
4. is the news on (TV)
5. 's a beautiful view, isn't it
6. horrible/awful weather

UNIT 69

69.1

3. It's a vegetable.
4. It's a game. / It's a board game.
5. They're musical instruments.
6. It's a (tall/high) building.
7. They're planets.
8. It's a flower.
9. They're rivers.
10. They're birds.
12. He was a writer / a poet / a playwright / a dramatist.
13. He was a scientist / a physicist.
14. They were U.S. presidents / American presidents / presidents of the U.S.
15. She was an actress / a movie actress / a movie star.
16. They were singers.
17. They were painters / artists.

69.2

2. 's a waiter.
3. 's a travel agent.
4. He's a surgeon.
5. He's a chef.
6. She's a journalist.
7. He's a plumber.
8. She's an interpreter.

69.3

4. a
5. an
6. – (Do you collect stamps?)
7. a
8. Some
9. – (Do you enjoy going to concerts?)
10. – (I've got sore feet.)
11. a
12. some
13. a . . . a
14. – (Those are nice shoes.)
15. some
16. a . . . some
17. a . . . – (Her parents were teachers, too.)
18. a . . . – (He's always telling lies.)

UNIT 70

70.1

1. . . . and **a** magazine. **The** newspaper is in my briefcase, but I can't remember where I put **the** magazine.
2. I saw **an** accident this morning. **A** car crashed into **a** tree. **The** driver of **the** car wasn't hurt, but **the** car was badly damaged.
3. . . . **a** blue one and **a** gray one. **The** blue one belongs to my neighbors; I don't know who **the** owner of **the** gray one is.
4. My friends live in **an** old house in **a** small town. There is **a** beautiful garden behind **the** house. I would like to have **a** garden like that.

70.2

1. b) the
   c) the
2. a) a
   b) a
   c) the
3. a) a
   b) the
   c) the
4. a) an . . . The
   b) the
   c) the
5. a) the
   b) a
   c) a

70.3

2. **the** dentist
3. **the** door
4. **a** mistake
5. **the** bus station
6. **a** problem
7. **the** post office
8. **the** floor
9. **the** book
10. **a** job at **a** bank
11. **a** small apartment near **the** hospital
12. **a** supermarket on **the** corner

70.4

解答例

3. About once a month.
4. Once or twice a year.
5. About 55 miles an hour.
6. About seven hours a night.
7. Two or three times a week.
8. About two hours a day.

UNIT 71

71.1

2. *A:* a; *B:* the
3. *A:* the; *B:* the
4. *A:* the; *B:* a
5. *A:* –; *B:* the
6. *A:* the; *B:* –
7. *A:* a; *B:* the
8. *A:* –; *B:* –
9. *A:* –; *B:* the
10. *A:* the; *B:* a

71.2

2. the . . . the
3. –
4. The
5. the
6. –
7. the . . . the . . . – . . .
8. the

71.3

2. in a small town in the country
3. The moon goes around the earth every 27 days.
4. the same thing
5. a very hot day . . . the hottest day of the year
6. usually have lunch . . . eat a good breakfast
7. live in a foreign country . . . learn the language
8. on the wrong platform
9. The next train . . . from Platform 3

71.4

2. the ocean
3. question 8
4. the movies
5. breakfast
6. the gate
7. Gate 21

UNIT 72

72.1

2. to school
3. at home
4. to work
5. in high school
6. in bed
7. to prison

72.2

1. c) school
   d) school
   e) . . . school . . . The school
   f) school
   g) the school
2. a) college
   b) college
   c) the college
3. a) church
   b) church
   c) the church
4. a) class
   b) the class

c) class
d) the class
5. a) prison
b) the prison
c) prison
6. a) bed
b) home
c) work
d) bed
e) work
f) work

UNIT 73

73.1

解答例

2.–5.

I like cats.
I don't like zoos.
I don't mind fast food restaurants.
I'm not interested in football.

73.2

3. spiders
4. meat
5. the questions
6. the people
7. History
8. lies
9. the hotels
10. The water
11. the grass
12. patience

73.3

3. Apples
4. the apples
5. Women . . . men
6. tea
7. The vegetables
8. Life
9. skiing
10. the people
11. people . . . aggression
12. All the books
13. the beds
14. war
15. The First World War
16. the Pyramids
17. the history . . . modern art
18. the marriage
19. Most people . . . marriage . . . family life . . . society

UNIT 74

74.1

1. b) the cheetah
c) the kangaroo (and the rabbit)
2. a) the swan
b) the penguin
c) the owl
3. a) the wheel
b) the laser
c) the telescope
4. a) the rupee
b) the (Canadian) dollar
c) the . . .

74.2

2. a
3. the
4. a
5. the
6. the
7. a
8. The

74.3

2. the injured
3. the unemployed
4. the sick
5. the rich . . . the poor

74.4

2. a German Germans
3. a Frenchman/Frenchwoman the French
4. a Russian Russians
5. a Chinese the Chinese
6. a Brazilian Brazilians
7. a Japanese man/woman Japanese

UNIT 75

75.1

2. the
3. the . . . the
4. – (President Kennedy was assassinated in 1963.)
5. the
6. – (Do you know Professor Brown's phone number?)

75.2

3. *OK*
4. the United States
5. The south of India. . . the north
6. *OK*
7. the Channel
8. the Middle East
9. *OK*
10. the Swiss Alps
11. The UK
12. The Seychelles . . . the Indian Ocean
13. *OK*
14. The Hudson River . . . the Atlantic Ocean

75.3

2. (in) South America
3. the Nile
4. Sweden
5. the United States
6. the Rockies
7. the Mediterranean
8. Australia
9. the Pacific
10. the Indian Ocean
11. the Thames
12. the Mississippi
13. Thailand
14. the Panama Canal
15. the Amazon

UNIT 76

76.1

2. Turner's on Carter Road
3. the Crown (Hotel) on Park Road
4. St. Paul's on Market Street
5. the City Museum on George Street
6. Blackstone's on Forest Avenue
7. Lincoln Park at the end of Market Street
8. The China House on Park Road *or* Mario's Pizza on George Street

76.2

2. The Eiffel Tower
3. the Taj Mahal
4. The White House
5. The Kremlin
6. Broadway
7. The Acropolis
8. Buckingham Palace

76.3

2. Central Park
3. St. James's Park
4. The Ramada . . . Main Street
5. O'Hare Airport
6. McGill University
7. Harrison's
8. the Ship Inn
9. The Statue of Liberty . . . New York Harbor
10. the Science Museum
11. IBM . . . General Electric
12. The Classic
13. the Great Wall
14. The Washington Post
15. Cambridge University Press

UNIT 77

77.1

3. shorts
4. a means
5. means
6. some scissors *or* a pair of scissors
7. a series
8. series
9. species

77.2

2. politics
3. economics
4. physics
5. gymnastics
6. electronics

77.3

2. don't
3. want
4. was
5. aren't
6. wasn't
7. isn't
8. they
9. are
10. Do
11. is

77.4

3. . . . wearing black jeans.
4. very nice people.
5. *OK*
6. . . . buy some new pajamas. *or* . . . buy a new pair of pajamas.
7. There was a police officer / a policeman / a policewoman . . .
8. *OK*
9. These scissors aren't . . .
10. . . . two days is enough . . .
11. Many people have . . .

UNIT 78

78.1

3. a computer magazine
4. (your) vacation pictures
5. milk chocolate
6. a factory inspector
7. a race horse
8. a horse race
9. a Los Angeles lawyer
10. (your) exam results
11. the dining room carpet
12. an oil company scandal
13. a five-story building
14. a traffic plan
15. a five-day course
16. a two-part question
17. a seven-year-old girl

78.2

2. room number
3. seat belt
4. credit card
5. weather forecast
6. newspaper editor
7. shop window

78.3

3. 20-dollar
4. 15-minute
5. 60 minutes
6. two-hour
7. five courses
8. two-year
9. 500-year-old
10. five days
11. six miles
12. six-mile

UNIT 79

79.1

3. your friend's umbrella
4. *OK*
5. Charles's daughter
6. Mary and Dan's son
7. *OK*
8. yesterday's newspaper
9. *OK*
10. *OK*
11. Your children's friends
12. Our neighbors' garden
13. *OK*
14. Bill's hair
15. Catherine's party
16. *OK*
17. Mike's parents' car
18. *OK*
19. *OK* (the government's economic policy も可)

79.2

2. a boy's name
3. children's clothes
4. a girls' school
5. a bird's nest
6. a women's magazine

79.3

2. week's storm caused a lot of damage.
3. town's only movie theater has closed down.
4. Chicago's weather is very changeable.
5. The region's main industry is tourism.

79.4

2. a year's salary
3. four weeks' pay
4. five hours' sleep
5. a minute's rest

UNIT 80

80.1

2. hurt himself
3. blame herself
4. Put yourself
5. enjoyed themselves
6. burn yourself
7. express myself

80.2

2. me
3. myself
4. us
5. yourself
6. you
7. ourselves
8. themselves
9. them

80.3

2. dried herself
3. concentrate
4. defend yourself
5. meeting
6. relax

80.4

2. themselves
3. each other
4. each other
5. themselves
6. each other
7. ourselves
8. each other
9. ourselves . . . each other

80.5

2. it himself.
3. mail/do it myself.
4. told me herself. / herself told me. / did herself.
5. call him yourself? / . . . do it yourself?

UNIT 81

81.1

2. relative of yours.
3. a book of mine.
4. some friends of hers to her place.
5. a neighbor of ours.
6. two friends of mine.
7. a friend of yours?
8. a friend of Amy's

81.2

2. his own opinions
3. her own business
4. its own (private) beach
5. our own words

81.3

2. your own fault
3. her own ideas
4. your own problems
5. his own decisions

81.4

2. makes her own clothes
3. bake/make our own bread
4. writes his own songs

81.5

2. my own
3. myself
4. himself
5. his own
6. herself
7. her own
8. yourself
9. our own
10. herself

UNIT 82

82.1

3. Is there . . . there's / there is
4. there was . . . It was
5. It was
6. There was
7. is it
8. It was
9. It's / It is
10. there wasn't
11. Is it . . . it's / it is
12. there was . . . There was
13. It was
14. There wasn't
15. There was . . . it wasn't

82.2

2. is a lot of salt
3. There was nothing
4. There was a lot of violence in the film. / There was a lot of fighting . . .
5. There were a lot of people in the stores / the mall.
6. There is a lot to do in this town. / There is a lot happening in this town.

82.3

2. There might be
3. there will be / there'll be *or* there are going to be
4. There's going to be / There is going to be
5. There used to be
6. there should be
7. there wouldn't be

82.4

2. and there was a lot of snow
3. There used to be a church here
4. There must have been a reason.
5. *OK*
6. There's sure to be a parking lot somewhere.
7. there will be an opportunity
8. *OK*
9. there would be somebody . . . but there wasn't anybody.
10. There has been no change.
11. *OK*

UNIT 83

83.1

2. some
3. any
4. any . . . some
5. some
6. any
7. any
8. some
9. any
10. any

83.2

2. somebody/someone
3. anybody/anyone
4. anything
5. something
6. somebody/someone . . . anybody/anyone
7. something . . . anybody/anyone
8. Anybody/Anyone
9. anybody/anyone
10. anywhere
11. somewhere
12. anywhere
13. anybody/anyone
14. something
15. Anybody/Anyone
16. something
17. anybody/anyone . . . anything

83.3

2. Any day
3. Anything
4. anywhere
5. Any job *or* Anything
6. Any time
7. Anybody/Anyone
8. Any newspaper *or* Any one

UNIT 84

84.1

3. no
4. any
5. None
6. none
7. No
8. any
9. any
10. none
11. no

84.2

2. Nobody/No one.
3. None.
4. Nowhere.
5. None.
6. Nothing.
8. I wasn't talking to anybody/anyone.
9. I don't have any luggage.
10. I'm not going anywhere.
11. I didn't make any mistakes.
12. I didn't pay anything.

84.3

2. nobody/no one
3. Nowhere
4. anything
5. Nothing. I couldn't find anything . . .
6. Nothing
7. anywhere
8. Nobody/No one said anything.

84.4

2. nobody
3. anyone
4. Anybody
5. Nothing
6. Anything
7. anything

UNIT 85

85.1

3. a lot of salt
4. *OK*
5. It cost a lot
6. *OK*
7. many people *or* a lot of people
8. I use the phone a lot
9. *OK*
10. a lot of money

85.2

2. plenty of money.
3. plenty of room.
4. plenty to learn.
5. are plenty of things to see.
6. There are plenty of hotels.

85.3

2. little
3. many
4. much
5. few
6. little
7. many

85.4

3. a few dollars
4. *OK*
5. a little time
6. *OK*
7. only a few words
8. a few months

85.5

2. a little
3. a few
4. few
5. little
6. a little
7. little
8. a few

UNIT 86

86.1

3. –
4. of
5. –
6. –
7. of
8. of
9. –
10. –

86.2
3. of my spare time
4. accidents
5. of the buildings
6. of her friends
7. of the population
8. birds
9. of my teammates
10. of her opinions
11. large cities
12. (of) my dinner

86.3
解答例
2. the time / the day
3. my friends
4. (of) the questions
5. the photos / the photographs / the pictures
6. (of) the money

86.4
2. All of them
3. none of us
4. some of it
5. none of them
6. None of it
7. Some of them
8. all of it

UNIT 87

87.1
2. Neither
3. both
4. Either
5. Neither

87.2
2. either
3. both
4. Neither of
5. neither . . . both / both the / both of the
6. both / both of

87.3
2. either of them
3. both of them
4. neither of us
5. neither of them

87.4
3. Both Joe and Sam are on vacation.
4. Neither Joe nor Sam has a car.
5. Brian neither watches TV nor reads newspapers.
6. The movie was both boring and long.
7. That man's name is either Richard or Robert.
8. I've got neither the time nor the money to go on vacation.
9. We can leave either today or tomorrow.

87.5
2. either
3. any
4. none
5. any
6. either
7. neither

UNIT 88

88.1
3. Everybody/Everyone
4. Everything
5. all/everything
6. everybody/everyone
7. everything
8. All
9. everybody/everyone
10. All
11. everything/all
12. Everybody/Everyone
13. All
14. everything

88.2
2. whole team played well.
3. the whole box (of chocolates).
4. searched the whole house.
5. whole family plays tennis.
6. Ann/She worked the whole day.
7. It rained the whole week.
8. worked all day.
9. It rained all week.

88.3
2. every four hours
3. every four years
4. every five minutes
5. every six months

88.4
2. every day
3. all day
4. The whole building
5. every time
6. all the time
7. all my luggage

UNIT 89

89.1
3. Each
4. Every
5. Each
6. every
7. each
8. every

89.2
3. Every
4. Each
5. every
6. every
7. each
8. every
9. every
10. each
11. Every
12. each

89.3
2. had 10 dollars each. / . . . and I each had 10 dollars.
3. postcards cost 40 cents each. / . . . postcards are 40 cents each.
4. paid $195 each. / . . . each paid $195.

89.4
2. everyone
3. every one
4. Everyone
5. every one

UNIT 90

90.1
2. who breaks into a house to steal things.
3. A customer is someone who buys something from a store.
4. A shoplifter is someone who steals from a store.
5. A coward is someone who is not brave.
6. An atheist is someone who doesn't believe in God.
7. A pessimist is someone who expects the worst to happen.
8. A tenant is someone who pays rent to live in a room or apartment.

90.2
2. waitress who/that served us was impolite and impatient.
3. building that/which was destroyed in the fire has now been rebuilt.
4. people who/that were arrested have now been released.
5. bus that/which goes to the airport runs every half hour.

90.3
2. who/that runs away from home
3. that/which were on the wall
4. that/which cannot be explained
5. who/that stole my car
6. that/which gives you the meaning of words
7. who/that invented the telephone
8. that/which can support life

90.4
3. that/which sells
4. who/that caused
5. *OK* (who took も可)
6. that/which is changing
7. *OK* (which were も可)
8. that/which won

UNIT 91

91.1

3. *OK* (the people who/that we met も可)
4. The people who/that work in the office
5. *OK* (the people who/that I work with も可)
6. *OK* (the money that/which I gave you も可)
7. the money that/which was on the table
8. *OK* (the worst film that/which you've ever seen も可)
9. the best thing that/which has ever happened to you

91.2

2. you're wearing *or* that/which you're wearing
3. you're going to see *or* that/which you're going to see
4. I/we wanted to visit *or* that/which I/we wanted to visit
5. I/we invited to the party *or* who/whom/that we invited . . .
6. you had to do *or* that/which you had to do
7. I/we rented *or* that/which I/we rented
8. Tom had recommended (to us) *or* that/which Tom had recommended . . .

91.3

2. we were invited to *or* that/which we were invited to
3. I work with *or* who/that I work with
4. you told me about *or* that/which you told me about
5. we went to last night *or* that/which we went to . . .
6. I applied for *or* that/which I applied for
7. you can rely on *or* who/that you can rely on
8. I saw you with *or* who/that I saw you with

91.4

3. – (that も可)
4. what
5. that
6. what
7. – (that も可)
8. what
9. – (that も可)

UNIT 92

92.1

2. whose wife is an English teacher
3. who owns a restaurant
4. whose ambition is to climb Everest
5. who have just gotten married / just got married
6. whose parents used to work in a circus

92.2

2. where I can buy some postcards
3. where I work
4. where Sue is staying
5. where I/we play baseball

92.3

2. where
3. who
4. whose
5. whom
6. where
7. whose
8. whom

92.4

解答例

2. I'll never forget the time we got stuck in an elevator.
3. The reason I didn't write to you was that I didn't know your address.
4. Unfortunately I wasn't at home the evening you called.
5. The reason they don't have a car is that they don't need one.
6. 1996 was the year Amanda got married.

UNIT 93

93.1

3. We often go to visit our friends in New York, which is not very far away.
4. I went to see the doctor, who told me to rest for a few days.
5. John, who/whom I've known for a very long time, is one of my closest friends.
6. Sheila, whose job involves a lot of travel, is away from home a lot.
7. The new stadium, which can hold 90,000 people, will be opened next month.
8. Alaska, where my brother lives, is the largest state in the United States.
9. A friend of mine, whose father is the manager of a company, helped me to get a job.

93.2

3. which began 10 days ago, is now over.
4. the book I was looking for this morning. *or* . . . the book that/which I was looking for.
5. which was once the largest city in the world, is now decreasing.
6. the people who/that applied for the job had the necessary qualifications.
7. a picture of her son, who is a police officer.

93.3

2. My office, which is on the second floor, is very small.
3. *OK* (The office that/which I'm using . . . も可)
4. Ben's father, who used to be a teacher, now works for a TV company.
5. *OK* (The doctor who examined me . . . も可)
6. The sun, which is one of millions of stars in the universe, provides us with heat and light.

UNIT 94

94.1

2. of which he's very proud
3. with whom we went on vacation
4. to which only members of the family were invited

94.2

2. most of which was useless
3. neither of which she has received
4. none of whom was suitable
5. one of which she hardly ever uses
6. half of which he gave to his parents
7. both of whom are teachers
8. only a few of whom I knew
9. (the) sides of which were lined with trees
10. the aim of which is to save money

94.3

2. doesn't have a phone, which makes it difficult to contact her.
3. Neil has passed his exams, which is good news.
4. Our flight was delayed, which meant we had to wait three hours at the airport.
5. Kate offered to let me stay at her house, which was very nice of her.
6. The street I live on is very noisy at night, which makes it difficult to sleep sometimes.
7. Our car has broken down, which means we can't take our trip tomorrow.

UNIT 95

95.1

2. the man sitting next to me on the plane
3. The taxi taking us to the airport
4. a path leading to the river
5. A factory employing 500 people
6. a brochure containing the information I needed

95.2

2. damaged in the storm
3. suggestions made at the meeting
4. paintings stolen from the museum
5. the man arrested by the police

95.3

3. living
4. offering
5. named
6. blown
7. sitting . . . reading
8. driving . . . selling

95.4

3. is somebody coming.
4. There were a lot of people traveling.
5. There was nobody else staying there.
6. There was nothing written on it.
7. There's a new course beginning next Monday.

UNIT 96

96.1

2. a) exhausting
   b) exhausted
3. a) depressing
   b) depressed
   c) depressed
4. a) exciting
   b) exciting
   c) excited

96.2

2. interested
3. exciting
4. embarrassing
5. embarrassed
6. amazed
7. astonishing
8. amused
9. terrifying . . . shocked
10. bored . . . boring
11. boring . . . interesting

96.3

2. bored
3. confusing
4. disgusting
5. interested
6. annoyed
7. boring
8. exhausted
9. excited
10. amusing
11. interesting

UNIT 97

97.1

2. an unusual gold ring
3. a beautiful old house
4. black leather gloves
5. an old Italian film
6. a long thin face
7. big black clouds
8. a lovely sunny day
9. an ugly yellow dress
10. a long wide avenue
11. a little old red car
12. a nice new green sweater
13. a small black metal box
14. a big fat black cat
15. a charming little old country inn
16. beautiful long black hair
17. an interesting old French painting
18. an enormous red and yellow umbrella

97.2

2. tastes/tasted awful
3. feel fine
4. smell nice
5. look wet
6. sounds/sounded interesting

97.3

2. happy
3. happily
4. violent
5. terrible
6. properly
7. good
8. slow

97.4

3. the last two days
4. the first two weeks of May
5. the next few days
6. the first three questions (in the exam)
7. the next two years
8. the last three days of our vacation

UNIT 98

98.1

2. badly
3. easily
4. patiently
5. unexpectedly
6. regularly
7. perfectly . . . slowly . . . clearly

98.2

3. selfishly
4. terribly
5. sudden
6. colorfully
7. colorful
8. badly
9. badly
10. safe

98.3

2. careful
3. continuously
4. happily
5. fluent
6. specially
7. complete
8. perfectly
9. nervous
10. financially *or* completely

98.4

2. seriously ill
3. absolutely enormous
4. slightly damaged
5. unusually quiet
6. completely changed
7. unnecessarily long
8. badly planned

UNIT 99

99.1

2. good
3. well
4. good
5. well
6. well
7. good
8. well
9. good
10. well

99.2

2. well known
3. well maintained
4. well written
5. well informed
6. well dressed
7. well paid

99.3

2. *OK*
3. *OK*
4. hard
5. *OK*
6. slowly

99.4

2. hardly hear
3. hardly slept
4. hardly speak
5. hardly said
6. hardly changed
7. hardly recognized

99.5

2. hardly any
3. hardly anything
4. hardly anybody/anyone
5. hardly ever
6. Hardly anybody/anyone
7. hardly anywhere
8. hardly *or* hardly ever
9. hardly any
10. hardly anything . . . hardly anywhere

UNIT 100

100.1

4. so
5. so
6. such a
7. so
8. such
9. such a
10. such a
11. so
12. so . . . such
13. so

14. such a
15. such a

100.2

3. I was so tired (that) I couldn't keep my eyes open.
4. We had such a good time on our vacation (that) we didn't want to come home.
5. She speaks English so well (that) you would think it was her native language. *or* She speaks such good English (that) . . .
6. I've got such a lot to do (that) I don't know where to begin. *or* I've got so much to do (that) . . .
7. The music was so loud (that) you could hear it from miles away.
8. I had such a big breakfast (that) I didn't eat anything else for the rest of the day.
9. It was such terrible weather (that) we spent the whole day indoors.
10. I was so surprised (that) I didn't know what to say.

100.3

解答例

2. a) friendly.
   b) a nice person.
3. a) lively.
   b) an exciting place.
4. a) exhausting.
   b) a difficult job.
5. a) long.
   b) a long time.

UNIT 101

101.1

3. enough money
4. enough milk
5. warm enough
6. enough room
7. well enough
8. enough time
9. qualified enough
10. big enough
11. enough cups

101.2

2. too busy to talk
3. too late to go
4. warm enough to sit
5. too shy to be
6. enough patience to be
7. too far away to hear
8. enough English to read

101.3

2. too hot to drink.
3. was too heavy to move.
4. aren't / are not ripe enough to eat.
5. is too complicated (for me) to explain.
6. was too high (for us) to climb over.
7. isn't / is not big enough for three people (to sit on).
8. things are too small to see without a microscope.

UNIT 102

102.1

2. stronger
3. smaller
4. more expensive
5. warmer/hotter
6. more interesting / more exciting
7. nearer/closer
8. more difficult / more complicated
9. better
10. worse
11. longer
12. more quietly
13. more often
14. farther/further
15. happier

102.2

3. more serious than
4. thinner
5. bigger
6. more interested
7. more important than
8. simpler / more simple
9. more crowded than
10. more peaceful than
11. more easily
12. higher than

102.3

2. longer by train than by car.
3. further/farther than Dave.
4. worse than Chris (on the test).
5. arrived earlier than I expected.
6. run more often than the trains. *or* The buses run more frequently than . . .
7. were busier than usual (at work today). *or* We were busier at work today than usual.

UNIT 103

103.1

2. much bigger
3. much more complicated than
4. a little cooler
5. far more interesting than
6. a little more slowly
7. a lot easier
8. slightly older

103.2

2. any sooner / any earlier
3. no higher than / no more expensive than
4. any farther/further
5. no worse than

103.3

2. bigger and bigger
3. heavier and heavier
4. more and more nervous
5. worse and worse
6. more and more expensive
7. better and better
8. more and more talkative

103.4

2. the more I liked him *or* the more I got to like him
3. the more profit you (will) make *or* the higher your profit (will be) *or* the more your profit (will be)
4. the harder it is to concentrate
5. the more impatient she became

103.5

2. older
3. older *or* elder
4. older

UNIT 104

104.1

2. as high as yours.
3. know as much about cars as me. *or* . . . as I do.
4. as cold as it was yesterday.
5. feel as tired as I did yesterday. *or* . . . as I felt yesterday.
6. lived here as long as us. *or* . . . as we have.
7. as nervous (before the interview) as I usually am. *or* . . . as usual.

104.2

3. as far as I thought.
4. less than I expected.
5. go out as much as I used to. *or* . . . as often as I used to.
6. have longer hair.
7. know them as well as me. *or* . . . as I do.
8. as many people at this meeting as at the last one.

104.3

2. as well as
3. as long as
4. as soon as
5. as often as
6. as quietly as
7. just as comfortable as
8. just as well-qualified as
9. just as bad as

104.4

2. is the same color as mine.
3. arrived at the same time as you did
4. birthday is the same day as Tom's. *or* birthday is the same as Tom's.

104.5

2. than him / than he does
3. as me / as I do
4. than us / than we were
5. than her / than she is
6. as them / as they have been

UNIT 105

105.1

2. the cheapest restaurant in the town.
3. the happiest day of my life.
4. 's the most intelligent student in the class.
5. 's the most valuable painting in the gallery.
6. 's the busiest time of the year.
8. of the richest men in the world.
9. 's one of the oldest houses in the city.
10. 's one of the best colleges in the state.
11. was one of the worst experiences of my life.
12. 's one of the most dangerous criminals in the country.

105.2

3. larger
4. the smallest
5. better
6. the worst
7. the most popular
8. . . . the highest mountain in the world . . . It is higher than . . .
9. the most enjoyable
10. more comfortable
11. the quickest
12. The oldest *or* The eldest

105.3

2. the funniest joke I've ever heard.
3. is the best coffee I've ever tasted.
4. 's the most generous person I've ever met.
5. 's the furthest/farthest I've ever run.
6. 's the worst mistake I've ever made. *or* was the worst . . .
7. 's the most famous person you've ever met?

UNIT 106

106.1

3. Jim doesn't like basketball very much.
4. *OK*
5. I ate my breakfast quickly and . . .
6. . . . a lot of people to the party?
7. *OK*
8. Did you go to bed late last night?
9. *OK*
10. I met a friend of mine on my way home.

106.2

2. We won the game easily.
3. I closed the door quietly.
4. Diane speaks Chinese quite well.
5. Tim watches TV all the time.
6. Please don't ask that question again.
7. Does Ken play golf every weekend?
8. I borrowed some money from a friend of mine.

106.3

2. go to the supermarket every Friday.
3. did you come home so late?
4. takes her children to school every day.
5. been to the movies recently.
6. write your name at the top of the page.
7. remembered her name after a few minutes.
8. walked around the town all morning.
9. didn't see you at the party on Saturday night.
10. found some interesting books in the library.
11. left her umbrella in a restaurant last night.
12. are building a new hotel across from the park.

UNIT 107

107.1

3. I usually take . . .
4. *OK*
5. Steve hardly ever gets angry.
6. . . . and I also went to the bank.
7. Jane always has to hurry . . .
8. *OK*
9. *OK*

107.2

2. a) We were all on vacation in Spain.
   b) We were all staying at the same hotel.
   c) We all enjoyed ourselves.
3. Catherine is always very generous.
4. I don't usually have to work on Saturdays.
5. Do you always watch TV in the evenings?
6. . . . is also studying Japanese.
7. a) The new hotel is probably very expensive.
   b) It probably costs a lot to stay there.
8. a) I can probably help you.
   b) I probably can't help you.

107.3

2. usually take
3. am usually
4. has probably gone
5. were both born
6. can also sing
7. often sleeps
8. have never spoken
9. always have to wait
10. can only read
11. will probably be leaving
12. probably won't be
13. is hardly ever
14. are still living
15. would never have met
16. am always

UNIT 108

108.1

3. He doesn't write poems anymore.
4. He still wants to be a teacher.
5. He isn't / He's not interested in politics anymore.
6. He's still single.
7. He doesn't go fishing anymore.
8. He doesn't have a beard anymore.

10.–12. （順不同）
He no longer writes poems.
He is / He's no longer interested in politics.
He no longer goes fishing.
He no longer has a beard.

108.2

2. hasn't left yet.
3. haven't finished (repairing the road) yet.
4. They haven't woken up yet.
5. Has she found a place to live yet?
6. I haven't decided (what to do) yet.
7. It hasn't taken off yet.

108.3

5. I don't want to go out yet.
6. she doesn't work there anymore
7. I still have a lot of friends there. *or* I've still got . . .
8. We've already met.
9. Do you still live in the same place
10. have you already eaten
11. He's not here yet.
12. he still isn't here (he isn't here yet も可)
13. are you already a member
14. I can still remember it very clearly
15. These pants don't fit me anymore.
16. "Have you finished with the paper yet?" "No, I'm still reading it." *or* Are you finished with . . . ?

UNIT 109

109.1

2. even Amanda
3. not even Julie
4. even Amanda
5. even Sarah
6. not even Amanda

109.2

2. even painted the floor.
3. 's even met the president. *or* even met . . .
4. could even hear it from two blocks away. *or* You could even hear the noise from . . .
6. I can't even remember her name.
7. There isn't even a movie theater.
8. He didn't even tell his wife (where he was going).
9. I don't even know the people next door.

109.3

2. even older
3. even better
4. even more difficult
5. even worse
6. even less

109.4

2. if
3. even if
4. even
5. even though
6. Even
7. even though
8. even if
9. Even though

UNIT 110

110.1

2. Although I had never seen her before
3. although it was pretty cold
4. although we don't like them very much
5. Although I didn't speak the language
6. Although the heat was on
7. although I'd met her twice before
8. although we've known each other a long time

110.2

2. a) In spite of (*or* Despite)
   b) Although
3. a) because
   b) although
4. a) because of
   b) in spite of (*or* despite)
5. a) although
   b) because of

解答例

6. a) he hadn't studied very hard
   b) he had studied very hard
7. a) I was hungry
   b) being hungry / my hunger / the fact (that) I was hungry

110.3

2. In spite of having very little money, they are happy. *or* In spite of the fact (that) they have very little money . . .
3. Although my foot was injured, I managed to walk to the nearest town. *or* I managed to walk to the nearest town although my . . .
4. I enjoyed the movie in spite of the silly story. / . . . in spite of the story being silly. / . . . in spite of the fact (that) the story was silly. *or* In spite of . . . , I enjoyed the movie.
5. Despite living on the same street, we hardly ever see each other. *or* Despite the fact (that) we live on . . . *or* We hardly ever see each other despite . . .
6. Even though I was only out for five minutes, I got very wet in the rain. *or* I got very wet in the rain even though I was . . .

110.4

2. It's very windy, though.
3. We ate it, though.
4. I don't like her husband, though.

UNIT 111

111.1

2.–5.

a map with you in case you get lost.

Take a raincoat with you in case it rains.

Take a camera with you in case you want to take some pictures

Take some water with you in case you're thirsty. *or* . . . you get thirsty.

111.2

2. in case I don't see you again (before you go).
3. check the list in case we forgot something? *or* . . . forgot anything?
4. your files in case the computer crashes.

111.3

2. the name (of the book) in case he forgot it.
3. my parents in case they were worried (about me).
4. (Liz) another e-mail in case she hadn't received the first one.
5. them my address in case they came to New York (one day).

111.4

3. If
4. if
5. in case
6. if
7. if
8. in case
9. in case

UNIT 112

112.1

2. unless you listen carefully.
3. I'll never speak to her again unless she apologizes to me. *or* Unless she apologises to me, I'll . . .
4. He won't be able to understand you unless you speak very slowly. *or* Unless you speak very slowly, he . . .
5. The company will have to close unless business improves soon. *or* Unless business improves soon, the company . . .

112.2

2. (to the party) unless you go too.
3. won't attack you unless you move suddenly.
4. won't speak to you unless you ask him something.
5. won't see you unless it's an emergency.

112.3

2. unless
3. providing
4. as long as
5. unless
6. unless
7. provided
8. Unless
9. unless
10. as long as

112.4

解答例

2. it's not too hot
3. there isn't too much traffic
4. it isn't raining
5. I'm in a hurry
6. you have something else to do
7. you pay it back next week
8. you take risks

UNIT 113

113.1

2. We all smiled as we posed for the photograph.
3. I burned myself as I was taking a hot dish out of the oven.
4. The crowd cheered as the two teams ran onto the field.
5. A dog ran out in front of the car as we were driving along the road.

113.2
3. because
4. at the same time as
5. at the same time as
6. because
7. because

解答例
9. Since I was tired, I went to bed early.
10. We decided to go out to eat since we had no food at home.
11. Since we don't use the car very often, we've decided to sell it.

113.3
3. *OK*
4. when I was asleep
5. When I finished high school
6. *OK*
7. when I was a child

113.4
解答例
1. you were getting into your car.
2. we started playing tennis.
3. I had to walk home.
4. somebody walked in front of the camera.

UNIT 114

114.1
3. like her mother
4. people like him
5. *OK*
6. like most of his friends
7. like talking to the wall
8. *OK*
9. *OK*
10. *OK*
11. like a bomb exploding
12. like a fish

114.2
2. like blocks of ice
3. like a beginner
4. as a tour guide
5. like a church
6. as a birthday present
7. like winter
8. like a child

114.3
2. like
3. as
4. like
5. like
6. as (like も可)
7. like
8. as
9. as
10. like
11. like
12. as
13. as
14. Like
15. as
16. As
17. like
18. as (like も可)

UNIT 115

115.1
2. look like you've seen a ghost.
3. sound like you're enjoying yourself.
4. feel like I've (just) run a marathon.

115.2
2. looks like it's going to rain.
3. It sounds like they're having an argument.
4. It looks like there's been an accident.
5. It looks like we'll have to walk.
6. It sounds like you should see a doctor.

115.3
2. as if he meant what he said
3. as if she hurt her leg
4. as if he hadn't eaten for a week
5. as if she was enjoying it
6. as if I'm going to be sick
7. as if she didn't want to come
8. as if I didn't exist

115.4
2. as if [I] was/were
3. as if she was/were
4. as if it was/were

UNIT 116

116.1
3. during
4. for
5. during
6. for
7. for
8. for
9. during
10. for
11. for
12. for
13. during
14. for

116.2
3. while
4. While
5. During
6. while
7. during
8. During
9. while
10. during
11. while
12. during
13. while
14. while

116.3
解答例
3. I was doing the housework.
4. I make a quick phone call?
5. the lesson.
6. the interview.
7. the car is moving.
8. we were having dinner.
9. the game.
10. we were walking home.

UNIT 117

117.1
2. by 8:30.
3. by Saturday whether you can come to the party.
4. you're here by 2:00.
5. we should arrive by lunchtime.

117.2
2. by
3. by
4. until
5. until 5:30 . . . by now
6. by
7. until
8. by
9. by
10. until
11. By
12. by

117.3
解答例
3. until I come back
4. by 5:00
5. by next Friday
6. until midnight

117.4
2. By the time I got to the station / By the time I'd gotten to the station
3. By the time I finished (my work) / By the time I'd finished (my work)
4. By the time the police arrived
5. By the time we got to the top / By the time we'd gotten to the top

UNIT 118

118.1
2. at night
3. in the evening
4. on July 21, 1969
5. at the same time
6. in the 1920s
7. in about 20 minutes
8. at the moment
9. in the Middle Ages
10. in 11 seconds
11. (on) Saturdays

118.2
2. on
3. in
4. On
5. on
6. in
7. in
8. at
9. on

10. at
11. in
12. at
13. on
14. in
15. On . . . at
16. at . . . in
17. on . . . in
18. on . . . in

118.3

3. a
4. 両方正しい
5. b
6. b
7. 両方正しい
8. a
9. b
10. a

UNIT 119

119.1

2. on time
3. in time
4. on time
5. in time
6. on time
7. in time
8. in time
9. on time

119.2

2. got home just in time.
3. stopped him just in time.
4. got to the theater just in time for the beginning of the film.

119.3

2. at the end of the month
3. at the end of the course
4. at the end of the race
5. at the end of the interview

119.4

2. In the end she resigned (from her job).
3. In the end I gave up (trying to learn German).
4. In the end we decided not to go (to the party). *or* In the end we didn't go (to the party).

119.5

2. In
3. at . . . at
4. in
5. in
6. at
7. in
8. at
9. in

UNIT 120

120.1

2. On his arm. *or* On the man's arm.
3. At the traffic light.
4. a) On the door.
   b) In the door.
5. On the wall.
6. In Paris.
7. a) At the front desk.
   b) On the desk.
8. On/At the beach.

120.2

2. on my guitar
3. at the next gas station
4. in your coffee
5. on that tree
6. in the mountains
7. on the island
8. at the window

120.3

2. on
3. at
4. on
5. in
6. on
7. at
8. in . . . in
9. on
10. in
11. on . . . in
12. at

UNIT 121

121.1

2. On the second floor.
3. At/On the corner.
4. In the corner.
5. At the top of the stairs.
6. In the back of the car.
7. In the front.
8. On the left.
9. In the back row.
10. On a farm.

121.2

2. on the right
3. in the world
4. on the way to work
5. on the West Coast
6. in the front row
7. in/at the back of the class
8. on the back of this card

121.3

2. in
3. in
4. in/at
5. in
6. on
7. At . . . on
8. in
9. in
10. on
11. in
12. on
13. in
14. on . . . on

UNIT 122

122.1

2. on a train
3. at a conference
4. in the hospital
5. at the hairdresser's
6. on his bike
7. in New York
8. at the Ford Theater

122.2

2. in a taxi
3. at the party
4. on the plane
5. at school
6. at the gym
7. in the hospital
8. in/at the airport
9. in prison

122.3

2. at
3. in
4. at
5. at/in . . . in
6. in
7. on
8. at
9. in
10. at
11. in
12. at . . . at
13. in
14. in . . . at

UNIT 123

123.1

3. at
4. to
5. to
6. into
7. at *or* –
8. to
9. into
10. to
11. at
12. to
13. into
14. to
15. – . . . to
16. to . . . in
17. in . . . to . . . in

123.2

解答例

2.–4.

I've been to Hong Kong once.
I've never been to Tokyo.
I've been to Paris a few times.

123.3

2. in
3. –
4. at
5. to
6. –

123.4

2. got on the bus.
3. I got out of the car.
4. I got off the train.
5. I got into the taxi. *or* I got in the taxi.
6. I got off the plane.

UNIT 124

124.1

2. in cold weather
3. in pencil
4. in love
5. in capital letters
6. in the shade
7. in my opinion

124.2

2. on strike
3. on a tour
4. on television
5. on purpose
6. on a diet
7. on business
8. on vacation
9. on the phone
10. on the whole

124.3

2. on
3. on
4. at
5. in
6. on
7. for
8. on
9. at
10. at
11. on
12. In . . . on
13. on
14. on
15. on
16. at
17. on
18. in

UNIT 125

125.1

2. by mistake
3. by hand
4. by credit card
5. by satellite

125.2

2. on
3. by
4. by . . . on
5. in
6. on
7. by

125.3

解答例

3.–5.

Ulysses is a novel by James Joyce.
"Yesterday" is a song by Paul McCartney.
Guernica is a painting by Pablo Picasso.

125.4

2. by
3. with
4. by
5. by
6. by . . . in
7. by . . . with . . . on it

125.5

2. traveling by bus *or* traveling on the bus *or* traveling on buses
3. taken with a very good camera
4. this music is by Beethoven
5. pay cash *or* pay in cash
6. a mistake by one of our players

125.6

2. by 25 cents.
3. by two votes.
4. her/Kate by five minutes.

UNIT 126

126.1

2. to the problem
3. with her brother
4. in the cost of living
5. to your question
6. for a new road
7. in/to working at home
8. in the number of people without jobs
9. for shoes like these any more
10. between your job and mine

126.2

2. invitation to
3. contact with
4. key to
5. cause of
6. reply to
7. connection between
8. pictures of
9. reason for
10. damage to

126.3

2. to
3. in
4. for
5. of
6. in *or* to
7. for
8. to *or* toward
9. with
10. in
11. to
12. of
13. for . . . in
14. to
15. with

UNIT 127

127.1

2. nice of
3. was generous of him.
4. wasn't very nice of them.
5. That's very kind of
6. That wasn't very polite of him.
7. That's a little childish of them.

127.2

2. kind to
3. sorry for
4. nervous about
5. upset about
6. impressed by / with
7. bored with
8. astonished at/by

127.3

2. of
3. to . . . to
4. of
5. of
6. with
7. to
8. with
9. at/by
10. with
11. about
12. about
13. for/about . . . at
14. at/with . . . for
15. about
16. about
17. at/by
18. by/with
19. about
20. about
21. for

UNIT 128

128.1

2. of furniture
3. for this mess
4. of time
5. at tennis
6. to a Russian (man)
7. of him / of Robert
8. from yours / than yours

128.2

2. similar to
3. afraid of
4. interested in
5. responsible for
6. proud of
7. different from/than

128.3

2. for
3. of
4. of
5. in
6. to
7. of . . . of
8. on
9. of
10. with
11. of
12. of
13. in
14. of
15. of
16. at
17. of
18. to
19. of

128.4

解答例

2. I'm hopeless at telling jokes.
3. I'm not very good at mathematics.
4. I'm pretty good at remembering names.

UNIT 129

129.1

3. this question to me? / Can you explain it to me?
4. you explain the problem to me? / Can you explain it to me?
5. Can you explain to me how this machine works?
6. Can you explain to me what I have to do?

129.2

3. to
4. –
5. to
6. to
7. –
8. –
9. to
10. –

129.3

3. speaking to
4. point . . . at
5. glanced at
6. listen to
7. throw . . . at
8. throw . . . to

129.4

2. at
3. at
4. to
5. to
6. at
7. at
8. to
9. at
10. at
11. to

UNIT 130

130.1

2. for
3. for
4. to
5. for
6. about
7. –
8. about
9. –
10. for
11. for
12. about
13. for
14. for

130.2

2. waiting for
3. talk about
4. asked . . . for
5. applied for
6. do . . . about
7. looks after *or* has looked after
8. left . . . for

130.3

2. for
3. about
4. of
5. for
6. of
7. about
8. –

130.4

2. looking for
3. looked after
4. looking for
5. look for
6. looks after

UNIT 131

131.1

2. about
3. to . . . about
4. of
5. of
6. about . . . about . . . about . . . about
7. of
8. about
9. about/of

131.2

2. complaining about
3. think about
4. warn . . . about
5. heard of
6. dream of
7. reminded . . . about
8. remind . . . of

131.3

2. hear about
3. heard from
4. heard of
5. hear from
6. hear about
7. heard of

131.4

2. think about
3. think of
4. think of
5. thinking of/about
6. think of
7. thought about
8. think . . . of
9. thinking about/of

UNIT 132

132.1

2. for the misunderstanding
3. on winning the tournament
4. from/against his enemies
5. of nine players
6. on bread and eggs

132.2

2. for everything
3. for the economic crisis
4. on television
5. is to blame for the economic crisis
6. television is to blame for the increase in violent crime

132.3

2. paid for
3. accused of
4. depends on
5. live on
6. congratulated . . . on
7. apologize to

132.4

2. from
3. on
4. of/from
5. for
6. for
7. –
8. on
9. on
10. – *or* on
11. from/against
12. of

UNIT 133

133.1

2. small towns to big cities.
3. with all the information I needed.
4. $70 on a pair of shoes.

133.2

2. happened to
3. invited to
4. divided into
5. believe in
6. fill . . . with
7. drove into
8. Concentrate on
9. succeeded in

133.3
2. to
3. on
4. in
5. to
6. in
7. with
8. into
9. in
10. on
11. into
12. to
13. –
14. into
15. on
16. from . . . into
17. to . . . on
18. into
19. with

133.4
解答例
2. on CDs
3. into a wall
4. to volleyball
5. into many languages

UNIT 134

134.1
2. sit down
3. flew away
4. get out
5. run out
6. get by
7. gone up
8. looked around

134.2
2. back at
3. up to
4. forward to
5. away with
6. up at
7. in through
8. along with

134.3
2. wake me up
3. get it out
4. give them back
5. turn it on
6. take them off

134.4
3. them back
4. the television off *or* off the television
5. it over
6. her up
7. 解答例
your coat on *or* on your coat
8. it out
9. my shoes off *or* off my shoes
10. the light(s) on *or* on the light(s)

UNIT 135

135.1
2. eats
3. moved
4. drop
5. checked
6. cut
7. plug
8. fit
9. fill
10. hand / turn
11. leave
12. dropped

135.2
2. into
3. in
4. out
5. into
6. out of

135.3
2. dropped out
3. moved in
4. left out
5. joined in
6. eating out *or* to eat out
7. fits in
8. dropped in
9. get out of

135.4
2. Fill them out
3. handed it in
4. left them out
5. let us in

UNIT 136

136.1
2. a mistake
3. a candle
4. an order
5. a campfire
6. a new product
7. a problem

136.2
2. works out
3. carried out
4. ran out
5. work out
6. find out
7. tried out
8. pointed out
9. work out
10. went out
11. turned out
12. figure out
13. find out
14. put out

136.3
2. giving/handing out
3. turned out nice/fine/sunny
4. working out
5. run out
6. figure out . . . use the camera / her new camera

136.4
2. try it out
3. figure him out
4. pointing it out

UNIT 137

137.1
2. put the heat on
3. put the radio on
4. put the light on
5. put a DVD on

137.2
2. going on
3. take off
4. turned off
5. drove off / went off
6. put on
7. had on
8. put off
9. called off
10. put on
11. see . . . off

137.3
2. took off
3. tried on a/the hat *or* tried a/the hat on
4. was called off
5. see him off
6. put them on

UNIT 138

138.1
2. went on
3. went on walking
4. dozed off / dropped off / nodded off
5. go on
6. went off
7. keeps on calling me

138.2
2. went off
3. dropped off
4. taken on
5. ripped off
6. goes on
7. dozed off / dropped off / nodded off
8. told off
9. lay off
10. going off
11. keep on
12. go on
13. showing off
14. hold on / hang on

138.3
2. dragging on
3. were ripped off
4. go off
5. move on / go on
6. go on with
7. tell them off
8. laid off

UNIT 139

139.1

2. turn it down
3. calm him down
4. put them up
5. let her down
6. turned it down

139.2

2. took them down
3. stand up
4. turned it up
5. put their bags down
6. were blown/knocked down
7. wrote it down
8. bent down . . . picked them up

139.3

2. calm down
3. slowed down
4. was turned down
5. broken down
6. cut down
7. let down
8. (has) closed down
9. be torn down
10. turned down
11. burned down
12. broken down

UNIT 140

140.1

2. went up to / walked up to
3. catch up with
4. keep up with

140.2

2. used up
3. backed up
4. grow up
5. turn up
6. gave up
7. taking up
8. give up
9. ended up
10. takes up
11. make up

140.3

3. set it up
4. keep up with
5. was brought up / grew up
6. keep it up
7. backed up
8. went up to
9. was made up of
10. backing me up

UNIT 141

141.1

2. D
3. E
4. C
5. G
6. A
7. B

141.2

2. held up
3. fixed it up
4. cheer him up

141.3

2. blew up
3. beaten up
4. broken up / split up
5. came up
6. clears up
7. mixed up

141.4

2. look it up
3. put up with
4. made it up
5. come up with
6. tear it up
7. saving up for
8. clean it up

UNIT 142

142.1

2. Pay
3. throw
4. gets
5. be
6. look
7. gave
8. get

142.2

2. be away / have gone away
3. be back
4. ran away
5. smile back
6. get away
7. Keep away

142.3

2. blew away
3. put it back
4. walked away
5. threw it back (to her)
6. threw them away

142.4

2. throw it away
3. take them back
4. pay you back / pay it back
5. gave them away
6. call back / call me back

補充問題解答

(p. 296より)

1

3. 'm getting / am getting
4. do you do
5. arrived . . . was raining
6. calls . . . didn't call
7. were thinking . . . decided
8. are you looking
9. doesn't rain
10. rang . . . were having
11. went . . . was studying . . . didn't want . . . didn't stay
12. told . . . didn't believe . . . thought . . . was joking

2

2. didn't go
3. is wearing
4. went
5. haven't heard
6. is being
7. wasn't reading
8. didn't have
9. It's beginning
10. got
11. wasn't
12. you've been
13. I've been doing
14. did she go
15. I've been playing
16. do you come
17. since I saw her
18. for 20 years

3

3. are you going
4. Do you watch
5. have you lived / have you been living / have you been
6. Did you have
7. Have you seen
8. was she wearing
9. Have you been waiting / Have you been here
10. does it take
11. Have you ridden
12. Have you (ever) been

4

2. 've known each other / have known each other *or* 've been friends / have been friends
3. I've ever had / I've ever been on / I've had in ages (*etc.*)
4. He left / He went home / He went out
5. I've worn it
6. I was playing
7. been swimming for *or* gone swimming for
8. since I've been / since I (last) went
9. did you buy / did you get

5

1. got . . . was already waiting . . . had arrived
2. was lying . . . wasn't watching . . . 'd fallen / had fallen . . . was snoring . . . turned . . . woke
3. 'd just gone / had just gone . . . was reading . . . heard . . . got . . . didn't see . . . went
4. missed . . . was standing . . . realized . . . 'd left / had left . . . had . . . got
5. met . . . was walking . . . 'd been / had been . . . 'd been playing / had been playing . . . were going . . . invited . . . 'd arranged / had arranged . . . didn't have

6

2. Sombody's taken it. / Somebody has taken it.
3. They'd only known / They had only known each other (for) a few weeks.
4. It's been raining / It has been raining all day. *or* It's rained / It has rained all day.
5. I'd been dreaming. / I had been dreaming.
6. I'd had / I had had a big breakfast.
7. They've been going / They have been going there for years.
8. I've had it / I have had it since I got up.
9. He's been training / He has been training very hard for it.

7

1. I haven't seen
2. You look *or* You're looking
3. are you going
4. are you meeting
5. I'm going
6. Do you travel a lot
7. are you going
8. I'm meeting
9. has been *or* was
10. I've been waiting
11. has just started *or* just started
12. is she doing *or* has she been doing
13. Does she like
14. she thinks
15. Are you working *or* Do you work
16. spoke
17. you were working
18. went
19. I started / I had started
20. I lost
21. you haven't had
22. I've had
23. have you seen
24. has he been
25. I saw
26. he left
27. He'd been
28. he decided / he'd decided
29. He was really looking forward
30. is he doing
31. I haven't heard
32. he left

8

1. invented
2. it's ended / it has ended / it ended
3. had gone . . . left
4. did you do . . . Did you go
5. have you had
6. was looking
7. She's been teaching / She has been teaching
8. I bought . . . I haven't worn
9. I saw . . . was . . . I'd seen / I had seen . . . I remembered . . . he was
10. Have you heard . . . She was . . . died . . . She wrote . . . Have you read
11. does this word mean . . . I've never seen
12. Did you get . . . it had already begun
13. knocked . . . was . . . she'd gone / she had gone . . . she didn't want
14. He'd never used / He had never used . . . he didn't know
15. went . . . She needed . . . she'd been sitting / she had been sitting

9

3. used to drive
4. was driving
5. were working
6. used to have
7. was living
8. was playing
9. used to play
10. was wearing

10

2. I'm going to the dentist.
3. we're going to rent a car.
4. I'll take care of the children.
5. I'm having lunch with Sue.
6. are you going to have?
7. I'll turn on the light.
8. I'm going to turn on the light.

11

2. I'll go
3. should/shall we meet
4. starts
5. I'll meet
6. I'm seeing
7. Should/Shall I ask
8. I'll see
9. are going
10. does the movie start
11. Are you meeting
12. I'll be

12

1. (2) Are you going to take
   (3) it starts
   (4) you'll enjoy
   (5) it will / it's going to be
2. (1) you're going
   (2) We're going
   (3) you have
   (4) I'll send
   (5) I'll get
   (6) I get
3. (1) I'm having / I'm going to have
   (2) are coming
   (3) they'll have left
   (4) they're
   (5) I won't be / I will not be
   (6) you know
   (7) I'll call
4. (1) should/shall we meet
   (2) I'll be waiting
   (3) you arrive
   (4) I'll be sitting
   (5) I'll be wearing
   (6) Is Agent 307 coming / Is Agent 307 going to come / Will Agent 307 be coming
   (7) Should/Shall I bring
   (8) I'll explain
   (9) I see
   (10) I'll try

13

1. I'll have
2. Are you going
3. should/shall I call
4. It's going to land
5. it's / it is
6. I'll miss / I'm going to miss . . . you go (*or* you've gone)
7. Should/Shall I give . . . I give . . . will you send
8. does it end
9. I'm going . . . is getting
10. I'll tell . . . I'm . . . I won't be
11. I'm going to have / I'm having
12. she apologizes
13. we'll be living
14. you finish

14

2. 've had
3. I bought *or* I got
4. 'll come
5. 've been *or* 've eaten
6. used to play
7. haven't been waiting *or* haven't been here
8. 'd been
9. 'm going
10. haven't seen *or* haven't heard from
11. 'll have gone *or* 'll have left

15

2. I've been traveling
3. I'm beginning
4. I've seen
5. has been
6. I've met
7. I left
8. I stayed *or* I was staying
9. I'd planned *or* I was planning
10. I ended up
11. I enjoyed
12. I took
13. met
14. I'm staying *or* I'm going to stay *or* I'll be staying *or* I'll stay
15. I continue
16. I'll get
17. I'm
18. I'll let
19. I know
20. I'm staying
21. we're going to visit *or* we're visiting
22. are building *or* have been building
23. it will be
24. I'll be

16

2. A
3. C
4. C
5. B
6. A *or* C
7. A *or* C
8. C
9. B *or* C
10. A *or* B
11. A *or* B
12. C
13. A *or* B
14. B *or* C
15. B

17

3. He must have forgotten.
4. You shouldn't have left so late.
5. It can't be changed now.
6. You could have gotten here earlier.
7. She may be watching television.
8. She must have been waiting for somebody.
9. He couldn't have done it.
10. I would have helped you.
11. You should have been warned about it.
12. He might not have been feeling very well. *or* He might not have felt . . .

18

3. could rain / might rain
4. might have gone / could have gone
5. couldn't go
6. couldn't have seen / can't have seen
7. should get
8. wouldn't recognize / might not recognize
9. must have heard
10. should have turned

19

4. rings
5. were
6. 's / is
7. was/were
8. had been
9. had
10. hadn't had
11. 'd driven / had driven *or* 'd been driving / had been driving
12. didn't read

20

2. came (to see us now).
3. wouldn't have disturbed you.
4. be upset . . . I told them what happened.
5. you hadn't frightened the dog, it wouldn't have attacked you.
6. wouldn't have gotten (so) wet if I'd had an umbrella. *or* . . . if I had had an umbrella.
7. hadn't been (so) nervous, he wouldn't have failed (his driver's test).

21

解答例

1. I wasn't feeling so tired
2. I hadn't had so much to do
3. I would have forgotten Jane's birthday
4. you hadn't taken so long to get ready
5. I would have gone to the concert
6. you were in trouble
7. there was less traffic
8. people would go out more

22

3. was canceled
4. has been repaired
5. is being restored
6. 's believed / is believed
7. 'd be fired / would be fired
8. might have been thrown
9. was taught
10. being arrested / having been arrested
11. Have you ever been arrested
12. are reported . . . have been injured *or* be injured

23

3. sold *or* 've sold / have sold
4. 's been sold / has been sold
5. are made
6. might be stolen
7. must have been stolen
8. must have taken
9. can be solved
10. should have left
11. is delayed
12. is being built . . . is expected

24

Fire at City Hall

2. was discovered
3. was injured
4. be rescued
5. are believed to have been destroyed
6. is not known

Convenience Store Robbery

1. was forced
2. being threatened
3. had been stolen
4. was later found
5. had been abandoned
6. has been arrested / was arrested
7. is still being questioned

Road Delays

1. is being resurfaced
2. are asked / are being asked / have been asked
3. is expected
4. will be closed
5. will be rerouted

Accident

1. was taken
2. was allowed
3. was blocked
4. be rerouted
5. have been killed

25

1. I told **her (that) Paul had gone out** and **I didn't know when he'd be back**. I asked **(her) if/whether she wanted to leave a message**, but she said **(that) she'd try again** later.
2. I had reserved a hotel room, but when I got to the hotel, they told **me (that) they had** no **record of a reservation in my name**. When I asked **(them) if/whether they had any rooms available anyway**, they said **(that) they were sorry**, but **the hotel was full**.
3. The immigration official asked us **why we were visiting the country**, and we told **him (that) we were on vacation**. Then he wanted to know **how long we intended to stay** and **where we would be staying during our visit**.
4. She said **(that) she'd call us from the airport when she arrived**. *or* She said **(that) she'll call us from the airport when she arrives**. No, she said **not to come to the airport**. She said **(that) she'd take the bus**. *or* She said **(that) she'll take the bus**.
5. He wanted to know **what my job was** and asked **(me) how much I made**. *or* He wanted to know **what my job is** and asked **(me) how much I made**. . . . so I told **him to mind his own business** and I put the phone down.
6. He said **(that) he'd be at the restaurant at 7:30**. He said **(that) he knew where the restaurant was**. And I told **him to call me if there was any problem**.
7. You just said **(that) you weren't hungry**. But you said **(that) you didn't like bananas**. You told **me not to buy any**.

26

3. changing
4. to change
5. change
6. being
7. saying
8. to call
9. drinking
10. to be
11. to see
12. to be
13. to think . . . making
14. living . . . to move
15. to be . . . playing
16. being stopped . . . to stealing . . . driving
17. work . . . pressing

27

3. We stopped watching after a while.
4. He tends to forget things.
5. Would you mind helping me? / Do you mind helping me?
6. Everybody seems to have gone out.
7. We're thinking of moving.
8. I was afraid to touch it.
9. He's / He is afraid of being robbed.
10. It's not worth seeing.
11. I'm not used to walking so far.
12. She seems to be enjoying herself.
13. He insisted on showing them to me.
14. I'd rather somebody else did it.

28

3. reading newspapers.
4. not go out tonight / . . . stay at home tonight.
5. walking
6. me to call you tonight?
7. anybody seeing me / . . . without being seen.
8. of being a liar/ . . . of lying.
9. to seeing them again.
10. to do?
11. to have gone out with you.
12. not taking your advice / . . . that I didn't take your advice.

29

2. – Tennis . . . twice **a** week . . . **a** very good player
3. for – dinner . . . after – work . . . to **the** movies
4. – Unemployment . . . for – people . . . find – work
5. **an** accident . . . going – home . . . taken to **the** hospital. I think – most accidents . . . by – people driving
6. **an** economist . . . in **the** investment department of – Lloyds Bank . . . for **an** American bank . . . in **the** United States
7. **the** name of **the** hotel . . . **The** Royal . . . on – West Street in **the** suburbs . . . near **the** airport.
8. **The** older one . . . **a** pilot with – Western Airlines . . . **The** younger one . . . in – high school. . . . he finishes – school . . . go to – college . . . study – engineering.

30

2. B
3. C
4. A *or* B
5. C
6. B
7. A *or* C

8. A
9. C
10. B *or* C
11. B
12. A
13. A *or* B
14. B

31

3. It's the most polluted place . . .
4. I was disappointed that . . .
5. *OK*
6. Joe works hard, but . . .
7. . . . in a large modern building.
8. *OK* (as fast as he can も可)
9. I missed the last three days . . .
10. *OK*
11. The weather has been unusually cold . . .
12. The water in the pool was too dirty to swim in.
13. . . . to wait such a long time. (so long も可)
14. *OK*
15. . . . I got up earlier than usual.

32

2. If
3. when
4. if
5. when
6. if
7. if
8. unless
9. if
10. as long as
11. in case
12. in case
13. if
14. even if
15. Although
16. Although
17. When
18. when

33

2. on
3. at . . . on
4. on
5. on
6. at
7. In
8. at
9. during
10. on . . . since
11. for
12. at
13. at . . . until
14. by
15. in

34

1. in
2. by
3. at
4. on
5. in
6. on
7. to . . . at
8. on
9. on
10. to . . . to
11. in . . . at
12. in . . . on
13. to . . . in
14. on . . . by
15. at
16. on
17. in . . . on
18. on
19. by
20. On . . . by
21. on . . . on
22. in
23. in . . . to
24. to
25. on

35

1. for
2. at
3. to
4. to
5. in
6. with
7. of
8. to
9. of
10. at/by
11. of
12. about

36

1. of
2. after
3. –
4. about
5. to
6. –
7. into
8. of
9. to
10. –
11. on
12. of
13. of
14. –
15. in
16. at (about も可)
17. on
18. – . . . for
19. to . . . for
20. – . . . for

37

2. h
3. e
4. g
5. a
6. k
7. c
8. j
9. b
10. f
11. i

38

2. D
3. B
4. B
5. A
6. B
7. D
8. C
9. C
10. B
11. A
12. D

39

2. out to
3. up with
4. forward to
5. up with
6. out of
7. on with
8. out of
9. up with
10. back on
11. out about
12. along with

40

3. went off
4. turned up / showed up
5. fill it out / fill it in
6. torn down / knocked down
7. taken on
8. give up
9. dozed off / dropped off / nodded off
10. split up / break up
11. put up with it
12. get by
13. went on
14. put it off

41

2. put
3. moving
4. put
5. fixed
6. turned / turns
7. find
8. Calm
9. drop
10. held
11. left *or* 've left / have left
12. drop
13. join
14. works
15. let
16. work
17. went . . . woke

診断テスト解答

(p. 319より)

現在形と過去形

1.1 A
1.2 B
1.3 C
1.4 B, C
1.5 C
1.6 A

現在完了形と過去形

2.1 C
2.2 A
2.3 A, C
2.4 A
2.5 A
2.6 C
2.7 A
2.8 C
2.9 A
2.10 B
2.11 A
2.12 D
2.13 C
2.14 C
2.15 D
2.16 C

未来

3.1 B
3.2 A
3.3 C
3.4 A, C
3.5 B
3.6 C
3.7 A

法助動詞

4.1 A, B
4.2 B
4.3 A, C, D
4.4 C
4.5 B
4.6 C, D
4.7 B
4.8 B
4.9 A
4.10 A
4.11 D
4.12 A

if と wish

5.1 B
5.2 C
5.3 B
5.4 D
5.5 A

受動態

6.1 C
6.2 B
6.3 D
6.4 A
6.5 A, B
6.6 C
6.7 D

間接話法

7.1 A
7.2 B
7.3 A

疑問文と繰り返しを避ける助動詞

8.1 C
8.2 A
8.3 D
8.4 A
8.5 B

動名詞（-ing）と不定詞（to＋動詞の原形）

9.1 A
9.2 B, D
9.3 B
9.4 A
9.5 A
9.6 A
9.7 C
9.8 D
9.9 C
9.10 C
9.11 B
9.12 C
9.13 B, D
9.14 B
9.15 A, B
9.16 A
9.17 A
9.18 B, C

冠詞と名詞

10.1 B
10.2 A
10.3 B, C
10.4 B
10.5 C
10.6 A
10.7 A
10.8 A
10.9 D
10.10 C
10.11 C
10.12 A
10.13 C
10.14 B

代名詞と限定詞

11.1 A
11.2 B
11.3 D
11.4 B
11.5 B
11.6 C
11.7 A, C
11.8 C
11.9 D
11.10 A, C
11.11 B

関係詞節

12.1 A, C
12.2 A, B
12.3 C
12.4 B
12.5 D
12.6 B, C

形容詞と副詞

13.1 B
13.2 C
13.3 B, C
13.4 A
13.5 A, D
13.6 B
13.7 C
13.8 C
13.9 B, C
13.10 D
13.11 A, B
13.12 B
13.13 D
13.14 D

接続詞と前置詞

14.1 A, D
14.2 C
14.3 B, C
14.4 B
14.5 B
14.6 C, D
14.7 B, C
14.8 A

前置詞

15.1 B, D
15.2 A
15.3 C
15.4 B
15.5 A
15.6 B, D
15.7 B
15.8 B
15.9 C
15.10 C
15.11 C
15.12 A
15.13 C
15.14 B
15.15 D
15.16 D
15.17 A

句動詞

16.1 B
16.2 A
16.3 D
16.4 C
16.5 C
16.6 B
16.7 A
16.8 A, D
16.9 B

索引

各項目の右に示した数字はユニットの番号を表します。ページ番号ではありません。

文法項目

注意の必要な文法用語については，簡単な説明を与えてあります。

重要語句

ILLUSTRATION CREDITS

Carlos Castellanos: 4, 9, 10, 14, 17, 21, 30, 34, 38, 58, 70, 72, 86, 87, 100, 118, 160, 190, 202, 222, 279, 283

Tim Foley: 6, 13, 22, 24, 28, 32, 40, 46, 47, 60, 64, 78, 89, 92, 96, 110, 130, 140, 192, 198, 220, 224, 226, 241, 248, 250, 270, 275, 281

Marty Harris: 36, 37, 80, 111, 148, 153, 154, 172, 234

Randy Jones: 11, 35, 44, 54, 65, 90, 91, 95, 97, 99, 103, 105, 107, 121, 185, 217, 219, 242

Kamae Designs: 311

Roger Penwill: 304, 305

Lisa Smith: 2, 12, 20, 26, 42, 46, 48, 52, 62, 68, 74, 88, 93, 102, 130, 131, 134, 144, 162, 164, 179, 208, 218, 230, 240, 243, 245, 273, 285, 306, 309

Simon Williams: 316, 317

Cambridge University Press thanks Izumi Walker for her work on 'Grammar in Use Intermediate with Answers 2nd Edition (Japan edition).'

訳者・協力者紹介

渡辺 雅仁（わたなべ・まさひと）
横浜国立大学 大学教育総合センター 英語教育部 教授
田島 祐規子（たしま・ゆきこ）
横浜国立大学 大学教育総合センター 英語教育部 准教授

マーフィーの
ケンブリッジ英文法（中級編）新訂版

2010年11月30日 第1版第1刷発行

著　者 Raymond Murphy
William R. Smalzer（執筆協力）
訳　者 渡辺 雅仁
田島 祐規子（日本語訳協力）
発行所 Cambridge University Press
79 Anson Road, #06-04/06, Singapore 079906
発売元 United Publishers Services Limited
〒140-0002 東京都品川区東品川 1-32-5
電話 (03) 5479-7281

組　版 東京リスマチック株式会社
編　集 K's counter　カバーデザイン 岡崎健二

ISBN 978-4-902290-23-3　Printed in Singapore by Craft Print International Ltd

SCREWDRIVER

technique: build | time total: 3 min | serves: 1

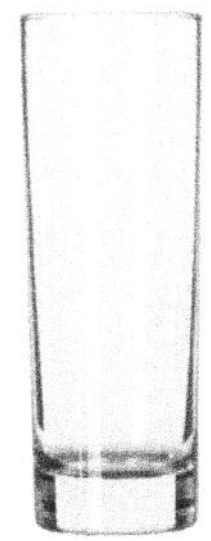

collins glass, jigger, bar spoon, drinking straws

- **2 oz. vodka**
- **5 oz. orange juice**
- **Ice**
- **Orange**

1. Fill a collins glass to the top with ice

2. Pour in 2 oz. of vodka

3. Top up with orange juice and stir gently

4. Garnish with an orange wheel

SEA BREEZE

technique: build | time total: 5 min | serves: 1

collins glass, jigger, bar spoon, drinking straws, cocktail skewer

- **2 oz. vodka**
- **2 oz. grapefruit juice**
- **4 oz. cranberry juice**
- **Ice**
- **Cranberry**
- **Orange**

1. Fill a collins glass to the top with ice

2. Pour in 2 oz. of grapefruit juice and 2 oz. of vodka

3. Top up with cranberry juice and stir gently

4. Garnish with cranberries and an orange wheel on a cocktail skewer

WHITE RUSSIAN

technique: build | time total: 5 min | serves: 1

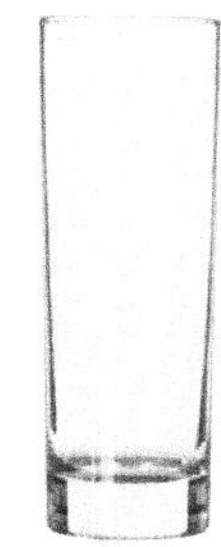

rocks glass, jigger, bar spoon, drinking straws

- **1 oz. vodka**
- **1 oz. coffee liqueur**
- **1 oz. light cream**
- **Ice**

1. Fill a rocks glass to the top with ice
2. Pour in 1 oz. of light cream, 1 oz. of coffee liqueur, 1 oz. of vodka
3. Stir until the sides of the glass begin to frost

ADONIS

technique: stir | time total: 5 min | serves: 1

cocktail glass, jigger, mixing glass, bar spoon, strainer

- **1½ oz. fino sherry**
- **1½ oz. sweet vermouth**
- **Orange bitters**
- **Ice**
- **Orange twist**

1. Pour 1½ oz. of sweet vermouth, 1½ oz. of fino sherry and 2 dashes of orange bitters into a mixing glass
2. Fill the glass with ice cubes and stir
3. Strain into a chilled cocktail glass
4. Garnish with orange twist

AVIATION

technique: stir | time total: 5 min | serves: 1

cocktail glass, mixing glass, squeezer, bar spoon, strainer, jigger

- **1½ oz. gin**
- **¾ oz. Maraschino liqueur**
- **¼ oz. violet liqueur**
- **½ oz. lemon juice**
- **Ice**
- **Lemon zest**

1. Pour ½ oz. of lemon juice, ¾ oz. of Maraschino liqueur, ¼ oz. of violet liqueur and 1½ oz. of gin into a mixing glass
2. Fill the glass with ice cubes and stir gently
3. Strain into a chilled cocktail glass
4. Garnish with lemon zest

BAMBOO

technique: stir | time total: 5 min | serves: 1

coupe glass, jigger, mixing glass, bar spoon, strainer

- **1½ oz. fino sherry**
- **½ oz. dry vermouth**
- **Ice**
- **Lemon zest**

1. Pour ½ oz. of dry vermouth and 1½ oz. of fino sherry into a mixing glass
2. Fill the glass with ice cubes and stir
3. Strain into a chilled coupe glass
4. Garnish with lemon zest

BIJOU

technique: stir | time total: 5 min | serves: 1

cocktail glass, jigger, mixing glass, bar spoon, strainer

- **1 oz. gin**
- **1 oz. sweet vermouth**
- **1 oz. green Chartreuse liqueur**
- **Orange bitters**
- **Ice**
- **Lemon twist**

1. Pour 1 oz. of sweet vermouth, 1 oz. of green Chartreuse liqueur, 1 oz. of gin and dash of orange bitters into a mixing glass
2. Fill the glass with ice cubes and stir
3. Strain into a chilled cocktail glass
4. Garnish with orange twist

BROOKLYN

technique: stir | time total: 5 min | serves: 1

cocktail glass, jigger, mixing glass, bar spoon, strainer, cocktail skewer

- **2 oz. rye whisky**
- **1 oz. dry vermouth**
- **¼ oz. maraschino liqueur**
- **Angostura bitters**
- **Ice**
- **Maraschino cherry**

1. Pour 1 oz. of dry vermouth, ¼ oz. of maraschino liqueur, 2 oz. of rye whisky and dash of Angostura bitters into a mixing glass
2. Fill the glass with ice cubes and stir
3. Strain into a chilled cocktail glass
4. Garnish with a maraschino cherry on a cocktail skewer

DRY MARTINI

technique: stir | time total: 5 min | serves: 1

cocktail glass, mixing glass, bar spoon, strainer, jigger, cocktail skewer

- **2 ½ oz. gin**
- **½ oz. dry vermouth Martini**
- **Ice**
- **Green olives**

1. Pour ½ oz. of dry vermouth and 2 ½ oz. of gin into a mixing glass
2. Fill the glass with ice cubes and stir gently
3. Strain into a chilled cocktail glass
4. Garnish with green olive on a cocktail skewer

MANHATTAN

technique: stir | time total: 5 min | serves: 1

cocktail glass, mixing glass, bar spoon, strainer, jigger

- **1½ oz. bourbon**
- **¾ oz. red vermouth**
- **Angostura bitters**
- **Maraschino cherry**
- **Ice**

1. Pour ¾ oz. of red vermouth and 1½ oz. of bourbon into a mixing glass
2. Add 1 dash of Angostura bitters
3. Fill the glass with ice cubes and stir gently
4. Strain into a chilled cocktail glass
5. Garnish with a Maraschino cherry

MARTINEZ

technique: stir | time total: 5 min | serves: 1

cocktail glass, mixing glass, bar spoon, strainer, jigger

- **2 oz. gin**
- **1 oz. red vermouth**
- **¼ oz. Maraschino liqueur**
- **Orange bitters**
- **Orange zest**
- **Ice**

1. Pour ¼ oz. of Maraschino liqueur, 1 oz. of red vermouth and 2 oz. of gin into a mixing glass
2. Add 1 dash of orange bitters
3. Fill the glass with ice cubes and stir gently
4. Strain into a chilled cocktail glass
5. Squeeze orange zest over the glass and put into the cocktail

OLD PAL

technique: stir | time total: 5 min | serves: 1

cocktail glass, jigger, mixing glass, bar spoon, strainer

- **1 oz. rye whisky**
- **1 oz. dry vermouth**
- **1 oz. red bitter**
- **Ice**
- **Lemon twist**

1. Pour 1 oz. of dry vermouth, 1 oz. of red bitter and 1 oz. of rye whisky into a mixing glass
2. Fill the glass with ice cubes and stir
3. Strain into a chilled cocktail glass
4. Garnish with a lemon twist

ROB ROY

technique: stir | time total: 5 min | serves: 1

cocktail glass, mixing glass, bar spoon, strainer, jigger, zest knife, clothespins

- **2 oz. Scotch whisky**
- **1½ oz. red vermouth**
- **Angostura bitters**
- **Ice**
- **Orange zest**

1. Pour 1½ oz. of red vermouth and 2 oz. of Scotch whisky into a mixing glass
2. Add 1 dash of Angostura bitters
3. Fill the glass with ice cubes and stir
4. Strain into a chilled cocktail glass
5. Garnish with orange zest on a clothespin

SAZERAC

technique: stir | time total: 5 min | serves: 1

rocks glass, jigger, muddler, mixing glass, bar spoon, strainer

- **2½ oz. Cognac**
- **½ oz. absinthe**
- **½ oz. still water**
- **Angostura bitters**
- **Peychaud's bitters**
- **Ice**
- **Sugar cubes**
- **Lemon zest**

1. Fill a rocks glass to the top with ice cubes
2. Pour in ½ oz. of absinthe and ½ oz. of still water, then set aside
3. Place a sugar cube into a mixing glass
4. Soak the sugar with 3 dashes of Angostura bitters and 3 dashes of Peychaud's bitters and muddle
5. Add 2½ oz. of Cognac
6. Fill the glass with ice cubes and stir until the sugar dissolves
7. Pour out still water, absinthe and ice from the rocks glass
8. Strain the cocktail into the aromatized glass
9. Garnish with a lemon zest

WHAT ABOUT: PEYCHAUD'S BITTERS

Peychaud's Bitters was originally created around 1830 by Antoine Amédée Peychaud, a Creole apothecary from the French colony of Saint-Domingue (now Haiti) who settled in New Orleans, Louisiana in 1795. It is a gentian-based bitters, comparable to Angostura bitters, but with a predominant anise aroma combined with a background of mint

TUXEDO

technique: stir | time total: 5 min | serves: 1

cocktail glass, jigger, mixing glass, bar spoon, strainer, cocktail skewer

- **1 oz. gin**
- **1 oz. dry vermouth**
- **¼ oz. maraschino liqueur**
- **¼ oz. absinthe**
- **Orange bitters**
- **Ice**
- **Lemon twist**
- **Maraschino cherry**

1. Pour 1 oz. of dry vermouth, ¼ oz. of maraschino liqueur, ¼ oz. of absinthe, 1 oz. of gin and 3 dashes of orange bitters into a mixing glass
2. Fill the glass with ice cubes and stir
3. Strain into a chilled cocktail glass
4. Garnish with a maraschino cherry and lemon twist on a cocktail skewer

VODKA MARTINI

technique: stir | time total: 3 min | serves: 1

cocktail glass, mixing glass, bar spoon, strainer, jigger, cocktail skewer

- **2½ oz. vodka**
- **½ oz. dry vermouth Martini**
- **Ice**
- **Green olives**

1. Pour ½ oz. of dry vermouth and 2½ oz. of vodka into a mixing glass
2. Fill the glass with ice cubes and stir gently
3. Strain into a chilled cocktail glass
4. Garnish with 3 green olives on a cocktail skewer

ANGEL FACE

technique: shake | time total: 3 min | serves: 1

cocktail glass, jigger, shaker, strainer

- **1 oz. gin**
- **1 oz. calvados**
- **1 oz. apricot brandy**
- **Ice**

1. Pour 1 oz. of calvados, 1 oz. of apricot brandy and 1 oz. of gin into a shaker

2. Fill the shaker with ice cubes and shake

3. Strain into a chilled cocktail glass

AIR MAIL

technique: shake | time total: 5 min | serves: 1

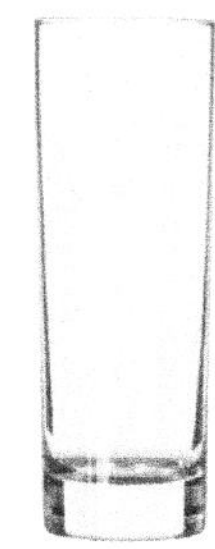

collins glass, jigger, squeezer, shaker, strainer

- **2 oz. white rum**
- **½ oz. fresh lime juice**
- **½ oz. fresh orange juice**
- **¼ oz. honey syrup**
- **5 oz. Brut Champagne**
- **Ice**
- **Mint sprig**

1. Pour ½ oz. of fresh lime juice, ½ oz. of fresh orange juice, ¼ oz. of honey syrup and 2 oz. of white rum into a shaker

2. Fill the shaker with ice cubes and shake

3. Strain into a chilled collins glass

4. Top up with Brut Champagne

5. Garnish with a mint sprig

BLOODY MARY

technique: shake | time total: 5 min | serves: 1

highball glass, shaker, strainer, jigger, squeezer, drinking straws

- **1½ oz. vodka**
- **3 oz. tomato juice**
- **½ oz. lemon juice**
- **Worcestershire Sauce**
- **Tabasco**
- **Celery salt**
- **Ground Black Pepper**
- **Ice**
- **Celery**

1. Fill a highball glass to the top with ice
2. Pour ½ oz. of lemon juice, 3 oz. of tomato juice into a shaker
3. Pour 1 ½ oz. of vodka into a shaker
4. Add 3 dashes of Tabasco and 2 dashes of Worcestershire sauce
5. Add a pinch of celery salt and a pinch of ground black pepper
6. Fill the shaker with ice, close it and roll vertically from one hand to another for a few minutes
7. Strain into the highball glass and garnish with a celery stalk

WHAT ABOUT: TABASCO

Tabasco is a brand of hot sauce made exclusively from tabasco peppers (Capsicum frutescens var. tabasco), vinegar, and salt. It is produced by McIlhenny Company of Avery Island, Louisiana

BLOOD AND SAND

technique: shake | time total: 3 min | serves: 1

coupe glass, jigger, shaker, strainer

- **1 oz. scotch whisky**
- **1 oz. red vermouth**
- **1 oz. cherry liqueur**
- **1 oz. orange juice**
- **Ice**

1. Pour 1 oz. of orange juice, 1 oz. of cherry liqueur, 1 oz. of red vermouth and 1 oz. of Scotch whisky into a shaker
2. Fill the shaker with ice cubes and shake
3. Strain into a chilled coupe glass

BRANDY ALEXANDER

technique: shake | time total: 3 min | serves: 1

cocktail glass, jigger, shaker, strainer, nutmeg grater

- **1½ oz. Cognac**
- **1 oz. dark cacao liqueur**
- **1 oz. light cream**
- **Ice**
- **Ground nutmeg**

1. Pour 1 oz. of light cream, 1 oz. of dark cacao liqueur and 1½ oz. of Cognac into a shaker
2. Fill the shaker with ice cubes and shake
3. Strain into a chilled cocktail glass
4. Garnish with ground nutmeg

BRONX

technique: shake | time total: 3 min | serves: 1

cocktail glass, jigger, shaker, strainer

- **1 oz. gin**
- **½ oz. red vermouth**
- **½ oz. dry vermouth**
- **¾ oz. orange juice**
- **Ice**

1. Pour ¾ oz. of orange juice, ½ oz. of red vermouth, ½ oz. of dry vermouth and 1 oz. of gin into a shaker
2. Fill the shaker with ice cubes and shake
3. Strain into a chilled cocktail glass

CLOVER CLUB

technique: shake | time total: 5 min | serves: 1

cocktail glass, squeezer, jigger, shaker, strainer

- **1½ oz. gin**
- **1 oz. raspberry syrup**
- **½ oz. lime juice**
- **1 egg white**
- **Ice**
- **Mint leaf**

1. Pour 1 egg white, ½ oz. of lime juice, 1 oz. of raspberry syrup and 2 oz. of gin into a shaker
2. Fill the shaker with ice cubes and shake thoroughly
3. Strain into a chilled cocktail glass
4. Garnish with a mint leaf

COSMOPOLITAN

technique: shake | time total: 5 min | serves: 1

cocktail glass, shaker, strainer, jigger, squeezer, zest knife, culinary torch

- **1½ oz. vodka**
- **¾ oz. triple sec liqueur**
- **2 oz. cranberry juice**
- **¼ oz. lime juice**
- **Orange zest**
- **Ice**

1. Pour ¼ oz. of lime juice, 2 oz. of cranberry juice ¾ oz. of triple sec liqueur and 1½ oz. of vodka into a shaker
2. Fill the shaker with ice cubes and shake
3. Strain into a chilled cocktail glass
4. Use a culinary torch to flambé the oils from the orange zest over the cocktail
5. Rim the sides of the glass with flamed orange zest and put it in the glass

DAIQUIRI

technique: shake | time total: 3 min | serves: 1

coupe glass, squeezer, jigger, shaker, strainer

- **2 oz. white rum**
- **½ oz. sugar syrup**
- **1 oz. lime juice**
- **Ice**

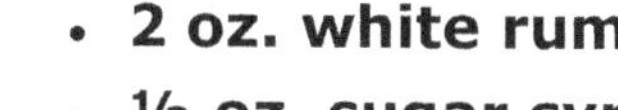

1. Pour 1 of lime juice, ½ oz. of sugar syrup and 2 oz. of white rum into a shaker
2. Fill the shaker with ice cubes and shake
3. Strain into a chilled coupe glass

FLORADORA

technique: shake | time total: 5 min | serves: 1

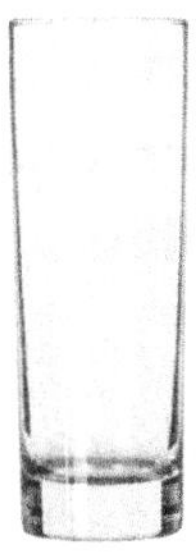

collins glass, jigger, squeezer, shaker, strainer

- **1½ oz. gin**
- **½ oz. fresh lime juice**
- **½ oz. crème de framboise liqueur**
- **4 oz. ginger ale**
- **Ice**
- **Lime wedge**

1. Pour ½ oz. of fresh lime juice, ½ oz. of crème de framboise liqueur and 1½ oz. of gin into a shaker
2. Fill the shaker with ice cubes and shake
3. Strain into a chilled collins glass
4. Top up with ginger ale
5. Garnish with a lime wedge

GIMLET

technique: shake | time total: 3 min | serves: 1

cocktail glass, squeezer, jigger, shaker, strainer

- **2 oz. gin**
- **1 oz. lime juice**
- **Ice**
- **Lime zest**

1. Pour 1 oz. of lime juice and 2 oz. of gin into a shaker
2. Fill the shaker with ice cubes and shake
3. Strain into a chilled cocktail glass
4. Garnish with lime zest

HURRICANE

technique: shake | time total: 5 min | serves: 1

hurricane glass, squeezer, jigger, shaker, strainer, drinking straws

- **2 oz. light rum**
- **2 oz. dark rum**
- **2 oz. passion fruit juice**
- **1 oz. orange juice**
- **1 oz. lime juice**
- **½ oz. sugar syrup**
- **½ oz. grenadine**
- **Maraschino cherry**
- **Orange slice**
- **Ice**

1. Pour 2 oz. of passion fruit juice, 1 oz. of orange juice, 1 oz. of lime juice, ½ oz. of sugar syrup, ½ oz. of grenadine, 2 oz. of light rum and 2 oz. of dark rum into a shaker
2. Fill the shaker with ice cubes and shake
3. Strain into a chilled hurricane glass
4. Garnish with a Maraschino cherry and orange wheel

JUNGLE BIRD

technique: shake | time total: 5 min | serves: 1

rocks glass, jigger, squeezer, shaker, strainer

- **1½ oz. dark rum**
- **¾ oz. red bitter**
- **½ oz. fresh lime juice**
- **1½ oz. pineapple juice**
- **½ oz. simple syrup**
- **Ice**
- **Pineapple wedge**

1. Pour ½ oz. of fresh lime juice, 1½ oz. of fresh pineapple juice, ¾ oz. of red bitter, ½ oz. of simple syrup and 1½ oz. of dark rum into a shaker
2. Fill the shaker with ice cubes and shake
3. Strain into a chilled rocks glass
4. Garnish with a pineapple wedge

KNICKERBOCKER

technique: shake | time total: 3 min | serves: 1

cocktail glass, squeezer, jigger, shaker, strainer

- **1½ oz. white rum**
- **¾ oz. dry orange liqueur**
- **½ oz. raspberry syrup**
- **½ oz. lime juice**
- **Ice**

1. Pour ½ oz. of lime juice, ½ oz. of raspberry syrup, ¾ oz. of dry orange liqueur and 1½ oz. of white rum into a shaker
2. Fill the shaker with ice cubes and shake
3. Strain into a chilled cocktail glass

HOW TO MAKE: RASPBERRY SYRUP

Ingredients:

- ½ cup raspberry juice
- ¾ cup caster sugar

Directions:

1. Muddle a few punnets of fresh raspberries in a bowl to make into a pulp
2. Push the raspberry pulp through a large fine sieve and collect the juice in a mug, filling it halfway
3. Pour the juice into a saucepan over a low heat
4. Add ¾ cup caster sugar
5. Be sure to only gently warm - just enough heat to help the sugar dissolve. Use elbow grease rather than too much heat or your syrup will have a cooked jammy flavour
6. Continue to stir until all the sugar is dissolved and then fine strain into a sterilised and still warm glass bottle. Seal, allow to cool and then store in the refrigerator until required. Keep for a maximum of 7 days

MAI TAI

technique: shake | time total: 5 min | serves: 1

rocks glass, squeezer, jigger, shaker, strainer, drinking straws

- **2 oz. aged rum**
- **¾ oz. dry orange liqueur**
- **½ oz. simple syrup**
- **½ oz. almond syrup**
- **¾ oz. lime juice**
- **Pineapple**
- **Mint**
- **Red maraschino cherry**
- **Crushed ice**
- **Ice cubes**

1. Fill a rocks glass to the top with crushed ice
2. Pour ¾ oz. of lime juice, ½ oz. of simple syrup, ½ oz. of almond syrup, ¾ oz. of dry orange liqueur and 2 oz. of aged rum into a shaker
3. Fill the shaker with ice cubes and shake
4. Strain into the rocks glass
5. Top up with crushed ice
6. Garnish with a Maraschino cherry, a pineapple wedge and a mint sprig

WHAT ABOUT: MAI TAI COCKTAIL

A Mai Tai is basically a Daiquiri based on aged rum with orange curaçao liqueur and orgeat syrup contributing to its flavour and sweetness. The Mai Tai is the king of Tiki cocktails and one of the most enduring of all vintage cocktails, but like most classic drinks there is controversy over its origin while its reputation is tarnished by poor renditions

MARGARITA

technique: shake | time total: 5 min | serves: 1

margarita glass, squeezer, jigger, shaker, strainer

- **1½ oz. silver tequila**
- **¾ oz. triple sec liqueur**
- **½ oz. simple syrup**
- **1 oz. lime juice**
- **Lime**
- **Salt**
- **Ice**

1. Salt the rim of the glass
2. Pour 1 oz. of lime juice, ¾ oz. of triple sec liqueur, ½ oz. of simple syrup and 1½ oz. of silver tequila into a shaker
3. Fill the shaker with ice cubes and shake gently
4. Strain into a chilled margarita glass
5. Garnish with a lime wheel

PEGU CLUB

technique: shake | time total: 5 min | serves: 1

cocktail glass, muddler, jigger, shaker, strainer

- **2 oz. gin**
- **¾ oz. triple sec liqueur**
- **1 oz. lime juice**
- **Orange bitters**
- **Angostura bitters**
- **Ice**
- **Lime**
- **Granulated cane sugar**

1. Salt the rim of the glass
2. Pour 1 oz. of lime juice, ¾ oz. of triple sec liqueur, ½ oz. of simple syrup and 1½ oz. of silver tequila into a shaker
3. Fill the shaker with ice cubes and shake gently
4. Strain into a chilled margarita glass
5. Garnish with a lime wheel

PLANTER'S PUNCH

technique: shake | time total: 7 min | serves: 1

highball glass, squeezer, jigger, shaker, strainer

- **1½ oz. dark rum**
- **1 oz. orange juice**
- **1 oz. pineapple juice**
- **¾ oz. lemon juice**
- **½ oz. grenadine syrup**
- **¼ oz. simple syrup**
- **1 dash Angostura bitters**
- **Ice**
- **Maraschino cherry**
- **Orange wheel**
- **Pineapple wedge**

1. Fill a highball glass to the top with ice
2. Pour 1 oz. of pineapple juice, 1 oz. of orange juice, ¾ oz. of lemon juice
3. Add ¼ oz. of simple syrup, ½ oz. of grenadine syrup,1 dash of Angostura bitters and 1½ oz. dark rum
4. Fill the shaker with ice cubes and shake
5. Strain into the highball glass
6. Sprinkle grated nutmeg on top
7. Garnish with an orange wheel, a pineapple wedge and a red Maraschino cherry

SIDECAR

technique: shake | time total: 5 min | serves: 1

cocktail glass, squeezer, jigger, shaker, strainer

- **1½ oz. Cognac**
- **1 oz. triple sec liqueur**
- **¼ oz. simple syrup**
- **¾ oz. lemon juice**
- **½ oz. still water**
- **Ice**

1. Pour ¾ oz. of lemon juice, ½ oz. of still water and ¼ oz. of simple syrup

2. Add 1 oz. of triple sec liqueur and 1½ oz. of Cognac into a shaker

3. Fill the shaker with ice cubes and shake

4. Strain into the chilled cocktail glass

WHAT ABOUT: SIDECAR COCKTAIL

The Sidecar is a classic cocktail made with Cognac, triple sec orange liqueur and lemon juice. Traditionally made to be on the slightly sour side of balanced, it is often served in a glass with a sugared rim to compensate. However, modern bartenders tend to forgo the sugared rim and balance when mixing with the addition of a dash of sugar syrup or other sweetener

There have been periods when it has been fashionable to coat the rim of the glass in which this drink is served with sugar. The earliest written reference to this is in 1934. Thankfully sugar rims are now out of vogue and, as Embury writes in his book, "A twist of lemon may be used if desired and the peel dropped into the glass. Otherwise no decoration."

SINGAPORE SLING

technique: shake | time total: 7 min | serves: 1

sling glass, jigger, shaker, strainer, squeezer, drinking straws, cocktail skewer

- **1 oz. gin**
- **½ oz. Benedictine**
- **½ oz. triple sec liqueur**
- **½ oz. cherry liqueur**
- **½ oz. cherry liqueur**
- **4 oz. pineapple juice**
- **½ oz. lime juice**
- **¼ oz. grenadine syrup**
- **Angostura bitters**
- **Ice**
- **Pineapple**
- **Red maraschino cherry**

1. Fill a sling glass to the top with ice cubes
2. Pour ½ oz. of lime juice, 4 oz. of pineapple juice, ¼ oz. of grenadine syrup, ½ oz. of cherry liqueur, ½ oz. of triple sec, ½ oz. of Benedictine and 1 oz. of gin into a shaker
3. Add 1 dash of Angostura bitters
4. Fill the shaker with ice cubes and shake
5. Strain into the chilled sling glass
6. Garnish with a small pineapple wedge and a maraschino cherry on a cocktail skewer

SOUTHSIDE

technique: shake | time total: 5 min | serves: 1

cocktail glass, jigger, squeezer, shaker, strainer

- **2 oz. gin**
- **½ oz. fresh lime juice**
- **¾ oz. simple syrup**
- **Ice**
- **Mint leaf**

1. Pour ½ oz. of fresh lime juice, ¾ oz. of simple syrup and 2 oz. of gin into a shaker
2. Fill the shaker with ice cubes and shake
3. Strain into a chilled cocktail glass
4. Garnish with a mint leaf

TOM COLLINS

technique: shake | time total: 5 min | serves: 1

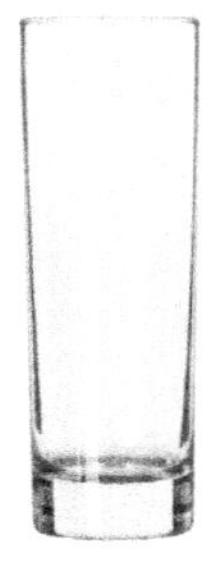

collins glass, squeezer, jigger, shaker, strainer, bar spoon, drinking straws

- **1½ oz. gin**
- **¾ oz. simple syrup**
- **¾ oz. lemon juice**
- **3½ oz. club soda**
- **Ice**
- **Orange, for garnish**
- **Maraschino cherry**

1. Fill a collins glass to the top with ice cubes
2. Pour ¾ oz. of lemon juice, ¾ oz. of simple syrup and 1½ oz. of gin into a shaker
3. Fill the shaker with ice cubes and shake
4. Strain into the collins glass
5. Top up with club soda and stir gently
6. Garnish with an orange wheel and a red Maraschino cherry

WHISKEY SOUR

technique: shake | time total: 5 min | serves: 1

rocks glass, squeezer, jigger, shaker, strainer, cocktail skewer

- **1½ oz. bourbon**
- **½ oz. simple syrup**
- **1 oz. lemon juice**
- **Angostura bitters**
- **Egg white**
- **Lemon**
- **Maraschino cherry**
- **Ice**

1. Fill a rocks glass to the top with ice cubes
2. Pour 1 egg white, 1 oz. of lemon juice, ½ oz. of simple syrup and 1½ oz. of bourbon into a shaker
3. Add 1 dash of Angostura bitters and shake
4. Fill the shaker with ice cubes and shake again
5. Strain into the rocks glass
6. Garnish with a lemon wheel and a Maraschino cherry on a cocktail skewer

PIÑA COLADA

technique: blend | time total: 6 min | serves: 1

hurricane glass, blender, bar spoon, squeezer, jigger, scoop, cocktail umbrella, drinking straws

- **1 oz. white rum**
- **1 oz. coconut cream**
- **3 oz. pineapple juice**
- **Ice**
- **Maraschino cherry**
- **Pineapple wedge**

1. Place 6 bar spoons of coconut cream into a blender

2. Pour in 3 oz. of pineapple juice and 1 oz. of white rum

3. Add a scoop of crushed ice and blend

4. Pour into a hurricane glass

5. Garnish with a pineapple wedge, a Maraschino cherry and a cocktail umbrella

MODERN

A cocktail's path towards popularity can be tricky and unpredictable. Earning the title of "classic" usually involves a unique situation in which an outstanding drink is in the right place at the right time. Sometimes, a cocktail will become ubiquitous and breaks free of any imposed limitations until it eventually goes on to define an era.

Whether the drink gains recognition via word of mouth or association with a seminal bar, it must meet other criteria in order to make the classic leap. And tasting delicious is just a start. Any modern classic should primarily consist of ingredients that are commonly stocked and easy to prepare.

This is why a recipe with ginger and grapefruit juice will always spread quicker and more ferociously than a cocktail with dehydrated Fernet salt (which I am pretty sure is not even a thing). In addition, it doesn't hurt for the drink has a standout name. There's no doubt that some of our favorite modern classics – such as the Cosmopolitan and the Penicillin – proliferated partly because of their memorable monikers.

Despite the odds, many cocktails of the modern era have managed to attain the classic title. Drinks such as the Old Cuban and the Bramble are made in bars around the world, and are so common that many imbibers mistake them for relics of a past age.

Yet, even with all the right boxes checked, for a drink to go from popular to classic is another feat all together, and every year countless creations put together by talented bartenders are lost in the annals of time. Too often these libations are interesting, but do not quite have what it takes to break through the endless barrage of new fads and trends.

AT FULL PARADE

technique: build | time total: 6 min | serves: 1

flute glass, jigger, squeezer, bar spoon

- **¾ oz. aged blended scotch**
- **½ oz. cherry liqueur**
- **¾ oz. cranberry juice**
- **¼ oz. lemon juice**
- **3½ Champagne**
- **Ice**
- **Cherry**

1. Pour ¼ oz. of lemon juice, ½ oz. of cherry liqueur, ¾ oz. of cranberry juice, 3½ of Champagne and ¾ oz. of aged blended scotch into a flute glass
2. Stir gently
3. Garnish with a Cherry

BATANGA

technique: build | time total: 5 min | serves: 1

highball glass, jigger, squeezer, bar spoon

- **2 oz. tequila**
- **½ oz. fresh lime juice**
- **5 oz. cola**
- **Ice**
- **Lime**

1. Rub the rim of highball glass with lime wedge and salt
2. Pour ½ oz. of fresh lime juice and 2 oz. of tequila into a highball glass
3. Add ice cubes and stir
4. Top up with cola
5. Garnish with a lime wheel

BERRY CLASH

technique: build | time total: 5 min | serves: 1

highball glass, squeezer, jigger, muddler, bar spoon

- **2 oz. vodka**
- **¾ oz. lemon juice**
- **¾ oz. agave nectar**
- **4 oz. soda water**
- **2 blackberries**
- **2 blueberries**
- **Ice**
- **Mint sprig**

1. Pour 2 blackberries and 2 blueberries into a highball glass and muddle
2. Add ¾ oz. of lime juice, ¾ oz. of agave nectar, 2 oz. of vodka and ice
3. Top up with soda water and stir gently
4. Garnish with a mint sprig

BRAMBLE

technique: build | time total: 5 min | serves: 1

rocks glass, jigger, squeezer, bar spoon, cocktail skewer, drinking straws

- **1¾ oz. gin**
- **¼ oz. crème de cassis liqueur**
- **½ oz. simple syrup**
- **¾ oz. lemon juice**
- **Blackberries**
- **Lemon zest**
- **Crushed ice**

1. Fill a rocks glass to the top with ice cubes
2. Pour in ¾ oz. of lemon juice and ½ oz. of simple syrup
3. Add 1¾ oz. of gin and mix carefully with a bar spoon
4. Pour in ¼ oz. of crème de cassis and add a little bit of crushed ice
5. Garnish with lemon zest and two blackberries on a cocktail skewer

DOLL DAGGER

technique: build | time total: 5 min | serves: 1

rocks glass, jigger, squeezer, bar spoon, drinking straws

- **1 oz. rum**
- **1½ oz. fino sherry**
- **1 oz. fresh lime juice**
- **½ oz. cane syrup**
- **¼ oz. vanilla syrup**
- **Angostura bitters**
- **Crushed ice**
- **Lime wedge**
- **Mint sprig**

1. Fill a rocks glass to the top with crushed ice

2. Pour in 1 oz. of fresh lime juice, 1½ oz. of fino sherry, ½ oz. of cane syrup, ¼ oz. of vanilla syrup and 1 oz. of rum and stir gently

3. Top up with crushed ice and add splash of Angostura bitters

4. Garnish with lime wedge and mint sprig

ENGLISH MOJITO

technique: build | time total: 5 min | serves: 1

rocks glass, jigger, squeezer, bar spoon, drinking straws

- **2 oz. gin**
- **½ oz. simple syrup**
- **1 oz. fresh lime juice**
- **3 oz. soda water**
- **10 mint lives**
- **2 oz. cucumber**
- **Crushed ice**
- **Mint sprig**

1. Pour ½ oz. of simple syrup, 1 oz. of fresh lime juice and 2 oz. of gin into a highball glass

2. Add 10 mint lives and 2 oz. of chopped cucumber and stir

3. Top up with soda water and crushed ice

4. Garnish with a mint sprig

PALOMA

technique: build | time total: 5 min | serves: 1

highball glass, squeezer, jigger, bar spoon, drinking straws

- **2 oz. silver tequila**
- **½ oz. lime juice**
- **5 oz. grapefruit soda**
- **Salt**
- **Lime**
- **Strawberry**
- **Mint**
- **Ice**

1. Rim a highball glass with salt
2. Fill the glass to the top with ice cubes
3. Pour in ½ oz. of lime juice and 2 oz. of silver tequila
4. Top up with grapefruit soda and stir gently
5. Garnish with a chopped strawberry, a lime wheel and a mint sprig

SABOTAGE

technique: build | time total: 5 min | serves: 1

highball glass, jigger, squeezer, bar spoon

- **2 oz. spiced rum**
- **½ oz. lime juice**
- **5 oz. cola**
- **Ice**
- **Lime**

1. Fill a highball glass to the top with ice cubes
2. Pour in ½ oz. of lime juice and 2 oz. of spiced rum
3. Top up with cola and stir gently
4. Garnish with 2 lime wheels

CABALLERO

technique: stir | time total: 5 min | serves: 1

cocktail glass, jigger, mixing glass, bar spoon, strainer

- **2 oz. reposado tequila**
- **½ oz. saffron liqueur**
- **1 oz. dry vermouth**
- **Angostura bitters**
- **Ice**
- **Cherry**

1. Pour ½ oz. of saffron liqueur, 1 oz. of dry vermouth, 2 oz. of reposado tequila and 2 dashes of Angostura bitters into a mixing glass
2. Add ice cubes and stir
3. Strain into a chilled cocktail glass
4. Garnish with a cherry

CAMPBELTOWN

technique: stir | time total: 5 min | serves: 1

cocktail glass, jigger, mixing glass, bar spoon, strainer

- **2 oz. aged blended scotch whisky**
- **1 oz. cherry liqueur**
- **1 oz. green Chartreuse liqueur**
- **Ice**
- **Lemon peel**

1. Pour 1 oz. of cherry liqueur, 1 oz. of green Chartreuse liqueur and 2 oz. of aged blended scotch whisky into a mixing glass
2. Add ice cubes and stir
3. Strain into a chilled cocktail glass
4. Express the oil of a lemon peel, and discard the peel

GALLO ROJO

technique: stir | time total: 5 min | serves: 1

cocktail glass, jigger, mixing glass, bar spoon, strainer

- 2 oz. whisky
- ¾ oz. Punt e Mes
- ¾ oz. sweet vermouth
- Pomegranate liqueur
- Ice
- Orange zest twist

1. Pour ¾ oz. of Punt e Mes, ¾ oz. of sweet vermouth, 2 dashes of pomegranate liqueur and 2 oz. of whisky into a mixing glass
2. Fill the mixing glass with ice cubes and stir
3. Strain into a chilled cocktail glass
4. Garnish with an orange zest twist

GUYANA GOLD

technique: stir | time total: 5 min | serves: 1

rocks glass, jigger, mixing glass, bar spoon, strainer

- 2 oz. aged rum
- ¾ oz. Pedro Ximénez sherry
- Angostura bitters
- Chocolate bitters
- Ice
- Orange zest
- Maraschino cherry

1. Pour ¾ oz. of Pedro Ximénez sherry, 1 dash of Angostura bitters, 2 dashes of chocolate bitters and 2 oz. of aged rum into a mixing glass
2. Fill the mixing glass with ice cubes and stir
3. Strain into a chilled rocks glass over ice
4. Garnish with orange zest and 2 Maraschino cherry

EAST INDIA COMPANY

technique: stir | time total: 5 min | serves: 1

cocktail glass, jigger, mixing glass, bar spoon, strainer

- **2 oz. dark rum**
- **1 oz. sweet sherry**
- **½ oz. amaro liqueur**
- **Chocolate bitters**
- **Ice**

1. Pour 1 oz. of sweet sherry, ½ oz. of amaro liqueur and 2 oz. of dark rum into a mixing glass
2. Fill the mixing glass with ice cubes and stir
3. Strain into a chilled cocktail glass

EL DON

technique: stir | time total: 5 min | serves: 1

Cognac glass, jigger, mixing glass, bar spoon, strainer

- **¾ oz. triple sec liqueur**
- **1½ oz. coffee liqueur**
- **Angostura bitters**
- **Orange bitters**
- **Ice**

1. Pour 1½ oz. of coffee liqueur, ¾ oz. of triple sec liqueur, 2 dashes of Angostura bitters and 2 dashes of orange bitters into a mixing glass
2. Fill the mixing glass with ice cubes and stir
3. Strain into a chilled Cognac glass

FIAMMATO

technique: stir | time total: 5 min | serves: 1

cocktail glass, jigger, mixing glass, bar spoon, strainer, sieve

- **2½ oz. vodka**
- **½ oz. sweet vermouth**
- **1 tsp. ground caraway seeds**
- **Ice**
- **Chili slice**

1. Pour ½ oz. of sweet vermouth, 1 tsp. of ground caraway seeds and 2½ oz. of vodka into a mixing glass
2. Fill the mixing glass with ice cubes and stir
3. Double strain into a chilled cocktail glass
4. Garnish with a chili slice

LEAF FALL

technique: stir | time total: 5 min | serves: 1

cocktail glass, jigger, mixing glass, bar spoon, strainer

- **2 oz. aged rum**
- **½ oz. ginger liqueur**
- **½ oz. coffee liqueur**
- **Orange bitters**
- **Ice**
- **Tobacco leaf**

1. Pour ½ oz. of ginger liqueur, ½ oz. of coffee liqueur, 2 dashes of orange bitters and 2 oz. of aged rum into a mixing glass
2. Add ice cubes and stir
3. Strain into a cocktail glass
4. Garnish with tobacco leaf

LOVELY PRINCE CHARLIE

technique: stir | time total: 5 min | serves: 1

rocks glass, jigger, squeezer, mixing glass, bar spoon, strainer

- **1 oz. Cognac**
- **¾ oz. Drambuie**
- **¼ oz. fresh lemon juice**
- **Orange bitters**
- **Ice**
- **Orange zest twist**

1. Pour ¾ oz. of Drambuie, ¼ oz. of fresh lemon juice and 1 oz. of Cognac into a mixing glass and stir
2. Strain into a chilled rocks glass over ice
3. Garnish with an orange zest twist

MADAM

technique: stir | time total: 5 min | serves: 1

cocktail glass, jigger, mixing glass, bar spoon, strainer

- **2 oz. vodka**
- **¾ oz. grapefruit liqueur**
- **¾ oz. rose syrup**
- **Himalayan pink salt**
- **White pepper**
- **Ice**
- **Pink petal**

1. Pour ¾ oz. of grapefruit liqueur, ¾ of rose syrup and 2 oz. of vodka into a mixing glass
2. Add a pinch of Himalayan pink salt, a pinch of white pepper and ice cubes and stir
3. Strain into a cocktail glass
4. Garnish with a pink petal

MANSFIELD

technique: stir | time total: 5 min | serves: 1

rocks glass, jigger, mixing glass, bar spoon, strainer

- **1½ oz. single malt whisky**
- **1 oz. Fernet-Branca**
- **½ oz. orgeat almond syrup**
- **Ice**
- **Lemon zest twist**

1. Pour 1 oz. of Fernet-Branca, ½ oz. of orgeat almond syrup and 1½ oz. of single malt whisky into a mixing glass and stir
2. Strain into a chilled rocks glass over ice
3. Garnish with a lemon zest twist

ONE 7 ONE

technique: stir | time total: 5 min | serves: 1

cocktail glass, jigger, squeezer, mixing glass, bar spoon, strainer

- **1 oz. gin**
- **1 oz. ginseng vodka**
- **¼ oz. orange bitters**
- **Ice**
- **Orange twist**

1. Pour ¼ oz. of orange bitters, 1 oz. of ginseng vodka and 1 oz. of gin into a mixing glass
2. Add ice cubes and stir
3. Strain into a chilled cocktail glass
4. Garnish with an orange twist

POLISH ARISTOCRAT

technique: stir | time total: 5 min | serves: 1

flute glass, jigger, squeezer, mixing glass, bar spoon, strainer, sieve

- **2 oz. vodka**
- **1 oz. grapefruit juice**
- **½ oz. ginger syrup**
- **¼ oz. honey**
- **3 oz. Champagne**
- **Angostura bitters**
- **Ice**
- **Grapefruit zest twist**

1. Pour 1 oz. of grapefruit juice, ½ oz. of ginger syrup, ¼ oz. honey, 2 dashes of Angostura bitters and 2 oz. of vodka into a mixing glass
2. Fill the mixing glass with ice cubes and stir
3. Double strain into a chilled flute glass
4. Top up with Champagne
5. Garnish with a grapefruit zest twist

QUEEN MOTHER

technique: stir | time total: 5 min | serves: 1

coupe glass, jigger, mixing glass, bar spoon, strainer

- **1½ oz. gin**
- **1 oz. Dubonnet**
- **1 oz. red bitter**
- **¼ oz. dark rum**
- **Ice**
- **Orange zest twist**

1. Pour 1 oz. of Dubonnet, 1 oz. of red bitter, ¼ oz. of dark rum and 1½ oz. of gin into a mixing glass
2. Add ice cubes and stir
3. Strain into a chilled coupe glass
4. Garnish with orange zest twist

SMOKED BEAR

technique: stir | time total: 5 min | serves: 1

rocks glass, jigger, mixing glass, bar spoon, strainer

- **2 oz. aged rum**
- **½ oz. mezcal**
- **½ oz. maple syrup**
- **Absinthe**
- **Angostura bitters**
- **Ice**
- **Lemon zest twist**

1. Pour ½ oz. of maple syrup, ½ oz. of mezcal, 2 dashes of absinthe, 2 dashes of Angostura bitters and 2 oz. of aged rum into a mixing glass
2. Add ice cubes and stir
3. Strain into a chilled rocks glass over ice
4. Garnish with lemon zest twist

VINE AND ORCHID

technique: stir | time total: 5 min | serves: 1

rocks glass, jigger, mixing glass, bar spoon, strainer

- **2 oz. Cognac**
- **½ oz. pear liquor**
- **Orange bitters**
- **Angostura bitters**
- **Ice**
- **Ground nutmeg**

1. Pour ½ oz. of pear liqueur, 2 dashes of orange bitters, 2 dashes of Angostura bitters and 2 oz. of Cognac into a mixing glass
2. Add ice cubes and stir
3. Strain into a rocks glass
4. Garnish with ground nutmeg

1879

technique: shake | time total: 5 min | serves: 1

coupe glass, jigger, squeezer, shaker, strainer

- **2 oz. vodka**
- **½ oz. Lilliet Blanc**
- **1 oz. apple juice**
- **½ oz. elderflower cordial**
- **1 oz. lime juice**
- **Orange bitters**
- **Ice**
- **Mint sprig**

1. Pour ½ oz. of Lilliet Blanc, 1 oz. of apple juice, 1 oz. of lime juice, ½ oz. of elderflower cordial, 2 oz. of vodka and dash of orange bitters into a shaker
2. Fill the shaker with ice cubes and shake
3. Strain into a chilled coupe glass
4. Garnish with a mint sprig

25th ELEMENT

technique: shake | time total: 5 min | serves: 1

rocks glass, jigger, squeezer, shaker, strainer

- **1 oz. gin**
- **¾ oz. grapefruit juice**
- **½ oz. simple syrup**
- **3 oz. prosecco**
- **1 egg white**
- **Ice**
- **White ostrich feather**

1. Pour ¾ oz. of grapefruit juice, ½ oz. of simple syrup, 1 egg white and 1 oz. of gin into a shaker
2. Fill the shaker with ice cubes and shake
3. Strain into a chilled rocks glass
4. Top up with prosecco
5. Garnish with a white ostrich feather

ALOEVERITA

technique: shake | time total: 5 min | serves: 1

rocks glass, jigger, squeezer, shaker, strainer

- **1½ oz. silver tequila**
- **½ oz. triple sec liqueur**
- **¼ oz. agava syrup**
- **½ oz. fresh lime juice**
- **Ice**
- **Lime wheel**

1. Pour ¼ oz. of agava syrup, ½ oz. of triple sec liqueur, ½ oz. of fresh lime juice and 1½ oz. of silver tequila into a shaker
2. Fill the shaker with ice cubes and shake
3. Strain into a chilled rocks glass over ice
4. Garnish with a lime wheel

ATOMIC DAIQUIRI

technique: shake | time total: 5 min | serves: 1

cocktail glass, jigger, squeezer, shaker, strainer

- **1 oz. white rum**
- **½ oz. velvet falernum syrup**
- **1 oz. green Chartreuse liqueur**
- **1 oz. fresh lime juice**
- **Ice**
- **Lime wedge**

1. Pour 1 oz. of green Chartreuse liqueur, ½ oz. of velvet falernum syrup, 1 oz. of fresh lime juice and 1 oz. of white rum into a shaker
2. Fill the shaker with ice cubes and shake
3. Strain into a chilled cocktail glass
4. Garnish with a lime wedge

AUTUMN SMOKE

technique: shake | time total: 5 min | serves: 1

cocktail glass, jigger, shaker, strainer

- **2 oz. single malt whisky**
- **¾ oz. crème de cacao liqueur**
- **1 oz. tangerine juice**
- **Ice**
- **Orange zest twist**

1. Pour ¾ oz. of crème de cacao liqueur, 1 oz. of tangerine juice and 2 oz. of single malt whisky into a shaker
2. Fill the shaker with ice cubes and shake
3. Strain into a chilled cocktail glass
4. Garnish with an orange zest twist

BLACKTHORN #4

technique: shake | time total: 5 min | serves: 1

cocktail glass, jigger, shaker, strainer

- **1½ oz. gin**
- **¾ oz. sweet vermouth**
- **¾ oz. irish whiskey**
- **½ oz. sherry amontillado**
- **Ice**
- **Orange zest twist**

1. Pour ¾ oz. of sweet vermouth, ¾ oz. of irish whiskey, ½ oz. of sherry amontillado and 1½ oz. of gin into a shaker
2. Fill the shaker with ice cubes and shake
3. Strain into a chilled cocktail glass
4. Garnish with an orange zest twist

CASSIS ROYAL

technique: shake | time total: 5 min | serves: 1

flute glass, jigger, shaker, strainer

- **½ oz. Cognac**
- **1 oz. crème de cassis liqueur**
- **½ oz. champagne**
- **Orange bitters**
- **Ice**
- **Orange zest twist**

1. Pour 1 oz. of crème de cassis liqueur, ½ oz. of Cognac into a shaker
2. Fill the shaker with ice cubes and shake
3. Strain into a chilled flute glass
4. Add ½ oz. of champagne and 2 dashes of orange bitters
5. Garnish with orange zest twist

CILANTRO

technique: shake | time total: 5 min | serves: 1

cocktail glass, jigger, squeezer, shaker, strainer

- **2 oz. silver tequila**
- **½ oz. triple sec liqueur**
- **1 oz. fresh lime juice**
- **¼ oz. elderflower cordial**
- **½ oz. honey**
- **Ice**
- **Cilantro leaf**

1. Pour ½ oz. of triple sec liqueur, 1 oz. of fresh lime juice, ¼ oz. of elderflower cordial, ½ oz. of honey and 2 oz. of silver tequila into a shaker
2. Fill the shaker with ice cubes and shake
3. Strain into a chilled cocktail glass
4. Garnish with a cilantro leaf

DAYDREAMER

technique: shake | time total: 5 min | serves: 1

cocktail glass, jigger, squeezer, shaker, strainer

- **1½ oz. vodka**
- **½ oz. Fernet-Branca**
- **¾ oz. fresh lime juice**
- **½ oz. cinnamon syrup**
- **1 egg white**
- **Chocolate bitters**
- **Ice**

1. Pour ¾ oz. of fresh lime juice, ½ oz. of Fernet-Branca, ½ oz. of cinnamon syrup and 1½ oz. of vodka into a shaker
2. Fill the shaker with ice cubes and shake
3. Strain into a chilled cocktail glass
4. Top with splash of chocolate bitters

DAY AND NIGHT

technique: shake | time total: 5 min | serves: 1

highball glass, jigger, muddler, squeezer, shaker, strainer

- **2 oz. vodka**
- **½ oz. lime juice**
- **¾ oz. cinnamon syrup**
- **Lemongrass**
- **Strawberry**
- **Crushed ice**

1. Fill a highball glass to the top with crushed ice
2. Place a half of finely chopped lemongrass stalk, 5 strawberries into a shaker and muddle
3. Pour in ½ oz. of lime juice, ¾ oz. of cinnamon syrup and 2 oz. of vodka
4. Fill the shaker with ice cubes and shake
5. Strain into a highball glass
6. Top up with crushed ice
7. Garnish with a stalk of lemongrass and strawberry

EMERALD

technique: shake | time total: 5 min | serves: 1

coupe glass, jigger, muddler, squeezer, shaker, strainer, sieve

- **1½ oz. aged whisky**
- **¾ oz. ginger liqueur**
- **¾ oz. simple syrup**
- **1 oz. lemon juice**
- **15 fresh blueberries**
- **Ice**
- **Foam of green apples**

1. Pour into 15 fresh blueberries a shaker and muddle
2. Add ¾ oz. of ginger liqueur, 1 oz. of lemon juice, ¾ oz. of simple syrup and 1½ oz. of lightly aged whisky into a shaker
3. Fill the shaker with ice cubes and shake
4. Double strain into a chilled coupe glass
5. Garnish with a foam of green apples

FANDANGO

technique: shake | time total: 5 min | serves: 1

flute glass, jigger, squeezer, shaker, strainer

- **1 oz. gin**
- **¾ oz. fresh lemon juice**
- **¼ oz. simple syrup**
- **4 oz. sparkling wine**
- **Lavender bitters**
- **Ice**
- **Lemon zest twist**
- **Cocktail cherry**

1. Pour ¾ oz. of fresh lemon juice, ¼ oz. of simple syrup and 1 oz. of gin into a shaker
2. Fill the shaker with ice cubes and shake
3. Strain into a chilled flute glass
4. Top with sparkling wine and splash of lavender bitters
5. Garnish with a lemon zest twist and cocktail cherry

GARAPITA

technique: shake | time total: 5 min | serves: 1

highball, jigger, squeezer, shaker, strainer

- **1½ oz. lightly aged rum**
- **½ oz. orange liqueur**
- **1 oz. mango puree**
- **1 oz. pineapple juice**
- **½ oz. lime juice**
- **½ oz. simple syrup**
- **Pulp of 1 passion fruit**
- **Ice**
- **Lime**
- **Passion fruit**

1. Pour ½ oz. of orange liqueur, ½ oz. of lime juice, 1 oz. of mango puree, 1 oz. pineapple juice, ½ oz. of simple syrup, pulp of 1 passion fruit and 1½ oz. of lightly aged rum into a shaker
2. Fill the shaker with ice cubes and shake
3. Strain into a chilled highball glass over ice
4. Garnish with a lime wedge and quarter of passion fruit

WHAT ABOUT: ORANGE & CURAÇAO LIQUEURS

Curaçao liqueurs are traditionally made from the dried peel of the small bitter Curaçao orange, named for the island of Curaçao. As Curaçao was a Dutch colony, it supplied oranges to the liqueur makers of Holland, but curaçao liqueurs are now also produced from bitter oranges of other origins.

Curaçao liqueurs can be translucent or coloured blue, red and orange. The colours are purely decorative and were developed for cocktail bartenders, although the flavour of each colour may differ slightly with a producer creating slightly different styles

HARVEST

technique: shake | time total: 5 min | serves: 1

coupe glass, jigger, muddler, squeezer, shaker, strainer

- **1 oz. vodka**
- **¼ oz. apricot brandy**
- **¼ oz. calvados**
- **¾ oz. fresh lemon juice**
- **½ oz. simple syrup**
- **3 oz. Champagne**
- **Pear**
- **Ice**

1. Pour ¼ of pear into a shaker and muddle
2. Add ¼ oz. of apricot brandy, ¼ oz. of calvados, ¾ oz. of fresh lemon juice, ½ oz. of simple syrup and 1 oz. of vodka
3. Fill the shaker with ice cubes and shake
4. Strain into a chilled coupe glass
5. Top up with Champagne

HULLABALOO

technique: shake | time total: 5 min | serves: 1

cocktail glass, jigger, squeezer, shaker, strainer, sieve

- **2 oz. whisky**
- **½ oz. fresh lime juice**
- **1 oz. fresh banana puree with cinnamon**
- **½ oz. vanilla syrup**
- **Ice**
- **Banana slices**

1. Pour ½ oz. of fresh lime juice, ½ oz. of vanilla syrup, 1 oz. of fresh banana puree with cinnamon and 2 oz. of whisky into a shaker
2. Fill the shaker with ice cubes and shake
3. Double strain into a chilled cocktail glass
4. Garnish with banana slices

ITALIANO

technique: shake | time total: 5 min | serves: 1

rocks glass, jigger, shaker, strainer

- **1 oz. aged whisky**
- **1 oz. red bitter**
- **1 oz. sweet vermouth**
- **Angostura bitters**
- **Ice**
- **Orange zest twist**

1. Pour 1 oz. of sweet vermouth, 1 oz. of red bitter, 1 oz. of aged whisky and 2 dashes of Angostura bitters into a shaker
2. Fill the shaker with ice cubes and shake
3. Strain into a chilled rocks glass over ice
4. Garnish with orange zest twist

LADY SPEYSIDE

technique: shake | time total: 5 min | serves: 1

coupe glass, jigger, shaker, strainer

- **1½ oz. gin**
- **1 oz. grapefruit liqueur**
- **1 oz. lemon juice**
- **½ oz. simple syrup**
- **½ egg white**
- **Ice**
- **Saffron threads**

1. Pour 1 oz. of grapefruit liqueur, 1 oz. of lemon juice, ½ oz. simple syrup, ½ egg white and 1 oz. of gin into a shaker
2. Fill the shaker with ice cubes and shake
3. Strain into a chilled coupe glass
4. Garnish with a saffron threads

MALECON

technique: shake | time total: 5 min | serves: 1

coupe glass, jigger, shaker, strainer

- **2 oz. white rum**
- **¾ oz. tawny porto**
- **½ oz. oloroso sherry**
- **Orange bitters**
- **Ice**

1. Pour ¾ oz. of tawny porto, ½ oz. of oloroso sherry, 2 dashes of orange bitters and 2 oz. of white rum into a shaker
2. Fill the shaker with ice cubes and shake
3. Strain into a chilled coupe glass

MEXICAN BREAKFAST

technique: shake | time total: 5 min | serves: 1

cocktail glass, jigger, muddler, shaker, strainer

- **2 oz. tequila**
- **1 tsp. superfine sugar**
- **Mandarine**
- **Crushed ice**

1. Pour 1 mandarine and 1 tsp. of superfine sugar into a shaker and muddle
2. Add 2 oz. of tequila and crushed ice and shake
3. Strain into a chilled cocktail glass

MEXICAN MAFIA

technique: shake | time total: 5 min | serves: 1

highball glass, jigger, squeezer, shaker, strainer

- **2 oz. reposado tequila**
- **¾ oz. fresh lemon juice**
- **¼ oz. simple syrup**
- **½ oz. limoncello liqueur**
- **½ oz. amaretto liqueur**
- **3 oz. soda water**
- **Ice**
- **Lemon wedge**

1. Pour ¾ oz. of fresh lemon juice, ½ oz. of limoncello liqueur, ½ oz. of amaretto liqueur, ¼ oz. of simple syrup and 2 oz. of reposado tequila into a shaker

2. Fill the shaker with ice cubes and shake

3. Strain into a chilled highball glass

4. Garnish with a lemon wedge

MOSCOWPOLITAN

technique: shake | time total: 5 min | serves: 1

cocktail glass, jigger, squeezer, muddler, shaker, strainer, cocktail skewer

- **2 oz. vodka**
- **1 oz. cranberry juice**
- **¾ oz. fresh lime juice**
- **1 oz. vanilla syrup**
- **2 tsp. apricot jam**
- **Blueberry**
- **Ice**

1. Pour 5 blueberries into a shaker and muddle

2. Add 1 oz. of cranberry juice, ¾ oz. of fresh lime juice, 1 oz. of vanilla syrup, 2 tsp. of apricot jam and 2 oz. of vodka

3. Fill the shaker with ice cubes and shake

4. Strain into a chilled cocktail glass

5. Garnish with 3 blueberries on a cocktail skewer

ORCHID BREEZE

technique: shake | time total: 5 min | serves: 1

sling glass, jigger, shaker, strainer, sieve

- **2 oz. vodka**
- **1 oz. elderflower liqueur**
- **1 oz. dry white wine**
- **3 oz. fresh apple juice**
- **Ice**
- **Apple**

1. Pour 1 oz. of elderflower liqueur, 1 oz. of dry white wine, 3 oz. fresh apple juice and 2 oz. of vodka into a shaker
2. Fill the shaker with ice cubes and shake
3. Double strain into a chilled sling glass
4. Garnish with an apple slices

OZ

technique: shake | time total: 5 min | serves: 1

coupe glass, jigger, shaker, strainer

- **1½ oz. Cognac**
- **1½ oz. plum wine**
- **½ oz. lemon juice**
- **½ oz. apple juice**
- **1 oz. sparkling wine**
- **Ice**
- **Lemon zest twist**

1. Pour ½ oz. of lemon juice, ½ oz. of apple juice, 1½ oz. plum wine and 1½ oz. of Cognac into a shaker
2. Fill the shaker with ice cubes and shake
3. Strain into a chilled coupe glass
4. Top with sparkling wine
5. Garnish with a lemon zest twist

PADDINGTON

technique: shake | time total: 5 min | serves: 1

coupe glass, jigger, squeezer, shaker, strainer

- **1½ oz. rum**
- **½ oz. absinthe**
- **½ oz. still water**
- **½ oz. Lillet Blanc**
- **½ oz. grapefruit juice**
- **½ oz. lemon juice**
- **¼ oz. apricot jam**
- **Ice**
- **Grapefruit zest**

1. Fill a coupe glass to the top with ice cubes
2. Pour in ¼ oz. of absinthe and ½ oz. of still water, then set aside
3. Pour ½ oz. of Lillet Blanc, ½ oz. of grapefruit juice, ½ oz. of lemon juice, ¼ oz. of apricot jam into a shaker
4. Fill the glass with ice cubes and shake
5. Pour out still water, absinthe and ice from the coupe glass
6. Strain the cocktail into the aromatized glass
7. Garnish with a grapefruit zest

WHAT ABOUT: LILLET BLANC

A French aperitif wine produced from a combination of the white wines from Bordeaux mixed with fruit liqueurs. While the wine matures, the peel of both sweet, bitter and sour oranges and green quinine are steeped in brandy spirits. Then everything is mixed together and kept in oak barrels for 8-12 months

PEPPY CUCUMBER

technique: shake | time total: 5 min | serves: 1

coupe glass, jigger, squeezer, shaker, strainer

- **2 oz. vodka**
- **1 oz. cucumber juice**
- **¼ oz. absinthe**
- **Lemon juice**
- **Elderflower cordial**
- **Ice**
- **Cucumber**

1. Pour 1 oz. of cucumber juice, 2 dashes of lemon juice, 2 dashes of elderflower cordial and 2 oz. of vodka into a shaker
2. Fill the shaker with ice cubes and shake
3. Strain into a chilled coupe glass
4. Add a splash of absinthe
5. Garnish with a peace of cucumber

PREVIEW COCKTAIL

technique: shake | time total: 5 min | serves: 1

coupe glass, jigger, squeezer, shaker, strainer

- **1¼ oz. sweet vermouth**
- **1¼ oz. tawny porto**
- **¼ oz. fresh lemon juice**
- **½ oz. simple syrup**
- **Angostura bitters**
- **Orange bitters**
- **Ice**
- **Lemon zest twist**

1. Pour 1¼ oz. of sweet vermouth, 1¼ oz. of tawny porto, ¼ oz. of fresh lemon juice, ½ oz. of simple syrup, 2 dashes of Angostura bitters and 2 dashes of orange bitters into a shaker
2. Fill the shaker with ice cubes and shake
3. Strain into a chilled coupe glass
4. Garnish with a lemon zest twist

ROUND HEELS

technique: shake | time total: 5 min | serves: 1

coupe glass, jigger, muddler, shaker, strainer

- **2 oz. white rum**
- **1 oz. pineapple juice**
- **¾ oz. lemon juice**
- **¾ oz. honey**
- **Mint leaves**
- **Ice**
- **Clove**

1. Pour 6 mint leaves into a shaker and muddle
2. Add 1 oz. of pineapple juice, ¾ oz. of lemon juice, ¾ oz. honey and 2 oz. of white rum
3. Fill the shaker with ice cubes and shake
4. Strain into a chilled coupe glass
5. Garnish with a mashed buds of cloves

TWINKLE

technique: shake | time total: 5 min | serves: 1

flute glass, jigger, shaker, strainer

- **1 oz. vodka**
- **¾ oz. elderflower liqueur**
- **4 oz. sparkling wine**
- **Ice**
- **Lemon zest twist**

1. Pour ¾ oz. of elderflower liqueur and 1 oz. of vodka into a shaker
2. Fill the shaker with ice cubes and shake
3. Strain into a chilled flute glass
4. Top up with sparkling wine
5. Garnish with a lemon zest twist

SUPERFLY

technique: shake | time total: 5 min | serves: 1

highball glass, jigger, squeezer, shaker, strainer

- **2 oz. aged rum**
- **4 oz. ale**
- **1 oz. fresh lemon juice**
- **1 oz. fresh pineapple juice**
- **1 oz. fresh orange juice**
- **½ oz. blueberry syrup**
- **¼ oz. ginger syrup**
- **Angostura bitters**
- **Ice**
- **Mint sprig**
- **Cherry**
- **Raspberry**

1. Fill the highball glass with ice and add 4 oz. of ale
2. Pour 1 oz. of fresh lemon juice, 1 oz. of pineapple juice, 1 oz. of fresh orange juice, ½ oz. of blueberry syrup, ¼ oz. of ginger syrup, 2 dashes of Angostura bitters and 2 oz. of aged rum into a shaker
3. Fill the shaker with ice cubes and shake
4. Strain into a highball glass
5. Garnish with a mint sprig, cherry and raspberry

WHAT ABOUT: GINGER SYRUP

A spicy Asian syrup produced by pasteurizing ginger extracts in sugar syrup spirits. Then everything is mixed together and kept in oak barrels for 8-12 months

WATERMELON & VODKA

technique: shake | time total: 5 min | serves: 1

cocktail glass, jigger, muddler, squeezer, shaker, strainer

- **2 oz. vodka**
- **1 oz. simple syrup**
- **¼ oz. fresh lemon juice**
- **½ oz. passion fruit puree**
- **Watermelon**
- **Ice**

1. Pour 3 pieces of watermelon into a shaker and muddle
2. Add 1 oz. of simple syrup, ½ oz. of passion fruit puree, ¼ oz. fresh lemon juice and 2 oz. of vodka into a shaker
3. Fill the shaker with ice cubes and shake
4. Strain into a chilled cocktail glass
5. Garnish with a peace of watermelon

MEAT LIQUEUR LAGERITA

technique: blend | time total: 5 min | serves: 1

highball glass, jigger, blender, strainer

- **1 oz. silver tequila**
- **¾ oz. triple sec liqueur**
- **½ oz. simple syrup**
- **2 oz. lager beer**
- **Ice**

1. Pour ¾ oz. of triple sec liqueur, ½ oz. of simple syrup and 1 oz. of silver tequila into a blender
2. Add ice cubes and blend
3. Strain into a chilled highball glass over ice
4. Top up with lager beer

HALLOWEEN SPECIALS

Although going all out on costumes can make every Halloween pregame feel extra, a signature cocktail will make your party feel totally creeeeepy (but, like, in a good way). Make up a bunch of these and you'll be the scariest host in your friend group (again, a good thing).

BLACK BARREL CIDER

technique: build | time total: 5 min | serves: 1

rocks glass, bar spoon, squeezer, jigger

- **1½ oz. tequila anejo**
- **¾ oz. apple cider**
- **¾ oz. cinnamon syrup**
- **1 oz. lemon juice**
- **Ice**
- **Angostura bitters**
- **Apple**

1. Pour 1 oz. of lemon juice, ¾ oz. of cinnamon syrup, ¾ oz. of apple cider, 2 dashes Angostura bitters and 1½ oz. tequila anejo into a chilled rocks glass
2. Fill the glass with ice cubes and stir gently
3. Garnish with a cinnamon stick and an apple wedge

KOMBUCHA DARK'N'STORMY

technique: build | time total: 5 min | serves: 1

highball glass, bar spoon, jigger

- **2 oz. dark rum**
- **4 oz. strong ginger kombucha**
- **Ice**
- **Lime**

1. Fill a highball glass to the top with ice
2. Pour in 2 oz. of dark rum
3. Add a squeeze of lime juice
4. Top up with strong ginger kombucha and stir gently
5. Garnish with a couple of thinly sliced lime wheels

LIKE GRIM REAPER

technique: build | time total: 5 min | serves: 1

rocks glass, bar spoon, jigger

- **1 oz. white rum**
- **1 oz. coffee liqueur**
- **¼ oz. grenadine syrup**
- **Ice**

1. Fill a rocks glass to the top with ice
2. Pour in 1 oz. of coffee liqueur and 1 oz. of white rum
3. Add two ice cubes and pour the dash of grenadine syrup over them for a red tint

RED NAIL

technique: build | time total: 5 min | serves: 1

cocktail glass, jigger

- **1 oz. vodka**
- **1 oz. red bitters**
- **Ice**

1. Pour a few ice cubes into a cocktail glass
2. Add 1 oz. of red bitters and 1 oz. of vodka
3. Sit for seven minutes before serving

WHAT ABOUT: COFFEE LIQUEUR

A famous invigorating liqueur produced by percolating coffee beans of different varieties with grain alcohol. The resulting mix is not filtered, but mixed directly with burnt sugar and diluted with water to the desired strength

SCARY BERRY

technique: build | time total: 5 min | serves: 1

wine glass, squeezer, jigger, bar spoon

- **1½ oz. coconut liqueur**
- **1½ oz. club soda**
- **1½ oz. prosecco**
- **½ oz. blueberry juice**
- **Crushed ice**

1. Fill a wine glass to the top with crushed ice

2. Add ½ oz. of blueberry juice, 1½ oz. of prosecco and 1½ oz. of coconut liqueur

3. Top up with club soda and stir gently

WHAT ABOUT: COCONUT LIQUEUR

A tropical tiki liqueur produced by macerating coconut pulp in rum. The resulting distillate is filtered, mixed with sugar and diluted with water to the desired strength

APPLE BOBBING

technique: stir | time total: 5 min | serves: 1

coupe glass, mixing glass, squeezer, strainer, jigger, bar spoon

- **1¼ oz. gin**
- **1 oz. apple juice**
- **½ oz. fresh lime juice**
- **½ oz. honey**
- **Ice**
- **Apple**

1. Pour 1 oz. of apple juice, ½ oz. of fresh lime juice, ½ oz. of honey and 1¼ oz. of gin into a mixing glass
2. Fill the glass with ice cubes and stir gently
3. Strain into a chilled coupe glass
4. Garnish with an apple slice

CARDINALE

technique: stir | time total: 5 min | serves: 1

rocks glass, mixing glass, strainer, jigger, bar spoon

- **1 oz. gin**
- **¾ oz. red bitters**
- **¾ oz. dry vermouth**
- **Ice**
- **Lemon**

1. Pour ¾ oz. of dry vermouth, ¾ oz. of red bitters and 1 oz. of gin into a mixing glass
2. Fill the glass with ice cubes and stir gently
3. Strain into a chilled cocktail glass
4. Express lemon twist over top and discard. Garnish with dehydrated lemon peel

DEVIL MARTINI

technique: stir | time total: 5 min | serves: 1

cocktail glass, mixing glass, strainer, jigger, bar spoon, cocktail skewer

- **2 oz. dark rum**
- **½ oz. dry vermouth**
- **Ice**
- **Orange sugar**
- **Black olive**

1. Rim a cocktail glass with orange sugar
2. Pour ½ oz. of dry vermouth and 2 oz. of dark rum into a mixing glass
3. Fill the glass with ice cubes and stir gently
4. Strain into a chilled cocktail glass
5. Garnish with black olive on a cocktail skewer

GOODBYE DAISY

technique: stir | time total: 5 min | serves: 1

cocktail glass, mixing glass, strainer, jigger, bar spoon

- **2 oz. vodka**
- **1 oz. limoncello**
- **1 oz. maple syrup**
- **Ice**

1. Pour 1 oz. of limoncello, 1 oz. of maple syrup and 2 oz. of vodka into a mixing glass
2. Fill the glass with ice cubes and stir gently
3. Strain into a chilled cocktail glass Garnish with black olive on a cocktail skewer

MASQUERADE

technique: stir | time total: 3 min | serves: 1

cocktail glass, mixing glass, bar spoon, strainer, jigger

- **1½ oz. vodka**
- **2 oz. black currant juice**
- **½ oz. Green chartreuse**
- **Ice**

1. Pour 2 oz. of black currant juice, ½ oz. of Green chartreuse and 1½ oz. of vodka into a mixing glass
2. Fill the glass with ice cubes and stir gently
3. Strain into a chilled cocktail glass

VAMPIRE'S DESIRE

technique: stir | time total: 5 min | serves: 1

cocktail glass, mixing glass, bar spoon, strainer, jigger, cocktail skewer

- **1½ oz. irish whiskey**
- **1 oz. red vermouth**
- **1 oz. sweet vermouth**
- **Ice**
- **Edible eyeball**

1. Pour 1 oz. of red vermouth, 1 oz. of sweet vermouth and 1½ oz. of irish whiskey into a mixing glass
2. Fill the glass with ice cubes and stir gently
3. Strain into a chilled cocktail glass
4. Garnish with edible eyeball on a cocktail skewer

HOW TO MAKE: EDIBLE EYEBALLS

Ingredients:

- Cake balls or doughnut holes
- Gummy Lifesavers
- Chocolate chips
- White Chocolate
- Red decorator's gel

Directions:

1. Melt white chocolate in a bowl set over simmering water
2. Dip cake balls or doughnut holes in white chocolate and set on parchment
3. Add gummy Lifesavers and chocolate chips to create iris and pupils before the chocolate sets
4. Decorate pupils with a dot of white chocolate to add the resemblance of light reflecting off the eye
5. Add blood vessels with red decorators gel and a toothpick

BLOODIED BELGIAN

technique: shake | time total: 5 min | serves: 1

cocktail glass, squeezer, jigger, shaker, strainer

- ¾ oz. scotch whisky
- ¾ oz. sweet vermouth
- 2 oz. fresh blood orange juice
- 4 oz. kriek lambic
- Ice
- 2 fresh cherries

1. Pour 2 oz. of fresh blood orange juice, ¾ oz. of sweet vermouth and ¾ oz. of scotch whisky into a shaker
2. Fill the shaker with ice cubes and shake
3. Strain into a chilled cocktail glass
4. Top with the kriek lambic, drop in the cherries for garnish

BLOOD ORANGE BLOOM

technique: shake | time total: 5 min | serves: 1

coupe glass, muddler, shaker, strainer, jigger, cocktail skewer

- 1 oz. gin
- ¾ oz. lemon juice
- ½ oz. simple syrup
- ½ oz. red bitters
- Ice
- Blood orange

1. Place 2 blood orange wedges and ½ simple syrup into a shaker and muddle
2. Add ¾ oz. of lemon juice, ½ oz. of red bitters and 1 oz. of gin
3. Fill the shaker with ice cubes and shake
4. Strain into a chilled coupe glass
5. Garnish with orange peel spiral

EVIL ONE

technique: shake | time total: 5 min | serves: 1

cocktail glass, jigger, shaker, strainer

- **1½ oz. reposado tequila**
- **½ oz. creme de cassis liqueur**
- **½ oz. lime juice**
- **4 oz. ginger beer**
- **Ice**
- **Grenadine syrup**

1. Pour ½ oz. of lime juice, ½ oz. of creme de cassis liqueur, 4 oz. of ginger beer and 1½ oz. of reposado tequila into a shaker

2. Fill the shaker with ice cubes and shake

3. Strain into a chilled cocktail glass

4. Add the splash of grenadine syrup

GLOWING JEKYLL

technique: shake | time total: 5 min | serves: 1

highball glass, squeezer, jigger, shaker, strainer, drinking straws

- **3 oz. gin**
- **½ oz. lemon juice**
- **¼ oz. grenadine syrup**
- **5 oz. tonic water**
- **Ice**
- **Glow stick**

1. Fill a highball glass to the top with ice

2. Pour ½ oz. of lemon juice, ¼ oz. of grenadine syrup and 3 oz. of gin into a shaker

3. Fill the shaker with ice cubes and shake

4. Strain into a chilled highball glass

5. Top with tonic water

6. Garnish with a glow stick

WHAT ABOUT: GLOW STICK

Glow sticks are essentially plastic tubes filled with dibutyl phthalate, a clear, oily liquid that (according to the Carolinas Poison Control Center) is "low in toxicity but can cause irritation to any part of the body that it comes into contact with." Of course, the irritant is locked in the plastic tube, so you're theoretically safe — if you trust your intoxicated self to prevent the thin plastic from even the slightest crack

HAUNTING HALLOWEEN

technique: shake | time total: 5 min | serves: 1

cocktail glass, jigger, shaker, strainer

- **1½ oz. black vodka**
- **2 oz. pomegranate juice**
- **¼ oz. orange bitters**
- **¼ oz. honey**
- **Ice**
- **Blackberries**
- **Black sanding sugar**

1. Rim a cocktail glass with honey and black sanding sugar
2. Pour 2 oz. of pomegranate juice, ¼ oz. of orange bitters and 1½ oz. of vodka into a shaker
3. Fill the shaker with ice cubes and shake
4. Strain into a chilled cocktail glass
5. Garnish with blackberries on a cocktail skewer

HELLISH CAULDRON

technique: shake | time total: 5 min | serves: 1

coupe glass, squeezer, jigger, shaker, strainer

- **1½ oz. gold tequila**
- **¾ oz. lemon juice**
- **¼ oz. agave syrup**
- **¼ oz. simple syrup**
- **Angostura bitters**
- **Ice**
- **1 capsule activated charcoal**
- **Lemon slice**

1. Pour ¾ oz. of lemon juice, ¼ oz. of agave syrup, ¼ oz. of simple syrup, 2 dashes Angostura bitters, and 1 capsule activated charcoal and 1½ oz. of gold tequila into a shaker
2. Fill the shaker with ice cubes and shake
3. Strain into a chilled coupe glass
4. Garnish with a lemon wedge

JACKHAMMER

technique: shake | time total: 5 min | serves: 1

cocktail glass, jigger, shaker, strainer

- **1 oz. Cognac**
- **½ oz. ginger ale**
- **1½ oz. orange juice**
- **½ oz. triple sec liqueur**
- **Ice**
- **Blueberries**

1. Pour 1½ oz. of orange juice, ½ oz. of ginger, ½ oz. of triple sec liqueur ale and 1 oz. of Cognac into a shaker
2. Fill the shaker with ice cubes and shake
3. Strain into a chilled cocktail glass
4. Garnish with blueberries

LACRIMOSA

technique: shake | time total: 5 min | serves: 1

cocktail glass, squeezer, jigger, shaker, strainer

- **3 oz. Pisco brandy**
- **1 oz. fresh lemon juice**
- **1 oz. fresh lime juice**
- **½ oz. simple syrup**
- **Angostura bitters**
- **Crushed ice**

1. Pour 1 oz. of fresh lemon juice, 1 oz. of fresh lemon juice, ½ oz. of simple syrup and 3 oz. of Pisco brandy into a shaker
2. Fill the shaker with crushed ice and shake
3. Strain into a chilled cocktail glass
4. Top with a few drops of bitters

LIQUEFIED SPIRIT

technique: shake | time total: 5 min | serves: 1

cocktail glass, jigger, shaker, strainer

- **2 oz. vodka**
- **1 oz. vanilla simple syrup**
- **1 oz. heavy cream**
- **2 oz. soda**
- **Ice**

1. Pour 1 oz. of vanilla simple syrup, 1 oz. of heavy cream, 2 oz. of soda and 2 oz. of vodka into a shaker
2. Fill the shaker with ice cubes and shake
3. Strain into a chilled cocktail glass

NECROMANCER

technique: shake | time total: 5 min | serves: 1

coupe glass, shaker, strainer, jigger, cocktail skewer

- **1 oz. gin**
- **¼ oz. absinthe**
- **1 oz. lillet blanc**
- **1 oz. triple sec liqueur**
- **1 oz. lemon juice**
- **Ice**
- **Cherries**

1. Pour 1 oz. of lillet blanc, 1 oz. of triple sec liqueur, 1 oz. of lemon juice, ¼ oz. of absinthe and 1 oz. of gin into a shaker
2. Fill the shaker with ice cubes and shake
3. Strain into a chilled coupe glass
4. Garnish with two cherries on a cocktail skewer

NECROPOLIS

technique: shake | time total: 5 min | serves: 1

highball glass, squeezer, jigger, shaker, strainer, drinking straws

- **1 oz. gin**
- **1 oz. light rum**
- **1 oz. silver tequila**
- **1 oz. vodka**
- **1½ oz. blue curacao liqueur**
- **2 oz. sour mix**
- **Sparkling water**
- **Ice**

1. Fill a highball glass to the top with ice
2. Pour 2 oz. of sour mix, 1½ oz. of blue curacao liqueur, 1 oz. of gin, 1 oz. of light rum, 1 oz. of silver tequila and 1 oz. of vodka into a shaker
3. Fill the shaker with ice cubes and shake
4. Strain into a chilled highball glass
5. Top with sparkling water

PUMPKIN MARTINI

technique: shake | time total: 5 min | serves: 1

cocktail glass, jigger, shaker, strainer

- 3 oz. vodka
- ½ oz. pumpkin spice liqueur
- ¼ oz. simple syrup
- Ice
- Cinnamon stick

1. Pour ¼ oz. of simple syrup, ½ oz. of pumpkin spice liqueur and 3 oz. of vodka into a shaker
2. Fill the shaker with ice cubes and shake
3. Strain into a chilled cocktail glass
4. Garnish with a cinnamon stick

PUMPKIN SPIKE

technique: shake | time total: 5 min | serves: 1

coupe glass, shaker, strainer, jigger

- 1¼ oz. gin
- ¾ oz. lemon juice
- 1 oz. pumpkin puree
- ½ oz. maple syrup
- 1 whole egg
- Ice
- Nutmeg

1. Pour ¾ oz. of lemon juice, ½ oz. of maple syrup, 1 oz. of pumpkin puree, 1 whole egg and 1¼ oz. of gin into a shaker
2. Fill the shaker with ice cubes and shake
3. Strain into a chilled coupe glass
4. Dust the top with nutmeg to garnish

SMASHING STING

technique: shake | time total: 5 min | serves: 1

rocks glass, shaker, strainer, jigger

- **1 oz. spiced rum**
- **¼ oz. grenadine syrup**
- **½ oz. blue curacao liqueur**
- **1 oz. white rum**
- **1 oz. sour mix**
- **Ice**

1. Pour 1 oz. of sour mix, ½ oz. of blue curacao liqueur 1 oz. of white rum and 1 oz. of spiced rum into a shaker
2. Fill the shaker with ice cubes and shake
3. Strain into chilled rocks glass
4. Drop the grenadine over an ice cube and serve quickly so it looks like blood in the water

TOXIC APPLE PIE

technique: shake | time total: 5 min | serves: 1

coupe glass, jigger, shaker, strainer

- **2 oz. dark rum**
- **2 oz. apple cider**
- **½ oz. cinnamon syrup**
- **½ oz. heavy cream**
- **1 egg white**
- **Ice**
- **Ground cinnamon**
- **1 capsule activated charcoal**

1. Pour ½ oz. cinnamon syrup, 2 oz. of apple cider, ½ oz. heavy cream, 2 oz. of dark rum and 1 medium egg white into a shaker and shake for 30 seconds
2. Add ice, and shake again to chill
3. Strain into a chilled coupe glass
4. Slowly pour 2 oz. of apple cider into the same glass
5. Sprinkle two pinches of activated charcoal powder and cinnamon on top to garnish

VAMPIRE RITUAL

technique: shake | time total: 5 min | serves: 1

cocktail glass, muddler, jigger, shaker, strainer

- **1½ oz. gin**
- **½ oz. triple sec**
- **1½ oz. blueberry-beet syrup**
- **¾ oz. lemon juice**
- **Ice**
- **Blueberries**
- **Lemon**

1. Place 10 blueberries and 1½ oz. blueberry-beet syrup into a shaker and muddle
2. Pour ¾ oz. of lemon juice, ½ oz. of triple sec and 1½ oz. of gin into a shaker
3. Fill the shaker with crushed ice and shake
4. Strain into a chilled cocktail glass
5. Garnish with a lemon slice colored with beets

VAMPIRE'S KISS

technique: shake | time total: 5 min | serves: 1

cocktail glass, jigger, squeezer, shaker, strainer

- **1½ oz. vodka**
- **1¼ oz. orange liqueur**
- **¾ oz. fresh lemon juice**
- **1 tsp. caster sugar**
- **Ice**
- **Red gel frosting**

1. Rim a cocktail glass with red gel frosting
2. Add two drips down the glass to mimic a vampire's favorite beverage
3. Pour 1 tsp. of caster sugar, ¾ oz. of fresh lemon juice, 1¼ oz. of orange liqueur and 1½ oz. of vodka into a shaker
4. Fill the shaker with ice cubes and shake
5. Strain into a chilled cocktail glass

WANDERING FIRE

technique: shake | time total: 5 min | serves: 1

cocktail glass, jigger, shaker, strainer

- **1 oz. Cognac**
- **2 oz. chardonnay**
- **½ oz. apple cider**
- **½ oz. simple syrup**
- **1 tsp. spiced pumpkin pie mix**
- **Ice**

1. Pour 1 tsp. of spiced pumpkin pie mix, ½ oz. of simple syrup, 2 oz. of chardonnay, ½ oz. of apple cider and 1 oz. of Cognac into a shaker
2. Fill the shaker with ice cubes and shake
3. Strain into a chilled cocktail glass

WITCH'S HEART

technique: shake | time total: 5 min | serves: 1

cocktail glass, jigger, shaker, strainer

- **2 oz. black rum**
- **½ oz. caramel syrup**
- **5 drops Angostura bitters**
- **Ice**

1. Pour ½ oz. of caramel syrup, 2 oz. of black rum and 5 drops of Angostura bitters into a shaker
2. Fill the shaker with ice cubes and shake
3. Strain into a chilled cocktail glass

CHRISTMAS SPECIALS

Baby, it's cold outside – and what better way to warm up than with a Christmas cocktail? (Okay, fine, two Christmas cocktails.) Here, we've rounded up our all-time favorite easy Christmas cocktails to serve your friends and family this season.

Whether you just need something with which to wash down all those Christmas cookies or you're looking for a more sophisticated recipe to serve at your annual Christmas party, we've probably got just the thing somewhere on our list. There are so many reasons to whip up a batch of divine winter drinks, after all: For starters, a festive spirit gives you a delicious and oh-so-necessary reason to celebrate the holiday season. But it's also a gorgeous accompaniment to the rest of your Christmas dinner menu, and the perfect, grown-up companion for, say, a batch of gingerbread cookies!

And if you're dreaming up a Netflix Christmas movie or Hallmark movie marathon this year (and let's face it – who isn't?), we can't imagine a more perfect accessory with which to toast your watch party. From Christmas pun-inspired names to irresistible, original flavors and even upgrades to classic cocktails you already know and love, there's something here for just about everyone. Cheers to you!

APPLE, VODKA AND GINGER BEER

technique: build | time total: 5 min | serves: 1

highball glass, bar spoon, strainer, jigger

- **1 oz. vodka**
- **4 oz. apple juice**
- **8 oz ginger beer**
- **Ice**
- **Apple slices**

1. Pour 4 oz. of apple juice, 8 oz of ginger beer and 1 oz. of vodka into a highball glass and stir gently
2. Top up with the ice
3. Garnish with 2 apple slices

CINNAMON WHISKEY HOT TODDY

technique: build | time total: 5 min | serves: 1

rocks glass, jigger, bar spoon

- **1½ oz. bourbon**
- **¼ oz. fresh lemon juice**
- **6 oz. hot water**
- **1 tsp. honey**
- **1 cinnamon stick**
- **Ice**
- **Lemon**

1. Pour ¼ oz. of lemon juice and 1 tsp. of honey into a glass
2. Pour in 1½ oz. of bourbon and stir together with cinnamon stick
3. Pour hot water over cinnamon stick into the glass. Let steep for 5-6 minutes
4. Drink while hot!

GINGERBREAD EGGNOG

technique: build | time total: 5 min | serves: 1

rocks glass, bar spoon, strainer, jigger

- **¾ oz. dark rum**
- **1 oz. Advocaat liqueur**
- **1½ oz. single cream**
- **2 oz. whole milk**
- **1 tsp golden syrup**
- **¼ tsp ground ginger**
- **¼ tsp ground cinnamon**
- **1 cinnamon stick**

1. Pour 3 oz. of pink grapefruit juice, 1 oz. of pomegranate juice, ¾ oz. of triple sec liqueur, ¼ oz. gin and ¾ oz. of vodka into a rocks glass
2. Garnish with a sprinkling of ground ginger and a cinnamon stick

MARMALADE MULE

technique: build | time total: 3 min | serves: 1

rocks glass, muddler, jigger, bar spoon, drinking straws

- **1 oz. vodka**
- **4 oz. orange juice**
- **½ tbsp orange marmalade**
- **1 tsp runny honey**
- **Thick slice of blood orange**

1. Place ½ tbsp of orange marmalade, 1 tsp of runny honey and 1 oz. of vodka into a rocks glass and muddle
2. Top up with the orange juice
3. Garnish with the blood orange slice in the liquid

SPICED CHERRY SPRITZ

technique: build | time total: 3 min | serves: 1

rocks glass, jigger, bar spoon

- **2 oz. amaro liqueur**
- **3 oz. sparkling wine**
- **3 oz. cherry soda**
- **1 maraschino cherry**
- **Ice**

1. Fill a rocks glass to the top with ice
2. Pour in 2 oz. of amaro liqueur and 3 oz. of sparkling wine
3. Top up with cherry soda and stir gently
4. Garnish with 1 maraschino cherry

WHITE PORT AND TONIC

technique: build | time total: 3 min | serves: 1

highball glass, jigger, bar spoon, drinking straws

- **2 oz. white port**
- **4 oz. tonic water**
- **Ice**
- **3 blackberries**
- **Lime**
- **Mint sprigs**

1. Fill the highball glass to the top with ice
2. Add 2 oz. of white port and 2 blackberries
3. Top up tonic water and stir gently
4. Garnish with a blackberry, lime slices and a small sprig of mint

CLEMENTINE PROSECCO

technique: stir | time total: 5 min | serves: 1

coupe glass, mixing glass, squeezer, bar spoon, strainer, jigger

- **3 oz. prosecco**
- **¾ oz. orange liqueur**
- **1 oz. clementine juice**
- **Ice**
- **Clementine wheel**

1. Pour 1 oz. of clementine juice, ¾ oz. of orange liqueur and 3 oz. of prosecco into a mixing glass
2. Fill the glass with ice cubes and stir gently
3. Strain into a chilled coupe glass
4. Garnish with a clementine wheel

GLIMPSE

technique: stir | time total: 5 min | serves: 1

coupe glass, mixing glass, bar spoon, strainer, jigger

- **1 oz. vodka**
- **3½ oz. prosecco**
- **½ oz. elderflower cordial**
- **Ice**

1. Pour ½ oz. of elderflower cordial , 3½ oz. of prosecco and 1 oz. of vodka into a mixing glass
2. Fill the glass with ice cubes and stir gently
3. Strain into a chilled coupe glass

MAPLE BRANDY PUNCH

technique: stir | time total: 10 min | serves: 2

two highball glasses, mixing glass, bar spoon, strainer, jigger

- **1½ oz. maple syrup**
- **2 oz. apple brandy**
- **2 oz. Cognac**
- **2 oz. spiced rum**
- **¼ oz. lemon juice**
- **10 oz carbonated water, chilled**
- **Red bitter**
- **Ice**
- **Thinly sliced apples**
- **Lemon twists**

1. Place syrup in a small saucepan, bring to a boil. Reduce heat; simmer, uncovered, for 5 minutes. Remove from the heat and set aside to cool
2. Combine ¼ oz. of lemon juice, 2 oz. of apple brandy, 2 oz. of Cognac, 2 oz. of spiced rum and dash of red bitter in a mixing glass
3. Stir in maple reduction
4. Add 10 oz of carbonated water and stir
5. Strain into a two chilled highball glasses
6. Garnish with apple slices and lemon twists

WHAT ABOUT: MAPLE SYRUP

A famous Christmastime syrup made from sugar maple sap, collected from maple trees in February and March. Produced by pasteurizing the sap along with cane sugar and water

PINK BAUBLE

technique: stir | time total: 5 min | serves: 1

cocktail glass, mixing glass, bar spoon, strainer, jigger

- **¾ oz. vodka**
- **¼ oz. gin**
- **¾ oz. triple sec liqueur**
- **3 oz. pink grapefruit juice**
- **1 oz. pomegranate juice**
- **Ice**
- **Pomegranate seeds**
- **Grapefruit slice**

1. Pour 3 oz. of pink grapefruit juice, 1 oz. of pomegranate juice, ¾ oz. of triple sec liqueur, ¼ oz. gin and ¾ oz. of vodka into a mixing glass
2. Fill the glass with ice cubes and stir gently
3. Drop a few pomegranate seeds into the bottom of chilled cocktail glass and pour over the mixture
4. Garnish with grapefruit slices

ANGEL'S DELIGHT

technique: shake | time total: 5 min | serves: 1

cocktail glass, jigger, shaker, strainer

- **¾ oz. gin**
- **1 oz. triple sec liqueur**
- **¼ oz. grenadine syrup**
- **1 oz. heavy cream**
- **Ice**
- **Grenadine syrup**

1. Pour 1 oz. of triple sec liqueur, 1 oz. of heavy cream, ¼ oz. grenadine syrup and ¾ oz. of gin into a shaker
2. Fill the shaker with ice cubes and shake
3. Strain into a chilled cocktail glass

BETWEEN THE SHEETS

technique: shake | time total: 5 min | serves: 1

cocktail glass, jigger, shaker, strainer

- **1 oz. Cognac**
- **1 oz. triple sec liqueur**
- **1 oz. white rum**
- **½ oz. lemon juice**
- **Ice**
- **Lemon peel twist**

1. Pour ½ oz. of lemon juice, 1 oz. of triple sec liqueur, 1 oz. of Cognac and 1 oz. of white rum into a shaker
2. Fill the shaker with ice cubes and shake
3. Strain into a chilled cocktail glass
4. Garnish with a twist of lemon peel

BLUSH MARTINI

technique: shake | time total: 5 min | serves: 1

cocktail glass, jigger, shaker, strainer

- **1½ oz. vodka**
- **½ oz. cranberry juice**
- **½ oz. lemon juice**
- **½ tsp pure maple syrup**
- **Angostura bitters**
- **Ice**
- **Lemon peel twist**

1. Pour ½ oz. of lemon juice, ½ oz. of cranberry juice, ½ tsp of pure maple syrup, 1½ oz. of vodka and dash of Angostura bitters into a shaker
2. Fill the shaker with ice cubes and shake
3. Strain into a chilled cocktail glass
4. Garnish with a twist of lemon peel

BRANDY MILK PUNCH

technique: shake | time total: 5 min | serves: 1

rocks glass, jigger, shaker, strainer

- **2 oz. brandy**
- **1½ oz. heavy cream**
- **1 oz. simple syrup**
- **½ tsp. vanilla extract**
- **Ice**
- **Freshly grated nutmeg**

1. Pour 1 oz. of simple syrup, 1½ oz. of heavy cream, ½ tsp. of vanilla extract and 2 oz. of brandy into a shaker
2. Fill the shaker with ice cubes and shake
3. Strain into a chilled rocks glass filled with ice
4. Garnish with a freshly grated nutmeg

CANDY CANE

technique: shake | time total: 5 min | serves: 1

cocktail glass, jigger, shaker, strainer

- **¾ oz. berry vodka**
- **¾ oz. peppermint schnapps**
- **¾ oz. creme de cacao liqueur**
- **¼ oz. grenadine syrup**
- **½ oz. heavy cream**
- **Ice**
- **Crushed hard peppermint candy**

1. Rim a cocktail glass with crushed hard peppermint candy
2. Pour ¾ oz. of peppermint schnapps, ¾ oz. of creme de cacao liqueur, ¼ oz. of grenadine syrup and ¾ oz. of berry vodka into a shaker
3. Fill the shaker with ice cubes and shake
4. Strain into a chilled cocktail glass
5. Top it off with heavy cream

DIRTY MANHATTAN

technique: shake | time total: 5 min | serves: 1

cocktail glass, jigger, shaker, strainer, cocktail stick

- **2 oz. whisky**
- **1 oz. dry vermouth**
- **Ice**
- **Angostura bitters**
- **Pitted green olive**
- **Twist of lemon zest**

1. Pour 1 oz. of dry vermouth, 2 oz. of whisky and a few dashes of Angostura Bitters into a shaker
2. Fill the shaker with ice cubes and shake
3. Strain into a chilled cocktail glass
4. Thread a pitted green olive onto a cocktail stick and place into the glass
5. Garnish with a twist of lemon zest

HOLIDAY RUM SPARKLER

technique: shake | time total: 5 min | serves: 1

rocks glass, jigger, shaker, strainer

- **2 oz. dark rum**
- **2 oz. sparkling wine**
- **1 oz. apple juice**
- **¼ oz. honey syrup**
- **Ice**
- **Apple slice**
- **Mint sprig**

1. Pour ¼ oz. of honey syrup, 1 oz. of apple juice and 2 oz. of dark rum into a shaker
2. Fill the shaker with ice cubes and shake
3. Strain into a chilled rocks glass filled with ice
4. Top with sparkling wine
5. Garnish with apple slice and mint sprig

MAE ROSE

technique: shake | time total: 5 min | serves: 1

coupe glass, jigger, shaker, strainer

- **1½ oz. gin**
- **1 oz. dry vermouth**
- **½ oz. red bitter**
- **½ oz. grapefruit liqueur**
- **Ice**
- **Grapefruit twist**

1. Pour 1 oz. of dry vermouth, ½ oz. of red bitter, ½ oz. of grapefruit liqueur and 1½ oz. of gin into a shaker
2. Fill the shaker with ice cubes and shake
3. Strain into a chilled coupe glass
4. Garnish with a grapefruit twist

MAPLE & SAGE GIN CREAM CHRISTMAS

technique: shake | time total: 5 min | serves: 1

coupe glass, muddler, jigger, shaker, strainer

- **2 oz. gin**
- **1 oz. maple syrup**
- **¾ oz. lemon juice**
- **½ oz. heavy cream**
- **Nutmeg**
- **Sage leaves**

1. Place two sage leaves into a shaker and muddle
2. Pour ¾ oz. of lemon juice, 1 oz. of maple syrup, ½ oz. of heavy cream and 2 oz. of gin into a shaker
3. Fill the shaker with ice cubes and shake
4. Strain into a chilled coupe glass
5. Grate nutmeg on top
6. Garnish with sage leaf

MERRY BERRY

technique: shake | time total: 5 min | serves: 1

cocktail glass, jigger, shaker, strainer

- **1 oz. vodka**
- **1 oz. gin**
- **2 oz. cranberry juice**
- **1 candy cane**
- **Ice**
- **Caster sugar**
- **Lemon wedge**
- **Orange zest**

1. Rub the rim of cocktail glass with lemon wedge and caster sugar
2. Pour 2 oz. of cranberry juice, 1 oz. of vodka and 1 oz. of gin into a shaker
3. Fill the shaker with ice cubes and shake
4. Strain into a rimmed cocktail glass
5. Garnish with the orange zest and a candy cane

MISTLETOE MARG

technique: shake | time total: 5 min | serves: 1

margarita glass, jigger, shaker, strainer

- **2 oz. reposado tequila**
- **2 oz. fresh blood orange juice**
- **1 oz. fresh lime juice**
- **½ oz. orange liqueur**
- **12 whole cloves**
- **Ice**
- **Orange wedges**

1. Pour 2 oz. of fresh blood orange juice, 1 oz. of fresh lime juice, ½ oz. of orange liqueur and 2 oz. of reposado tequila into a shaker, along with half of the whole cloves
2. Fill the shaker with ice cubes and shake
3. Strain into a chilled margarita glass
4. Garnish with an orange wedge studded with a few whole cloves alone the peel

PAPER PLANE

technique: shake | time total: 5 min | serves: 1

coupe glass, jigger, squeezer, shaker, strainer

- **¾ oz. bourbon**
- **¾ oz. amaro liqueur**
- **¾ oz. red bitter**
- **¾ oz. fresh lemon juice**
- **Ice**

1. Pour ¾ oz. of amaro liqueur, ¾ oz. of red bitters, ¾ oz. of fresh lemon juice and ¾ oz. of bourbon into a shaker
2. Fill the shaker with ice cubes and shake
3. Strain into a chilled coupe glass

PINK LADY

technique: shake | time total: 5 min | serves: 1

cocktail glass, muddler, jigger, shaker, strainer

- **1½ oz. gin**
- **1 oz. triple sec liqueur**
- **¾ oz. lemon juice**
- **Ice**
- **Raspberries**
- **Lemon peel twist**

1. Pour 5 raspberries into a cocktail shaker and muddle
2. Add ¾ oz. of lemon juice, 1 oz. of triple sec liqueur and 1½ oz. of gin
3. Fill the shaker with ice cubes and shake
4. Strain into a chilled cocktail glass
5. Garnish with a twist of lemon peel and raspberry

REINDEER TRACKS MARTINI

technique: shake | time total: 5 min | serves: 1

cocktail glass, jigger, shaker, strainer

- **2 oz. chocolate vodka**
- **1 oz. Frangelico**
- **½ oz. creme de cacao liqueur**
- **¼ oz. heavy cream**
- **Ice**
- **Crushed Oreos**

1. Rim a chilled cocktail glass with crushed Oreos
2. Fill a cocktail shaker with ice cubes and pour in 1 oz. of Frangelico, ½ oz. of creme de cacao liqueur, ¼ oz. of heavy cream and 2 oz. of chocolate vodka
3. Shake vigorously
4. Strain into a chilled cocktail glass
5. Add more cookie crumbles over top of the drink

SANTA HAT MARTINI

technique: shake | time total: 5 min | serves: 1

cocktail glass, jigger, shaker, strainer

- **2 oz. white rum**
- **1 oz. vanilla vodka**
- **½ oz. coconut syrup**
- **4 oz. cranberry juice**
- **Ice**
- **Caster sugar**
- **Grated coconut**

1. Rim a cocktail glass with the extra coconut syrup, caster sugar, and grated coconut
2. Pour 4 oz. of cranberry juice, ½ oz. of coconut syrup, 2 oz. of white rum and 1 oz. of vanilla vodka into a shaker
3. Fill the shaker with ice cubes and shake
4. Strain into a rimmed cocktail glass

TRICK NOG CHRISTMAS

technique: shake | time total: 5 min | serves: 1

rocks glass, jigger, shaker, strainer

- **2½ oz. bourbon**
- **¼ oz. cherry liqueur**
- **½ oz. orange juice**
- **½ oz. heavy cream**
- **¼ oz. brown simple syrup**
- **1 whole egg**
- **Ice**
- **Nutmeg**
- **Orange zest**
- **Cinnamon sticks**

1. Pour ¼ oz. of cherry liqueur, ½ oz. of orange juice, ½ oz. of heavy cream, ¼ oz. of brown simple syrup and 2½ oz. of bourbon into a shaker
2. Fill the shaker with ice cubes and shake
3. Strain into a chilled rocks glass
4. Grate cinnamon on top
5. Garnish with orange peel and cinnamon stick

VERY CHERRY CHRISTMAS

technique: shake | time total: 5 min | serves: 1

cocktail glass, jigger, shaker, strainer, cocktail skewer

- **2 oz. cherry vodka**
- **½ oz. Irish cream liqueur**
- **½ oz. chocolate liqueur**
- **¼ oz. heavy cream**
- **Ice**
- **Maraschino cherries**

1. Fill a shaker with ice cubes and pour in ½ oz. of Irish cream liqueur, ½ oz. of chocolate liqueur, ¼ oz. heavy cream and 2 oz. of cherry vodka
2. Shake well until chilled
3. Strain into a chilled cocktail glass
4. Garnish with cherries on a cocktail skewer

VERY CHERRY CHRISTMAS

technique: shake | time total: 5 min | serves: 1

cocktail glass, jigger, shaker, strainer

- **1 oz. vodka**
- **1 oz. amaretto liqueur**
- **1 oz. heavy cream**
- **Ice**
- **Nutmeg (grated)**

1. Pour 1 oz. of amaretto liqueur, 1 oz. of heavy cream and 1 oz. of vodka into a shaker
2. Fill the shaker with ice cubes and shake
3. Strain into a chilled cocktail glass
4. Garnish with grated nutmeg on top

WINTER SEA BREEZE

technique: shake | time total: 5 min | serves: 1

goblet glass, jigger, shaker

- **1 oz. vodka**
- **1 oz. grapefruit juice**
- **2 oz. tonic water**
- **Crushed ice**
- **Pomegranate seeds**
- **Cranberries**
- **Mint leaves**

1. Pour 1 oz. of grapefruit juice, 2 oz. of tonic water and 1 oz. of vodka into a shaker and shake

2. Fill a goblet glass with crushed ice and pour in the drink mixture

3. Garnish with the pomegranate seeds, cranberries and mint

CHRISTMAS JONES

technique: blend | time total: 5 min | serves: 2

two highball glasses, blender, bar spoon, jigger, drinking straws

- **1½ oz. vodka**
- **5 oz. pineapple juice**
- **5 oz. lemon-lime soda**
- **2 tsp. superfine sugar**
- **4 fresh strawberries**
- **Ice**
- **Mint sprigs**

1. Place 4 fresh strawberries, 5 oz. of pineapple juice and 1½ oz. of vodka into a blender

2. Add 2 tsp. of superfine sugar and blend

3. Pour the mix equally into two highball glasses

4. Top with lemon-lime soda

5. Garnish with a sprig mint

VALENTINE'S SPECIALS

Whether you're planning a date night or girls night this Valentine's Day, it's always a good idea to add a fun cocktail into the mix. In honor of the most romantic day of the year, here are 30 Valentine's Day cocktail recipes you'll fall in love with.

CHAMPAGNE COCKTAIL

technique: build | time total: 3 min | serves: 1

flute glass

- **6 oz. Champagne**
- **1 sugar cube**
- **Angostura bitters**
- **Lemon peel twist**

1. Place 1 sugar cube in a flute glass
2. Add 3 dashes Angostura bitters over the cube
3. Fill the glass slowly with Champagne
4. Garnish with a lemon peel twist

GOOD NIGHT KISS

technique: build | time total: 3 min | serves: 1

flute glass, jigger

- **4 oz. sparkling wine**
- **1 oz. red bitter**
- **1 sugar cube**
- **Angostura bitters**

1. Add 1 dash Angostura bitters onto 1 sugar cube and drop it into a flute glass
2. Add 4 oz. of sparkling wine
3. Top with 1 oz. of red bitter

STRAWBERRY CRUSH

technique: build | time total: 5 min | serves: 1

highball glass, jigger, muddler, bar spoon, drinking straws

- **1 oz. vodka**
- **4 oz. lemonade**
- **Crushed ice**
- **Strawberries**
- **Basil leaves**

1. Pour 2 strawberries into a highball glass and muddle
2. Add 3 basil leaves, 4 oz. of lemonade and 1 oz. of vodka and stir
3. Top up with crushed ice
4. Garnish with a few basil leaves

THE HEARTBREAKER

technique: build | time total: 3 min | serves: 1

rocks glass, jigger, bar spoon

- **1 oz. vodka**
- **1½ oz. espresso**
- **¼ oz. simple syrup**
- **1 oz. heavy cream**
- **Ice**

1. Pour ¼ oz. of simple syrup, 1½ oz. of espresso, 1 oz. of heavy cream and 1 oz. of vodka into a rocks glass
2. Fill the glass with ice cubes stir gently

THE SEDUCTRESS

technique: build | time total: 3 min | serves: 1

flute glass, jigger, bar spoon

- **4 oz. brut wine**
- **½ oz. passion fruit puree**
- **½ oz. ginger syrup**
- **1 oz. red bitter**
- **Red rose petal**

1. Chill all ingredients and champagne flute
2. Pour 4 oz. of brut wine, ½ oz. of passion fruit puree, ½ oz. of ginger syrup and 1 oz. of red bitter into a flute glass and stir gently
3. Garnish with a red rose petal

VALENTINE'S SPARKLER

technique: build | time total: 3 min | serves: 1

flute glass, jigger, bar spoon

- **1½ oz. aged light rum**
- **1½ oz. vanilla simple syrup**
- **½ oz. unsweetened fresh cranberry juice**
- **2 oz. sparkling wine**
- **Orange peel**

1. Pour 1½ oz. of vanilla simple syrup, ½ oz. of unsweetened fresh cranberry juice, 2 oz. of sparkling wine and 1½ oz. of aged light rum into a flute glass and stir gently
2. Garnish with an orange peel cut in the shape of a heart

ABSOLUT GOLD

technique: stir | time total: 5 min | serves: 1

flute glass, jigger, mixing glass, bar spoon, strainer

- **1 oz. vodka**
- **½ oz. Lillet Blanc**
- **½ oz. peach liqueur**
- **3 oz. sparkling wine**
- **Ice**
- **Edible gold flakes**

1. Pour ½ oz. of Lillet Blanc, ½ oz. of peach liqueur and 1 oz. of vodka into a mixing glass
2. Fill the glass with ice cubes and stir gently
3. Strain into a chilled flute glass
4. Top up with sparkling wine
5. Garnish with edible gold flakes

ALL THAT GLITTERS

technique: stir | time total: 5 min | serves: 1

coupe glass, jigger, mixing glass, bar spoon, strainer

- **1½ oz. vodka**
- **1 oz. Lillet Blanc**
- **¼ oz. limoncello liqueur**
- **¼ oz. red bitter**
- **Ice**
- **Lemon twist**
- **Edible gold glitter**

1. Pour 1 oz. of Lillet Blanc, ¼ oz. of limoncello liqueur, ¼ oz. of red bitter and 1½ oz. of vodka into a mixing glass
2. Sprinkle in a small amount of edible gold glitter
3. Fill the glass with ice cubes and stir gently
4. Strain into a chilled coupe glass
5. Garnish with lemon twist

MEDITERRANEAN SANGRIA

technique: stir | time total: 5 min | serves: 1

highball glass, jigger, mixing glass, bar spoon, strainer

- **½ oz. peach schnapps**
- **½ oz. triple sec**
- **½ oz. apricot brandy**
- **½ oz. apple pucker**
- **½ oz. orange juice**
- **½ oz. pineapple juice**
- **1 oz. pomegranate juice**
- **5 oz. of red wine**
- **3 oz. Champagne**
- **Ice**

1. Pour ½ oz. of peach schnapps, ½ oz. of triple sec, ½ oz. of apricot brandy, ½ oz. of apple pucker, ½ oz. of orange juice, ½ oz. of pineapple juice, 1 oz. of pomegranate juice, and 5 oz. of red wine into a mixing glass
2. Fill the glass with ice cubes and stir gently
3. Strain into a chilled highball glass

BUBBLE BOUQUET

technique: shake | time total: 5 min | serves: 1

flute glass, jigger, shaker, strainer

- 1½ oz. vodka
- ½ oz. simple syrup
- 4 oz. Champagne
- Ice

Rose petals

1. Pour ½ oz. of simple syrup and 1½ oz. of vodka into a shaker
2. Fill the shaker with ice cubes and shake
3. Strain into a chilled flute glass
4. Top up with Champagne
5. Garnish with rose petals

DOLCE VITA

technique: shake | time total: 5 min | serves: 1

wine glass, jigger, shaker, strainer

- ½ oz. raspberry eau-de-vie
- ¾ oz. creme de cacao liqueur
- ¾ oz. red bitter
- ½ oz. raspberry preserves
- 1 oz. half & half
- Ice
- Dark chocolate

1. Pour ¾ oz. creme de cacao liqueur, ¾ oz. of red bitter, 1 oz. of half & half, ½ oz. raspberry preserves and ½ oz. of raspberry eau-de-vie into a shaker
2. Fill the shaker with ice cubes and shake
3. Strain into a chilled wine glass
4. Garnish with shavings of dark chocolate

ENDLESS LOVE

technique: shake | time total: 5 min | serves: 1

coupe glass, jigger, shaker, strainer, cocktail stick

- **2 oz. vodka**
- **½ oz. maraschino liqueur**
- **1 oz. lemon juice**
- **¼ oz. cranberry juice**
- **¾ oz. simple syrup**
- **Ice**
- **Cherry**
- **Lemon twist**

1. Pour ½ oz. of maraschino liqueur, ¾ oz. of simple syrup, 1 oz. of lemon juice and 2 oz. of vodka into a shaker
2. Fill the shaker with ice cubes and shake
3. Strain into a chilled coupe glass
4. Add a splash of cranberry juice
5. Garnish with a cherry and lemon twist on a cocktail stick

FRENCH MARTINI

technique: shake | time total: 5 min | serves: 1

cocktail glass, jigger, shaker, strainer

- **1½ oz. vodka**
- **¾ oz. pineapple juice**
- **¾ oz. creme de cassis liqueur**
- **¼ oz. lemon juice**
- **Ice**
- **Lemon zest**

1. Pour ¾ oz. of pineapple juice, ¾ oz. of creme de cassis liqueur, ¼ oz. of lemon juice and 1½ oz. of vodka into a shaker
2. Fill the shaker with ice cubes and shake
3. Strain into a chilled cocktail glass
4. Garnish with lemon zest

GEORGIA PEACH FLOAT

technique: shake | time total: 7 min | serves: 1

large wine glass, jigger, shaker, strainer

- **1½ oz. vodka**
- **4 oz. sparkling juice peach**
- **2 oz. peach puree**
- **Ice**
- **Ice cream**
- **Sea salt**
- **Peach slice**
- **Basil sprig**

1. Pour 4 oz. of sparkling juice peach, 2 oz. of peach puree and 1½ oz. of vodka into a shaker
2. Fill the shaker with ice cubes and shake
3. Strain into a large wine glass filled with 3 scoops of ice cream
4. Sprinkle with sea salt
5. Garnish with peach slice and sprig of fresh basil

HEART DAY

technique: shake | time total: 5 min | serves: 1

rocks glass, jigger, shaker, strainer, cocktail skewer

- **1½ oz. vanilla vodka**
- **½ oz. agave syrup**
- **¾ oz. lime juice**
- **1 oz. pineapple juice**
- **Ice**
- **Brown sugar**
- **Raspberries**

1. Rim glass with brown sugar
2. Pour ½ oz. of agave syrup, ¾ oz. of lime juice, 1 oz. of pineapple juice and 1½ oz. of vanilla vodka into a shaker
3. Fill the shaker with ice cubes and shake
4. Strain into a chilled rocks glass over fresh ice
5. Garnish with 3 raspberries on a cocktail skewer

HEMINGWAY IN LOVE DAIQUIRI

technique: shake | time total: 5 min | serves: 1

cocktail glass, jigger, shaker, strainer, cocktail skewer

- **1½ oz. light rum**
- **¼ oz. loganberry liqueur**
- **½ oz. grapefruit juice**
- **¾ oz. lime juice**
- **¼ oz. simple syrup**
- **Ice**
- **Lime wedge**
- **Blackberry**

1. Pour ¼ oz. of loganberry liqueur, ¾ oz. of lime juice, ½ oz. of grapefruit juice, ¼ oz. of simple syrup and 1½ oz. of light rum into a shaker
2. Fill the shaker with ice cubes and shake
3. Strain into a chilled cocktail glass over fresh ice
4. Garnish with lime wedge and blackberry on a cocktail skewer

JASMINE KISS

technique: shake | time total: 5 min | serves: 1

coupe glass, jigger, shaker, strainer

- **1½ oz. gin**
- **¾ oz. triple sec liqueur**
- **½ oz. red bitter**
- **¾ oz. lemon juice**
- **½ oz. simple syrup**
- **Ice**
- **Edible pansy flower**

1. Pour ¾ oz. of triple sec liqueur, ¾ oz. of lemon juice, ½ oz. of simple syrup, ½ oz. of red bitter and 1½ oz. of gin into a shaker
2. Fill the shaker with ice cubes and shake
3. Strain into a chilled coupe glass
4. Garnish with an edible pansy flower

JUST BEET IT

technique: shake | time total: 5 min | serves: 1

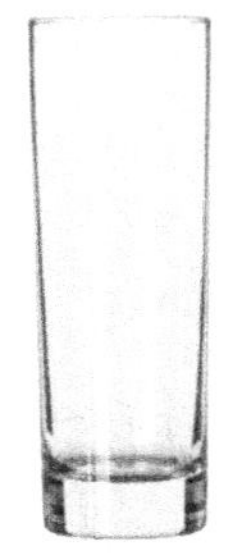

collins glass, jigger, shaker, strainer

- **1 oz. gold tequila**
- **1 oz. pimms**
- **1 oz. beet juice**
- **¼ oz. ginger juice**
- **¼ oz. lemon juice**
- **¼ oz. simple syrup**
- **4 oz. ginger beer**
- **Ice**
- **Mint sprig**

1. Pour 1 oz. of pimms,1 oz. of beet juice, ¼ oz. of ginger juice, ¼ oz. of lemon juice, ¼ oz. of simple syrup and 1 oz. of gold tequila into a shaker
2. Fill the shaker with ice cubes and shake
3. Strain into a chilled collins glass
4. Top up with ginger beer
5. Garnish with mint sprig

LADY IN RED

technique: shake | time total: 5 min | serves: 1

coupe glass, jigger, squeezer, shaker, strainer

- **2 oz. gin**
- **¼ oz. crème de cassis liqueur**
- **½ oz. fresh lemon juice**
- **½ oz. strawberry puree**
- **3 oz. sparkling wine**
- **Ice**
- **Lemon twist**

1. Pour ½ oz. of strawberry puree, ½ oz. of fresh lemon juice, ¼ oz. of crème de cassis liqueur and 2 oz. of gin into a shaker
2. Fill the shaker with ice cubes and shake
3. Strain into a chilled coupe glass
4. Top up with sparkling wine
5. Garnish with a twist of lemon

LA VELA

technique: shake | time total: 5 min | serves: 1

goblet glass, jigger, muddler, shaker, strainer

- **1½ oz. silver tequila**
- **½ oz. rosemary syrup**
- **1 oz. rosé wine**
- **¾ oz. grapefruit juice**
- **¼ oz. lime juice**
- **Crushed ice**
- **Watermelon**
- **Chili**
- **Rosemary sprig**

1. Pour 2 pieces of watermelon and 1 slice of chili into a shaker and muddle
2. Add ¾ oz. of grapefruit juice, ½ oz. of rosemary syrup, ¼ oz. of lime juice and 1½ oz. of silver tequila into a shaker
3. Shake and strain into a goblet glass over crushed ice
4. Top up with rosé wine
5. Garnish with a rosemary sprig

LOVE BUZZ

technique: shake | time total: 5 min | serves: 1

coupe glass, jigger, shaker, strainer

- **½ oz. crème de cacao liqueur**
- **1 oz. raspberry puree**
- **1 oz. room-temperature espresso**
- **1½ oz. vodka**
- **Ice**
- **Chocolate tuile**

1. Pour 1 oz. of raspberry puree, ½ oz. of crème de cacao liqueur, 1 oz. of room-temperature espresso and 1½ oz. of vodka into a shaker
2. Fill the shaker with ice cubes and shake
3. Strain into a chilled coupe glass
4. Garnish with chocolate tuile

LOVE POTION

technique: shake | time total: 5 min | serves: 1

coupe glass, jigger, shaker, strainer

- **3 oz. gin**
- **1 oz. lime juice**
- **1 oz. elderflower liquor**
- **3 oz. rosé wine**
- **Ice cubes**
- **Crushed ice**

1. Pour 1 oz. of elderflower liquor, 1 oz. of lime juice and 3 oz. of gin into a shaker
2. Fill the shaker with ice cubes and shake
3. Strain into a chilled coupe glass over crushed ice
4. Top up with rosé wine

QUEEN OF HEARTS

technique: shake | time total: 5 min | serves: 1

wine glass, jigger, shaker, strainer

- **1 ½ oz. gin**
- **¾ oz. hibiscus syrup**
- **¾ oz. lemon juice**
- **2 oz. sparkling wine**
- **Ice**
- **Edible flower**
- **Lemon twist**

1. Pour ¾ oz. of hibiscus syrup, ¾ oz. of lemon juice and 1½ oz. of gin into a shaker
2. Fill the shaker with ice cubes and shake
3. Strain into a chilled wine glass
4. Top up with sparkling wine
5. Garnish with edible flower and lemon twist

RASPBERRY KISS

technique: shake | time total: 7 min | serves: 1

rocks glass, jigger, shaker, strainer, cocktail skewer

- **1½ oz. vodka**
- **½ oz. raspberry liqueur**
- **½ oz. simple syrup**
- **2 oz. raspberry lemonade**
- **Ice cubes**
- **Crushed ice**
- **Raspberry**
- **Caster sugar**
- **Heart-shaped candy**

1. Rub the rim of rocks glass with raspberry and caster sugar
2. Pour ½ oz. of simple syrup, ½ oz. of raspberry liqueur, 2 oz. of raspberry lemonade and 1½ oz. of vodka into a shaker
3. Fill the shaker with ice cubes and shake
4. Strain into a rimmed rocks glass over crushed ice
5. Garnish with fresh raspberry and heart-shaped candy on cocktail skewer

WHAT ABOUT: RASPBERRY LIQUEUR

A berry dessert liqueur produced by macerating wild raspberries in neutral spirits with water for up to two months. The juice is filtered without pressing and mixed with sugar

SHERRY COBBLER SPRITZ

technique: shake | time total: 5 min | serves: 1

sling glass, jigger, muddler, shaker, strainer

- **3½ oz. sherry**
- **½ oz. lemon juice**
- **½ oz. simple syrup**
- **Ice cubes**
- **Crushed ice**
- **Blackberries**
- **Raspberries**
- **Lemon wheel**
  Mint sprig

1. Pour 4 raspberries and 2 blackberries into a shaker and muddle
2. Add 3½ oz. of sherry, ½ oz. of lemon juice and ½ oz. of simple syrup
3. Fill the shaker with ice cubes and shake
4. Strain into a chilled sling glass filled with fresh crushed ice
5. Garnish with blackberries, raspberries, lemon wheel, and mint sprig

TEQUILA SPARKLER

technique: shake | time total: 5 min | serves: 1

coupe glass, jigger, shaker, strainer

- **1 oz. silver tequila**
- **½ oz. lime juice**
- **½ oz. simple syrup**
- **4 oz. sparkling wine**
- **Ice**

1. Pour ½ oz. of simple syrup, ½ oz. of lime juice and 1 oz. of silver tequila into a shaker
2. Fill the shaker with ice cubes and shake
3. Strain into a chilled coupe glass
4. Top up with sparkling wine

THE KING CUATRO

technique: shake | time total: 5 min | serves: 1

coupe glass, jigger, shaker, strainer

- **1½ oz. aged rum**
- **½ oz. elderflower liqueur**
- **3 oz. prosecco**
- **¾ oz. lemon juice**
- **¼ oz. honey**
- **Ice**
- **Blackberries**

1. Pour ¾ oz. of lemon juice, ½ oz. of elderflower liqueur, ¼ oz. of honey and 1½ oz. of aged rum into a shaker
2. Fill the shaker with ice cubes and shake
3. Strain into a chilled coupe glass
4. Top up with prosecco
5. Garnish with a blackberry-speared purple orchid

THE SWEETEST THING

technique: shake | time total: 5 min | serves: 1

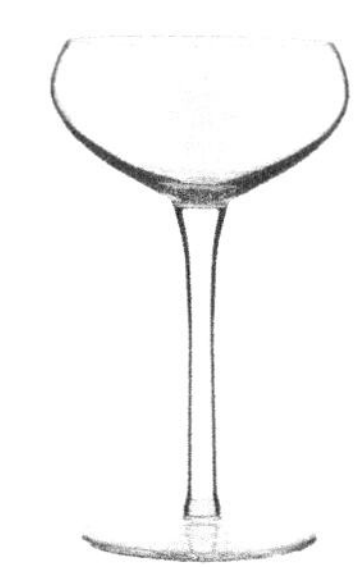

coupe glass, jigger, shaker, strainer

- **½ oz. silver tequila**
- **½ oz. maple syrup**
- **3 oz. red sparkling wine**
- **1 tsp. unsweetened chocolate powder**
- **1 oz. almond milk Ice**
- **Raspberry**
- **Powdered sugar**
- **Squish marshmallows**

1. Rub the rim of cocktail glass with raspberry and powdered sugar
2. Pour ½ oz. of maple syrup, 1 oz. of almond milk, 1 tsp. of unsweetened chocolate powder and ½ oz. of silver tequila into a shaker
3. Fill the shaker with ice cubes and shake
4. Strain into a rimmed cocktail glass
5. Top up with red sparkling wine
6. Garnish with red sparkling squish marshmallows

WHITE LADY

technique: shake | time total: 5 min | serves: 1

cocktail glass, jigger, squeezer, shaker, strainer

- **2 oz. gin**
- **1 oz. triple sec liqueur**
- **1 oz. fresh lemon juice**
- **Egg white**
- **Ice**
- **Lemon twist**

1. Pour 1 oz. of triple sec liqueur, 1 oz. of fresh lemon juice, 1 egg white and 2 oz. of gin into a shaker
2. Fill the shaker with ice cubes and shake
3. Strain into a chilled cocktail glass
4. Garnish with a lemon twist

YOUNG LUST

technique: shake | time total: 5 min | serves: 1

rocks glass, jigger, shaker, strainer, cocktail skewer

- **1½ oz. vodka**
- **1 oz. pomegranate liqueur**
- **¾ oz. lime juice**
- **½ oz. agava syrup**
- **Ice**
- **Lime wheel**

1. Pour ¾ oz. of lime juice, ½ oz. of agava syrup, 1 oz. of pomegranate liqueur and 1½ oz. of vodka into a shaker
2. Fill the shaker with ice cubes and shake
3. Strain into a chilled rocks glass
4. Garnish with a lime wheel on a cocktail skewer

INDEX

1

2

A

B

P

Q

R

S

T

V

W

Y

Made in the USA
Monee, IL
16 November 2019

16899181R00077